THE DICTIONARY OF WAR QUOTATIONS

Other books by Justin Wintle

Reference

Dictionary of Biographical Quotation
(with Richard Kenin)

Makers of Nineteenth Century Culture

Makers of Modern Culture

The Dragon's Almanac
(Chinese, Japanese and other Far Eastern Proverbs)

A Dictionary of Arabic and Islamic Proverbs
(with Paul Lunde)

Novels

Paradise For Hire

Mortadella

Other

The Fun Art Bus
(with Ed Berman)

The Pied Pipers
(with Emma Fisher)

Heat Treatment: Travels Beyond the Orient

THE DICTIONARY OF WAR QUOTATIONS

Compiled and edited by

JUSTIN WINTLE

A John Curtis Book

Hodder & Stoughton

LONDON SYDNEY AUCKLAND TORONTO

First published in Great Britain 1989

British Library Cataloguing in Publication Data
Wintle, Justin, *1949–*
The dictionary of war quotations. –
(A John Curtis book).
1. War
I. Title
355'.02
ISBN 0-340-48560-4

Published by Hodder and Stoughton,
a division of Hodder and Stoughton Ltd,
Mill Road, Dunton Green, Sevenoaks, Kent TN13 2YA
Editorial Office: 47 Bedford Square, London WC1B 3DP

Design by Behram Kapadia

Photoset by Rowland Phototypesetting Ltd,
Bury St Edmunds, Suffolk

Printed in Great Britain by St Edmundsbury Press Ltd,
Bury St Edmunds, Suffolk

CONTENTS

for Peter Yapp

FOREWORD

This book of quotations is divided into three parts: Generalities, Particularities and Personalities.

Part One, Generalities, deals chronologically (by author) with general statements about war. It includes the pronouncements of such theorists as Sun Tzu, Machiavelli and Clausewitz.

Part Two, Particularities, deals, again chronologically, with individual wars and engagements.

Part Three, Personalities, deals alphabetically with the captains of war, the heroes and the villains.

In addition there are two Indexes: an Index of Authors quoted and a Main Index, both at the back.

The Main Index is the key to this dictionary. It should be used to locate particular wars, battles and other events in both Parts Two and Three. It also supplies references to all the military figures and other proper names as they occur throughout the book.

For example, although there is a sub-section, in Part Two, on the Battle of Waterloo, at the end of the section on 'The French Revolution and Wars of Napoleon', further references to Waterloo occur in the entries for Napoleon and Wellington in Part Three, and elsewhere. By looking up 'Waterloo' in the Main Index the reader can satisfy his or her curiosity more fully.

As for the book itself, and the materials it contains, it needs to be said that *The Dictionary of War Quotations* is, like any anthology of quotations, highly selective. This is so for two reasons. First, the literature of war is enormous. Second, I have my own views about war. For these I make no apology.

My aim, throughout the period spent gathering materials, was to produce a book that would be sufficiently broad-based to reflect the changing nature of warfare down the ages, yet not so large that it necessarily became a piece of furniture in the reading rooms of libraries, from whence it was too bulky to be removed.

By the same token, I have endeavoured to produce something that can be consulted and dipped into, yet which may also engage the reader for several hours at a time.

To this end I have included two kinds of quotation: the familiar or well-known, what might be called the lore of war, often pithy statements; and longer passages that may or may not have been anthologised before, which add in-depth illumination to the business of war.

The business of war is a serious one, the most serious there is. This compilation reflects that fact. I have however incorporated some lighter, humorous material, when it has presented itself, to show that man, even at his most deadly, sometimes reveals aspects of his friendlier nature. In other respects too I have striven for balance. For example, I have attempted to balance the historian's approach to war, generally focusing on the significance of armed conflict in terms of the jockeying of peoples and nations for survival and domination, against the actual experience of war, as witnessed by participants of all ranks. Again, I have endeavoured to give the peace-seekers a say among the warmongers – since that is where my own heart lies. But, inevitably, achieving such balances on each and every page has not proved possible. One must be limited by the sources that are available. The voices of war have changed just as much as warfare itself. The hard, deadpan style of the contemporary war reporter, engendered by Russell in the Crimea, has no exact equivalent in either classical times or the Middle Ages. Again, the modern media have ensured that much of the sick, flip humour one suspects must accompany any war surfaces far more profusely today than it did in times past. The Peloponnesian Wars and the Wars in Vietnam are very different kinds of war; but that difference is compounded by the way in which they have been recorded.

Conversely something may also have been lost. The standards of impartiality set by the best of the ancient military historians – Thucydides – have seldom been emulated, and never excelled.

Yet to praise Thucydides in such terms indicates editorial prejudice. I have relied heavily on certain historians – Sallust, Caesar, Gibbon, Oman, Fuller – not just on account of the ground they cover, but because of the way in which they cover it. Because I believe that war is best understood in a historical context, I have naturally made room for those writers whose grasp of history seems to me the surest.

The fascination with war is indeed to learn how much and how little it has changed down the centuries, and to discover what, in individual cases, motivates war. It is from this that the meaning of war emerges.

For these reasons I have preferred a chronological structure, at least as regards Parts One and Two, even at the risk of exposing my flanks. Just how selective I have been will be readily apparent to any serious student of either war or history. Because this is a book of quotations, and therefore must have a regard for the way in which its primary language, English, has been used to describe war, I have neglected many important contests fought between those who speak and write in 'foreign' tongues. Nonetheless my hope is that this *Dictionary of War Quotations* gives an impression of the evolution of war, as well as of its tastes and smells. If I have succeeded at all, then perhaps a little of the somewhat awesome education I have had in compiling it will pass on to others.

A part of that education was furnished by Lieutenant-Colonel M. J. G. Martin, MBE, in London, and by Professor Calvin Christman, in Texas. Their many suggestions have made this a richer book. To each of them I give thanks, while stressing that any shortcomings are entirely my responsibility.

Justin Wintle,
Milford Haven, 1989

A NOTE ON TRANSLATIONS

It has not been possible to identify the translator of every foreign-language source, particularly where I have extracted materials from secondary sources; and in a handful of cases I have either provided my own original translation, or amended existing translations. However, as regards what might be called 'standard works', the following is a list of those translations used.

AGATHIAS: *History of His Own Time*, trans. Charles Oman, in *A History of the Art of War in the Middle Ages*, 1924 (2nd edition)
AMMIANUS: *The Roman History*, trans. C. D. Yonge, 1862
The ANGLO-SAXON CHRONICLE: trans. G. N. Garmonsway, 1953
ANONYMOUS: *Battle of Maldon*, trans. Kevin Crossley-Holland, 1965
Charles ARDANT DU PICQ: *Battle Studies*, trans. John Greely and Robert Cotton, 1921
ARISTOTLE: *Politics*, trans. John Warrington, 1959
ARRIANUS: *The Anabasis of Alexander*, trans. E. J. Chinnock, 1884
St AUGUSTINE: *City of God*, trans. Henry Nettenson, 1972
BEDE: *Ecclesiastical History of the English People*, trans. Leo Sherley-Price, 1955
The BIBLE: the Authorized King James version
Carlo G. G. BOTTA: *The American War*, trans. G. A. Otis, 1839 (9th edition)
Bertolt BRECHT: *Mother Courage*, trans. Eric Bentley, 1963
Julius CAESAR: *Commentaries on the Civil War*, trans. W. A. M'Devitte, 1853, revised W. C. Bohn, 1902; *Commentaries on the Gallic Wars*, trans. T. Rice Holmes, 1908
Karl von CLAUSEWITZ: *On War*, trans. J. J. Graham, 1908
Philip CONTAMINE: *War in the Middle Ages*, trans. Michael Jones, 1984
DEMOSTHENES: translations of his speeches taken from *Greek Political Oratory*, trans. A. N. W. Saunders, 1970
Giulio DOUHET: *The Command of the Air*, trans. Dino Ferrari, 1943
Nadezhda DUROVA: *The Cavalry Maiden*, trans. Mary Fleming Zurin, 1988
Franz FANON: *The Wretched of the Earth*, trans. Constance Farrington, 1964
Anne FRANK: *The Diary of a Young Girl*, trans. B. M. Mooyaart-Doubleday, 1952
FREDERICK the Great: *Particular Instructions of the King of Prussia to the Officers of His Army* and *Military Instructions of the Late King of Prussia to His Generals*, trans. Thomas Foster, 1796 and 1797
FROISSART: *Chronicles*, trans. Thomas Johnes, 1839

L. P. GACHARD: *Collection des voyages des souverains des Páys-Bas*, trans. Michael Jones: see above, Philip CONTAMINE
GERALD of Wales: *The Description of Wales*, trans. Lewis Thorpe, 1978
André GIDE: *Journals*, trans. Justin O'Brien, 1953
Jean GIRAUDOUX: *Tiger at the Gates*, trans. Christopher Fry, 1955
J. W. von GOETHE: *The Campaign in France*, trans. Robert Farie, 1849
HENRY of HUNTINGDON: *History of England*, trans. T. Forrester, 1853
HERODOTUS: *Histories*, trans. George Rawlinson, 1858
Adolf HITLER: *Mein Kampf*, trans. James Murphy, 1939
Prince Kraft zu HOHENLOHE-INGELFINGEN: *Letters on Artillery*, trans. N. L. Walford, 1890
HOMER: *Iliad*, trans. T. A. Buckley, 1879
ISOCRATES: translations of his speeches taken from *Greek Political Oratory*, trans. A. N. W. Saunders, 1970
Antoine Henri de JOMINI: *Précis of the Art of War*, trans. G. H. Mendell and W. P. Craighill, 1879
JOSEPHUS: *The Wars of the Jews*, trans. William Whiston, no date
LAO TZU: *Tao Te Ching*, trans. D. C. Lau, 1963
Abraham LEWIN: *A Cup of Tears*, trans. Christopher Hutton, 1988
LI PO: 'Fighting South of the Ramparts', trans. Arthur Waley, in *The Poetry and Career of Li Po*, 1950
LIVY: *The History of Rome*, Everyman Library translation, no translator given, 1912
Konrad LORENZ: *The Waning of Humaneness*, trans. R. W. Kickert, 1987
LUCAN: *Pharsalia*, trans. Robert Graves, 1956
Niccolò MACHIAVELLI: *The Prince*, trans. Luigi Ricci, revised E. R. P. Vincent, 1936; *The Art of War*, trans. Ellis Farneworth, 1775
MAO TSE-TUNG: various, all trans. Foreign Language Press, Peking, 1966
Walter MAP: *De Nugis Curialum*, trans. F. Tupper and M. B. Ogle, 1924
MIYAMOTO MUSASHI: *A Book of Five Rings*, trans. Victor Harris, 1974
The Prophet MOHAMMED: *Koran*, trans. J. M. Rodwell, 1861
Helmuth von MOLTKE: *The Franco-Prussian War*, trans. C. Bell and H. W. Fischer, 1891
ONOSANDER: *The General*, trans. Illinois Greek Club, 1923
PLATO: *The Republic*, trans. Benjamin Jowett, 1888
PLUTARCH: *Lives*, trans. Aubrey Stewart and George Long, 1892
POLYBIUS: *Histories*, trans. E. S. Shuckburgh, 1889
RICHARD of Devizes: *Chronicle*, trans. J. T. Appleby, 1963
SALLUST: *The Jugurthine War* and *The Conspiracy of Catiline*, trans. S. A. Handford, 1963
Maurice de SAXE: *Rêveries*, trans. Thomas R. Phillips
Albert SPEER: *Inside the Third Reich*, trans. Richard and Clara Winston, 1970
SUN TZU: *The Art of War*, trans. Lionel Giles, 1910
Marshal SUVOROV: *The Art of Victory*, trans. Philip Longworth, 1963
TACITUS: *Annals*, *Histories*, and *Treatise on the Manners of the Germans*, the 'Oxford Translation', 1872–74

THUCYDIDES: *History of the Peloponnesian Wars*, trans. Benjamin Jowett, 1881
Leo TOLSTOY: *War and Peace*, trans. Louise and Alymer Maude, 1942
VEGETIUS: *De Re Militari*, trans. T. R. Phillips, 1943
WILLIAM of Poitiers: *Chronicle*, trans. Charles Oman, in *History of the Art of War in the Middle Ages*, 1924; *Life of William I*, trans. G. W. Greenaway, in *English Historical Documents*, vol. II, 1953
XENOPHON: *Cyropaedia*, trans. J. S. Watson and Henry Dale, 1870

PART ONE: GENERALITIES

General statements about war, arranged chronologically by author

The BIBLE: Old Testament, from the 10th century BC

Whoso sheddeth man's blood, by man shall his blood be shed: for in the image of God made he man.

Genesis 9.vi

And by thy sword shalt thou live, . . .

Genesis 27.xl

The Lord is a man of war: the Lord is his name.

Exodus 15.iii

Thou shalt not kill.

Exodus 20.xiii

When thou goest out to battle against thine enemies, and seest horses, and chariots, and a people more than thou, be not afraid of them: for the Lord thy God is with thee, which brought thee up out of the Land of Egypt. And it shall be, when ye are come nigh unto the battle, that the priest shall approach and speak unto the people, And shall say unto them, Hear, O Israel, ye approach this day unto battle against your enemies: let not your hearts faint, fear not, and do not tremble, neither be ye terrified, because of them; for the Lord your God is he that goeth with you, to fight for you against your enemies, to save you. And the officers shall speak unto the people, saying, What man is there that hath built a new house, and hath not dedicated it? let him go and return to his house, lest he die in the battle, and another man dedicate it. And what man is he that hath planted a vineyard, and hath not yet eaten of it? let him also go and return unto his house, lest he die in the battle, and another man eat of it. And what man is there that hath betrothed a wife, and hath not taken her? let him go and return unto his house, lest he die in the battle, and another man take her. And the officers shall speak further unto the people, and they shall say, What man is there that is fearful and fainthearted? let him go and return unto his house, lest his brethren's heart faint as well as his heart.

Deuteronomy 20.i–viii

How are the mighty fallen in the midst of the battle!

II Samuel 1.xxv

He saith among the trumpets, Ha, ha; and he smelleth the battle afar off, the thunder of the captains, and the shouting.

Job 39.xxv

Thine hand shall find out all thine enemies; thy right hand shall find those that hate thee. Thou shalt make them as a fiery oven in the time of thine anger: the Lord shall swallow them up in his wrath, and the fire shall devour them. Their fruit shalt thou destroy from the earth, and their seed from among the children of men. For they intended evil against thee: they imagined a mischievous device, which they are not able to perform. Therefore shalt thou make them turn their back, when thou shalt make ready thine arrows upon thy strings against the face of them. Be thou exalted, Lord, in thine own strength: so we will sing and praise thy power.

Psalms 21.viii–xiii

Who is this King of glory? The Lord of hosts, he is the King of glory. Selah.

Psalms 24.x

He maketh wars to cease unto the end of the earth; he breaketh the bow, and cutteth the spear in sunder; he burneth the chariot in the fire.

Psalms 46.ix

They that dwell in the wilderness shall bow before him; and his enemies shall lick the dust.

Psalms 72.ix

I am for peace: but when I speak, they are for war.

Psalms 120.vii

A wise man is strong; yea, a man of knowledge increaseth strength. For by wise counsel thou shalt make thy war: and in multitude of counsellors there is safety.

Proverbs 24.v–vi

And he shall judge among the nations, and shall rebuke many people: and they shall beat their swords into plowshares, and their spears into pruninghooks: nation shall not lift up sword against nation, neither shall they learn war any more.

Isaiah 2.iv

They have healed also the hurt of the daughter of my people slightly, saying, Peace, peace; when there is no peace.

Jeremiah 6.xiv

But if the watchman see the sword come, and blow not the trumpet, and the people be not warned; if the sword come, and take any person from among them, he is taken away in his iniquity; but his blood will I require at the watchman's hand.

Ezekiel 33.vi

For they have sown the wind, and they shall reap the whirlwind: it hath no stalk: the bud shall yield no meal: if so be it yield, the strangers shall swallow it up.

Hosea 8.vii

Proclaim ye this among the Gentiles; Prepare war, wake up the mighty men, let all the men of war draw near; let them come up: Beat your plowshares into swords, and your pruninghooks into spears: let the weak say, I am strong.

Joel 3.ix–x

He that dasheth in pieces is come up before thy face: keep the munitions, watch the way, make thy loins strong, fortify thy power mightily. For the Lord hath turned away the excellency of Jacob, as the excellency of Israel: for the emptiers have emptied them out, and marred their vine branches. The shield of his mighty men is made red, the valiant men are in scarlet: the chariots shall be with flaming torches in the day of his preparation, and the fir trees shall be terribly shaken. The chariots shall rage in the streets, they shall justle one against another in the broad ways: they shall seem like torches, they shall run like the lightnings.

Nahum 2.i–iv

HOMER, 8th century BC

Tribeless, lawless, homeless is he, who loves horrid civil war.

Iliad, Bk IX

Of all things is there satiety, – of sleep, of love, of sweet singing, and of faultless dancing, with which one would much more readily satisfy his desire, than with war; . . .

Iliad, Bk XIII

The sword itself often incited a man to fight.

Odyssey, Bk XVI

SOLON of Athens, 638–559 BC

Learn to obey before you command.

Maxim

ALCAEUS, *c.* 600 BC

Brave men are a city's strongest tower of defence.

Attributed

HERACLITUS, 6th century BC

War is the father of all things.

Fragment

LAO TZU, 6th century BC

It is because arms are instruments of ill omen and there are Things that detest them that one who has the way does not abide by their use.

Tao Te Ching

Arms are instruments of ill omen, not the instruments of the gentleman. When one is compelled to use them, it is best to do so without relish. There is no glory in victory, and to glorify it despite this is to exult in the killing of men.

Tao Te Ching

When great numbers of people are killed, one should weep over them with sorrow. When victorious in war, one should observe the rites of mourning.

Tao Te Ching

One who excels as a warrior does not appear formidable;
One who excels in fighting is never roused in anger;

One who excels in defeating his enemy does not join issue;
One who excels in employing others humbles himself before them.
This is known as the virtue of non-contention;
This is known as making use of the efforts of others;
This is known as matching the sublimity of heaven.

Tao Te Ching

SIMONIDES of Ceos, 556–468 BC

We count it death to falter, not to die.

Epigram

CONFUCIUS *c.* 550–479 BC

Tzu-lu said, 'If you were leading the Three Armies whom would you take with you?'

The Master said, 'I would not take with me anyone who would try to fight a tiger with his bare hands or to walk across the [Yellow] River and die in the process without regrets. If I took anyone it would have to be a man who, when faced with a task, was fearful of failure and who, while fond of making plans, was capable of successful execution.'

The Analects, Bk VII

The Master said, 'The Three Armies can be deprived of their commanding officer, but even a common man cannot be deprived of his purpose.'

The Analects, Bk IX

Tzu-kung asked about government. The Master said, 'Give them enough food, give them enough arms, and the common people will have trust in you.'

Tzu-kung said, 'If one had to give up one of these . . . which should one give up first?'

'Give up arms.'

The Analects, Bk XII

SUN TZU, fl. 490 BC

The art of war is of vital importance to the State. It is a matter of life and death, a road either to safety or to ruin. Hence it is a subject of inquiry which can on no account be neglected.

The art of war, then, is governed by five constant factors, to be taken into account in one's deliberations, when seeking to determine the conditions obtaining in the field. These are: 1. The Moral Law; 2. Heaven; 3. Earth; 4. The Commander; 5. Method and discipline.

The Moral Law causes the people to be in complete accord with their ruler, so that they will follow him regardless of their lives, undismayed by any danger. Heaven signifies night and day, cold and heat, times and seasons. Earth comprises distances, great and small; danger and security; open ground and narrow passes; the chances of life and death. The Commander stands for the virtues of wisdom, sincerity, benevolence, courage and strictness. By Method and discipline are to be understood the marshalling of the army in its proper subdivisions, the gradations of rank among the officers, the maintenance of roads by which supplies may reach the army, and the control of military expenditure.

The Art of War, 490 BC

All warfare is based on deception. Hence, when able to attack, we must seem unable; when using our forces, we must seem inactive; when we are near, we must make the enemy believe we are far away; when far away, we must make him believe we are near. Hold out baits to entice the enemy. Feign disorder and crush him. If he is secure in all points, be prepared for him. If he is in superior strength, evade him.

The Art of War, 490 BC

There is no instance of a country having benefited from prolonged warfare.

The Art of War, 490 BC

In the practical art of war, the best thing of all is to take the enemy's country whole and intact; to shatter and destroy it is not so good. So, too, it is better to capture an army entire than to destroy it, to capture a regiment, a detachment or a company entire than to destroy them.

Hence to fight and conquer in all your battles is not supreme excellence; supreme excellence consists in breaking the enemy's resistance without fighting.

The Art of War, 490 BC

. . . The worst policy of all is to besiege walled cities.

The Art of War, 490 BC

There are three ways in which a ruler can bring misfortune upon his army: 1. By commanding the army to advance or to retreat, being ignorant of the fact that it cannot obey. This is called hobbling the army. 2. By attempting to govern an army in the same way he administers a kingdom, being ignorant of conditions which obtain in an army. This causes restlessness in the soldiers' minds. 3. By employing the officers of his army without discrimination, through ignorance of the military principle of adaptation to circumstances. This shakes the confidence of the soldiers.

The Art of War, 490 BC

The general who is skilled in defence hides in the most secret recesses of the earth; he who is skilled in attack flashes forth from the topmost heights of heaven.

The Art of War, 490 BC

To lift an autumn hair is no sign of great strength; to see sun and moon is no sign of sharp sight; to hear the noise of thunder is no sign of a quick ear. What the ancients called a clever fighter is one who not only wins, but excels in winning with ease.

The Art of War, 490 BC

Fighting with a large army under your command is nowise different from fighting with a small one; it is merely a question of instituting signs and signals.

The Art of War, 490 BC

Do not repeat the tactics that have gained you one victory, but let your methods be regulated by the infinite variety of circumstances.

The Art of War, 490 BC

Let your rapidity be that of the wind, your compactness that of the forest. In raiding and plundering be like fire, in immovability like a mountain. Let your plans be dark and impenetrable as night, and when you move, fall like a thunderbolt.

The Art of War, 490 BC

Camp in high places, facing the sun. Do not climb heights in order to fight. So much for mountain warfare.

The Art of War, 490 BC

When there is dust rising in a high column, it is the sign of chariots advancing; when the dust is low, but spread out over a wide area, it betokens the approach of infantry. When it branches out in different directions, it shows that parties have been sent to collect firewood. A few clouds of dust moving to and fro signify that the army is encamping.

The Art of War, 490 BC

The general who advances without coveting fame and retreats without fearing disgrace, whose only thought is to protect the country and do good service to his sovereign, is the jewel of the kingdom.

The Art of War, 490 BC

Knowledge of the enemy's dispositions can only be obtained from other men. Hence the use of spies, of whom there are five classes: 1. Local spies; 2. inward spies; 3. converted spies; 4. doomed spies; 5. surviving spies. When these five kinds of spy are all at work, none can discover the secret system. This is called 'divine manipulation of the threads'. It is the sovereign's most precious faculty.

The Art of War, 490 BC

ANONYMOUS

The general must be first in the toils and fatigue of the army. In the heat of summer he does not spread his parasol nor in the cold of winter don thick clothing. In dangerous places he must dismount and walk. He waits until the army's wells have been dug and only then drinks; until the army's food is cooked before he eats; until the army's fortifications have been completed, to shelter himself.

Ping Fa (Military Code), 5th century BC

SOPHOCLES, 496–406 BC

War prefers its victims young.

Scyrii (fragment 507)

ANONYMOUS

Peace is best secured by those who use their strength justly and who show they have no intention of submitting to injustice.

Address of the Corinthians to the Athenians, 433 BC

HERODOTUS, 484–424 BC

When you have passed this portion of the [Nile] in the space of forty days, you go on board another boat, and proceed by water for twelve days more, at the end of which time you reach a great city called Meroë, which is said to be the capital of the other Ethiopians. The only gods worshipped by the inhabitants are Jupiter and Bacchus; to whom great honours are paid. There is an oracle of Jupiter in the city, which directs the warlike expeditions of the Ethiopians; when it commands they go to war, and in whatever direction it bids them march, thither straightway they carry their arms.

Histories, *c.* 450 BC: Bk II

In what concerns war, their customs are the following. The Scythian soldier drinks the blood of the first man he overthrows in battle. Whatever number he slays, he cuts off all their heads, and carries them to the king; since he is thus entitled to a share of the booty, whereto he forfeits all claim if he does not produce a head. In order to strip the skull of its covering, he makes a cut round the head above the ears, and, laying hold of the scalp, shakes the skull out; then with the rib of an ox he scrapes the scalp clean of flesh, and softening it by rubbing between the hands, uses it thenceforth as a napkin.

Histories, *c.* 450 BC: Bk IV

EURIPIDES, 480–406 BC

The God of War hates the man who hesitates.

Heraclidae, *c.* 425 BC

HIPPOCRATES, late 5th century BC

War is the surgeon's most proper school.

Wounds To The Head, *c.* 415 BC

THUCYDIDES, *c.* 460–395 BC

Many will always judge the war in which they happen to be fighting the greatest in history.

History of the Peloponnesian Wars, *c.* 404 BC: Bk I

Wise men refuse to move until they are wronged, but brave men as soon as they are wronged go to war, and when there is a good opportunity make peace again. They are not intoxicated by military success; but neither will they tolerate injustice from a love of peace and ease.

History of the Peloponnesian Wars, *c.* 404 BC: Bk I

To famous men, all the earth is a sepulchre.

History of the Peloponnesian Wars, *c.* 404 BC: Bk II

That war is an evil is something that we all know, and it would be pointless to go on cataloguing all the disadvantages involved in it. No one is forced into war by ignorance, nor, if he thinks he will gain from it, is he kept out of it by fear. The fact is that one side thinks that the profits to be won outweigh the risks to be incurred, and the other side is ready to face danger rather than accept an immediate loss.

History of the Peloponnesian Wars, *c.* 404 BC: Bk IV

A collision at sea can ruin an entire day.

Attributed

WU CH'I, 430–381 BC

A general good at commanding troops is like one sitting in a leaking boat or lying beneath a burning roof: there is no time for the wise to offer counsel, or for the brave to be angry.

Quoted in Robert Debs Heinl Jr, *Dictionary of Military and Naval Quotations*, 1966

PLATO, 428–347 BC

Socrates: . . . The country which was enough to support the original inhabitants will be too small now, and not enough.
Glaucon: Quite true.
Socrates: Then a slice of our neighbour's land will be wanted by us for pasture and tillage, and they will want a slice of ours, if, like ourselves, they exceed the limit of necessity, and give themselves up to the unlimited accumulation of wealth?
Glaucon: That, Socrates, will be inevitable.
Socrates: And so we shall go to war, Glaucon. Shall we not?
Glaucon: Most certainly . . .
Socrates: Then, without determining as yet whether war does good or harm, thus much may we affirm, that now we have discovered war to be derived from causes which are also the causes of almost all the evils in States, private as well as public.

The Republic, *c.* 354 BC

Many victories have been and will be suicidal to the victors.

Laws, *c.* 352 BC

CHABRIAS, 410–357 BC

An army of deer led by a lion is more to be feared than an army of lions led by a deer.

Attributed

LYCURGUS of Sparta, 396–324 BC

A third *rhetra* of Lycurgus is mentioned, which forbids the Spartans to make war frequently with the same people, lest by constant practice they too should become warlike.

Plutarch, *Lives: Lycurgus*, *c.* AD 110

To brave men, the prizes that war offers are freedom and renown.
Attributed

DEMOSTHENES of Athens, 384–322 BC

Our country has been engaged in numerous wars, against democracies as well as oligarchies. You know this well enough. But the motive of each of these encounters is perhaps a thing on which no one reflects. What is that motive? Against popular governments it has either been a matter of private grievance which could not be solved by public negotiation, or of partition of land, of boundaries, of community feeling or of leadership. Against oligarchies none of these considerations has applied; it has been an ideological matter or a question of liberty. Indeed, I would not hesitate to maintain that I think it better that all Greeks should be our enemies under democracy than our friends under oligarchy.
'On The Liberty Of Rhodes', 351 BC

ARISTOTLE, 384–322 BC

Just as there are four chief divisions of the mass of the population – farmers, mechanics, shopkeepers and day labourers – so there are also four kinds of military force – cavalry, heavy infantry, light-armed troops and the navy. Where a territory is suitable for the use of cavalry, there is a favourable ground for the construction of a strong form of oligarchy: the inhabitants of such a territory need a cavalry force for security, and it is only men of large means who can afford to breed and keep horses. Where a territory is suitable for the use of heavy infantry, the next and less exclusive form of oligarchy is natural: service in the heavy infantry is a matter for the well-to-do rather than for the poor. Light-armed troops and the navy are drawn from the mass of the people and are thus wholly on the side of democracy – with the light-armed troops and naval forces as large as they are, the oligarchical side is generally worsted in any civil dispute.

This situation should be met, and remedied, by following the practice of some military commanders who combine and appropriate numbers of light-armed troops with the cavalry and infantry. The reason why the masses can defeat the wealthier classes, in any civil dissension, is that a light-armed and mobile force finds it easy to copy with a force of cavalry and heavy infantry. An oligarchy which builds up a force of light-armed men exclusively from the masses is thus only building up a challenge to itself.
Politics and the Athenian Constitution

War, as the saying goes, is full of false alarms.
Ethics, *c.* 340 BC: Bk III

MENCIUS, *c.* 370–290 BC

And so it is certain that a small country cannot contend with a great, that a few cannot contend with many; that the weak cannot contend with the strong.
Ya Sheng

POLYBIUS, 200–118 BC

A good general not only sees the way to victory; he knows when victory is beyond him.

Histories, c. 125 BC

Peace, with justice and honour, is the best and most profitable of possessions; but with shame and cowardice, it is the worst and most harmful of all.

Histories, c. 125 BC

Among those who are placed at the head of armies, there are some who are so deeply immersed in sloth and indolence that they lose all attention both to the safety of their country and their own. Others are immoderately fond of wine, so that their senses are always disordered by it before they sleep. Others abandon themselves to the love of women – a passion so infatuating that those whom it has once possessed will often sacrifice even their honour and their lives to the indulgence of it.

Histories, c. 125 BC

TERENCE (Publius Terentius Afer), 185–159 BC

Fortune favours the brave.

Pharmio, c. 161 BC

Marcus Tullius CICERO, 106–43 BC

Laws are dumb in time of war.

Pro Milone, 51 BC

Boundless money is the sinew of war.

Philippics V, 44 BC

An army is of little value in the field unless wise counsels prevail at home.

De Officiis, 44 BC

Yield, ye arms, to the toga.

De Officiis, 44 BC

All things are wretched in civil war.

Epistolae ad Familiares, 42 BC

ONOSANDER, 1st century BC

A shrewd general who sees that the enemy has many troops when he himself is about to engage with fewer will select, or rather make it his practice to find, localities where he may prevent an encircling movement of the enemy, either by arranging his army along the bank of a river, or, by choosing a mountainous district he will use the mountains themselves to block off those who wish to outflank him, placing a few men on the summits to prevent the enemy from climbing above the heads of the main army. Not alone does knowledge of military science play a part in this matter but luck as well: for it is necessary to have the luck to find such places; one cannot prepare the terrain for oneself. To choose the better positions, however, from those at hand, and to know which will be advantageous, is the part of the wise general.

The General, c. AD 52

When passing through the country of an ally, the general must order his troops not to lay hands on the country, nor to pillage and destroy; for every army under arms is ruthless, when it has the opportunity of exercising power, and the close view of desirable objects entices the thoughtless to greediness; while small reasons alienate allies or make them quite hostile. But the country of his enemy he should ruin and burn and ravage, for loss of money and shortage of crops reduce warfare as abundance nourishes it. But first he should let the enemy know what he intends to do; for often the expectation of impending terror has brought those who have been endangered, before they have suffered at all, to terms which they previously would not have wished to accept; but when they have once suffered a reverse, in the belief that nothing can be worse they are careless of future perils.

The General, c. AD 52

Soldiers do not enjoy being commanded by one who is not of good birth.

The General, c. AD 52

Gaius Julius CAESAR, 100–44 BC

It is the right of war for the conquerors to treat the conquered according to their pleasure.

Commentaries on the Gallic War, c. 51 BC

PUBLILIUS Syrus, mid-1st century BC

What is left when honour is lost?

Sententiae, c. 43 BC

Necessity knows no law except to conquer.

Sententiae, c. 43 BC

No pain is felt from a wound sustained in the moment of victory.

Sententiae, c. 43 BC

VIRGIL (Publius Vergilius Maro), 70–19 BC

Of arms and the man I sing.

Aeneid, 19 BC: Bk I

Being mad, I take to arms, even though there is little reason in arms.

Aeneid, 19 BC: Bk II

HORACE (Quintus Horatius Flaccus), 65–8 BC

My life's amusement have been just the same
Before and after standing armies came.

Satires, 30 BC: II.ii

It is sweet and befitting to die for one's country.
(Dulce et decorum est pro patria mori.)
Odes, 23 BC: III.ii

Octavius Caesar AUGUSTUS, 63 BC–AD 14

A battle or a war ought never to be undertaken, unless the prospect of gain outweighs the fear of loss. For men who pursue small advantages with no small hazard, resemble those who fish with a golden hook, the loss of which, if the line should happen to break, could never be compensated by all the fish they might take.
Quoted in Suetonius, *The Lives Of The Twelve Caesars*, *c.* 117

LIVY (Titus Livius), 59 BC–AD 17

It is the nature of a Roman to do and suffer bravely.
The History of Rome, from 29 BC: Bk II

To those to whom war is necessary it is just; and a resort to arms is righteous for those to whom no other hope remains.
The History of Rome, from 29 BC: Bk IX

Certain peace is preferable to a projected victory.
The History of Rome, from 29 BC

DIONYSIUS of Helicarnassus, fl. 20 BC

Only the brave enjoy noble and glorious deaths.
Antiquities of Rome, *c.* 20 BC

Albius TIBULLUS, 54–19 BC

Who was the first who forged the deadly blade?
Of ragged steel his savage soul was made.
Elegies, *c.* 19 BC: I.xi

SENECA, 4 BC–AD 65

Worse than war is the fear of war.
Thyestes

Of war men will ask its outcome, not its cause.
Hercules Furens

JESUS CHRIST, 4 BC?–AD 30

Blessed are the peacemakers: for they shall be called the children of God.
The Gospel According to St Matthew, late 1st century: 5.ix

But I say unto you, Love your enemies, . . .
The Gospel According to St Matthew, late 1st century: 5.xliv

Think not that I am come to send peace on earth: I came not to send peace, but a sword.

The Gospel According to St Matthew, late 1st century: 10.xxxiv

And Jesus answered and said unto them, Take heed that no man deceive you. For many shall come in my name, saying, I am Christ; and shall deceive many. And ye shall hear of wars and rumours of wars: see that ye be not troubled: for all these things must come to pass, but the end is not yet. For nation shall rise against nation, and kingdom against kingdom: and there shall be famines, and pestilences, and earthquakes, in divers places. All these are the beginning of sorrows. Then shall they deliver you up to be afflicted, and shall kill you: and ye shall be hated of all nations for my name's sake. And then shall many be offended, and shall betray one another, and shall hate one another. And many false prophets shall arise, and shall deceive many. And because iniquity shall abound, the love of many shall wax cold. But he that shall endure unto the end, the same shall be saved.

The Gospel According to St Matthew, late 1st century: 24.iv–xiii

Put up again thy sword into his place: for all they that take the sword shall perish with the sword.

The Gospel According to St Matthew, late 1st century: 26.lii

St PAUL THE APOSTLE, *c.* AD 10–65

Put on the whole armour of God, that ye may be able to stand against the wiles of the devil. For we wrestle not against flesh and blood, but against principalities, against powers, against the rulers of the darkness of this world, against spiritual wickedness in high places. Wherefore take unto you the whole armour of God, that ye may be able to withstand in the evil day, and having done all, to stand. Stand therefore, having your loins girt about with truth, and having on the breastplate of righteousness; And your feet shod with the preparation of the gospel of peace; Above all, taking the shield of faith, wherewith ye shall be able to quench all the fiery darts of the wicked. And take the helmet of salvation, and the sword of the Spirit, which is the word of God: . . .

Epistle to the Ephesians, *c.* AD 60: 6.xi–xvii

Flavius JOSEPHUS, AD 37–100

The Romans are certain of victory . . . because their exercises are battles without bloodshed, and their battles bloody exercises.

History of the Jewish War, AD 75–79

PLUTARCH, 46–120

Extraordinary rains pretty generally fall after great battles.

Lives: Marcus Cato, *c.* 110

No profession makes men such passionate lovers of peace as that of a man who farms his own land; for he retains enough of the warlike spirit to fight fiercely in defence of his own property, but has lost all desire to despoil and wrong his neighbours.

Lives: Numa, *c.* 110

For neither is avoidance of death blameable, if a man does not cling to life from dishonourable motives; nor is exposure to peril honourable, if it springs from carelessness of life. For this reason Homer always brings the most daring and warlike heroes into battle well and beautifully armed, . . .

Lives: Pelopidas, *c.* 110

That was a clever saying of Antisthenes, who answered, when he heard that Ismenias was a capital flute-player, 'But he must be a worthless man, for if he were not, he would not be such a capital flute-player!' and King Philip of Macedon, when his son played brilliantly on the harp at an entertainment, said to him, 'Are you not ashamed to play so well?'

Lives: Pericles, *c.* 110

Cornelius TACITUS, 56–120

Fortune can give no greater advantage than discord among the enemy.

A Treatise on the Manners of the Germans, AD 98

It is just as fitting for a soldier to be ignorant of some things, as that he should know others.

The Histories, *c.* 109, Bk I

In the course of the debate, Caecina Severus proposed, 'that no magistrate should go into any province accompanied by his wife.' He introduced this motion with a long preface, 'that he lived with his own in perfect concord, by her he had six children; and what he was establishing as a law for all, he had observed at home, having during forty years' service confined her to Italy. It was not, indeed, without cause established of old, that women should not be taken into allied nations or foreign. A train of women introduced luxury in peace, by their fears retarded war, and made a Roman army resemble in their march the stately progress of Barbarians. The sex was not only delicate and unequal to fatigue, but, if suffered, cruel, aspiring, and greedy of authority: that they walked among the troops, and had the centurions at their beck. A woman had lately presided at the exercises of the troops, and at the decursions of the legions. The senate themselves should consider that as often as any of the magistrates were charged with plundering the provinces, their wives were the chief offenders. To the ladies the most profligate in the province immediately attached themselves; by them all affairs were undertaken and transacted: that two persons were to be attended when they went out, and there were two courts of justice; but the orders of the ladies were the more peremptory and capricious. Such excesses were formally restrained by the Oppian and other laws; but now these barriers removed, women ruled all things, their families, the courts of justice, and, at length, even the armies.'

The Annals, *c.* 115, Bk III

Quintus Curtius RUFUS, 2nd century AD

Fear tempts men to fear the worst.

The Deeds of Alexander the Great, *c.* 180: IV

Flavius VEGETIUS Renatus, late 4th century

One excellent and general rule must be observed. If you intend to engage with your right wing only, it must be composed of your best troops. And the same method must be taken with respect to the left. Or, if you intend to penetrate the enemy's line, the wedges which you form for that purpose before your centre, must consist of the best disciplined soldiers. Victory in general is gained by a small number of men. Therefore the wisdom of a general appears in nothing more than in such choice of disposition of his men as is most consonant with reason and service.

De Re Militari, *c.* 378: Bk I

. . . It is not profusion of riches or excess of luxury that can influence our enemies to court or respect us. This can only be effected by fear of our arms.

De Re Militari, *c.* 378: Bk I

The young soldier should have a lively eye and carry his head erect; his chest should be broad, his shoulders muscular and brawny, his fingers long, his arms strong, his waist small, his build compact, his legs and feet wiry rather than fleshy. When all these qualities are found in a recruit, a little height may be dispensed with.

De Re Militari, *c.* 378: Bk I

Let who desires peace prepare for war.

De Re Militari, *c.* 378: Bk III

Famine makes greater havoc in an army than the enemy, and is more terrible than the sword.

De Re Militari, *c.* 378: Bk III

St AUGUSTINE of Hippo, 354–430

There are . . . certain exceptions to the law against killing, made by the authority of God himself. There are some whose killing God orders, either by a law, or by an express command to a particular person at a particular time. In fact one who owes a duty of obedience to the giver of the command does not himself 'kill' – he is an instrument, a sword in its user's hand. For this reason the commandment forbidding killing was not broken by those who have waged wars on the authority of God, or those who have imposed the death-penalty on criminals when representing the authority of the State in accordance with the laws of the State, the justest and most reasonable source of power.

City Of God, 427: I.xxii

It is a wicked prayer to ask to have someone to hate or to fear, so that he may be someone to conquer.

City Of God, 427: IV.xv

It rests with the decision of God in his just judgement and mercy either to afflict or console mankind, so that some wars come to an end more speedily, some more slowly.

City Of God, 427: V.xxii

. . . The wise man, they say, will wage just wars. Surely, if he remembers that he is a human being, he will rather lament the fact that he is faced with the necessity of waging just wars; for if they were not just, he would not have to engage in them, and consequently there would be no wars for a wise man. For it is the injustice of the opposing side that lays on the wise man the duty of waging wars; and this injustice is assuredly to be deplored by a human being, since it is the injustice of human beings, even though no necessity for war should arise from it.

City Of God, 427: XIX.vii

Anyone who joins me in an examination, however slight, of human affairs, and the human nature we all share, recognizes that just as there is no man who does not wish for joy, so there is no man who does not wish for peace. Indeed, even when men choose war, their only wish is for victory; which shows that their desire in fighting is for peace and glory. For what is victory but the conquest of the opposing side? And when that is achieved, there will be peace. Even wars, then, are waged with peace as their object, even when they are waged by those who are concerned to exercise their warlike prowess, either in command or in actual fighting. Hence it is an established fact that peace is the desired end of war.

City Of God, 427: XIX.xii

LI CHING, 571–649

Attacking does not merely consist in assaulting walled cities or striking at an army in battle array: it must include the art of assailing the enemy's mental equilibrium.

Quoted by Lionel Giles in his translation of Sun Tzu, *The Art of War*

The Prophet MOHAMMED, 570–632

War is prescribed to you: but from this you are averse.

Yet haply ye are averse from a thing, though it be good for you, and haply ye love a thing, though it be bad for you: and God knoweth; but ye, ye know not.

They will ask thee concerning war in the Sacred Month. Say: To war therein is bad, but to turn aside from the cause of God, and to have no faith in Him, and in the Sacred Temple, and to drive out its people, is worse in the sight of God; and civil strife is worse than bloodshed. They will not cease to war against you until they turn you from your religion, if they be able: but whoever of you shall turn from his religion and die an infidel, their works shall be fruitless in this world, and in the next: they shall be consigned to fire; therein to abide for aye.

But who believe, and who fly their country, and fight in the cause of God may hope for God's mercy: and God is gracious, Merciful.

The Koran, sura 2

The *Koran* is a manifesto to man, and a guidance, and a warning to the God-fearing!

And be not fainthearted, and be not sorrowful: for ye shall gain the upper hand if ye be believers.

If a wound hath befallen you, a wound like it hath already befallen others: we alternate these days of successes and reverses among men, that God may know those who have believed, and that He may take martyrs from among you, – but God loveth not the wrongful doers –

And that God may test those who believe, and destroy the infidels.

The Koran, sura 3

And when ye go forth to war in the land, it shall be no crime in you to cut short your prayers, if ye fear lest the infidels come upon you: Verily the infidels are your undoubted enemies!

And when thou, O apostle, shalt be among them, and shalt pray with them, then let a party of them rise up with thee, but let them take their arms; and when they shall have made their prostrations, let them retire to your rear: then let another party that hath not prayed come forward, and let them pray with you; but let them take their precautions and their arms.

Pleased would the infidels be for you to neglect your arms and your baggage, that they might turn upon you at once! And it shall be no crime in you to lay down your arms if rain annoy you, or if ye be sick. But take your precautions. Verily, God hath made ready a shameful torment for the infidels.

The Koran, sura 4

Slacken not in pursuit of the foe. If ye suffer, assuredly they suffer also as ye suffer; but ye hope from God for what they cannot hope! And God is Knowing, Wise!

The Koran, sura 4

When ye encounter the infidels, strike off their heads till ye have made a great slaughter among them, and of the rest make fast the fetters.

And afterwards let there be either free dismissals or ransomings, till the war hath laid down its burdens. Thus do. Were such the pleasure of God, he could himself take vengeance upon them: but He would rather prove the one of you by the other. And whoso fight for the cause of God, their works he will not suffer to miscarry;

He will vouchsafe them guidance, and dispose their hearts aright; And he will bring them into Paradise, of which he hath told them.

The Koran, sura 47

It shall be no crime on the part of the blind, the lame or the sick, if they go not out to fight. But whoso obey God and His Apostle, he shall bring him into the gardens 'neath which the rivers flow: but who so shall turn back, He will punish him with a sore punishment.

The Koran, sura 48

Hast thou not seen how thy Lord dealt with the army of the elephants?
Did he not cause their stratagem to miscarry?
And he sent against them birds in flocks,

Clay stones did they hurl down upon them,
And he made them like stubble eaten down.
The Koran, sura 105

TU MU, 803–52

The commander must acquaint himself beforehand with the maps so that he knows dangerous places for chariots and carts, where the water is too deep for wagons; passes in famous mountains, the principal rivers, the locations of highlands and hills; where rushes, forests and reeds are luxuriant; the road distances; the size of cities and towns; well-known cities and abandoned ones, and where there are flourishing orchards. All this must be known, as well as the way boundaries run in and out. All these facts the general must store in his mind.
Wei Liao Tzu, *c.* 845

A general unable to estimate his capabilities or comprehend the arts of expediency or flexibility when faced with the opportunity to engage the enemy will advance in a tumbling and hesitant manner, looking anxiously first to his right and then to his left, and be unable to produce a plan. Credulous, he will place confidence in unreliable reports, believing at one moment this, and at another that. As timorous as a fox in advancing and retiring, his groups will be scattered about. What is the difference between this and driving innocent people into boiling water or fire? Is this not exactly like driving cows and sheep to feed wolves or tigers?
Wei Liao Tzu, *c.* 845

The General is the Minister of Death, and cannot be responsible to the heavens above, to the earth below, to the enemy in front, or to the emperor in his rear.
Wei Liao Tzu, *c.* 845

TS'AO SUNG, *c.* 870–920

The hills and rivers of the lowland country
You have made your battle-ground.
How do you suppose the people who live there
Will procure 'firewood and hay'?
Do not let me hear you talking together
About titles and promotions;
For a single general's reputation
Is made out of ten thousand corpses.
'A Protest In The Sixth Year of Ch'ien Fu'

GENGHIS KHAN, *c.* 1162–1227

Happiness lies in conquering one's enemies, in driving them in front of oneself, in taking their property, in savoring their despair, in outraging their wives and daughters.
Quoted in Witold Rodzinski, *A History of China*, 1979

KUSUNOKI MASASHIGE, 1294–1336

The outcome of a battle depends not upon numbers, but upon the united hearts of those who fight.

Attributed saying

KUSUNOKI MASASUE, d. 1336

I should like to be reborn seven times into this world of men, so that I might destroy the enemies of the Court.

In the *Taiheiki*, *c.* 1370

Jean FROISSART, 1337–1410

It often happens, that fortune in war and love turns out more favourable and wonderful than could have been hoped for or expected.

Chronicles, 1369–1404: I.clxiii

Geoffrey CHAUCER, 1343–1400

First on the wal was peynted a forest,
In which ther dwelleth neither man ne beast,
With knotty, knarry, bareyne trees olde,
Of stubbes sharpe and hidouse to biholde,
In which ther ran a rumbel in a swough,
As though a storm sholde bresten every bough.
And dounward from an hille, under a bente,
Ther stood the temple of Mars armypotente,
Wroght al of burned steel, of which the entree
Was long and streit, and gastly for to see.
And therout came a rage and swich a veze
That it made al the gate for to rese.
The northern lyght in at the dores shoon,
For wyndowe on the wal ne was ther noon,
Thurgh which men myghten any light discerne.
The door was al of adamant eterne,
Yclenched overthwart and endelong
With iren tough; and for to make it strong,
Every pyler, the temple to sustene,
Was tonne-greet, of iren bright and shene.
Ther saugh I first the derke ymaginyng
Of Felonye, and al the compassyng;
The crueel Ire, reed as any gleede;
The pykepurs, and eek the pale Drede;
The smylere with the knyf under the cloke;
The shepne brennynge with the blake smoke;
The tresoun of the mordrynge in the bedde;
The open werre, with woundes al bibledde;

Contek, with blody knyf and sharp manace.
Al ful of chirkyng was that sory place.
The Canterbury Tales: The Knight's Tale, c. 1387: the 'Temple of Mars'.

And al above, depeynted in a tour,
Saugh I Conquest, sittynge in greet honour,
With the sharp swerd over his heed
Hangynge by a soutil twynes threed.
Depeynted was the slaughtre of Julius,
Of grete Nero, and of Antonius;
Al be that thilke tyme they were unborn,
Yet was hir deth depeynted ther-biforn
By manasynge of Mars, right by figure.
So was it shewed in that portreiture,
As is depenyted in the sterres above,
Who shal be slayn or elles deed for love.
The Canterbury Tales: The Knight's Tale, c. 1387

The statue of Mars upon a carte stood
Armed, and looked grym as he were wood;
And over his heed ther shynen two figures
Of sterres, that been cleped in scriptures,
That oon Puella, that oother Rubeus –
This god of armes was arrayed thus.
A wolf ther stood biforn hym at his feet
With eyen rede, and of a man he eet;
With soutil pencel depeynted was this storie
In redoutynge of Mars and of his glorie.
The Canterbury Tales: The Knight's Tale, c. 1387

Desiderius ERASMUS, 1467–1536

The most disadvantageous peace is better than the most just war.
Adagia, 1500

It is a sign of a soldier to believe that there is nothing left of man after death except a corpse.
Hippeas Anippos, 1517

Niccolò MACHIAVELLI, 1469–1527

. . . It is to be noted, that in taking a state the conqueror must arrange to commit all his cruelties at once, so as not to have to recur to them every day, and so as to be able, by not making fresh changes, to reassure people and win them over by benefiting them. Whoever acts otherwise, either through timidity or bad counsels, is always obliged to stand with knife in hand, and can never depend on his subjects, because they, owing to continually fresh injuries, are unable to depend upon him.
The Prince, 1513: viii

The chief foundations of all states, whether new, old, or mixed, are good laws and good arms. And as there cannot be good laws where there are not good arms, and where there are good arms there must be good laws, I will not now discuss the laws, but will speak of arms.

I say, therefore, that the arms by which a prince defends his possessions are either his own, or else mercenaries, or auxiliaries, or mixed. The mercenaries and auxiliaries are useless and dangerous, and if any one supports his state by the arms of mercenaries, he will never stand firm or sure, as they are disunited, ambitious, without discipline, faithless, bold amongst friends, cowardly amongst enemies, they have no fear of God, and keep no faith with men. Ruin is only deferred as long as the assault is postponed; in peace you are despoiled by them, and in war by the enemy. The cause of this is that they have no love or other motive to keep them in the field beyond a trifling wage, which is not enough to make them ready to die for you. They are quite willing to be your soldiers so long as you do not make war, but when war comes, it is either fly or decamp altogether.

The Prince, 1513: xii

A prince . . . should have no other aim or thought, nor take up any other thing for his study, but war and its organization and discipline, for that is the only art that is necessary to one who commands, and it is of such virtue that it not only maintains those who are born princes, but often enables men of private fortune to attain to that rank.

The Prince, 1513: xiv

For among other evils caused by being disarmed, it renders you contemptible; which is one of those disgraceful things which a prince must guard against, . . .

The Prince, 1513: xiv

[The prince] ought . . . never to let his thoughts stray from the exercise of war; and in peace he ought to practise it more than in war, which he can do in two ways: by action and by study. As to action, he must, besides keeping his men well disciplined and exercised, engage continually in hunting, and thus accustom his body to hardships; and meanwhile learn the nature of the land, how steep the mountains are, how the valleys debouch, where the plains lie, and understand the nature of rivers and swamps. To all this he should devote great attention. This knowledge is useful in two ways. In the first place, one learns to know one's country, and can better see how to defend it. Then by means of the knowledge and experience gained in one locality, one can easily understand any other that it may be necessary to observe; for the hills and valleys, plains and rivers of Tuscany, for instance, have a certain resemblance to those of other provinces, so that from a knowledge of the country in one province one can easily arrive at a knowledge of others. And that prince who is lacking in this skill is wanting in the first essentials of a leader; for it is this which teaches how to find the enemy, take up quarters, lead armies, plan battles and lay siege to towns with advantage.

The Prince, 1513: xiv

But when the prince is with his army and has a large number of soldiers under his control, then it is extremely necessary that he should not mind being thought cruel; for without this reputation he could not keep an army united or disposed to any duty.

The Prince, 1513: xvii

Without doubt princes become great when they overcome difficulties and opposition, and therefore fortune, especially when it wants to render a new prince great, who has greater need of gaining a great reputation than a hereditary prince, raises up enemies and compels him to undertake wars against them, so that he may have cause to overcome them, and thus climb up higher by means of that ladder which his enemies have brought him. There are many who think therefore that a wise prince ought, when he has the chance, to foment astutely some enmity, so that by suppressing it he will augment his greatness.

The Prince, 1513: xx

Only those defences are good, certain and durable, which depend on yourself alone and your own ability.

The Prince, 1513: xxiv

Many are now of opinion, My Dear Lorenzo, that no two things are more discordant and incongruous than a civil and a military life. Hence we see daily, that when a man goes into the army, he presently changes, not only his dress, but his behaviour, his company, his air, his manner of speaking, and affects to throw off all appearance of any thing that may look like common life and conversation. For a man that is to be ready equipped for any kind of violence, despises the formal garb of a Citizen, and thinks no dress fit for his purpose but a suit of armour: and as to civility and politeness, how can we expect to find any such thing in one who imagines it would make him look effeminate, and rather be a hindrance to his preferment than otherwise; especially when he thinks it his duty, instead of talking and looking like other men, to fright every body he meets with a volley of oaths, and a terrible pair of whiskers? This indeed gives some countenance to such an opinion, and makes people look upon a soldier as a different sort of creature from all other men.

The Art of War, 1520: Preface

Fabrizio: I would take some of the Roman arms and armour, and some of the German; half of my men should be armed with one, and half with the other; for if in every six thousand foot, three thousand were provided with swords and shields like the Romans, two thousand with pike, and one thousand with muskets, like the Germans, it would be sufficient for my purpose, . . . For I would place my Pikemen either in the front of the battle, or where I thought the enemy's cavalry were most likely to make an impression: and the others I would post in such a manner as to support the Pikemen, and push forwards when a way was opened for them: which I think would be a better method of arming and drawing up a body of Infantry, than any other that is used at present.

The Art of War, 1520: Bk II

Cosimo: What exercises would you recommend to such as are to compose our Infantry at present?
Fabrizio: Most of those which I have already mentioned, as running, wrestling,

leaping, carrying heavy arms, the use of the cross-bow, the long-bow, and the musket; which last is a new weapon, you know, but a very useful one. To these exercises I would accustom all the youth in the country, but those in particular who are destined to be Soldiers: and for this purpose I would set aside all holidays and idle times. I would likewise have them taught to swim, which is very necessary; for all rivers have not bridges over them, nor can they expect to find boats always ready to transport them; so that if your Soldier cannot swim, you will lose many advantages and opportunities of doing great things. The reason why the Romans exercised their youth in the Campus Martius was because the Tiber ran close to it; that so when they were fatigued they might refresh themselves in the river, and learn to swim.

The Art of War, 1520: Bk II

Fabrizio: If any Prince or Republic . . . would make their armies respectable, they should accustom their Generals to harangue the men, and the men to listen to their Generals.

The Art of War, 1520: Bk IV

Fabrizio: Flights of birds, and clouds of dust, have frequently discovered an enemy: for whenever the enemy approaches they must of course raise a great dust, which should serve you therefore as a sufficient warning to prepare for an attack. It has often happened likewise, that when Generals have observed a great number of pigeons or other birds, that usually fly together in flocks, suddenly take wing, and hover about in the air a great while without lighting again, they have suspected there was an Ambuscade thereabout; in which case, by sending out parties to discover it, they have sometimes escaped the enemy, and sometimes defeated them. – To avoid being drawn into an Ambuscade by the enemy, you must be very cautious of trusting to flattering appearances: for instance, if the enemy should leave a considerable booty in your way, you should suspect there is a hook in the bait; or if a strong party of the enemy should fly before a few of your men, or a few of their men should attack a strong party of your army; or if the enemy runs away on a sudden, without any apparent cause, it is reasonable to imagine there is some artifice in it, and that they know very well what they are about: so that the weaker and remiss they seem to be, the more it behoves you to be upon your guard, if you are to avoid falling into their Snares.

The Art of War, 1520: Bk V

Francesco GUICCIARDINI, 1483–1540

It is fighting against a great disadvantage to fight against those who have nothing to lose.

Storia d'Italia, 1564

Martin LUTHER, 1483–1546

War is the greatest plague that afflicts mankind; it destroys religion, it destroys nations, it destroys families. Any other scourge is preferable.

Table Talk, 1569

If Adam had seen in a vision the horrible instruments his children were to invent, he would have died of grief.

Table Talk, 1569

Pietro ARETINO, 1492–1556

Since both are slaves to desperation the art of war and the art of the courtesan are sisters.

Letter to Ambrogio Eusebio, November 1537

François RABELAIS, 1494–1533

Coin is the sinews of war.

Works, I.46

Niccolò Fontana TARTAGLIA, 1499–1557

Every gunner should know that it is good for him to drink, and eat a little meat, before he discharges any piece of artillery, otherwise the fumes of the saltpetre and brimstone may damage his brain.

Colloquies Concerning the Art of Shooting in Great and Small Pieces of Artillery, *c.* 1538

A gunner should be sober, wakeful, lusty, hardy, patient, cautious and quick-witted; he should also have keen eyesight, good judgement, know perfectly where to position himself in action, inflict the most damage on the enemy, and be least disturbed by him.

Colloquies Concerning the Art of Shooting in Great and Small Pieces of Artillery, *c.* 1538

Anonymous

The air was cut by purple sabres,
Into solid ruby the blades were turned.

Mogul war song, 16th century

The first shot is for the Devil, the second is for God, the third is for the King.

Gunners' saying, English 16th century

KHAYR AD-DIN (BARBAROSSA), d. 1546

Who rules the sea will shortly rule the land.

Attributed

William Cecil, Lord BURGHLEY, 1520–98

Soldiers in peace are like chimneys in summer.

Advice to His Son, *c.* 1555

Michel Eyquem de MONTAIGNE, 1533–92

So many goodly cities ransacked and razed; so many nations destroyed and made desolate; so infinite millions of harmless people of all sexes, states and ages massacred, ravaged, and put to the sword; and the richest, the fairest, the best part of the world overturned, and defaced for the traffic of pearls and pepper: Oh, base conquest!

Essays, 1588: iii

Peter WHITEHORNE, fl. 1573

These balles, after they are fired and well kindeled, and having blowen a little, must be quickly thrown, lest they hurte such as hurtle them.

Certayne Wayes for the Ordering of Soldiours in Battleray, 1573

Sir Francis DRAKE, 1540–96

The wings of man's life are plumed with the feathers of death.

Attributed

Barnaby RICH, 1540–1617

When service happeneth we disburthen the prisons of thieves, we rob the taverns and alehouses of tosspots and ruffians, we scour both town and country of rogues and vagabonds.

A Pathway To Military Practice, 1587

The Prince or Council sendeth down their warrant to certain Commissioners, of every such shire when they mind to have such a number of soldiers levied and appointed; the Commissioner he sendeth his precept to the High Constable of every Hundred; the High Constable of every Hundred, he giveth knowledge to every petty Constable of every Parish within his circuit that upon such a day, he must bring two or three able and sufficient men, to serve the Prince, before such Commissions, to such a place; the petty Constable when he perceiveth the wars are at hand, forseeing the toils, the infinite perils and troublesome travails that is incident to soldiers, is loth that any honest man should hazard himself amongst so many dangers, wherefore if within his office there hap to remain any idle fellow, some drunkard, or seditious quarreller, a privy picker or some such one as hath some skill in stealing a goose, these shall be presented to the service of the Prince.

A Right Excellent and Pleasant Dialogue between Mercury and an English Soldier, 1587

They say soldiers and lawyers could never thrive both together in one shire.

The Anatomy of Ireland, 1615

Miguel de CERVANTES, 1547–1616

Nothing is so subject to the inconstancy of fortune as war.

Don Quixote, 1605–15

Blessed be those happy ages that were strangers to the dreadful fury of those devilish instruments of artillery, whose inventor I am satisfied is now in hell, receiving the reward of his cursed invention, which is the cause that very often a cowardly base hand takes away the life of the bravest gentleman.

Don Quixote, 1605–15

Francis BACON, Viscount St Albans, 1561–1626

A just fear of imminent danger, though there be no blow given, is a lawful cause of war.

Essays, 1625: 'Of Empire'

Who shows mercy to an enemy, denies it to himself.

De Augmentis Scientiarum, 1623

William SHAKESPEARE, 1564–1616

Reignier: I am a soldier, and unapt to weep
Or to exclaim on Fortune's fickleness.

Henry VI Part One, *c.* 1593: Act V sc. iii

Hotspur: But I remember, when the fight was done,
When I was dry with rage and extreme toil,
Breathless and faint, leaning upon my sword,
Came there a certain lord, neat, and trimly dress'd,
Fresh as a bridegroom; and his chin, new reap'd,
Show'd like a stubble-land at harvest-home:
He was perfumed like a milliner,
And 'twixt his finger and his thumb he held
A pouncet-box, which ever and anon
He gave his nose and took't away again;
Who therewith angry, when it next came there,
Took it in snuff: and still he smil'd and talk'd;
And as the soldiers bore dead bodies by,
He call'd them untaught knaves, unmannerly,
To bring a slovenly unhandsome corpse
Betwixt the wind and his nobility.
With many holiday and lady terms
He question'd me; among the rest, demanded
My prisoners in your majesty's behalf.
I then all smarting with my wounds being cold,
To be so pester'd with a popinjay,
Out of my grief and my impatience
Answer'd neglectingly, I know not what,
He should, or he should not; for he made me mad
To see him shine so brisk and smell so sweet
And talk so like a waiting-gentlewoman
Of guns, and drums, and wounds, – God save the mark! –

And telling me the sovereign'st thing on earth
Was parmaceti for an inward bruise;
And that it was great pity, so it was,
This villainous saltpetre should be digg'd
Out of the bowels of the harmless earth,
Which many a good tall fellow had destroy'd
So cowardly; and but for these vile guns,
He would himself have been a soldier.

Henry IV Part One, 1597: Act I sc. iii

Falstaff: If I be not ashamed of my soldiers, I am a soused gurnet. I have misused the king's press damnably. I have got, in exchange of a hundred and fifty soldiers, three hundred and odd pounds. I press me none but good householders, yeomen's sons; inquire me out contracted bachelors, such as had been asked twice on the banns; such a commodity of warm slaves, as had as lief hear the devil as a drum; such as fear the report of a caliver worse than a struck fowl or a hurt wild-duck. I pressed me none but such toasts-and-butter, with hearts in their bellies no bigger than pins' heads, and they have bought out their services; and now my whole charge consists of ancients, corporals, lieutenants, gentlemen of companies, slaves as ragged as Lazarus in the painted cloth, where the glutton's dogs licked his sores; and such as indeed were never soldiers, but discarded unjust serving-men, younger sons to younger brothers, revolted tapsters and ostlers trade-fallen, the cankers of a calm world and a long peace; ten times more dishonourable ragged than an old-faced ancient: and such have I, to fill up the rooms of them that have bought out their services, that you would think that I had a hundred and fifty tattered prodigals, lately come from swine-keeping, from eating draff and husks. A mad fellow met me on the way and told me I had unloaded all the gibbets and pressed the dead bodies. No eye hath seen such scare-crows.

Henry IV Part One, 1597: Act IV sc. ii

Falstaff: And this same half-faced fellow, Shadow, give me this man: he presents no mark to the enemy; the foeman may with as great aim level at the edge of a penknife.

Henry IV Part Two, 1598: Act III sc. ii

Jaques: Then a soldier,
Full of strange oaths, and bearded like the pard,
Jealous in honour, sudden and quick in quarrel,
Seeking the bubble reputation
Even in the cannon's mouth.

As You Like It, 1599: Act II sc. vii

Gower: Why, 'tis a gull, a fool, a rogue, that now and then goes to the wars to grace himself at his return into London under the form of a soldier. And such fellows are perfect in the great commanders' names, and they will learn you by rote where services were done; at such and such a sconce, at such a breach, at such a convoy; who came off bravely, who was shot, who disgraced, what terms the enemy stood on; and this they con perfectly in the phrase of war, which they trick up with new-tuned oaths: and what a beard of the general's cut and a horrid suit of the camp will do among foaming bottles and ale-washed wits, is wonderful to be thought on. But you must learn to know such slanders of the age, or else you may be marvellously mistook.

Henry V, 1599: Act III sc. vi

Williams: But if the cause be not good, the king himself hath a heavy reckoning to make; when all those legs and arms and heads, chopped off in a battle, shall join together at the latter day, and cry all, 'We died at such a place'; some swearing, some crying for a surgeon, some upon their wives left behind them, some upon the debts they owe, some upon their children rawly left. I am afeard there are few die well that die in battle; for how can they charitably dispose of any thing when blood is their argument? Now, if these men do not die well, it will be a black matter for the king that led them to it, whom to disobey were against all proportion of subjection.

Henry V, 1599: Act IV sc. i

King Henry: But this is not so: the king is not bound to answer the particular endings of his soldiers, the father of his son, nor the master of his servant; for they purpose not their death when they purpose their services. Besides, there is no king, be his cause never so spotless, if it come to the arbitrement of swords, can try it out with all unspotted soldiers. Some, peradventure, have on them the guilt of premeditated and contrived murder; some, of beguiling virgins with the broken seals of perjury; some, making wars their bulwark, that have before gored the gentle bosom of peace with pillage and robbery. Now, if these men have defeated the law and outrun native punishment, though they can outstrip men, they have no wings to fly from God: war is his beadle, war is his vengeance; so that here men are punished for before-breach of the king's laws in now the king's quarrel: where they feared the death they have borne life away, and where they would be safe they perish. Then, if they die unprovided, no more is the king guilty of their damnation than he was before guilty of those impieties for the which they are now visited. Every subject's duty is the king's; but every subject's soul is his own.

Henry V, 1599: Act IV sc. i

The painful warrior famoused for fight,
After a thousand victories once foil'd,
Is from the book of honour razed quite,
And all the rest forgot for which he toil'd: . . .

Sonnet XXV, *c.* 1599

Caesar: Cowards die many times before their deaths:
The valiant never taste of death but once.
Of all the wonders that I yet have heard,
It seems to me most strange that men should fear;
Seeing that death, a necessary end,
Will come when it will come.

Julius Caesar, *c.* 1600: Act II sc. ii

Antony: And Caesar's spirit, raging for revenge,
With Ate by his side come hot from hell,
Shall in these confines with a monarch's voice
Cry 'Havoc!' and let slip the dogs of war.
Julius Caesar, *c.* 1600: Act III sc. i

Rosencrantz: Many wearing rapiers are afraid of goose-quills.
Hamlet, 1602: Act II sc. ii

Iago: But he, as loving his own pride and purposes,
Evades them, with a bombast circumstance
Horribly stuff'd with epithets of war; . . .
Othello, 1604: Act I sc. i

Othello: . . . 'tis the soldiers' life,
To have their balmy slumbers wak'd with strife.
Othello, 1604: Act II sc. iii

Ventidius: Who does i' the wars more than his captain can
Becomes his captain's captain; and ambition,
The soldier's virtue, rather makes choice of loss
Than gain which darkens him.
Antony and Cleopatra, 1607: Act III sc. i

2nd Servant: Why, then we shall have a stirring world again. This peace is nothing but to rust iron, increase tailors, and breed ballad-makers.
1st Servant: Let me have war, say I; it exceeds peace as far as day does night; it's spritely, waking, audible, and full of vent. Peace is a very apoplexy, lethargy; mulled, deaf, sleepy, insensible; a getter of more bastard children than war's a destroyer of men.
2nd Servant: 'Tis so: and as war, in some sort, may be said to be a ravisher, so it cannot be denied but peace is a great maker of cuckolds.
1st Servant: Ay, and it makes men hate one another.
Coriolanus, 1608: Act IV sc. v

Thomas DEKKER, 1570?–1632

And though mine arm should conquer twenty worlds,
There's a lean fellow beats all conquerors.
Old Fortunates, 1600

John DONNE, 1572–1631

As peace is of all goodness, so war is an emblem, a hieroglyphic, of all misery.
Devotions, 1622: xii

Any man's death diminishes me, because I am involved in Mankind; and therefore never send to know for whom the bell tolls; it tolls for thee.
Devotions, 1662: xvii

Robert FLUDD, 1574–1637

Of the English I would say, they stand by one another, and are often seen to die together. They are spirited enough and have plenty of boldness. . . . They are brave in fighting and have plenty of resolution. They are the best of archers. Abroad, if things are going in favour of the enemy, they preserve good military discipline; and at all times are jovial yet quick in pride.

1617, quoted in John Laffin, *Tommy Atkins*, 1966

Robert BURTON, 1577–1640

How much more cruel the pen may be than the sword.

Anatomy of Melancholy, 1621

John FLETCHER, 1579–1625

O great corrector of enormous times,
Shaker of o'er-rank states, thou grand decider
Of dusty and old titles, that heal'st with blood
The earth when it is sick, and cure'st the world
O' the pleurisy of people.

Two Noble Kinsmen, most probably written in collaboration with Shakespeare, *c.* 1613

Philip MASSINGER, 1583–1640

If e'er my son
Follow the war, tell him it is a school
Where all the principles tending to honour
Are taught, if truly followed.

The Maid of Honour, 1627

Hugo GROTIUS (Huigh de Groot), 1583–1645

War is not one of the acts of life. On the contrary it is a thing so vile that nothing but the highest necessity or the deepest charity can make it right.

De Jure Belli ac Pacis, 1625

Peace made on any condition whatever is, by all means, to be kept, on account of the sacredness of good faith, of which we speak; and care must be taken not only to avoid perfidy but anything which may exasperate the mind of the other party.

De Jure Belli ac Pacis, 1625

If someone is commanded to join in a war, as often happens, knowing that the war is unlawful, then they should abstain. That God is to be obeyed rather than men not only have the Apostles decreed but Socrates as well.

De Jure Belli ac Pacis, 1625

And even if there can be no questioning the justice of a war it does not seem equitable that unwilling Christians should be compelled to become soldiers.

De Jure Belli ac Pacis, 1625

If . . . an enemy comes with the intention not to spare the lives of his adversary's subjects when he might spare them, then those subjects have the right to defend themselves by the law of nature, which no law of nations can deprive them of.
De Jure Belli ac Pacis, 1625

MIYAMOTO MUSASHI, 1584–1645

It is said that the warrior's is the twofold Way of pen and sword, and he should have a taste for both Ways. Even if a man has no natural ability he can be a warrior by sticking assiduously to both divisions of the Way. Generally speaking the Way of the warrior is resolute acceptance of death. Although not only warriors but priests, women, peasants and lowlier folk have been known to die readily in the cause of duty or out of shame, this is a different thing. The warrior is different in that studying the Way of strategy is based on overcoming men. By victory gained in crossing swords with individuals, or enjoining battle with large numbers, we can attain power and fame for ourselves or our lord. This is the virtue of strategy.
A Book Of Five Rings, *c.* 1643

Students of the Ichi school Way of strategy should train from the start with the sword and long sword in each hand. This is a truth: when you sacrifice your life, you must make fullest use of your weaponry. It is false not to do so, and to die with a weapon yet undrawn.
A Book Of Five Rings, *c.* 1643

If he attains the virtue of the long sword, one man can beat ten men. Just as one man can beat ten, so a hundred men can beat a thousand, and a thousand can beat ten thousand. In my strategy, one man is the same as ten thousand, so this strategy is the complete warrior's craft.
A Book Of Five Rings, *c.* 1643

One of the virtues of the bow is that you can see the arrows in flight and correct your aim accordingly, whereas gunshot cannot be seen. You must appreciate the importance of this.
A Book Of Five Rings, *c.* 1643

You should not have a favourite weapon. To become over familiar with one weapon is as much a fault as not knowing it sufficiently well. You should not copy others, but use weapons which you can handle properly. It is bad for commanders and troopers to have likes and dislikes. These are things you must learn thoroughly.
A Book Of Five Rings, *c.* 1643

Adopt a stance with the head erect, neither hanging down, nor looking up, nor twisted. Your forehead and the space between your eyes should not be wrinkled. Do not roll your eyes nor allow them to blink, but slightly narrow them. With your features composed, keep the line of your features straight with a feeling of slightly flaring your nostrils. Hold the line of the rear of the neck straight: instil vigour into your hairline, and in the same way from the shoulders down through your entire body. Lower both shoulders and, without the buttocks jutting out, put strength in your legs from the knees to the tips of your toes. Brace your abdomen so that you do not bend at the hips. Wedge your companion sword in your belt against your abdomen, so that your belt is not slack – this is called 'wedging in'.

In all forms of strategy it is necessary to maintain the combat stance in everyday life and to make your everyday stance your combat stance. You must research this well.

A Book Of Five Rings, *c.* 1643

To stab at the face means, when you are in confrontation with the enemy, that your spirit is intent on stabbing at his face, following the line of the blades with the point of your long sword. If you are intent on stabbing at his face, his face and body will become rideable. When the enemy becomes as if rideable, there are various opportunities for winning. You must concentrate on this. When fighting and the enemy's body become rideable, you can win quickly, so you ought not to forget to stab at the face.

A Book Of Five Rings, *c.* 1643

Today is victory over yourself of yesterday; tomorrow is your victory over lesser men.

A Book Of Five Rings, *c.* 1643

Nathaniel FIELD, 1587–1633

As many are soldiers that are not captains
So many are captains that are not soldiers.

'A Woman Is A Weather-Cock', 1609

Thomas HOBBES, 1588–1679

Hereby it is manifest that during the time men live without a common Power to keep them all in awe, they are in that condition which is called War, and such a war as is of every man, against everyman. For War consisteth not in Battle only, of the act of fighting; but in a tract of time, wherein only the Will to contend by battle is sufficiently known: and therefore the notion of time is to be considered in the nature of War, as it is in the nature of Weather. For as the nature of Foul Weather lieth not in a shower or two of rain, but in an inclination thereto of many days together, so the nature of war consisteth not in actual fighting, but in the known disposition thereto during all the time there is no assurance to the contrary. All other time is Peace.

Whatsoever, therefore, is consequent to a time of War, where everyman is Enemy to every man, the same is consequent to the time wherein men live without other security than what their own strength and their own invention shall furnish them withal. In such condition there is no place for Industry, because the fruit thereof is uncertain: and consequently no Culture of the Earth; no Navigation, nor use of the commodities that may be imported by the Sea, no commodious Building, no Instruments of moving – and removing – such things as require much force; no knowledge of the face of the Earth; no account of Time, no Arts, no Letters; no Society; and, which is worst of all, continual fear and danger of violent death; and the life of man solitary, poor, nasty, brutish, and short.

Leviathan, 1651

In the nature of man, we find three principal causes of quarrel. First, competition; secondly, diffidence; thirdly, glory. The first maketh man invade for gain; the second, for safety; the third, for reputation.

Leviathan, 1651

Force, and fraud, are in war the two cardinal virtues.

Leviathan, 1651

It is a general rule of reason, that every man ought to endeavour Peace, as far as he has hope of obtaining it; and when he cannot obtain it, that he may seek and use all helps and advantages of War.

Leviathan, 1651

Covenants without swords are but words.

Leviathan, 1651

Francis QUARLES, 1592–1644

Our God and soldier we alike adore,
When at the break of ruin, not before;
After deliverance, both alike requited,
Our God forgotten, and our soldiers slighted.

Epigram, 1640

Robert HAYMAN, d. 1631?

Peace makes plenty, plenty makes pride.
Pride breeds quarrel, and quarrel brings war:
War brings spoil, and spoil poverty,
Poverty patience, and patience peace:
So peace brings war, and war brings peace.

Quodlibets: 'The World's Whirlegigge', 1630

George HERBERT, 1593–1633

He that will have peace, God gives him war.

Outlandish Proverbs, 1640

For want of a nail the shoe is lost; for want of a shoe the horse is lost; for want of a horse the rider is lost; for want of a rider the battle is lost; for want of a battle the kingdom is lost.

Outlandish Proverbs, 1640

One sword keeps another in the sheath.

Jacula Prudentum, 1651

James HOWELL, 1594–1666

Soldiers and travellers lie by authority.
Proverbs, 1659

Oliver CROMWELL, 1599–1658

A man-of-war is the best ambassador.
Attributed

Baltasar GRACIAN Y MORALES, 1601–58

You may be obliged to wage war, but you are not obliged to use poisoned arrows.
The Art of Worldly Wisdom, 1647

William HOOKE, 1601–78

A day of battle is a day of harvest for the Devil.
Sermon at Taunton, Massachusetts, 1640

John MILTON, 1608–74

Peace hath her victories
No less renowned than war.
'To The Lord General Cromwell', 1652

To overcome in Battle, and subdue
Nations, and bring home spoils with infinite
Man-slaughter, shall be held the highest pitch
Of human Glory, and for Glory done
Of triumph, to be styl'd great Conquerors,
Patrons of Mankind, Gods, and Sons of Gods,
Destroyers rightlier call'd and Plagues of men.
Thus Fame shall be achiev'd, renown on Earth,
And what most merits fame in silence hid.
Paradise Lost, 1667: Bk XI

Raimondo MONTECUCULI, 1609–80

Without the pike, which is the queen of foot arms, any infantry attacked by a squadron or battalion of pike cannot remain entire or offer long resistance.
c. 1674, quoted in M. le Blond, *Elémens de Tactique*, 1758

Marshal TURENNE, Henri de la Tour d'Auvergne, 1611–75

Speak to me of a general who has made no mistakes in war, and you speak of one who has seldom made war.
Quoted in Sir William Napier, *History of the War in the Peninsula*, 1862

Few sieges, and many combats.
Maxim

God is always on the side of the big battalions.
Attributed

Anonymous

Good worship, cast your eyes
Upon a soldier's miseries:
Let not my lean cheeks, I pray,
Your bounty from a soldier stay,
But like a noble friend
Some silver lend,
And Jove will pay you in the end.
I pray your worship think of me,
That am what I seem to be,
No rooking rascal, nor no cheat,
But a soldier in every way compleat:
I have wounds to show
That prove it so.
'The Maunding Soldier, or The Fruit of War is Beggary', *c.* 1652

Samuel BUTLER, 1612–80

For his Religion, it was fit
To match his learning and his wit:
'Twas Presbyterian true blue,
For he was of that stubborn crew
Of errant saints, whom all men grant
To be the true church militant:
Such as do build their faith upon
The holy text of pike and gun;
Decide all controversy by
Infallible artillery;
And prove their doctrine orthodox
By apostolic blows and knocks;
Call fire, and sword, and desolation
A godly-thorough-Reformation,
Which always must be carried on,
And still be doing, never done: . . .
Hudibras, 1663: Part I

There's but the twinkling of a star
Between a man of peace and war.
Hudibras, 1663: Part II

Duc de ROCHEFOUCAULD, François, 1613–80

Courage in soldiers is a dangerous profession they follow to earn their living.
Maxims, 1665

Sir James TURNER, 1615–86

The most honourable death for a delinquent soldier is beheading, the next to that is shooting, with pistols if he be a horseman, with muskets if a foot soldier.

Pallas Armata, 1683

Those who condemn the profession or art of soldiery smell rank of Anabaptism and Quakery.

Pallas Armata, 1683

Richard LOVELACE, 1618–56

Tell me not, sweet, I am unkind,
That from the nunnery
Of thy chaste breast and quiet mind,
To wars and arms I fly.

True, a new mistress now I chase,
The first foe in the field;
And with a stronger faith embrace
A sword, a horse, a shield.

Yet this inconstancy is such
As you too shall adore;
I could not love thee, dear, so much,
Loved I not honour more.

'To Lucasta, On Going to the Wars', 1648

Jean de LA FONTAINE, 1621–95

There is no road of flowers leading to glory.

Fables, 1668–94: x

Blaise PASCAL, 1623–62

The cause of some going to war, and of others avoiding it, is the same desire in both, attended with different views.

Pensées, 1670

John DRYDEN, 1631–1700

Peace itself is war in masquerade.

'Absalom and Achitophel', 1682

War seldom enters but where wealth allures.

'The Hind And The Panther', 1687

The trumpet's loud clangor
Excites us to arms,
With shrill notes of anger
And mortal alarms.

The double, double beat
Of the thundering drum
Cries Hark! the foe is come!
'A Song For St Cecilia's Day', 1687

Raw in the fields, the rude militia swarms,
Mouths without hands, maintain'd at vast expense.
In peace a charge, in war a weak defense.
'Cymon and Iphigenia', 1699

Benedict de SPINOZA, 1632–77

Minds are conquered not by arms, but by love and magnanimity.
Ethics, 1677

George Savile, Marquess of HALIFAX, 1633–95

To the question, What shall we do to be saved in this world? there is no answer but this, Look to your moat.
A New Model At Sea, 1694

Gentlemen shall not be capable of bearing office at sea, except they be tarpaulins too; that is to say, except they are so trained up by a continued habit of living at sea, that they have a right to be admitted free denizens of Wapping. When a gentleman is preferred at sea, the tarpaulin is very apt to impute it to friend or favour: but if that gentleman hath before his preferment passed through all the steps that lead to it, so that he smelleth as much of pitch and tar, as those that were swaddled in sailing-cloth; his having an escutcheon will be far from doing him any harm.
A New Model At Sea, 1694

The third part of an army must be destroyed, before a good one can be made out of it.
Works

Jean-Baptiste RACINE, 1639–99

No pay, no Swiss.
Les Plaideurs, 1668

William PENN, 1644–1718

No man is fit to command another that cannot command himself.
No Cross, No Crown, 1669

Anonymous

Some talk of Alexander and some of Hercules,
Of Conon and Lysander and some of Miltiades,
But of all the world's brave heroes there's none can compare
With a tow row row row row
To the British Grenadier.

None of those ancient heroes e'er saw a cannon ball,
Or knew the force of powder to slay their foes with all,
But our brave boys do know it and banish all their fears,
With a tow row row, etc.

When'er we are commanded to storm the palisades
Our leaders march with fuses and we with hand grenades.
We throw them from the glacis about our enemies' ears,
With a tow row row, etc.

The god of war was pleased and great Bellona smiles,
To see these noble heroes of our British Isles,
And all the gods celestial descending from their spheres,
With a tow row row, etc.

Then let us crown a bumper and drink a health to those
Who carry caps and pouches, that wear the louped clothes.
May they and their commanders live happy all their years,
With a tow row row, etc.

British Grenadiers (song), late 17th century

YAMAMOTO TSUNENORI, 17th century

There is no way to describe what a warrior should do other than that he should adhere to the Way of the warrior [Bushido]. I find that all men are negligent of this. There are few men who can quickly reply to the question, 'What is the Way of the warrior?' This is because they do not know in their hearts. From this we can see that they do not follow the Way of the warrior. By the Way of the warrior is meant death. It means choosing death whenever there is a choice between life and death. It means nothing more than this. It means to see things through, being resolved.

Ha Gakure, 17th century

Lord GALWAY, Massue de Ruvigny, 1648–1720

Good engineers are so scarce, that one must bear with their humours and forgive them because we cannot be without them.

Dispatch from Spain, 1704

WILLIAM III of England, 1650–1702

Every bullet has its billet.

Quoted in John Wesley, *Journal*, 6th June 1765

There is one certain means by which I can be sure never to see my country's ruin: I will die in the last ditch.

Attributed

John Churchill, Duke of MARLBOROUGH, 1650–1722

No soldier can fight unless he is properly fed on beef and beer.

Attributed

Charles DAVENANT, 1656–1714

War is quite changed from what it was in the days of our forefathers; when in a hasty expedition and a pitch'd field, the matter was decided by courage; but now the whole art of war is in a manner reduced to money; and nowadays that prince who can best find money to feed, clothe and pay his army, not he that hath the most valiant troops, is surest to success and conquest.

Essay on Ways and Means of Supplying the War, 1695

Jacques-François PUYSÉGUR, 1656–1743

Firearms, and not cold steel, now win battles.

Principles and Rules of the Art of War, 1748

Anne Finch, Countess of WINCHILSEA, 1661–1721

Trail all your pikes, dispirit every drum,
March in a slow procession from afar,
Be silent, ye dejected Men of War!
Be still the hautboys, and the flute be dumb!
Display no more, in vain, the lofty banner;
For see! where on the bier before ye lies
The pale, the fall'n, the untimely Sacrifice
To your mistaken Shrine, to your false idol Honour.

The Soldier's Death, *c.* 1713

Daniel DEFOE, 1661–1731

Now it is frequent to have armies of 50,000 men a side standing at bay within sight of one another, and spend the whole campaign in dodging – or, as it is genteely called, observing one another – and then march off into winter quarters.

An Enquiry Upon Projects, 1697

PRINCE François EUGÈNE de Savoie-Carignan, 1663–1736

It was a saying of Prince Eugene, 'that if a General did not wish to fight, he had nothing more to do than hold a council of war.'

Frederick the Great, *Military Instruction To His Generals*, *c.* 1745

Jonathan SWIFT, 1667–1745

War is the child of pride, and pride the daughter of riches.

The Battle of the Books, 1697

The motives that may engage a wise prince or state in war, I take to be one or more of these: either to check the overgrown power of some ambitious neighbour; to recover what has been unjustly taken from them; to revenge some injury they have received, which all political casuists allow; to assist some ally in a just quarrel, or, lastly, to defend themselves when they are invaded. In all these cases, the writers upon politics admit a war to be justly undertaken.

The last is, what has usually been called *pro aris et focis*; where no expense or endeavour can be too great, because all we have is at stake, and consequently our utmost force to be exerted; and the dispute is soon determined, either in safety or in utter destruction. But in the other four, I believe, it will be found that no monarch or commonwealth did ever engage beyond a certain degree; never proceeding so far as to exhaust the strength and substance of their country by anticipation and loans, which, in a few years, must put them in a worse condition than any they could reasonably apprehend from those evils, for the preventing of which they first entered into the war; because this would be to run into real infallible ruin only in hope to remove what might, perhaps, appear so, by a probable speculation.

The Conduct of the Allies, 1711

The soldier smiling hears the widow's cries,
And stabs the son before the mother's eyes.
With like remorse his brother of the trade,
The butcher, fells the lamb beneath his blade.

'On Dreams', 1724

Giambattista VICO, 1668–1744

Wherever a people has grown savage in arms, so that human laws no longer have their place, the only effective means of reducing it is religion.

The New Science, 1725–44

Richard STEELE, 1672–1729

There is no weapon too short for a brave man.

In the *Guardian*, 25th August 1713

William SOMERVILLE, 1675–1742

. . . The chase, the sport of kings;
Image of war, without its guilt.

The Chase, 1735

George FARQUAR, 1678–1707

If any gentlemen, soldiers or others have a mind to serve Her Majesty, and pull down the French King; if any prentices have severe masters, any children have undutiful parents; if any servants have too little wages, or any husband too much wife, let them repair to the noble Sergeant Kite, at the sign of the Raven in this good town of Shrewsbury, and they shall receive present relief and entertainment. Gentlemen, I don't beat my drum here to ensnare or inveigle any man; for you must know, Gentlemen, that I am a man of honour! Besides, I don't beat up for common soldiers: No, I list only grenadiers – *grenadiers*, gentlemen!

The Recruiting Officer, 1704

I take a bold Step, a rakish toss, a smart Cock, and an impudent air to be the principal ingredients in the Composition of a Captain.

The Recruiting Officer, 1704

Anonymous

Grenadoes are small shells, concave Globes or hollow Balls, some made of Iron, some of Tin, others of Wood, and even of Pasteboard; but most commonly of Iron, because the splinters of it do most Execution. This Globe or Hollow is fill'd with Fine Powder, and into the touch-hole of it is stuck a Fuze, full of powder, beaten and tempered with charcoal dust, that it may not flash, but burn gently till it come to the Charge. These are thrown by hand into places where Men stand thick, and particularly into Trenches and Lodgments the enemy make, and are of good use.

A Military Dictionary, by An Officer, 1702

Alexander POPE, 1688–1744

Whose bosom beats not in his country's cause?

Prologue to Addison's *Cato*, 1713

Heroes are much the same, the point's agreed,
From Macedonia's madman to the Swede;
The whole strange purpose of their lives to find,
Or make, an enemy of all mankind!

Essay on Man, 1733–34

Charles-Louis de Secondat MONTESQUIEU, 1689–1755

The true strength of a prince consists not so much in his ability to conquer his neighbours, but in their inability to conquer him.

The Spirit of the Laws, 1748

Philip Dormer Stanhope, LORD CHESTERFIELD, 1694–1773

That silly, sanguine notion, which is firmly entertained here, that one Englishman can beat three Frenchmen, encourages, and has sometimes enabled, one Englishman, in reality to beat two.

Letters, 7th February 1749

Even war is pusillanimously carried on in this degenerate age; quarter is given; towns are taken, and the people spared; even in a storm, a woman can hardly hope for the benefit of a rape.

Letters, 12th January 1757

One of the greatest difficulties in civil war is, that more art is required to know what should be concealed from our friends than what ought to be done against our enemies.

Miscellaneous Pieces, 1777

VOLTAIRE (François-Marie Arouet), 1694–1778

Men appear to prefer to ruin one another's fortunes, and to cut each other's throats over a few miserable villages, than to extend the means of human happiness.

Philosophical Dictionary, 1764

It is forbidden to kill; therefore only those murderers are punished who do not kill in company, and to the sound of trumpets.

Philosophical Dictionary, 1764

Allow soldiers to marry and they will no longer desert. Bound to their families they will also be bound to their country.

Philosophical Dictionary, 1764

Hermann Maurice, Comte DE SAXE, 1696–1750

Many commanding generals only spend their time on the day of battle in making their troops march in a straight line, in seeing that they keep their proper distances, in answering questions which their aides de camp come to ask, in sending them hither and thither, and in running about incessantly themselves. In short, they try to do everything and, as a result, do nothing. They appear to me like men with their heads turned, who no longer see anything and who are only able to do what they have done all their lives, which is to conduct troops methodically under the orders of a commander. How does this happen? It is because very few men occupy themselves with the higher problems of war. They pass their lives drilling troops and believe that this is the only branch of the military art. When they arrive at the command of armies they are totally ignorant, and, in default of knowing what should be done, they do what they know.

Reveries, 1757

I have seen very good colonels become very bad generals. I have known others who were great takers of villages, excellent for manoeuvers within an army, but who outside of that, were not even able to lead a thousand men in war, who lost their heads completely and were unable to make any decision.

Reveries, 1757

I do not favor pitched battles, especially at the beginning of a war, and I am convinced that a skillful general could make war all his life without being forced into one. Nothing so reduces the enemy to absurdity as this method; nothing advances affairs better. Frequent small engagements will dissipate the enemy until he is forced to hide from you.

Reveries, 1757

The circumstances of war are sensed rather than explained.

Reveries, 1757

Benjamin FRANKLIN, 1706–90

There never was a good war or a bad peace.

Letter to Josiah Quincy, September 1773

Five thousand balloons, capable of raising two men each, could not cost more than five ships of the line; and where is the prince who can afford so to cover his country with troops for its defence as that 10,000 men descending from the clouds might not in many cases do an infinite deal of mischief before a force could be brought together to repel them?

Letter to Jan Ingenhousz, 1784

Sir John PRINGLE, 1707–82

The *lues Venerea* and the itch are infections of a different kind. The first, not being more incident to soldiers than to other men, I shall pass over. But the latter, being so frequent in camp, barracks and hospitals, may be reckoned one of the military diseases.

Observations on Diseases of the Army, 1768

Samuel JOHNSON, 1709–84

The festal Blazes, the triumphal Show,
The ravish'd Standard, the captive Foe,
The Senate's Thanks, the Gazette's pompous Tale,
With Force resistless o'er the Brave prevail.

'The Vanity of Human Wishes', 1749

Among the calamities of war may be justly numbered the diminution of the love of truth by the falsehoods which interests dictate and credulity encourages. A peace will equally leave the warrior and the relater of wars destitute of employment; and I know not whether more is to be dreaded from streets filled with soldiers accustomed to plunder, or from garrets filled with scribblers accustomed to lie.

The Idler, 11th November 1758

What would be the security of the good, if the bad could at pleasure invade them from the sky? Against an army sailing through the clouds neither walls, nor mountains, nor seas could afford any security. A flight of northern savages might hover in the wind and light at once with irresistible violence upon the capital of a fruitful region that was rolling under them.

Rasselas, 1759

An officer is much more respected than any other man who has as little money.

In conversation with James Boswell, 3rd April 1776

Every man thinks meanly of himself for not having been a soldier.

In conversation with James Boswell, 10th April 1778

It is mutual cowardice that keeps us in peace. Were one-half of mankind brave, and one-half cowards, the brave would always be beating the cowards. Were all brave, they would lead a very uneasy life; all would be continually fighting: but being all cowards, we go on very well.

In conversation with James Boswell, 28th April 1778

Thomas Augustine ARNE, 1710–78

Britain's best bulwarks are her wooden walls.

'Britain's Best Bulwarks', *c.* 1760

Captain JENEY, mid 18th century

I know that straight swords deal a more deadly blow, but they are not nearly as effective in combat. If you need convincing, I will explain the mechanism of the two kinds of weapon. When he is at a full gallop and a cavalryman attacks his enemy with the point, he will invariably pierce him. But then he must stop his horse and break off his part in the action, so as to pull the sword out. During an equivalent amount of time a dragoon with a curved sabre will have wounded three or four enemy, without having to stop his horse or stop fighting. The enemy will not be mortally wounded, but at least they will be disabled, which is what we ought to look for in battle.

Le Partisan, ou l'art de faire la petite guerre, 1759

Jean-Jacques ROUSSEAU, 1712–78

The right of conquest has no basis except in the right of might.

The Social Contract, 1762

FREDERICK THE GREAT (Frederick II of Prussia), 1712–86

Don't forget your great guns, which are the most respectable arguments of the rights of kings.

Letter to his brother, Prince Henry, April 1721

It is the fashion these days to make war, and presumably it will last a while yet.

Letter to Voltaire, 1742

Every officer should bear in mind that the true point of honour alone *may* prove the foundation of his fortune: he should therefore constantly regard it as the *main spring* of all his actions, and be fully persuaded, that it is the only road by which he can arrive at those honourable distinctions which are the just reward of real desert. The true point of honour will ever induce him, not only to avoid all imputation of *blame*, but also to endeavour to procure esteem by his own personal merit: it is this, which will convince him that it is not only necessary to signalize himself when an occasion offers, but that it is the duty of every intelligent Officer to search and be on the look-out for such opportunity.

Particular Instruction of the King of Prussia to the Officers of His Army, *c.* 1745: Preface

Nothing injures an Officer more in the opinion of a soldier than the suspicion of fraud: this is often induced by a passion for Play, the fatal consequences of which too often extend much farther: his money had much better be expended in the purchase of good arms or good horses, on which the life and reputation of a man so often depend.

Particular Instruction of the King of Prussia to the Officers of His Army, *c.* 1745: Preface

If an [cavalry] Officer wish to signalize himself by engaging in an affair with an enemy of superior force, he should propose to himself an attack on a quarter that is occupied by hussars, as being the most agreeable, easy, and certain way of acquiring reputation.

Particular Instruction of the King of Prussia to the Officers of His Army, *c.* 1745: xii

An army is composed for the most part of idle and inactive men, and unless the General has a constant eye upon them, and obliges them to do their duty, this artificial machine, which with greatest care cannot be made perfect, will very soon fall to pieces, and nothing but the bare idea of a disciplined army will remain.

Military Instruction from the King of Prussia to his Generals, *c.* 1745: i

A General, who with other nations would be regarded as being rash or half mad, would with us be only acting by established rules.

Military Instruction from the King of Prussia to his Generals, *c.* 1745: i

Protection must be afforded to the sutlers, especially in a country whose inhabitants are fled, and where provisions cannot be had for money. At such a time we are justified in not being over nice with respect to the peasantry.

Military Instruction from the King of Prussia to his Generals, *c.* 1745: iii

Convoys for the army should ever be followed by herds of cattle, for the support and nourishment of the soldier.

Military Instruction from the King of Prussia to his Generals, *c.* 1745: iii

Our cavalry, being designed to act with velocity, can only be made use of on a plain, whereas the infantry may be employed in every possible variety of ground. Their fire is for defence, and their bayonet for attack.

Military Instruction from the King of Prussia to his Generals, *c.* 1745: vii

It is only repeating an ancient maxim of war to say, 'that he who divides his force, will be beaten in detail'. If you are about to give battle, strain every nerve to get together as many troops as you possibly can, for they never can be employed to better purpose.

Military Instruction from the King of Prussia to his Generals, *c.* 1745: x

The best stratagem is, to lull the enemy into security at the time when the troops are about to disperse and go into winter quarters, so that by retiring, you may be enabled to advance on them to some good purpose. With this view, the troops should be so distributed, as to assemble again very readily, in order to force the enemy's quarters. If this measure succeed, you may recover in a fortnight the misfortunes of a whole campaign.

Military Instruction from the King of Prussia to his Generals, *c.* 1745: xi

There is yet another way to gain intelligence of the enemy when milder methods fail, though I confess it to be an harsh and cruel practice. We find out a rich citizen who has a large family and good estate, and allow him a man who understands the language of the country dressed as a servant, whom we force him to take along with him into the enemy's camp, as his valet or coachman, under pretence of complaining of some injuries which he has received; he is to be threatened also at the same time, that if he does not return after a certain period, and bring the man with him, that his houses shall be burned, and his wife and children hacked to pieces.

Military Instruction from the King of Prussia to his Generals, c. 1745: xii

If glory were my only object, I would never make war but in my own country, by reason of its manifold advantages, as every man *there* acts as a spy, nor can the enemy stir a foot without being betrayed.

Military Instruction from the King of Prussia to his Generals, c. 1745: xiv

For my own part I am determined never to attack by night, on account of the confusion which darkness necessarily occasions, and because the major part of the soldiery require the eye of their Officers, and the fear of punishment, to induce them to do their duty.

Military Instruction from the King of Prussia to his Generals, c. 1745: xxii

So many men are lost in the attacks on villages, that I have vowed never to undertake them, unless obliged by absolute necessity, for you run the hazard of losing the flower of your infantry.

Military Instruction from the King of Prussia to his Generals, c. 1745: xxii

I would burn every village which is at the head or on the wings of the army, if the wind did not drive the smoke into the camp.

Military Instruction from the King of Prussia to his Generals, c. 1745: xxii

The most certain way of insuring victory is, to march briskly and in good order against the enemy, always endeavouring to gain ground.

Military Instruction from the King of Prussia to his Generals, c. 1745: xxii

Generals are much more to be pitied than is generally imagined. All the world condemns them unheard. They are exposed in the gazette to the judgement of the meanest plebeian, whilst amongst many thousand readers there is not one perhaps who knows how to conduct the smallest detachment.

Military Instruction from the King of Prussia to his Generals, c. 1745: xxiv

It must be observed here, that we are not to trust too much in the security of mountains, but remember the proverb, 'that wherever a goat can pass, a soldier can'.

Military Instruction from the King of Prussia to his Generals, c. 1745: xxvii

A well-disciplined regiment is as well-behaved as a community of monks.

Testament Politique, written 1752

It seems to me that in all periods there have been two basic methods of conducting war, and each has its own advantages. The Romans followed one way, and all the peoples of Asia and Africa have followed the other. The first procedure supposes exact discipline and gains permanent conquest. The second is carried out through raids, and passes in an instant.

Works, 1846–57: vol. XVII

Long service and good service are the same thing.
Attributed

When an officer comes on parade, every man in the barrack square should tremble in his boots.
Attributed

Diplomacy without arms is like music without instruments.
Attributed

Laurence STERNE, 1713–68

The history of a soldier's wound beguiles the pain of it.
Tristram Shandy, 1759

A soldier, cried my uncle Toby, interrupting the corporal, is no more exempt from saying a foolish thing, Trim, than a man of letters – But not so often, an' please your honour, replied the corporal
Tristram Shandy, 1759

Emmerich de VATTEL, 1714–87

At the present time war is carried on by regular armies; the people, the peasantry, the townsfolk play no part in it, and generally have nothing to fear from the sword of the enemy.
The Law of Nations, 1758

Luc de Clapier, Marquis de VAUVENARGUES, 1715–47

Vice foments war: virtue fights. Were there no virtue, we should have peace forever.
Reflections And Maxims, 1746

What we dignify with the name of peace is really only a short truce, in accordance with which the weaker party renounces his claims, whether just or unjust, until such time as he can find an opportunity to assert them with the sword.
Reflections And Maxims, 1746

Claude Adrien HELVETIUS, 1715–71

Discipline is simply the art of making the soldiers fear their officers more than the enemy.
De l'Esprit, 1758

David GARRICK, 1717–79

Hearts of oak are our ships,
Jolly tars are our men,
We always are ready, steady, boys, steady,
We'll fight and we'll conquer again and again.
'Hearts Of Oak', 1759

Horace WALPOLE, 1717–97

Soldiers only make risings and riots; they are generals and colonels who make rebellions.

Letter to Mrs Carter, 25th July 1789

Henry LLOYD, 1723–85

Land forces are nothing. Marines are the only species of troops proper for this nation: they alone can defend and protect it effectively.

A Political and Military Rhapsody on the Invasion and Defence of Great Britain and Ireland, 1770

Adam SMITH, 1723–90

The security of every society must always depend, more or less, upon the martial spirit of the great body of the people . . . Martial spirit alone, and unsupported by a well-disciplined army, would not perhaps be sufficient for the defence and security of any society. But where every citizen had the spirit of a soldier, a smaller standing army would surely be necessary.

The Wealth of Nations, 1776

Defence is superior to opulence.

The Wealth of Nations, 1776

Immanuel KANT, 1724–1804

There is no state whose leader does not wish to secure permanent peace by conquering all the universe . . .

Perpetual Peace, 1795

James WOLFE, 1727–59

. . . Experience shows me that, in affairs depending on vigour and despatch, the Generals should settle their plan of operations, so that no time may be lost in idle debate and consultations when the sword should be drawn; that pushing on smartly is the road to success, and more particularly so in affairs of this nature; that nothing is to be reckoned an obstacle to your undertaking which is not found really to be so upon trial; that in war something must be allowed to chance and fortune, seeing it is in its nature hazardous, and an option of difficulties; that the greatness of an object should come under consideration, opposed to the impediments that lie in the way; that the honour of one's country is to have some weight; and that, in particular circumstances and times, the loss of a thousand men is rather an advantage to a nation than otherwise, seeing that gallant attempts raise its reputation and make it respectable; whereas the contrary appearances sink the credit of a country, ruin the troops, and create infinite uneasiness and discontent at home.

Letter to Major Rickson, 5th November 1757

Edmund BURKE, 1729–97

Civil wars strike deepest of all into the manners of the people. They vitiate their politics; they corrupt their morals; they pervert even the natural taste and relish of equity and justice. By teaching us to consider our fellow citizens in a hostile light, the whole body of our nation becomes gradually less dear to us.

Letter to the Sheriffs of Bristol, 3rd April 1777

. . . A rapacious and licentious soldiery. . . .

Speech, 1st December 1783

An armed, disciplined body is, in its essence, dangerous to liberty. Undisciplined, it is ruinous to society.

Speech on the Army Estimates, 1790

John SCOTT, 1730–83

I hate that drum's discordant sound,
Parading round, and round, and round:
To thoughtless youth it pleasure yields,
And lures from cities and from fields,
To sell their liberty for charms
Of tawdry lace, and glittering arms;
And when Ambition's voice commands,
To march, and fight, and fall, in foreign lands.

I hate that drum's discordant sound,
Parading round, and round, and round:
To me it talks of ravag'd plains,
And burning towns, and ruin'd swains,
And mangled limbs, and dying groans,
And widows' tears, and orphans' moans;
And all that Misery's hand bestows,
To fill the catalogue of human woes.

'The Drum', *c.* 1770

Alexander Vasilevich SUVOROV, 1730–1800

Fire seldom but accurately. Thrust the bayonet with force. The bullet misses, the bayonet doesn't. The bullet's an idiot, the bayonet's a fine chap. Stab once, and throw the Turk off the bayonet. Bayonet another, bayonet a third; a real warrior will bayonet half a dozen and more. Keep a bullet in the barrel. If three should run at you, bayonet the first, shoot the second, and lay out the third with your bayonet.

In Philip Longworth, *The Art of Victory*, 1963

[On storming a town:] Break through the abatis, throw hurdles over the wolf traps, jump over the palisade, throw down your fascines, go down into the ditch, place the ladders. Marksmen, cover the column. Fire at the heads appearing on the battlements. Columns, jump across the wall onto the parapet. Stick to the parapet. Form a line; put a guard on the powder magazines. Open the gates for the cavalry. The enemy runs into the town, turn his guns against him. Fire hard down the streets. Give them a lively bombardment. Don't go after them until ordered down into the town. Then cut up the enemy on the streets. Cavalry, cut them down. Don't go into the houses. Hit them in the open: storm the places where they have gathered, occupy the square and mount a guard.

In Philip Longworth, *The Art of Victory*, 1963

There is an enemy greater than the hospital: the damned fellow who 'doesn't know'. The hint-dropper, the riddle-poser, the deceiver, the word-spinner, the prayer-skimper, the two-faced, the mannered, the incoherent. The fellow who 'doesn't know' has caused a great deal of harm.

In Philip Longworth, *The Art of Victory*, 1963

Francis GROSE, 1731–91

A Commander in Chief is to the army under his command what the soul is to the body: it can neither think nor act without him; and in short, is as perfect a non-entity without its commander, as a wife is without her husband. You must, therefore, through pure goodwill and affection for your troops, take care of your own sacred person, and never expose it to any dangers. You have not arrived at this rank without knowing the folly of knocking one's head against a post, when it can be avoided.

Advice to the Officers of the British Army, 1782, sometimes ascribed to John Williamson: 'To General Officers, commanding in Chief'

As you probably did not rise to your present distinguished rank by your own merit, it cannot reasonably be expected that you should promote others on that score.

Advice to the Officers of the British Army, 1782: 'To General Officers, commanding in Chief'

If upon service you have any ladies in your camp, be valiant in your conversation before them. There is nothing pleases the ladies more than to hear of storming breaches, attacking the covert-way sword in hand, and such-like martial exploits. This, however, I only recommend at night over the bottle; it cannot be expected that you should be so valiant and bloodthirsty, upon mature deliberation, the next morning; that, indeed, would be murder in cold blood.

Advice to the Officers of the British Army, 1782: 'To General Officers, commanding in Chief'

Nothing is so commendable as generosity to the enemy. To follow up a victory, would be taking advantage of his distress. It will be sufficient therefore for you to shew, that you can beat him when you think proper. Besides, giving your enemy too severe a drubbing may put an end to the war, before you have feathered your nest handsomely, and provided for your relations and dependents.

Advice to the Officers of the British Army, 1782: 'To General Officers, commanding in Chief'

When an inferior general is to be detached upon an expedition, be sure to send the most ignorant, and inexperienced; for he stands most in need of a lesson.

Advice to the Officers of the British Army, 1782: 'To General Officers, commanding in Chief'

Keep two lancets: a blunt one for the soldiers, and a sharp one for the officers: this will be making a proper distinction between them.

Advice to the Officers of the British Army, 1782: 'To the Surgeon'

When on leave of absence, never come back to your time; as that might cause people to think that you had nowhere to stay, or that your friends were tired of you.

Advice to the Officers of the British Army, 1782: 'To Young Officers'

You are first painter to the regiment, and your principal duty is, to instruct the young academicians in the art. Your pencils indeed are none of the softest; and though you do not aim at the grace of *Raphael*, or the grandeur of *Michael Angelo*, yet you must not yield to *Titian* in colouring.

Advice to the Officers of the British Army, 1782: 'To the Drum-Major'

William COWPER, 1731–1800

But war's a game, which were their subjects wise,
Kings would not play at.

The Task, 1785

George WASHINGTON, 1732–99

To place any dependence upon militia is assuredly resting upon a broken staff.

Letter to the President of Congress, 24th September 1776

An army formed of good officers moves like clockwork.

Letter to the President of Congress, 24th September 1776

To be prepared for war is one of the most effectual means of preserving peace.

First Annual Address to Congress, 8th January 1790

To lean on the militia is to lean on a broken reed. Being familiar with the use of the musket they will fight under cover, but they will not attack or stand in the open field.

Quoted in E. M. Lloyd, *A Review of the History of Infantry*, 1908

Edward GIBBON, 1737–94

. . . As long as mankind shall continue to bestow more liberal applause on their destroyers than on their benefactors, the thirst of military glory will ever be the vice of the most exalted characters.

The History Of The Decline And Fall Of The Roman Empire, 1776–88: i

The power of the sword is more sensibly felt in an extensive monarchy, than in a small community. It has been calculated by the ablest politicians that no state, without being soon exhausted, can maintain above a hundredth part of its members in arms and idleness. But although this relative proportion may be uniform, the influence of the army over the rest of society will vary according to the degree of its positive strength. The advantages of military science cannot be exerted, unless a proper number of soldiers are united in one body, and actuated by one soul. With a handful of men, such a union would be ineffectual; with an unwieldy host, it would be impracticable; and the powers of the machine would be alike destroyed by the extreme minuteness, or the excessive weight, of its springs. To illustrate this observation, we need only reflect, that there is no superiority of natural strength, artificial weapons, or acquired skill, which could enable one man to keep in constant subjection one hundred of his fellow-creatures: the tyrant of a single town or small district, would soon discover that a hundred armed followers were a weak defence against ten thousand peasants or citizens; but an hundred thousand well-disciplined soldiers will command, with despotic sway, ten millions of subjects; and a body of ten or fifteen thousand guards will strike terror into the most numerous populace that ever crowded the streets of an immense capital.

The History Of The Decline And Fall Of The Roman Empire, 1776–88: iv

Drunkenness, the most illiberal, but not the most dangerous, of *our* vices, was sometimes capable, in a less civilized state of mankind, of occasioning a battle, a war, or a revolution.

The History Of The Decline And Fall Of The Roman Empire, 1776–88: ix

. . . The experience of the world, from China to Britain, has exposed the vain attempt of fortifying any extensive tract of country. An active enemy, who can select and vary his points of attack, must, in the end, discover some feeble spot, or some unguarded moment. The strength, as well as the attention, of the defenders is divided; and such are the blind effects of terror on the firmest troops, that a line broken in a single place is almost instantly deserted. The fate of the wall which Probus erected [*c.* AD 278], may confirm the general observation. Within a few years of his death it was overthrown by the Alemanni. Its scattered ruins, universally ascribed to the power of the Daemon, now serve only to excite the wonder of the Swabian peasant.

The History Of The Decline And Fall Of The Roman Empire, 1776–88: xii

. . . The historian may content himself with an observation, which seems to be justified by experience, that man has much more to fear from the passions of his fellow-creatures, than from the convulsions of the elements.

The History Of The Decline And Fall Of The Roman Empire, 1776–88: xxvi

The attentive study of the military operations of Xenophon, or Caesar, or Frederic, when they are described by the same genius which conceived and executed them, may tend to improve (if such improvement can be wished) the art of destroying the human species.

The History Of The Decline And Fall Of The Roman Empire, 1776–88: xxxv

Thomas PAINE, 1737–1809

He who is the author of a war lets loose the whole contagion of hell and opens a vein that bleeds a nation to death.

The American Crisis, 1776–83

War involves in its progress such a train of unforeseen and unsupposed circumstances that no human wisdom can calculate the end. It has but one thing certain, and that is to increase taxes.

Prospects On The Rubicon, 1787

To make war with those who trade with us is like setting a bulldog upon a customer at the shop-door.

The Age of Reason, 1794

Jacques Antoine Hyppolite, Comte de GUIBERT, 1743–90

What I want to avoid is that my supplies should command me.

Essay on Tactics, 1770

Thomas JEFFERSON, 1743–1826

A naval force can never endanger our liberties, nor occasion bloodshed; a land force would do both.

Letter to James Monroe, 1786

If there be one principle more deeply rooted than any other in the mind of every American, it is that we should have nothing to do with conquest.

Letter to William Short, 1791

The spirit of this country [the United States] is totally adverse to a large military force.

Letter to Chandler Price, 1807

The creator has not thought proper to mark those in the forehead who are of the stuff to make good generals. We are first, therefore, to seek them blindfold, and let them learn the trade at the expense of great losses.

Letter to General Bailey, February 1813

A little rebellion now and then is a good thing, and as necessary in the political world as storms in the physical.

Works, vol. VI

John Paul JONES, 1747–92

A Captain of the Navy ought to be a man of Strong and well connected Sense with a tolerable education, a Gentleman as well as a Seaman both in Theory and Practice.

Letter to Joseph Hewes, 19th May 1776

The rules of conduct, the maxims of action, and the tactical instincts that serve to gain small victories may always be expanded into the winning of great ones with suitable opportunity; because in human affairs the sources of success are ever to be found in the fountains of quick resolve and swift stroke; and it seems to be a law inflexible and inexorable that he who will not risk cannot win.

Letter to Vice-Admiral Kersaint, 1791

Robert JACKSON, 1750–1827

The value of the American people as soldiers consists in skill in the use of fire-arms. That skill, it is presumed, arises from the practice of firing at birds and wild beasts in the rivers, ponds, and woods, of an extensive continent.

A View of the Formation, Discipline and Economy of Armies, 1845

Joseph JOUBERT, 1754–1824

The noise of the drum drives out thought; for that very reason it is the most military of instruments.

Pensées, 1842

Charles-Maurice de TALLEYRAND-Périgord, 1754–1838

Avoid too much zeal!

Attributed

War is much too serious a business to be left to military men.

Attributed

Alexander HAMILTON, 1755–1804

The steady operations of war against a regular and disciplined army can only be successfully conducted by a force of the same kind.

The Federalist, 1787: XXV

William BLAKE, 1757–1827

Nought can deform the human race
Like to the armour's iron brace.

'Auguries of Innocence', 1789

Horatio, Lord NELSON, 1758–1805

Frigates are the eyes of a fleet.

Letter, 1804

Robert BURNS, 1759–96

The sodger's wealth is honour.

'The Soldier's Return', 1793

Ye hypocrites! are these your pranks?
To murder men, and give God thanks?
Desist for shame! Proceed no further:
God won't accept your thanks for Murther.

'On Thanksgiving for a National Victory', 1794

Jean Paul RICHTER, 1763–1825

A battlefield is at once the playroom of all the gods and the dancehall of all the furies.

Titan, 1803

William COBBETT, 1763–1835

I like soldiers, as a class in life, better than any other description of men. Their conversation is more pleasing to me; they have generally seen more than other men; they have less of vulgar prejudices about them. Amongst soldiers less than amongst any other description of men, have I observed the vices of lying and hypocrisy.

The Progress of a Ploughboy to a Seat in Parliament, 1834

John Quincy ADAMS, 1767–1848

Wherever the standard of freedom and independence has been or shall be unfurled, there will be America's heart, her benedictions, and her prayers. But she goes not abroad in search of monsters to destroy.

Speech in Washington DC, 4th July 1821

NAPOLEON BONAPARTE (Napoleon I), 1769–1821

First I engage, then I see what can be done.

Remark made during the Italian war of 1796

In war, moral considerations account for three-quarters, the balance of actual forces only for the other quarter.

Letter, 27th August 1808

Plans of campaign may be modified, ad infinitum, according to circumstances, the genius of the general, the character of the troops, and the features of the country.

Military Maxims, selected and translated by Colonel D'Aguilar, 1831: ii

When the conquest of a country is undertaken by two or three armies, which have each their separate line of operation, until they arrive at a point fixed upon for their concentration, it should be laid down as a principle, that the junction should never take place near the enemy, because the enemy in uniting his forces, may not only prevent it, but beat the armies in detail.

Military Maxims, selected and translated by Colonel D'Aguilar, 1831: iv

All wars should be governed by certain principles, for every war should have a definite object, and be conducted according to the rules of art. War should only be undertaken with forces proportioned to the obstacles to be overcome.

Military Maxims, selected and translated by Colonel D'Aguilar, 1831: v

At the commencement of a campaign, to *advance* or *not to advance*, is a matter for grave consideration, but when once the offensive has been assumed, it must be sustained to the last extremity. However skilful the manoeuvres, a retreat will always weaken the *morale* of an army, because in losing the chances of success, these last are transferred to the enemy. Besides retreats always cost more men and *matériel*, than the most bloody engagements; with this difference, that in battle, the enemy's loss is nearly equal to your own, whereas in retreat, the loss is on your side only.

Military Maxims, selected and translated by Colonel D'Aguilar, 1831: vi

A general in chief should ask himself frequently in the day, what should I do if the enemy's army appeared now in my front, or on my right, or my left? If he have any difficulty in answering these questions, he is ill posted, and should seek to remedy it.

Military Maxims, selected and translated by Colonel D'Aguilar, 1831: viii

The strength of an army, like the power in mechanics, is estimated by multiplying the mass by the rapidity; a rapid march augments the *morale* of an army, and increases all the chances of victory.

Military Maxims, selected and translated by Colonel D'Aguilar, 1831: ix

In mountain warfare, the assailant has always the disadvantage. Even in offensive warfare in the open field, the great secret consists in defensive combats, and in obliging the enemy to attack.

Military Maxims, selected and translated by Colonel D'Aguilar, 1831: xiv

The first consideration with a General who offers battle, should be the glory and honour of his arms; the safety and preservation of his men is only the second; . . .

Military Maxims, selected and translated by Colonel D'Aguilar, 1831: xv

The transition from the defensive to the offensive, is one of the most delicate operations in war.

Military Maxims, selected and translated by Colonel D'Aguilar, 1831: xix

Infantry, cavalry, and artillery, are nothing without each other. They should always be so disposed in cantonments, as to assist each other in case of surprise.

Military Maxims, selected and translated by Colonel D'Aguilar, 1831: xlvii

Charges of cavalry are equally useful at the beginning, the middle, and the end of a battle. They should be made always, if possible, on the flanks of the infantry, especially when this last is engaged in front.

Military Maxims, selected and translated by Colonel D'Aguilar, 1831: l

The first qualification of a soldier is fortitude under fatigue and privation. Courage is only the second; hardship, poverty and want are the best school for a soldier.

Military Maxims, selected and translated by Colonel D'Aguilar, 1831: lviii

There are five things the soldier should never be without, his firelock, his ammunition, his knapsack, his provisions, (for at least four days,) and his entrenching tool. The knapsack may be reduced to the smallest size possible, but the soldier should always have it with him.

Military Maxims, selected and translated by Colonel D'Aguilar, 1831: lix

Every means should be taken to attach the soldier to his colours. This is best accomplished by showing consideration to the old soldier. His pay likewise should increase with his length of service. It is the height of injustice to give a veteran no greater advantages than a recruit.

Military Maxims, selected and translated by Colonel D'Aguilar, 1831: lx

It is not set speeches at the moment of battle, that render soldiers brave. The veteran scarcely listens to them, and the recruit forgets them at the first discharge. If discourses and harangues are useful, it is during the campaign; to do away unfavourable impressions, to correct false reports, to keep alive a proper spirit in the camp, and to furnish materials and amusement for the bivouac. All printed orders of the day should keep in view these objects.

Military Maxims, selected and translated by Colonel D'Aguilar, 1831: lxi

Nothing is so important in war as an undivided command; for this reason, when war is carried on against a single power, there should be only one army, acting upon one base, and conducted by one chief.

Military Maxims, selected and translated by Colonel D'Aguilar, 1831: lxiv

In war the general alone can judge of certain arrangements. It depends on him alone to conquer difficulties by his own superior talents and resolution.

Military Maxims, selected and translated by Colonel D'Aguilar, 1831: lxvi

To authorize generals or other officers to lay down their arms in virtue of a particular capitulation, under any other circumstances than when they are composing the garrison of a fortress, affords a dangerous latitude. It is destructive of all military character in a nation to open such a door to the cowardly, the weak, or even the misdirected brave. Great extremities require extraordinary resolution. The more obstinate the resistance of an army, the greater the chances of assistance or of success.

How many seeming impossibilities have been accomplished by men whose only resource was death!

Military Maxims, selected and translated by Colonel D'Aguilar, 1831: lxvii

There is but one honourable mode of becoming a prisoner of war. That is, by being taken separately; by which is meant, by being cut off entirely, and when we can no longer make use of our arms. In this case there can be no conditions, for honour can impose none. We yield to an irresistible necessity.

Military Maxims, selected and translated by Colonel D'Aguilar, 1831: lxix

The first qualification in a general in chief, is a cool head – that is, a head which receives just impressions, and estimates things and objects at their real value. He must not allow himself to be elated by good fortune, or depressed by bad.

The impressions he receives either successively or simultaneously in the course of the day, should be so classed as to take up only the exact place in his mind which they deserve to occupy; since it is upon a just comparison and consideration of the weight due to different impressions, that the power of reasoning and of right judgement depends.

Some men are so physically and morally constituted as to see everything through a highly coloured medium. They raise up a picture in the mind of every slight occasion, and give to every trivial occurrence a dramatic interest. But whatever knowledge or talent, or courage, or other good qualities such men may possess, nature has not formed them for the command of armies, or the direction of great military operations.

Military Maxims, selected and translated by Colonel D'Aguilar, 1831: lxxiii

Peruse again and again the campaigns of Alexander, Hannibal, Caesar, Gustavus Adolphus, Turenne, Eugene and Frederick. Model yourself upon them. This is the only means of becoming a great captain, and of acquiring the secret of the art of war. Your own genius will be enlightened and improved by this study, and you will learn to reject all maxims foreign to the principles of these great commanders.

Military Maxims, selected and translated by Colonel D'Aguilar, 1831: lxxviii

In war, as in love, we must come into contact before we can triumph.

Maximes de Napoléon, ed. A. G. De Liancourt, 1842

Better a known enemy than a forced ally.

Political Aphorisms, 1848

Marriage is good for nothing in the military profession.

Political Aphorisms, 1848

Conscription is the vitality of a nation, the purification of its morality, and the real foundation of all its habits.

Political Aphorisms, 1848

A great people may be killed, but they cannot be intimidated.

Political Aphorisms, 1848

The best generals are those who have served in the artillery.

In conversation with Gaspard Gourgard, 1815

War is a singular art. I assure you that I have fought sixty battles, and I learned nothing but what I knew when I fought the first one.

In conversation with Gaspard Gourgard, 1815

In order to have good soldiers, a nation must be always at war.

In conversation with Barry E. O'Meara, 26th October 1816

A battle sometimes decides everything; and sometimes the merest trifle decides a battle.

Letter to Barry E. O'Meara, 9th November 1816

The mind of a general ought to resemble and be as clear as the field-glass of a telescope.

In conversation with Barry E. O'Meara, 20th September 1817

Soldiers are made on purpose to be killed.

In conversation with Gaspard Gourgard, 1818

Generals should mess with the common soldiers. The Spartan system was a good one.

In conversation with Gaspard Gourgard, 1818

War is made possible by biscuits.
Attributed

Four hostile newspapers are more to be feared than a thousand rapiers.
Attributed

War is a business of positions.
Attributed

There are no bad regiments, only bad colonels.
Attributed

Every French soldier carries in his cartridge pouch the baton of a marshal of France.
Attributed

I made all my generals out of mud.
Attributed

Arthur Wellesley, Duke of WELLINGTON, 1769–1852

The history of a battle is not unlike the history of a ball. Some individuals may recollect all the little events of which the great result is the battle won or lost; but no individual can recollect the order in which, or the exact moment at which, they occurred, which makes all the difference . . . But if a true history is written, what will become of the reputation of half of those who have acquired reputations, and who deserve it for their gallantry, but who, if their mistakes and casual misconduct were made public, would not be so well thought of?
Letter, 8th August 1815

A great country cannot wage a little war.
Speech in the House of Lords, 16th January 1838

Nobody in the British Army ever reads a regulation or an order as if they were going to be a guide for his conduct, or in any other manner than an amusing novel.
Quoted in Norman F. Dixon, *On the Psychology of Military Incompetence*, 1977

There is no such thing as a little war for a great nation.
Comment made to Fitzroy Somerset

There is nothing so stupid as a gallant officer.
Attributed

There are no manifestos like cannon and musketry.
Attributed

William WORDSWORTH, 1770–1850

Who is the happy Warrior? Who is he
That every man in arms should wish to be?
– It is the generous Spirit, who, when brought
Among the tasks of real life, hath wrought
Upon the plan that pleased his boyish thought:

Whose high endeavours are an inward light
That makes the path before him always bright:
Who, with a natural instinct to discern
What knowledge can perform, is diligent to learn:
Abides by this resolve, and stops not there,
But makes his moral being his prime care;
Who, doomed to go in company with Pain,
And Fear, and Bloodshed, miserable train!
Turns his necessity to glorious gain;
In face of these doth exercise a power
Which is our human nature's highest dower;
Controls them and subdues, transmutes, bereaves
Of their bad influence, and their good receives:
By objects, which might force the soul to abate
Her feeling, rendered more compassionate;
Is placable – because occasions rise
So often that demand such sacrifice;
More skilful in self-knowledge, even more pure,
As tempted more; more able to endure,
As more exposed to suffering and distress;
Thence, also, more alive to tenderness.

'Character of the Happy Warrior', 1807

But Thy most dreaded instrument,
In working out a pure intent,
Is Man – arrayed for mutual slaughter,
Yea, Carnage is thy daughter.

'Ode', 1815: early draft

Sir Walter SCOTT, 1771–1823

Leave untended the herd,
The flock without shelter;
Leave the corpse uninterred,
The bride at the altar;
Leave the deer, leave the steer,
Leave nets and barges;
Come with your fighting gear,
Broadswords and targes.

'Pibroch of Donald Dhu', 1816

Tell that to the Marines – the soldiers won't believe it.

Redgauntlet, 1824

Samuel Taylor COLERIDGE, 1772–1834

And 'mid this tumult Kubla heard from far
Ancestral voices prophesying war!

'Kubla Khan', 1797

Robert SOUTHEY, 1774–1843

The offender is sometimes sentenced to receive a thousand lashes – a surgeon stands by to feel his pulse during the execution and determine how long the flogging can continue without killing him. When human nature can stand no more he is remanded to hospital. His wound, for from shoulders to loins it leaves him one wound, is dressed, and as soon as it is sufficiently healed to be laid open in the same manner, he is brought out to undergo the remainder of his sentence. And this is repeatedly and openly practised in a country where they read in their churches, and in their houses, *that Bible*, in their own language, which saith, 'Forty stripes may the judge inflict upon the offender, and not exceed.'

On flogging in the British Army, *Espriella's Letters*, 1807

Anonymous

The military profession is not designed for debauchees.

The Military Mentor: Being a Series of Letters Recently Written by a General Officer to His Son, 1804

Thomas CAMPBELL, 1777–1844

Ye Mariners of England
That guard our native seas!
Whose flag has braved, a thousand years,
The battle and the breeze!
Your glorious standard launch again
To match another foe:
And sweep through the deep
While the stormy winds do blow;
While the battle rages loud and long
And the stormy winds do blow.

The spirits of your fathers
Shall start from every wave –
From the deck it was their field of fame,
And Ocean was their grave:
Where Blake and mighty Nelson fell
Your manly hearts shall glow,
As ye sweep through the deep,
While the stormy winds do blow; . . .

'Ye Mariners of England', 1800

Britannia needs no bulwarks
No towers along the steep;
Her march is o'er the mountain-waves,
Her home is on the deep.
With thunders from her native oak
She quells the floods below –

As they roar on the shore,
When the stormy winds do blow; . . .
'Ye Mariners of England', 1800

The meteor flag of England
Shall yet terrific burn;
Till danger's troubled sign depart
And the star of peace return.
'Ye Mariners of England', 1800

Our bugles sang truce, for the night-cloud had lower'd,
And the sentinel stars set their watch in the sky;
And thousands had sunk on the ground overpower'd,
The weary to sleep, and the wounded to die.

When reposing that night on my pallet of straw
By the wolf-scaring faggot that guarded the slain,
At the dead of the night a sweet Vision I saw;
And thrice ere the morning I dreamt it again.

Methought from the battlefield's dreadful array
Far, far, I had roam'd on a desolate track:
'Twas Autumn, – and sunshine arose on the way
To the home of my fathers, they welcomed me back.

I flew to the pleasant fields traversed so oft
In life's morning march, when my bosom was young;
I heard my own mountain-goats bleating aloft,
And knew the sweet strain that the corn-reapers sung.

Then pledged we the wine-cup, and fondly I swore
From my home and my weeping friends never to part:
My little ones kiss'd me a thousand times o'er,
And my wife sobb'd aloud in her fulness of heart.

'Stay – stay with us! – rest! – thou art weary and worn!' –
And fain was their war-broken soldier to stay; –
But sorrow return'd with the dawning of morn,
And the voice in my dreaming ear melted away.
'The Soldier's Dream', 1804

There is a victory in dying well.
'Stanzas to the Memory of the Spanish Patriots', 1808

Henry CLAY, 1777–1852

An honourable peace is obtainable only by an efficient war.
Speech in the House of Representatives, 1813

Grand Duke CONSTANTINE of Russia (Konstantin Pavlovich), 1779–1831

I detest war. It ruins armies.
Attributed

Antoine Henri de JOMINI, 1779–1869

War in its ensemble is not a science, but an art.
Précis of the Art of War, 1838

Of all the theories on the art of war, the only reasonable one is that which, founded upon the study of military history, admits a certain number of regulating principles but leaves to natural genius the greatest part of the general conduct of a war without tramelling it with exclusive rules.
Précis of the Art of War, 1837

The new inventions of the last twenty years seem to threaten a great revolution in army organization, armament and tactics. Strategy alone will remain unaltered, with its principles the same as under the Scipios and Caesars, Frederick and Napoleon, since they are independent of the nature of arms and the organization of the troops.
Précis of the Art of War, 1838

Battles have been stated by some writers to be the chief and deciding features of war. This assertion is not strictly true, as armies have been destroyed by strategic operations without the occurrence of pitched battles, merely by a succession of inconsiderable affairs. It is also true that a complete and decided victory may bring similar results even though there may have been no grand strategic combination. But it is the morale of the armies, as well as of nations, more than anything else, which makes victories and their results decisive. Clausewitz commits a grave error in asserting that a battle not characterized by a manoeuvre to turn the enemy cannot result in a complete victory.
Précis of the Art of War, 1838

An observer is doubtless more at his ease in a clock tower than in a frail basket floating in mid-air, but steeples are not always at hand in the vicinity of battle-fields, and they cannot be transported at pleasure.
Précis of the Art of War, 1838

A general should be capable of making all the resources of the invaded country contribute to the success of his enterprise.
Précis of the Art of War, 1838

The second [result of this treatise] will be, perhaps, the doubling of material and personnel of the artillery and the adoption of all improvements capable of augmenting the destructive effect. As artillerists will be among the first victims, it will be necessary to instruct in the infantry men chosen to serve in the ranks of the artillery. Finally it will be necessary to seek means of neutralizing the effects of this carnage; the first seems to be the modification of the armament and the equipment of troops, then the adoption of new tactics which will yield results as promptly as possible.

This task will be for the rising generation, when we shall have tested by experience all the inventions with which we are occupied in the schools of artillery. Happy will be those who, in the first encounters, shall have plenty of shrapnel howitzers, many guns charged at the breech and firing thirty shots a minute; many pieces ricocheting at the height of a man and never failing their mark; finally, the most improved rockets – without counting even the famous steam guns of Perkins, reserved to the defence of ramparts but which (if the written statement of Lord Wellington is to be believed) will be able to make cruel ravages. What a beautiful text for preaching universal peace and the exclusive reign of railroads!

Précis of the Art of War, 1838

Karl von CLAUSEWITZ, 1780–1831

Now, philanthropists may easily imagine there is a skilful method of disarming and overcoming an enemy without causing great bloodshed, and that this is the proper tendency of the Art of War. However plausible this may appear, still it is an error which must be extirpated; for in such dangerous things as War, the errors which proceed from a spirit of benevolence are the worst. As the use of physical power to the utmost extent by no means excludes the cooperation of the intelligence, it follows that he who uses force unsparingly, without reference to the bloodshed involved, must obtain a superiority if his adversary uses less vigour in its application. The former then dictates the law to the latter, and both proceed to extremities to which the only limitations are those imposed by the amount of counteracting force on each side.

On War, 1832: I.i

The worst condition in which a belligerent can be placed is that of being completely disarmed. If, therefore, the enemy is to be reduced to submission by an act of War, he must either be positively disarmed or placed in such a position that he is threatened with it. From this it follows that the disarming or overthrow of an enemy, whichever we call it, must always be the aim of Warfare.

On War, 1832: I.i

The Art of War has to deal with living and with moral forces, the consequence of which is that it can never attain the absolute and positive. There is therefore everywhere a margin for the accidental, and just as much in the greatest things as in the smallest. As there is room for this accidental on the one hand, so on the other there must be courage and self-reliance in proportion to the room available. If these qualities are forthcoming in a high degree, the margin left may likewise be great. Courage and self-reliance are, therefore, principles quite essential to War; consequently, theory must only set up such rules as allow ample scope for all degrees and varieties of these necessary and noblest of military virtues.

On War, 1832: I.i

We see, therefore, that War is not only a political act, but also a real political instrument, a continuation of political commerce, a carrying out of the same by other means. All beyond this which is strictly peculiar to War relates merely to the peculiar nature of the means which it uses. That the tendencies and views of policy shall not be incompatible with these means, the Art of War in general and the Commander in each particular case may demand, and this claim is truly not a trifling one. But however powerfully this may react on political views in particular cases, still it must always be regarded as only a modification of them; for the political view is the object, War is the means, and the means must always include the object in our conception.

On War, 1832: I.i

War is . . . not only chameleon-like in character, because it changes its colour in some degree in each particular case, but it is also, as a whole, in relation to the predominant tendencies which are in it, a wonderful trinity, composed of the original violence of its elements, hatred and animosity, which may be looked upon as a blind instinct; of the play of probabilities and chance, which make it a free activity of the soul; and of the subordinate nature of a political instrument, by which it belongs purely to reason.

On War, 1832: I.i

If, in the next place, we keep once more to the pure conception of War, then we must say that the political object properly lies out of its province, for if War is an act of violence to compel the enemy to fulfil our will, then in every case all depends on our overthrowing the enemy, that is, disarming him, and on that alone.

On War, 1832: I.ii

The decision by arms is, for all operations in War, great and small, what cash payment is in bill transactions. However remote from each other these relations, however seldom the realization may take place, still it can never entirely fail to occur.

On War, 1832: I.ii

War is the province of uncertainty: three-fourths of those things upon which action in War must be calculated, are hidden more or less in the clouds of great uncertainty. Here, then, above all a fine and penetrating mind is called for, to search out the truth by the tact of its judgement.

On War, 1832: I.iii

Of the noble feelings which fill the human heart in the exciting tumult of battle, none, we must admit, are so powerful and constant as the soul's thirst for honour and renown, which the German language treats so unfairly and tends to depreciate by the unworthy associations in the words *Ehrgeiz* (greed of honour) and *Ruhmsucht* (hankering after glory). No doubt it is just in War that the abuse of these proud aspirations of the soul must bring upon the human race the most shocking outrages, but by their origins they are certainly to be counted amongst the noblest feelings which belong to human nature, and in War they are the vivifying principle which gives the enormous body a spirit.

On War, 1832: I.iii

. . . A strong mind is not one that is merely susceptible of strong excitement, but one which can maintain its serenity under the most powerful excitement, so that, in spite of the storm in the breast, the perception and judgement can act with perfect freedom, like the needle of the compass of a storm-tossed ship.

On War, 1832: I.iii

Let us accompany the novice to the battlefield. As we approach, the thunder of cannon becoming plainer and plainer is soon followed by the howling of shot, which attracts the attention of the inexperienced. Balls begin to strike the ground close to us, before and behind. We hasten to the hill where stands the General and his numerous Staff. Here the close striking of the cannon balls and the bursting of shells is so frequent that the seriousness of life makes itself visible through the youthful picture of imagination. Suddenly someone known to us falls – a shell strikes amongst the crowd and causes some involuntary movements: we begin to feel that we are no longer perfectly at ease and collected; even the bravest is at least to some degree confused. Now, a step farther into the battle which is raging before us like a scene in a theatre. We get to the nearest General of Division; here ball follows ball, and the noise of our own guns increases the confusion. From the General of Division to the Brigadier. He, a man of acknowledged bravery, keeps carefully behind a rising ground, a house, or a tree – a sure sign of increasing danger. Grape rattles on the roofs of the houses and in the fields; cannon balls howl over us, and plough the air in all directions, and soon there is a frequent whistling of musket balls. A step further towards the troops, to that sturdy infantry which for hours has maintained its firmness under this heavy fire; here the air is filled with the hissing of balls which announce their proximity by a short sharp noise as they pass within an inch of the ear, the head or the breast.

To add to all this, compassion strikes the beating heart with pity at the sight of the maimed and the fallen. The young soldier cannot reach any of these different strata of danger without feeling that the light of reason does not move here in the same medium, that it is not refracted in the same manner as in speculative contemplation. Indeed, he must be a very extraordinary man who, under these impressions for the first time, does not lose the power of making any instantaneous decisions.

On War, 1832: i.iv

Like an obelisk towards which the principal streets of a town converge, the strong will of a proud spirit stands prominent and commanding in the middle of the Art of War.

On War, 1832: I.vii

Activity in War is movement in a resistant medium. Just as a man immersed in water is unable to perform with ease and regularity the most natural and simplest movement, that of walking, so in War, with ordinary powers, one cannot keep even the line of mediocrity. This is the reason why a correct theorist is like a swimming master, who teaches on dry land movements which are required in water, which must appear grotesque and ludicrous to those who forget about the water. This is also why theorists, who have never plunged in themselves, or who cannot deduce any generalities from their experience, are unpractical and even absurd, because they only teach what every one knows – how to walk.

On War, 1832: I.vii

According to our classification . . . tactics is the theory of the use of military forces in combat. Strategy is the theory of the use of combats for the object of the War.

On War, 1832: II.i

. . . State policy is the womb in which War is developed, in which its outlines lie hidden in a rudimentary state, like the qualities of living creatures in their germs.

On War, 1832: II.iii

. . . It is neither necessary nor desirable that criticism should completely identify itself with the person acting. In War, as in all matters of skill, there is a certain natural aptitude required which is called talent. This may be great or small. In the first case it may easily be superior to that of the critic, for what critic can pretend to the skill of a Frederick or a Buonaparte? Therefore, if criticism is not to abstain altogether from offering an opinion where eminent talent is concerned, it must be allowed to make use of the advantage which its enlarged horizon affords. Criticism must not, therefore, treat the solution of a problem by a great General like a sum in arithmetic; it is only through the results and through the exact coincidences of events that it can recognize with admiration how much is due to the exercise of genius, and that it first learns the essential combination which the glance of that genius devised.

On War, 1832: II.v

The national spirit of an Army (enthusiasm, fanatical zeal, faith, opinion) displays itself most in mountain warfare, where every one down to the common soldier is left to himself. On this account a mountainous country is the best campaigning ground for popular levies.

Expertness of an Army through training, and that well-tempered courage which holds the ranks together as if they had been cast in a mould, show their superiority in an open country.

On War, 1832: III.iv

An Army which preserves its usual formations under the heaviest fire, which is never shaken by imaginary fears, and in the face of real danger disputes the ground inch by inch, which, proud in the feeling of its victories, never loses its sense of obedience, its respect for and confidence in its leaders, even under the depressing effects of defeat; an Army with all its physical powers, inured to privations and fatigue by exercise, like the muscles of an athlete; an Army which looks upon all its toils as the means to victory, not as a curse which hovers over its standards, and which is always reminded of its duties and virtues by the short catechism of one idea, namely the *honour of its arms*: Such an Army is imbued with the true military spirit.

On War, 1832: III.v

. . . Where the conduct of War spins out the time with a number of small flourishes, with skirmishes at outposts, half in earnest, half in jest, with long dispositions which end in nothing, with positions and marches, which afterwards

are designated as skilful only because their infinitesimally small causes are lost, and common sense can make nothing of them, here on this field many theorists find the real Art of War at home: in these feints, parades, half and quarter thrusts of former Wars, they find the aim of all theory, the supremacy of mind over matter, and modern Wars appear to them mere savage fisticuffs, from which nothing is to be learnt, and which must be regarded as mere retrograde steps towards barbarism. This opinion is as frivolous as the objects towards which it relates. Where great forces and great passions are wanting, it is certainly easier for a practised dexterity to show its game; but is then the command of great forces not in itself a higher exercise of the intelligent faculties? Is then that kind of conventional sword-exercise not comprised in and belonging to the other mode of conducting War? Does it not bear the same relation to it as the motions upon a ship to the motion of the ship itself? Truly it can take place only under the tacit condition that the adversary does no better. And can we tell, how long he may choose to respect those conditions? Has not the French Revolution fallen upon us in the midst of the fancied security of our old system of War, and driven us from Châlons to Moscow? And did not Frederick the Great in like manner surprise the Austrians reposing in their ancient habits of War, and make their Monarchy tremble? Woe to the cabinet which, with a shilly-shally policy, and a routine-ridden military system, meets with an adversary who, like the rude element, knows no other law than that of his intrinsic force.
On War, 1832: III.xvi

All War supposes human weakness, and against that it is directed.
On War, 1832: IV.x

Let us not hear of Generals who conquer without bloodshed. If a bloody slaughter is a horrible sight, then that is ground for paying more respect to War, but not for making the sword we wear blunter and blunter by degrees from feeling of humanity, until someone steps in with one that is sharp and lops off the arm from our body.
On War, 1832: IV.xi

Does the cessation of diplomatic notes stop the political relations between different Nations and Governments? Is not War merely another kind of writing and language for political thoughts? It has certainly a grammar of its own, but its logic is not peculiar to itself.
On War, 1832: V.vi

If War belongs to policy, it will naturally take its character from thence. If policy is grand and powerful, so also will be the War, and this may be carried to the point at which War attains to *its absolute form*.
On War, 1832: V.vi

George Caleb COLTON, 1780–1832

War is a game in which princes seldom win, the people never.
Lacon, 1825

(Marie Henri Beyle) STENDHAL, 1783–1842

The King who rules the Cossacks rules the world.
A Life of Napoleon, 1818

There is only one defence against the Russians and that is a very hot climate.
A Life of Napoleon, 1818

Washington IRVING, 1783–1859

It is but seldom that any one overt act produces hostilities between two nations; there exists, more commonly, a previous jealousy and ill will, a predisposition to take offense.
The Sketch Book of Geoffrey Crayon, 1820

Nadezhda DUROVA, 1783–1866

The cavalryman gallops up, gallops away, wounds, rushes past, turns back again, and sometimes kills, but his every motion is eloquent of mercy for the enemy; all this is merely the harbinger of death. But the infantry formation is death itself, dreadful, inevitable death.
The Cavalry Maiden, 1836

James Henry Leigh HUNT, 1784–1859

Military talent is greatly overrated by the world, because the means by which it shows itself are connected with brute force and the most terrible results; and men's faculties are dazzled and beaten down by a thunder and lightning so formidable to their very existence. If playing a game of chess involved the blowing up of gunpowder and the hazard of laying waste a city, men would have the same grand idea of chess.
The Companion, 1828

Henry John Temple, Lord PALMERSTON, 1784–1865

Officers of the army are apt in general to write like kitchen maids.
Letter to Florence Nightingale, 1857

George Gordon, Lord BYRON, 1788–1824

Such be the sons of Spain, and strange her fate!
They fight for freedom who were never free,
A Kingless people for a nerveless state;
Her vassals combat when her chieftains flee,
True to the veriest slaves of Treachery:
Fond of a land which gave them nought but life,
Pride points the path that leads to Liberty;
Back to the struggle, baffled in the strife,
War, war is still the cry, 'War even to the knife!'
Childe Harold's Pilgrimage, 1813: Canto I

Even good men like to make the public stare.

Don Juan, 1823

Revolutions are not to be made with rosewater.

Letters and Journals, 1898–1901

Basil HALL, 1788–1844

The words Marine and Mariner differ by one small letter only; but no two races of men, I had well nigh said no two animals, differ from one another more completely.

Journal, 1832

Frederick MARRYAT, 1792–1848

No names can be too fine for a pretty girl or a fine frigate.

Peter Simple, 1834

Thaddeus STEVENS, 1792–1868

Though the President is Commander-in-Chief, Congress is his commander; and, God willing, he shall obey.

In the House of Representatives, 3rd July 1867

Thomas CARLYLE, 1795–1881

Oh ye kind Heavens, there is in every Army a fittest, wisest, bravest, best; whom, could we find and make Commander, all were in truth well – by what art discover him – for our need for him is great!

Sartor Resartus, 1834

Have I not myself known five hundred living soldiers sabred into crows' meat for a piece of glazed cotton which they call their flag; which, had you sold it in any market-cross, would not have brought above three groschen?

Sartor Resartus, 1834

Under the sky there is no uglier spectacle than two men with clenched teeth and hellfire eyes, hacking one another's flesh; converting precious living bodies, and priceless living souls, into nameless masses of putrescence useful only for turnip-manure.

Past and Present, 1843

NICHOLAS I of Russia, 1796–1855

Russia has two generals whom she can trust: General Janvier and General Février.

Quoted in *Punch*, 10th March 1853

Alfred de VIGNY, 1797–1863

An army is a nation within a nation; it is one of the vices of our age.

Servitude et grandeur militaire, 1835

Thomas HOOD, 1799–1845

Ben Battle was a soldier bold,
And used to war's alarms:
But a cannon-ball took off his legs,
So he laid down his arms.

'Faithless Nelly Gray', 1826

Anonymous

The only title to an officer's commission shall be in time of peace, education and professional knowledge; in time of war, distinguished valor and perception. From the entire nation, therefore, all individuals who possess these qualities are eligible for the highest military posts. All previously existing class preference in the military establishment is abolished, and every man, without regard to his origins, has equal duties and equal rights.

Decree of the Prussian Army, 1808

Colonel J. G. D. TUCKER, fl. 1826

Many of the greatest military commanders owe their exaltation and celebrity to the Art of letter writing.

Advice To Young Officers, 1826

Thomas Babington MACAULAY, 1800–59

The reluctant obedience of distant provinces generally costs more than it is worth.

Essays: Hallam's Constitutional History, 1828

Helmuth von MOLTKE (the 'Elder'), 1800–91

Very large concentrations of troops are in themselves a calamity. The army which is concentrated at one point is difficult to supply and can never be billeted; it cannot march, it cannot operate, it cannot at all exist for any length of time; it can only fight. To keep all the forces concentrated without a distinct object or otherwise than for a decisive battle is, therefore, a mistake. For that decisive battle we can certainly never be too strong, and therefore it is absolutely necessary to summon even the last battalion to the battlefield. But anyone who wishes to close with his enemy must not intend to advance in one body on one or few roads.

Instructions for the Commanders of Large Formations, 1869

Without war the world would sink into materialism.

Letter to J. K. Bluntschli, 11th December 1880

The consecutive achievements of a war are not premeditated but spontaneous and guided by military instinct.

Quoted in Sir Basil Liddell Hart, *The Sword and the Pen*, 1978

You will usually find that the enemy has three courses open to him, and of these he will adopt the fourth.

Quoted in Robert Debs Heinl Jr, *Dictionary of Military and Naval Quotations*, 1966

Order, counterorder, disorder.
Favourite saying

An order that can be misunderstood will be misunderstood.
Attributed

The military commander is the fate of the nation.
Attributed

No plan survives contact with the enemy.
Attributed

Edward George Earle, Lord BULWER-LYTTON, 1803–73

Rank is a great beautifier.
The Lady of Lyons, 1838

The pen is mightier than the sword.
Richelieu, 1839

Ralph Waldo EMERSON, 1803–82

Every hero becomes a bore at last.
Representative Men, 1849

The peace of the man who has forsworn the use of the bullet seems to me not quite peace, but a canting impotence.
Journal, 1839

The god of Victory is said to be one-handed, but Peace gives victory to both sides.
Journal, 1867

Was it Buonaparte who said that he found the vices very good patriots? – 'he got five millions from the love of brandy, and he should be glad to know which of the virtues would pay him as much.' Tobacco and opium have broad backs, and will cheerfully carry the load of armies.
Society and Solitude, 1870

War is on its last legs; and a universal peace is as sure as is the prevalence of civilization over barbarism, of liberal governments over feudal forms. The question for us is only how soon?
Miscellanies, 1884

War educates the senses, calls into action the will, perfects the physical constitution, brings men into such swift and close collision in critical moments that man measures man.
Miscellanies, 1884

War, to the sane men at the present day, begins to look like an epidemic insanity, breaking out here and there like the cholera or influenza, infecting men's brains, instead of their bowels.
Miscellanies, 1884

He who loves the bristle of bayonets only sees in their glitter what beforehand he feels in his heart.

Miscellanies, 1884

Benjamin DISRAELI, Earl of Beaconsfield, 1804–81

The Services in war time are fit only for desperadoes, but in peace are fit only for fools.

Vivian Grey, 1827

Henry Wadsworth LONGFELLOW, 1807–82

He loved the twilight that surrounds
The border-land of old romance;
Where glitter hauberk, helm and lance,
And banner waves, and trumpet sounds,
And ladies ride with hawk on wrist,
And mighty warriors sweep along,
Magnified by the purple mist,
The dust of centuries and of song.

'Tales of a Wayside Inn', 1863

Better like Hector in the field to die,
Than like a perfumed Paris turn and fly.

'Morituri Salutamus', 1875

Charles Louis Bonaparte, NAPOLEON III, 1808–73

The history of artillery is the history of progress in the sciences, and is therefore the history of civilization.

Attributed

George S. HILLARD, 1808–79

No man can be a great officer who is not infinitely patient of details, for an army is an aggregation of details.

The Life and Campaigns of George B. McClellan, 1874

Abraham LINCOLN, 1809–65

Military glory – that attractive rainbow rises in showers of blood, that serpent's eye that charms to destroy.

In the House of Representatives, 12th January 1848

The ballot is stronger than the bullet.

Speech, 19th May 1856

John Adolphus Bernard DAHLGREN, 1809–70

The officer should wear his uniform as the judge his ermine, without a stain.

Attributed last words, 12th July 1870

Charles Robert DARWIN, 1809–82

A struggle for existence inevitably follows from the high rate at which all organic beings tend to increase. Every being, which during its natural lifetime produces several eggs or seeds, must suffer destruction during some period of its life, and during some season or occasional year, otherwise, on the principle of geometrical increase, its numbers would quickly become so inordinately great that no country could support the product. Hence, as more individuals are produced than can possibly survive, there must in every case be a struggle for existence, either one individual with another of the same species, or with the individuals of distinct species, or with the physical conditions of life.

The Origin of Species, 1859

. . . the war of nature . . .

The Origin of Species, 1859

Alfred, Lord TENNYSON, 1809–92

I dipt into the future far as human eye could see,
Saw the vision of the world, and all the wonder that would be;
Saw the heavens fill with commerce, argosies of purple sails,
Pilots of the purple twilight, dropping down with costly bales;
Heard the heavens filled with shouting, and there rain'd a ghastly dew
From the nations' airy navies grappling in the central blue.

'Locksley Hall', 1842

William Makepeace THACKERAY, 1811–63

A military gent, I see . . .

The Newcomes, 1854

Charles DICKENS, 1812–70

Any animated description of a modern battle, any private soldier's letter published in the newspapers, any page of the records of the Victoria Cross, will show that in the ranks of the Army there exists under all disadvantages as fine a sense of duty as to be found in any station on earth. Who doubts that if we did our duty as faithfully as the soldier does his, this world would be a better place? There may be greater difficulties in our way than in the soldier's. Not disputed. But let us at least do our duty toward *him*.

Preface to *The Uncommercial Traveller*, 1861

Robert BROWNING, 1812–89

Our wearisome pedantic art of war,
By which we prove retreat may be success,
Delay best speed, half loss, at times, whole gain.

Luria, 1846

James Anthony FROUDE, 1812–94

Wild animals never kill for sport. Man is the only one to whom the torture and death of his fellow-creatures is amusing in itself.

Oceana, 1886

Henry Ward BEECHER, 1813–87

It is not merely cruelty that leads men to love war, it is excitement.

Proverbs From Plymouth Pulpit, 1887

Joseph HOOKER, 1814–79

No one will consider the day as ended, until the duties it brings have been discharged.

General order, given on taking command of the United States's Northwest Department

Henry Wager HALLECK, 1815–72

The Bible nowhere prohibits war. In the Old Testament we find war and even conquest positively commanded, and although war was raging in the time of Christ and His Apostles, still they said not a word of its unlawfulness and immorality.

Elements of Military Art and Science, 1846

Otto von BISMARCK, 1815–98

Pointed bullets are better than pointed speeches.

Speech, 1850

Not by speechifying and counting majorities are the great questions of the times to be resolved – that was the error of 1848 and 1849 – but by iron and blood.

In the Prussian Diet, 1862

Henry David THOREAU, 1817–62

Where a battle has been fought, you will find nothing but the bones of men and beasts; where a battle is being fought, there are hearts beating.

Quoted in Robert Debs Heinl Jr, *Dictionary of Military and Naval Quotations*, 1966

Karl MARX, 1818–83

The history of all hitherto existing society is the history of class struggles. Freeman and slave, patrician and plebeian, lord and serf, guildmaster and journeyman, in a word, oppressor and oppressed, stood in constant opposition to each other, carried on an uninterrupted, now hidden, now open fight, a fight that each time ended, either in a revolutionary reconstitution of society at large, or in the common ruin of the contending classes.

The Communist Manifesto, 1848, with Friedrich Engels [*see p. 91*]

James Russell LOWELL, 1819–91

Ninepunce a day fer killin' folks comes kind o' low fer murder.
The Biglow Papers, 1848

Ef you want peace, the thing you've got tu du
Is jes' to show you're up to fightin', tu.
The Biglow Papers, 1848

Herman MELVILLE, 1819–91

When shall the time come, how much longer will God postpone it, when the clouds, which at times gather over the horizons of nations, shall not be hailed by any class of humanity, and invoked to burst as a bomb? Standing navies, as well as standing armies, serve to keep alive the spirit of war even in the meek heart of peace. In its very embers and smoulderings they nourish that fatal fire, and half-pay officers, as priests of Mars, yet guard the temple though no God be there.
White-Jacket, 1850

Walt WHITMAN, 1819–92

Know'st thou not, there is but one theme for ever-enduring bards?
And that is the theme of war, the fortune of battles,
The making of perfect soldiers.
'As I ponder'd in Silence', 1870

The whole present system of the officering and personnel of the Army and Navy of these States, and the spirit and letter of their trebly-aristocratic rules and regulations, is a monstrous exotic, a nuisance and revolt, and belongs here just as much as orders of nobility or the Pope's council of cardinals. I say that if the present theory of our Army and Navy is possible and true, then the rest of America is an unmitigated fraud.
Democratic Vistas, 1870

John RUSKIN, 1819–1900

No great art yet rose on earth but among a nation of soldiers.
The Crown of Wild Olive, 1866

All great nations learned their truth of word, and strength of thought, in war; they were nourished in war, and wasted by peace; taught by war, and deceived by peace; trained by war, and betrayed by peace; – in a word, they were born in war, and expired in peace.
The Crown of Wild Olive, 1866

Anonymous

The needle gun, the needle gun,
The death-defying needle gun;
It does knock over men like fun –
What a formidable weapon is the needle gun!
In *Punch*, 1866

William Tecumseh SHERMAN, 1820–91

War, like the thunderbolt, follows its laws and turns not aside even if the beautiful, the virtuous and charitable stand in its path.

Letter to Charles Dana, April 1864

You cannot qualify war in harsher terms than I will. War is cruelty, and you cannot refine it.

Memoirs, 1875

To be at the head of a strong column of troops, in the execution of some task that requires brain, is the highest pleasure of war.

Memoirs, 1875

I would define true courage to be a perfect sensibility of the measure of danger, and a mental willingness to incur it.

Memoirs, 1875

I am tired and sick of war. Its glory is all moonshine . . . War is hell.

Address to the Michigan Military Academy, 19th June 1879

The legitimate object of war is a more perfect peace.

Epigram composed on 23rd February 1883

Friedrich ENGELS, 1820–95

Fighting is to war what cash payment is to trade, for however rarely it may be necessary for it actually to occur, everything is directed toward it.

Letter to Karl Marx, 25th September 1857

Florence NIGHTINGALE, 1820–1910

It has been said by officers enthusiastic in their profession that there are three causes which make a soldier enlist, viz. being out of work, in a state of intoxication, or, jilted by a sweetheart. Yet the incentives to enlistment, which we desire to multiply, can hardly be put by Englishmen of the nineteenth century in this form, viz. more poverty, more drink, more faithless sweethearts.

Notes on Matters Affecting the Health, Efficiency, and Hospital Administration of the British Army, 1858

Charles ARDANT DU PICQ, 1821–70

The man is the first weapon of battle; let us then study the soldier in battle, for it is he who brings reality to it. Only study of the past can give us a sense of reality and show us how the soldier will fight in the future.

Battle Studies, 1871

In battle, two moral forces, even more than two material forces, are in conflict. The strongest conquers. The victor has often lost by fire more than the vanquished. Moral effect does not come entirely from destructive power, real and effective as it may be. It comes, above all, from its presumed, threatening power, present in the form of reserves threatening to renew the battle, of troops that appear on the flank, even of a determined frontal attack.

Battle Studies, 1871

The moral effect must be a terrible thing. A body advances to meet another. The defender has only to remain calm, ready to aim, each pitted against a man before him. The attacking body comes within deadly range. Whether or not it halts to fire, it will be a target for the other body which awaits it, calm, ready, sure of its effect. The whole first rank of the assailant falls, smashed. The remainder, little encouraged by their reception, disperse automatically or before the least indication of an advance on them. Is this what happens? Not at all! The moral effect of the assault worries the defenders. They fire in the air if at all. They disperse immediately before the assailants who are even encouraged by this fire now that it is over. It quickens them in order to avoid a second salvo.

Battle Studies, 1871

Ulysses Simpson GRANT, 1822–85

The art of war is simple enough. Find out where your enemy is. Get at him as soon as you can. Strike at him as hard as you can, and keep moving on.

Quoted in Robert Debs Heinl Jr, *Dictionary of Military and Naval Quotations*, 1966

I had rather lose one man in marching than five in fighting.

Attributed

Henry James Sumner MAINE, 1822–88

War appears to be as old as mankind, but peace is a modern invention.

Early History of Institutions, 1875

Thomas Jonathan ('Stonewall') JACKSON, 1824–63

Duty is ours, consequences are God's.

Quoted in Robert Debs Heinl Jr, *Dictionary of Military and Naval Quotations*, 1966

Count Lev (Leo) Nikolaevich TOLSTOY, 1828–1910

The Austro–Prussian war [of 1866] appears to us undoubtedly the result of the crafty conduct of Bismarck, and so on. The Napoleonic wars still seem to us, though already questionably, to be the outcome of their heroes' will. But in the crusades we already see an event occupying its definite place in history, and without which we cannot imagine the modern history of Europe, though to the chroniclers of the Crusades that event appeared as merely due to the will of certain people. In regard to the migration of peoples it does not enter any one's head to-day to suppose that the renovation of the European world depended on Attila's caprice. The farther back in history the object of our observation lies, the more doubtful does the freewill of those concerned in the event become, and the more manifest the law of inevitability.

War and Peace, 1868–69

In descriptions of battles it is generally said that such and such armies were sent to attack such and such points, and were then ordered to retire and so on, as if assuming that discipline, which subjects tens of thousands of men to the will of one man on a parade-ground, will have the same effect where it is a question of life and death. Any one who has been in a war knows how untrue that is, yet the reports are based on that assumption, and on them the military descriptions. Make a round of the troops immediately after a battle, or even next day or the day after, before the reports have been drawn up, and ask any of the soldiers and senior and junior officers how the affair went: you will be told what all these men experienced and saw, and you will form a majestic, complex, infinitely varied, depressing and indistinct impression; and from no one – least of all from the commander-in-chief – will you learn what the whole affair was like. Two or three days after the reports begin to be handed in. Talkers begin to narrate how things happened which they did not see; finally a general report is drawn up, and on this report the general opinion of the army is formed. Everyone is glad to exchange his own doubts and questionings for this deceptive, but clear and always flattering, presentation. Question a month or two later a man who was in the battle, and you will no longer feel in his account the raw, vital material that was there before, but he will answer according to the report.

Some Words About 'War and Peace', 1868

Emily DICKINSON, 1830–86

A Bayonet's contrition
Is nothing to the Dead.

'My Triumph Lasted till the Drums', *c.* 1870

Mikhail Ivanovich DRAGOMIROV, 1830–1905

To make war, to kill without being killed, is an illusion.

Notes for Soldiers, *c.* 1890

If your bayonet breaks, strike with the stock; if the stock gives way, hit with your fists; if your fists are hurt, bite with your teeth.

Notes for Soldiers, *c.* 1890

Lewis CARROLL (Charles Lutwidge Dodgson), 1832–98

'You know,' he said gravely, 'it's one of the most serious things that can happen to one in battle – to get one's head cut off.'

Alice Through the Looking Glass, 1872

Alfred von SCHLIEFFEN, 1833–1913

The modern commander-in-chief is no Napoleon who stands with his brilliant suite upon a hill. . . . The commander is further to the rear in a house with roomy offices, where telegraph and wireless, telephone and signalling instruments are at hand, while a fleet of automobiles and motorcycles, ready for the longest trips, wait for orders. Here, in a comfortable chair before a large table, the modern Alexander overlooks the entire battlefield on a map. From here he telephones inspiring words, and here he receives the reports from army and corps commanders and from balloons and dirigibles which observe the enemy's movements and detect his positions.

Cannae, 1913

John Singleton MOSBY, 1833–1916

The military value of a partisan's work is not measured by the amount of property destroyed, or the number of men killed or captured, but by the number he keeps watching.

War Reminiscences, 1887

Heinrich von TREITSCHKE, 1834–96

War is elevating, because the individual disappears before the great conception of the state.

Politik, 1897

What a perversion of morality to wish to abolish heroism among men!

Politik, 1897

God shall see to it that war shall always recur, as a drastic remedy for ailing humanity.

Politik, 1897

Mark TWAIN (Samuel Langhorne Clemens), 1835–1910

The pitifulest thing out is a mob; that's what an army is – a mob; they don't fight with courage that's born in them, but with courage that's borrowed from their mass, and from their officers.

The Adventures of Huckleberry Finn, 1884

Ivan Stanislavovich BLOCH, 1836–1902

. . . Instead of war fought out to the bitter end in a series of decisive battles we shall have as a substitute a long period of continually increasing strain upon the resources of the combatants. . . . Everybody will be entrenched in the next war. The spade will be as indispensable to a soldier as his rifle.

Is War Impossible?, 1899

Soldiers may fight as they please; the ultimate decision is in the hand of famine . . .

Is War Impossible?, 1899

The modern rifle has immense power, and its use is simple and convenient. It will be extremely difficult to overcome the resistance of infantry in sheltered positions. Driven from position it will quickly find natural obstacles – hillocks, pits and groups of trees – which may serve as points for fresh opposition. The zone of deadly fire is much wider than before, the battles will be more stubborn and prolonged. Of such a sudden sweeping away of an enemy in the course of a few minutes as took place at Rosbach it is absurd even to think.

Modern Weapons and Modern War, 1900

It was Marshal St Cyr who declared that 'a brave army consists of one third of soldiers actually brave, one third of those who might be brave under special circumstances, and a remaining third consisting of cowards.' With the increase of culture and prosperity nervousness has also increased, and in modern, especially in Western European armies, a considerable proportion of men will be found unaccustomed to heavy physical labour and to forced marches. To this category the majority of manufacturing labourers will belong. Nervousness will be the more noticeable since night attacks are strongly recommended by many military writers, and undoubtedly these will be made more often than in past wars. Even the expectation of battle by night will cause alarm and give birth to nervous excitement.

Modern Weapons and Modern War, 1900

It is true that ancient history presents examples of immense hordes entering upon war. But these wars were generally decided by a few blows, for there existed neither rapid communications for the purpose of reinforcement, nor regular defensive lines. Modern history shows many instances of prolonged wars. But it must be remembered that the Thirty Years' and the Seven Years' wars were not uninterrupted, and that the armies engaged went into winter quarters where they were regularly provisioned, and in spring recommenced operations resulting only in partial successes, the gaining of a battle, the taking of a fortress, followed by another stoppage of operations. Thus the long wars of modern history may be regarded as a series of short campaigns.

Modern Weapons and Modern War, 1900

W(illiam) S(chwenk) GILBERT, 1836–1911

Stick close to your desks and never go to sea,
And you may all be rulers of the Queen's Navee!

HMS Pinafore, 1878

I am the very model of a modern major-general,
I've information vegetable, animal and mineral;
I know the kings of England, and I quote the fights historical,
From Marathon to Waterloo, in order categorical.

The Pirates of Penzance, 1879

Grover CLEVELAND, 1837–1908

The United States is not a nation to which peace is a necessity.

Annual Message to Congress, 7th December 1896

Benjamin CONSTANT, 1838–91

The army is the people in uniform.

Quoted in Robert Debs Heinl Jr, *Dictionary of Military and Naval Quotations*, 1966

Alfred Thayer MAHAN, 1840–1914

The United States in her turn may have the rude awakening of those who have abandoned their share in the common birthright of all people, the sea.

The Influence of Sea Power upon History, 1892

... Self-preservation, the first law of states even more than of men; for no government is empowered to assent to that last sacrifice, which the individual may make for the noblest motives.

The Influence of Sea Power upon History, 1892

Navies do not dispense with fortifications nor with armies, but when wisely handled they may save a country the strain which comes when these have to be called into play.

The Influence of Sea Power upon the French Revolution, 1892

Peace, indeed, is not adequate to all progress; there are resistances that can be overcome only by explosion.

The Peace Conference, 1899

Force does not exist for mobility but mobility for force. It is of no use to get there first unless, when the enemy arrives, you have also the most men – the greater force.

Lessons of the War with Spain, 1899

Communications dominate war; broadly considered, they are the most important single element in strategy, political, or military.

The Problem of Asia, 1900

In its proper manifestation the jealousy between civil and military spirits is a healthy symptom.

Naval Administration and Warfare, 1903

The habit of the arm-chair easily prevails over that of the Quarter-deck; it is more comfortable.

Naval Administration and Warfare, 1903

In giving up the offensive the Navy gives up its proper sphere.

Naval Strategy, 1911

When it is remembered that the United States, like Great Britain and like Japan, can be approached only by sea, we can scarcely fail to see that upon the sea primarily must be found our power to secure our own borders and to sustain our external policy.

Naval Strategy, 1911

Thomas HARDY, 1840–1928

Yes; quaint and curious war is!
You shoot a fellow down
You'd treat if met where any bar is,
Or help to half-a-crown.
'The Man He Killed', 1902

My argument is that War makes rattling good history; but Peace is poor reading.
The Dynasts, 1906

Sir John FISHER, 1841–1920

The whole principle of naval fighting is to be free to go anywhere with every damned thing the Navy possesses.
Memories, 1919

Rashness in war is prudence.
Memories, 1919

The best scale for an experiment is 12 inches to a foot.
Memories, 1919

Georges CLEMENCEAU, 1841–1929

War is too important to be left to the generals.
Attributed

Oliver Wendell HOLMES Jr, 1841–1935

War is an organized bore.
Remark made when recuperating from a wound, 1862

As long as man dwells upon the globe, his destiny is battle.
Letter, 1914

Ambrose Gwinett BIERCE, 1842–1914

Battle, n. A method of untying with the teeth a political knot that would not yield to the tongue.
The Devil's Dictionary, 1911

Cannon, n. An instrument employed in the rectification of national boundaries.
The Devil's Dictionary, 1911

Peace, n. In international affairs, a period of cheating between two periods of fighting.
The Devil's Dictionary, 1911

Prince Peter Alexeivich KROPOTKIN, 1842–1921

War is the usual condition of Europe. A thirty years' supply of the causes of war is always to hand.
Paroles d'un Révolté, 1884

George Morris Cohen BRANDES, 1842–1927

The appalling thing about war is that it kills all love of truth.

Letter to Georges Clemenceau, March 1915

Anonymous

There's a boy across the river
With a bottom like a peach,
But alas I cannot swim.

Sung by British troops in India, from *c.* 1890 onwards, and based originally on a Pushtu love song, 'Zakmi Dil' (Wounded Heart)

Friedrich Wilhelm von NIETZSCHE, 1844–1900

Against war it may be said that it makes the victor stupid and the vanquished revengeful.

The Dawn, 1881

Man shall be framed for War, and Woman for the entertainment of the Warrior; all else is folly.

Thus Spake Zarathustra, 1885

Ye shall love peace only as a means to new wars – and the short peace more than the long.

Thus Spake Zarathustra,1885

Paul von HINDENBURG, 1847–1934

Loyalty is the marrow of honour.

Out Of My Life, 1920

Hans DELBRÜCK, 1848–1929

To discover in the abstract, with the benefit of hindsight and the knowledge of all the facts, the best possible source of action is not really so difficult. Great military ideas are actually extremely simple. The most celebrated manoeuvres, counted by history as the work of true genius, for instance the Prussian withdrawal from Ligny *towards* Waterloo, could be invented on the map by a regimental clerk. Greatness lies in the freedom of the intellect and spirit at moments of pressure and crisis, and in the willingness to take risks.

History of the Art of War, 1900

James Anson FARRER, 1849–95

The first striking difference between military and naval warfare is that, while – in theory at least – the military forces of a country confine their attacks to the persons and power of their enemy, the naval forces devote themselves primarily to the plunder of his property and commerce.

Military Manners and Customs, 1885

Thomas Miller MAGUIRE, 1849–1920

All movements in the battlefield have but one end in view, the development of fire in greater volume and more effectively than that of the opposing force.

The Development of Tactics, 1904

Friedrich von BERNHARDI, 1849–1930

War is a biological necessity of the first importance.

Germany and the Next War, 1911

Robert Louis STEVENSON, 1850–94

Bring the comb and play upon it!
Marching, here we come!
Willie cocks his highland bonnet,
Johnnie beats the drum.

Mary Jane commands the party,
Peter leads the rear;
Feet in time, alert and hearty,
Each a Grenadier!

All in the most martial manner
Marching double-quick;
While the napkin like a banner
Waves upon the stick!

Here's enough of fame and pillage,
Great commander Jane!
Now that we've been round the village,
Let's go home again.

'Marching Song', from *A Child's Garden of Verses*, 1885

Ferdinand FOCH, 1851–1929

That is good sport, but for the Army the aeroplane is of no value.

Said while watching an aeronautics display in 1910

No study is possible on the battlefield; one does there simply what one can in order to apply what one knows. Therefore, in order to do even a little, one has already to know a great deal and know it well.

Principles of War, 1919

The unknown is the governing condition of war.

Principles of War, 1919

There can never be too many guns, there are never enough of them.

Principles of War, 1919

The most solid moral qualities melt away under the effect of modern arms.

Principles of War, 1919

It takes fifteen thousand casualties to train one major-general.
Attributed.

Emperor MEIJI of Japan, 1852–1912

Death is lighter than a feather, duty heavy as a mountain.
Imperial Rescript to Soldiers and Sailors, January 1883

Reginald Baliol, Lord ESHER, 1852–1930

History is written for schoolmasters and armchair strategists. Statesmen and warriors pick their way through the dark.
Diary, 15th March 1915

Robert Bontine CUNNINGHAME-GRAHAM, 1852–1936

A steed, a steed of matchless speed!
A sword of metal keen!
All else to noble hearts is dross,
All else on earth is mean.
'Cavalier's Song', *c.* 1920

Ian Standish Monteith HAMILTON, 1853–1947

The ideal General Staff should, in peace time, do nothing! They deal in an intangible stuff called thought. Their main business consists in thinking out what an enemy may do and what their Commanding Generals ought to do, and the less they clank their spurs the better.
The Soul and Body of an Army, 1921

Oscar WILDE, 1854–1900

As long as war is regarded as wicked it will always have its fascination. When it is looked upon as vulgar, it will cease to be popular.
The Critic As Artist, 1891

George Francis Robert HENDERSON, 1854–1903

Life in the British Islands, except perhaps on the moors and in the forests of the north, was, and is, no preparation for war whatsoever.
The Science of War, 1905

Woodrow WILSON, 1856–1924

There is no question what the roll of honor in America is. The roll of honor consists of the names of men who have squared their conduct by ideals of duty.
Speech in Washington, 27th February 1916

Militarism does not consist in the existence of an army, nor even in the existence of a very great army. Militarism is a spirit. It is a point of view. It is a system. It is a purpose. The purpose of militarism is to use armies for aggression.
Speech at West Point, 13th June 1916

Sigmund FREUD, 1856–1939

The warring state permits itself every misdeed, every act of violence, as would disgrace the individual man.

Civilization, War and Death, 1930

George Bernard SHAW, 1856–1950

You can always tell an old soldier by the inside of his holsters and cartridge boxes. The young men carry pistols and cartridges; the old ones, grub.

Arms and the Man, 1894

Soldiering, my dear madam, is the coward's art of attacking mercilessly when you are strong, and keeping out of harm's way when you are weak. That is the whole secret of successful fighting. Get your enemy at a disadvantage; and never, on any account, fight on equal terms.

Arms and the Man, 1894

The British soldier can stand up to anything except the British War Office.

The Devil's Disciple, 1897

A soldier is an anachronism of which we must get rid.

The Devil's Disciple, 1897

When the military man approaches, the world locks up its spoons and packs off its womankind.

Man and Superman, 1903

Nothing is ever done in this world until men are prepared to kill one another if it is not done.

Major Barbara, 1905

He who bears the brand of Cain shall rule the earth.

Back to Methuselah, 1921

Henri Philippe Omer PÉTAIN, 1856–1951

One does not fight with men against material; it is with material served by men that one makes war.

In Alistair Horne, *The Price of Glory*, 1962

John DAVIDSON, 1857–1909

From fear in every guise,
From sloth, from love of pelf,
By war's great sacrifice
The world redeems itself.

'War Song', 1898

Theodore ROOSEVELT, 1858–1919

Again and again we have owed peace to the fact that we were prepared for war.

Speaking at the Naval War College, 2nd June 1897

Peace is a goddess only when she comes with sword girt on thigh.
Speaking at the Naval War College, 2nd June 1897

If the American nation will speak softly and yet build and keep at a pitch of the highest training a thoroughly efficient Navy, the Monroe Doctrine will go far.
Speech, 2nd September 1901

A man who is good enough to shed his blood for his country is good enough to be given a square deal afterwards. More than that no man is entitled to, and less than that no man shall have.
Speech at Springfield, Illinois, 4th June 1903

War is a dreadful thing, and unjust war is a crime against humanity. But it is such a crime because it is unjust, not because it is war.
Speech at the Sorbonne, 23rd April 1910

Speak softly and carry a big stick; you will go far.
Derived from an African proverb, and frequently used by Roosevelt

Andrew BONAR LAW, 1858–1923

In war it is necessary not only to be active but to seem active.
Quoted in Robert Debs Heinl Jr, *Dictionary of Military and Naval Quotations*, 1966

William Lee HOWARD, 1860–1918

A boy who hears a history lesson ended by the beauty of peace, and how Napoleon brought ruin upon the world and that he should be forever cursed, will not have much confidence in his teacher. He wants to hear more about the fighting and less about the peace negotiations.
Dolls and Pugnacity, 1903

Henry NEWBOLT, 1862–1938

The sand of the desert is sodden red, –
Red with the wreck of a square that broke; –
The Gatling's jammed and the Colonel dead,
And the regiment blind with dust and smoke,
The river of death has brimmed his banks,
And England's far, and Honour a name,
But the voice of a schoolboy rallies the ranks:
'Play up! play up! and play the game!'
'Vitaï Lampada', 1897

Broken and pierced, hung on the bitter wire,
By their most precious death the Sons of Man
Redeem for us the life of our desire
O Christ how often since the world began!
'A Perpetual Memory', 1915

George SANTAYANA, 1863–1925

To call war the soil of courage and virtue is like calling debauchery the soil of love.

The Life of Reason, 1905–6

To delight in war is a merit in the soldier, a dangerous quality in the captain, and a positive crime in the statesman.

The Life of Reason, 1905–6

Frederick Scott OLIVER, 1864–1934

The real difficulty which besets the philanthropist in his endeavour to exorcise the spirit of war is caused, not by the vices of this spirit, but by its virtues. In so far as it springs from vainglory or cupidity, it is comparatively easy to deal with. In so far as it is base, there is room for a bargain. It can be compounded with or bought off, as we have seen before now, with some kind of material currency. It will not stand out for very long against promises of prosperity and threats of death. But where, as at most crises, the spirit is not base, where its impulse is not less noble, but more noble than those which influence men, day by day in the conduct of their worldly affairs, where the contrast which presents itself to their imagination is between duty on the one hand and gain on the other, between self-sacrifice and self-interest, between their country's need and their own ease, it is not possible to quench the fires by appeals proceeding from a lower plane. The philanthropist, if he is to succeed, must take still higher ground, and higher ground than this it is not a very simple matter to discover.

Ordeal by Battle, 1915

Guy DU MAURIER, 1865–1915

Democracy is the best system of government yet devised, but it suffers from one great defect – it does not encourage those military virtues upon which, in an envious world, it must frequently depend for survival.

Quoted in Robert Debs Heinl Jr, *Dictionary of Military and Naval Quotations*, 1966

Rudyard KIPLING, 1865–1936

We have fed our sea for a thousand years
And she calls us, still unfed,
Though there's never a wave of all her waves
But marks our English dead.

'A Song of the English', 1893

The strength of twice three thousand horse,
That serve in one command;
The hand that heaves the headlong force,
The hate that backs the hand:
The doom-bolt in the darkness freed,
The mine that splits the main;
The white-hot wake, the 'wildering speed –
The Choosers of the Slain!

'The Destroyers', 1898

God of our fathers, known of old,
  Lord of our far-flung battle-line,
Beneath whose awful Hand we hold
  Dominion over palm and pine –
Lord God of Hosts, be with us yet,
Lest we forget – lest we forget!

The tumult and the shouting dies;
  The Captains and the Kings depart;
Still stands Thine ancient sacrifice,
  An humble and a contrite heart.
Lord God of Hosts, be with us yet,
Lest we forget – lest we forget!

Far-called, our navies melt away;
  On dune and headland sinks the fire:
Lo, all our pomp of yesterday
  Is one with Nineveh and Tyre!
Judge of the Nations, spare us yet,
Lest we forget – lest we forget!
'Recessional', 1897

I went into a public-'ouse to get a pint o' beer,
The publican 'e up an' sez, 'We serve no redcoats here'.
The girls be'ind the bar they laughed an' giggled fit to die,
I outs into the street again an' to myself sez I:
  O it's Tommy this, an' Tommy that, an' 'Tommy go away';
  But it's 'Thank you, Mister Atkins', when the band begins to play –
  The band begins to play, my boys, the band begins to play,
  O it's 'Thank you, Mister Atkins', when the band begins to play.
Tommy, 1907

We aren't no thin red 'eroes, nor we aren't no blackguards too,
But single men in barricks, most remarkable like you;
An' if sometimes our conduck isn't all your fancy paints,
Why, single men in barricks don't grow into plaster saints;
  While it's Tommy this, an' Tommy that, an' 'Tommy fall be'ind',
  But it's 'Please to walk in front, sir', when there's trouble in the wind –
  There's trouble in the wind, my boys, there's trouble in the wind,
  O it's 'Please to walk in front, sir', when there's trouble in the wind.
Tommy, 1907

A good soldier is always a bit of an old maid.
The New Army, 1915

Erich LUDENDORFF, 1865–1937

War is the highest expression of the racial view of life.
Meine Kriegserinnerungen, 1919

William Butler YEATS, 1865–1939

The dews drop slowly and dreams gather: unknown spears
Suddenly hurtle before my dream-awakened eyes,
And then the clash of fallen horsemen and the cries
Of unknown perishing armies beat about my ears.
We who still labour by the cromlech on the shore,
The grey cairn on the hill, when day sinks drowned in dew,
Being weary of the world's empires, bow down to you,
Master of the still stars and of the flaming door.

'The Valley of the Black Pig', 1899

Romain ROLLAND, 1866–1944

I find war detestable, but even more detestable are those who praise war without participating in it.

Inter Arma Caritas, 30th October 1914

H(erbert) G(eorge) WELLS, 1866–1946

'I'll call my article,' meditated the war-correspondent, 'Mankind *versus* Iron-mongery.'

'The Land Ironclads', 1901

The third peculiarity of aerial warfare was that it was at once enormously destructive and entirely indecisive.

The War in the Air, 1908

The army ages men sooner than law and philosophy; it exposes them more freely to germs, which undermine and destroy, and it shelters them more completely from thought, which stimulates and preserves.

'Bealby', 1915

We want to get rid of the militarist not simply because he hurts and kills, but because he is an intolerable thick-voiced blockhead who stands hectoring and blustering in our way to achievement.

The Outline of History, 1920

The professional military mind is by necessity an inferior and unimaginative mind; no man of high intellectual quality would willingly imprison his gifts in such a calling.

The Outline of History, 1920

Richard LE GALLIENNE, 1866–1947

The cry of the Little Peoples goes up to God in vain,
For the world is given over to the cruel sons of Cain.

'The Cry of the Little Peoples', 1892

John Joseph PERSHING, 1866–1948

All a soldier needs to know is how to shoot and salute.

Attributed

Charles Edward MONTAGUE, 1867–1928

The number of medals on an officer's breast varies in inverse proportion to the square of the distance of his duties from the front line.
Fiery Particles, 1915

War hath no fury like a noncombatant.
Disenchantment, 1922

Anonymous

Hostilities must not be begun without previous and explicit warning in the form of a reasoned declaration of war, or of an ultimatum embracing a conditional declaration.
The Hague Convention, 1907

Old soldiers never die –
They simply fade way.
British Army song, *c.* 1915

You're in the Army now,
You're not behind a plow.
You'll never get rich,
You son of a bitch,
You're in the Army now.
US, *c.* 1916

Me no likee English sailor
When Yankee sailor come ashore.
English sailor plenty money,
Yankee sailor plenty more.
Yankee sailor call me ducky darling,
English sailor call me Chinese whore.
Yankee sailor only shag for short time,
English sailor shag for evermore.
Royal Navy, traditional

The Infantry, the Infantry, with dirt behind their ears,
The Infantry, the Infantry, can drink their weight in beers!
The Cavalry, the Artillery, and the God-damned Engineers
Can never beat the Infantry in a hundred thousand years.
US, early 20th century

From the halls of Montezuma to the shores of Tripoli
We fight our country's battles in the air, on land and sea,
First to fight for right and freedom,
And to keep our honor clean.
We are proud to claim the title
Of United States Marine . . .
US, 'The Marines' Hymn', early 20th century

If the Army and the Navy
Ever gaze on Heaven's scenes
They will find the streets are guarded
By United States Marines.

US, 'The Marines' Hymn', early 20th century

Cavalry will never be scrapped to make room for the tanks; in the course of time cavalry may be reduced as the supply of horses in this country diminishes. This depends greatly on the life of fox-hunting.

Unsigned contribution, *Journal of the Royal United Services Institution*, February 1921

Bombardment from the air is legitimate only when directed at a military objective, the destruction of which could constitute a distinct military disadvantage to the belligerent.

The Hague Convention of Jurists, 1923

The next war may well start in the air, but in all probability it will wind up, as did the last war, in the mud.

Report of the President's Board to Study Development of Aircraft for the National Defense, 1925

Giulio DOUHET, 1869–1930

To have command of the air means to be in a position to prevent the enemy from flying while retaining the ability to fly oneself. Planes capable of carrying moderately heavy loads of bombs already exist, and the construction of enough of them for national defence would not require exceptional resources. The active ingredients of bombs or projectiles, the explosives, the incendiaries, the poison gases, are already being produced. An aerial fleet capable of dumping hundreds of tons of such bombs can easily be organized; therefore the striking force and magnitude of aerial offensives, considered from the standpoint of either material or moral significance, are far more effective than those of any other offensive yet known.

The Command of the Air, 1921

I have mathematical certainty that the future will confirm my assertion that aerial warfare will be the most important element in future wars, and that in consequence not only will the importance of the Independent Air Force rapidly increase, but the importance of the army and the navy will decrease in proportion.

The Command of the Air, 1921

A people who are bombed today as they were bombed yesterday, and who know that they will be bombed again tomorrow and see no end of their martyrdom, are bound to call for peace at length.

The Command of the Air, 1921

Every development or improvement in firearms favours the defensive.

The Command of the Air, 1921

Neville CHAMBERLAIN, 1869–1940

In war, whichever side may call itself the victor, there are no winners, but all are losers.

Speech at Kettering, 3rd July 1938

Mahatma (Mohandas Karamchand) GANDHI, 1869–1948

Non-violence is not a garment to be put on and off at will. Its seat is in the heart, and it must be an inseparable part of our very being.

Non-Violence in Peace and War, 1948

War is an unmitigated evil. But it certainly does one good thing. It drives away fear and brings bravery to the surface.

Non-Violence in Peace and War, 1948

What difference does it make to the dead, the orphans and the homeless whether the mad destruction is wrought under the name of totalitarianism or the holy name of liberty or democracy?

Non-Violence in Peace and War, 1948

André-Paul-Guillaume GIDE, 1869–1951

It is essential to persuade the soldier that those he is being urged to massacre are bandits who do not deserve to live; before killing other good, decent fellows like himself, his gun would fall from his hands.

Journals, 10th February 1943

Vladimir Ilyich LENIN (Vladimir Ulyanov), 1870–1924

We are not pacifists. We are against imperialist wars, but it is absurd for the proletariat to oppose revolutionary wars that are indispensable for the victory of socialism.

Farewell Letter to the Swiss workers, 8th April 1917

Socialists have always condemned wars as barbarous and brutal. Our attitude towards war, however, is fundamentally different from that of the bourgeois pacifists (supporters and advocates of peace) and of the anarchists. We differ from the former in that we understand the inevitable connection between wars and class struggles within a country; we understand that wars cannot be abolished unless classes are abolished and socialism is created; we also differ in that we regard civil wars, i.e. wars waged by an oppressed class against the oppressing class, by a slave against slave-holders, by serf against landowners, and by wage-earners against the bourgeoisie, as fully legitimate, progressive and necessary.

War and Socialism, 1915

Stephen CRANE, 1871–1900

They were going to look at war, the red animal – war, the blood-swollen god.

The Red Badge of Courage, 1895

At times he regarded the wounded soldiers in an envious way. He conceived persons with torn bodies to be peculiarly happy. He wished that he, too, had a wound, a red badge of courage.

The Red Badge of Courage, 1895

Do not weep, maiden, for war is kind.
Because your lover threw wild hands towards the sky
And the affrighted steed ran on alone,
Do not weep.
War is kind.

'War Is Kind', 1899

Do not weep, babe, for war is kind.
Because your father tumbled in the yellow trenches,
Raged at his breast, gulped and died,
Do not weep.
War is kind.

'War Is Kind', 1899

Paul VALÉRY, 1871–1945

There could be real peace only if everyone were satisfied. That means that there is not often real peace. There are only actual states of peace which, like wars, are mere expedients.

Reflections on the World Today, 1931

Calvin COOLIDGE, 1872–1933

The nation which forgets its defenders will itself be forgotten.

Speech, 21st July 1920

Bertrand RUSSELL, 1872–1970

People who are vigorous and brutal often find war enjoyable, provided that it is a victorious war and that there is not too much interference with rape and plunder. This is a great help in persuading people that wars are righteous.

Unpopular Essays, 1950

Patriots always talk about dying for their country, and never about killing for their country.

Attributed

Alexander Graham BELL, 1874–1922

The nation that secures control of the air will ultimately control the world.

Letter, 1909

Amy LOWELL, 1874–1925

For the man who should loose me is dead,
Fighting with the Duke in Flanders,
In a pattern called a war.
Christ! What are patterns for?

'Patterns', 1916

G(ilbert) K(eith) CHESTERTON, 1874–1936

It's not the world that's got so much worse, but the news coverage that's got so much better.

Attributed

Gertrude STEIN, 1874–1946

Two things are always the same the dance and war. One might say anything is the same but the dance and war are particularly the same because one can see them. That is what they are for.

Everybody's Autobiography, 1938

George Ivanovich GURDJIEFF, 1874–1949

There is a war going on at the present moment. What does it signify? It signifies that several millions of sleeping people are trying to destroy several millions of other sleeping people. They would not do this of course, if they were to wake up.

Quoted in P. D. Ouspensky, *In Search of the Miraculous*, 1949

Winston Leonard Spencer CHURCHILL, 1874–1965

Nothing is more exhilarating than to be shot at without result.

The Malakand Field Force, 1898

Fanaticism is not the cause of war. It is the means which helps savage peoples to fight.

The River War, 1899

Countless and inestimable are the chances of war.

The River War, 1899

There is required for the composition of a great commander not only passive common sense and reasoning power, not only imagination, but also an element of legerdemain, an original and sinister touch, which leaves the enemy puzzled as well as beaten.

The World Crisis, 1923

War, which used to be cruel and magnificent, has now become cruel and squalid. It has all been the fault of democracy and science. From the moment that either of these meddlers and muddlers was allowed to take part in actual fighting, the doom of War was sealed. Instead of a small number of well-trained professionals championing their country's cause with ancient weapons and a beautiful intricacy of archaic movement, we now have entire populations, including even women and children, pitted against each other in brutish mutual extermination, and only a set of blear-eyed clerks left to add up the butcher's bill. From the moment when Democracy was admitted to, or rather forced itself upon, the battlefield, War ceased to be a Gentleman's pursuit.

My Early Life, 1930

Never, never, never believe any war will be smooth and easy.

A Roving Commission, 1930

It is the greatest possible mistake to mix up disarmament with peace. When you have peace, you will have disarmament.

In the House of Commons, 13th July 1934

Traditions of the Royal Navy? I'll give you traditions of the Navy: rum, buggery, and the lash.

Remark made at the Board of Admiralty, 1939

In my experience, based on many years' observation, officers with high athletic qualifications are not usually successful in the higher ranks.

Memorandum to the Secretary of State for War, 4th February 1941

The late M. Venizelos observed that in all her wars England – he should have said Britain, of course – always wins one battle, the last.

Speech at the Lord Mayor's Banquet, 10th November 1942

No one can guarantee success in war, but only deserve it.

The Second World War: Their Finest Hour, 1949

It is dangerous to meddle with Admirals when they say they can't do things. They have always got the weather or fuel or something to argue about.

The Second World War: Their Finest Hour, 1949

I hear that my Generals are selling their Lives dearly.

Attributed, in old age

Carl SANDBURG, 1878–1964

Sometime they'll give a war and nobody will come.

The People, Yes, 1936

John Frederick Charles FULLER, 1878–1966

It is war that shapes peace, and armament that shapes war.

Armament and History, 1945

The soldier cannot be a fighter and a pack animal at one and the same time, any more than a field piece can be a gun and a supply vehicle combined.

Letter to S. L. A. Marshall, 1948

Sir John FORTESCUE, 1879–1933

. . . that sorely tried institution, the British Army.

History of the British Army, 1930

Will (William Penn Adair) ROGERS, 1879–1935

You can't say civilization don't advance, however, for in every war they kill you a new way.

Autobiography, 1928

Leon TROTSKY, 1879–1940

Every great revolution brings ruin to the old army.

c. 1921, attributed

Insurrection is an art, and like all arts it has its laws.

History of the Russian Revolution, 1931

Armed insurrection stands in the same relation to revolution that revolution as a whole does to evolution. It is the critical point when accumulating quantity turns with an explosion into quality.

History of the Russian Revolution, 1931

Patriotism to the Soviet State is a revolutionary duty, whereas patriotism to a bourgeois State is treachery.

Quoted in Fitzroy Maclean, *Disputed Barricade*, 1957

An ally has to be watched just like an enemy.

Quoted in A. Ulam, *Expansion and Coexistence*, 1968

Joseph Vissarionovich STALIN, 1879–1953

History shows that there are no invincible armies.

Radio broadcast, 3rd July 1941

A single death is a tragedy. A million deaths are a statistic.

Quoted in Harold Coyle, *Sword Point*, 1988

Albert EINSTEIN, 1879–1955

The man who enjoys marching in line and file to the strains of music falls below my contempt; he received his great brain by mistake – the spinal cord would have been amply sufficient.

What I Believe, 1930

Nationalism is an infantile disease, . . .

The World As I See It, 1949

E(dward) M(organ) FORSTER, 1879–1970

I hate the idea of causes, and if I had to choose between betraying my country and betraying my friend, I hope I should have the guts to betray my country.

Two Cheers for Democracy, 1951: 'What I Believe'

Thomas Michael KETTLE, 1880–1916

I have seen war, and faced modern artillery, and I know what an outrage it is against simple men.

The Ways of War, 1915

Guillaume APOLLINAIRE, 1880–1918

Ah God! how pretty war is
With its songs and its rests.

'L'Adieu du Cavalier', 1918

Kurt von HAMMERSTEIN, d. 1945

I divide officers into four classes – the clever, the lazy, the stupid and the industrious. Each officer possesses at least two of these qualities. Those who are clever and industrious are fitted for the high staff appointments. Use can be made of those who are stupid and lazy. The man who is clever and lazy is fit for the very highest command. He has the temperament and the requisite nerves to deal with all situations. But whoever is stupid and industrious must be removed immediately.

Quoted in Robert Debs Heinl Jr, *Dictionary of Military and Naval Quotations*, 1966

H(enry) L(ouis) MENCKEN, 1880–1956

There is no record in history of a nation that ever gained anything valuable by being unprepared to defend itself.

Prejudices: Series V, 1926

War is the only sport that is genuinely amusing. And it is the only sport that has any intelligible use.

Prejudices: Series V, 1926

The military caste did not originate as a party of patriots, but as a party of bandits.

Minority Report, 1956

George C(atlett) MARSHALL, 1880–1959

If man does find the solution for world peace it will be the most revolutionary reversal of his record we have ever known.

Biennial Report of the Chief of Staff, US Army, September 1945

Douglas MacARTHUR, 1880–1964

In no other profession are the penalties for employing untrained personnel so appalling and so irrevocable as in the military.

Annual Report of the Chief of Staff, US Army, 1933

There is no security on this earth. Only opportunity.

Quoted in Courtney Whitney, *MacArthur: His Rendezvous with History*, 1955

The soldier, above all other people, prays for peace, for he must suffer and bear the deepest wounds and scars of war.

Speaking at West Point, 12th May 1962

Jean GIRAUDOUX, 1882–1944

Ask any soldier. To kill a man is to merit a woman.

Tiger at the Gates, 1935

There's a kind of permission for war which can only be given by the world's mood and atmosphere, the feel of its pulse. It would be madness to undertake a war without that permission.

Tiger at the Gates, 1935

During war we imprison the rights of man.

Tiger at the Gates, 1935

Franklin D(elano) ROOSEVELT, 1882–1945

I have seen war. I have seen war on land and sea. I have seen blood running from the wounded. I have seen men coughing out their gassed lungs. I have seen the dead in the mud. I have seen cities destroyed. I have seen two hundred limping, exhausted men come out of the line – the survivors of a regiment of a thousand that went forward 48 hours before. I have seen children starving. I have seen the agony of mothers and wives. I hate war.

Speech in Chautauqua, NY, 14th August 1936

You cannot organize civilization around the core of militarism and at the same time expect reason to control human destinies.

Radio broadcast, 26th October 1938

Franz KAFKA, 1883–1924

Every revolution evaporates, leaving behind only the slime of a new bureaucracy.

Attributed

Benito MUSSOLINI, 1883–1945

Neutrals never dominate events. They always sink. Blood alone moves the wheels of history.

Speech in Parma, 13th December 1914

Archibald Percival, Lord WAVELL, 1883–1950

The real way to get value out of the study of military history is to take particular situations, and as far as possible get inside the skin of the man who made a decision, realize the conditions in which the decision was made, and then see in what way you could have improved it.

Lecture, Aldershot, *c.* 1930

Interior lines at night are the general's delight. Exterior lines at morning are the general's warning.

Lecture, Aldershot, *c.* 1930

Speed is unfortunately a most expensive commodity: alike in battleships, motor cars, racehorses and women, a comparatively small increase in speed may double the price of the article.

The Palestine Campaigns, 1931

But above them all towers the indomitable figure of the British soldier, the finest all-round fighting man the world has seen . . . whose humorous endurance of time and chance lasts always to the end.

The Good Soldier, 1931

The advantages are nearly all on the side of the guerilla in that he is bound by no rules, tied by no transport, hampered by no drill-books, while the soldier is bound by many things, not the least by his expectation of a full meal every so many hours. The soldier usually wins in the long run, but very expensively.

Speaking at Blackdown, 30th August 1932

One well-known Brigadier always phrases his requirements of the ideal infantryman as 'athlete, stalker, marksman'. I always feel a little inclined to put it on a lower plane and say that the qualities of a successful poacher, cat burglar and gunman would content me.

The Training of the Army for War, 1933

Sorting out muddles is really the chief job of a commander.

In the *Journal of the Royal United Services Institution*, February 1933

Efficiency in a general, his soldiers have a right to expect; geniality they are usually right to suspect.

Generals and Generalship, 1939

The more I see of war, the less I think that general principles of strategy count as compared with administrative problems and the gaining of intelligence. The main principles of strategy, i.e. to attack the other fellow in the flank or in the rear in preference to the front, to surprise him by any means in one's power and to attack his morale before you attack him physically are really things that every savage schoolboy knows. But it is often outside the power of the general to act as he would have liked owing to lack of adequate resources and I think that military history very seldom brings this out. In fact it is almost impossible that it should do so without a detailed study which is often unavailable. For instance, if Hannibal had had another twenty elephants, it might have altered his whole strategy against Italy.

Letter to B. H. Liddell Hart, 1942

When things are going badly in battle the best tonic is to take one's mind off one's own troubles by considering what a rotten time one's opponent must be having.

Other Men's Flowers, 1944

Note, too, with what economy most of Shakespeare's characters get their dying done: Hamlet ('the rest is silence'); Romeo and Juliet; Antony and Cleopatra;

Arthur ('Heaven take my soul and England keep my bones' – a precocious last line for a young one!); Caesar, Cassius and Brutus; the principal exception is, I regret to say, a Commander-in-Chief, Othello – but he was an Oriental.

Footnote in *Other Men's Flowers*, 1944

The best confidential report I ever heard of was also the shortest. It was by one Horse Gunner of another, and ran, 'Personally I would not breed from this officer.'

Attributed

José ORTEGA Y GASSET, 1883–1955

Today, violence is the rhetoric of the period.

The Revolt of the Masses, 1930

Harry S. TRUMAN, 1884–1972

The Marine Corps is the Navy's police force and as long as I am President that is what it will remain. They have a propaganda machine that is almost equal to Stalin's.

Letter to Gordon L. McDonough, 29th August 1950

I sincerely regret the unfortunate choice of language which I used in my letter of August 29 to Congressman McDonough concerning the Marine Corps.

Letter to General C. B. Cates, 6th September 1950

D(avid) H(erbert) LAWRENCE, 1885–1930

A soldier! – a common soldier! – nothing but a body that makes movements when it hears a shout.

Sons and Lovers, 1913

George S(mith) PATTON Jr, 1885–1945

Untutored courage is useless in the face of educated bullets.

In *Cavalry Journal*, April 1922

War will be won by Blood and Guts alone.

Comment made to officers at Fort Benning, Georgia, 1940

A piece of spaghetti or a military unit can only be led from the front end.

Attributed remark, 1942

The most vital quality a soldier can possess is self-confidence, utter, complete and bumptious.

Letter to his son, 6th June 1944

A pint of sweat will save a gallon of blood.

War As I Knew It, 1947

There is only one tactical principle which is not subject to change. It is: to use the means at hand to inflict the maximum amount of wounds, death and destruction on the enemy in the minimum of time.

War As I Knew It, 1947

Use steamroller strategy; that is, make up your mind on the course and direction of action, and stick to it. But in tactics, do not steamroller. Attack weakness. Hold them by the nose and kick them in the pants.

War As I Knew It, 1947

It is sad to remember that, when anyone has fairly mastered the art of command, the necessity for that art usually expires – either through the termination of the war or through the advanced age of the commander.

War As I Knew It, 1947

There are more tired corps and division commanders than there are tired corps and divisions.

War As I Knew It, 1947

All very successful commanders are prima donnas, and must be so treated.

War As I Knew It, 1947

There is a great deal of talk about loyalty from the bottom to the top. Loyalty from the top down is even more necessary and much less prevalent.

War As I Knew It, 1947

One of the great defects of our military establishment is the giving of weak sentences for military offences. The purpose of military law is administrative rather than legal . . . Injustice to other men, soldiers who go to sleep on post, who go absent for an unreasonable time during combat, who shirk battle, should be executed; and Army or Corps commanders should have the authority to approve the death sentence. It is utterly stupid to say that General Officers, as a result of whose orders thousands of gallant and brave men have been killed, are not capable of knowing how to remove the life of one poltroon.

War As I Knew It, 1947

If you can't get them to salute when they should salute, and wear the clothes you tell them to wear, how are you going to get them to die for their country?

Quoted in Robert Debs Heinl Jr, *Dictionary of Military and Naval Quotations*, 1966

Bernard Law, Lord MONTGOMERY, 1887–1979

An extensive use of weedkiller is needed in the senior ranks after a war; this will enable the first class young officers who have emerged during the war to be moved up.

Memoirs, 1958

The morale of the soldier is the greatest single factor in war and the best way to achieve a high morale in wartime is by success in battle.

Memoirs, 1958

Most official accounts of past wars are deceptively well written, and seem to omit many important matters – in particular, anything which might indicate that any of our commanders ever made the slightest mistake. They are therefore useless as a source of instruction.

Memoirs, 1958

T(homas) E(dward) LAWRENCE, 1888–1935

Guerilla war is far more intellectual than a bayonet charge.

The Science of Guerilla Warfare, 1929

Rebellions can be made by two per cent active in a striking force, and 98 per cent sympathetic.

The Science of Guerilla Warfare, 1929

The greatest commander is he whose intuitions most nearly happen.

The Science of Guerilla Warfare, 1929

I hope you have kept the enemy always in the picture. War-books so often leave them out.

Letter to Archibald Wavell, 9th February 1928

With 2,000 years of examples behind us we have no excuse when fighting, for not fighting well.

Quoted in B. H. Liddell Hart, *Memoirs*, 1965

John Foster DULLES, 1888–1959

The ability to get to the verge without getting to the war is the necessary art. If you cannot master it, you inevitably get into war. If you try to run away from it, if you are scared to go to the brink, you are lost.

Quoted in *Life* magazine, January 1956

Hoffman NICKERSON, 1888–1965

Air power is a thunderbolt launched from an eggshell invisibly tethered to a base.

Arms and Policy, 1945

Irving BERLIN, b. 1888

Oh! how I hate to get up in the morning,
Oh! how I'd love to remain in bed;
For the hardest blow of all
Is to hear the bugle call,
'You've got to get up, you've got to get up,
You've got to get up this morning!'

Song, 1918

Philip GUEDALLA, 1889–1944

The conversation of military men upon political topics is a rare stimulant for civilians.

Fathers of the Revolution, 1926

Adolf HITLER, 1889–1945

I know that fewer people are won over by the written word than by the spoken word and that every great movement on this earth owes its growth to great speakers and not to great writers.

Mein Kampf, 1924–6: Preface

Man has become great through perpetual struggle. In perpetual peace his greatness must decline.

Mein Kampf, 1924–6

. . . Every attempt to combat a *Weltanshauung* by means of force will turn out futile in the end if the struggle fails to take the form of an offensive for the establishment of an entirely new spiritual order of things. It is only in the struggle between two *Weltanshauungen* that physical force, consistently and ruthlessly applied, will eventually turn the scales in its own favour.

Mein Kampf, 1924–6

Any alliance whose purpose is not the intention to wage war is senseless and useless.

Mein Kampf, 1924–6

He who would live must fight. He who does not wish to fight in this world, where permanent struggle is the law of life, has not the right to exist.

Mein Kampf, 1924–6

The little affair of operational command is something that anybody can do.

Quoted in Alan Bullock, *Hitler*, 1971

Walter LIPPMANN, 1889–1974

It is for all practical purposes impossible to win a guerilla war if there is a privileged sanctuary behind the guerilla fighters.

In the *Washington Post*, 5th September 1963

Nobody has yet found a way of bombing that can prevent foot soldiers from walking.

In the *Washington Post*, 18th February 1965

Revolutions are always the work of a conscious minority.

In the *Washington Post*, 12th April 1966

Dwight D(avid) EISENHOWER, 1890–1969

In the final analysis a soldier's pack is not so heavy a burden as a prisoner's chains.

Inaugural Address, 20th January 1953

HO CHI MINH, 1890–1969

Military action without politics is like a tree without roots.

Attributed

Charles André Joseph Marie DE GAULLE, 1890–1970

The graveyards are full of indispensable men.

Attributed

Anonymous

I don't know what'll be the most important weapon in the next war, but in the war after that it'll be the bow and arrow.

Common saying, *c.* 1945

Erwin ROMMEL, 1891–1944

One must not judge everyone in the world by his qualities as a soldier: otherwise we should have no civilization.

Advice to his son, *c.* 1943

David LOW, 1891–1966

I have never met anyone who wasn't against War. Even Hitler and Mussolini were, according to themselves.

In the *New York Times*, 10th February 1964

William Joseph, Viscount SLIM, 1891–1970

Nothing is easier in jungle or dispersed fighting than for a man to shirk. If he has no stomach for advancing, all he has to do is to flop into the undergrowth; in retreat he can slink out of the rear guard, join up later, and swear he was the last to leave. A patrol leader can take his men a mile into the jungle, hide there, and return with any report he fancies.

Defeat Into Victory, 1956

Long ago I had learned that in conversation with an irate senior, a junior should confine himself to the three remarks, 'Yes, sir', 'No, sir' and 'Sorry, sir'. Repeated in the proper sequence, they will get him through the most difficult interview with the minimum discomfort.

Unofficial History, 1959

I find I have liked all of the soldiers of different races who have fought with me and most of those who have fought against me. This is not strange, for there is a freemasonry among fighting soldiers that helps them to understand one another even if they are enemies.

Unofficial History, 1959

While the battles the British fight may differ in the widest possible ways, they have invariably two common characteristics: they are always fought uphill and always at the junction of two or more map sheets.

Unofficial History, 1959

Henry MILLER, 1891–1980

How different the new order would be if we could consult the veteran instead of the politician.

The Wisdom of the Heart, 1941

Ugo BETTI, 1892–1953

Perhaps there is nothing in the whole of creation which knows the meaning of peace.

The Fugitives, 1953

MAO TSE-TUNG (Mao Zedong), 1893–1976

A revolution is not a dinner party, or writing an essay, or painting a picture, or doing embroidery; it cannot be so refined, so leisurely and gentle, so temperate, kind, courteous, restrained, and magnanimous. A revolution is an insurrection, an act of violence by which one class overthrows another.

Report on an Investigation of the Peasant Movement in Hunan, 1927

War is the highest form of struggle for resolving contradictions, when they have developed to a certain stage, between classes, nations, states, or political groups, and it has existed ever since the emergence of private property and of classes.

Problems of Strategy in China's Revolutionary War, 1936

War, this monster of mutual slaughter among men, will be finally eliminated by the progress of human society, and in the not too distant future too. But there is only one way to eliminate it and that is to oppose war with war, to oppose counter-revolutionary war with revolutionary war, to oppose national counter-revolutionary war with national revolutionary war, and to oppose counter-revolutionary class war with revolutionary class war.

Problems of Strategy in China's Revolutionary War, 1936

Many people think it is impossible for the guerilla to exist for long in the enemy's rear. Such a belief reveals lack of comprehension of the relationship that should exist between the people and the troops. The former may be likened to water and the latter to the fish that inhabit it.

On Guerilla Warfare, 1937

It is incorrect to hold a theory of equality in all things, but there must be equality of existence in accepting the hardships and dangers of war.

On Guerilla Warfare, 1937

Revolutionary war is an antitoxin which not only eliminates the enemy's poison but also purges us of our own filth.

On Protracted War, 1938

In ancient warfare, the spear and the shield were used, the spear to attack and destroy the enemy, and the shield to defend and preserve oneself. To the present day, all weapons are still an extension of the spear and the shield. The bomber, the machine-gun, the long-range gun and poison gas are developments of the spear, while the air-raid shelter, the steel helmet, the concrete fortification and the gas mask are developments of the shield. The tank is a new weapon combining the functions of both spear and shield.

On Protracted War, 1938

Every communist must grasp the truth, 'Political power grows out of the barrel of a gun.'

Problems of War and Strategy, 1938

To get rid of the gun we must first grasp it in our own hands.

Problems of War and Strategy, 1938

I hold that it is bad as far as we are concerned if a person, a political party, an army or a school is not attacked by the enemy, for in that case it would definitely mean that we have sunk to the level of the enemy. It is good if we are attacked by the enemy, since it proves that we have drawn a clear line of demarcation between the enemy and ourselves.

To Be Attacked by the Enemy Is Not a Bad Thing but a Good Thing, 1939

The ability to run away is the essence of the guerilla.

Strategic Problems in the Anti-Japanese Guerilla War, 1939

We should support whatever the enemy opposes, and oppose whatever the enemy supports.

Interview, in *Sao Tang Pao*, 16th September 1939

All men must die, but death can vary in its significance. The ancient Chinese writer Szuma Chien said, 'Though death befalls all men alike, it may be weightier than Mount Tai or lighter than a feather.' To die for the people is weightier than Mount Tai, but to work for the fascists and die for the exploiters and oppressors is lighter than a feather.

Serve the People, 1944

An army without culture is a dull-witted army, and a dull-witted army cannot defeat the enemy.

The United Front in Cultural Work, 1944

Without a people's army the people have nothing.

On Coalition Government, 1945

Everything reactionary is the same; if you don't hit it, it won't fall. This is also like sweeping the floor; as a rule, where the broom does not reach, the dust will not vanish of itself.

The Situation and Our Policy After the Victory in the War of Resistance Against Japan, 1945

As for the method of training, we should unfold the mass training movement in which officers teach soldiers, soldiers teach officers and the soldiers teach each other.

Policy for Work in the Liberation Areas for 1946, 1945

Be united, alert, earnest and lively.

Motto, Anti-Japanese Military and Political College

Aldous HUXLEY, 1894–1964

The most shocking fact about war is that its victims and its instruments are individual human beings, and that these individual beings are condemned by the monstrous conventions of politics to murder or be murdered in quarrels not their own.

The Olive Tree, 1937

Jean ROSTAND, b. 1894

Kill one man and you are a murderer. Kill millions and you are a conqueror. Kill everybody and you are God.

Pensées d'un biologiste, 1939

Nikita Sergeyevich KHRUSHCHEV, 1894–1971

I would say that only a child and an idiot do not fear war – the child because he cannot yet understand, and the idiot because he has been deprived by God of this possibility.

Speech in Kazincharcika (Hungary), 6th April 1964

(Maurice) Harold MACMILLAN, 1894–1986

Jaw-jaw is better than war-war.

Speaking in Canberra, 30th January 1958

Charles Turner JOY, 1895–1956

Every battle has a turning point when the slack water of uncertainty becomes the ebb tide of defeat or the flood water of victory.

Quoted in Robert Debs Heinl Jr, *Dictionary of Military and Naval Quotations*, 1966

Lewis MUMFORD, b. 1895

War is both the product of an earlier corruption and a producer of new corruption.

The Conduct of Life, 1951

Basil Henry LIDDELL HART, 1895–1970

The practical value of history is to throw the film of the past through the material projector of the present onto the screen of the future.

Thoughts on War, 1944

The large ground organization of a modern air force is its Achilles' heel.

Thoughts on War, 1944

Armies are temples of ancestor worship.

Thoughts on War, 1944

Smooth answers smooth the path to promotion.
Thoughts on War, 1944

There are only two classes who, as categories, show courage in war – the front-line soldier and the conscientious objector.
Thoughts on War, 1944

Darkness is a friend to the skilled infantryman.
Thoughts on War, 1944

The Army, for all its good points, is a cramping place for a thinking man.
Thoughts on War, 1944

An important difference between a military operation and a surgical operation is that the patient is not tied down. But it is a common fault of generalship to assume that he is.
Thoughts on War, 1944

Official manuals, by the nature of their compilation, are mainly registers of prevailing practice, not the log-books of a scientific study of war.
Thoughts on War, 1944

The only thing harder than getting a new idea into the military mind is to get an old one out.
Thoughts on War, 1944

Movement is the safety-valve of fear.
Thoughts on War, 1944

Two fundamental lessons of war experience are – never to check momentum; never to resume mere pushing.
Thoughts on War, 1944

There is no blitzkrieg possible in naval warfare – no lightning flash over the seas, no striking down an opponent. Seapower acts more like radium, beneficial to those who use it and are shielded, it destroys the tissues of those who are exposed to it.
Defence of the West, 1950

It is amazing to find how much time many rising soldiers spend in studying the Army List and its bearing on their own promotional prospects. One prominent general, Ironside, even kept a large ledger in which he kept the details of the service record of all the officers above him in the list and other people's views on their performance, health and prospects.
Memoirs, 1965

Bernard NEWMAN, 1897–1968

I have never met or heard of troops who can withstand a night attack from the rear.
The Cavalry Came Through, 1930

Bertolt BRECHT, 1898–1956

What they could do with round here is a good war. What else can you expect with peace running wild all over the place? You know what the trouble with peace is? No organization.

Mother Courage, 1939: Act I

When a soldier sees a clean face, there's one more whore in the world.

Mother Courage, 1939: Act III

I say, you can't be sure the war will ever end. Of course, it may have to pause occasionally – for breath as it were – it can even meet with an accident – nothing on this earth is perfect – a war of which we could say it left nothing to be desired will probably never exist.

Mother Courage, 1939: Act VI

War is like love, it always finds a way.

Mother Courage, 1939: Act VI

Don't tell me peace has broken out.

Mother Courage, 1939: Act VIII

A good soldier has his heart and soul in it. When he receives an order, he gets a hard-on, and when he sends his lance into the enemy's guts, he comes.

The Caucasian Chalk Circle, 1944

Robert Edward Shelford BIDWELL, 1899–1968

No general ever won a war whose conscience troubled him or who did not want 'to beat his enemy too much'.

Modern Warfare

Marie-Antoine-Roger de SAINT-EXUPÉRY, 1900–44

It is as a soldier that you make love, and as a lover that you make war.

Wind, Sand and Stars, 1939

In a civil war the firing line is invisible: it passes through the hearts of men.

Wind, Sand and Stars, 1939

The soldier's body becomes a stock of accessories that are no longer his property.

Flight to Arms, 1942

Daniel Vincent GALLERY, b. 1901

The Pentagon Whiz Kids are, I think, conscientious, patriotic people who are experts at calculating odds, figuring cost-effectiveness and squeezing the last cent out of contract negotiations. But they are heavy-handed butchers in dealing with that delicate, vital thing called 'morale'. This is the stuff that makes ships like the *Enterprise*, puts flags on top of Iwo Jima and wins wars. But I doubt if Mr McNamara and his crew have any morale setting on their computers.

Eight Bells and All's Well, 1965

George ORWELL (Eric Blair), 1903–50

War is war. The only good human being is a dead one.
Animal Farm, 1945

The quickest way of ending a war is to lose it.
Shooting an Elephant, 1950

Cyril CONNOLLY, 1903–74

There is always a raw and intolerant nation eager to destroy the tolerant and mellow.
The Unquiet Grave, 1945

Konrad LORENZ, 1903–89

A few decades ago one could . . . still accept the expression 'My Country right or wrong' as a proper expression of patriotism; today this standpoint can be regarded as lacking in moral responsibility.
The Waning of Humaneness, 1983

Albert SPEER, 1905–81

Now we know that we do not live in an earthquake-proof structure. The build-up of negative impulses, each reinforcing the other, can inexorably shake to pieces the complicated apparatus of the modern world. There is no halting this process by will alone. The danger is that the automatism of progress will depersonalize man further and withdraw more and more of his self-responsibility.
Note written in prison, 1947

Arthur KOESTLER, 1905–83

The most persistent sound which reverberates through men's history is the beating of war drums.
Janus: A Summing Up, 1978

Samuel Blair GRIFFITH, b. 1906

In the United States, we go to considerable trouble to keep soldiers out of politics, and even more to keep politics out of soldiers.
'Introduction' to Mao Tse-tung, *Guerilla Warfare*, 1961

Curtis Emerson LeMAY, b. 1906

A man should have dinner with his friends, and the commanding officer has no friends.
Refusing to dine with his fellow officers, quoted in *Look*, November 1965

Lyndon Baines JOHNSON, 1908–73

We must be constantly prepared for the worst and constantly acting for the best – strong enough to win a war and wise enough to prevent one.
State of the Union Message, 8th January 1964

The guns and the bombs, the rockets and the warships, are all symbols of human failure. They are necessary symbols. They protect what we cherish.

Speech at The Johns Hopkins University, 7th April 1965

J. K. GALBRAITH, b. 1908

All successful revolutions are the kicking in of a rotten door. The violence of revolutions is the violence of men who charge into a vacuum.

The Age of Uncertainty, 1976

Bernard BRODIE, 1910–78

Thus far the chief purpose of our military establishment has been to win wars. From now on its chief purpose must be to avert them. It can have almost no other useful purpose.

The Absolute Weapon: Atomic Power and World Order, 1946

Alan MOOREHEAD, b. 1910

Wars in the main start with textbooks.

The Blue Nile, 1962

Charles Wheller THAYER, b. 1910

Guerillas never win wars but their adversaries often lose them.

Guerilla, 1963

Barbara TUCHMAN, 1912–89

Nothing so comforts the military mind as the maxim of a great but dead general.

The Guns of August, 1962

Albert CAMUS, 1913–60

All modern revolutions have ended in a reinforcement of the power of the state.

The Rebel, 1951

Henry REED, b. 1914

It was, I think, a *good war*, one of the best there have so far been. I've often advanced the view that it was a war deserving of better generalship than it received on either side.

Not a Drum was Heard: The War Memoirs of General Gland (Radio play)

In a civil war, a general must know – and I'm afraid it's a thing rather of instinct than of practice – he must know exactly when to move over to the other side.

Not a Drum was Heard: The War Memoirs of General Gland (Radio play)

(George) Orson WELLES, 1915–85

In Italy for thirty years under the Borgias they had warfare, terror, murder, bloodshed – they produced Michelangelo, Leonardo da Vinci and the Renaissance. In Switzerland they had brotherly love, five hundred years of democracy and peace, and what did they produce? The cuckoo clock!

Speech added to Graham Greene's script for *The Third Man*, 1949

John MASTERS, b. 1915

Command doth make actors of us all.

The Road Past Mandalay, 1961

The Army in my day was not a nine-to-five occupation. One worked very hard for a time, then very little. Above the lowest ranks a man had certain responsibilities but how he discharged them was his responsibility.

In *Harper's Magazine*, March 1963

John F(itzgerald) KENNEDY, 1917–63

It is unfortunate that we can secure peace only by preparing for war.

Campaign speech, Seattle, 16th November 1960

What you have chosen to do for your country by devoting your life to the service of your country is the greatest contribution that any man could make.

Addressing the Graduate Class, US Naval Academy, 6th June 1961

No man who witnessed the tragedies of the last war, no man who can imagine the unimaginable possibilities of the next war, can advocate war out of irritability or frustration or impatience.

Veterans' Day Address, Arlington National Assembly, 11th November 1961

There is another type of warfare – new in its intensity, ancient in its origin – war by guerillas, subversives, insurgents, assassins; war by ambush instead of by combat, by infiltration instead of by aggression, seeking victory by eroding and exhausting the enemy instead of engaging him. It is a form of warfare uniquely adapted to what have been strangely called 'wars of liberation', to undermine the efforts of new and poor countries to maintain the freedom they have finally achieved. It preys on unrest and ethnic conflicts.

Addressing the Graduate Class, US Naval Academy, 6th June 1962

The mere absence of war is not peace.

State of the Union Message, 14th January 1963

Peace is a daily, a weekly, a monthly process, gradually changing opinions, slowly eroding old barriers, quietly building new structures. And however undramatic the pursuit of peace, that pursuit must go on.

Speech to the United Nations General Assembly, 20th September 1963

Victory has a thousand fathers but defeat is an orphan.

Attributed

'Dickey' (Georgette Marie Louise) CHAPELLE, 1919–65

Being a lady war correspondent is like being a lady wrestler: you can be one at a time, but not both simultaneously.

Attributed remark, made shortly before she was killed in Vietnam, November 1965

Jean DOUTARD, b. 1920

The role of the army is to march to the sound of the guns.

Taxis of the Marne, 1957

William H. (Bill) MAULDIN, b. 1921

Look at an infantryman's eyes and you can tell how much war he has seen.

Up Front, 1944

Peter USTINOV, b. 1921

And here is the lesson I learned in the Army. If you want to do a thing badly, you have to work at it as though you wanted to do it well.

Romanoff and Juliet, 1965

Norman F. DIXON, b. 1922

While modern war becomes increasingly swift and deadly, and the means by which it is waged increasingly complex, the intellectual level of those entering the armed services as officers could well be on the wane. This tentative supposition is based on the fact that fewer and fewer of the young consider the military to be a worthwhile career. One has only to look at contemporary recruiting advertisements to realize the evident difficulties of finding officer-material. They spare nothing in their efforts to convince an unresponsive youth. The services are depicted as glittering toyshops, where handsome young men enjoy themselves with tanks and missiles while basking in the respect of lower ranks hardly less godlike than themselves. In their eagerness to drum up applicants these calls to arms attempt the mental contortion of presenting the services as a classless society in which officers nevertheless remain gentlemen.

On the Psychology of Military Incompetence, 1976

Upon reflection it is hardly surprising that the horse became the *sine qua non* of the military life. For a thousand years man has found in it enormous advantages. There was nothing better for transportation and load-hauling. Horses raised morale and enhanced egos. Horses took the weight off feet and enabled people to go to war sitting down. When they lay down you could hide behind them. When it was cold you could borrow their warmth, and when they died you could eat them!

On the Psychology of Military Incompetence, 1976

A comparison of the best with the worst of military commanders supports the view that military incompetence results from those defects of personality associated with authoritarianism and disordered achievement-motivation. When all that is natural, creative, flexible, warm and outgoing in the human spirit becomes crushed and restricted, such qualities of leadership as compassion, bold decisions and military flair give way to conformity, sycophantism, indecision and fear of failure.

On the Psychology of Military Incompetence, 1976

In one American training establishment alone two new versions of compulsive 'bull' have been discovered: rectilinear movement, and eating by numbers. In this place where future controllers of nuclear weaponry receive their basic training, cadets must always walk *parallel* to the walls of buildings: diagonal or other directions of locomotion are forbidden. The old belief that a straight line is the shortest distance between two points is evidently a property of subversive geometry! An interesting feature of eating by numbers, wherein officer cadets are constrained to handle their cutlery with measured uniformity – *up* one-two, *across* one-two, *enter mouth* one-two, *withdraw* one-two, *reload* one-two – is that the drill can never be completed if a junior speaker is spoken to in midstream by a senior member of the mess. As a result of this delicately controlled sadism, it is quite possible for a potential future general to die of starvation.

On the Psychology of Military Incompetence, 1976

Kurt VONNEGUT, b. 1922

One of the main effects of war . . . is that people are discouraged from being characters.

Slaughterhouse 5, 1969

Joseph HELLER, b. 1923

There was only one catch and that was Catch-22, which specified that a concern for one's own safety in the face of dangers that were real and immediate was the process of a rational mind. Orr was crazy and could be grounded. All he had to do was ask; and as soon as he did he would no longer be crazy and would have to fly more missions . . . If he flew them he was crazy and didn't have to; but if he didn't want to he was sane and had to.

Catch-22, 1955

Marc Lindsay PARROT, b. 1923

Glamor, caste and unpopularity are among the gifts of the sea, and their influence on Marines is not dead yet.

Hazard, 1962

Frantz FANON, 1925–61

The native intellectual, who takes up arms to defend his nation's legitimacy and who wants to bring proofs to bear out that legitimacy, who is willing to strip himself naked to study the history of his body, is obliged to dissect the heart of his body.

The Wretched of the Earth, 1961

In guerilla warfare the struggle no longer concerns the place where you are, but the place where you are going. Each fighter carries his warring country between his toes.

The Wretched of the Earth, 1961

When I search for Man in the technique and the style of Europe, I see only a succession of negations of man, and an avalanche of murders.

The Wretched of the Earth, 1961

Correlli BARNETT, b. 1927

War is the great auditor of institutions.

The Swordbearers, 1964

The importance of war and military institutions has been generally neglected in British historical writing, whose tone has been set up by the Whig and liberal emphasis on peaceful constitutional progress. In this liberal view war appears as an aberration, an interruption of a 'natural' condition of peace: almost as a form of delinquency unworthy of intellectual attention.

Britain and Her Army, 1509–1970, 1970

(Ernesto) Che GUEVARA, 1928–1967

Nothing helps a fighting force more than correct information. Moreover it should be in perfect order, and done well by capable personnel.

Memorandum, 1963

Stanley KUBRICK, b. 1928

The great nations have always acted like gangsters, and the small nations like prostitutes.

Quoted in the *Guardian*, 5th June 1963

Alan BENNETT, b. 1934

I have never understood this liking for war. It panders to instincts already catered for within the scope of any respectable domestic establishment.

Forty Years On, 1969: Act I

Edward LUTTWAK, b. 1942

As the French *Événements* of May 1968 have shown yet again, insurrection – even if successful – no longer leads to revolution in developed countries. The defence apparatus of the modern state with its professional personnel, with its independent transport and communications and with its extensive sources of information, cannot be defeated by mere civilian agitation, even if intense and prolonged. The general strike can swamp the system temporarily, but cannot defeat it, since in a modern economic setting the civilians will remain without food and fuel well before the military and police organizations. Any attempt to use the masses for a direct attack will be neutralized by the efficient equipment available to the police;

if an armed attack is attempted modern automatic weapons in the hands of trained men will equalize any mass of civilians with improvised means.

The modern state is therefore almost invulnerable to direct assault. Two possible threats remain: revolutionary war and the *coup d'état.*

Coup d'État: a Practical Handbook, 1968

Harold LASSWELL, 20th century

Soldiers are the tradesmen of killing, but officers are the managers of violence.

In Gwynne Dyer, *War*, 1986

Anonymous

Join the Army, see the world, meet interesting people and kill them.

Pacifist slogan, early 1970s

The R.A.F. [Royal Air Force] do not have traditions, they only have habits.

Unnamed naval officer, in *The Times*, 1977

[Note: for further quotations about the nature of modern warfare, see Part II: 'Nuclear Weapons and the Cold War', pp. 354–58]

PROVERBS AND OTHER SAYINGS OF WAR

Never say die so long as there's a shot in the locker.

American, 18th century

I can't get 'em up,
I can't get 'em up,
I can't get 'em up in the morning;
I can't get 'em up,
I can't get 'em up,
I can't get 'em up at all.
Corporal's worse than privates;
Sergeant's worse than corporals;
Lieutenant's worse than sergeants;
And Captain's worst of all!

American, reveille

R.H.I.P. (Rank Hath Its Privileges)

American

Nervous in the service.

American, for cowardice

It ain't the size of the dog in the fight that counts: it's the size of the fight in the dog.

American

Safety lies forward.

American

When the going gets tough, the tough get going.
American

Train hard, fight easy.
American

A battery seen is a battery lost.
American: artillery saying

Snafu – Situation Normal, All Fucked Up
Fubar – Fucked Up Beyond All Recognition
American (World War II)

The difficult we do immediately. The impossible takes a little longer.
American: slogan of the US Armed Services

Hey diddle diddle, right up the middle.
American: US Marine saying

Fighting for peace is like fucking for chastity.
American: graffito, *c.* 1976

Make love, not war.
American: hippy slogan

Military solutions are problems.
American, carsticker, contemporary

Numbers overcome the brave.
Arabic

Fight for honour, for dishonour is easily won.
Arabic

The world began with war and will end with war.
Arabic

A brass hat is anybody at least one rank senior to you.
British

If it moves, salute it.
If it doesn't move, pick it up.
If you can't pick it up, paint it.
British

When will blood stop running down the mountains? When sugar cane grows in the snows!
Caucasian

If you know the enemy and know yourself, you need not fear the result of a hundred battles. If you know yourself but not the enemy, for every victory gained you will also suffer a defeat. If you know neither the enemy nor yourself, you will succumb in every battle.
Chinese

To make nails do not waste good iron; to make soldiers do not waste good men.
Chinese

It is an ignorant scholar who preaches politeness to a soldier.
Chinese

If you are planning to hunt a tiger or going to the wars, take some relatives.
Chinese

It is easier to find a large army than a good general.
Chinese

Drawing near the enemy, the tigers in our hearts become lambs.
Chinese

Armies kept for three years are deployed in one morning.
Chinese

Better a dog in time of peace than a man in time of war.
Chinese

When the cat is at the rat-hole, ten thousand rats dare not come out. When a tiger guards the ford, ten thousand deer cannot cross.
Chinese

Wars are caused either by women or priests.
Czech

He that fights and runs away
May live to fight another day.
English, 17th century

All is fair in love and war.
English

The Legion is our Fatherland.
(Legio patria nostra.)
Foreign Legion motto

The soup makes the soldier.
French

One bad general is better than two good generals.
French

The enemy never sleeps.
French

The attack, always the attack.
French

With the stick comes peace.
French

Arms, women and books need to be looked at every day.
Dutch

In time of war the devil makes more room in hell.
German

Young soldiers, old beggars.
German

A soldier should be well paid and well hanged.
German

Better to die than be a coward.
Gurkha

When the war is over, make alliances.
Ancient Greek

Sons of heroes are a plague.
Ancient Greek

Wars are not sugar plums.
Hindi

He who has land will have war.
Italian

Better to live like a lion for a day than live like a sheep for a hundred days.
Italian

Many who return from war cannot give account of the battle.
Italian

The best armour is to keep out of gun-shot.
Italian

Warriors and gold may be idle, but they never rust.
Japanese

Even if he has nothing to eat a warrior should still pick his teeth.
Japanese

At the sound of the bridle the soldier's child always starts.
Japanese

Nobody can blunder twice in war.
Latin

The brave may fall, but they do not yield.
Latin

Victory loves prudence.
Latin

A coward's mother doesn't weep.
Latin

If you wish to destroy a people, pray that they have many leaders.
Lebanese

It is easy to watch a war through field-glasses.
Lebanese

When one generation is warlike, the ten that succeed are pusillanimous.
Mongolian

An unarmed horseman is like a bird without wings.
Moroccan

Eternal peace lasts until the next war.
Russian

War, hunting and love offer a thousand pains for one pleasure.
Spanish

The best soldiers come from the plough.
Spanish

Let him who does not know what war is go to war.
Spanish

Even to command a flock of sheep is pleasant.
Spanish

A bayonet is a weapon with a worker at each end.
Socialist slogan, early 20th century

My enemy's liver is my sword's scabbard.
Tibetan

A weapon is an enemy even to its owner.
Turkish

Distant drum, sweet music.
Turkish

When the flag is flying, all reason is in the trumpet.
Ukrainian

Divide and conquer.
Universal

Force binds for a time, education binds forever.
Vietnamese

It is easy to be brave behind a castle wall.
Welsh

PART TWO: PARTICULARITIES

Quotations about individual wars and battles, arranged chronologically

THE STONE AGE

The poisoned arrow was the Stone Age equivalent of a nuclear deterrent . . . The slow action of the poison left a stricken adversary ample time in which to avenge the suffering that lay ahead of him.

A. Warneburg, *The Bushman*, 1979

THE WARS OF THE ISRAELITES, from the 13th century BC

And the Lord said unto Moses, Wherefore criest thou unto me? speak unto the children of Israel, that they go forward: But lift thou up thy rod, and stretch out thine hand over the sea, and divide it: and the children of Israel shall go on dry land through the midst of the sea. And I, behold, I will harden the hearts of the Egyptians, and they shall follow them: and I will get me honour upon Pharaoh, and upon all his host, upon his chariots, and upon his horsemen. And the Egyptians shall know that I am the Lord, when I have gotten me honour upon Pharaoh, upon his chariots, and upon his horsemen. And the angel of God, which went before the camp of Israel, removed and went behind them; and the pillar of the cloud went from before their face, and stood behind them: And it came between the camp of the Egyptians and the camp of Israel; and it was a cloud and darkness to them, but it gave light by night to these: so that the one came not near the other all the night. And Moses stretched out his hand over the sea; and the Lord caused the sea to go back by a strong east wind all that night, and made the sea dry land, and the waters were divided. And the children of Israel went into the midst of the sea upon the dry ground: and the waters were a wall unto them on their right hand, and on their left. And the Egyptians pursued, and went in after them to the midst of the sea, even all Pharaoh's horses, his chariots and his horsemen. And it came to pass, that in the morning watch the Lord looked unto the host of the Egyptians through the pillar of fire and of cloud, and troubled the host of the Egyptians. And took off their chariot wheels, that they drave them heavily: so that the Egyptians said, Let us flee from the face of Israel; for the Lord fighteth for them against the Egyptians. And the Lord said unto Moses, Stretch out thine hand over the sea, that the waters may come again upon the Egyptians, upon their chariots and upon their horsemen. And Moses stretched forth his hand over the sea, and the sea returned to his strength when the morning appeared; and the Egyptians fled against it; and the Lord overthrew the Egyptians in the midst of the sea.

Exodus 14.xv–xxvii

And when king Arad the Canaanite, which dwelt in the south, heard tell that Israel came by the way of the spies; then he fought against Israel, and took some of them prisoners. And Israel vowed a vow unto the Lord, and said, If thou wilt indeed deliver this people into my hand, then I will utterly destroy their cities. And the Lord hearkened to the voice of Israel, and delivered up the Canaanites; and they utterly destroyed them and their cities: and he called the name of the place Hormah.

Numbers 21.i–iii

And the Lord spake unto Moses, saying, Avenge the children of Israel of the Midianites: afterward shalt thou be gathered unto thy people. And Moses spake unto the people, saying, Arm some of yourselves unto the war, and let them go against the Midianites, and avenge the Lord of Midian. Of every tribe a thousand, throughout all the tribes of Israel, shall ye send to the war. So there were delivered out of the thousands of Israel, a thousand of every tribe, twelve thousand armed for war. And Moses sent them to the war, a thousand of every tribe, them and Phinehas the son of Eleazar the priest, to the war, with the holy instruments, and the trumpets to blow in his hand. And they warred against the Midianites, as the Lord commanded Moses; and they slew all the males. And they slew the kings of Midian, beside the rest of them that were slain; namely, Evi, and Rekem, and Zur, and Hur, and Reba, five kings of Midian: Balaam also the son of Beor they slew with the sword. And the children of Israel took all the women of Midian captives, and their little ones, and took the spoil of all their cattle, and all their flocks, and all their goods. And they burnt all their cities wherein they dwelt, and all their goodly castles, with fire. And they took all the spoil, and all the prey, both of men and of beasts.

Numbers 31.i–xi

Moreover the Lord thy God will send the hornet among them, until they that are left, and hide themselves from thee, be destroyed. Thou shalt not be affrighted at them: for the Lord thy God is among you, a mighty God and terrible. And the Lord thy God will put out those nations before thee little by little: thou mayest not consume them at once, lest the beasts of the field increase upon thee.

Deuteronomy 7.xx–xxii

And Joshua the son of Nun sent out of Shittim two men to spy secretly, saying, Go view the land, even Jericho. And they went, and came into an harlot's house, named Rahab, and lodged there.

Joshua 2.i

Now Jericho was straitly shut up because of the children of Israel: none went out, and none came in. And the Lord said unto Joshua, See, I have given into thine hand Jericho, and the king thereof, and the mighty men of valour. And ye shall compass the city, all ye men of war, and go round about the city once. Thus shalt thou do six days. And seven priests shall bear before the ark seven trumpets of rams' horns: and the seventh day ye shall compass the city seven times, and the priests shall blow with the trumpets. And it shall come to pass that when they make a long blast with the ram's horn, and when ye hear the sound of the trumpet, all the people shall shout with a great shout; and the wall of the city shall fall down flat, and the people shall ascend up every man straight before him.

Joshua 6.i–v

Joshua made war a long time with all those kings. There was not a city that made peace with the children of Israel, save the Hivites the inhabitants of Gibeon: all other they took in battle. For it was of the Lord to harden their hearts, that they should come against Israel in battle, that he might destroy them utterly, and that they might have no favour, but that he might destroy them, as the Lord commanded Moses.

Joshua 11.xviii–xx

And the Lord said unto Gideon, The people that are with thee are too many for me to give the Midianites into their hands, lest Israel vaunt themselves against me, saying, Mine own hand hath saved me. Now therefore go to, proclaim in the ears of the people, saying, Whosoever is fearful and afraid, let him return and depart early from Mount Gilead. And there returned of the people twenty and two thousand; and there remained ten thousand. And the Lord said unto Gideon, The people are yet too many; bring them down unto the water, and I will try them for thee there: and it shall be, that of whom I say unto thee, This shall go with thee, the same shall go with thee; and of whomsoever I say unto thee, This shall not go with thee, the same shall not go. So he brought down the people unto the water: and the Lord said unto Gideon, Every one that lappeth of the water with his tongue, as a dog lappeth, him shalt thou set by himself; likewise every one that boweth down upon his knees to drink. And the number of them that lapped, putting their hand to their mouth, were three hundred men; but all the rest of the people bowed down upon their knees to drink water. And the Lord said unto Gideon, By the three hundred men that lapped will I save you, and deliver the Midianites into thine hand: and let all the other people go every man unto his place.

Judges 7.ii–vii

And [Gideon] divided the three hundred men into three companies, and he put a trumpet in every man's hand, with empty pitchers, and lamps within the pitchers. And he said unto them, Look on me, and do likewise: and behold, when I come to the outside of the camp, it shall be that, as I do, so shall ye do. When I blow with a trumpet, I and all that are with me, then blow ye the trumpets also on every side of all the camp, and say, The sword of the Lord, and of Gideon. So Gideon, and the hundred men that were with him, came unto the outside of the camp in the beginning of the middle watch; and they had but newly set the watch: and they blew the trumpets, and brake the pitchers that were in their hands. And the three companies blew the trumpets, and brake the pitchers, and held the lamps in their left hands and the trumpets in their right hands to blow withal: and they cried, The sword of the Lord, and of Gideon. And they stood every man in his place round about the camp: and all the host ran, and cried, and fled. And the three hundred blew their trumpets, and the Lord set every man's sword against his fellow, even throughout all the host: . . .

Judges 7.xvi–xxii

And when he came unto Lehi, the Philistines shouted against him: and the Spirit of the Lord came mightily upon him, and the cords that were upon his arms became as flax that was burnt with fire, and his bands loosed from off his hands.

And he found a new jawbone of an ass, and put forth his hand, and took it, and slew a thousand men therewith. And Samson said, With the jawbone of an ass, heaps upon heaps, with the jaw of an ass have I slain a thousand men.

Judges 15.xiv–xvi

And the Philistines stood on a mountain on one side, and Israel stood on a mountain on the other side: and there was a valley between them. And there went out a champion out of the camp of the Philistines, named Goliath, of Gath, whose height was six cubits and a span. And he had an helmet of brass upon his head, and he was armed with a coat of mail; and the weight of the coat was five thousand shekels of brass. And he had greaves of brass upon his legs, and a target of brass between his shoulders. And the staff of his spear was like a weaver's beam; and his spear's head weighed six hundred shekels of iron: and one bearing a shield went before him. And he stood and cried unto the armies of Israel, and said unto them, Why are ye come out to set your battle in array? am I not a Philistine, and ye servants to Saul? choose you a man for you, and let him come down to me. If he be able to fight with me, and to kill me, then will we be your servants: but if I prevail against him, and kill him, then shall ye be our servants, and serve us . . . David girded his sword upon his armour, and he assayed to go; for he had not proved it. And David said unto Saul, I cannot go with these; for I have not proved them. And David put them off him. And he took his staff in his hand, and chose him five smooth stones out of the brook, and put them in a shepherd's bag which he had, even in a scrip; and his sling was in his hand: and he drew near to the Philistine. And the Philistine came on and drew near unto David; and the man that bare the shield went before him. And when the Philistine looked about, and saw David, he disdained him: for he was but a youth, and ruddy, and of a fair countenance. And the Philistine said unto David, Am I a dog, that thou comest to me with staves? And the Philistine cursed David by his gods. And the Philistine said to David, Come to me, and I will give thy flesh unto the fowls of the air, and to the beasts of the field. Then said David unto the Philistine, Thou comest to me with a sword, and with a spear, and with a shield: but I come to thee in the name of the Lord of hosts, the God of the armies of Israel, whom thou hast defied. This day will the Lord deliver thee into mine hand; and I will smite thee, and take thine head from thee; and I will give the carcases of the host of the Philistines this day unto the fowls of the air, and to the wild beasts of the earth; that all the earth may know that there is a God in Israel. And all this assembly shall know that the Lord saveth not with sword and spear: for the battle is the Lord's, and he will give you into our hands. And it came to pass, when the Philistine arose, and came and drew nigh to meet David, that David hasted, and ran toward the army to meet the Philistine. And David put his hand in his bag, and took thence a stone, and slang it, and smote the Philistine in his forehead, that the stone sunk into his forehead; and he fell upon his face to the earth.

I Samuel 17. iii–ix and xxxix–xlix

Now the Philistines fought against Israel: and the men of Israel fled from before the Philistines, and fell down slain in mount Gilboa. And the Philistines followed hard upon Saul and upon his sons; and the Philistines slew Jonathan, and

Abinadab, and Malchi-shua, Saul's sons. And the battle went sore against Saul, and the archers hit him; and he was sore wounded of the archers. Then said Saul unto his armourbearer, Draw thy sword, and thrust me through therewith; lest these uncircumcised come and thrust me through, and abuse me. But his armourbearer would not; for he was sore afraid. Therefore Saul took a sword and fell upon it. And when his armourbearer saw that Saul was dead, he fell likewise upon his sword, and died with him.

I Samuel 31. i–v

And when all the Moabites heard that the kings were come up to fight against them, they gathered all that were able to put on armour, and upward, and stood in the border. And they rose up early in the morning, and the sun shone upon the water, and the Moabites saw the water on the other side as red as blood: And they said, This is blood: the kings are surely slain, and they have smitten one another: now therefore, Moab, to the spoil. And when they came to the camp of Israel, the Israelites rose up and smote the Moabites, so that they fled before them: but they went forward smiting the Moabites, even in their country. And they beat down the cities, and on every good piece of land cast every man his stone, and filled it; and they stopped all the wells of water, and felled all the good trees: only in Kirharaseth left they the stones thereof; howbeit the slingers went about it, and smote it. And when the king of Moab saw the battle was too sore for him, he took with him seven hundred men that drew swords, to break through even unto the king of Edom: but they could not. Then he took his eldest son that should have reigned in his stead, and offered him for a burnt offering upon the wall. And there was great indignation against Israel: and they departed from him, and returned to their own land.

II Kings 3. xxi–xxvii

When the posterity of Abraham had multiplied like the sands of the sea, the Deity, from whose mouth they received a system of laws and ceremonies, declared himself the proper and as it were the national God of Israel; and with the most jealous care separated his favourite people from the rest of mankind. The conquest of the land of Canaan was accompanied with so many wonderful and so many bloody circumstances, that the victorious Jews were left in a state of irreconcilable hostility with all their neighbours.

Edward Gibbon, *The History Of The Decline And Fall Of The Roman Empire*, 1776–88: xv

It could be claimed . . . that the most influential book on the conduct, as well as on the occurrence of war has been the Holy Bible. It has been testified that the Old Testament contains useful military information, especially for those who, as circumstances frequently demand, are required to campaign in the area. Lloyd George provided Allenby with a biblical commentary, remarking that he would find it more helpful than any war office manual.

Adrian Liddell Hart, Introduction to B. H. Liddell Hart, *The Sword and the Pen*, 1978

Defeat of Sennacherib, King of Assyria, *c.* 700 BC

And the Lord sent an angel, which cut off all the mighty men of valour, and the leaders and captains in the camp of the king of Assyria. So he returned with shame of face to his own land. And when he was come into the house of his god, they that came forth of his own bowels slew him there with the sword.

II Chronicles 32. xxi

The Assyrian came down like the wolf on the fold,
And his cohorts were gleaming in purple and gold;
And the sheen of their spears was like stars on the sea,
When the blue wave rolls nightly on deep Galilee.

Like the leaves of the forest when Summer is green,
That host with their banners at sunset was seen:
Like the leaves of the forest when Autumn hath blown,
That host on the morrow lay withered and strown.

For the Angel of Death spread his wings on the blast,
And breathed in the face of the foe as he passed;
And the eyes of the sleepers waxed deadly and chill,
And their hearts but once heaved, and for ever grew still!

And there lay the steed with his nostril all wide,
But through it there rolled not the breath of his pride:
And the foam of his gasping lay white on the turf,
And cold as the spray of the rock-beating surf.

And there lay the rider distorted and pale,
With the dew on his brow, and the rust on his mail;
And the tents were all silent, the banners alone,
The lances unlifted, the trumpet unblown.

Lord Byron, 'The Destruction of Sennacherib', *c.* 1815

THE TROJAN WAR, *c.* 1100 BC

. . . So fell the heads of the flying Trojans, at the hand of Agamemnon, son of Atreus, and many lofty-necked steeds rattled their empty chariots through the ranks of the battle, longing for their faultless charioteers; but they lay upon the earth, far more agreeable to the vultures than to their wives.

Homer, *Iliad*, Bk XI

In the midst noble Achilles was armed, and there was a gnashing of his teeth, and his eyes shone like a blaze of fire; but intolerable grief entered his heart within him, and, enraged against the Trojans, he put on the gifts of the god, which Vulcan, toiling, had fabricated for him. First around his legs he placed the beautiful greaves, joined with silver clasps, next he put on the corslet round his breast, and suspended from his shoulders the brazen, silver-studded sword; then he seized the shield, large and solid, the sheen of which went to a great distance, as of the moon. And as when from the sea the blaze of a burning fire shines to mariners, which is lit aloft amongst the mountains in a solitary place; but the storm bears them against their inclination away from their friends over the fishy deep; so from the shield of Achilles, beautifully and skilfully made, the brightness reached the sky. But raising it, he placed the strong helmet upon his head; and the helmet, crested with horse-hair, shone like a star; and the golden tufts which Vulcan had diffused thick around the cone were shaken. Then noble Achilles tried himself in his arms if they would fit him, and if his fair limbs would move freely in them; but they were like wings to him, and lifted up the shepherd of the people. And from its sheath he drew forth his paternal spear, heavy, great, and stout, which no other of the Greeks was able to brandish, but Achilles alone knew how to hurl it – a Pelian ash, which Chiron had cut for his father from the top of Pelion, to be a destruction to heroes.

Homer, *Iliad*, Bk XI

Now as for the carrying off of women, it is the deed, they say, of a rogue; but to make a stir about such as are carried off, argues a man a fool. Men of sense care nothing for such women, since it is plain that without their own consent they would never be forced away. The Asiatics, when the Greeks ran off with their women, never troubled themselves about the matter; but the Greeks, for the sake of a single Lacedaemonian girl, collected a vast armament, invaded Asia, and destroyed the kingdom of Priam.

Herodotus, *Histories*, *c.* 450 BC: Bk I

I am inclined to think that Agamemnon succeeded in collecting the expedition, not because the suitors of Helen had bound themselves to Tyndareus, but because he was the most powerful king of the time.

Thucydides, *The Peloponnesian Wars*, 401 BC: Bk I

There are empty fields now where Troy once was.

Ovid, *Epistolae Heroidum*, *c.* 17 BC

Because Cassandra was not believed, Troy fell.

Phaedrus, *Fables*, *c.* AD 45

And it was not because Troy lost Minerva that Troy perished. What loss did Minerva herself first incur, that led to her own disappearance? Was it, perhaps, the loss of her guards? There can be no doubt that their death made her removal possible – the image did not preserve the men; the men were preserving the image. Why then did they worship her, to secure her protection for their country and its citizens? She could not guard her own keepers.

St Augustine, *City Of God*, 427: I.iii

Faustus: Was this the face that launcht a thousand shippes?
And burnt the toplesse Towres of Ilium?
Sweete Helen, make me immortall with a kisse:
Her lips sucke forth my soule, see where it flies:
Come Helen, come give mee my soule againe.
Here wil I dwel, for heaven be in these lips,
And all is drosse that is not Helena:

I wil be Paris, and for love of thee,
Insteede of Troy shal Wertenburge be sackt,
And I wil combate with weake Menelaus,
And weare thy colours on my plumed Crest:
Yea I wil wounde Achillis in the heele,
And then returne to Helen for a kisse.

Christopher Marlowe, *The Tragicall History of Doctor Faustus*, *c.* 1592

Marcus: The story of that baleful burning night
When subtle Greeks surpris'd King Priam's Troy; . . .

William Shakespeare, *Titus Andronicus*, 1594

Achilles, though invulnerable, never went into battle but completely armed.

Lord Chesterfield, Letter, 15th January 1753

Troy owes to Homer what whist owes to Hoyle.

Lord Byron, *Don Juan*, 1820: Canto III

A shudder in the loins engenders there
The broken wall, the burning roof and tower
And Agamemnon dead.

W. B. Yeats, *Leda and the Swan*, 1928

The only war I ever approved of was the Trojan war; it was fought over a woman and the men knew what they were fighting for.

William Lyon Phelps, sermon, 25th June 1933

In the early days of the city kings, battles were little more than duels between selected heroes, as depicted by Homer, in which valour was the supreme virtue, value and virtue being expressed by the same word. It is out of valour that European history rises; the spear and the sword, and not, as in Asia, the bow and the arrow, are its symbols. The bravest and not the most crafty are the leaders of men, and it is their example rather than their skill which dominates battle. Fighting is a contest between man and man more than between brain and brain. The spearman Achilles, and not Paris the archer, is the typical hero. Psychologically the *arme blanche* dominates the missile.

J. F. C. Fuller, *The Decisive Battles of the Western World*, 1954–56

THE WARS OF CYRUS THE GREAT, 550–529 BC

The particulars which he [Cyrus] specified were these: for the private man, to render himself obedient to his commanders, ready to undergo labour, willing to face dangers consistently with good order, skilful in military exercises, fond of having his arms in good condition, and desirous of praise in all such matters. For the captain of five, to make himself such as it became an able private man to be; and to do his utmost to make his five likewise such. For the captain of ten, to make his ten such; for the captain of twenty-five, to do the same for his twenty-five; and for the centurion, to be himself unexceptionable in conduct, and to keep watch over those who commanded under him, that they might make those whom they commanded fulfil their duties. The rewards that he proposed were, for the centurions, that those who appeared to have brought their companies into the best condition, should be made commanders of a thousand; for the captains of twenty-five, that those who appeared to exhibit the best companies, should be promoted to the places vacated by the centurions; for the captains of ten, that such as were most meritorious should be put into the places of the captains of twenty-five; for the captains of five, in like manner, to be advanced to the places of the captains of ten; and for the private men that behaved best, to be promoted to the rank of captains of five.

Xenophon, *Cyropaedia*, *c.* 360 BC: II.i

Cyrus, on one occasion, invited an entire company, together with their centurion, to sup with him. This invitation he gave him, from having seen him form half the men of his company against the other half, in order to attack each other; both parties having their corslets on, and their shields in their left hands; but to one half he had given thick sticks in their right hands, and the others he had ordered to pick up clods of earth to throw. When they stood thus ready prepared, he gave them a signal to engage; when some of those who threw the clods hit the corslets or shields of the opposite party, others their thighs or legs; but when they came to close quarters, they who had the sticks applied their blows to the thighs of some, the hands and legs of others, and the necks and backs of such as were stooping for clods; and, at last, those who had the sticks put the others to rout, and pursued them, laying on their blows with much laughter and diversion. Then the others, in their turn, taking the sticks, assailed in the same manner their opponents, who took their turn in throwing clods. Cyrus was much struck with these proceedings, with the contrivance of the officer, and the obedience of the men, and was glad that they were at the same time both exercised and diverted, and that those men gained the victory who were armed in a manner like that of the Persians.

Xenophon, *Cyropaedia*, *c.* 360 BC: II.iii

Battle of Sardis, 546 BC

The reason why Cyrus opposed his camels to the enemy's horse was, because the horse has a natural dread of the camel, and cannot abide either the sight or the smell of that animal. By this stratagem he hoped to make Croesus's horse useless to him, the horse being what he chiefly depended upon for victory. The two armies then joined battle, and immediately the Lydian war-horses, seeing and smelling the camels, turned round and galloped off; and so it came to pass that all Croesus's hopes withered away.

Herodotus, *Histories*, *c.* 450 BC: Bk I

Battle of Pteria, 545 BC

In this battle, the Egyptians only, of all the enemy's people, at all distinguished themselves; and of those on the side of Cyrus, the Persian cavalry were thought to have been the best; hence the same sort of arms, with which Cyrus then equipped his cavalry, continue in use to this day. The chariots armed with scythes, too, were greatly approved; so that that engine of war continues still to be used by the successive kings of Persia. The camels did no more than frighten the horses; they that mounted them did no execution upon the cavalry, nor were any of the men themselves killed by the cavalry, for no horse would come near them. This animal, then, was reckoned of use; but no respectable man will breed camels for his own riding, nor exercise them with a view to fighting on their backs; so that, returning to their old condition, they continue in the baggage train.

Xenophon, *Cyropaedia*, *c.* 360 BC: VII.ii

Capture of Babylon, 538 BC

Cyrus was now reduced to great perplexity, as time went on and he made no progress against the place. In this distress either someone made the suggestion, or he bethought himself of a plan, which he proceeded to put in execution. He placed a portion of his army at the point where the river enters the city, and another body at the back of the place where it issues forth, with orders to march into the town by the bed of the stream, as soon as the water became shallow enough: he then himself drew off the unwarlike portion of his host, and made for the place where Nitocris dug the basin for the river, where he did exactly what she had done formerly: he turned the Euphrates by a canal into the basin, which was then a marsh, on which the river sank to such an extent that the natural bed of the stream became fordable.

Herodotus, *Histories*, *c.* 450 BC: Bk I

Measuring out, accordingly, the ground around the wall, and leaving a space by the side of the river sufficient to hold large towers, he dug on each side of the wall a very deep trench, and the men threw up the earth toward themselves. He then, in the first place, built towers on the bank of the river, laying their foundation with palm-trees not less than a hundred feet in length; for there are some that grow even to a yet greater length; and palm-trees that are pressed by a weight, bend up under it, like asses used to carrying loads. He placed these below, with this object, that he might make it appear, as much as possible, that he was preparing to blockade the city, and in order that, if the river forced its way into the ditch, it might not carry off the towers. He raised likewise a great many other towers upon the earth which was thrown up, that he might have as many places as possible for stationing men on guard. Thus the troops of Cyrus enjoyed themselves. But those who were on the walls laughed at this blockade, as being furnished with provisions for more than twenty years. Cyrus, hearing this, divided his army into twelve parts, as if he intended that each part should keep guard one month a year. When the Babylonians heard this, they laughed yet more than before; reflecting that Phrygians, Lydians, Arabians, and Cappadocians were to keep guard over them, men who were affected to them more than to the Persians.

The trenches were now dug; and Cyrus, when he heard that there was a festival in Babylon, in which all the Babylonians drunk and revelled the whole night, took, during the time of it, a number of men with him, and, as soon as it was dark, opened the trenches on the side towards the river. When this was done, the water ran off in the night into the trenches, and the bed of the river through the city allowed men to walk on it. When the river was thus prepared, Cyrus gave orders to the Persian captains of thousands, of infantry and cavalry, to attend him, each with his thousand drawn up two abreast, and the rest of the allies to follow in the rear, ranged as they used to be before. They accordingly came; and he, causing those that attended his person, both foot and horse, to go down into the dry channel of the river, ordered them to try whether the bed of the river was passable . . .

Xenophon, *Cyropaedia*, *c.* 360 BC: VII.v

Death of Cyrus, *c.* 529 BC

Tomyris, when she found that Cyrus paid no heed to her advice, collected all the forces of her kingdom, and gave him battle. Of all the combats in which the barbarians have engaged among themselves, I reckon this to have been the fiercest. The following, as I understand, was the manner of it: – First, the two armies stood apart and shot their arrows at each other; then, when their quivers were empty, they closed and fought hand-to-hand with lances and daggers; and thus they continued fighting for a length of time, neither choosing to give ground. At length the Massagetae prevailed. The greater part of the army of the Persians was destroyed and Cyrus himself fell, after reigning nine and twenty years. Search was made among the slain by order of the queen for the body of Cyrus, and when it was found she took a skin, and, filling it full of human blood, she dipped the head of Cyrus in the gore, saying, as she thus insulted the corpse, 'I live and have conquered thee in fight, and yet by thee am I ruined, for thou tookest my son with guile; but thus I make good my threat, and give thee thy fill of blood.'

Herodotus, *Histories*, *c.* 450 BC: Bk I

PERSIAN CONQUEST OF EGYPT, 525 BC

Battle of Pelusium, 525 BC

On the field where this battle was fought I saw a very wonderful thing which the natives pointed out to me. The bones of the slain lie scattered on the field in two lots, those of the Persians in one place by themselves, as the bodies lay at the first – those of the Egyptians in another place apart from them: if, then, you strike the Persian skulls, even with a pebble, they are so weak, that you break a hole in them; but the Egyptian skulls are so strong, that you may smite them with a stone and you will scarcely break them in.

Herodotus, *Histories*, *c.* 450 BC: Bk III

ROME'S WARS WITH THE SABINES, late 6th/early 5th century BC

Spurius Tarpeius was in command of the Roman citadel. Whilst his daughter had gone outside the fortifications to fetch water for some religious ceremonies, Tatius bribed her to admit his troops within the citadel. Once admitted, they crushed her to death beneath their shields, either that the citadel might appear to have been taken by assault, or that her example might be left as a warning that no faith should be kept with traitors. A further story runs that the Sabines were in the habit of wearing heavy gold armlets on their left arms and richly jewelled rings, and that the girl made them promise to give her 'what they had on their left arms', accordingly they piled their shields upon her instead of golden gifts. Some say that in bargaining for what they had in their left hands, she expressly asked for their shields, and being suspected of wishing to betray them, fell a victim to her own bargain.

Livy, *The History of Rome*, from 29 BC: Bk I

Then it was that the Sabine women, whose wrongs had led to the war, throwing off all womanish fears in their distress, went boldly into the midst of the flying missiles with dishevelled hair and rent garments. Running across the space between the two armies they tried to stop any further fighting and calm the excited passions by appealing to their fathers in the one army and their husbands in the other not to bring upon themselves a curse by staining their hands with the blood of a father-in-law or a son-in-law, nor upon their posterity the taint of parricide. 'If,' they cried, 'you are weary of these ties of kindred, these marriage-bonds, then turn your anger upon us; it is we who are the cause of the war, it is we who have wounded and slain our husbands and fathers. Better for us to perish rather than live without the one or the other of you, as widows or as orphans.'

The armies and their leaders were alike moved by this appeal. There was a sudden hush and silence. Then the generals advanced to arrange terms of a treaty.

Livy, *The History of Rome*, from 29 BC: Bk I

THE GRAECO-PERSIAN WARS OF 490–479 BC

According to the Persians best informed in history, the Phoenicians began the quarrel.

Herodotus, *Histories*, *c.* 450 BC: Bk I

The idea was afloat in the air that the Trojan war was an earlier act in the same drama, – that the warriors of Salamis and Plataea were fighting in the same cause as the heroes who had striven with Hector on the plain of Troy.

J. B. Bury, *A History of Greece*, 1900

In tactics, the mistakes made were those which have since pursued the soldier over many a battlefield, notably reliance on masses of semi-trained men, expecting that quantity can make good a deficit in quality, and a lack of appreciation of weapon power as well as the misapplication of weapons to ground and the tactical conditions of the moment. But above all, the whole war shows that the psychological factor, loss or gain of morale by the soldier and loss or gain of prestige by the supreme command was, as it still remains, the determining factor in war.

J. F. C. Fuller, *The Decisive Battles of the Western World*, 1954–56

Battle of Marathon, September 490 BC

. . . In the mid battle, where the Persians themselves and the Sacae had their place, the barbarians were victorious, and broke and pursued the Greeks into the inner country; but on the two wings the Athenians and the Plataeans defeated the enemy. Having done so, they suffered the routed barbarians to fly at their ease, and joining the two wings in one, fell upon those who had broken their own centre, and fought and conquered them. These likewise fled, and now the Athenians hung upon the runaways and cut them down, chasing them all the way to the shore, on reaching which they laid hold of the ships and called aloud for fire.

Herodotus, *Histories*, *c.* 450 BC: Bk VI

That man is little to be envied, whose patriotism would not gain force upon the plain of Marathon, . . .

Samuel Johnson, *A Journey to the Western Isles*, 1775

The flying Mede, his shaftless broken bow;
The fiery Greek, his red pursuing spear;
Mountains above, Earth's, Ocean's plain below;
Death in the front, Destruction in the rear!

Lord Byron, *Childe Harold's Pilgrimage*, 1812–18

The mountains look on Marathon –
And Marathon looks on the sea;
And musing there an hour alone,
I dream'd that Greece might still be free;
For standing on the Persians' grave
I could not deem myself a slave.

Lord Byron, *Don Juan*, 1819–24: Canto III

Larger forces and heavier slaughter, than had been seen at Marathon, signalised the conflicts of Greeks and Persians at Artemisium, Salamis, Plataea, and the Eurymedon. But mighty and momentous as these battles were, they rank not with Marathon in importance. They originated no new impulse. They turned back no current of fate. They were merely confirmatory of the already existing bias which Marathon had created. The day of Marathon is the critical epoch in the history of the two nations. It broke for ever the spell of Persian invincibility, which had previously paralysed men's minds. It generated among the Greeks the spirit which beat back Xerxes, and afterwards led on Xenophon, Agesilaus, and Alexander, in terrible retaliation through their Asiatic campaigns. It secured for mankind the intellectual treasures of Athens, the growth of free institutions, the liberal enlightenment of the Western world, and the gradual ascendancy for many ages of the great principles of European civilization.

E. S. Creasy, *The Fifteen Decisive Battles of the World*, 1851

Truth-loving Persians do not dwell upon
The trivial skirmish fought near Marathon.

Robert Graves, *The Persian Version*, 1948

Marathon was the birth cry of Europe.

J. F. C. Fuller, *The Decisive Battles of the Western World*, 1954–56

Xerxes at Abydos, 481 BC

. . . As he looked and saw the whole Hellespont covered with the vessels of his fleet, and all the shore and every plain about Abydos as full as could be of men, Xerxes congratulated himself on his good fortune; but after a little while, he wept.

Then Artabanus, the king's uncle, . . . when he heard that Xerxes was in tears, went to him, and said –

'How different, sire, is what thou art now doing, from what thou didst a little while ago! Then thou didst congratulate thyself, and now, behold! thou weepest.'

'There came upon me,' replied he, 'a sudden pity, when I thought of the shortness of man's life, and considered that of all of this host, so numerous as it is, not one will be alive when a hundred years are gone by.'

Herodotus, *Histories*, *c.* 450 BC: Bk VII

Battle of Thermopylae, August 480 BC

Go tell the Spartans, thou that passeth by,
That here, obedient to their laws, we lie.

Simonides of Ceos, Epitaph for the Spartan army

Now, as the king was in a great strait, and knew not how he should deal with the emergency, Ephialtes, the son of Eurydemus, a man of Malis, came to him and was admitted to a conference. Stirred by the hope of receiving a rich reward at the king's hands, he had come to tell him of the pathway which led across the mountain to Thermopylae; by which disclosure he brought destruction on the band of Greeks who had there withstood the barbarians.

Herodotus, *Histories*, *c.* 450 BC: Bk VII

Thus nobly did the whole body of Lacedaemonians and Thespians behave, but nevertheless one man is said to have distinguished himself above all the rest, to wit Dieneces the Spartan. A speech which he made before the Greeks engaged the Medes, remains on record. One of the Trachinians told him, 'such was the number of barbarians, that when they shot forth their arrows the sun would be darkened by their multitude'. Dieneces, not at all frightened at these words, but making light of the Median numbers, answered, 'Our Trachinian friend brings us excellent tidings. If the Medes darken the sun, we shall have our fight in the shade.'

Herodotus, *Histories*, *c.* 450 BC: Bk VII

Earth! render back from out thy breast
  A remnant of thy Spartan dead!
Of the three hundred grant but three,
To make a new Thermopylae.

Lord Byron, *Don Juan*, 1819–24: Canto III

Every great crisis of human history is a pass of Thermopylae, and there is always a Leonidas and his three hundred to die in it, if they cannot conquer.

George William Curtis, *The Call of Freedom*, 1869

Battle of Salamis, 480 BC

The event proved undeniably that the fate of Hellas depended on her navy. And the three chief elements of success were contributed by us; namely, the greatest number of ships, the ablest general, the most devoted patriotism.

Address of the Athenians to the Spartans, 432 BC, in Thucydides, *The Peloponnesian Wars*, 401 BC: Bk I

At this crisis, Themistokles, despairing of influencing the populace by human reasoning, just as a dramatist has recourse to supernatural machinery, produced signs and wonders and oracles. He argued that it was a portent that the sacred snake during those days deserted his usual haunt. The priests, who found their daily offerings to him of the first fruits of the sacrifices left untouched, told the people, at the instigation of Themostokles, that the goddess Athena (Minerva) had left the city, and was leading them to the sea. He also swayed the popular mind by the oracle, in which he argued that by 'wooden walls' ships were alluded to; and that Apollo spoke of Salamis as 'divine', not terrible or sad, because Salamis would be the cause of great good fortune to the Greeks. Having thus gained his point, he proposed a decree, that the city be left to the care of the tutelary goddess of the Athenians, that all able-bodied men should embark in the ships of war, and that each man should take the best measures in his power to save the women and children and slaves.

Plutarch, *Lives: Themistocles*, *c.* AD 110

Tactically, Salamis was not a superlatively great victory, but strategically it was shattering. It knocked the bottom out of the Persian plan, which, for success, depended on the closest co-operation of fleet and army. It was not the loss of ships which was so serious for Xerxes, it was the loss of prestige. The one could be replaced, the other could not be in a conglomerate empire held together by the autocracy of its universal monarch.

J. F. C. Fuller, *The Decisive Battles of the Western World*, 1954–56

Battle of Plataea, 479 BC

Salamis was the turning-point of the war. Plataea was the consummation of Salamis.

G. B. Grundy, *The Great Persian War*, 1901

THE PELOPONNESIAN WARS, 432–404 BC

Whoever is strongest at sea, make him your friend.

Address of the Corcyraeans to the Athenians, 433 BC

I am more afraid of our mistakes than our enemies' designs.

Pericles, speech to the Athenians, 432 BC

Only the love of honour stays young for ever.

Pericles, Funeral Oration, 431 BC

. . . Though men will always judge any war in which they are actually fighting to be the greatest at the time, but, after it is over, revert to their admiration of some other which has preceded, still the Peloponnesian, if estimated by the actual facts, will certainly prove to have been the greatest ever known.

Thucydides, *The Peloponnesian Wars*, 401 BC: Bk I

And you have never considered what manner of men are these Athenians with whom you will have to fight, and how utterly unlike yourselves. They are revolutionary, equally quick in conception and in the execution of every new plan; while you are conservative – careful only to keep what you have, originating nothing, and not acting even when action is most necessary.

Address of the Corinthians to the Spartans, 432 BC, in Thucydides, *The Peloponnesian Wars*, 401 BC: Bk I

When troubles had once begun in the cities, those who followed carried the revolutionary spirit further and further, and determined to outdo the report of all who had preceded them by the ingenuity of their enterprises and the atrocity of their revenges. The meaning of words had no longer the same relation to things, but was changed by them as they thought proper. Reckless daring was thought to be loyal courage; prudent delay was the excuse of a coward; moderation was the disguise of unmanly weakness; to know everything was to do nothing. Frantic energy was the true quality of a man. A conspirator who wanted to be safe was a recreant in disguise. The lover of violence was always trusted, and his opponent suspected. He who succeeded in a plot was deemed knowing, but a still greater master in craft was he who detected one.

Thucydides, *The Peloponnesian Wars*, 401 BC: Bk III

The Spartans (Lacedaemonians)

The Spartans are not wont to ask how many the enemies are, but where they are.

Agis II of Sparta, *c.* 415 BC

The Lacedaemonians have temples dedicated not only to Fear, but to Death, and Laughter, and the like. They honour Fear, not as a malevolent divinity to be shunned, but because they think that the constitutions of states are mainly upheld by Fear. For this reason, Aristotle tells us that the Ephors, when they enter upon their office, issue a proclamation ordering the citizens to shave off their moustache and obey the laws that the laws might not be hard upon them. The injunction about shaving the moustache is inserted, I imagine, in order to accustom the young to obedience even in the most trivial matters. It seems to me that the ancient Spartans did not regard bravery in consisting of the absence of fear, but in the fear of shame and dread of dishonour; for those who fear the laws are the bravest in battle; and those who most fear disgrace care least for their own personal safety.

Plutarch, *Lives: Cleomenes*, *c.* AD 110

During a campaign they made the men perform less severe gymnastic exercises, and allowed them to live a freer life in other respects, so that, for them alone of all mankind, war was felt as a relief from preparation for war. When their army was formed and the enemy were in sight, the king used to sacrifice a kid, and bid them all put on garlands, and the pipers to play the hymn to Kastor; then he himself began to sing the paean for the charge, so that it was a magnificent and terrible spectacle to see the men marching in time to the flutes, making no gap in their lines, with no thought of fear, but quietly and steadily moving to the sound of the music against the enemy. Such men were not likely to be either panic-stricken or over-confident, but had a cool and cheerful confidence, believing that the gods were with them.

Plutarch, *Lives: Lycurgus*, *c.* AD 110

In Sparta those ex-generals who have accomplished their purpose by persuasion or fraud sacrifice an ox, while those who have done it by battle offer a cock. For, though warlike to excess, they thought that a victory gained by clever negotiation was greater and more befitting human beings than one gained by force and courage. Which is to be preferred, I leave to my readers' consideration.

Plutarch, *Lives: Marcellus*, *c.* AD 110

The Spartans made war their chief study. They are affirmed to be the first who reasoned on the events of battles, and committed their conclusions to paper with such success as to reduce the art of war, which until then was considered dependent on courage and fortune alone, to fixed rules and principles.

Vegetius, *De Re Militari*, *c.* 378: Bk III

A Lacedemonian was once rallied with having painted a fly on his shield, as if he wished to avoid being known, by adopting so small a mark of distinction. 'You are deceived,' said the brave Lacedemonian, 'I shall go so near my enemies, that they will easily recognize me.'

The Percy Anecdotes, 1823

Commencement of Hostilities, 431 BC

On neither side were there any mean thoughts; they were both full of enthusiasm; and no wonder, for all men are energetic when they are making a beginning. At that time the youth of Peloponnesius and the youth of Athens were numerous; they had never seen war, and were therefore very willing to take up arms. All Hellas was excited by the coming conflict between her two chief cities. Many were the prophecies circulated and many the oracles chanted by diviners, not only in the cities about to engage in the struggle, but throughout Hellas. Quite lately the island of Delos had been shaken by an earthquake for the first time within the memory of the Hellenes; this was interpreted and generally believed to be a sign of coming events. And everything of the sort which occurred was curiously noted.

Thucydides, *The Peloponnesian Wars*, 401 BC: Bk II

Burial of the Heroes, Athens 431 BC

I have dwelt upon the greatness of Athens because I want to show you that we are contending for a higher prize than those who enjoy none of these privileges, and to establish by manifest proof the merit of these men whom I am now commemorating. Their loftiest praise has already been spoken. For in magnifying the city I have magnified them, and men like them whose virtues made her glorious. And of how few Hellenes can it be said as of them, that their deeds when weighed in the balance have been found equal to their fame? Methinks that a death such as theirs has been gives the true measure of a man's worth; it may be the first revelation of his virtues, but is at any rate their final seal. For even those who come short in other ways may justly plead the valour with which they have fought for their country; they have blotted out the evil with the good, and have benefited the state more by their public services than they have injured her by their private actions.

Pericles, 'Funeral Oration', in Thucydides, *The Peloponnesian Wars*, 401 BC: Bk II

Massacre of the Oligarchs at Corcyra, 427 BC

And, during the seven days which Eurymedon after his arrival remained with his sixty ships, the Corcyraeans continued slaughtering those of their fellow-citizens whom they deemed their enemies; they professed to punish them for their designs against the democracy, but in fact some were killed from motives of personal enmity, and some because money was owing to them, by the hands of their debtors. Every form of death was to be seen, and everything, and more than everything that commonly happens in revolutions, happened then. The father slew the son, and the suppliants were torn from the temples and slain near them; some of them were even walled up in the temple of Dionysus, and there perished. To such extremes of cruelty did revolution go; and this seemed to be the worst of revolutions, because it was the first.

Thucydides, *The Peloponnesian Wars*, 401 BC: Bk III

Battle of Pylos, 425 BC

It was a singular turn of fortune which drove the Athenians to repel the Lacedaemonians, who were attacking them by sea, from the Lacedaemonian coast, and the Lacedaemonians to fight for a landing on their own soil, now hostile to them, in the face of the Athenians. For in those days it was the great glory of the Lacedaemonians to be an inland people distinguished for their military prowess, and of the Athenians to be a nation of sailors and the first naval power in Hellas.

Thucydides, *The Peloponnesian Wars*, 401 BC: Bk IV

Siege of Delium, 424 BC

The Boeotians now marched against Delium and attacked the rampart, employing among other military devices an engine, with which they succeeded in taking the place; it was of the following description. They sawed in two and hollowed out a great beam, which they joined together again very exactly, like a flute, and suspended by chains a vessel at the end of the beam; the iron mouth of a bellows directed downwards into the vessel was attached to the beam, of which a great part itself was overlaid with iron. This machine they brought from a distance on carts to various points of the rampart where vine stems and wood had been most extensively used, and when it was quite near the wall they applied the bellows to their own end of the beam, and blew through it. The blast, prevented from escaping, passed into the vessel which contained burning coals and sulphur and pitch; these made a huge flame and set fire to the rampart, so that no one could remain upon it. The garrison took flight, and the fort was taken.

Thucydides, *The Peloponnesian Wars*, 401 BC: Bk IV

Battle of Mantinea, 418 BC

The Athenians were told that it was glorious to be fighting side by side with a host of brave allies and to be found equal to the bravest. If they could conquer the Lacedaemonians in Peloponnese, they would both extend and secure their dominion, and need never fear an invader again. Such were the exhortations addressed to the Argives and their allies. But the Lacedaemonians, both in their war-songs and in the words a man spoke to his comrade, did but remind one another of what their brave spirits already knew. For they had learned that true safety was to be found in long previous training, and not in eloquent exhortations uttered when they were going into action.

Thucydides, *The Peloponnesian Wars*, 401 BC: Bk V

The Lacedaemonians moved slowly and to the music of many flute-players, who were stationed in their ranks, and played, not as an act of religion, but in order that the army might march evenly and in true measure, and that the line might not break, as often happens in great armies when they go into battle.

Thucydides, *The Peloponnesian Wars*, 401 BC: Bk V

Interim Truce, 416 BC

A truce for one year had already been arranged between them, and during this they conversed freely with one another, and, enjoying a life of leisure and freedom from the restraints and alarms of war, began to long for an unbroken period of peace, and to sing:

'My spear the spider's home shall be',

remembering with pleasure the proverb that in time of peace men are awakened not by trumpets, but by crowing cocks.

Plutarch, *Lives: Nicias*, *c.* AD 110

The Siege and Battle of Syracuse, 415–413 BC

It has been, and continues to be the ruin of our crews, that the sailors, having to forage and fetch water and wood from a distance, are cut off by the Syracusan horse, while our servants, since we have been reduced to an equality with the enemy, desert us. Of the foreign sailors, some who were pressed into the service run off at once to the Sicilian cities; others, having been originally attracted by high pay, and fancying that they were going to trade and not to fight, astonished at the resistance which they encounter, and especially at the naval strength of the enemy, either find an excuse for deserting to the Syracusans, or they effect their escape into the country; and Sicily is a large place.

Nicias, Letter to the Athenian Assembly, 414 BC, in Thucydides, *The Peloponnesian Wars*, 401 BC: Bk VII

More nations met at Syracuse than ever gathered around a single city, although not so many as the whole number of nations enrolled in this war under the Athenians and Lacedaemonians.

Thucydides, *The Peloponnesian Wars*, 401 BC: Bk VII

While the naval engagement hung in the balance the two armies on shore had great trial and conflict of soul. The Sicilian soldier was animated by the hope of increasing the glory which he had already won, while the invader was tormented by the fear that his fortunes might sink lower still. The last chance of the Athenians lay in their ships, and their anxiety was dreadful. The fortune of the battle varied; and it was not possible that the spectators on the shore should all receive the same impression of it. Being quite close and having different points of view, they would some of them see their own ships victorious; their courage would then revive, and they would earnestly call upon the Gods not to take from them their hope of deliverance. But others, who saw their ships worsted, cried and shrieked aloud, and were by the sight alone more utterly unnerved than the defeated combatants themselves. Others again, who had fixed their gaze on some part of the struggle, were in a state of excitement still more terrible; they kept swaying their bodies to and fro in an agony of hope and fear as the stubborn conflict went on and on; for at every instant they were all but saved or all but lost.

Thucydides, *The Peloponnesian Wars*, 401 BC: Bk VII

. . . The whole [Athenian] army was in tears, and such was their despair that they could hardly make up their minds to stir, although they were leaving an enemy's country, having suffered calamities too great for tears already, and dreading miseries yet greater in the unknown future. There was already a general feeling of shame and self-reproach, – indeed they seemed, not like an army, but like the fugitive population of a city captured after a siege; and of a great city too.

Thucydides, *The Peloponnesian Wars*, 401 BC: Bk VII

The moon was behind the backs of the Athenians: and this circumstance was greatly against them, for it made it hard for them to see the numbers of their own friends, but shone plainly on the glittering shields of their antagonists, making them look taller and more terrible than they were.

Plutarch, *Lives: Nicias*, *c.* AD 110

Nikias . . . opposed the idea of retreat, not because he did not fear the Syracusans, but because he feared the Athenians more, and the treatment which, as an unsuccessful general, he would probably meet with. He declared that he saw no reason for alarm, and that even if there was, that he would rather perish by the hands of the enemy than those of his countrymen. A very different sentiment to that which was afterwards uttered by Leon the Byzantine, who said, 'My countrymen, I had rather be put to death by you than to be put to death together with you.'

Plutarch, *Lives: Nicias*, *c.* AD 110

GALLIC INVASION OF ROME, *c.* 390 BC

While these proceedings were taking place at Veii, the Citadel and Capitol of Rome were in imminent danger. The Gauls had either noticed the footprints left by the messenger from Veii, or had themselves discovered a comparatively easy ascent up the cliff to the temple of Carmentis. Choosing a night when there was a faint glimmer of light, they sent an unarmed man in advance to try the road; then handing one another their arms where the path was difficult, and supporting each other or dragging each other up as the ground required, they finally reached the summit. So silent had their movements been that not only were they unnoticed by the sentinels, but they did not even wake the dogs, an animal peculiarly sensitive to nocturnal sounds. But they did not escape the notice of the geese, which were sacred to Juno and had been left untouched in spite of the extremely scanty supply of food. This proved the safety of the garrison, for their clamour and the noise of their wings aroused M. Manlius, the distinguished soldier, who had been consul three years before. He snatched up his weapons and ran to call the rest to arms, and while the rest hung back he struck with the boss of his shield a Gaul who had got a foothold on the summit and knocked him down. He fell on those behind and upset them, and Manlius slew others who had laid aside their weapons and were clinging to the rocks with their bare hands. By this time others had joined him, and they began to dislodge the enemy with volleys of stones and javelins till the whole body fell helplessly down to the bottom.

Livy, *The History of Rome*, from 29 BC: Bk V

A conference took place between Q. Sulpicius, the consular tribune, and Brennus, the Gaulish chieftain, and an agreement was arrived at by which 1000 lbs of gold was fixed as the ransom of a people destined ere long to rule the world. The humiliation was great enough as it was, but it was aggravated by the despicable meanness of the Gauls, who produced unjust weights, and when the tribune protested, the insolent Gaul threw his sword into the scale, with an exclamation intolerable to Roman ears, *'Woe to the vanquished!'*

Livy, *The History of Rome*, from 29 BC: Bk V

SECOND CARTHAGINIAN INVASION OF SICILY, 387 BC

Siege of Syracuse, 387 BC

. . . Dionysius was inspired with resolution to abide the storm, that so he might fulfil that purpose of God's providence, which designed the Greek power in Sicily to stand as a breakwater against the advances of Carthage, and to afford a shelter to the yet unripened strength of Rome.

Thomas Arnold, *History of Rome*, 1838

WARS OF THE GREEK CITY STATES, 4th century BC

Battle of Tegyra, 373 BC

At Tegyra, then, Pelopidas and the Thebans retiring from Orchomenus met the Lacedaemonians marching back from Lokris, in the opposite direction. When they first descried them coming out of the narrow gorges of the hills, some one ran to Pelopidas, and cried out, 'We have fallen into the midst of the enemy!' 'Why so,' asked he, 'more than they into the midst of us?'

Plutarch, *Lives: Pelopidas*, *c.* 110

Battle of Leuctra, 371 BC

When news of the defeat at Leuctra arrived at Sparta, the city was celebrating the festival of the Gymnopaedia, and the chorus of grown men were going through its usual solemnity in the theatre. The Ephors, although the news clearly proved that all was lost and the state utterly ruined, yet would not permit the chorus to abridge its performance, and forbade the city to throw off its festal appearance. They privately communicated the names of the slain to their relatives, but they themselves calmly continued to preside over the contest of the choruses in the theatre, and brought the festival to a close as though nothing unusual had occurred. Next morning, when all men knew who had fallen and who had survived, one might see those whose relations had been slain, walking about in public with bright and cheerful countenances: but of those whose relatives survived, scarce one showed himself in public, but they sat at home with the women, as if mourning for the dead; or if any one of them was forced to come forth, he looked mournful and humbled, and walked with downcast eyes. Yet more admirable was the conduct of the women, for one might see mothers receiving their sons who had survived the battle with silence and sorrow, while those whose children had fallen proceeded to the temples to return thanks to the gods, and walked about the city with a proud and cheerful demeanour.

Plutarch, *Lives: Agesilaus*, *c.* 110

Second Battle of Mantinea, 362 BC

Many brave men on their [the Athenian] side were killed; and they themselves killed many brave men on that of the enemy [the Thebans]; for none on either side had weapons so short that they could not reach one another.

Xenophon, *Hellenics*, *c.* 365 BC: VII

THE CONQUESTS OF ALEXANDER THE GREAT, 334–323 BC

... It was reported that the statue of Orpheus, son of Oeagrus the Thracian, which was in Pieris, sweated incessantly. Various were the explanations of this prodigy given by the soothsayers; but Aristander, a man of Telmissus, a soothsayer, bade Alexander take courage; for he said it was evident from this that there would be much labour for the epic and lyric poets, and for the writers of odes, to compose and sing about Alexander and his achievements.

Arrian, *The Anabasis of Alexander*, *c.* 160: Bk I

Battle of the Grancius, May 334 BC

[Alexander] also buried the Persian commanders and the Greek mercenaries who were killed fighting on the side of the enemy. But as many of them as he took prisoners he bound in fetters and sent them away to Macedonia to till the soil, because, though they were Greeks, they were fighting against Greece on behalf of the foreigners in opposition to the decrees which the Greeks had made in their federal council. To Athens also he sent 300 suits of Persian armour to be hung up in the Acropolis as a votive offering to Athens, and ordered this inscription to be fixed over them: 'Alexander, son of Philip, and all the Greeks except the Lacedaemonians, present this offering from the spoils taken from the foreigners inhabiting Asia.'

Arrian, *The Anabasis of Alexander*, *c.* 160: Bk I

Alexander at Gordium, 332 BC

In addition to this the following report was current concerning the wagon, that whosoever could loosen the cord with which the yoke of the wagon was tied, was destined to be the ruler of Asia. The cord was made of cornel bark, and neither end nor beginning to it could be seen. It is said by some that when Alexander could find out no way to loosen the cord and yet was unwilling to allow it to remain unloosened, lest it should exercise some disturbing influence on the multitude, he struck the cord with his sword and cut it through, saying it had been untied by him. But Aristobulus says that he pulled out the pin of the wagon-pole, which was a wooden peg driven right through it, holding the cord together. Having done this he drew out the yoke from the wagon-pole.

Arrian, *The Anabasis of Alexander*, *c.* 160: Bk II

Battle of Arbela (Gaugamela), 1st October 331 BC

It is said that Parmenio came to him in his tent, and urged him to make a night attack upon the Persians; saying that thus he would fall upon them unprepared and in a state of confusion, and at the same time more liable to a panic in the dark. But the reply which he made, as others were listening to their conversation, was, that it would be mean to steal a victory, and that Alexander was to conquer in open daylight, and without any artifice. This vaunting did not appear any arrogance on his part, but rather to indicate self-confidence amid dangers.

Arrian, *The Anabasis of Alexander*, *c.* 160: Bk III

Alexander's victory at Arbela not only overthrew an Oriental dynasty, but established European rulers in their stead. It broke the monotony of the Eastern world by the impression of Western energy and superior civilization; even as England's present mission is to break up the mental and moral stagnation of India and Cathay, . . .

E. S. Creasy, *The Fifteen Decisive Battles of the World*, 1851

The Punishment of Bessus

Then Alexander gathered a conference of those who were then at hand, and led Bessus in before them. Having accused him of the betrayal of Darius, he ordered his nose and ears to be cut off, and that he should be taken to Ecbatana to be put to death there in the council of the Medes and Persians. I do not commend this excessive punishment; on the contrary, I consider that the mutilation of the prominent features of the body is a barbaric custom, and I agree with those who say that Alexander was induced to indulge his desire by emulating the Median and Persian wealth and to treat his subjects as inferior beings according to the custom of the foreign kings.

Arrian, *The Anabasis of Alexander*, *c.* 160: Bk IV

Alexander Among the Indians

After this, Alexander, who had suffered great losses from the Indian mercenary troops who flocked to defend the cities which he attacked, made a treaty of alliance with them in a certain town, and afterwards, as they were going away, set upon them while they were on the road and killed them all. This is the greatest blot upon his fame; for in all the rest of his wars, he always acted in good faith, as became a king. He was also much troubled by the philosophers who attended him, because they reproached those native princes who joined him, and encouraged the free states to revolt and regain their independence. For this reason, he caused not a few of them to be hanged.

Plutarch, *Lives: Alexander*, *c.* 110

Battle of the Hydaspes, 326 BC

Alexander, seeing his opportunity, at the very moment the cavalry was wheeling round in the other direction, made an attack on those opposed to him with such vigour that the Indians could not sustain the charge of his cavalry, but were scattered and driven to the elephants, as to a friendly wall, for refuge. Upon this, the drivers of the elephants urged forward the beasts against the cavalry; but now the phalanx itself of the Macedonians was advancing against the elephants, the men casting darts at the riders and also striking the beasts themselves, standing round them on all sides. The action was unlike any of the previous contests; for wherever the beasts could wheel round, they rushed forth against the ranks of the infantry and demolished the phalanx of the Macedonians, dense as it was. The Indian cavalry also, seeing that the infantry were engaged in the action, rallied again and advanced against the Macedonian cavalry. But when Alexander's men, who far excelled both in strength and military discipline, got the mastery over them the second time, they were again repulsed towards the elephants and cooped up among them. By this time the whole of Alexander's cavalry had collected into one squadron, not by any command of his, but having settled into this arrangement by the mere effect of the struggle itself; and wherever it fell upon the ranks of the Indians they were broken up with great slaughter. The beasts being now cooped up into a narrow space, their friends were no less injured by them than their foes, being trampled down in their wheeling and pushing about. Accordingly there ensued a great slaughter of the cavalry, cooped up as it was in a narrow space around the elephants. Most of the keepers of the elephants had been killed by the javelins, and some of the elephants themselves had been wounded, while others no longer kept apart in the battle on account of their sufferings or being destitute of keepers. But, as if frantic with pain, rushing forward at friends and foes alike, they pushed about, trampled down and killed them in every kind of way. However, the Macedonians retired whenever they were assailed, and they rushed in at the beasts in a more open space, and in accordance with their own plan; and when they wheeled round to return, they followed them closely and hurled javelins at them; whereas the Indians retreating among them were now receiving greater injury from them. But when the beasts were tired out, and they were no longer able to charge with any vigour, they began to retire, facing the foe like ships backing water, merely uttering a shrill piping sound.

Arrian, *The Anabasis of Alexander*, *c.* 160: Bk V

The March through Gadrosia, 324 BC

They were far on the journey, and Alexander himself, though oppressed with thirst, was nevertheless with great pain and difficulty leading the army on foot, so that his soldiers, as is usual in such a case, might more patiently bear their hardships by the equalization of the distress. At this time some of the light-armed soldiers, starting away from the army in quest of water, found some collected in a shallow cleft, a small and mean spring. Collecting this water with difficulty, they came with all speed to Alexander, as if they were bringing him some great boon. As soon as they approached the king, they poured the water into a helmet and carried it to him. He took it and, commending the men who brought it, immediately poured it upon the ground in sight of all. As a result of this action the entire army was reinvigorated to so great a degree that any one would have imagined that the water poured away by Alexander had furnished a draught to every man.

Arrian, *The Anabasis of Alexander*, *c.* 160, Bk VI

PYRRHUS'S INVASION OF ITALY, 279 BC

The Battle of Asculum

The armies separated after the battle, and it is said that Pyrrhus, when congratulated on his victory by his friends, said in reply: 'If we win one more such victory over the Romans, we shall be ruined.'

Plutarch, *Lives: Pyrrhus*, *c.* AD 110

THE PUNIC WARS: 264–241 BC, 218–201 BC and [*see p. 170*] 149–146 BC

I, too, feel as much relief in having reached the end of the Punic War as if I had taken a personal part in its toils and dangers. It ill befits one who has had the courage to promise a complete history of Rome to find the separate sections of such an extensive work fatiguing. But when I consider that the sixty-three years from the beginning of the First Punic War to the end of the Second take up as many books as the four hundred and eighty-seven years from the foundation of the City to the consulship of Appius Claudius under whom the First Punic War commenced, I see that I am like people who are tempted by the shallow water along the beach to wade out to sea; the further I progress, the greater the depth, as though it were a bottomless sea, into which I am carried. I imagined that as I completed one part after another the task before me would diminish; as it is, it almost becomes greater.

Livy, *The History of Rome*, from 29 BC: Bk XXXI

... How many smaller kingdoms were wiped out! How many spacious and famous towns were razed, how many communities suffered disaster or utter ruin! How many wide regions and countries endured widespread devastation! How frequent were the interchanges of defeat and victory! What loss of life occurred among both the combatants and the civil population! What a huge total of ships was lost, either destroyed in sea-battles or sunk by storm or various kinds of bad weather! If I were to recall and relate those calamities, I should turn into just another chronicler.

St Augustine, *City Of God*, 427: III.xviii

The Roman combination of the heavy javelin with the sword ... produced similar results ... to those attained in modern warfare by the introduction of bayonet muskets; the volley of javelins prepared the way for the sword encounter, exactly in the same way as a volley of musketry now precedes a charge with the bayonets.

J. F. C. Fuller, *The Decisive Battles of the Western World*, 1954–56

... The conflict between Rome and Carthage was as close as classical civilization ever got to the concept of total war.

Gwynne Dyer, *War*, 1986

THE SECOND PUNIC WAR, 218–201 BC

I am not come to fight against Italians, but on behalf of Italians against Rome.

Hannibal, in Polybius, *Histories*, 125 BC, IX

I consider myself at liberty to commence what is only a section of my history with a prefatory remark such as most writers have placed at the very beginning of their works, namely, that the war I am about to describe is the most memorable of any that have ever been waged, I mean the war with the Carthaginians, under Hannibal's leadership, waged with Rome. No states, no nations ever met in arms greater in strength or richer in resources; these Powers themselves had never been in so high a state of efficiency or better prepared to stand the strain of a long war; they were no strangers to each other's tactics after their experience in the first Punic War; and so variable were the fortunes and so doubtful the issue of the war that those who were ultimately victorious were in the earlier stages brought nearest to ruin. And yet, great as was their strength, the hatred they felt toward each other was almost greater. The Romans were furious with indignation because the vanquished had dared to take the offensive against their conquerors; the Carthaginians bitterly resented what they regarded as the tyrannical and rapacious conduct of Rome.

Livy, *The History of Rome*, from 29 BC: Bk XXI

Of all that befell the Romans and Carthaginians, good or bad, the cause was one man and one mind, Hannibal.

Polybius, *Histories*, 125 BC, IX

Even the historians who set out to sing the praises of the Roman Empire, rather than to recount Rome's wars, have to admit that the victory resembled a defeat.

St Augustine, *City Of God*, 427: III.xix

The unsuccessful expedition of Hannibal served only to display the character of the senate and people; of a senate degraded, rather than ennobled, by the comparison of an assembly of kings; and of a people, to whom the ambassador of Pyrrhus ascribed the inexhaustible resources of a hydra.

Edward Gibbon, *The History Of The Decline And Fall Of The Roman Empire*, 1776–88: xxxi

Hannibal Crosses the Alps

Accordingly, at early dawn he began the ascent as though determined to force the pass in broad daylight, and spent the day in movements designed to conceal his real intentions and in fortifying the camp on the spot where they had halted. As soon as he observed that the natives had left the heights and were no longer watching his movements, he gave orders, with a view to deceiving the enemy, for a large number of fires to be lighted, larger in fact than would be required by those remaining in camp. Then, leaving the baggage with the cavalry and the greater part of the infantry in camp, he himself with a specially selected body of troops in light marching order rapidly moved out of the defile and occupied the heights which the enemy had held.

Livy, *The History of Rome*, from 29 BC: Bk XXI

The next day, as the savages attacked with less vigour, the column closed up, and the pass was surmounted, not without loss, more, however, of baggage animals than of men. From that time the natives made their appearance in smaller numbers and behaved more like banditti than regular soldiers; they attacked either front or rear just as the ground gave them opportunity, or the advance or halt of the column presented a chance of surprise. The elephants caused considerable delay, owing to the difficulty of getting them through narrow or precipitous places; on the other hand, they rendered that part of the column safe from attack where they were, for the natives were unaccustomed to the sight of them and had a great dread of going too near them.

Livy, *The History of Rome*, from 29 BC: Bk XXI

Battle of Trebbia, December 218 BC

The infantry battle, as far as the Romans were concerned, was maintained more by courage than by physical strength, for the Carthaginians, who had shortly before been getting themselves into trim, brought their powers fresh and unimpaired into action, whilst the Romans were fatigued and hungry and stiff with cold. Still, their courage would have kept them up had it been only infantry that they were fighting against. But the light infantry, after repulsing the cavalry, were hurling their missiles on the flanks of the legions; the elephants had now come up against the centre of the Roman line, and Mago and his Numidians, as soon as it had passed their ambuscade, rose up in the rear and caused terrible disorder and panic. Yet in spite of all the dangers that surrounded them, the ranks stood firm and immovable for some time, even, contrary to all expectations, against the elephants. Some skirmishers who had been placed where they could attack these animals flung darts at them and drove them off, and rushed after them, stabbing them under their tails, where the skin is soft and easily penetrated.

Livy, *The History of Rome*, from 29 BC: Bk XXI

Portents in Rome in the Winter of 218–217 BC

A six-month-old child, of freeborn parents, is said to have shouted 'Io Triumphe' in the vegetable market, whilst in the Forum Boarium an ox is reported to have climbed up of its own accord to the third storey of a house, and then, frightened by the noisy crowd which gathered, it threw itself down. A phantom navy was seen shining in the sky; the temple of Hope in the vegetable market was struck by lightning; at Lanuvium Juno's spear had moved of itself, and a crow had flown down to her temple and settled upon her couch; in the territory of Amiternum beings in human shape and clothed in white were seen at a distance, but no one came close to them; in the neighbourhood of Picenum there was a shower of stones; at Caere the oracular tablets had shrunk in size; in Gaul a wolf had snatched a sentinel's sword from its scabbard and run off with it.

Livy, *The History of Rome*, from 29 BC: Bk XXI

Battle of Lake Trasimenus (Trasimeno), 217 BC

At last, when the battle was over and the sun's heat had dispelled the fog, mountain and plain revealed in the clear light the disastrous overthrow of the Roman army and showed only too plainly that all was lost. Fearing lest they should be seen in the distance and cavalry be sent against them, they hurriedly took up their standards and disappeared with all possible speed. Maharbal pursued them through the night with the whole of his mounted force, and on the morrow, as starvation, in addition to all their other miseries, was threatening them, they surrendered to Maharbal, on condition of being allowed to depart with one garment apiece. The promise was kept with Punic faith by Hannibal, and he threw them all into chains.

Livy, *The History of Rome*, from 29 BC: Bk XXII

Battle of Cannae, 3rd August 216 BC

. . . But the fighting was slack at first, owing to a Carthaginian stratagem. About 500 Numidians, carrying, besides their usual arms and missiles, swords concealed under their coats of mail, rode out from their own line with their shields slung behind their backs as though they were deserters, and suddenly leaped from their horses and flung their shields and javelins at the feet of the enemy. They were received into their ranks, conducted to the rear, and ordered to remain quiet. While the battle was spreading to the various parts of the field they remained quiet, but when the eyes and minds of all were wholly taken up with the fighting they seized the large Roman shields which were lying everywhere amongst the heaps of slain and commenced a furious attack upon the rear of the Roman line. Slashing away at backs and hips, they made a great slaughter and still greater panic and confusion.

Livy, *The History of Rome*, from 29 BC: Bk XXII

Hannibal's officers all surrounded him and congratulated him on his victory, and urged that after such a magnificent success he should allow himself and his exhausted men to rest for the remainder of the day and following night. Maharbal, however, the commandant of the cavalry, thought that they ought not to lose a moment. 'That you may know,' he said to Hannibal, 'what has been gained by this battle I prophesy that in five days you will be feasting as victor in the Capitol. Follow me; I will go in advance with the cavalry; they will know that you are come before they know that you are coming.' To Hannibal the victory seemed too great and too joyous for him to realise all at once. He told Maharbal that he commended his zeal, but he needed time to think out his plans. Maharbal replied: 'The gods have not given all their gifts to one man. You know how to win victory, Hannibal, but not how to use it.' That day's delay is believed to have saved the City and the empire.

Livy, *The History of Rome*, from 29 BC: Bk XXII

The next day, as soon as it grew light, they set about gathering the spoils on the field and viewing the carnage, which was a ghastly sight even for an enemy. There all those thousands of Romans were lying, infantry and cavalry indiscriminately as chance had brought them together in the battle or the flight. Some covered with blood raised themselves from amongst the dead around them, tortured by their wounds which were nipped by the cold of the morning, and were promptly put an end to by the enemy. Some they found lying with their thighs and knees gashed but still alive; these bared their throats and necks and bade them drain what blood they still had left. Some were discovered with their heads buried in the earth, they had evidently suffocated themselves by making holes in the ground and heaping the soil over their faces. What attracted the attention of all was a Numidian who was dragged alive from under a dead Roman lying across him; his ears and nose were torn, for the Roman with hands too powerless to grasp his weapon had, in his mad rage, torn his enemy with his teeth, and while doing so expired.

Livy, *The History of Rome*, from 29 BC: Bk XXII

Siege of Syracuse, 213–12 BC

Marcellus . . . sarcastically said to his own engineers: 'Are we to give into this Briareus of a geometrician, who sits at his ease by the sea-shore and plays at upsetting our ships, to our lasting disgrace, and surpasses the hundred-handed giant of fable by hurling so many weapons at us at once?' For indeed all the other Syracusans were merely the limbs of Archimedes, and his mind alone directed and guided everything. All other arms were laid aside and the city trusted to his weapons solely for defence and safety. At length Marcellus, seeing that the Romans had become so scared that if only a rope or small beam were seen over the wall they would turn and fly, crying out that Archimedes was bringing some engine to bear upon them, ceased assaulting the place, and trusted to time alone to reduce it.

Plutarch, *Lives: Marcellus*, *c.* AD 110

Battle of the Metaurus, 207 BC

To this part of the field the elephants too had been driven, and at their first onset they threw the front ranks into confusion and forced the standards to give way. Then as the battle became hotter and the noise and shouting more furious, it became impossible to control them, they rushed about between the two armies as though they did not know to which side they belonged, just like ships drifting rudderless.

Livy, *The History of Rome*, from 29 BC: Bk XXVII

More elephants were killed by their drivers than by the enemy. They had a carpenter's chisel and a mallet, and when the maddened beasts rushed among their own side the driver placed the chisel between the ears just where the head is joined to the neck and drove it home with all his might. This was the quickest method that had been discovered of putting these huge animals to death when there was no hope of controlling them, and Hasdrubal was the first to introduce it.

Livy, *The History of Rome*, from 29 BC: Bk XXVII

Success the most complete had crowned [Claudius] Nero's enterprise. Returning as rapidly as he had advanced, he was again facing the inactive enemies in the south before they even knew of his march. But he brought with him a ghastly trophy of what he had done. In the true spirit of that savage brutality which deformed the Roman national character, Nero ordered Hasdrubal's head to be flung into his brother's camp. Ten years had passed since Hannibal had last gazed on those features. The sons of Hamilcar had then planned their system of warfare against Rome, which they had so nearly brought to successful accomplishment. Year after year had Hannibal been struggling in Italy, in the hope of one day hailing the arrival of him who had left Spain; and of seeing his brother's eye flash with affection and pride at the junction of their irresistible hosts. He now saw that eye glazed in death, and in the agony of his heart the great Carthaginian groaned aloud that he recognized his country's destiny.

E. S. Creasy, *The Fifteen Decisive Battles of the World*, 1851

The Fall of Astapa, 205 BC

. . . A much more horrible butchery took place in the city, where a weak and defenceless crowd of women and children were massacred by their own people, and their still writhing bodies flung on the lighted pile which was again almost extinguished by the streams of blood. And last of all, the men themselves, exhausted by the pitiful slaughter of those dear to them, flung themselves arms and all into the midst of the flames. All had perished by the time the Romans came on the scene. At first they stood horror-struck at such a fearful sight, then, seeing the melted gold and silver flowing amongst the other articles which made up the heap, the greediness common to human nature impelled them to try and snatch what they could out of the fire. Some were caught by the flames, others were scorched by the heated air, for those in front could not retreat owing to the crowd pressing on behind.

Livy, *The History of Rome*, from 29 BC: Bk XXVIII

Battle of Zama, 202 BC

To the Carthaginians it was a struggle for their own lives and the sovereignty of Libya; to the Romans for universal dominion and supremacy.

Polybius, *Histories*, *c.* 120 BC: Bk V

On the morrow they went into battle – the two most brilliant generals and the two strongest armies that the two most powerful nations possessed – to crown on that day the many honours they had won, or for ever lose them. The soldiers were filled with alternate hopes and fears as they gazed at their own and then the opposing lines and measured their comparative strength with the eye rather than the mind, cheerful and despondent in turn. The encouragement which they could not give to themselves their generals gave them in their exhortations. The Carthaginian reminded his men of their sixteen years' successes on Italian soil, of all the Roman generals who had fallen and all the armies that had been destroyed, and as he came to each soldier who had distinguished himself in any battle, he recounted his gallant deeds. Scipio recalled the conquest of Spain and the recent battles in Africa and showed up the enemies' confession of weakness, since their fears compelled them to sue for peace and their innate faithlessness prevented them from abiding by it. He turned to his own purpose his conference with Hannibal, which being private allowed free scope for invention. He drew an omen and declared that the gods had vouchsafed the same auspices on them as those under which their fathers fought at the Aegates. The end of the war and of their labours, he assured them, had come; the spoils of Carthage were in their hands, and the return home to their wives and children and household gods. He spoke with uplifted head and a face so radiant that you might suppose he had already won the victory.

Livy, *The History of Rome*, from 29 BC: Bk XXX

THE GREAT WALL OF CHINA, *c.* 215 BC

In the third century before the christian aera, a wall of fifteen hundred miles in length was constructed, to defend the frontiers of China against the inroads of the Huns; but this stupendous work, which holds a conspicuous place in the map of the world, has never contributed to the safety of an unwarlike people. The cavalry of the Tanjou frequently consisted of two or three hundred thousand men, formidable by the matchless dexterity with which they managed their bows and their horses; by their hardy patience in supporting the inclemency of the weather; and by the incredible speed of their march, which was seldom checked by torrents, or precipices, by the deepest rivers, or by the most lofty mountains.

Edward Gibbon, *The History Of The Decline And Fall Of The Roman Empire*, 1776–88: xxvi

THIRD MACEDONIAN WAR, 172–168 BC

In any crowd and at every table you will find someone to lead the army in Macedonia, who knows where the camp should be made, what ports held by the troops, where the territory is best entered, where magazines should be established, how provisions moved, by land or by sea, where the enemy should be engaged, and when to hold back. And these people not only tell us how the campaign should be conducted, but what's wrong with the actual campaign, accusing the consul as though he were on trial. Well then, if there is anyone who thinks he is properly qualified to give me advice, let him come with me to Macedonia. But what he mustn't do is think the toils of war too much, and, preferring the repose of city life, assume the office of a pilot on land.

Lucius Aemilius Paulus, speech in the Roman Senate, 169 BC

Battle of Pydna, 22nd June 168 BC

. . . The result was not the decay of Greece, but the victory of Hellenism; for the Greeks were the Chinese of the ancient world and always conquered their conquerors. What they needed, in order to exorcise the excessive individualism which had kept them fractionized and mutually antagonistic, was the authority of a strong and stable world government. And what Rome needed, in order to become a civilizing world power, was the culture of the Hellenistic world. These two things and not plunder and tribute were the true booty of Pydna . . .

J. F. C. Fuller, *The Decisive Battles of the Western World*, 1954–56

THIRD PUNIC WAR, 149–146 BC

The Sack of Carthage, 146 BC

To destroy that for which a war is undertaken seems an act of madness, and madness of a very violent kind.

Polybius, *Histories*, *c.* 125 BC

The last of [Cato's] political acts is said to have been the destruction of Carthage. This was actually brought to pass by Scipio the Younger, but it was chiefly owing to the counsels of Cato that the war was begun. He was sent on a mission to Africa to investigate the grounds of a quarrel which existed between the Carthaginians and Masinissa, the king of the Numidians. Masinissa had always been the friend of Rome, whereas the Carthaginians, after their defeat by Scipio, had been subjected to hard conditions, having lost their sovereignty over the neighbouring tribes, and having been compelled to pay a large sum of tribute to Rome. Cato, however, found the city, not, as the Romans imagined it to be, crushed by its recent overthrow, but full of young men, overflowing with wealth, well provided with arms and munitions of war, and, as may be expected, full of warlike spirit. He concluded that it was no time for the Romans to arbitrate about the grievances of Masinissa and his Numidians, but that, unless they destroyed the city which bore them an undying hatred and which had recovered its strength in an incredibly short space of time, they would have as much to fear from Carthage as ever.

Plutarch, *Lives: Marcus Cato*, *c.* AD 110

ROME'S WAR AGAINST JUGURTHA OF NUMIDIA, 112–105 BC

After passing through the gates of Rome, it is said that [Jugurtha] looked back at the city several times in silence, and finally exclaimed: 'Yonder is a city put up for sale, and its days are numbered if it finds a buyer.'

Sallust, *The Jugurthine War*, *c.* 42 BC

For Jugurtha was so crafty, so well acquainted with the country, and so experienced in warfare, that one never knew which was the more deadly – his presence or his absence, his offers of peace or his threats of hostilities.

Sallust, *The Jugurthine War*, *c.* 42 BC

These were the only men available: for with the exception of the cavalry of the royal bodyguard, no Numidian, after a rout, returns to his post in the king's army; every man goes off where he pleases, and this is not regarded as a shameful thing for a soldier to do, because it is the custom of the country.

Sallust, *The Jugurthine War*, *c.* 42 BC

Massacre of the Roman Garrison at Vaga, 109 BC

Disconcerted by the sudden peril and not knowing what best to do, the Roman soldiers were much alarmed. They could not reach the citadel where their standards and shields were, because the way was barred by a hostile force; flight was out of the question because the gates had been shut before the attack. Moreover women and children perched on the edges of the housetops were pelting them as hard as they could with stones and anything else they could find there. Unable to guard against dangers threatening from two directions at once, the bravest men could do nothing even against such feeble assailants: good soldiers and bad soldiers, courageous and cowardly, were cut down together with none to avenge them. In this massacre, perpetrated by a savage enemy in a completely closed city, the commander Turpilius was the only Italian who got away unhurt. Whether he owed his escape to his host's compassion, or to a secret bargain, or simply to luck, I have not discovered. In any case, a man who in such a calamity could prefer dishonourable survival to an untarnished name must have been a detestable wretch.

Sallust, *The Jugurthine War*, *c.* 42 BC

Siege of Thala, 108 BC

When Metellus saw that the defenders of Thala were bent on fighting it out and that the place was protected both by its situation and by fortifications, he encircled the walls with a stockade and trench. Then, in the two best spots available, he moved forward mantlets and threw up a mound, on which towers were erected to provide cover for his siegeworks and the workmen. The besieged were equally prompt with their counter-measures. Both sides strained every nerve. Eventually, after six weeks' exhausting labour and fighting, the Romans got possession of the town, but were cheated of the booty they had hoped for, because it was all destroyed by their own deserters. These men, when they saw the walls being breached by the battering-rams and realized that all was lost, carried the gold, silver, and other valuables to the royal palace. There, after gorging themselves with food and wine, they made a bonfire of the treasure and the palace and allowed the flames to consume their own bodies as well, thus inflicting upon themselves the very punishment they feared from the hands of their foes in case of defeat.

Sallust, *The Jugurthine War*, *c.* 42 BC

REVOLT OF CATILINE, 64–63 BC

Battle of Pistoia, 63 BC

In battle, those who are most afraid are always in the greatest danger.

Lucius Sergius Catilina, exhorting his troops, attributed

Of that whole army which fought and fled, not a single free-born citizen was taken prisoner: all were as careless as of their enemies' lives. The victory of the government forces, however, was not gained without blood and tears: all the best fighters had either been killed in the action or come out of it badly wounded. Many who came from the camp to view the battlefield or to loot, as they went about turning over the rebels' corpses, found friends, relatives or men who had been their guests or their hosts. Some also recognized the face of an enemy. Thus diverse feelings affected all the army: gladness and rejoicing were tempered by grief and lamentation.

Sallust, *The Conspiracy of Catiline*, *c.* 41 BC

CAESAR'S GALLIC WARS, 61–51 BC

About the same time the Gauls inflicted upon our commanders Quintus Caepio and Gnaeus Manlius a defeat that made all Italy tremble with terror and inspired in the Romans a belief which persisted even to our own day – what while all other peoples could easily be subjected by their valour, a war against Gauls was a struggle for very existence and not just a matter of making a bid for glory.

Sallust, *The Jugurthine War*, *c.* 42 BC

Campaign Against the Helvetii, 61–58 BC

While he was halting for a few days close to the Vesontio to collect corn and other supplies, a violent panic seized the whole army, completely paralysing every one's judgement and nerve. It arose from the inquisitiveness of our men and the chatter of the Gauls and the traders, who affirmed that the Germans were men of huge stature, incredible valour, and practised skill in war: many a time they had themselves come across them, and had not been able even to look them in the face or meet the glare of their piercing eyes. The panic began with the tribunes, the auxiliary officers, and others who had left the capital to follow Caesar in the hope of winning his favour, and had little experience in war. Some of them applied for leave of absence, alleging various urgent reasons for their departure, though a good many, anxious to avoid the imputation of cowardice, stayed behind for very shame. They were unable, however, to assume an air of unconcern, and sometimes even to restrain their tears; shutting themselves up in their tents, they bemoaned their own fate or talked dolefully with their intimates of the peril that threatened the army. All over the camp men were making their wills. Gradually even legionaries, centurions and cavalry officers, who had long experience of campaigning, were unnerved by these alarmists. Those who did not want to be thought cowards said that it was not the enemy they were afraid of, but the narrow roads and the huge forests which separated them from Ariovistus, or the difficulty of bringing up grain.

Julius Caesar, *Commentaries*, 51 BC: Bk I

Campaign Against the Venetii, 56 BC

After taking several strongholds, Caesar saw that all his labour was being expended in vain, and that, by merely capturing their forts, he could neither prevent the enemy from escaping nor cripple them. He decided, therefore, that it would be best to wait for his fleet. As soon as it arrived and was sighted by the enemy, their ships, numbering about two hundred and twenty, ready for sea and fully equipped, stood out of harbour and ranged opposite ours. Brutus, who commanded the fleet, and the tribunes and centurions, each of whom had been entrusted with a single ship, did not quite know what to do, or what tactics to adopt. They had ascertained that it was impossible to injure the enemy's ships by ramming. The turrets were run up; but even then they were overtopped by the foreigners' lofty sterns, so that, from the lower position, it was impossible to throw javelins with effect, while the missiles thrown by the Gauls fell with increased momentum. Our men, however, had a very effective contrivance ready, – namely hooks sharpened at the ends and fixed to long poles shaped somewhat like grappling-hooks. By means of these the halyards were seized and pulled taut: the galley rowed hard; and the ropes snapped. When they were cut, the yards of course fell down; and as the efficiency of the Gallic ships depended altogether upon their sails and rigging, when they were gone the ships were no longer of any use. Thenceforward the struggle turned upon sheer courage, in which our soldiers easily had the advantage, especially as the fighting went on under the eyes of Caesar and the whole army, so that no act of courage at all remarkable could escape notice; for all the cliffs and high ground which commanded a near view over the sea were occupied by the army.

Julius Caesar, *Commentaries*, 51 BC: Bk III

First Invasion of Britain, 55 BC

The natives knew what the Romans intended. Sending on ahead the cavalry and charioteers – a kind of warrior whom they habitually employ in action – they followed with the rest of their force and attempted to prevent our men from disembarking. It was very difficult to land, for these reasons. The size of the ships made it impossible to ground except in deep water; the soldiers did not know the ground, and with their hands loaded, and weighted by their heavy, cumbrous armour, they had to jump down from the ships, keep their foothold in the surf, and fight the enemy all at once; while the enemy had all their limbs free, they knew the ground perfectly, and standing on dry land or moving forward a little into the water, they threw their missiles boldly and drove their horses into the sea, which they were trained to enter. Our men were unnerved by the situation; and having no experience of this kind of warfare, they did not show the same dash and energy that they generally did in battles on dry land.

Caesar, noticing this, ordered the galleys, with the look of which the natives were not familiar, and which were easier to handle, to sheer off a little from the transports, row hard and range alongside the enemy's flank, and slingers, archers, and artillery to shoot from their decks and drive the enemy out of the way.

Julius Caesar, *Commentaries*, 51 BC: Bk IV

Chariots are used in action in the following way. First of all the charioteers drive all over the field, the warriors hurling missiles; and generally they throw the enemy's ranks into confusion by the mere terror inspired by their horses and the clatter of the wheels. As soon as they have penetrated between troops and cavalry, the warriors jump off the chariots and fight on foot. The drivers meanwhile gradually withdraw from the action, and range the cars in such a position that, if the warriors are hard pressed by the enemy's numbers, they may easily get back to them. Thus they exhibit in action the mobility of cavalry with the steadiness of infantry; and they become so efficient from constant practice and training that they will drive their horses at full gallop, keeping them well in hand, down a steep incline, check and turn them in an instant, run along the pole, stand on the yoke, and step backwards again to the cars with the greatest nimbleness.

Julius Caesar, *Commentaries*, 51 BC: Bk IV

Second Invasion of Britain, 54 BC

All the Britons, without exception, stain themselves with woad, which produces a bluish tint; and this gives them a wild look in battle. They wear their hair long and shave the whole of their body except the head and the upper lip.

Julius Caesar, *Commentaries*, 51 BC: Bk V

. . . The emperor Julius Caesar was the first of the Romans to invade Britain, and hard pressed the Britons in Battle and overcame them, but could not gain a kingdom there.

The Anglo-Saxon Chronicle

Rebellion of Vercingetorix, 52 BC

His adherents saluted him as king. He sent out envoys in every direction, adjuring the confederates to remain true. He quickly secured the adhesion of the Senones, Parisii, Pictones, Cadurci, Turoni, Aulerci, Lemovices, Andi and all the other maritime tribes; and the chief command was conferred upon him unanimously. Armed with this power, he ordered all these tribes to give hostages and bring him speedily a definite quota of troops. He fixed a date by which each tribe was to turn out a specified quantity of arms from its own workshops, and devoted special attention to his cavalry. With the utmost diligence he combined the utmost severity in the exercise of his command, coercing waverers by heavy penalties. Thus he punished serious misdemeanours by death at the stake with all kinds of tortures, while he sent home minor offenders with their ears lopped off or one eye gouged out, that they might serve as a warning to the rest and that the severity of their punishment make others quail.

Julius Caesar, *Commentaries*, 51 BC: Bk VII

Sometimes, indeed, the Gauls attempted to storm our works and made furious sallies from the town (Alesia) by several gates. Caesar therefore thought it necessary to strengthen the works still further, in order to render the lines defensible by a smaller force. Accordingly trees or very stout branches were cut down and their ends stripped of their bark and sharpened to a point; continuous trenches were then dug, five feet deep, in which the logs were planted and fastened down at the bottom to prevent them being dragged out, while the boughs projected above. There were five rows in each trench, connected with one another and interlaced; and all who stepped in would impale themselves on the sharp stakes. The men called them 'grave-stones'. In front of them, arranged in slanting rows in the form of a quincunx, pits were dug, three feet deep, which tapered gradually towards the bottom. Smooth logs, as thick as a man's thigh, sharpened at the top and hardened by fire, were planted in them, projecting not more than four fingers above the ground. At the same time the earth was trampled down to the depth of one foot above the bottom, to keep them firmly in position; while the rest of the pit was covered with twigs and brushwood to hide the trap. There were eight rows of this kind, three feet apart. The men called them lilies, from their resemblance to that flower. In front of them blocks of wood a foot long, with barbed iron spikes let into them, were completely buried in the earth and scattered about in all directions at moderate intervals. The men called them 'spurs'.

Julius Caesar, *Commentaries*, 51 BC: Bk VII

Attempted Relief of Alesia, 52 BC

. . . but it is most worthy of admiration that Caesar engaged with so many thousands outside of the town and defeated them without it being known to those in the city; and still more admirable, that this was unknown to the Romans who were guarding the wall towards the city. For they knew nothing of the victory till they heard the weeping of the men in Alesia and the wailing of the women, when they saw on the other side many shields adorned with silver and gold, and many breastplates smeared with blood, and also cups and Gallic tents conveyed by the Romans to their camp. So quickly did so mighty a force, like a phantom or a dream, vanish out of sight and disperse, the greater part of the men having fallen in battle.

Plutarch, *Lives: Caesar*, *c.* 110

PARTHIAN WAR, 53 BC

Battle of Carrhae, 53 BC

The Parthians, dispersing themselves at considerable distances from one another, began by discharging their arrows from all points at once, not taking any very exact aim (for the close and compact ranks of the Romans did not give a man the opportunity of missing if he had wished it), but sending their arrows with vigorous and forcible effect from bows which were strong and large, and, owing to their great degree of bending, discharged the missiles with violence. Now the condition of the Romans was pitiable from the beginning: for, if they kept their position, they were exposed to be wounded, and if they attempted to close with the enemy, they were just as far from doing the enemy any harm, and they suffered just as much; for the Parthians while retreating still discharged their arrows, and they do this most effectively next to the Scythians; and it is a most subtle device to make their escape from danger while they are still fighting, and to take away the disgrace of flight.

Plutarch, *Lives: Caesar*, *c.* 110

WARS OF THE FIRST TRIUMVIRATE, 49–47 BC

In whatever part of Italy I stamp the earth with my foot, there will spring up forces both men and foot.

Pompeius Magnus, in Plutarch, *Lives: Pompeius*, *c.* 110

. . . 'Civil War' is an understatement, since Pompey and Caesar, the opposing leaders, were not only fellow-citizens but relatives: the whole struggle was indeed no better than one of licensed fratricide.

Lucan, *Pharsalia*, AD 65: I

Pompey and Caesar met on unequal terms. Pompey, now past middle age, had not taken the field for some years. His main preoccupation was to keep his fame alive by courting the favour of the common people; he distributed largesse, provided costly spectacles, and exulted in the applause that greeted him when he entered the great theatre which he himself had built. Resting on his well-earned laurels, he made no attempts to win fresh ones, but basked in the glory of his surname, 'the Great', which had been officially bestowed on him by the Senate. It was as when an oak towering above a lush meadow – the repository of votive offerings and enemy spoils hung on its branches by bygone tribal chieftains – ceases to derive any support from the roots, but relies merely on its bulk to keep it upright . . . Caesar, on the other hand, had not only won the reputation of a successful general, but was burned with so restless a desire for conquest that he felt disgraced by inactivity. Headstrong, fierce, and never hesitating to flesh his sword, he stood prepared to lead his troops wherever hope of glory or personal resentment offered a battlefield. Confident in Fortune's continued favours, he would follow up each advantage gained; thrusting aside all obstacles that barred his march to supreme power, and rejoicing in the havoc he occasioned. Caesar may, indeed, be justly compared to lightning. Discharged by the winds from a pack of clouds, it darts out jaggedly with a crash that splits the daylight skies, dazzling every eye, striking terror into every heart, and blasting its own airy seats. Nothing may stand against it, either during that furious progress through the clouds, or when it bursts against the earth and at once recomposes its scattered fires.

Lucan, *Pharsalia*, AD 65: I

Caesar had long ago resolved to put down Pompeius, as Pompeius also had fully resolved to do towards him. For now that Crassus had lost his life among the Parthians, who kept a watch over both of them, in order to be the chief, to put down him who was, and to him who was the chief, to take off the man whom he feared, in order that this might not befall him. But it had only recently occurred to Pompeius to take alarm, and hitherto he had despised Caesar, thinking it would be no difficult thing for the man whom he had elevated to be again depressed by him; but Caesar, who had formed his design from the beginning, like an athlete, removed himself to a distance from his antagonists, and exercised himself in the Celtic wars, and thus disciplined his troops and increased his reputation, being elevated by his exploits to an equality with the victories of Pompeius; also laying hold of pretexts, some furnished by the conduct of Pompeius himself, and others by the times and the disordered state of the administration at Rome, owing to which, those who were candidates for magistracies placed tables in public and shamelessly bribed the masses, and the people being hired went down to show their partisanship not with votes on behalf of their briber, but with bows and swords and slings. And after polluting the Rostra with blood and dead bodies, they separated, leaving the city to anarchy, like a ship carried along without a pilot, so that sensible men were well content if matters should result in nothing worse than a monarchy after such madness and such tempest.

Plutarch, *Lives: Caesar*, *c.* 110

Caesar Crosses the Rubicon, 10th January 49 BC

When intelligence, therefore, was received, that the interposition of the tribunes in his favour had been utterly rejected, and that they themselves had fled from the city, he immediately sent forward some cohorts, but privately, to prevent any suspicion of his design; and, to keep up appearances, attended at a public spectacle, examined the model of a fencing-school which he proposed to build, and, as usual, sat down to table with a numerous party of his friends. But after sun-set, mules being put to his carriage from a neighbouring mill, he set forward on his journey with all possible privacy, and a small retinue. The lights going out, he lost his way, and wandered about a long time, until at length, by the help of a guide, whom he found towards day-break, he proceeded on foot through some narrow paths, and again reached the road. Coming up with his troops on the bank of the Rubicon, which was the boundary of his province, he halted for a while, and, revolving in his mind the importance of the step he was on the point of taking, he turned to those about him, and said: 'We may still retreat; but if we pass this little bridge, nothing is left for us but to fight it out with arms.'

While he was thus hesitating, the following incident occurred. A person remarkable for his noble mien and graceful aspect appeared close at hand, sitting and playing upon a pipe. When, not only the shepherds, but a number of soldiers also flocked from their posts to listen to him, and some trumpeters among them, he snatched a trumpet from one of them, ran to the river with it, and sounding the advance with a piercing blast, crossed to the other side. Upon this, Caesar exclaimed, 'Let us go whither the omens of the Gods and the iniquity of our enemies call us. The die is now cast.'

Suetonius, *Lives of the Twelve Caesars*, *c.* 117

Caesar's First Spanish Expedition, 49 BC

After the defeat Nonnius observed that they ought to have good hopes, for that seven eagles were left in the camp of Pompeius. 'Your advice would be good,' said Cicero, 'if we were fighting with jackdaws.'

Plutarch, *Lives: Cicero*, *c.* AD 110

[Caesar] then set out for Spain, in which province Pompey had a numerous army, under the command of three lieutenants, Marcus Petreius, Lucius Afranius, and Marcus Varro; declaring amongst his friends, 'That he was going against an army without a general, and should return thence against a general without an army.'

Suetonius, *Lives of the Twelve Caesars*, *c.* 117

Encampments and Battle of Dyrrachium, 48 BC

Vibullius, as soon as the alarm, which Caesar's unexpected arrival had raised, was over, began again to deliver Caesar's message in the presence of Libo, Lucius Lucceius, and Theophanes, to whom Pompey used to communicate his most confidential secrets. He had scarcely entered on the subject when Pompey interrupted him, and forbade him to proceed. 'What need,' says he, 'have I of life or Rome, if the world shall think I enjoy them by the bounty of Caesar?'

Julius Caesar, *Commentaries: The Civil War*, 44 BC: iii

In this new kind of war, new methods of managing it were invented by both generals. Pompey's men, perceiving by our fires at night, at what part of the works our cohorts were on guard, coming silently upon them discharged their arrows at random among the whole multitude, and instantly retired to their camp: as a remedy against which our men were taught by experience, to light their fires in one place, and keep guard in another.

Julius Caesar, *Commentaries: The Civil War*, 44 BC: iii

But in the fort, not a single soldier escaped without a wound; and in one cohort, four centurions lost their eyes. And being desirous to produce testimony of the fatigue they underwent, and the danger they sustained, they counted to Caesar above thirty thousand arrows which had been thrown into the fort; and in the shield of the centurion Scaeva, which was brought to him, were found two hundred and thirty holes.

Julius Caesar, *Commentaries: The Civil War*, 44 BC: iii

Pompey's party were so elated with confidence and spirit at this success, that they thought no more of the method of conducting the war, but thought that they were already conquerors. They did not consider that the smallness of our numbers, and the disadvantage of the place and the confined nature of the ground occasioned by their having first possessed themselves of the camp, and the double danger both from within and without the fortifications, and the separation of the army into two parts, so that the one could not give relief to the other, were the cause of our defeat. They did not consider, in addition, that the contest was not decided by a vigorous attack, nor a regular battle; and that our men had suffered greater loss from their own numbers and want of room, than they had sustained from the enemy. In fine, they did not reflect upon the common casualties of war; how trifling causes, either from groundless suspicions, sudden affright, or religious scruples, have oftentimes been productive of considerable losses; how often an army has been unsuccessful either by the misconduct of the general, or the oversight of a tribune; but as if they had proved victorious by their valour, they published the success of the day throughout the world by reports and letters.

Julius Caesar, *Commentaries: The Civil War*, 44 BC: iii

Battle of Pharsalus, 9th August 48 BC

There was in Caesar's army a volunteer of the name of Crastinus, who the year before had been first centurion of the tenth legion, a man of pre-eminent bravery. He, when the signal was given, says, 'Follow me, my old comrades, and display such exertions on behalf of your general as you have determined to do; this is our last battle, and when it shall be won, he will recover his dignity, and we our liberty.' At the same time he looked back to Caesar, and said, 'General, I will act in such a manner today, that you will feel grateful to me, living or dead.'

Julius Caesar, *Commentaries: The Civil War*, 44 BC: iii

There was so much space left between the two lines, as sufficed for the onset of the hostile armies: but Pompey had ordered his soldiers to await Caesar's attack, and not to advance from their position, or suffer their line to be put into disorder. And he is said to have done this by the advice of Caius Triarius, that the impetuosity of the charge of Caesar's soldiers might be checked, and their line broken, and that Pompey's troops remaining in their ranks, might attack them while in disorder; and he thought that the javelins would fall with less force if the soldiers were kept in their ground, than if they met them in their course; at the same time he trusted that Caesar's soldiers, after running over double the usual ground, would become weary and exhausted by the fatigue. But to me Pompey seems to have acted without sufficient reason: for there is a certain impetuosity of spirit and an alacrity implanted by nature in the hearts of all men, which is inflamed by a desire to meet the foe. This a general should endeavour not to repress, but to increase; nor was it a vain institution of our ancestors, that the trumpets should sound on all sides, and a general shout be raised; by which they imagined that the enemy were struck with terror, and their own army inspired with courage.

Julius Caesar, *Commentaries: The Civil War*, 44 BC: iii

While he was performing a lustration of the army, as soon as he had sacrificed the first victim, the soothsayer said that within three days there would be a decisive battle with the enemy. Upon Caesar asking him, if he saw any favourable sign in the victims as to the result of the battle, he replied, 'You can answer this better for yourself: the gods indicate a great change and revolution of the actual state of things to a contrary state, so that if you think yourself prosperous in your present condition, expect the worse fortune; but if you do not, expect the better.'

Plutarch, *Lives: Caesar*, *c.* 110

The infantry having thus rushed together in the centre and being engaged in the struggle, the cavalry of Pompeius proudly advanced from the wing, extending their companions to enclose Caesar's right; but before they could fall upon the enemy, the cohorts sprang forth from among Caesar's troops, not, according to the usual fashion of war, throwing their spears nor yet holding them in their hands and aiming at the thighs and legs of the enemy, but pushing them against their eyes and wounding them in the face; and they had been instructed to do this by Caesar, who was confident that men who had no great familiarity with battles or wounds, and were young and very proud of their beauty and youth, would dread such wounds and would not keep their ground both through fear of the present danger and the future disfigurement. And it turned out so; for they could not stand the spears being pushed up at them nor did they venture to look at the iron that was presented against their eyes, but they turned away and covered their faces to save them; and at last, having thrown themselves into confusion, they turned to flight most disgracefully and ruined the whole cause.

Plutarch, *Lives: Caesar*, *c.* 110

Battle of Zela, 2nd August 47 BC

I came, I saw, I conquered. (*Veni, vidi, vici.*)

Julius Caesar, in a dispatch to the Roman Senate, 47 BC

WARS OF THE SECOND TRIUMVIRATE, 36–31 BC

Battle of Actium, 2nd September 31 BC

While the sea fight was still undecided and equally favourable to both sides, all at once the sixty ships of Cleopatra were seen raising their sails for the purpose of making off, and flying through the centre of the combatants; for they were stationed behind the large vessels and they caused confusion by making their way through them. The enemy looked on with wonder, seeing them take advantage of the wind and shaping their course toward the Peloponnesus. On this occasion Antonius clearly showed that he was not governed by the considerations that befit either a commander or a man, or even by his own judgement, but, as someone observed in jest, that the soul of the lover lives in another person's body, so was he dragged along by the woman as if he had grown to her and moved together with her. For no sooner did he see her ship sailing away, than, forgetting everything, and deserting and skulking away from those who were fighting and dying in his cause, he got into a five-oared galley with only Alexas the Syrian and Skellius to attend him, and followed after her who had already ruined him and was destined to complete his ruin.

Plutarch, *Lives: Antonius*, *c.* 110

ROME AND GERMANY, early 1st century AD

Battle of the Teutoburger Wald, AD 9

Caecina having been sent before to explore the gloomy recesses of the forest, and to lay bridges and causeways over the watery portions of the morasses and insecure places in the plains, they enter[ed] the doleful scene, hideous in appearance and association. The first camp of Varus appeared in view. The extent of ground, and the measurement of the principia, left no doubt that the whole was the work of three legions. After that, a half-decayed rampart with a shallow foss, where their remains, now sadly reduced, were understood to have sunk down. In the intervening portion of the plain were whitening bones, either scattered or accumulated, according as they had fled or made a stand. Near them lay fragments of javelins and limbs of horses. There were also skulls fixed upon the trunks of trees. In the adjacent groves were the savage altars, where they had immolated the tribunes and centurions of the first rank.

Tacitus, *The Annals*, *c.* 115: Bk I

In all his wars [Augustus] never received any signal or ignominious defeat, except twice in Germany, under his lieutenants Lollius and Varus. The former had in it indeed more of dishonour than disaster; but that of Varus threatened the security of the empire itself; three legions, with the commander, his lieutenants, and all the auxiliaries, being cut off. Upon receiving intelligence of this disaster, he gave orders for keeping a strict watch over the city, to prevent any public disturbance, and prolonged the appointments of the prefects in the provinces, that the allies might be kept in order by the experience of persons to whom they were used. He made a vow to celebrate the great games in honour of Jupiter, Optimus, Maximus, 'if he would be pleased to restore the state to more prosperous circumstances'. This had formerly been resorted to in the Cimbrian and Marsian wars. In short, we are informed that he was in such consternation at this event, that he let the hair of his head and beard grow for several months, and sometimes knocked his head against the door-posts, crying out, 'O, Quintilius Varus! Give me back my legions!'

Suetonius, *Lives of the Twelve Caesars*, *c.* 117

Roman Revenge, AD 16

Meanwhile an omen of happiest import appeared; eight eagles, seen to fly toward the wood, and to enter it, caught the eye of the general [Germanicus]: 'Advance!' he cried, 'follow the Roman birds; follow the tutelar deities of the legions!' At once the foot charged, and the cavalry sent forward attacked their flank and rear: and strange to relate, the two divisions of their army fled opposite ways; that in the woods ran to the plain, that in the plain rushed into the woods. The Cheruscans between both were driven from the hills; amongst them Arminius formed a conspicuous object, while with his hand, his voice, and the exhibition of his wounds, he strove to sustain the fight: he had vigorously assaulted the archers, and would have broken through them, had not the cohorts of the Rhaetians, the Vindelicians, and the Gauls, advanced to oppose him: however, by his own personal effort, and the impetus of his horse, he made good his passage; his face besmeared with his own blood to avoid being known. Some have related that the Chaucians, who were amongst the Roman auxiliaries, knew him, and let him go: the same bravery or stratagem procured Iguiomer his escape: the rest were slain on all hands; great numbers attempting to swim the Visurgis, perished either by the darts showered after them, or the violence of the current; or if they escaped these, they were overwhelmed by the weight of the rushing crowd, and the banks which fell upon them: some seeking an ignominious refuge climbed to the tops of trees, and concealing themselves amongst the branches, were shot in sport by the archers, who were brought up for the purpose; others were dashed against the ground as the trees were felled.

Tacitus, *The Annals*, *c.* 115: Bk II

The German Tribes

Against these people mistrust was the surest defence; for those who were trusted effected the most mischief.

Strabo, *The Geography*, *c.* AD 23

Their line of battle is disposed in wedges. To give ground, provided they rally again, is considered rather as a prudent strategem, than cowardice. They carry off their slain even while the battle remains undecided. The greatest disgrace that can befall them is to have abandoned their shields. A person branded with this ignominy is not permitted to join in their religious rites, or enter their assemblies; so that many, after escaping from battle, have put an end to their infamy by the halter.

Tacitus, *A Treatise On The Manners Of The Germans*, AD 98

. . . nor are they so easily persuaded to cultivate the earth, and await the produce of the seasons, as to challenge the foe, and expose themselves to wounds; nay, they even think it base and spiritless to earn by sweat what they might purchase with blood.

Tacitus, *A Treatise On The Manners Of The Germans*, AD 98

The Suevi, even till they are hoary, continue to have their hair growing stiffly backwards, and often it is fastened on the very crown of the head. The chiefs dress it with still greater care: and in this respect they study ornament, though of an undebasing kind. For their design is not to make love, or inspire it: they decorate themselves in this manner as they proceed to war, in order to seem taller and more terrible; and dress for the eyes of their enemies.

Tacitus, *A Treatise On The Manners Of The Germans*, AD 98

The Bructeri: . . . they even gratified us with the spectacle of a battle, in which above sixty thousand Germans were slain, not by Roman arms, but, what was still grander, by mutual hostilities, as it were for our pleasure and entertainment.

Tacitus, *A Treatise On The Manners Of The Germans*, AD 98

The Arii: Their shields are black; their bodies painted; they choose the darkest nights for an attack; and strike terror by the funereal gloom of their sable bands – no enemy being able to sustain their singular, and, as it were, infernal appearance; since in every combat the eyes are the first part subdued.

Tacitus, *A Treatise On The Manners Of The Germans*, AD 98

THE ROMAN ARMY OF EARLY IMPERIAL TIMES

Now here one cannot but admire at the precaution of the Romans, in providing themselves of such household servants, as might not only serve at other times for the common offices of life, but might also be of advantage to them in their wars; and indeed, if any one does but attend to the other parts of their military discipline, he will be forced to confess that their obtaining so large a dominion, hath been the acquisition of their valour, and not the bare gift of Fortune; for they do not begin to use their weapons first in time of war, nor do they then put their hands first into motion, while they avoided so to do in times of peace; but, as if their weapons did always cling to them, they have never any truce from warlike exercises; nor do they stay till times of war admonish them to use them; for their military exercises differ not at all from the real use of their arms, but every soldier is every day exercised, and that with real diligence, as if it were in time of war, which is the reason why they bear the fatigue of battles so easily; for neither can any disorder remove them from their usual regularity, nor can fear affright them out of it, nor can labour tire them; which firmness of conduct makes them always to overcome those that have not the same firmness; nor would he be mistaken that would call those their exercises unbloody battles, and their battles bloody exercises.

Flavius Josephus, *The Wars of the Jews*, AD 75–79: II.xiii

It was an inflexible maxim of Roman discipline that a good soldier should dread his own officers far more than the enemy.

Edward Gibbon, *The History Of The Decline and Fall Of The Roman Empire*, 1776–88: i

THE CONQUEST OF BRITAIN, early to mid-1st century

After a war of about forty years, undertaken by the most stupid, maintained by the most dissolute, and terminated by the most timid, of all the emperors, the far greater part of the island submitted to the Roman yoke. The various tribes of Britons possessed valour without conduct, and the love of freedom without the spirit of union. They took up arms with savage fierceness; they laid them down, or turned them against each other, with wild inconsistency; and while they fought singly they were successively subdued. Neither the fortitude of Caractacus, nor the despair of Boadicea, nor the fanaticism of the druids, could avert the slavery of their country, or resist the steady progress of the imperial generals, who maintained the national glory, when the throne was disgraced by the weakest, or the most vicious, of mankind.

Edward Gibbon, *The History Of The Decline And Fall Of The Roman Empire*, 1776–88: i

Skirmish on the Island of Mona (Anglesey), AD 60

On the shore stood the forces of the enemy, a dense array of arms and men, with women dashing through the ranks like furies; their dress funereal, their hair dishevelled, and carrying torches in their hands. The druids around the host, pouring forth dire imprecations, with their hands uplifted towards the heavens, struck terror into the soldiers by the strangeness of the sight; insomuch that, as if their limbs were paralysed, they exposed their bodies to the weapons of the enemy, without an effort to move.

Tacitus, *The Annals*, *c.* 115, Bk XIV

Battle of Fenny Stratford, AD 60

Boadicea, seated in a chariot, with her two daughters before her, traversed the field, and as she came up to each nation, she called them to witness 'that it was usual for Britons to war under the conduct of women: but on that occasion she entered the field not as one descended from ancestors so illustrious to recover her kingdom and her treasure; but as one of the humblest among them, to take vengeance for liberty extinguished, her own body lacerated with stripes, the chastity of her daughters defiled; that the Romans, in the fury of their inordinate passions, had proceeded to such extremes, that the persons of those within their reach were not safe; they would not leave old age unmolested, nor virginity uncontaminated; that the gods, however, aided their righteous revenge; a legion, which dared an engagement, had already fallen; the rest skulked behind their intrenchments, or were looking about for a way of escape: they would not be able to endure the clangour and shouts of so many thousands; much less their spirit and their strength . . . Such was the fixed resolve of a woman; the men might live if they pleased, and be the slaves of Romans.'

Tacitus, *The Annals*, *c.* 115, Bk XIV

In the time of Nero, when the bondage of the Romans became so oppressive, that the Britons were determined to resist, Boadicea animated them to shake it off by an eloquent address, which she concluded in these words: 'Let the Romans, who are not better than hares and foxes, understand, that they make a wrong match with wolves and greyhounds.' As she said this, she let a hare out from her lap, as a token of the fearfulness of the Romans. The result of the battle, however, proved that there was more wit than truth in the comparison.

The Percy Anecdotes, 1823

THE JEWISH REVOLT AD 66–70

It is true, these writers have the confidence to call their accounts histories; wherein yet they seem to me to fail of their own purpose, as well as to relate nothing that is found; for they have a mind to demonstrate the greatness of Romans, while they still diminish and lessen the actions of the Jews, as not discerning how it cannot be that those must appear to be great who have only conquered those that were little; . . .

Flavius Josephus, *The Wars of the Jews*, AD 75–79: II.xiii

Siege and Fall of Jerusalem, March–8th September AD 70

And Jesus went out, and departed from the temple: and his disciples came to him for to shew him the buildings of the temple. And Jesus said unto them, See ye not all these things? verily I say unto you, There shall not be left here one stone upon another, that shall not be thrown down.

Gospel According to St Matthew: 24.i–ii

. . . The famine was too hard for all other passions, and it is destructive to nothing so much as to modesty; for what was otherwise worthy of reverence was in this case despised; insomuch that children pulled the very morsels that their fathers were eating out of their very mouths, and what was still more to be pitied, so did the mothers do as their infants; and when those that were most dear were perishing under their hands, they were not ashamed to take from them the very last drops that might preserve their lives; and while they ate after this manner, yet were they not concealed in so doing; but the seditious everywhere came upon them immediately, and snatched away from them what they had gotten from others; for when they saw any house shut up, this was to them a signal that the people within had gotten some food; whereupon they broke open the doors, and ran in, and took pieces of what they were eating, almost out of their very throats, and this by force: the old men who held fast their food were beaten; and if the women hid what they had within their hands, their hair was torn for so doing; neither was there any commiseration shown either to the aged or to infants, but they lifted up children from the ground as they hung upon the morsels they had gotten, and shook them down upon the floor; . . .

Flavius Josephus, *The Wars of the Jews*, AD 75–79: V.x

There was a certain woman that dwelt beyond Jordan, her name was Mary; . . . She then attempted a most unnatural thing; and, snatching up her son, who was a child sucking at her breast, she said, 'O thou miserable infant! for whom shall I preserve thee in this war, this famine and this sedition? As to the war with the Romans, if they preserve our lives, we must be slaves! This famine also will destroy us, even before that slavery comes upon us; – yet are these seditious rogues more terrible than both the others. Come on; be thou my food, and be thou a fury to these seditious varlets and a by-word to the world, which is all that is now wanting to complete the calamities of the Jews.' And soon as she had said this she slew her son; and then roasted him, and ate the one half of him, and kept the other half by her concealed.

Flavius Josephus, *The Wars of the Jews*, AD 75–79: VI.iii

ROMAN CIVIL WAR OF AD 69

Battle of Bedriacum, 19th April AD 69

Sweet is the smell of a dead enemy.

Alus Vitellius, attributed

The Sack of Cremona by Antonius Primus, December AD 69

Antonius, by his fame and brilliant success, eclipsed all other commanders: the attention of all was fixed on him alone. He hastened to the baths to wash off the blood; and on observing that the water was not hot enough, he said that they would soon grow hotter. The expression was caught up: a casual word among slaves had the effect of throwing upon him the whole odium of having given a signal for setting fire to Cremona, which was already in flames.

Forty thousand men had poured into it. The number of drudges and camp followers was still greater, and more abandoned to lust and cruelty. Neither age nor dignity served as a protection; deeds of lust were perpetrated amid scenes of carnage, and murder was added to rape. Aged men and women that had passed their prime, and who were useless as booty, were made the objects of brutal sport. If a mature maiden, or any one of comely appearance, fell in their way, after being torn piecemeal by the rude bands of contending ruffians, they at last were the occasion of their turning their swords against each other. While eagerly carrying off money or massy gold from the temples, they were butchered by others stronger than themselves.

Tacitus, *Histories*, *c.* 109, Bk III

ROMAN INCURSION INTO SCOTLAND, AD 84

Battle of the Grampians, AD 84

To plunder, to slaughter, to steal, these things they [i.e. the Romans] misname empire; and where they make a desert, they call it peace.

Calgacus, addressing his troops before the battle, in Tacitus, *Agricola*, *c.* 110

THE DECLINE OF THE ROMAN EMPIRE, 180–455

The thicker the grass, the more easily it is cut.

Alaric, King of the Visigoths, *c.* 409, attributed

The Romans conquered all peoples by their discipline. In the measure that it became corrupted their success decreased. When the Emperor Gratian permitted the legions to give up their cuirasses and helmets because the soldiers complained that they were too heavy, all was lost.

Maurice de Saxe, *Mes Rêveries*, 1732

It was scarcely possible that the eyes of contemporaries should discover in the public felicity the latent causes of decay and corruption. This long peace, and the uniform government of the Romans, introduced a slow and secret poison into the vitals of the empire. The minds of men were gradually reduced to the same level, the fire of genius was extinguished, and even the military spirit evaporated. The natives of Europe were braced and robust. Spain, Gaul, Britain and Illyricum, supplied the legions with excellent soldiers, and constituted the real strength of the monarchy. Their personal valour remained, but they no longer possessed the public courage which is nourished by the love of independence, the sense of national honour, the presence of danger, and the habit of command. They received laws and governors from the will of their sovereign, and trusted for their defence to a mercenary army. The posterity of their boldest leaders was contented with the rank of citizens and subjects. The most aspiring spirits resorted to the court or standard of the emperors; and the deserted provinces, deprived of political strength or union, insensibly sunk into the languid indifference of private life.

Edward Gibbon, *The History Of The Decline And Fall Of The Roman Empire*, 1776–88: ii

The barbarians who broke up the Roman empire did not arrive a day too soon.

Ralph Waldo Emerson, *Conduct of Life: Considerations by the Way*, 1860

The Persian Army, *c.* 240

The Persians, long since civilized and corrupted, were very far from possessing the martial independence, and the intrepid hardiness, both of mind and body, which have rendered the northern barbarians masters of the world. The science of war, that constituted the more rational force of Greece and Rome, as it now does of Europe, never made any considerable progress in the East. Those disciplined evolutions which harmonize and animate a confused multitude, were unknown to the Persians. They were equally unskilled in the arts of constructing, besieging, or defending regular fortifications. They trusted more to their numbers than to their courage; more to their courage than to their discipline. The infantry was a half-armed spiritless crowd of peasants, levied in haste by the allurements of plunder, and as easily dispersed by a victory as by a defeat. The monarch and his nobles transported into the camp the pride and luxury of the seraglio. Their military operations were impeded by a useless train of women, eunuchs, horses and camels; and in the midst of a successful campaign, the Persian host was often separated or destroyed by an unexpected famine.

Edward Gibbon, *The History Of The Decline And Fall Of The Roman Empire*, 1776–88: viii

The Germanic Bards

It was in the hour of battle, or in the feast of victory, that the bards celebrated the glories of heroes of ancient days, the ancestors of those warlike chieftains, who listened with transport to their artless but animated strains. The view of arms and of danger heightened the effect of the military song; and the passions which it tended to excite, the desire of fame, and the contempt of death, were the habitual sentiments of a German mind.

Edward Gibbon, *The History Of The Decline And Fall Of The Roman Empire*, 1776–88: ix

The Goths Cross the Danube, 250

This is the first considerable occasion in which history mentions that great people, who afterwards broke the Roman power, sacked the capital, and reigned in Gaul, Spain and Italy. So memorable was the part which they acted in the subversion of the Western empire, that the name of Goths is frequently but improperly used as a general appellation of rude and warlike barbarism.

Edward Gibbon, *The History Of The Decline And Fall Of The Roman Empire*, 1776–88: x

The Romans Cross Themselves, *c.* 325

An instrument of the tortures which were inflicted only on slaves and strangers, became an object of horror in the eyes of a Roman citizen; and the ideas of guilt, of pain, and of ignominy, were closely united with the cross. The piety, rather than the humanity, of Constantine soon abolished in his dominions the punishment which the Saviour of mankind had condescended to suffer; but the emperor had already learned to despise the prejudices of his education, and of his people, before he could erect in the midst of Rome his own statue, bearing a cross in its right hand; with an inscription, which referred, to the victory of his arms, and the deliverance of Rome, to the virtue of that salutary sign, the true symbol of force and courage. The same symbol sanctified the arms of the soldiers of Constantine; the cross glittered on their helmets, was engraved on their shields, was interwoven with their banners; and the consecrated emblems which adorned the person of the emperor himself, were distinguished only by richer materials and more exquisite workmanship.

Edward Gibbon, *The History Of The Decline And Fall Of The Roman Empire*, 1776–88: xx

The Huns, *c.* 375

Sometimes, when provoked, they fight; and when they go into battle, they form in a solid body, and utter all kinds of terrific yells. They are very quick in their operations, of exceeding speed, and fond of surprising their enemies. With a view to this, they suddenly disperse, then reunite, and again, after having inflicted vast loss upon the enemy, scatter themselves over the whole plain in irregular formations: always avoiding a fort or an intrenchment. And in one respect you may pronounce them the most formidable of all warriors, for when at a distance they use missiles of various kinds tipped with sharpened bones instead of the usual points of javelins, and these bones are admirably fastened into the shaft of the javelin or arrow; but when they are at close quarters they fight with the sword, without any regard for their own safety; and often while their antagonists are warding off their blows they entangle them with twisted cords, so that, their hands being fettered, they lose all power of either riding or walking.

Ammianus Marcellinus, *The Roman History*, *c.* 390: xxxi

The numbers, the strength, the rapid motions, and the implacable cruelty of the Huns, were felt, and dreaded, and magnified, by the astonished Goths; who beheld their fields and villages consumed with flames, and deluged with indiscriminate slaughter. To these real terrors they added, the surprise and abhorrence which were excited by the shrill voice, the uncouth gestures, and the strange deformity, of the Huns. These savages of Scythia were compared (and the picture had some resemblance) to the animals who walk very awkwardly on two legs; and to the misshapen figures, the *Termini*, which were often placed on the bridges of antiquity. They were distinguished from the rest of humanity by their broad shoulders, flat noses, and small black eyes, deeply buried in the head; and as they were almost destitute of beards, they never enjoyed either the manly graces of youth, or the venerable aspect of age. A fabulous origin was assigned, worthy of their form and manners; that the witches of Scythia, who, for their foul, and deadly practices, had copulated in the desert with infernal spirits; and that the Huns were the offspring of this execrable conjunction.

Edward Gibbon, *The History Of The Decline And Fall Of The Roman Empire*, 1776–88; xxvi

Battle of Hadrianople (Adrianople), 9th August 378

But when the barbarians, rushing on with their enormous host, beat down our horses and men, and left no spot to which our ranks could fall back to deploy, while they were so closely packed that it was impossible to escape by forcing a way through them, our men at last began to despise death, and again took to their swords and slew all they encountered, while with mutual blows of battle-axes, helmets and breastplates were dashed to pieces. Then you might see the barbarian towering in his fierceness, hissing or shouting, fall with his legs pierced through, or his right hand cut off, sword and all, or his side transfixed, and still, in the last gasp of life, casting around him defiant glances.

Ammianus Marcellinus, *The Roman History*, *c.* 390: xxxi

The emperor was persuaded to send an ambassador to the Gothic camp; the zeal of Richomer, who alone had courage to accept the dangerous commission, was applauded; and the count of the domestics, adorned with the splendid ensigns of his dignity, had proceeded some way in the space between the two armies, when he was suddenly recalled by the alarm of battle. The hasty and imprudent attack was made by Bacurius the Iberian, who commanded a body of archers and targeteers; and as they advanced with rashness, they retreated with loss and disgrace. In the same moment, the flying squadrons of Alatheus and Saphrax, whose return was anxiously expected by the general of the Goths, descended like a whirlwind from the hills, swept across the plain, and added new terrors to the tumultuous, but irresistible, charge of the barbarian host. The event of the battle Hadrianople, so fatal to Valens and to the empire, may be described in a few words: the Roman cavalry fled; the infantry was abandoned, surrounded, and cut in pieces.

Edward Gibbon, *The History Of The Decline And Fall Of The Roman Empire*, 1776–88: xxvi

A Gothic chief was heard to declare, with insolent moderation, that, for his own part, he was fatigued with slaughter; but he was astonished how a people, who fled before him like a flock of sheep, could still presume to dispute the possession of their treasures and provinces.

Edward Gibbon, *The History Of The Decline And Fall Of The Roman Empire*, 1776–88: xxvi

The military importance of Adrianople was unmistakable; it was a victory of cavalry over infantry. The Imperial army had developed its attack on the great *laager* in which the Goths lay encamped, arrayed in the time-honoured formation of Roman hosts – with the legions and cohorts in the centre, and the squadrons on the wings. The fight was raging hotly all along the barricade, when suddenly a great body of horsemen charged in upon the Roman left. It was the main strength of the Gothic cavalry, which had been foraging at a distance; receiving news of the fight, it had ridden straight for the battlefield, and fell upon the exposed flank of the Imperial host, 'like a thunderbolt which strikes on a mountain top, and dashes away all that stands in its path.' [Ammianus]

Charles Oman, *A History of the Art of War in the Middle Ages*, 1924

The Sack of Rome, 410

All the devastation, the butchery, the plundering, the conflagrations, and all the anguish which accompanied the recent disaster at Rome were in accordance with the general practice of warfare. But there was something which established a new custom, something which changed the whole aspect of the scene; the savagery of the barbarians took on such an aspect of gentleness that the largest basilicas were selected and set aside to be filled with people to be spared by the enemy. No one was to be violently used there, no one snatched away. Many were to be brought there for liberation by merciful foes; none were to be taken from there into captivity even by cruel enemies. This is to be attributed to the name of Christ and the influence of Christianity. Anyone who fails to see this is blind; anyone who sees it and fails to give praise for it is thankless; anyone who tries to stop another from giving praise is a madman.

St Augustine, *City Of God*, 427: I.vii

In the pillage of Rome, a just preference was given to gold and jewels, which contain the greatest value in the smallest compass and weight: but, after these portable riches had been removed by the more diligent robbers, the palaces of Rome were rudely stripped of their splendid and costly furniture. The sideboards of massy plate and variegated wardrobes of silk and purple, were irregularly piled in waggons, that always followed the march of a Gothic army. The most exquisite works of art were roughly handled, or wantonly destroyed: many a statue was melted for the sake of the precious materials; and many a vase, in the division of the spoil, was shivered into fragments by the stroke of a battle-axe. The acquisition of riches served only to stimulate the avarice of the rapacious barbarians, who proceeded, by threats, by blows, and by tortures, to force from their prisoners the confessions of hidden treasure. Visible splendour and expense were alleged as a proof of a plentiful fortune: the appearance of poverty was imputed to a parsimonious disposition; and the obstinacy of some misers, who endured the most cruel torments before they would discover the secret object of their affection, was fatal to many unhappy wretches, who expired under the lash, for refusing to reveal their imaginary treasures.

Edward Gibbon, *The History Of The Decline And Fall Of The Roman Empire*, 1776–88: xxxi

Battle of Châlons, 451

The number of the slain amounted to one hundred and sixty-two thousand, or, according to another account, three hundred thousand persons; and these incredible exaggerations suppose a real and effective loss, sufficient to justify the historian's remark, that whole generations may be swept away, by the madness of kings, in the space of a single hour.

Edward Gibbon, *The History Of The Decline And Fall Of The Roman Empire*, 1776–88: xxxv

The Huns were undoubtedly vanquished, since Attila was compelled to retreat. He had exposed his person with the rashness of a private soldier; but the intrepid troops of the centre had pushed forward beyond the rest of the line; their attack was faintly supported; their flanks were unguarded; and the conquerors of Scythia and Germany were saved by the approach of the night from a total defeat. They retired within the circle of waggons that fortified their camp; and the dismounted squadrons prepared themselves for a defence, to which neither their arms, nor their temper, was adapted. The event was doubtful: but Attila had secured a last and honourable resource. The saddles and rich furniture of the cavalry were collected, by his order, into a funeral pile; and the magnanimous barbarian had resolved, if his intrenchments should be forced, to rush headlong into the flames, and deprive his enemies of the glory which they might have acquired, by the death or captivity of Attila.

Edward Gibbon, *The History Of The Decline And Fall Of The Roman Empre*, 1776–88: xxxv

It was not a Roman victory or a Teutonic victory, but a victory of both peoples combined over Asiatics, as Salamis had been a victory of both Athenians and Spartans over Persians.

J. F. C. Fuller, *The Decisive Battles of the Western World*, 1954–56

The Siege of Aquileia, 452

Three months were consumed without effect in the siege of Aquileia; till the want of provisions, and the clamours of his army, compelled Attila to relinquish the enterprise; and reluctantly to issue his orders, that the troops should strike their tents next morning, and begin their retreat. But as he rode round the walls, pensive, angry, and disappointed, he observed a stork, preparing to leave her nest, in one of the towers, and to fly with her infant family toward the country. He seized, with the ready penetration of a statesman, this trifling incident, which chance had offered to superstition; and exclaimed, in a loud and cheerful tone, that such a domestic bird, so constantly attached to human society, would never have abandoned her ancient seat, unless those towers had been devoted to impending ruin and solitude. The favourable omen inspired an assurance of victory; the siege was renewed, and prosecuted with fresh vigour; a large breach was made in the part of the wall from whence the stork had taken her flight; the Huns mounted to the assault with irresistible fury; and the succeeding generation could scarcely discover the ruins of Aquileia.

Edward Gibbon, *The History Of The Decline And Fall Of The Roman Empire*, 1776–88: xxxv

The Vandals Take Rome, June 455

. . . and, at the end of four hundred years, the spoils of Jerusalem were transferred from Rome to Carthage by a barbarian [Ganseric] who derived his origin from the shores of the Baltic.

Edward Gibbon, *The History Of The Decline And Fall Of The Roman Empire*, 1776–88: xxxvi

THE FRANKS, *c.* 500

The arms of the Franks are very rude; they wear neither mail-shirt nor greaves, and their legs are only protected by strips of linen and leather. They have hardly any horsemen, but their foot-soldiery are bold and well practised in war. They bear swords and shields, but never use the sling or bow. Their missiles are axes and barbed javelins. These last are not very long, they can be used either to cast or to stab. The iron of the head runs so far down the stave that very little of the wood remains unprotected. In battle they hurl these javelins, and if they strike an enemy the barbs are so firmly fixed in his body that it is impossible for him to draw the weapon out. If it strikes a shield, it is impossible for the enemy to get rid of it by cutting off its head, for the iron runs too far down the shaft. At this moment the Frank rushes in, places his foot on the butt as it trails on the ground, and so, pulling the shield downwards, cleaves his uncovered adversary through the head, or pierces his breast with a second spear.

Agathias, *History of His Own Times*, *c.* 580

THE SPREAD OF ISLAM, from 622

In the constitution of Europe, the right of peace and war is now confined to a small, and the actual exercise to a much smaller, list of respectable potentates; but each Arab, with impunity and renown, might point his javelin against the life of his countryman. The union of the nation consisted only in a vague resemblance of language and manners; and in each community, the jurisdiction of the magistrate was mute and impotent. Of the time of ignorance which preceded Mahomet, seventeen hundred battles are recorded by tradition; hostility was embittered with the rancour of civil faction; and the recital, in prose or verse, of an obsolete feud, was sufficient to rekindle the same passion among the descendants of the hostile tribes. In private, every man, at least every family, was the judge and avenger of his own cause. The nice sensibility of honour, which weighs the insult rather than the injury, sheds its deadly venom on the quarrels of the Arabs: the honour of their women, and of their *beards*, is most easily wounded; an indecent action, a contemptuous word, can be expiated only by the blood of the offender; and such is their patient inveteracy, that they expect whole months and years the opportunity of revenge.

Edward Gibbon, *The History Of The Decline And Fall Of The Roman Empire*, 1776–88:1

And like a cloud of locusts, whom the South
Wafts from the plains of wasted Africa,
The Musselmen upon Iberia's shore
Descend. A countless multitude they came;
Syrian, Moor, Saracen, Greek renegade,
Persian and Copt and Tatar, in one bond
Of erring faith conjoin'd . . . strong in the youth
And heat of zeal, . . . a dreadful brotherhood,
In whom all turbulent vices were let loose;
While Conscience, with their impious creed accurst,
Drunk as with wine, had sanctified to them
All bloody, all abominable things.

Robert Southey, *Roderick, The Last of the Goths*, 1814

Battle of Beder, 623

O Allah, if these troops are destroyed, by whom wilt Thou be worshipped on Earth?

Mohammed (Mahomet), attributed

Battle of Aiznadin, 13th July 633

In the presence of both armies, a venerable Greek advanced from the ranks with a liberal offer of peace; and the departure of the Saracens would have been purchased by a gift to each soldier, of a turban, a robe, and a piece of gold; ten robes and a hundred pieces to their leader; one hundred robes and a thousand pieces to the caliph. A smile of indignation expressed the refusal of Caled. 'Ye christian dogs, you know your option: the Koran, the tribute, or the sword.'

Edward Gibbon, *The History Of The Decline And Fall Of The Roman Empire*, 1776–88: li

Battle of Kadisiya, 637

Paradise is under the shadow of our swords!

Caliph Omar Ibn Alkhattab, quoted in Robert Debs Heinl Jr, *Dictionary of Military and Naval Quotations*, 1966

The Two Sieges of Constantinople, 668–75 and 716–18

In the two sieges, the deliverance of Constantinople may chiefly be ascribed to the novelty, the terrors, and the real efficacy of *Greek fire*. The important secret of compounding and directing this artificial flame was imparted by Callinicus, a native of Heliopolis in Syria, who deserted from the service of the caliph to that of the emperor. The skill of a chemist and an engineer was equivalent to the succour of fleets and armies; and this discovery or improvement of the military art was fortunately reserved for the distressful period, when the degenerate Romans of the east were incapable of contending with the warlike enthusiasm and youthful vigour of the Saracens. The historian who presumes to analyse this extraordinary composition, should suspect his own ignorance and that of his Byzantine guides, so prone to the marvellous, so careless, and in this instance, so jealous, of the truth. From their obscure, and perhaps fallacious, hints, it should seem that the principal ingredient of the Greek fire was the *naptha*, or liquid bitumen, a light, tenacious and inflammable oil, which springs from the earth, and catches fire as soon as it comes in contact with the air.

Edward Gibbon, *The History Of The Decline And Fall Of The Roman Empire*, 1776–88: lii

Battle of Tours, October 732

The men of the north stood as motionless as a wall; they were like a belt of ice frozen together, and not to be dissolved, as they slew the Arabs with the sword. The Austrasians, vast of limb, and iron of hand, hewed on bravely in the thick of the fight; it was they who found and cut down the Saracen king.

Isidorus Pacensis, *Chronicle*, late 8th century

The epithet *Martel*, the *Hammer*, which has been added to the name of Charles, is expressive of his weighty and irresistible strokes: the valour of Eudes was excited by resentment and emulation: and their companions, in the eye of history, are the true peers and paladins of French chivalry.

Edward Gibbon, *The History Of The Decline And Fall Of The Roman Empire*, 1776–88: lii

A victorious line of march had been prolonged above a thousand miles from the rock of Gibraltar to the banks of the Loire; the repetition of an equal space would have carried the Saracens to the confines of Poland and the Highlands of

Scotland: the Rhine is not more impassable than the Nile or Euphrates, and the Arabian fleet might have sailed without a naval combat into the mouth of the Thames. Perhaps the interpretation of the Koran would now be taught in the schools of Oxford, and her pupils might demonstrate to a circumcised people the sanctity and truth of the revelation of Mahomet.

Edward Gibbon, *The History Of The Decline And Fall Of The Roman Empire*, 1776–88: lii

Gibbon's sneering remark, that if the Saracen conquests had not then been checked, 'Perhaps the interpretation of the Koran would now be taught in the schools of Oxford, and her pulpits might demonstrate to a circumcised people the sanctity and truth of the revelation of Mahomet', has almost an air of regret.

E. S. Creasy, *The Fifteen Decisive Battles of the World*, 1851

It was not that Charles [Martel]'s victory saved Western Europe from Arab rule, and, therefore, prevented the Koran from being taught at Oxford, but that it made Charles supreme in Gaul and enabled him to establish his dynasty.

J. F. C. Fuller, *The Decisive Battles of the Western World*, 1954–56

The Siege of Salerno, 873

It was the amusement of the Saracens to profane, as well as to pillage, the monasteries and churches. At the siege of Salerno a mussalman chief spread his couch on the communion-table, and on that altar sacrificed each night the virginity of a christian nun. As he wrestled with a reluctant maid, a beam in the roof was accidentally or dexterously thrown down on his head; and the death of the lustful emir was imputed to the wrath of Christ, which was at length awakened to the defence of his faithful spouse.

Edward Gibbon, *The History Of The Decline And Fall Of The Roman Empire*, 1776–88: lvi

THE HUNS ATTACK CHINA, 8th century

Last year we were fighting at the source of the Sang-kan;
This year we are fighting on the Onion River Road.
We have washed our swords in the surf of Parthian seas;
We have pastured our horses among the snows of the T'ien Shan,
The King's armies have grown grey and old
Fighting ten thousand leagues away from home.
The Huns have no trade but battle and carnage;
They have no fields or ploughlands,
But only wastes where white bones lie among yellow sands.
Where the House of Ch'in built the great wall that was to keep away the Tartars,
There, in turn, the House of Han lit beacons of war.
The beacons are always alight, fighting and marching never stop.
Men die in the field, slashing sword to sword;
The horses of the conquered neigh piteously to Heaven.

Crows and hawks peck for human guts,
Carry them in their beaks and hang them on the branches of withered trees.
Captains and soldiers are smeared on the bushes and grass;
The General schemed in vain.
Know therefore that the sword is a cursed thing
Which the wise man uses only if he must.

Li Po, 'Fighting South of the Ramparts', *c.* 750

ASSAULT OF BAGHDAD, 900

In the year 900, the Carmathians, led by Abu Taher, made a daring inroad beyond the Tigris, and advanced to the gates of Bagdad with no more than five hundred horses. By the special order of Moctader, the Caliph of Bagdad, the bridges had been broken down, and the person or head of the rebel was expected every hour. The Caliph's lieutenant, from a motive of fear or pity, apprised Abu Taher of his danger, and recommended a speedy escape. 'Your master,' said the intrepid Carmathian to the messenger, 'is at the head of fifty thousand soldiers; three such men as these are wanting to his host.' Then turning to three of his companions, he commanded the first to plunge a dagger into his breast; the second to leap into the Tigris; and the third to cast himself headlong down a precipice. They obeyed without a murmur. 'Relate,' continued Abu Taher, 'what you have seen; and before evening, your general shall be chained among my dogs.' Before the evening, the camp was surprised, and the menace was executed.

The Percy Anecdotes, 1823

THE VIKINGS, 9th–11th centuries

. . . The wagon-folk of the seas.

J. F. C. Fuller, *The Decisive Battles of the Western World*, 1954–56

Offensive of 878

In this year the host went secretly in midwinter after Twelfth Night to Chippenham, and rode over Wessex and occupied it, and drove a great deal of the inhabitants oversea, and of the rest of the greater part they reduced to submission, except Alfred the king; and he with a small company moved under difficulties through woods and into inaccessible places in marshes.

The Anglo-Saxon Chronicle: 878

Offensive of 896

This same year the hosts in East Anglia and Northumbria greatly harassed Wessex along the south coast with predatory bands, most of all with the warships they had built many years before. Then king Alfred ordered warships to be built to meet the Danish ships: they were almost twice as long as the others, some had sixty oars, some more; they were both swifter, steadier, and with more freeboard than the others; they were built neither after the Frisian design nor after the Danish, but as it seemed to himself that they could be more serviceable. Then on one occasion the same year came six ships to the Isle of Wight and did much harm there, both in Devon and almost everywhere along the coast. Then the king ordered nine of the new ships to put out, and he blockaded the entrance from the open sea against their escape. Then the Danes sailed out with three ships against them, and three of their ships were beached on dry land at the upper end of the harbour, and the crews had gone off inland. Then the English seized two of the three ships at the entrance to the estuary, and slew the men, but the other escaped; in her also all but five were slain; and they escaped because the ships of the others were aground; they were also very awkwardly aground; three had gone aground on the side of the channel where the Danish ships were aground, and the others all on the other side, so that none of them could reach the others. But, when the tide had ebbed many furlongs from the ships, the Danes went from the three ships to the other three which were stranded on their side, and then there they fought. There was slain Lucumon, the king's reeve, and Wulfheard the Frisian, and Aebbe the Frisian, and Aethelhere the Frisian, and Aethelfrith of the king's household, totalling sixty-two killed of English and Frisians, and one hundred and twenty of the Danes. The tide however came first to the Danish ships, before the Christians could push off theirs, and hence they rowed away out to sea.

The Anglo-Saxon Chronicle: 896

Battle of Brunanburh, 937

In this year king Aethelstan, lord of warriors,
Ring-giver of men, with his brother prince Edmund,
Won undying glory with the edges of swords,
In warfare around *Brunanburh*.
With their hammered blades, the sons of Edward
Clove the shield-wall and hacked the linden bucklers,
As was instinctive in them, from their ancestry,
To defend their land, their treasures, and their homes,
In frequent battle against each enemy.
The foemen were laid low: the Scots
And the host from the ships fell doomed. The field
Grew dark with the blood of men after the sun,
That glorious luminary, God's bright candle,
Rose high in the morning above the horizon,
Until the noble being of the Lord Eternal
Sank to its rest. There lay many a warrior
Of the men of the North, torn by spears,
Shot o'er his shield; likewise many a Scot
Sated with battle, lay lifeless.
All through the day the West Saxons in troops
Pressed on in pursuit of the hostile peoples,
Fiercely, with swords sharpened on grindstone,
They cut down the fugitives as they fled.
Nor did the Mercians refuse hard fighting

To any of Anlaf's warriors, who invaded
Our land across the tossing waters,
In the ship's bosom, to meet their doom
In the fight.

The Anglo-Saxon Chronicle: 'The Battle of Brunanburh': 937

Battle of Maldon, 991

Then Byrhtnoth spoke. He grasped his shield
And brandished his slender ashen spear,
Resentful and resolute he shouted his reply:
'Can you hear, you pirate, what these people say?
They will pay you a tribute of whistling spears,
Of deadly darts and proven swords,
Weapons to pay you, pierce, slit and slay you in storming battle.
Listen, messenger! Take back this reply:
Tell your people the unpleasant tidings
That over here there stands a noble earl with his troop –
Guardians of the people and of the country,
The home of Ethelred, my prince – who'll defend this land
To the last ditch. We'll sever the heathens' heads
From their shoulders. It would be much to our shame
If you took our tribute and embarked without battle
Since you've intruded so far
And so rudely into this country.
No! You'll never get your treasure so easily.
The spear's point and the sword's edge, savage battle-play,
Must teach us first that we have to yield tribute.'

Anonymous, 'The Battle Of Maldon', *c.* 1000

Battle of Thetford, 1004

In this year Swein came with his fleet to Norwich, and completely sacked the borough and burnt it down. Then Ulfcytel and the chief men from East Anglia decided that it would be better for them to buy peace from the enemy before they did too much damage in that district, since they had come unexpectedly, and he had not had time to gather his levies together. However, under cover of the truce which was to have been observed between them, the host came up secretly from the ships and made their way to Thetford. When Ulfcytel discovered this, he sent men to hew their ships to pieces, but those detailed for it failed in their duty, so he mobilized in secret as strong a force of levies as he could. The host reached Thetford within three weeks of sacking Norwich, and spent a night in the borough, pillaging and burning it to the ground. The next morning, when they planned to retire to their ships, Ulfcytel came up with his force, and there was a fierce encounter and great slaughter on each side. There were slain the chief men of East Anglia, but if they had been up to full strength the enemy would never have got back to their ships, as they themselves admitted.

The Anglo-Saxon Chronicle: 1004

Battle of Stamford Bridge, 25th September 1066

The details of the fight are absolutely lost – we cannot unfortunately accept one word of the spirited narrative of the *Heimkringla*, for all the statements in it that can be tested are obviously incorrect. Harold *may* have offered his rebel brother pardon and an earldom, and have promised his Norse ally no more than the famous 'seven feet of English earth, since his stature is greater than that of other men'. The Vikings *may* have fought for long hours in their shield ring, and have failed at evening only, when their king had been slain by a chance arrow. But we cannot trust a saga which says that Morkar was King Harold Godwineson's brother, and fell at Fulford; that Earl Waltheof (then a child) took part in the fight, and that the English army was mostly composed of cavalry and archers. The whole tale of the *Heimkringla* reads like a version of the battle of Hastings transported to Stamford Bridge by some incredible error.

Charles Oman, *A History of the Art of War in the Middle Ages*, 1924

A battle which was a Flodden to Norway.

E. S. Creasy, *The Fifteen Decisive Battles of the World*, 1851

WARFARE IN THE MIDDLE AGES

The thesis which we have asserted merely lays down the rule, that with any reasonable proportion of resources between the besiegers and the besieged, it was the latter who during the early Middle Ages had the best chance of success. Hence come two of the main characteristics of these centuries – the long survival of small States placed among greedy and powerful neighbours, and the extraordinary power of resistance shown by rebellious nobles or cities of very moderate strength in dealing with their suzerains. These features persist till the invention and improvement of artillery made the fall of strongholds a matter of days instead of months. In the fourteenth century the change begins, in the fifteenth it is fully developed, in the sixteenth the feudal fastness has become an anachronism.

Charles Oman, *A History of the Art of War in the Middle Ages*, 1924

Once it became numerous, cavalry played the principal role. The lord wore full armour and was well mounted. All his life was passed on horseback in arms; war was his profession, occupation and hobby. The army never had such a uniform and exclusive recruitment, yet at the same time, never was the art of war so imperfect or so primitive, startling proof that a martial spirit and individual valour can achieve nothing without good organization and solid discipline.

R. van Overstraeten, *Des Principes de la guerre à travers les âges*, 1926

All the lords were equal, none consented to fight in the second rank. The army was formed into a single line; the knights charged without order, each choosing an adversary whom he judged worthy of his blows. The battle was a collection of individual combats in which the commander of the army participated as a single combatant.

R. van Overstraeten, *Des Principes de la guerre à travers les âges*, 1926

In the West during the Middle Ages the military spirit of feudal 'chivalry' was inimical to art, although the drab stupidity of its military course is lightened by a few bright gleams. King John of England had a real insight into grand strategy, and Prince Edward, later Edward I, produced a masterly example of mobility in exploiting a central position in the Evesham campaign.

B. H. Liddell Hart, in *Encyclopaedia Britannica*, 1937

Reflections on the art of war have long been the concern of historians who, conscious of long-term developments, have attempted to compare the medieval period with Antiquity and modern times. Almost without exception they have concluded that the art of war in the Middle Ages was very mediocre, rudimentary, simple, even non-existent as a deliberate, organized and established discipline, applicable at different levels by officers according to their rank and function. Many of these historians, sometimes serving or retired officers, work more or less consciously within the framework of pragmatic or utilitarian teaching designed for future officers or military schools. They have thus drawn the conclusion that there is practically nothing to be gathered or learnt from the study of medieval campaigns, battles or sieges. In short, as far as war is concerned, just as with the history of philosophic thought, between Antiquity and the Renaissance there is a thousand-year gap.

Philippe Contamine, *War in the Middle Ages*, 1980

Two considerations should be taken into account . . .: first, the feeble financial means of states, which meant that collection and payment of a large army for more than four or five months was, even for a powerful monarchy at the end of the Middle Ages, a fairly remarkable achievement; and second, that for all sorts of reasons it was very much easier and far more pleasant to wage war during the summer: 'When the soft season of summer had returned and it was good to wage war and stay in the fields' is a remark by Froissart which was a commonplace, almost an axiom.

Philippe Contamine, *War in the Middle Ages*, 1980

The values of chivalric warfare were not simply abstract ideals; incontestable examples show how they were applied in practice. After the murder of Count Charles the Good in 1127, war was waged for more than a year throughout the county of Flanders. In all about 1,000 knights were involved. Yet the day-to-day narration of these events by Galbert of Bruges mentions a total of seven dead, of whom five were nobles or knights. And of these only one was killed by an enemy during a chase – the other four were accident victims (a fall from a horse, a slip while climbing a wall, the collapse of a ceiling and too much enthusiasm in blowing a horn).

Philippe Contamine, *War in the Middle Ages*, 1980

THE NORMAN CONQUEST OF ENGLAND, from 1066

. . . The Normans and other foreigners, who followed the standard of William, while they made the vanquished kingdom the seat of government, were yet so far advanced in arts as to be acquainted with the advantages of a large property; and having totally subdued the natives, they pushed the rights of conquest (very extensive in the eyes of avarice and ambition, however narrow in those of reason) to the utmost extremity against them. Except the former conquest of England by the Saxons themselves, who were induced, by peculiar circumstances, to proceed even to the extermination of the natives, it would be difficult to find in all history a revolution more destructive, or attended with a more complete subjection of the ancient inhabitants. Contumely seems even to have been wantonly added to oppression; and the natives were universally reduced to such a state of meanness and poverty, that the English name became a term of reproach; . . .

David Hume, *The History of England*, 1754–62: vol i

Arletta's pretty feet twinkling in the brook made her the mother of William the Conqueror. Had she not thus fascinated Duke Robert the Liberal of Normandy, Harold would not have fallen at Hastings, no Anglo-Norman dynasty could have arisen, no British Empire.

E. S. Creasy, *The Fifteen Decisive Battles of the World*, 1851

Once he had decided to challenge Harold, William recognized that his project was no feudal affair of overlord against vassal or vassal against overlord, but an international undertaking, and that, in consequence, it had to be placed on an international footing. And because in his day the two great international authorities were the Pope and the Emperor, it was essential to gain their sanction and, if possible, their support. His first step was, therefore, to open negotiations with both, as well as to send envoys to the principal courts of Europe, to set forth his claim to the English crown. Through the diplomatic skill of his confidant and adviser, the learned Lanfranc, Prior of Bec, he won the support of Archdeacon Hildebrand (later Pope Gregory VII), who in his turn persuaded Pope Alexander II to bless the Norman cause and to send William a consecrated banner. From the Emperor Henry IV William obtained a promise of German help, should he need it, and Swein Estrithson, king of the Danes, also pledged his support, but did not keep his word.

J. F. C. Fuller, *The Decisive Battles of the Western World*, 1954–56

Battle of Hastings, 14th October 1066

Then duke William sailed from Normandy into Pevensey, on the eve of Michaelmas. As soon as his men were fit for service, they constructed a castle at Hastings. When king Harold was informed of this, he gathered together a great host, and came to oppose him at the grey apple-tree, and William came upon him unexpectedly before his army was set in order. Nevertheless the king fought against him most resolutely with those men who wished to stand by him, and there was great slaughter on both sides. King Harold was slain, and Leofwine, his brother, and earl Gurth, his brother, and many good men. The French had possession of the place of slaughter, as God granted them because of the nation's sins.

The Anglo-Saxon Chronicle

A strange manner of battle, where the one side works by constant motion and ceaseless charges, while the other can but endure passively as it stands fixed to the sod. The Norman arrow and sword worked on: in the English ranks the only movement was the dropping of the dead: the living stood motionless.

William of Poitiers, *Chronicle*

Seeing a large part of the hostile host pursuing his own troops, the prince [William I] thrust himself in front of those in flight, shouting at them and threatening them with his spear. Staying their retreat he took off his helmet, and standing before them bare-headed, he cried: 'Look at me well. I am still alive and by the grace of God I shall yet prove victor. What is this madness that makes you fly, and what way is open for you to retreat? You are allowing yourselves to be pursued by men whom you could slaughter like cattle. You are throwing away victory and lasting glory, rushing into ruin and incurring lasting disgrace. And all for naught since by flight none of you can escape destruction.' With these words he restored their courage, and leaping to the front and wielding his death-dealing sword, he defied the enemy who merited death for their disloyalty to him their prince.

William of Poitiers, *Life of William I*

The Saxon mass was subjected to exactly the same trial which befell the British squares in the battle of Waterloo – incessant charges by a gallant cavalry mixed with a destructive hail of missiles. Nothing could be more maddening than such an ordeal to the infantry-soldier, rooted to the spot by the necessities of his formation. The situation was frightful: the ranks were filled with wounded men unable to retire to the rear through the dense mass of their comrades, unable to sink to the ground for the hideous press. The enemy was now attacking on both flanks: shields and mail had been riven: the supply of missile spears had given out: the English could but stand passive, waiting for the night or the utter exhaustion of the enemy. The cavalry onsets must have been almost a relief compared with the desperate waiting between the acts, while the arrow-shower kept beating in on the thinning host.

Charles Oman, *A History of the Art of War in the Middle Ages*, 1924

Now was Harold's chance, and he failed to seize it. He has often been blamed for not having rigidly maintained his shield-wall throughout the battle. Though to have done so might have saved him from defeat, it could not have gained a victory. Had he now seized his chance, he would have ordered a general advance, and pouring down the slope on both sides of the Hastings road would, almost certainly, have annihilated the Norman archers and infantry. True, the Norman cavalry would have got away, but bereft of their infantry, in all probability they would not have drawn rein until they had found security behind the stockade at Hastings. The victory would have been Harold's, and it might well have been decisive enough to have compelled William to re-embark and abandon the campaign.

J. F. C. Fuller, *The Decisive Battles of the Western World*, 1954–56

Revolt of Hereward the Wake, 1070–71

The military drama of the conquest closed with the vast siege operations conducted by William against the Isle of Ely defended by Hereward. Hereward was a man of the Fenland district, with a genius for amphibious guerilla warfare in that difficult country. But his resistance only began after the rest of England had been conquered, and the event was therefore never in doubt. It was but the last and noblest of a series of regional revolts undertaken too late.

G. M. Trevelyan, *History of England*, 1926

Anarchy: The Reign of King Stephen, 1135–54

For every great man built himself castles and held them against the king; and they filled the whole land with these castles. They sorely burdened the unhappy people of the country with forced labour on the castles; and when the castles were built, they filled them with devils and wicked men. By night and by day they seized those whom they believed to have any wealth, whether they were men or women; and in order to get their gold and silver, they put them into prison and tortured them with unspeakable tortures, for never since were martyrs tortured as they were. They hung them up by the feet and smoked them with foul smoke. They strung them up by the thumbs, or by the head, and hung coats of mail on their feet. They tied knotted cords round their heads and twisted it till it entered the brain. They put them in dungeons wherein were adders and snakes and toads, and so destroyed them. Some they put into a 'crucethus': that is to say, into a short, narrow, shallow chest into which they put sharp stones; and they crushed the man in it until they had broken every bone in his body. In many of the castles were instruments of torture so that two or three men had enough to do to carry one. It was made in this way: a weight was fastened to a beam which was attached to a sharp iron put round the man's throat and neck so that he could move in no direction, and could neither sit, nor lie, nor sleep, but had to bear the whole weight of the iron. Many thousands they starved to death.

The Anglo-Saxon Chronicle

THE CRUSADES, 1095–1464

War and exercise were the reigning passions of the Franks or Latins; they were enjoined, as a penance, to gratify those passions.

Edward Gibbon, *The History Of The Decline And Fall Of The Roman Empire*, 1776–88: lviii

However splendid it may seem, a regular story of the crusades would exhibit the perpetual return of the same causes and effects; and the frequent attempts for the defence or recovery of the Holy Land, would appear so many faint and unsuccessful copies of the original.

Edward Gibbon, *The History Of The Decline And Fall Of The Roman Empire*, 1776–88: lix

Among the causes that undermined the Gothic edifice, a conspicuous place must be allowed to the crusades. The estates of barons were dissipated, and their race was often extinguished, by these costly and perilous expeditions. Their poverty extorted from their pride those charters of freedom which unlocked the fetters of the slave, secured the farm of the peasant and the shop of the artificer, and gradually restored a substance and a soul to the more numerous and useful part of the community. The conflagration which destroyed the tall and barren trees of the forest gave air and scope to the vegetation of the smaller and nutritive plants of the soil.

Edward Gibbon, *The History Of The Decline And Fall Of The Roman Empire*, 1776–88: lxi

And the spear was a Desert Physician who cured not a few of ambition
And drave not a few to perdition with medicine bitter and strong,
And the shield was a grief to the fool and as bright as a desolate pool,
And as straight as the rock of Stamboul when our cavalry thundered along,
For the coward was drowned with the brave when our battle sheered like a wave,
And the dead to the desert we gave, and the glory to God in our song.

James Elroy Flecker, 'War Song of the Saracen', 1913

From the strategical, as distinguished from the political or commercial or religious point of view, the Crusades had two main objects. The first was to relieve the pressure of the Turks on Constantinople, which had been so dangerous ever since the days of Manzikert. The second was to conquer the Holy Land and to restore its shrines to the custody of Christendom. Both of these purposes were to a certain extent accomplished: the Turkish frontier in Asia Minor was thrust back many scores of miles, and nearly two centuries elapsed before the Seljouk Sultans were able to recover their lost ground. Jerusalem was stormed, and for ninety years remained in the hands of the Franks. But these ends were achieved in the most wasteful manner, by the most blundering methods, and at the maximum cost of life and material.

Charles Oman, *A History of the Art of War in the Middle Ages*, 1924

Whether we regard them as the most tremendous and most romantic of Christian adventures or as the last of the barbarian invasions, the Crusades form a central fact in medieval history. Before their inception the centre of our civilization was placed in Byzantium and in the lands of the Arab Caliphate. Before they faded out the hegemony in civilization had passed to western Europe. Out of this transference modern history was born; . . .

Steven Runciman, *A History of the Crusades*, 1951–54: Preface

Seen in the perspective of history the whole Crusading movement was a vast fiasco. The almost miraculous success of the First Crusade set up Frankish states in Outremer; and a century later, when all seemed lost, the gallant effort of the Third Crusade preserved them for another hundred years. But the tenuous kingdom of Jerusalem and its sister principalities were a puny outcome from so much energy and enthusiasm.

Steven Runciman, *A History of the Crusades*, 1951–54: vol. III

The real disaster of the Crusades was the inability of Western Christendom to comprehend Byzantium.

Steven Runciman, *A History of the Crusades*, 1951–54: vol. III

The triumphs of the Crusades were the triumphs of faith. But faith without wisdom is a dangerous thing. By the inexorable laws of history the whole world pays for the crimes and follies of each of its citizens. In the long sequence of interaction and fusion between Orient and Occident out of which our civilization has grown, the Crusades were a tragic and destructive episode. The historian as he gazes back across the centuries at their gallant story must find his admiration overcast by sorrow at the witness that it bears to the limitations of human nature. There was so much courage and so little honour, so much devotion and so little understanding. High ideals were besmirched by cruelty and greed, enterprise and endurance by a blind and narrow self-righteousness; and the Holy War itself was nothing more than a long act of intolerance in the name of God, which is the sin against the Holy Ghost.

Steven Runciman, *A History of the Crusades*, 1951–54: vol. III

Turkish Conquest of Jerusalem, 1076–96

The pilgrims who, through innumerable perils, had reached the gates of Jerusalem, were the victims of private rapine or public oppression, and often sunk under the pressure of famine and disease, before they were allowed to salute the holy sepulchre. A spirit of native barbarism, or recent zeal, prompted the Turkmans to insult the clergy of every sect: the patriarch was dragged by the hair along the pavement, and cast into a dungeon, to extort a ransom from the sympathy of his flock; and the divine worship in the church of the resurrection was often disturbed by the savage rudeness of its masters. The pathetic tale excited the millions of the west to march under the standard of the cross to the relief of the Holy Land: and yet how trifling is the sum of these accumulated evils compared with the single act of the sacrilege of Hakem, which had been so patiently endured by the Latin christians! A slighter provocation inflamed the more irascible temper of their descendants: a new spirit had arisen of religious chivalry and papal dominion: a nerve was touched of exquisite feeling: and the sensation vibrated to the heart of Europe.

Edward Gibbon, *The History Of The Decline And Fall Of The Roman Empire*, 1776–88: lviii

Council of Clermont, 1095

It is indeed the will of God, and let this memorable word, the inspiration surely of the Holy Spirit, be for ever adopted as your cry of battle, to animate the devotion and courage of the champion of Christ. His cross is the symbol of your salvation: wear it, a red, a bloody cross, as an external mark, on your breasts or shoulders, as a pledge of your sacred and irrevocable engagement.

Urban II, inaugurating the Crusades, in Edward Gibbon, *The History Of The Decline And Fall Of The Roman Empire*, 1776–88: lviii

The First Crusade: the Capture of Jerusalem, July 1099

The massacre of Jerusalem profoundly impressed all the world. No one can say how many victims it involved; but it emptied Jerusalem of its Moslem and Jewish inhabitants. Many even of the Christians were horrified by what had been done; and amongst the Moslems, who had been ready hitherto to accept the Franks as another factor in the tangled politics of the time, there was henceforward a clear determination that the Franks must be driven out. It was this bloodthirsty proof of Christian fanaticism that recreated the fanaticism of Islam. When, later, wiser Latins in the East sought to find some basis on which Christian and Moslem could work together, the memory of the massacre always stood in their way.

Steven Runciman, *A History of the Crusades*, 1951–54: vol. I

The Third Crusade, 1187–92

Those who are unwilling to rescue, are unworthy to view, the sepulchre of Christ!

Richard I of England, before Jerusalem, attributed

The Infidels, not weighed down with heavy armour like our knights, but always able to outstrip them in pace, were a constant trouble. When charged they are wont to fly, and their horses are more nimble than any others in the world; one may liken them to swallows for swiftness. When they see that you have ceased to pursue them, they no longer fly but return upon you; they are like tiresome flies which you can flap away for a moment, but which come back the instance you have stopped hitting at them: as long as you beat about they keep off: the moment you cease, they are on you again. So the Turk, when you wheel about after driving him off, follows you home without a second's delay, but will fly again if you turn on him. When the king rode at them they always retreated, but they hung about our rear, and sometimes did us mischief, not infrequently disabling some of our men.

Itinerarium Regis Ricardi, contemporary

Richard and Philip were, by the situation and extent of their dominions, rivals in power; by their age and inclinations, competitors for glory; and these causes of emulation which, had the princes been employed in the field against the common enemy, might have stimulated them to martial enterprises, soon excited, during the present leisure and repose, quarrels between monarchs of such a fiery character. Equally haughty, ambitious, intrepid, and inflexible, they were irritated with the least appearance of injury, and were incapable, by mutual condescensions, to efface those causes of complaint which unavoidably arose between them. Richard, candid, sincere, undesigning, impolitic, violent, laid himself open, on every occasion, to the designs of his antagonist; who, provident, interested, intriguing, failed not to take all advantages against him: And thus, both the circumstances of their disposition in which they were similar, and those in which they differed, rendered it impossible for them to persevere in that harmony which was so necessary to the success of their undertaking.

David Hume, *The History of England*, 1754–62: vol. II

When the Crusaders under King Richard of England defeated the Saracens, the Sultan seeing his troops fly, asked what was the number of Christians who were making all this slaughter? He was told that it was only King Richard and his men, and that they were all on foot. 'Then,' said the Sultan, 'God forbid that such a fellow as King Richard should march on foot,' and sent him a noble charger. The messenger took it, and said, 'Sire, the Sultan sends you this charger, that you may not be on foot.' The king was as cunning as his enemy, and ordered one of his squires to mount the horse in order to try him. The squire obeyed; but the animal proved fiery; and the squire being unable to hold him in, he set off at full speed to the Sultan's pavilion. The Sultan expected he had got King Richard; and was not a little mortified to discover his mistake.

The Percy Anecdotes, 1823

A fiasco of self-seeking kings.

J. F. C. Fuller, *The Decisive Battles of the Western World*, 1954–56

The Battle of Tiberias, 4th July 1187

When the king of the Franks and his knights found themselves pressed together on a hillock on the side of the hill of Kurn-Hattin, I was with my father [Saladin]. I saw the Franks make a gallant charge at those of the Moslems who were nearest them, and drive them back close to the spot where we stood. I looked at my father and saw that he was deeply moved; he changed colour, grasped his beard in his hand, and moved forward crying, 'Let us prove the devil a liar!' At these words our men precipitated themselves upon the Franks, and drove them back up the hillside. I began myself to be overjoyed, and to cry, 'They fly! They fly!' But the enemy presently came back to the charge, and for a second time cut their way to the foot of the hill; when they were again driven back, I began to cry afresh, 'They fly! They fly!' Then my father looked at me and said, 'Hold your tongue and do not say that they are really routed till you see the king's banner fall.' Shortly after we saw the flag come down; then my father dismounted, prostrated himself on the earth in thanks to God, and wept tears of joy.

Malek-el-Afdal, in Charles Oman, *A History of the Art of War in the Middle Ages*, 1924

The Battle of Arsouf, 7th September 1191

All over the face of the land you could see the well-ordered bands of the Turks, myriads of parti-coloured banners, marshalled in troops and squadrons; of mailed men alone there appeared to be more than twenty thousand. With unswerving course, swifter than eagles, they swept down upon our line of march. The air was turned black by the dust that their hoofs cast up. Before the face of each emir went his musicians, making a horrid din with horns, trumpets, drums, cymbals and all manner of brazen instruments, while the troops behind pressed on with howls and cries of war. For the Infidels think that the louder the noise, the bolder grows the spirit of the warrior. So did the cursed Turk beset us before, behind, and on the flank, and they pressed in so close that for two miles around there was not a spot of the bare earth visible; all was covered by the thick array of the enemy.

Itinerarium Regis Ricardi, contemporary

In order to deter Godfrey of Bouillon from his siege of Arsouf, the Moslems tied up one of his friends, Gerard, and slung him over the wall. Gerard shouted down to Godfrey begging him to spare him, but Godfrey claimed he would attack even if his own brother were hanging there. After being punctured by twelve arrows, Gerard was reeled in by the Moslems and, amazingly enough, was able to recover, thanks to Moslem medical care. The next year Godfrey rewarded him with the fief of Hebron as compensation for those terrifying moments spent as a wriggling target.

Ronald Finucane, *Soldiers of the Faith*, 1983

The Albigensian Crusade, 1208–13

The Albigensian War, in the beginning of the thirteenth century, commenced with the storming of Bezieres, and a massacre in which fifteen thousand persons, or according to some accounts sixty thousand, were put to the sword. Not a living soul escaped, as witnesses assure us. It was here that a Cistercian monk, being asked how the Catholics were to be distinguished from heretics, answered, 'Kill them all! God will know his own.'

The Percy Anecdotes, 1823

ANGLO-FRENCH WAR 1214

Battle of Bouvines, 27th July 1214

The hardest fight, but not the longest.

Jean de Ypres, *Chronicle*, 13th century

We cannot ascribe much influence on the fate of the day to the French king. Philip [Augustus] showed courage and decision in offering battle; a further retreat would inevitably have led to the destruction of his rearguard, and the chances of an engagement were far more preferable to such a disaster. But during the fighting we look in vain for proof that he exercised any sort of command over his host. He did nothing more than conduct into battle the cavalry of the centre: he bore himself as a good knight, not as a general. Bishop Garin was the only Frenchman on the field who seems to have possessed a military eye.

Charles Oman, *A History of the Art of War in the Middle Ages*, 1924

If Bouvines had been won, John [of England] would have been the dominant power in Europe. With Philip Augustus humbled there would have been little chance that Otto's enemies could destroy his imperial power. The papacy would have had to bow to the victorious cousins. And the English baronage, appeased by the recovery of their continental lands, would hardly have considered revolt against so powerful a monarch.

Sidney Painter, *The Reign of King John*, 1949

THE MONGOL EXPANSION, 13th century

After the Moguls had subdued the northern provinces of China, it was seriously proposed, not in the hour of victory and passion, but in calm deliberate council, to exterminate all the inhabitants of that populous country, that the vacant land might be converted to the pasture of cattle. The firmness of a Chinese mandarin, who insinuated some principles of rational policy into the mind of Zingis [sic], diverted him from the execution of this horrible design. But in the cities of Asia, which yielded to the Moguls, the inhuman abuse of the rights of war was exercised, with a regular form of discipline, which may, with equal reason, though not with equal authority, be imputed to the victorious Huns. The inhabitants, who had submitted to their discretion, were ordered to evacuate their houses, and to assemble in some plain adjacent to the city; where a division of the vanquished was made into three parts. The first class consisted of the soldiers of the garrison, and of the young men capable of bearing arms; and their fate was instantly decided: they were either enlisted among the Moguls, or they were massacred on the spot by the troops, who, with pointed spears and bended bows, had formed a circle round the captive multitude. The second class, composed of the young and beautiful women, of the artificers of every rank and profession, and of the wealthy or more honourable citizens, from whom a private ransom might be expected, was distributed in equal or proportionable lots. The remainder, whose life or death was alike useless to the conquerors, were permitted to return to the city; which, in the meantime, had been stripped of its valuable furniture; and a tax was imposed on those wretched inhabitants for the indulgence of breathing their native air.

Edward Gibbon, *The History Of The Decline And Fall Of The Roman Empire*, 1776–88: xxxiv

Fall of Baghdad, 1259

The Asiatic Christians everywhere rejoiced. They wrote in triumph of the fall of the Second Babylon and hailed Hulagu and Dokuz Khatun as the new Constantine and Helena, God's instruments for vengeance on the enemies of Christ. To the Moslems it was a ghastly shock and a challenge. The Abbasid Caliphate had for centuries been shorn of much material power, but its moral prestige was still great. The elimination of the dynasty and the capital left the leadership of Islam vacant, for any ambitious Moslem leader to seize. The Christian satisfaction was short-lived. It was not long before Islam conquered its conquerors. But the unity of the Moslem world had suffered a blow from which it could never recover. The fall of Baghdad, following half a century after the fall of Constantinople in 1204, put an end for ever to that old balanced dyarchy between Byzantium and the Caliphate under which Near Eastern humanity had flourished for so long. The Near East was never again to dominate civilization.

Steven Runciman, *A History of the Crusades*, 1951–54: vol. III

CONQUEST OF WALES BY EDWARD I, 1277–95

Any prince who is really determined to conquer the Welsh and to govern them in peace must proceed as follows. He should first of all understand that for a whole year he must devote his every effort and give his undivided attention to the task which he has undertaken. He can never hope to conquer in one single battle a people which will never draw up its forces to engage an enemy army in the field, and will never allow itself to be besieged inside fortified strong-points. He can beat them only by patient and unremitting pressure applied over a long period. Knowing the spirit of hatred and jealousy which usually prevails among them, he must sow dissension in their ranks and do all he can by promises and bribes to stir them up against each other. In the autumn not only the marches but certain carefully chosen localities must be fortified with castles, and these he must supply with ample provisions and garrison with families favourable to his cause. In the meantime he must make every effort to stop the Welsh buying the stocks of cloth, salt and corn which they usually import from England. Ships manned with picked troops must patrol the coast, to make sure that these goods are not brought by water across the Irish Sea or the Severn Sea, to ward off enemy attacks and to secure his own supply-lines. Later on, when wintry conditions have really set in, or perhaps towards the end of winter, in February and March, by which time the trees have lost their leaves, and there is no more pasturage to be had in the mountains, a strong force of infantry must have the courage to invade their secret strongholds, which lie deep in the woods and are buried in the forests.

Gerald of Wales, *The Description of Wales*, *c.* 1190

Ruin seize thee, ruthless King!
Confusion on thy banners wait;
Tho' fann'd by Conquest's crimson wing
They mock the air with idle state.
Helm, nor hauberk's twisted mail,
Nor e'en thy virtues, tyrant, shall avail
To save thy secret soul from nightly fears,
From Cambria's curse, from Cambria's tears!

Thomas Gray, 'The Bard', 1757

Battle of Orewin Bridge, 11th December 1282

Llewellyn took up a strong position above the banks of the river Yrfon, a tributary of the Wye, blocking Orewin Bridge. It was a bare steep hillside, only accessible, as it appeared, if the bridge were forced. The Welsh stood in solid array of spearmen, out of bowshot from the farther bank. A local 'friendly', however, showed the Marchers a ford some way upstream, by which their infantry crossed at dawn unseen, and fell upon the flank of the Welsh position. Llewellyn, by some chance of war, was not on the spot when the fighting began: he was some miles away, at a conference with certain chiefs of doubtful loyalty, according to the native version of the story. At any rate his troops were without a commander when the action started. They clustered together on the hilltop, abandoning the bridge in front, and thus suffering the English cavalry to pass the Yrfon. Giffard and Mortimer brought up their archers against the mass of spearmen, who offered only a passive but an obstinate defence. When a great many of them had fallen, the men-at-arms charged uphill, and broke into the gaps in the mass. The majority were cut to pieces, the rest fled over the hills. Llewellyn, hurrying back at the rumour of battle, was too late to join his men – he chanced to fall in, somewhere on the outskirts of the fight, with an isolated Shropshire man-at-arms, one Stephen de Frankton, who slew him in single combat, not knowing who he was. His death was discovered only when the corpses were being stripped after the battle.

Charles Oman, *A History of the Art of War in the Middle Ages*, 1924

There prevails a vulgar story, which, as it well suits the capacity of the monkish writers, is carefully recorded by them: That Edward, assembling the Welsh, promised to give them a prince of unexceptionable manners, a Welshman by birth, and one who could speak no other language. On their acclamations of joy, and promise of obedience, he invested in the principality his second son Edward, then an infant, who had been born at Carnarvon. The death of his eldest son Alfonso soon after made young Edward heir to the monarchy: The principality of Wales was fully annexed to the crown; and henceforth gives a title to the eldest son of the kings of England.

David Hume, *History of England*, 1754–62: vol. II

ANGLO-SCOTTISH WARS, from 1296

On fut suld be all Scottis weire,
By hyll and mosse themselff to reare.
Lat woods for wallis be bow and speire,
That innymeis do them na deire.
In strait placis gar keip all store,
And byrnen ye planeland thaim before.
Thane sall thai pass away in haist
When that thai find na thing but waist.
With wyles and waykings of the nyght
And mekill noyis maid on hytht,
Thaim sall ye turnen with gret affrai,
As thai were chassit with swerd away.
This is the consall and intent
Of gud King Robert's testiment.

The 'Testament' of Robert Bruce, *c.* 1314

Battle of Falkirk, 22nd July 1298

The whole Scottish army was broken, and chased off the field with great slaughter; which the historians, attending more to the exaggerated relations of the populace than to the probability of things, make amount to fifty or sixty thousand men. It is only certain that the Scots never suffered a greater loss in any action, nor one which seemed to threaten more inevitable ruin to their country.

David Hume, *The History of England*, 1754–62: vol. II

The whole hope of Wallace lay in the solidity of his impenetrable masses of spears; he was resolved to fight a thoroughly defensive battle, and knew that all depended on the steadiness of his followers. 'I have brought you to the ring,' he is reported to have said; 'now hop if ye may.'

Charles Oman, *A History of the Art of War in the Middle Ages*, 1924

Battle of Bannockburn, 24th June 1314

The English arrived in sight on the evening, and a bloody conflict immediately ensued between the two bodies of cavalry; where Robert, who was at the head of the Scots, engaged in single combat with Henry de Bohun, a gentleman of the family of Hereford, and at one stroke cleft his adversary to the chin with a battle-ax, in sight of the two armies. The English horse fled with precipitation to the main body.

David Hume, *The History of England*, 1754–62: vol. II

. . . Sir James Douglas, who commanded the Scottish cavalry, gave the enemy no leisure to rally, but pushed them off the field with considerable loss, and pursued them in sight of their whole line of infantry. While the English army were alarmed with this unfortunate beginning of the action, which commonly proves decisive, they observed an army on the heights towards the left, which seemed to be marching leisurely in order to surround them; and they were distracted by their multiplied fears. This was a number of waggoners and sumpter-boys, whom Robert had collected; and having supplied them with military standards, gave them the appearance, at a distance, of a formidable body. The strategem took effect: A panic seized the English: They threw down their arms and fled: . . .

David Hume, *The History of England*, 1754–62: vol. II

Lay the proud usurpers low!
Tyrants fall in every foe!
Liberty's in every blow!
Let us do or die!

Robert Burns, 'Robert Bruce's March to Bannockburn', 1793

Edward III's First Expedition Against the Scots, August 1327

The first night that the English were posted on this second mountain, the lord James Douglas took with him about two hundred men at arms, and at midnight crossed the river, at such a distance from the camp that he was not noticed, and fell upon the English army, shouting 'Douglas for ever! Ye shall die, ye thieves of England!' He and his companions killed more than three hundred; and he galloped up to the king's tent, and cut two or three of its cords, crying, at the same time, 'Douglas! Douglas for ever!' when he set off; and in his retreat he lost some of his followers, but not many; – he returned to his friends on the mountain. Nothing more of the sort was attempted from that time; but the English in future kept a strong and attentive guard, for they were fearful of another attack from the Scots, and had placed sentinels and scouts to give notice of the smallest movement of the enemy; the chief lords also slept in their armour.

Jean Froissart, *Chronicles*, 1369–1404: I.xviii

Battle of Halidon Hill, 19th July 1333

Scottes out of Berwick and out of Aberdeen,
At the Burn of Bannock ye were far too keen,
King Edward has avenged it now, and fully too, I ween.

English ballad, contemporary

Sack of Durham, 1342

During this time, the king of Scotland [David II] made so many violent attacks with the engines he had constructed upon the city of Durham, that those who were within could not prevent it from being taken, pillaged, and burnt. All were put to death without mercy, and without distinction of persons or ranks, men, women, children, monks, canons, and priests; no one was spared, neither was there house nor church left standing. It was a pity thus to destroy, in Christendom, the churches wherein God was served and honoured.

Jean Froissart, *Chronicles*, 1369–1404: I.lxxv

Battle of Neville's Cross, 17th October 1346

The Queen of England [Philippa] then came to the place where her army was, and remained until it was drawn out in four battalions. The first was under the command of the bishop of Durham, and the lord Percy; the second, under the archbishop of York, and the lord Neville; the third, under the bishop of Lincoln, and Lord Mowbray; the fourth was commanded by lord Baliol, governor of Berwick, the archbishop of Canterbury, and the lord Roos.

Jean Froissart, *Chronicles*, 1369–1404: I.cxxxvi

Battle of Flodden, 9th September 1513

Dool and wae for the order, sent out lads to the Border!
The English, for ance, by guile wan the day;
The Flowers of the Forest, that fought aye the foremost,
The prime of our land, are cauld in the clay.

We'll hear nae mair lilting at the ewe-milking;
Women and bairns are heartless and wae;
Sighing and moaning on ilka green loaning –
The Flowers of the Forest are a' wede away.

Jane Elliott, 'Lament for Flodden', 1776

Still from the sire the son shall hear
Of the stern strife, and carnage drear
Of Flodden's fatal field,
Where shiver'd was fair Scotland's spear,
And broken was her shield!

Walter Scott, 'Marmion', 1808

THE HUNDRED YEARS WAR 1337–1453

An English army of the 14th century, unlike its French counterpart, was the mirror of a nation, not a class. There now appeared for the first time upon the battlefields of the continent that sturdy British infantry, drawn from the humbler regions of society, which again and again has disconcerted the calculations of brilliant commanders.

H. A. L. Fisher, *A History of Europe*, 1934

The greatest tourney of the middle ages.

J. F. C. Fuller, *The Decisive Battles of the Western World*, 1954–56

Stand-off at Vironfosse, 1339

It was a matter of much wonder how two such fine armies could separate without fighting. But the French were of contrary opinions among themselves, and each spoke out his thoughts. Some said it would be a great shame, and very blameable, if the king did not give battle when he saw his enemies so near him, and drawn up in his own kingdom in battle array, in order to fight with him according to his promise: others said it would exhibit a singular instance of madness to fight, as they were not certain that some treachery was not intended; besides, if fortune should be unfavourable, the king would run a great risk of losing his kingdom, and if he should conquer his enemies, he would not be the nearer to gain possession of England, or of the land of the allies. Thus the day passed until near twelve o'clock in disputes and debates. About noon a hare was started in the plain, and ran among the French army, who began to make a great shouting and noise, which caused those in [the] rear to imagine the combat was begun in the front, and many put on their helmets, and made ready their swords. Several new knights were made, especially by the earl of Hainault, who knighted fourteen, and they were ever after called *knights of the hare*.

Jean Froissart, *Chronicles*, 1369–1404: I.xlii

Battle of Sluys, 24th June 1340

This battle was very murderous and horrible. Combats at sea are more destructive and obstinate than upon land, for it is not possible to retreat or flee – every one must abide his fortune, and exert his prowess or valour.

Jean Froissart, *Chronicles*, 1369–1404: I.l

The importance of the Battle of Sluys does not lie in the influence it had on Edward's second Flanders campaign, which ended in as great a fiasco as his first, but on the war as a whole. It was so complete that for the space of a generation it gave to England the command of the Channel, without which it is highly improbable that the war would have continued for long or that the psychologically decisive battle of Crécy would ever have been fought.

J. F. C. Fuller, *The Decisive Battles of the Western World*, 1954–56

The Order of St George, 1344

. . . The king of England [Edward III] resolved to rebuild and embellish the great castle of Windsor, which king Arthur had first founded in time past, and where he had erected and established the great round table from whence so many gallant knights had issued forth, and displayed the valiant prowess of their deeds at arms over the world. King Edward, therefore, determined to establish an order of knighthood, consisting of himself, his children, and the most gallant knights in Christendom, to the number of forty. He ordered it to be denominated 'knights of the blue garter', and that the feast should be celebrated every year, at Windsor, upon St George's Day. He summoned, therefore, all the earls, barons and knights of his realm, to inform them of his intentions; they heard it with great pleasure; for it appeared to them highly honourable, and capable of increasing love and friendship.

Jean Froissart, *Chronicles*, 1369–1404: I.c

Edward III lands in Normandy, 1346

When the fleet of England was all safely arrived at la Hogue, the king leaped on shore first; but by accident he fell, and with such violence that the blood gushed out of his nose: the knights that were near him said, 'Dear sir, let us entreat you to return to your ship, and not think of landing to-day, for this is an unfortunate omen.' The king instantly replied, 'For why? I look upon it as very favourable, and a sign that the land is desirous of me.'

Jean Froissart, *Chronicles*, 1369–1404: I.cxxi

Battle of Crécy, 26th August 1346

You must know, that these kings, earls, barons and lords of France, did not advance in any regular order, but one after the other, or any way most pleasing to themselves. As soon as the king of France came in sight of the English, his blood began to boil, and he cried out to his marshals, 'Order the Genoese forward, and begin the battle, in the name of God and St Denis.' There were about fifteen thousand Genoese cross-bowmen; but they were quite fatigued, having marched on foot that day six leagues, completely armed, and with their cross-bows. They told the constable, they were not in a fit condition to do any great things that day in battle. The earl of Alençon, hearing this, said, 'This is what one gets by employing such scoundrels, who fall off when there is any need for them.' During this time a heavy rain fell, accompanied by thunder and a very terrible eclipse of the sun; and before this rain a great flight of crows hovered in the air over all the battalions, making a loud noise. Shortly afterwards it cleared up, and the sun shone very bright; but the Frenchmen had it in their faces, and the English in their backs. When the Genoese were somewhat in order, and approached the English, they set up a great shout, in order to frighten them; but they remained quite still, and did not seem to attend it. They then set up a second shout, and advanced a little forward; but the English never moved. They hooted a third time, advancing with their cross-bows presented, and began to shoot. The English archers then advanced one step forward, and shot their arrows with such force and quickness, that it seemed as if it snowed. When the Genoese felt these arrows, which pierced their arms, heads, and through their armour, some of them cut the strings of their cross-bows, others flung them on the ground, and all turned about and retreated quite discomfited. The French had a large body of men at arms on horseback, richly dressed, to support the Genoese. The king of France, seeing them thus fall back, cried out, 'Kill me those scoundrels; for they step up our road, without any reason.' You would then have seen the above-mentioned men at arms lay about them, killing all they could of these runaways.

Jean Froissart, *Chronicles*, 1369–1404: I.cxxix

Early in the day, some French, Germans, and Savoyards had broken through the archers of the [Black] prince's battalion, and had engaged with the men at arms; upon which the second battalion came to his aid, and it was time, for otherwise he would have been hard pressed. The first division, seeing the danger they were in, sent a knight in great haste to the king of England, who was posted upon an eminence, near a windmill. On the knight's arrival, he said, 'Sir, the earl of Warwick, the lord Stafford, the lord Reginald Cobham, and the others who are about your son, are vigorously attacked by the French; and they entreat that you would come to their assistance with your battalion, for, if their numbers should increase, they fear he will have too much to do.' The king replied, 'Is my son dead, unhorsed or so badly wounded that he cannot support himself?' 'Nothing of the sort, thank God,' rejoined the knight; 'but he is in so hot an engagement that he has great need of your help.' The king answered, 'Now, sir Thomas, return back to those that sent you, not to send again for me this day, or expect that I shall come, let what will happen, as long as my son has life; and say, that I command them to let the boy win his spurs; for I am determined, if it please God, that all the glory and honour of this day shall be given to him, and to those into whose care I have intrusted him.'

Jean Froissart, *Chronicles*, 1369–1404: I.cxxix

The battle was ended at the hour of vespers.

Jean Froissart, *Chronicles*, 1369–1404: I.cxxix

It was contrary to all expectation and likelihood that with the odds of three to one against them [the English] should easily discomfit the most formidable chivalry of Europe. But the moral of their victory was not fully grasped at first. It was obvious that they had won partly by their splendid archery, partly by the steadiness of their dismounted men-at-arms. The real secret was that King Edward [III] had known how to combine the two forms of military efficiency. But that it was the combination that had been his stroke of genius, was not altogether understood by his enemies.

Charles Oman, *A History of the Art of War in the Middle Ages*, 1924

. . . The most pronounced influence of Crécy on the war was that it made the English a military nation. Henceforth England's fighting prestige was held so high that it had to be maintained by the English.

J. F. C. Fuller, *The Decisive Battles of the Western World*, 1954–56

Settlement of a Ransom, *c.* 1346

About this time, sir Walter Manny had a conversation with a great knight from Normandy, whom he detained as his prisoner, and asked him, what sum he was willing to pay for his ransom? The knight replied, 'Three thousand crowns.' Upon this, sir Walter said, 'I know you are related to the duke of Normandy, much beloved by him, and one of his privy councillors. I will let you free upon your honour, if you will go to the duke, and obtain from him a passport for myself and twenty others, that we may ride through France, as far as Calais, paying courteously for whatever we may want: if therefore you obtain this from the king, I shall hold you free from your ransom, and also be much obliged to you; for I have a great desire to see the king of England, and will not remain in any town more than one night. If you cannot accomplish it, you will return in a month to this fortress, as to your prison.' The knight set out for Paris, and, having obtained from the duke the passport, returned with it to sir Walter at Aiguillon, who acquitted him of his ransom.

Jean Froissart, *Chronicles*, 1369–1404: I.cxxxiv

Siege and Capitulation of Calais, August 1346–4th August 1347

Gonners, to schew their arte,
Into the towne in many a parte
Schote many a full grete stone.
Thankyd be God and Mary myld,
They hurt nothir man, woman, ne chyld,
To the howsis thow they did harm.

Contemporary ballad

When sir Walter Manny had presented these six citizens to the king, they fell upon their knees, and, with uplifted hands, said, 'Most gallant king, see before you six citizens of Calais, who have been capital merchants, and who bring you the keys of the castle and of the town. We surrender ourselves to your absolute will and pleasure, in order to save the remainder of the inhabitants of Calais, who have suffered much distress and misery. Condescend therefore, out of nobleness of mind, to have mercy and compassion upon us.' All the barons, knights and squires, that were assembled there in great numbers, wept at this sight. The king eyed them with angry looks, (for he hated much the people of Calais, for the great losses he had formerly suffered from them at sea,) and ordered their heads to be stricken off. All present entreated the king, that he would be more merciful to them, but he would not listen to them. Then sir Walter Manny said, 'Ah, gentle king, let me beseech you to restrain your anger: you have the reputation of great nobleness of soul, do not therefore tarnish it by such an act as this, nor allow anyone to speak in a disgraceful manner of you. In this instance, all the world will say you have acted cruelly, if you put to death six such respectable persons, who, of their own free will, have surrendered themselves to your mercy, in order to save their fellow-citizens.' Upon this the king gave a wink, saying, 'Be it so,' and ordered the headsman to be sent for; for that the Calesians had done him so much damage, it was proper they should suffer for it. The queen of England, who at the time was very big with child, fell on her knees, and with tears said, 'Ah, gentle sir, since I have crossed the sea with great danger to see you, I have never asked you one favour; now, I must humbly ask as a gift, for the sake of the Son of the blessed Mary, and for your love to me, that you will be merciful to these six men.' The king looked at her for some time in silence, and then said, 'Ah, lady, I wish you had been anywhere else but here: you have entreated in such a manner that I cannot refuse you; I therefore give them to you, to do as you please with them.' The queen conducted the six men to her apartments, and had the halters taken from around their necks, after which she new clothed them, and served them with a plentiful dinner; . . .

Jean Froissart, *Chronicles*, 1369–1404: I.clxv

Battle of Poitiers, 19th September 1356

The engagement now began on both sides: and the battalion of the marshals was advancing before those who were intended to break the battalion of archers; who, as soon as they saw them fairly entered, began shooting with their bows in such an excellent manner, from each side of the hedge, that the horses, smarting under the pain of the wounds made by their bearded arrows, would not advance, but turned about, and, by their unruliness, threw their masters, who could not manage them, nor could those that had fallen get up again for the confusion: so that this battalion of the marshals could never approach that of the [Black] prince: however, there were some knights and squires so well mounted, that, by the strength of their horses, they passed through, and broke the hedge, but, in spite of their efforts, could not get up to the battalion of the prince. The lord James Audley, attended by his four squires, had placed himself, sword in hand, in front of this battalion, much before the rest, and was performing wonders. He had advanced, through his eagerness, so far, that he engaged the lord Arnold d'Andreghen, marshal of France, under his banner, when they fought a considerable time, and the lord Arnold was roughly enough treated. The battalion of the marshals was soon put to rout by the arrows of the archers, and the assistance of the men at arms, who rushed among them as they were struck down, and seized and slew them at their pleasure.

Jean Froissart, *Chronicles*, 1369–1404: I.clxi

When evening was come, the prince of Wales [Edward, the Black Prince] gave a supper in his pavilion to the king of France, and to the greater part of the princes and barons who were prisoners. The prince seated the king of France and his son the lord Philip at an elevated and well-covered table: with them were, sir James de Bourbon, the lord John d'Artois, the earls of Tancarville, of Estampes, of Dammartin, of Graville, and the lord of Partenay. The other knights and squires were placed at different tables. The prince himself served the king's table, as well as the others, with every mark of humility, and would not sit down at it, in spite of all his entreaties for him so to do, saying, that 'he was not worthy of such an honour, nor did it appertain to him to sit at the table of so great a king, or of so valiant a man as he had shown himself to be that day.' He added also with a noble air, 'Dear sir, do not make a poor meal because the Almighty God has not gratified your wishes in the event of this day; for be assured that my lord and father will show you every honour and friendship in his power, and will arrange your ransom so reasonably, that you will henceforward always remain friends. In my opinion you have cause to be glad that the success of this battle did not turn out as you desired; for you have this day acquired such high renown for prowess, that you have surpassed all the best knights on your side. I do not, dear sir, say this to flatter you, for all those of our side who have seen and observed the actions of each party, have unanimously allowed this to be your due, and decree you the prize and garland for it.' At the end of this speech there were murmurs of praise heard from every one; and the French said, the prince had spoken nobly and truly, and that he would be one of the most gallant princes in Christendom, if God should grant him life to pursue his career of glory.

Jean Froissart, *Chronicles*, 1369–1404: I.clxvii

The Jacquerie of Beauvoisis, 1358

These wicked people, without leader and without arms, plundered and burnt all the houses they came to, murdered every gentleman, and violated every lady and damsel they could find. He who committed the most atrocious actions, and such as no human creature would have imagined, was the most applauded, and considered as the greatest man amongst them. I dare not write the horrible and inconceivable atrocities they committed on the persons of the ladies. Among other infamous acts, they murdered a knight; and, having fastened him to a spit, roasted him before the eyes of his wife and his children, and, after ten or twelve had violated her, they forced her to eat some of her husband's flesh, and then knocked her brains out.

Jean Froissart, *Chronicles*, 1369–1404: I.clxxxi

Edward III in France, 1359

I must inform you, that the king of England and his rich lords were followed by carts laden with tents, pavilions, mills, and forges, to grind their corn and make shoes for their horses, and every thing of that sort which might be wanting. For this purpose there were upwards of six thousand carts, each of them drawn by four good and strong horses which had been transported from England. Upon these carts were also many vessels and small boats, made surprisingly well of boiled leather: they were large enough to contain three men, to enable them to fish any lake or pond, whatever might be its size: and they were of great use to the lords and barons during Lent: but the commonalty made use of what provisions they could get. The king had, besides, thirty falconers on horseback, laden with hawks: sixty couple of strong hounds, and as many greyhounds; so that every day he took the pleasure of hunting or fishing either by land or water.

Jean Froissart, *Chronicles*, 1369–1404: I.ccx

Battle of Auray, 27th September 1364

Battalions and banners rushed against each other, and sometimes were overthrown, and then up again. Among the knights, sir John Chandos shewed his ability, valorously fighting with his battle-axe: he gave such desperate blows, that all avoided him; for he was of great stature and strength, well made in all his limbs. He advanced to attack the battalion of the Earl of Auxerre and the French. Many bold actions were performed; and, through the courage of himself and people, he drove this battalion before him, and threw it into such disorder that, in brief, it was discomfited. All their banners and pennons were thrown on the ground, torn and broken: their lords and captains were in the greatest danger; for they were not succoured by any, their people being fully engaged in fighting and defending themselves. To speak truly, when once an army is discomfited, those who are defeated are so much frightened, that if one fall, three follow his example, and to these three ten, and to ten thirty; and also, should ten run away, they will be followed by a hundred. Thus it was at the battle of Auray.

Jean Froissart, *Chronicles*, 1369–1404: I.ccxxvii

The Battle of Navarrete, 3rd April 1367

It was delightful to see and examine these banners and pennons, with the noble army that was under them. The two armies began to move a little, and to approach nearer each other; but, before they met, the prince of Wales, with eyes and hands uplifted toward heaven, exclaimed: 'God of truth, the Father of Jesus Christ, who has made and fashioned me, condescend, through thy benign grace, that the success of the battle of this day may be for me and my army; for thou knowest, that in truth I have been solely emboldened to undertake it in support of justice and reason, to reinstate this king upon his throne, who has been disinherited and driven from it, as well as from his country.' After these words, he extended his right arm, took hold of don Pedro's hand, who was by his side, and added, 'Sir king, you shall know this day whether you will have anything in the kingdom of Castille or not.' He then cried out, 'Advance, banners, in the name of God and St George!'

Jean Froissart, *Chronicles*, 1369–1404: I.ccxli

The Battle of Rosbecque, 1382

. . . The oriflamme was a most excellent banner, and had been sent from heaven with great mystery: it is a sort of ganfanon, and is of much comfort in the day of battle to those who see it. Proof was made of its virtues at this time; for all morning there was so thick a fog, that with difficulty could they see each other, but the moment the knight had displayed it, and raised his lance in the air, this fog instantly dispersed, and the sky was as clear as it had been during the whole year. The lords of France were much rejoiced when they saw this clear day, and the sun shine, so that they could look about them on all sides.

Jean Froissart, *Chronicles*, 1369–1404: II.cxxiv

I was told that if all the armourers of Paris and Bruxelles had been there working at their trade, they could not have made a greater noise than these combatants did on the helmets of their enemies; for they struck with all their force, and set to their work with the greatest good will.

Jean Froissart, *Chronicles*, 1369–1404: II.cxxiv

Henry V of England Resumes the War, 1415

In the year of our lord 1415, Henry V King of England called together the prelates and lords of his kingdom, and asked their advice, on peril of their souls, whether he had a better grievance against the kingdom of Scotland, or against the kingdom of France, to go to war about.

The Book of Pluscarden

For these Frenchmen, puffed up with pride and lacking in foresight, hurling mocking words at the ambassadors of the King of England, said foolishly to them that as Henry was but a young man, they would send him little balls to play with and soft cushions to rest on until he should have grown to a man's strength. When the king heard these words he was much moved and troubled in spirit; yet he addressed these short, wise and honest words to those standing around him: 'If God wills, and if my life shall be prolonged with health, in a few months I will play with such balls in the Frenchmen's court-yards that they will lose the game eventually and for their game win but grief. And if they shall sleep too long on their cushions in their chambers, I will awake them, before they wish it, from their slumbers at dawn by beating on their doors.'

John Strecche, *The Chronicle for the Reign of Henry V*

Siege of Harfleur, 1415

Henry V: Once more unto the breach, dear friends, once more;
Or close the wall up with your English dead!
In peace there's nothing so becomes a man
As modest stillness and humility:
But when the blast of war blows in our ears,
Then imitate the action of a tiger;
Stiffen the sinews, summon up the blood,
Disguise fair nature with hard-favour'd rage;
Then lend the eye a terrible aspect;
Let it pry through the portage of the head
Like the brass cannon; let the brow o'erwhelm it
As fearfully as does a galled rock
O'erhang and jutty his confounded base,
Swill'd with the wild and wasteful ocean.
Now set the teeth and stretch the nostril wide,
Hold hard the breath, and bend up every spirit
To his full height! On, on, you noblest English!
Whose blood is fet from fathers of war-proof;
Fathers that, like so many Alexanders,
Have in these parts from morn till even fought,
And sheath'd their swords for lack of argument.

William Shakespeare, *Henry V*, 1599: Act III sc. i

Henry V: I see you stand like greyhounds in the slips,
Straining upon the start. The game's afoot:
Follow your spirit; and, upon this charge,
Cry 'God for Harry! England and Saint George!'

William Shakespeare, *Henry V*, Act III sc. i

Battle of Agincourt, 25th Ocober 1415

Henry V: Rather proclaim it, Westmoreland, through my host,
That he which hath no stomach for this fight,
Let him depart; his passport shall be made,

And crowns for convoy put into his purse:
We would not die in that man's company
That fears his fellowship to die with us.
This day is call'd the feast of Crispian:
He that outlives this day, and comes safe home,
Will stand a tip-toe when this day is nam'd,
And rouse him at the name of Crispian.
He that shall live this day, and see old age,
Will yearly on the vigil feast his neighbours,
And say, 'Tomorrow is Saint Crispian':
Then will he strip his sleeve and show his scars,
And say, 'These wounds I had on Crispin's day.'
Old men forget: yet all shall be forgot,
But he'll remember with advantages
What feats he did that day. Then shall our names,
Familiar in his mouth as household words,
Harry the king, Bedford, and Exeter,
Warwick and Talbot, Salisbury and Gloucester,
Be in their flowing cups freshly remembered.
This story shall the good man teach his son;
And Crispin Crispian shall ne'er go by,
From this day to the ending of the world,
But we in it shall be remember'd;
We few, we happy few, we band of brothers;
For he today that sheds his blood with me
Shall be my brother; be he ne'er so vile
This day shall gentle his condition:
And gentlemen in England now a-bed
Shall think themselves accurs'd they were not here,
And hold their manhoods cheap whiles any speaks
That fought with us upon Saint Crispin's day.

William Shakespeare, *Henry V*, 1599, Act IV sc. iii

Fair stood the wind for France,
When we our sails advance,
Nor now to prove our chance,
Longer will tarry.

Michael Drayton, 'Ballad of Agincourt', 1627

Upon Saint Crispin's Day
Fought was this noble fray,
Which fame did not delay,
To England to carry.
O when shall English men
With such acts fill a pen,
Or England breed again
Such a King Harry?

Michael Drayton, 'Ballad of Agincourt', 1627

The English victory was all the more astonishing because Henry was not able to receive battle in the original position, but had been forced to advance out of it, in order to get the enemy to take the offensive. The fight was on perfectly open, flat ground, not on a hillside or behind hedges – the archers' stakes were useful, but not a decisive item in the causes of victory, for the main struggle ended in a hand-to-hand mêlée. Perhaps the most striking moral of the affair was that armour had become so tiresome that in close contest the archer, with his steel cap and jack or brigandine, had many advantages over a fully equipped man-at-arms. The archer was effective not only with his bow but with his axe or mallet, when once his adversary was tired out and hampered in the mire.

Charles Oman, *A History of the Art of War in the Middle Ages*, 1924

Agincourt is one of the most instantly and vividly visualized of all epic passages in English history, and one of the most satisfactory to contemplate. It is a victory of the weak over the strong, of the common soldier over the mounted knight, of resolution over bombast, of the desperate, cornered and far from home, over the proprietorial and cocksure. Visually it is pre-Raphaelite, perhaps better a Medici Gallery print battle – a composition of strong verticals and horizontals and a conflict of rich dark reds and Lincoln greens against fishscale greys and arctic blues. It is a school outing to the Old Vic, Shakespeare is fun, *son-et-lumière*, blank verse, Laurence Olivier in battle armour; it is an episode to quicken the interest of any schoolboy bored by a history lesson, a set-piece demonstration of English moral superiority and cherished ingredient of a fading national myth. It is also a story of slaughter-yard behaviour and of outright atrocity.

John Keegan, *The Face of Battle*, 1976

[On the massacre of French prisoners:] If Henry could give the order and, as he did, subsequently escape the reproval of his peers, of the Church and of the chroniclers, we must presume it was because the battlefield itself was still regarded as a sort of moral no-man's land and the hour of battle as a legal *dies non*.

John Keegan, *The Face of Battle*, 1976

Siege of Orléans, 1428–29

That the appearance of Joan of Arc was the turning-point in the whole matter is clear; her influence was of course moral rather than strategic. Attempts have been made to show that she was not only a genuine and honest enthusiast (which most people save M. Anatole France now grant), but also a Heaven-sent general. These, I think, are exaggerated. It cannot be said, as a rule, that she exhibited any great tactical skill in her operations: her talent was that she inspired her soldiery to fight with an energy and confidence that had been unknown before. That she raised the siege of Orleans seemed astonishing to her contemporaries, but can hardly appear so to anyone who looks dispassionately upon the military situation. An army of five thousand men, which has strung itself out to the thinnest of lines in order to besiege a large town, and is divided in halves by a broad river like the Loire, is in a most desperate condition.

Charles Oman, *A History of the Art of War in the Middle Ages*, 1924

RICHARD II'S EXPEDITION TO IRELAND, 1399

To tell you the truth, Ireland is one of the worst countries to make war in, or to conquer; for there are such impenetrable and extensive forests, lakes and bogs, there is no knowing how to pass them, and carry on war advantageously; it is so thinly inhabited, that, whenever the Irish please, they desert the towns, and take refuge in these forests, and live in huts made of boughs, like wild beasts; and whenever they perceive any parties advancing with hostile dispositions, and about to enter their country, they fly to such narrow passes, it is impossible to follow them. When they find a favourable opportunity to attack their enemies to advantage, which frequently happens, from their knowledge of the country, they fail not to seize it; and no man at arms, be he ever so well mounted, can overtake them, so light are they of foot. Sometimes they leap from the ground behind a horseman, and embrace the rider (for they are very strong in their arms) so tightly, that he can no way get rid of them. The Irish have pointed knives, with broad blades, sharp on both sides like a dart-head, with which they kill their enemies; but they never consider them dead until they have cut their throats like sheep, opened their bellies and taken out their hearts, which they carry off with them, and some say, who are well acquainted with their manners, that they devour them as delicious morsels. They never accept of ransom for their prisoners; and when they find they have not the advantage in any skirmishes, they instantly separate, and hide themselves in hedges, bushes, or holes under ground, so that they seem to disappear, no one knows whether.

Jean Froissart, *Chronicles*, 1369–1404: IV.lxiv

THE FALL OF CONSTANTINOPLE, 29th May 1453

Cannot there be found a Christian to cut off my head?

Emperor Constantine Palaeologus, attributed, shortly before he was cut down by the Turks

The primitive Romans would have drawn their swords in the resolution of death or conquest. The primitive christians might have embraced each other, and awaited in patience and charity the stroke of martyrdom. But the Greeks of Constantinople were animated only by the spirit of religion, and that spirit was productive only of animosity and discord.

Edward Gibbon, *The History Of The Decline And Fall Of The Roman Empire*, 1776–88: lxviii

THE WARS OF THE ROSES, 1455–85

Battle of Tewkesbury, 4th May 1471

Lord Wenlocke not having advanced to the support of the first line, but remaining stationary, contrary to the expectations of Somerset, the latter, in a rage, rode up to him, reviled him, and beat his brains out with an axe.

Richard Brooke, *Visits to Fields of Battle in England of the Fifteenth Century*, 1857

Battle of Bosworth, 22nd August 1485

King Richard III: . . . I have set my life upon a cast,
And I will stand the hazard of the die.
I think there be six Richmonds in the field;
Five have I slain today, instead of him, –
A horse! a horse! my kingdom for a horse!

William Shakespeare, *The Tragedy of King Richard the Third*, 1594, Act V, sc. iii

They came with banner, spear and shield;
And it was proved in Bosworth-field,
Not long the Avenger was withstood –
Earth helped him with the cry of blood.

William Wordsworth, 'Song at the Feast of Brougham Castle', 1807

The first persons who attended the king, were Lovell, the Lord Chamberlain; Catesby, the Attorney-General; and Sir Richard Ratcliffe, all privy councillors, to whom he uttered the ill-bodings of his heart. Issuing from his tent, by twilight, he observed a centinel asleep, and is said to have stabbed him, with this remark, 'I found him asleep, and have left him as I found him.' Perhaps this was the only person Richard ever put to death, who deserved it.

William Hulton, *The Battle of Bosworth Field*, 1813

THE ITALIAN WARS OF THE LATE FIFTEENTH CENTURY

Because our Italian Princes were scourged by the Ultramontanes, they thought it sufficient for a Prince to write a handsome letter, or return a civil answer; to excel in drollery and repartee; to undermine and deceive; and to set themselves off with jewels and lace; to eat and sleep in greater magnificence and luxury than their neighbours; to spend their time in wanton dalliance and lascivious pleasures; to keep up a haughty kind of State, and grind the faces of their Subjects; to indulge themselves in indolence and inactivity; to dispose of their military honours and preferments to Princes and Parasites; to neglect and despise merit of every kind; to browbeat those that endeavoured to point out any thing that was salutary or praise-worthy; to have their words and sayings looked upon as oracles; not forseeing (weak and infatuated as they were) that by such conduct they were making a rod for their own backs, and exposing themselves to the mercy of the first invader. To this were owing the dreadful alarms, and disgraceful defeats, and the astonishing losses they sustained in the year one thousand four hundred and ninety four: and hence it came to pass that three of the most powerful States in Italy were so often ravaged and laid waste in those times.

Niccolò Machiavelli, *The Art of War*, 1520: VII

EMPEROR CHARLES V's INVASION OF ITALY, 1525

Battle of Pavia, 25th February 1525

There is nothing left to me but honour, and my life, which is saved.

Francis I, Letter to his mother, 24th February 1525

THE LOSS OF CALAIS, 6th January 1558

When I am dead and opened, you shall find 'Calais' lying in my heart.

Queen Mary Tudor, in *Holinshed's Chronicle*, 1577

Sponge me dry and keep me clean,
And I'll fire a shot to Calais Green.

Inscription on a field gun, sometimes called Queen Elizabeth's Pocket Pistol, *c.* 1570

FRENCH WARS OF RELIGION, 1562–98

Battle of Ivry, 14th March 1590

Before the battle of Ivry, Henry [IV] made an address to his soldiers; it was brief, but singularly impressive.

'Enfans, je suis votre Roi, vous êtes Français, voilà l'ennemi, donnons.'

['Soldiers, I am your king; you are Frenchmen. Behold the enemy; let us charge.']

The Percy Anecdotes, 1823

DUTCH WAR OF INDEPENDENCE, 1568–1609

Siege of Ostend, July 1601

An English officer, in a sally from Ostend, had one of his arms shot off with a cannon ball, which, taking up with him, he carried into the town to the surgeon, to whom he said, 'Behold the arm, which but at dinner did help its fellow.'

The Percy Anecdotes, 1823

THE CYPRUS WAR: BATTLE OF LEPANTO, 7th October 1571

In that enormous silence, tiny and unafraid,
Comes up along a winding road the noise of the Crusade.
Strong gongs groaning as the guns boom far,
Don John of Austria is going to the war;
Stiff flags straining in the night-blasts cold,
In the gloom black-purple, in the glint, old gold,
Torchlight crimson on the copper kettle-drums,
Then the tuckets, then the trumpets, then the cannon, and he comes.

G. K. Chesterton, 'Lepanto', from *The Collected Poems*, 1927

BATTLE OF NAGASHINO, 1575

They have not more than five hundred matchlock-men, and if you reckon on them all hitting at the first volley, and also at the second, for after that men shoot wildly, we shall not lose more than a thousand killed and wounded, and that is nothing much.

General Atobe Oinosuke's advice to Lord Takeda Katsuyori, in A. R. Sadler, *Life of Tokugawa Ieyasu*, 1937

ANGLO-SPANISH WAR OF 1587–88

English Attack on Cadiz, 29th April 1587

My very good Lords, next under God's mighty protection, the advantage and gain of time and place will be the only and chief means for our good; wherein I most humbly beseech your good Lordships to persevere as you have begun, for that with fifty sail of shipping we shall do more good upon their own coast, than a great many more will do here at home; and the sooner we are gone, the better we shall be able to impeach them.

Francis Drake, Letter to the Queen's Council, 30th March 1587

As for the Expedition of Sir Francis Drake in the year 1587, for the Destroying of the Spanish Shipping and Provision upon their own Coast, as I cannot say that there intervened in that Enterprise any sharp Fight or Encounter, so nevertheless it did straightly discover, either that Spain is very weak at home, or very slow to move, when they suffered a small fleet of English to make an hostile Invasion or Incursion upon their Havens and Roads from Cadiz to Cape Sacre, and thence to Cascous, and to fire, sink, and carry away at the least ten thousand Ton of their greater Shipping, besides fifty or sixty of their smaller Vessels, and that in the sight and under the favour of their Forts, and almost under the Eye of their great Admiral, the best Commander of Spain by Sea, the Marquis of Santa Cruce, without ever being disputed with in any Fight of Importance: I remember Drake, in the vaunting Stile of a Soldier, would call the Enterprise the Singeing of the King of Spain's Beard.

Francis Bacon, *Considerations Touching A War With Spain*, 1629

Defeat of the Spanish Armada, 21st–30th July 1588

There must be a beginning of any great matter, but the continuing unto the end until it be thoroughly finished yields the true glory.

Sir Francis Drake, Letter to Lord Walsingham, 17th May 1588

There is plenty of time to win this game, and to thrash the Spaniards too.

Sir Francis Drake, attributed, 20th July 1588, playing bowls at Plymouth

I know I have the body of a weak and feeble woman, but I have the heart and stomach of a king, and of a King of England too; and think foul scorn that Parma or Spain, or any prince of Europe should dare to invade the borders of my realm.

Queen Elizabeth I, speech at Tilbury, July 1588

Their force is wonderful, great and strong, yet we pluck their feathers little by little.

Sir William Howard, attributed

If you had seen that which I have seen, of the simple service that hath been done by the merchant and coast ships, you would have said that we have been little holpen by them, otherwise than that they did make a show.

Sir William Wynter, Letter to Lord Walsingham, 1st August 1588

Great thanks do I render Almighty God, by whose hand I am gifted with such power, that I could easily, if I chose, place another fleet upon the sea. Nor is it of very great importance that a running stream should be sometimes intercepted, so long as the fountain from which it flows remains inexhaustible.

Philip II of Spain, on hearing that the Spanish Admiral, Medina Sidonia, had returned home, September 1588, in J. L. Motley, *History of the United Netherlands*, 1860

Upon Tuesday, which was the three and twenty of July, the navy being come over against Portland, the wind began to turn Northerly, insomuch that the Spaniards had a fortunate and a fit gale to invade the English. But the Englishmen having lesser and nimbler Ships, recovered again the vantage of the wind from the Spaniards, whereat the Spaniards seemed to be more incensed to fight than before. But when the English Fleet had continually and without any intermission from morning to night, beaten and battered them with all their shot both great and small: the Spaniards uniting themselves, gathered their whole Fleet close together into a roundel, so that it was apparent that they meant not as yet to invade others, but only to defend themselves and to make haste unto the place prescribed unto them, which was near unto Dunkirk, that they might join forces with the Duke of Parma, who was determined to have proceeded secretly with his small ships under the shadow and protection of the great ones, and so had intended circumspectly to perform the whole expedition.

This was the most furious and bloody fight skirmish of all, in which the lord Admiral of England continued fighting amidst his enemies' Fleet and, seeing one of his Captains afar off, he spake unto him in these words: Oh George what doest thou? Wilt thou now frustrate my hope and opinion conceived of thee? Wilt thou forsake me now? With which words he, being enflamed, approached forthwith, encountered the enemy, and did the part of a most valiant Captain. His name was George Fenner, a man that had been conversant in many Sea-fights.

Richard Hakluyt, *Navigations and Voyages*, 1598–1600

For the perpetual memory of this matter, the Zealanders caused new coin of Silver and bars to be stamped: which on the one side contained the arms of Zealand, with this inscription: GLORY TO GOD ONLY; and on the other side, the pictures of certain great ships, with these words: THE SPANISH FLEET: and in the circumference about the ships: IT CAME, IT WENT, IT WAS, ANNO 1588. That is to say, the Spanish fleet came, went, and was vanquished this year; for which, glory be given to God only.

Richard Hakluyt, *Navigations and Voyages*, 1598–1600

While this wonderful and puissant Navy was sailing along the English coasts and all men did now plainly see and hear that which before they would not be persuaded of, all people throughout England prostrated themselves with humble prayers and supplications unto God: but especially the outlandish Churches (who had greatest cause to fear, and against whom by name, the Spaniards had threatened most grievous torments) enjoined to their people continual fastings and supplications, that they might turn away God's wrath and fury now imminent upon them for their sins: knowing right well, that prayer was the only refuge against all enemies, calamities, and necessities, and that it was the only solace and relief for mankind, being visited with affliction and misery.

Richard Hakluyt, *Navigations and Voyages*, 1598–1600

The England of our own days is so strong, and the Spain of our own days is so feeble, that it is not easy, without some reflection and care, to comprehend the full extent of the peril which England then ran from the power and ambition of Spain, or to appreciate the importance of that crisis in the History of the World. We had then no Indian or Colonial Empire, save the feeble germs of our North American settlements, which Raleigh and Gilbert had recently planted. Scotland was a separate kingdom; and Ireland was then even a greater source of weakness, and a worse nest of rebellion than she has been in after times. Queen Elizabeth had found at her accession an incumbered revenue, a divided people, and an unsuccessful foreign war, in which the last remnant of our possessions in France had been lost; she had also a formidable pretender to her crown, whose interests were favoured by all the Roman Catholic powers; and even some of her subjects were warped by religious bigotry to deny her title, and to look on her as an heretical usurper.

E. S. Creasy, *The Fifteen Decisive Battles of the World*, 1851

The Spanish Armada was a convoy of transports rather than a fleet of battleships, and when Drake singed the Spanish King's beard at Cadiz, he was not hurling an impudent insult at imposing dignity but demonstrating the effectiveness of naval guns which were almost as good as Nelson's at Trafalgar.

A. F. Pollard, *The Elizabethans and the Empire*, 1922

The defeat of the Armada whispered the imperial secret into England's ear; that in a commercial age the winning of the sea is more profitable than the winning of the land, and though this may not have been clearly understood in 1588, during the following century the whisper grew louder and louder until it became the voice of every Englishman.

J. F. C. Fuller, *The Decisive Battles of the Western World*, 1954–56

SIEGE OF BOMMEL, 1599

Two Spaniards, brothers, who although they had for a long series of years always sought each other, were never able to meet, at last accidentally came in contact at the siege of Bommel, then the seat of war, where they served in two different companies. Being unknown to each other at first, some little explanation made their relationship known, when they fell on each other's neck. While they were thus locked in an affectionate embrace, a cannon ball took off both their heads, without separating their bodies, which fell clasped together into the arms of Death, who thus summoned them away in the happiest moment of their lives.

The Percy Anecdotes, 1823

THE THIRTY YEARS WAR, 1618–48

All the wars that are on foot in Europe have been fused together, and have become a single war.

Gustavus Adolphus, Letter to Axel Oxenstierna, 1630

War should feed war.

Maxim of Albrecht von Wallenstein

Whose house doth burn, soldier must turn.

Popular saying of the War

The deputies of a great metropolis in Germany once offered the great Turenne one hundred thousand crowns not to pass with his army through their city. 'Gentlemen,' said he, 'I can't in conscience accept your money, as I had no intention to pass that way.'

The Percy Anecdotes, 1823

Sack of Magdeburg, 20th May 1631

Three hours' plundering is the shortest rule of war. The soldier must have something for all his toil and trouble.

Johann Tilly, attributed

Battle of Breitenfeld (Leipzig), 17th September 1631

Those tactics were, after all, but the military expression of the religious and political system in defence of which they were used. Those solid columns just defeated were the types of what human nature was to become under the Jesuit organization. The individual was swallowed up in the mass. As Tilly had borne down by sheer weight of his veterans, adventurers like Mansfeld and Christian of Brunswick, so the renewed Catholic discipline had borne down the wrangling theologians who had stepped into the places of Luther and Melanchthon. But now an army had arisen to prove that order and obedience were weak unless they were supported by individual intelligence. The success of the principle upon which its operations were based could not be confined to mere fighting. It would make its way in morals and politics, in literature and science.

Anton Gindely, *A History of the Thirty Years' War*, 1884

Battle of Lützen, 16th November 1632

I cannot bear to have Wallenstein under my nose and not make a swoop at him.

Gustavus Adolphus, attributed

THE ENGLISH CIVIL WAR, 1642–51

Captain or Colonel, or Knight in Arms,
Whose chance on these defenceless doors may seize,
If ever deed of honour did these please,
Guard them, and him within protect from harms;
He can requite thee, for he knows the charms
That call Fame on such gentle acts as these
And he can spread thy Name o'er Lands and Seas,
Whatever clime the Sun's bright circle warms.
Lift not thy spear against the Muses Bow'r:
The great Emathian Conqueror bid spare
The house of Pindarus, when Temple and Tow'r
Went to the ground; and the repeated air
Of sad *Electra's* Poet had the pow'r
To save th'Athenian Walls from ruin bare.

John Milton, 'When The Assault Was Intended To The City', 1642

I should most gladly wait on you according to your desire, but that I look upon you as engaged in that party, beyond a possibility of retreat and consequently uncapable of being wrought upon by persuasion. And I know the conference could never be so close between us, but that it would take wind and receive a construction to my dishonour; That great God, which is the searcher of my heart, knows with what a sad sense I go upon this service, and with what a perfect hatred I detest this war without an Enemy, but I look upon it as *Opus Domini*, which is enough to silence all passion in me. The God of peace in his good time send us peace, and in the meantime fit us to receive it: We are both upon the stage and must act those parts assigned us in this Tragedy: Let us do it in a way of honour, and without personal animosities, whatever the issue be, I shall never relinquish the dear title of

Your most affectionate friend and faithful servant, . . .

Sir William Waller, Letter to Sir Ralph Hopton, 16th June 1643

I have a lovely company; you would respect them, did you know them. They are no Anabaptists, they are honest sober Christians: they expect to be used as men!

Oliver Cromwell, Letter to Oliver St John, 11th September 1643

If you choose godly, honest men to be captains of Horse, honest men will follow them.

Oliver Cromwell, Letter to Sir William Springer, September 1643

Know that unless you bring to me the monthly contribution for six months you are to expect an unsanctified troop of horse among you, from whom, if you hide yourselves, they shall fire your houses without mercy, hang up your bodies wherever they find them, and scare your ghosts.

Royalist Proclamation, issued by the Governor of Worcester, sent to a local parish, 1643

Earl of Manchester: If we beat the King ninety-nine times, yet he is King still and so will his posterity be after him; but if the King beat us once we shall be hanged, and our posterity be made slaves.

Cromwell: My Lord, if this be so, why did we take up arms at first? This is against fighting ever hereafter. If so, let us make peace, be it never so base.

Calender of State Papers, entry for 10th November 1644

Q: What profession are you?
A: I am a Christian and a souldier.
Q: Is it lawfull for Christians to be souldiers?
A: Yes doubtlesse: we have Arguments enough to warrant it.

1. God calls himself a man of war, and Lord of Hosts.
2. Abraham had a Regiment of 318 Trained men.
3. David was employed in fighting the Lords battels.
4. The Holy Ghost makes honourable mention of Davids worthies.
5. God himself taught David to fight.
6. The noble gift of valour is given for this purpose.

Anonymous, *A Souldier's Catechism*, 1644

Till you have an army of your own, that you may command, it is impossible to do anything of importance.

Sir William Waller, address to the House of Commons, 1645

The poorest he that is in England hath a life to live as the greatest he.

Thomas Rainborowe, in the Putney Debates, October 1647

To give a further character of the court, though they were neat and gay in their apparell, yet they were very nasty and beastly, leaving at their departure their excrements in every corner, in chimneys, studies, cole-houses, cellars. Rude, rough, whoremongers: vaine, empty, careless.

Anthony Wood, describing a party of Royalists billeted at Oxford University, in *The Life and Times of Anthony à Wood*, 1891

Atrocities were few; the Puritans vented their wrath on Gothic images in churches and by smashing stained glass, while towns were not sacked but subjected to Puritan teaching, perhaps a subtler punishment.

Correlli Barnett, *Britain and Her Army 1509–1970*, 1970

Battle of Edgehill, 24th October 1642

O Lord! Thou knowest how busy I must be this day: If I forget Thee, do not Thou forget me.

Sir Jacob Astley, before the battle, attributed

Battle of Marston Moor, 2nd July 1644

Put your trust in God, my boys, and keep your powder dry.

Oliver Cromwell, attributed address to his troops

Those who most exactly describe that unfortunate battle, and more unfortunate abandoning that whole country (when there might have been means found to have drawn a good army together), by prince Rupert's hasty departure with all his troops, and the marquis of Newcastle's as hasty departure to the sea-side, and taking ships and transporting himself out of the kingdom, and all the ill consequences thereupon, give so ill account of any conduct, courage, or discretion, in the managery of that affair, that, as I can take no pleasure in the draught of it, so posterity would receive little pleasure or benefit in the most particular relation of it.

Earl of Clarendon, *The History of the Rebellion and Civil Wars in England*, 1702–4

Battle of Naseby, 14th June 1645

I can say this of Naseby, that when I saw the enemy draw up and march in gallant order towards us, and we a company of poor, ignorant men, to seek how to order our battle – the General having commanded me to order all the horse – I could not (riding alone about my business) but smile out to God in praises, in assurance of victory, because God would, by things that are not, bring to naught things that are. Of which I had great assurance; and God did it. O that men would therefore praise the Lord, and declare the wonders that He doth for the children of men!

Oliver Cromwell, in L. F. Solt, *Saints in Arms*, 1959

Those under the King's commanders grew insensibly into all the licence, disorder and impiety with which they had reproached the rebels; and they again into a great discipline, diligence and sobriety: which begat courage and resolution in them, and notable dexterity in achievement and enterprises. Insomuch as one side seemed to fight for monarchy with the weapons of confusion, and the other to destroy the King and government with all the principles and regularity of monarchy.

Earl of Clarendon, *The History of the Rebellion and Civil Wars in England*, 1702–4

Capture of King Charles I, 2nd June 1647

The same morning that Cromwell left London, Cornet Joyce, who was one of the agitators in the army, a tailor, a fellow who had two or three years before served in a very inferior employment in Mr Hollis's house, came with a squadron of fifty horse to Holmby, where the King was, about the break of day; and, without any interruption by the guard of horse or foot which waited there, came with two or three more, and knocked at the King's chamber door and said 'he must presently speak with the King'. His Majesty, surprised at the manner of it, rose out of his bed; and half dressed, caused the door to be opened, which he knew otherwise would be quickly broken open; they who waited in the chamber being persons of whom he had little knowledge, and less confidence. As soon as the door was opened, Joyce and two or three more came into the chamber, with their hats off and pistols in their hands. Joyce told the King 'that he must go with him'. His Majesty asked, 'whither?', he answered 'to the army'. The King asked him, 'where the army was?' he said 'they would carry him to the place where it was'. His Majesty asked 'by what authority they came?' Joyce answered 'by this'; and shewed him his pistol.

Earl of Clarendon, *The History of the Rebellion and Civil Wars in England*, 1702–4

Execution of Charles I, 30th January 1649

He nothing common did nor mean
Upon that memorable scene,
  But with his keener eye
  The axe's edge did try; . . .

Andrew Marvell, 'An Horatian Ode upon Cromwell's Return from Ireland', 1650

If ever a lawless act was defensible on the principle of self-preservation, the murther of Charles might be defended.

Samuel Taylor Coleridge, *Notes on the English Divines: Richard Baxter*, ed. D. Coleridge, 1854

Battle of Dunbar, 3rd September 1650

It is easy to say the Lord hath done this; it would do you good to see our poor foot go up and down making their boast to God. But, Sir, it is in your hands, and by these eminent mercies of God puts it more in your hands, to give glory to him to improve your power and his blessings to his praise. We that serve you beg of you not to own us, but God alone; we pray you own his people more and more, for they are the chariots and horse men of Israel. Disown yourselves, but own your authority, and improve it to curb the proud and the insolent, such as would disturb the tranquility of England, though under what specious pretences soever.

Relieve the oppressed, hear the groans of poor prisoners in England, be pleased to reform the abuses of all professions; and if there be anyone that makes many men poor to make a few rich, that suits not a commonwealth.

Oliver Cromwell, Letter to William Lenthall, Speaker of the House of Commons, 4th September 1650

Battle of Worcester, 3rd September 1651

It is for aught I know the crowning mercy.

Oliver Cromwell, Letter, 4th September 1651

MASSACRE OF THE WALDENSIANS IN PIEDMONT, 24th April 1655

Avenge, O Lord, thy slaughter'd Saints, whose bones
  Lie scatter'd on the Alpine mountains cold,
  Ev'n them who kept thy truth so pure of old
  When all our Fathers worship't Stocks and Stones,
Forget not: in thy book record their groans
  Who were thy Sheep in their ancient Fold
  Slain by the bloody Piemontese that roll'd
  Mother with Infant down the Rocks. Their moans
The Vales redoubl'd to the Hills, and they
  To Heav'n. Their martyr'd blood and ashes sow
  O'er all th'Italian fields, where still doth sway

The triple Tyrant: that from these may grow
A hundredfold, who having learnt thy way
Early may fly the Babylonian woe.
John Milton, 'On the Late Massacre in Piemont', 1655

ANGLO-SPANISH WAR, 1655–58

The Lord Himself hath a controversy with your enemies; even with that Romish Babylon of which the Spaniard is the great underpropper. In that respect we fight the Lord's battles.
Oliver Cromwell, Instructions to his Admirals in the West Indies, 1655

THE ENGLISH NAVY UNDER CHARLES II

There were gentlemen and there were seamen in the Navy of Charles II. But the seamen were not gentlemen, and the gentlemen were not seamen.
T. B. Macaulay, *History of England*, 1848: I

AUSTRO-TURKISH WAR 1682–99

Battle of Vienna, 12th September 1683

I came, I saw, God conquered.
John Sobieski III of Poland, message to the Pope after crushing the Turks.

Siege of Belgrade, 1688

I am not unaware of the fact that the gentlemen of the artillery are not always in agreement with their brethren in the engineers as to the employment of work parties, and that they get hold of them on their respective accounts whenever they can if they have any works in hand.
J. M. de la Colonie, in J. C. Horsley (ed.), *The Chronicles of an Old Campaigner*, 1904

WAR OF THE LEAGUE OF AUGSBERG, 1686–97

Battle of Fleurus, 1st July 1690

During this action, a lieutenant-colonel of a French regiment, whose name well-merited preservation, was on the point of charging. Not knowing how to animate his men, who were very discontented with having commenced the campaign without being clothed, he said to them, 'My friends, I congratulate you, that you have the good fortune to be in the presence of a regiment newly clothed. Charge them vigorously, and we will clothe ourselves.' This pleasantry so inspirited his soldiers, that they rushed on the regiment, destroyed it, and completely dressed themselves on the field of battle.
The Percy Anecdotes, 1823

IRISH REBELLION of 1690

Siege of Ballymore, 1690

. . . Here the miserable effects of war appeared in a very melancholy manner; for the enemy, to prevent a famine among themselves, had drove all useless mouths from among them the last winter, to our side of the Shannon; and we, for the same reason, would not suffer them to come within our frontiers, so between both they lay in a miserable starving condition. These wretched came flocking in great numbers to our camp, devouring all the filth they could meet with. Our dead horses crawling with vermin, as the sun had parched them, were delicious food to them; while their infants sucked their carcasses with as much eagerness as if they were at their mothers' breasts.

Robert Parker, *Memories of the Most Memorable Military Transactions*, 1746

WAR OF THE SPANISH SUCCESSION, 1701–14

Battle of Blenheim, 13th August 1704

'They say it was a shocking sight
After the field was won;
For many thousand bodies here
Lay rotting in the sun;
But things like that, you know, must be
After a famous victory.

'Great praise the Duke of Marlbro' won,
And our good prince Eugene.'
'Why 'twas a very wicked thing!'
Said little Wilhelmine.
'Nay . . . nay . . . my little girl,' quoth he,
'It was a famous victory.

'And everybody praised the Duke
Who this great fight did win.'
'But what good came of it at last?'
Quoth little Peterkin.
'Why that I cannot tell,' said he,
'But 'twas a famous victory.'

Robert Southey, 'The Battle of Blenheim', 1798

So tight was the press that my horse was carried along some three hundred paces without getting hoof to ground – right to the edge of a deep ravine: down we plunged a good twenty feet into a swampy meadow; my horse stumbled and fell. A moment later several more men and horses fell on top of me as the remains of my cavalry swept by all intermingled with the hotly pursued foes. I spent several minutes trapped beneath my horse.

Comte de Mérode-Westerloo, *Memoirs*, 1840

Battle of Ramillies, 23rd May 1706

Have particular attention to that part of the line which will endure the first shock of the English troops.

Louis XIV, advice to Villeroi, 1706

The great art of distributing troops on the field is, so to place them, that all have room to act and be uniformly useful. Villeroi, who perhaps was not acquainted with this rule, deprived himself of the assistance of the whole of his left wing on the plain of Ramillies, by having posted them behind a morass, where it was morally impossible that they could manoeuvre, or render any sort of support to his right wing.

Frederick the Great, *Military Instruction to His Generals, c.* 1745

Siege of Lille, 1708

Our men seized their arms and opened fire; this made several sparks set fire to some of the enemy's powder-bags; in an instant several hundred of them were hurled into the air amidst a terrifying explosion which shook the earth. As it turned out between six and seven hundred of the men in the centre and van of the column reached the city, but those in the rear turned about and made for Douai. As their powder-bags were made of linen and not of leather, several sprung leaks, leaving a trail of powder along the road behind them. As they rode their horseshoes made the sparks fly which set fire to the powder-trail and this in turn ignited the sacks, blowing up a number of men and horses with an infernal din. It was a horrible spectacle to see the remains of men and horses, whose legs, arms and torsoes even had been flung into the trees.

Comte de Mérode-Westerloo, *Memoirs*, 1840

Battle of Malplaquet, 11th September 1709

In that tremendous combat near upon two hundred and fifty thousand men were engaged, more than fifty thousand of whom were slain or wounded (the Allies lost twice as many men as they killed of the French, whom they conquered); and this dreadful slaughter very likely took place because a great General's credit was shaken at home, and he thought to restore it by a victory. If such were the motives that induced the Duke of Marlborough to venture that prodigious stake, and desperately sacrifice thirty thousand brave lives, so that he might figure once more in a *Gazette*, and hold his place and pensions a little longer, the event defeated that dreadful and selfish design, for the victory was purchased at a cost which no nation, greedy of glory as it may be, would willingly pay for any triumph.

William Makepeace Thackeray, *Henry Esmond*, 1852

THE BRITISH NAVY, *c.* 1715

Continual destruction in the foretop, the pox above board, the plague within decks, hell in the forecastle, and the devil at the helm.

Robert Parker, quoted in R. E. Scouller, *The Armies of Queen Anne*, 1966

WAR OF THE AUSTRIAN SUCCESSION 1740–48

Troops always ready to act, my well-filled treasury, and the liveliness of my disposition – these were my reasons for making war on Maria Theresa.

Frederick the Great, Letter to Voltaire, 1741

Kalckstein: Your Majesty, am I right in thinking there is going to be a war?
Frederick: Who can tell!
Kalckstein: The movement seems to be directed on Silesia.
Frederick: Can you keep a secret? (Taking him by the hand.)
Kalckstein: Oh yes, Your Majesty.
Frederick: Well, so can I!

Anonymous, *Beyträgge zu den Anecdoten und Charakterügen aus dem Leben Friedrichs des Zeiten*, 1788–89

If I did not succeed in the winter campain which I made in the year 1742 to relieve the country from the Elector of Bavaria, it was because the French behaved like fools, and the Saxons like traitors.

Frederick the Great, *Military Instruction to His Generals c.* 1745

Charles, Elector of Bavaria, pretended that he had a right to a large part of the inheritance which the Pragmatic Sanction gave to the Queen of Hungary; but he was not sufficiently powerful to move without support. It might, therefore, not unreasonably be expected that, after a short period of restlessness, all the potentates of Christendom would acquiesce in the arrangements made by the late Emperor. But the selfish rapacity of the King of Prussia gave the signal to his neighbours. His example quieted their sense of shame. His success led them to underrate the difficulty of dismembering the Austrian monarchy. The whole world sprang to arms. On the head of Frederic is all the blood which was shed in a war which raged during many years and in every quarter of the globe, the blood of the column of Fontenoy, the blood of the mountaineers who were slaughtered at Culloden. The evils produced by his wickedness were felt in lands where the name of Prussia was unknown; and, in order that he might rob a neighbour whom he had promised to defend, black men fought on the coast of Coromandel, and red men scalped each other by the Great Lakes of North America.

T. B. Macaulay, *Essays: Frederic the Great*, 1846

Battle of Fontenoy, 11th May 1745

Lord Charles Hay: Gentlemen of the French Guard, fire first!
Comte d'Auterrches: Sir – the French Guards never fire first. After you!

Attributed exchange

Battle of Hohenfriedberg, 4th June 1745

If you wish to come to an action, and the enemy seems disposed to avoid it, you must appear to be in dread of the force which is opposed to you, or spread a report that your army is much weakened. We played this game before the battle of Hohen-Friedberg. I caused all the roads to be repaired as if I meant, at the approach of Prince Charles, to march to Breslau in four columns: his self-confidence seconding my design, he followed me into the plain, and was defeated.

Frederick the Great, *Military Instruction to His Generals c.* 1745

To describe the Battle which ensued, Battle named of Striegau or Hohenfriedberg, excels the power of human talent, – if human talent had leisure for such employment. It is the huge shock and clash of 70,000 against 70,000, placed in the way we said. An enormous *simulatus* (or 'both-at-once', as the Latins phrase it), spreading over ten square miles. Rather say, a wide congeries of electric simultaneities; all *electric*, playing madly into one another; most loud, most mad; the aspect of which is smoky, thunderous, abtrusive; the true *sequences* of which, who shall unravel?

Thomas Carlyle, *Frederick the Great*, 1858–65

Battle of Kesselsdorf, 14th December 1745

Oh God, let me not be disgraced in my old age. Or if Thou wilt not help me, do not help those scoundrels, but leave us to try it ourselves.

Leopold I of Anhalt-Dessau ('Old Dessauer'), aged seventy, attributed

PRUSSIA AND HER ARMY, mid-18th century

The world does not rest as securely on the shoulders of Atlas as Prussia relies on her army.

Frederick the Great, attributed remark, June 1745

All the tall men with moustaches are placed in the first rank, with due attention being paid in the dressing to uniformity of appearance – thus we do not like to place an old soldier next to a much younger one, or someone with a thin, half-starved face next to an individual with a strong countenance. The flanks are most in evidence when the soldiers march past, and so they must be covered by our most handsome men with good faces. Men who have moustaches, but who are less good-looking, are placed in the second rank, but if there are not enough moustaches to fill the whole rank, they must be positioned on one side of the flanks. The shortest men go to the third rank, and the tallest men without moustaches to the fourth.

Prussian drill-book, 1751

War is the national industry of Prussia.

Count Mirabeau, *De La Monarchie Prussienne*, 1788

Prussia was hatched from a cannon-ball.

Napoleon Bonaparte, attributed

An anecdote of a Silesian girl is recorded, which serves in a striking manner to shew the general feeling which pervaded the country [Prussia]. Whilst her neighbours and family were contributing in different ways to the expenses of the war, she was for some time in the greatest distress at her inability to manifest her patriotism, as she possessed nothing which she could dispose of for that purpose.

At length the idea struck her that her hair, which was of great beauty, and pride to her parents, might be of some value; and she accordingly set off one morning privately for Breslau, and disposed of her tresses for a couple of dollars. The hairdresser, however, with whom she had negotiated the bargain, being touched with the girl's conduct, reserved his purchase for the manufacture of bracelets and other ornaments; and, as the story became public, he in the end sold so many, that he was enabled, by this fair maiden's locks alone, to subscribe a hundred dollars to the exigencies of the state.

The Percy Anecdotes, 1823

Frederick William I of Prussia asked Sir Robert Sutton, at a review of his tall grenadiers, if he thought an equal number of Englishmen could beat them? 'Sir,' replied Sir Robert, 'I do not venture to assert that; but I know that half the number would try.'

A Book of Naval and Military Anecdotes, 1824

It was customary with Frederick the Great of Prussia, whenever a new soldier appeared in his guards, to ask three questions, viz., 'How old are you? How long have you been in my service? Are you satisfied with your pay and treatment?' It happened that a young soldier, a native of France, who had served in his own country, desired to enlist into the Prussian service, and his figure was such as to cause him to be immediately accepted. He was, however, totally ignorant of the German language, but his captain gave him notice that the King would ask him certain questions in that language the first time he saw him, and therefore instructed him to learn by heart the three answers which he was to make to the King. The soldier learned them by the next day; and as soon as he appeared in the ranks Frederick came up to interrogate him. His Majesty, however, happened to begin with the second question first; and asked him 'How long have you been in my service?' 'Twenty-one years', answered the soldier. The King, struck with his youth, which contradicted his answer, said to him much astonished, 'How old are you?' 'One year, an't please your Majesty.' Frederick, still more astonished, cried, 'You or I must certainly be bereft of his senses.' The soldier, who took this for the third question about 'pay and conditions', replied firmly, 'Both, an't please your Majesty.'

A Book of Naval and Military Anecdotes, 1824

SCOTTISH, or JACOBITE REBELLION, 1745–46

Battle of Culloden, 16th April 1746

The lovely lass o' Inverness,
Nae joy nor pleasure can she see;
For e'en and morn she cries, Alas!
And aye the saut tear blin's her ee;

Drumossie moor – Drumossie day –
A waefu' day it was to me!
For there I lost my father dear,
My father dear, and brethren three.

Their winding-sheet the bluidy clay,
Their graves are growing green to see:
And by them lies the dearest lad
That ever blest a woman's e'e!

Now wae to thee, thou cruel lord,
A bluidy man I trow thou be;
For mony a heart thou hast made said
That ne'er did wrong to thine or thee.

Robert Burns, 'The Lovely Lass o' Inverness', 1794

SEVEN YEARS WAR, 1756–63

Annapolis! Oh! yes Annapolis must be defended; to be sure, Annapolis should be defended – pray where is Annapolis?

Duke of Newcastle, 1756, quoted in F. W. Longman, *Frederick the Great and the Seven Years War*, 1881

When the army is landed, the business is half done.

James Wolfe, Letter to his father, 20th May 1758

I am sorry I can give Mrs Moss no other account of her husband than that he died at Münster. As to his things, what he had is lost. When a man goes into hospital, his wallet, with his necessaries, are sent with him, but nothing ever returns. Those that recover, seldom bring anything back, but those that die are stripped of all. I have lost nine men and have not heard of anything that belonged to them. It is a common practice for a nurse, when a man is in danger, to put him on a clean shirt, that he may die in it, and that it may become her perquisite.

Major Richard Davenport, Letter to his brother, 1759

On the subject of this so-called 'cannon-fever' I have often talked with officers of all ranks, as well as with valiant private soldiers. They assure me with one voice that anyone who maintains he has gone through battle, and never experienced this appalling fear, must be accounted a braggart or a liar. But they all talked about something which I have noted myself, namely that such a sensation is spread in such a way over the early, middle and final stages of the battle that the stronger men bear up the weaker ones, and that a general flight sets in only when this disabling fear affects the morale of the majority of the army, and the weak men carry the strong along with them.

Carl Daniel Cüster, *Bruchstück seines Campagnelebens im siebenjahrigen Kriege*, 1791

Some states have been enabled, by their geographical position, to defend themselves with advantage against immense force. The sea has repeatedly protected England against the fury of the whole continent. The Venetian government, driven from its possessions on the land, could still bid defiance to the confederates of Cambray from the Arsenal amidst the lagoons. More than one great and one well-appointed army, which regarded the shepherds of Switzerland as an easy prey, has perished in the passes of the Alps. Frederic had no such advantage. The form of his states, their situation, the nature of the ground, all were against him. His long, scattered, straggling territory, seemed to have been shaped with an express view to the convenience of invaders, and was protected by no sea, by no chain of hills. Scarcely any corner of it was a week's march from the territory of the enemy. The capital itself, in the event of war, would be constantly exposed to insult. In truth there was hardly a politician or a soldier in Europe who doubted that the conflict would be terminated in a very few days by the prostration of the house of Brandenburg.

T. B. Macaulay, *Essays: Frederic the Great*, 1846

By the fourth and fifth years of the war Frederick no longer commanded love, respect or even fear among the nearest and most intimate members of his suite. I can say this because I saw it with my own eyes. When we rode behind him there was a mischievous young brigade-major of the cavalry, called Wodtke, who set out to amuse us by going into comic contortions behind his back, imitating the way he sat in the saddle, pointing at him and so on. Wodtke bestowed on Frederick the nickname 'Grave Digger'. Later on he abbreviated it to 'Digger', and this is what he called the great hero when we came together in private and engaged in jokes and malicious talk.

G. H. Berenhörst, *Auch dem Nachlasse von Georg Heinrich von Berenhörst*, 1845–47

Two captains of the Champagne regiment, La Fenestre and d'Agay, had been mortal enemies for twenty-eight years, and had met seven times on the field of honour. La Fenestre had his head blown off by a cannon ball at Vellinghausen, but his partisans noted with a point of pride that a fragment of his skull put out d'Agay's right eye.

L. Kennett, *The French Armies in the Seven Years War*, 1969

Battle of Prague, 6th May 1757

By push of bayonets – no firing till you see the whites of their eyes.

Frederick the Great, battlefield order, 6th May 1757

Prague was one battle where a genuine cavalry shock took place. Afterwards I showed my officers 150 Prussian and Austrian cavalrymen who were lodged in a barn; nearly all of them had been wounded in the right arm between the hand and elbow.

C. E. Warnery, *Das Herrn Generalmajor von Warnery samliche Schriften*, 1785–91

He (Frederick the Great) walked around the Austrians like a cooper round a tub.

E. D. B. Hamley, *Operations of War*, 1923

Battle of Kölin, 18th June 1757

The incident is this: never whispered-of for near fifty years (so silent were the three); and endlessly tossed about since that; the sense of it not understood till almost now. The three parties were: King Frederick; Moritz of Dessau, leading-on the centre here; Moritz's young Nephew Franz, Heir of Dessau, a brisk lad of seventeen, learning War here as Aide-de-Camp to Moritz: the exact spot is not known to me, – probably the ground near that Inn of Slatislunz, or Golden Sun; between the foot of Frederick's-Berg and that: – fact indubitable, though kept dark so long. Moritz is marching with the centre, or main battle, that way, intending to wheel and turn hillwards, Kreczor-wise, as per order, certain furlongs ahead; when Frederick (having, so I can conceive it, seen from his Hill-top, how Hülsen had done Kreczor, altogether prosperous there; and what endless capability there was of prospering to all lengths and speeding the general winning, were Hülsen but supported soon enough, were there any safe short-cut to Hülsen) dashed from the Hill-top in hot haste towards Prince Moritz, General of the centre, intending to direct him upon such short-cut: and hastily said, with Olympian brevity and fire, 'Face to right *here*!' With Jove-like brevity, and in such blaze of Olympian fire as we may imagine. Moritz himself is of brief, crabbed, fiery mind, brief in temper; and answers to the effect, 'Impossible to attack the enemy here, your Majesty; postured as they are; and we with such orders gone abroad!' – 'Face to right, I tell you!' said the King, still more Olympian, and too emphatic for explaining. Moritz, I hope, paused, but rather think he did not, before remonstrating the second time; neither perhaps was his voice so low as it should have been: it is certain Frederick dashed quite up to Moritz at this second remonstrance, flashed out his sword (the only time he ever drew his sword in battle): and now, gone all to mere Olympian lightning and thunder-tone, asks in *this* attitude, '*Will Er* (Will He) obey orders then?' – Moritz fallen silent of remonstrance, with gloomy rapidity obeys.

Thomas Carlyle, *Frederick The Great*, 1858–65

Battle of Plassey, 23rd June 1757

It is scarcely hyperbole to say that tomorrow the whole Moghul empire is in our power.

Robert Clive, Letter, 24th June 1757

The battle commenced with a cannonade in which the artillery of the Nabob did scarcely any execution, while the few field-pieces of the English produced great effect. Several of the most distinguished officers in Surajah Dowlah's service fell. Disorder began to spread through his ranks. His own terror increased every moment. One of the conspirators urged on him the expediency of retreating. The insidious advice, agreeing as it did with what his own terrors suggested, was readily received. He ordered his army to fall back, and this order decided his fate. Clive snatched the moment, and ordered his troops to advance. The confused and dispirited multitude gave way before the onset of disciplined valour. No mob attacked by regular soldiers was ever more completely routed. The little band of Frenchmen, who alone ventured to confront the English, were swept away down the stream of fugitives. In an hour the forces of Surajah Dowlah were dispersed, never to reassemble. Only five hundred of the vanquished were slain. But their camp, their guns, their baggage, innumerable wagons, innumerable cattle, remained in the power of the conqueror. With the loss of twenty-two soldiers killed and fifty wounded, Clive had scattered an army of near sixty thousand men, and subdued an empire larger and more populous than Great Britain.

T. B. Macaulay, *Essays: Lord Clive*, 1840

There never was a battle in which the consequences were so vast, so immediate and so permanent.

Colonel Malleson, *The Decisive Battles of India*, 1883

It is not too much to say that the destiny of Europe hinged upon the conquest of Bengal.

Brooks Adams, *The Law of Civilization and Decay*, 1895

... Out of the field of Plassey and the victors' 18 dead there sprouted forth the power of the nineteenth century. Mammon now rode into supremacy to become the unchallenged god of the western world. Once in the lands of the rising sun western man had sought the Holy Sepulchre. That sun had long set, and now in those spiritually arid regions he found the almighty sovereign. What the Cross had failed to achieve, in a few blood-red years the trinity of piston, sword and coin accomplished: the subjection of the East and for a span of nearly 200 years the economic serfdom of the Oriental world.

J. F. C. Fuller, *The Decisive Battles of the Western World*, 1954–56

Battle of Rossbach, 5th November 1757

Strictly speaking, the battle of Rossbach merely afforded me the freedom to go in search of new dangers in Silesia.

Frederick the Great, *Works*, vol. IV

Battle of Leuthen, 5th December 1757

Gentlemen: The enemy stands behind his entrenchments armed to the teeth. We must attack him and win, or else perish. Nobody must think of getting through in any other way. If you don't like this you may resign and go home.

Frederick the Great, addressing his officers before the battle

I will attack them [the Austrians] even if they stood on the steeples of Breslau.

Frederick the Great, 1757, quoted in F. W. Longman, *Frederick the Great and the Seven Years War*, 1881

The victory of Leuthen is, to this day, the proudest on the Prussian roll of fame. Leipsic indeed, and Waterloo, produced consequences more important to mankind. But the glory of Leipsic must be shared by the Prussians with the Austrians and Russians; and at Waterloo the British infantry bore the burden and heat of the day. The victory of Rosbach was, in a military point of view, less honourable than that of Leuthen; for it was gained over an incapable general and a disorganized army; but the moral effect which it produced was immense. All the preceding triumphs of Frederic had been triumphs over Germans, and could excite no emotions of national pride among the German people. It was impossible that a Hessian or a Hanoverian could feel any patriotic exultation at hearing that Pomeranians had slaughtered Moravians, or that Saxon banners had been hung in the churches of Berlin. Indeed, though the military character of the Germans justly stood high throughout the world, they could boast of no great day which belonged to them as a people; of no Agincourt, of no Bannockburn. Most of their victories had been gained over each other; and their most splendid exploits against foreigners had been achieved under the command of Eugene, who was himself a foreigner. The news of the battle of Rosbach stirred the blood of the whole of the mighty population from the Alps to the Baltic, and from the borders of Courland to those of Loraine. Westphalia and Lower Saxony had been deluged by a great host of strangers, whose speech was unintelligible, and whose petulant and licentious manners had excited the strongest feelings of disgust and hatred. That great host had been put to flight by a small band of German warriors, led by a prince of German blood on the side of father and mother, and marked by the fair hair and clear blue eyes of Germany. Never since the dissolution of the empire of Charlemagne, had the Teutonic race won such a field against the French. The tidings called forth a general burst of delight and pride from the whole of the great family which spoke the various dialects of the ancient language of Arminius. The fame of Frederic began to supply, in some degree, the place of a common government and of a common capital. It became a rallying point for all true Germans, a subject of mutual congratulation to the Bavarian and the Westphalian, to the citizen of Frankfort and the citizen of Nuremburg. Then first it was manifest that the Germans were truly a nation. Then first was discernible the patriotic spirit which, in 1813, achieved the great deliverance of central Europe, which still guards, and long will guard, against foreign ambition the old freedom of the Rhine.

T. B. Macaulay, *Essays: Frederic the Great*, 1846

Battle of Zorndorf, 25th August 1758

During this litany the king chatted with Seydlitz, who was looking on with an amused and detached air. In due course Forcade [reading back Frederick's Orders on the eve of the battle] came to the sentence 'Tomorrow, by the grace of God, we shall have a battle!' Frederick was apparently concerned that Seydlitz might think he had turned to God in his time of trial, and he muttered to him: 'That's only for the baggage drivers!'

Field-Marshal F. A. Kalkreuth, *Kalkreuth zun seinem Leben und zu seiner Zeit*, 1840

My flank man's head was blown off, and his brains flew in my face. My spontoon was snatched out of my hand, and I received a canister ball on my gorget, smashing the enamelled medallion. I drew my sword, and the tassel of the sword knot was shot away. A ball went through the skirts of my coat, and another knocked my hat aside, stripping the knot from the band in the process.

C. Hülsen, *Unter Friedrich dem Grossen*, 1890

Was there ever seen such a fight of Theseus and the Minotaur! Theseus, rapid, dextrous, with Heaven's lightning in his eyes, seizing the Minotaur; lassoing him by the hinder feet, then by the right horn; pouring steel and destruction into him, the very dust darkening all the air. Minotaur refusing to die when killed; tumbling to and fro upon its Theseus; the two lugging and tugging, flinging one another about, and describing figures of 8 round each other for three days before it ended.

Thomas Carlyle, *Frederick The Great*, 1858–65

Frederick: That was a diabolical day. Did you understand what was going on?
Catt: Your Majesty, I had a good grasp of the preliminary march, and the first arrangements for the battle. But all the rest escaped me. I could make no sense of the various movements.
Frederick: You were not the only one, my dear friend. Console yourself, you weren't the only one!

Heinrich de Catt, *Unterhaltüngen mit Friedrich der Grossen*, 1884

Battle of Hochkirk, 14th October 1758

Lord Keith: If the Austrians leave us unmolested in this camp, they deserve to be hanged.
Frederick the Great: It is to be hoped they are more afraid of us than of the gallows.

F. W. Longman, *Frederick the Great and the Seven Years War*, 1881

Battle of Minden, 1st August 1759

I have seen what I never thought to be possible: a single line of infantry break through three lines of cavalry ranked in order of battle, and tumble them to ruin.

Marquis de Contades, in John Laffin, *Tommy Atkins*, 1966

. . . A corps of French grenadiers, commanded by M. N. Perer, were exposed to a battery that carried off whole files at once. N. Perer wishing them not to fall back, rode slowly in front of the line with his snuff-box in his hand, and said, 'Well, my boys, what's the matter? Eh, cannon! Well, it kills you, it kills you, that's all, my boys; march on, and never mind it.'

The Percy Anecdotes, 1823

Quebec: Battle on the Plains of Abraham, 13th September 1759

Let not my brave soldiers see me drop. The day is ours. Keep it.

James Wolfe, after he had been mortally wounded

After our late worthy General, of renowned memory, was carried off wounded to the rear of the front line, he desired those who were about him to lay him down; being asked if he would have a surgeon, he replied, 'it is needless; it is all over with me.' One of them cried out, 'They run, see how they run.' 'Who runs?' demanded our hero with great earnestness, like a person aroused from sleep. The Officer answered, 'The Enemy, Sir; Egad, they give way everywhere.' Thereupon the General rejoined, 'Go one of you, my lads, to Colonel Burton; tell him to march Webb's regiment with all speed down to Charles's river, to cut off the retreat of the fugitives from the bridge.' Then, turning to one side, he added, 'Now, God be praised, I will die in peace'; and thus expired.

Captain John Knox, quoted in J. Freeman, *The Englishman at War*, 1941

Peace of Hubertsburg, February 1763

The war was over. Frederic was safe. His glory was beyond the reach of envy. If he had not made conquests as vast as those of Alexander, of Caesar, and of Napoleon, if he had not, on fields of battle, enjoyed the constant success of Marlborough and Wellington, he had yet given an example unrivalled in history of what capacity and resolution can effect against the greatest superiority of power and the utmost spite of fortune. He entered Berlin in triumph, after an absence of more than six years. The streets were brilliantly lighted up, and, as he passed along in an open carriage, with Ferdinand of Brunswick at his side, the multitude saluted him with loud praises and blessings. He was moved by those marks of attachment, and repeatedly exclaimed, 'Long live my dear people! Long live my children!' Yet, even in the midst of that gay spectacle, he could not but perceive every where the traces of destruction and decay. The city had been more than once plundered. The population had considerably diminished. Berlin, however, had suffered little when compared with most parts of the kingdom. The ruin of private fortunes, the distress of all ranks, was such as might appal the firmest mind. Almost every province had been the seat of war, and of war conducted with merciless ferocity. Clouds of Croatians had descended on Silesia. Tens of thousands of Cossacks had been let loose on Pomerania and Brandenburg. The mere contributions levied by invaders amounted, it was said, to more than a hundred millions of dollars; and the value of what they extorted was probably much less than the value of what they destroyed. The fields lay uncultivated. The very seed-corn had been devoured in the madness of hunger. Famine, and contagious maladies produced by famine, had swept away the herds and flocks; and there was reason to fear that a great pestilence among the human race was likely to follow in the train of that tremendous war. Near fifteen thousand houses had been burned to the ground. The population of the kingdom had in seven years decreased to the frightful extent of ten per cent. A sixth of the males capable of bearing arms had actually perished on the field of battle. In some districts no labourers, except women, were seen in the fields of harvest-time. In others, the traveller passed shuddering through a succession of silent villages, in which not a single inhabitant remained. The currency had been debased; the authority of laws and magistrates had been suspended; the whole social system was deranged. For, during that convulsive struggle, every thing that was not military violence was anarchy.

T. B. Macaulay, *Essays: Frederic the Great*, 1846

THE AMERICAN REVOLUTION and WAR OF INDEPENDENCE, 1775–83

Indeed, my lord, I don't know whether the neighbourhood of the French to our North American colonies was not the greatest security for their dependence on the mother country, which I feel will be slighted by them when their apprehension of the French is removed.

Duke of Bedford, Letter to the Duke of Newcastle, 9th May 1761

I conclude saying, I wish there was a war.

Alexander Hamilton, aged 12, Letter to a classmate, 1767

Four or five frigates will do the business without any military force.

Lord North, in the House of Commons, 1774

The use of force alone is but temporary. It may subdue for a moment; but it does not remove the necessity of subduing again: and a nation is not governed which is perpetually to be conquered.

Edmund Burke, speech, 22nd March 1775

The battle is not to the strong alone; it is to the vigilant, the active, the brave.

Patrick Henry, to the Virginia Convention, 23rd March 1775

If you think ten thousand men enough, send twenty; if a million is thought enough, give two; you will save both blood and Treasure in the end.

General Gage, message to the British Government, April 1775

There is a time to pray and a time to fight. This is the time to fight.

John Peter Gabriel Mühlenberg, sermon at Woodstock, Virginia, 1775

And there we see a swampin' gun
As big as a log of maple,
Upon a deuced little cart,
A load for father's cattle.
And every time they shoot it off
It takes a horn of powder,
And makes a noise like father's gun,
Only a nation louder.

Edward Bangs, 'Yankee Doodle', 1775

I rejoice that America has resisted. Three millions of people, so dead to all feelings of liberty, as voluntarily to submit to be slaves, would have been fit instruments to make slaves of the rest.

Lord Chatham, in the House of Commons, 14th January 1776

A Freeman contending for Liberty on his own ground is superior to any slavish mercenary on earth.

George Washington, General Order to the Continental Army, 2nd July 1776

I only regret that I have but one life to lose for my country.

Nathan Hale, prior to being hanged as a spy by the British, 22nd September 1776

Without a respectable Navy – alas America!

John Paul Jones, Letter to Robert Morris, 17th October 1776

These are the times that try men's souls. The summer soldier and the sunshine patriot will, in this crisis, shrink from the service of their country; but he that stands it now deserves the love and thanks of man and woman.

Thomas Paine, *The Crisis*, 1776

Don't Tread On Me
Motto on the flag of the *Rattlesnake*

The officers will take all proper opportunities to inculcate in their men's minds a reliance on the bayonet; men of their bodily strength and even a coward may be their match in firing. But a bayonet in the hands of the valiant is irresistible.
General Burgoyne, General Orders, June 1777

If I were an American, as I am an Englishman, while a foreign troop was landed in my country, I would never lay down my arms – never – never – never!
Lord Chatham (Pitt the Elder), in the House of Lords, 18th November 1777

Yr Excellency will have observed that whatever efforts are made by the Land Armies, the Navy must have the casting vote in the present contest.
George Washington, Letter to the Comte de Grasse, 28th October 1781

It follows then as certain as night follows day, that without a decisive naval force we can do nothing definite, and with it everything honourable and glorious.
George Washington, Letter to the Marquis de Lafayette, 15th November 1781

Oh God! It is all over!
Lord George Germain, receiving news of Cornwallis's surrender, 25th November 1781

I have seen enough of one war never to wish to see another.
Thomas Jefferson, Letter to John Adams, 1794

When Patrick Henry, who gave the first impulse to the ball of the American revolution, introduced his celebrated resolution on the stamp act into the House of Representatives in Virginia (May, 1765), he exclaimed, when descanting on the tyranny of the obnoxious act, 'Caesar had his Brutus; Charles the First his Cromwell; and George the Third' – 'Treason!' cried the Speaker; 'treason! treason!' echoed from every part of the house. It was one of those trying moments which are decisive of character. Henry faultered not for an instant; but rising to a loftier attitude, and fixing on the speaker an eye flashing with fire, continued, '*may profit by their example*. If this be treason, make the most of it.'
The Percy Anecdotes, 1823

A meeting was called in Boston, in consequence of some new inroads upon the rights and liberties of the people. [Samuel] Adams, who sat silent, at last rose, and after a few remarks, concluded with saying, 'A Grecian philosopher, who was lying asleep on the grass, was roused by the bite of some animal upon the palm of his hand. He closed his hand suddenly, as he awoke, and found that he had caught a field mouse. As he was examining the little animal who dared to attack him, it unexpectedly bit him a second time; he dropped it, and it made its escape. Now, fellow-citizens, what do you think was the reflection he made upon this trifling circumstance? It was this: that there is no animal, however weak and contemptible, which cannot defend its liberty, if only it will *fight* for it.
The Percy Anecdotes, 1823

If the military merit of the American people, as it appeared during the revolutionary war, be estimated fairly, it does not stand high even in partizan war. The Americans were soldiers from necessity – not from genius or inclination. They did not proceed to the combat with a mind inflamed with ideas of national glory. They had little of military enterprize in the constitution originally; and they made little scientific progress in the military art during the continuance of the contest. They advanced boldly to action in several instances; they maintained no combat obstinately. The cover of a bank, a tree, or a fence, was necessary to give them confidence to look at their antagonist. They exercised the firelock with effect while they were under cover; they retired when the enemy approached near, that is, they split and squandered, according to the cant phrase, to rally at an assigned point in the rear.

Robert Jackson, *A View of the Formation, Discipline and Economy of Armies*, 1845

The war which rent away the North American colonies from England is, of all subjects in history, the most painful for an Englishman to dwell on. It was commenced and carried on by the British ministry in iniquity and folly, and it was concluded in disaster and shame. But the contemplation of it cannot be evaded by the historian, however much it may be abhorred.

Edward Creasy, *The Fifteen Decisive Battles of the World*, 1851

Woe to the English soldiery,
That little dreads us near!
On them shall come at midnight
A strange and sudden fear;
When, waking to their tents on fire,
They grasp their arms in vain,
And they who stand to face us
Are beat to earth again;
And they who fly in terror deem
A mighty host behind,
And hear the tramp of thousands
Upon the hollow wind.

William Cullen Bryant, 'Song of Marion's Men', 1832

It was a blameless insurrection, founded on equity and quotations from Blackstone, a sedate rebellion, a sedition of the highest principles.

Philip Guedalla, *Fathers of the Revolution*, 1926

Skirmish at Concord, 19th April 1775

By the rude bridge that arched the flood,
  Their flag to April's breeze unfurled,
Here once the embattled farmers stood,
  And fired the shot heard round the world.

The foe long since in silence slept;
  Alike the conqueror silent sleeps;
And Time the ruined bridge has swept
  Down the dark stream which seaward creeps.

On this green bank, by this soft stream,
  We set today a votive stone;
That memory may their deed redeem,
  When like our sires, our sons are gone.

Spirit, that made these heroes dare
  To die, and leave their children free,
Bid Time and Nature gently spare
  The shaft we raise to them and thee.

Ralph Waldo Emerson, 'Concord Hymn', 1836

It was two by the village clock,
When he came to the bridge in Concord town.
He heard the bleating of the flock,
And the twitter of birds among the trees,
And felt the breath of the morning breeze
Blowing over the meadows brown.
And one was safe and asleep in his bed
Who at the bridge would be first to fall,
Who that day would be lying dead,
Pierced by a British musket-ball.
  You know the rest. In the books you have read,
How the British Regulars fired and fled –
How the farmers gave them ball for ball,
From behind each fence and farm-yard wall,
Chasing the Red-coats down the lane,
Then crossing the fields to emerge again
Under the trees at the turn of the road,
And only pausing to fire and load.
  So through the night rode Paul Revere;
And so through the night went his cry of alarm
To every Middlesex village and farm –
A cry of defiance and not of fear,
A voice in the darkness, a knock at the door,
And a word that shall echo for evermore!
For, borne on a night-wind of the Past,
Through all our history, to the last,
In the hour of darkness and peril and need,
The people will waken and listen to hear
The hurrying hoof-beats of that steed,
And the midnight message of Paul Revere.

Henry Wadsworth Longfellow, 'Paul Revere's Ride', 1863

Battle of Lexington Green, 19th April 1775

Stand your ground, men. Don't fire unless fired upon. But if they mean to have a war, let it begin here.

Captain Jonas Parker, addressing the Minute Men after British troops had deployed against them.

Surrender of Fort Ticonderoga, 10th May 1775

I ordered the Commander, Captain de la Place, to come forth instantly, or I would sacrifice the whole garrison; at which the Captain came immediately to the door, with his breeches in his hand, when I ordered him to deliver the fort instantly. He asked by what authority I demanded it, I answered him, 'In the name of the great Jehovah, and the Continental Congress.' The authority of the Congress being very little known at that time, he began to speak again, I interrupted him, and, with my drawn sword over his head, again demanded an immediate surrender of the garrison, with which he then complied.

Ethan Allen, Report, 1775

Battle of Bunker's Hill, 17th June 1775

Don't one of you fire until you see the whites of their eyes.

Israel Putnam, attributed

Let our object be, our country, our whole country, and nothing but our country.

Daniel Webster, laying the corner-stone of the Bunker Hill Monument, 17th June 1825

Now deeper roll the maddening drums,
And the mingling host like ocean heaves:
While from the midst a horrid wailing comes,
And high above the fight, the lonely bugle grieves.

Granville Mellen, 'Ode on the Celebration of the Battle of Bunker Hill', 1825

Battle of White Plains, 28th October 1776

Some of the bodies had been so slightly buried that the dogs or pigs, or both, had dug them out of the ground. The skulls and other bones and hair were scattered about the place. Here were Hessian skulls as thick as a bombshell. Poor fellows! They were left unburied in a foreign land.

J. P. Martin, *Private Yankee Doodle*, 1962

Princeton – skirmish, 3rd January 1777

An old fashioned Virginia fox-hunt, Gentlemen.

George Washington, attributed

Staten Island – skirmish, 22nd June 1777

When they were about 100 yards apart from each other both parties fired, but I did not observe any fall. They still advanced to a distance of 40 yards or less, and fired again. Our people then rushed upon them with their bayonets and the others took to their heels; I heard one of them call out *Murder!* lustily.

Nicholas Cresswell, *The Journal of Nicholas Cresswell 1774–1777*, 1924

Battle of Bennington, 16th August 1777

There, my boys, are your enemies, red-coats and Tories. We beat them today – or Molly Stark's a widow.

General John Stark, addressing his troops.

Their muskets were charged with old nails and angular pieces of iron, and from most of the men being wounded in the legs I am inclined to believe it was their design, not wishing to kill the men, to leave them as burdens on us, to exhaust their provisions, as well as to intimidate the rest of the soldiery.

Unidentified English surgeon, 1777, in F. Moore, *Diary of the American Revolution*, 1860

Battle of Stillwater (Saratoga), 7th October 1777

Towards midnight the body of General Frazer was buried in the British camp. His brother officers assembled sadly round while the funeral service was read over the remains of their brave comrade, and his body was committed to the hostile earth. The ceremony, always mournful and solemn of itself, was rendered even more terrible by the sense of recent losses, of present and future dangers, and of regret for the deceased. Meanwhile the blaze and roar of the American artillery amid the natural darkness and stillness of the night came on the senses with startling awe. The grave had been dug within range of the enemy's batteries; and while the service was proceeding a cannon-ball struck the ground close to the coffin and spattered earth over the face of the officiating chaplain.

Carlo G. G. Botta, *The American War*, 1812–13: Bk viii

The American Army at Valley Forge, Winter 1777–78

You might have attacked the army from White Marsh to Valley Forge by the blood of their feet.

George Washington, attributed

Imitating bird calls suggests that the troops' sense of humour saw them through the worst of their sufferings. They had their hatreds, too, and these also may have helped sustain them. One was firecake, a thin bread made of flour and water and baked over the campfire. Another was the commissaries who were supposed to provide food for the army. [Albigence] Waldo reconstructed a number of conversations along the following lines: 'What have you for your dinners, boys?' 'Nothing but firecake and water, Sir.' At night: 'Gentlemen, the supper is ready. What is your supper, lads?' 'Firecake and water, Sir.' In the morning: 'What have you got for breakfast, lads?' 'Firecake and water, Sir.' And from Waldo, the snarl: 'The Lord send that our Commissary of Purchases may live firecake and water till their glutted guts are turned to pasteboard.'

Robert Middlekauft, *The Glorious Cause: The American Revolution 1763–89*, 1982

The snow lies thick on Valley Forge,
The ice on Delaware,
But the poor dead soldiers of King George
They neither know nor care.

Rudyard Kipling, 'The American Rebellion', 1906

Siege of Savannah, 1779

An English aunt sent [Samuel Warren] word that if the report was true she hoped he would have an arm or a leg shot off in his first battle. She had her wish, as he lost one on 9th October. After the war, he placed the leg bone in an elephant mahogany case to which he affixed a plate bearing the date of the loss. This Warren sent to his aunt with a note to the effect that, while her wish had been fulfilled, he would rather be a rebel with one leg than a royalist with two.

William B. Stevens, in A. L. Lawrence, *Storm Over Savannah*, 1951

Siege of Yorktown, September–October 1781

The bombshells from the besiegers and the besieged are incessantly crossing each other's path in the sky. They are clearly in the form of a black ball in the day, but in the night, they appear like a fiery meteor with a blazing trail, most beautifully brilliant, ascending majestically from the mortar to a certain altitude, and gradually descending to the spot where they are destined to execute their work of destruction.

James Thacher, *Military Journal of the American Revolution*, 1862

Surrender of Yorktown and End to Hostilities, 19th October 1781

The play, sir, is over. Washington has given a dinner for British General O'Hara.

Lafayette, Letter to a friend, 22nd October 1781

THE FRENCH REVOLUTION AND THE WARS OF NAPOLEON, 1789–1815

But let us suppose that a vigorous people were to arise in Europe: a people of genius, of resources and of political understanding: a people who united with these sterling virtues and with a national militia a fixed plan of aggrandizement, and never lost sight of it: a people who know how to make war cheaply and sustain itself on its victories. Such a people would not be compelled to limit their fighting by financial calculations. One would see this people subjugate their neighbours, and overthrow our feeble constitutions, like the north wind bends the frail reeds.

Comte de Guibert, *Essai Général de Tactique*, 1773

Louis XVI: Is this a revolt?
Duke of Rochefoucauld-Liancourt: No, sir, it's a revolution.

Attributed exchange, after the fall of the Bastille, 1789

Liberté! Égalité! Fraternité!
[Liberty! Equality! Brotherhood!]

Slogan adopted by the Revolutionaries, 1789

War to the castles, peace to the cottages.

Nicolas Chamfort, Motto for the Revolution, 1790

Whenever our neighbour's house is on fire, it cannot be amiss for the engines to play a little on our own.

Edmund Burke, *Reflections on the French Revolution*, 1790

The young men shall fight. The married man shall forge weapons and transport supplies. The women shall make tents and clothes and will serve in the hospitals. The children shall convert old linen into lint. The old men shall have themselves carried into the public squares to arouse the courage of the fighting men, to preach hatred against kings and the unity of the Republic. Public buildings shall be turned into barracks, the squares converted into munitions factories.

Promulgation of the National Convention, 23rd August 1793

A war of all peoples against all kings.

Decree issued by the Directory, 1793

Oh Liberty! Liberty! what crimes are committed in your name!

Madame Roland, on her way to be guillotined, 1793

Laurels grow in the Bay of Biscay – I hope a bed of them may be found in the Mediterranean.

Horatio Nelson, Letter to Sir George Elliot, 4th August 1794

Our wives are now about going to church, but we will ring about these Frenchmen's ears a peal which will drown their bells.

Cuthbert Collingwood, aboard HMS *Barfleur*, 1st June 1794

No price is too great to preserve the health of the fleet.

Lord St Vincent, Letter to the Admiralty, 1796

A fleet of British ships of war are the best negotiators in Europe.

Horatio Nelson, Letter to Lady Hamilton, March 1801

I do not say the Frenchman will not come; I only say he will not come by sea.

Lord St Vincent, at the British Admiralty, 1803

A stands for ATTENTION, the first word he knows,
And B stands for BULLET, to tickle his foes.
C stands for a CHARGE, which the Frenchmen all dread;
And D stands for DISCHARGE, which soon lays them dead.
Next E begins EASE, at which sometimes he stands;
And F bids to FIGHT, when our enemy lands.
G stands for GENERAL, GRAPESHOT and GUN,
Which together combined must make Buonaparte run.
Then H begins HONOUR, to soldiers full dear;
And J stands for JUSTICE, which next they revere.
But K bids them KILL, for their country and King,
For whose health each true Briton doth joyfully sing.
L is LOVE, which the soldier will often times feel,
And M bids him MERCY, when conqu'ror, to deal.
N stands for a NATION, of Englishmen free;
And O for OUTPOST – but ours is the sea.
The P stands for PICKET, and for PIONEER;
And Q shows our enemies QUAKING with fear.
Next R stands for REGIMENT and ROLL of the drums;
And S for SALUTE when the general comes.

So T both for TOUCH-HOLE and TRIGGER may stand:
And V for the brave VOLUNTEERS of this land.
Then W whispers that WAR soon may cease:
And X, Y and Z will rejoice at the peace.

Anonymous, *Britannic Magazine*, 1804

England has saved herself by her exertions; and will, I trust, save Europe by her example.

William Pitt (the Younger), in the House of Commons, 9th November 1805

I have destroyed the enemy merely by marching.

Napoleon Bonaparte, attributed, 1805, after the end of his Austrian Campaign

You can't stop me. I spend thirty thousand men a month.

Napoleon Bonaparte, to Metternich, 1810

Antwerp is a pistol pointed at the heart of England.

Napoleon Bonaparte, attributed, *c.* 1810

Bad luck to this marching,
Pipe-claying and starching;
How neat one must be to be killed by the French!

British soldier's song, from the Peninsula, 1811

The British infantry is the best in the world. Fortunately it is not numerous.

Marshal Bugeaud, in the Peninsula, attributed, 1812

You must hate a Frenchman as you hate the devil.

Horatio Nelson, in Robert Southey, *Life of Nelson*, 1813

France is invaded: I go to place myself at the head of my troops.

Napoleon Bonaparte, in Paris, 23rd January 1814

How much might have been done with a hundred thousand soldiers such as these.

Napoleon Bonaparte, inspecting the guard of Marines aboard HMS *Bellerophon*, 15th July 1815

Wherever wood can swim, there I am sure to find this flag of England.

Napoleon Bonaparte, at Rochefort, July 1815

The English conquered us; but they are far from being our equals.

Napoleon Bonaparte, Letter to Gaspard Gourgaud, from St Helena, 1815

In these operations, and especially in the campaigns of Buonaparte, the conduct of War attained to that unlimited degree of energy which we have represented as the natural law of the element. This degree is therefore possible, and if it is possible then it is necessary.

Karl von Clausewitz, *On War*, 1832: III

We may therefore say, that the twenty years' victories of the Revolution are chiefly to be ascribed to the erroneous policy of the Governments by which it was opposed.

Karl von Clausewitz, *On War*, 1832: V

France was long a despotism tempered by epigrams.

Thomas Carlyle, *History of the French Revolution*, 1837

The whiff of grapeshot can, if needful, become a blast and tempest.

Thomas Carlyle, *History of the French Revolution*, 1837

Battles, even in these ages, are transacted by mechanism; men now even die, and kill one another, in an artificial manner.

Thomas Carlyle, *History of the French Revolution*, 1837

Pile the bodies high at Austerlitz and Waterloo,
Shovel them under and let me work –
I am the grass; I cover all.

Carl Sandburg, 'Grass', 1916

So impressive was the aggrandizement of England beyond the seas, that some writers have regarded the augmentation of the British Empire as the most important result of Napoleon's career.

H. A. L. Fisher, in *The Cambridge Modern History*, 1934

The scope and intensity of war is determined by its social and political frame. The wars of the eighteenth century had been fought by small ruling groups – the king, the court, even in parliamentary England by the gentry. War had been a matter of limited liability and limited purpose. The new doctrine of liberty and equality burst this narrow frame. With the Revolution, the masses with all their passions, frustrations, ignorance and idealism stepped into politics. The French armies were no longer the instrument of a limited materialistic policy, but of an ideological crusade. They were now the vehicle of all the physical and emotional resources of the French nation. Ruthless leadership was to enlist these resources by means impossible to the *ancien régime*: conscription, requisition, central direction. The objectives of war became no less far-reaching: instead of a town or a colony or a province, the very survival of opposed ideologies and social systems. The French Revolution imparted to war a new and appalling power.

Correlli Barnett, *Britain and Her Army, 1509–1970*, 1970

The Battle of Valmy, 20th September 1792

I had now arrived quite in the region where the balls were playing across me: the sound of them is curious enough, as if it were composed of the humming of tops, the gurgling of water, and the whistling of birds. They were less dangerous by reason of the wetness of the ground; wherever one fell, it stuck fast. And thus my foolish experimental ride was secured at least against the danger of the balls rebounding.

J. W. von Goethe, *Campaign in France*, 1792

In the midst of these circumstances I was soon able to remark that something unusual was taking place within me: I paid close attention to it, and still the sensation can be described only by similitude. It appeared as if you were in some extremely hot place, and at the same time quite penetrated by the heat of it, so that you feel yourself, as it were, quite one with the element in which you are. The eyes lose nothing of their strength or clearness; but it is as if the world had a kind of brown-red tint, which makes the situation, as well as the surrounding objects, more impressive. I was unable to perceive any agitation of the blood; but every thing seemed rather to be swallowed up in the glow of which I speak. From this, then, it is clear in what sense this condition can be called a fever. It is remarkable, however, that the horrible uneasy feeling arising from it is produced in us solely through the ears. For the cannon-thunder, the howling, whistling, crashing of the balls through the air is the real cause of these sensations.

J. W. von Goethe, *Campaign in France*, 1792

At last I was called upon to say what I thought of it; for I had been in the habit of enlivening and amusing the troop with short sayings. This time I said: 'From this place and from this day forth commences a new era in the world's history, and you can all say that you were present at its birth.'

J. W. von Goethe, *Campaign in France*, 1792

All these preparations were made contrary to the wish of the colonel, who made us observe that the French had a battery standing upon a hill opposite to us, behind a copsewood, with which they could bury us in real earnest, and annihilate us at their pleasure. But we could not abandon the sheltered spot and our sagaciously invented snuggery; and this was not the last time that I remarked, that people do not shun danger to escape from inconvenience.

J. W. von Goethe, *Campaign in France*, 1792

. . . I may as well mention that, in the midst of all this wretchedness, I made this whimsical vow: I swore that if we escaped, and I reached home in safety, nobody should ever hear me complain of the interruption to the view from my chamber-window caused by the projecting gable of the next house, which now, on the contrary, I ardently longed to behold; further, I would never complain of want of comfort in the German theatre, where you can always thank God, at least, that you are under cover, whatever may be taking place on the stage.

J. W. von Goethe, *Campaign in France*, 1792

After Valmy, every Frenchman who held a sword or musket in his hand looked on himself as the champion of a cause destined to triumph.

Arthur Chuquet, *Les guerres de la révolution*, *c.* 1793

Battle of Cape St Vincent, 14th February 1797

Westminster Abbey or Victory!

Horatio Nelson, in Robert Southey, *Life of Nelson*, 1813

Battle of the Pyramids, 21st July 1798

Soldiers! Think how from the tops of these pyramids forty centuries look down upon you!

Napoleon Bonaparte, addressing his army before the battle

Battle of the Nile, 1st August 1798

Before this time tomorrow I shall have gained a peerage, or Westminster Abbey.

Horatio Nelson, before the battle, in Robert Southey, *Life of Nelson*, 1813

In this battle the French had a superiority over the British of one hundred and eighty-four guns, and three thousand one hundred and eighty-two men; yet they lost five sail taken, three sail burnt, one driven on shore and fired, and three frigates. 'A victory,' said the gallant Nelson, 'is not a word strong enough for such an achievement; it should be called a conquest.' From Bonaparte it drew this acknowledgment. 'The destinies have wished to prove by this event, as by all others, that if they have given us a great preponderance on the Continent, they have given the empire of the sea to our rivals.'

The Percy Anecdotes, 1823

The boy stood on the burning deck,
Whence all but he had fled;
The flame that lit the battle's wreck
Shone round him o'er the dead.

Felicia Hemans, referring to the son of the *Orient*'s captain, 'Casabianca', *c.* 1820

Battle of Marengo, 14th June 1800

This battle is lost, but there is still time to gain another.

Marshal Desaix, to Napoleon, at about 4.00 p.m.

We have retired far enough for today; you know I always sleep on the field of battle.

Napoleon Bonaparte, attributed

Battle of Hohenlinden, 3rd December 1800

The combat deepens. On, ye brave,
Who rush to glory, or the grave!
Wave, Munich! all thy banners wave,
  And charge with all thy chivalry!

Few, few shall part, where many meet!
The snow shall be their winding-sheet,
And every turf beneath their feet
  Shall be a soldier's sepulchre.

Thomas Campbell, 'Hohenlinden', 1802

Battle of Copenhagen, 2nd April 1801

While the negotiation is going on, the Dane should see our flag every moment he lifts his head.

Horatio Nelson, to Sir Hyde Parker, 20th March 1801

It is warm work; and this day may be the last to any of us at a moment. But mark you! I would not be elsewhere for thousands!

Horatio Nelson, in Robert Southey, *Life of Nelson*, 1813

'Do you know,' said he [Nelson] to Mr Ferguson, 'what is shown on board the commander-in-chief? No. 39!' Mr Ferguson asked what that meant? – 'Why, to leave off action! Now damn me if I do! You know, Foley,' turning to the captain, 'I have only one eye, – I have a right to be blind sometimes,' – and then putting the glass to his blind eye, in that mood of mind which sports with bitterness, he exclaimed, 'I really do not see the signal!' Presently he exclaimed, 'Damn the signal! Keep mine for closer battle flying! That's the way I answer such signals. Nail mine to the mast!'

Robert Southey, *Life of Nelson*, 1813

Of Nelson and the North,
Sing the glorious day's renown,
When to battle fierce came forth
All the might of Denmark's crown,
And her arms along the deep proudly shone;
By each gun the lighted brand
In a bold determined hand,
And the Prince of all the land
Led them on.

Like leviathans afloat
Lay their bulwarks on the brine;
While the sign of battle flew
On the lofty British line:
It was ten of April morn by the chime:
As they drifted on their path
There was silence deep as death;
And the boldest held his breath
For a time.

But the might of England flush'd
To anticipate the scene;
And her van the fleeter rush'd
O'er the deadly space between.
'Hearts of oak!' our captains cried, when each gun
From its adamantine lips
Spread a death-shade round the ships,
Like the hurricane eclipse
Of the sun.

Thomas Campbell, 'Battle of the Baltic', 1808

Battle of Trafalgar, 21st October 1805

I trust you are now at Brest. Sail, do not lose a moment, and with my squadrons reunited enter the Channel. England is ours. We are ready and embarked. Appear for forty-eight hours, and all will be ended.

Napoleon Bonaparte, dispatch to Villeneuve, 22nd August 1805

But, in case signals can neither be seen or perfectly understood, no Captain can do very wrong if he places his ship alongside that of an enemy.
Horatio Nelson, to his captains, 9th October 1805

May the great God, whom I worship, grant to my country and for the benefit of Europe in general, a great and glorious victory, and may no misconduct in anyone tarnish it, and may humanity after the victory be the predominant feature of the British fleet.
Horatio Nelson, diary entry, 21st October 1805

England expects every man will do his duty.
Horatio Nelson, flag signal to the British Fleet

Any captain who isn't within the line of fire isn't where he should be.
Admiral Villeneuve, flag signal to the French Fleet

[Death of Nelson] Presently, calling Hardy back, he said to him, in a low voice, 'Don't throw me overboard'; and he desired that he might be buried by his parents, unless it should please the king to order otherwise. Then, reverting to his private feelings: 'Take care of my dear Lady Hamilton, Hardy; take care of poor Lady Hamilton. – Kiss me, Hardy,' said he. Hardy knelt down and kissed his cheek: and Nelson said, 'Now I am satisfied. Thank God, I have done my duty.'
Robert Southey, *Life of Nelson*, 1813

Lover of England, stand awhile and gaze
With thankful heart, and lips refrained from praise;
They rest beyond the speech of human pride
Who served with Nelson and with Nelson died.
Henry Newbolt, 'For a Trafalgar Cenotaph', 1898

Without Trafalgar there could have been no Peninsular War, and without the Peninsular War it is hard to believe there would ever have been a Waterloo.
J. F. C. Fuller, *The Decisive Battles of the Western World*, 1954–56

Battle of Jena, 14th October 1806

The wine is poured and we must drink it.
Marshal Ney, order to French troops to advance, 14th October 1806

When soldiers brave death they drive him into the lines of the enemy.
Napoleon Bonaparte, attributed, shortly after Jena

Another year! – another deadly blow!
Another mighty empire overthrown!
And we are left, or shall be left alone;
The last that dare to struggle with the foe.
William Wordsworth, 'November, 1806', 1806

Battle of Friedland, 14th June 1807

Over half of our brave regiment fell in this fierce and unsuccessful battle. Several times we attacked, several times we repulsed the enemy, and in turn we ourselves were driven back more than once. We were showered with caseshot and smashed by cannonballs, and the shrill whine of the hellish bullets has completely deafened me. Oh, I cannot bear them! The ball is a different matter. It roars so majestically at least, and there are always brief intervals in between. After some hours of heated battle, the remnants of our regiment were ordered to pull back a little to rest. I took advantage of it to go watch the operations of our artillery, without stopping to think that I might get my head torn off for no good reason. Bullets were showering me and my horse, but what do bullets matter beside the savage, increasing roar of the cannons?

Nadezhda Durova, *The Cavalry Maiden*, 1836

The Peninsular War, or War of Spanish Independence, 1808–14

I don't know what effect these men will have on the enemy, but, by God, they frighten me.

Duke of Wellington, 1809, receiving a fresh draft of troops from Britain.

Ours [the British Army] is composed of the scum of the earth – the mere scum of the earth. The British soldiers are fellows who have all enlisted for drink – that is the plain fact – they have all enlisted for drink.

Duke of Wellington, Letter from Portugal, 1809

I shall see that no officer under my command is debarred by attending to the futile quill-driving in your Lordship's office, from attending to his first duty, which is, and always has been, so to train the private men under his command that they may without question beat any force opposed to them in the field.

Duke of Wellington, Letter to the Secretary of State for War, 1810

You, sir, have an army; we have a travelling brothel.

Remark allegedly made by a captured French officer, to Wellington, Spain, 1810

. . . Our ministers may depend upon it that they cannot establish anywhere such a system as they have here; that they cannot anywhere keep in check so large a proportion of Buonaparte's army, with such small comparative British means; that they cannot anywhere be principals, and carry on the war upon their own responsibility, at so cheap a rate of men and means as they can here; that no seat of operations holds out such prospects of success, whatever may happen elsewhere, even for the attainment of those objects which would be in view in transferring the seat of war to the north of Europe.

Duke of Wellington, Letter to Lord Sydenham, from Freneda, 7th December 1811

Do the business of the day on the day.

Duke of Wellington, attributed, 1811

Napoleon's troops fought in bright fields, where every helmet caught some beams of glory; but the British soldier conquered under the old shoe of aristocracy, . . .

Sir William Napier, *History of the War in the Peninsula*, 1850

Thus the war terminated, and with it all remembrance of the veteran's service.

Sir William Napier, *History of the War in the Peninsula*, 1850

– Siege of Saragossa, June 1808

War even to the knife!

José de Palafox, when called to surrender to the French, June 1808

– Battle of Vimeiro, 21st August 1808

Thus in a loud voice clearly audible to his staff Wellesley [Wellington] exclaimed: 'Sir Harry, now is your time to advance. The enemy are completely beaten, we shall be in Lisbon in three days.' Sir Harry [General Burrard] hesitated and Wellesley pressed him again, adding the bait of Sir Harry himself taking part in the victorious campaign ... The French had in fact fled eastwards, leaving Torres Vedras and the road to Lisbon open. But Sir Harry had said No once and said it again. Enough was enough. He had been created a baronet for doing nothing much at Copenhagen in 1807. Before Junot's attack he had said to Wellesley, 'Wait for Moore'. He repeated it. It was not a pun but a fatuity. Wellesley turned away in disgust, remarking to his officers that they might as well go and shoot red-legged partridges.

Elizabeth Longford, *Wellington: The Years of the Sword*, 1969

– Battle of Talavera, 28th July 1809

The English, silent and impassive, with grounded arms, loomed like a long red wall.

Marshal Bugeaud, quoted in Robert Debs Heinl Jr, *A Dictionary of Military and Naval Quotations*, 1966

I saw [Wilson] engaged hand to hand with a French dragoon; I saw him – for I was by this time disabled by a severe wound, and stretched at length beside others of my suffering comrades – give and receive more than one pass, with equal skill and courage. Just then a French officer delivered a thrust at poor Harry Wilson's body, and delivered it effectually. I firmly believe that Wilson died on the instant; yet, though he felt the sword in its progress, he, with characteristic self-command, kept his eye still on the enemy in his front, and raising himself in his stirrups, let fall upon the Frenchman's helmet such a blow, that the brass and skull parted before it, and the man's head was cloven asunder to the chin. It was the most tremendous blow I ever saw struck; and both he who gave, and his opponent who received it, dropped dead together. The brass helmet was afterwards examined by order of an officer, who, as well as myself, was astonished at the exploit; and the cut was found to be as clean as if the sword had gone through a turnip, not so much as a dent being left on either side of it.

J. H. Stocqueler, *The British Soldier*, 1857

– Battle of Fuentes de Onero, 5th May 1811

The village of Fuentes de Onero, having been the field of battle, has not been much improved by the circumstance.

Duke of Wellington, dispatch, 6th May 1811

The mass was rent asunder, and Norman Ramsay burst forth sword in hand at the head of his battery, his horses breathing fire, stretched like greyhounds along the plain, the guns bounded behind them like things of no weight, and the mounted gunners followed close, with heads bent low and pointed weapons, in desperate career.

Sir William Napier, *History of the War in the Peninsula*, 1850

– Battle of Albu(h)era, 16th May 1811

Die hard, 57th! Die hard!

Lieutenant-Colonel Inglis, attributed, on receiving a wound

There is no beating these troops, in spite of their generals. I always thought them bad soldiers, now I am sure of it. For at Albuhera I turned their right, pierced their centre, broke them everywhere; the day was mine, and yet they did not know it, and would not run.

Marshal Soult, quoted in John Laffin, *Tommy Atkins*, 1966

Every individual nobly did his duty; and it is observed that our dead . . . were lying as they fought, in ranks, and every wound was in the front.

Sir William Beresford, Report, May 1811

You could not be successful in such an action without a large loss. We must make up our minds to affairs of this kind sometimes, or give up the game.

Duke of Wellington, Letter to Sir William Beresford, 19th May 1811

It was possible to destroy a well-trained and disciplined British infantry battalion, but, as Albuhera proved, it was not possible to break one. And before it could be destroyed it could do an incredible amount of damage. The killing power of the British infantry battalion exceeded anything to be found on the battlefields of the early nineteenth century. The Germans found the same thing in 1914 and 1944.

Sir Arthur Bryant, in *Illustrated London News*, 20th May 1950

– Assault of Badajoz, 6th–7th April 1812

Rangers of Connaught. It is not my intention to expend any powder this evening. We'll do this business with cold iron.

Sir Thomas Picton, to the 88th Foot Regiment, 6th April 1812, attributed.

The Walcheren Expedition, July 1809

The Earl of Chatham with sword drawn
Was waiting for Sir Richard Strachan;
Sir Richard, longing to be at 'em,
Was waiting for the Earl of Chatham.

George Canning, Epigram, 1809

Napoleon's Russian Campaign of 1812

War will occur in spite of me, in spite of the Emperor Alexander, in spite of the interests of France and the interests of Russia. I have so often seen this that it is my experience of the past which unveils the future to me . . . It is all a scene of the opera and the English control the machinery.

Napoleon Bonaparte, 1811, quoted in J. F. C. Fuller, *The Decisive Battles of the Western World*, 1954–56

There rises the sun of Austerlitz.
Napoleon, before Moscow, 1812

It is the beginning of the end.
Charles-Maurice de Talleyrand, attributed

The flames of Moscow were the aurora of the liberty of the world.
Benjamin Constant, *Esprit de Conquête*, 1813

In the campaign of 1812, a distinguished general officer of the French army was severely wounded in the leg. The surgeons, on consulting, declared that amputation was indispensable. The general received the intelligence with much composure. Among the persons who surrounded him, he observed his valet-de-chambre, who shewed by his profound grief the deep share which he took in the melancholy accident. 'Why dost thou weep, Germain?' said his master smilingly, to him. 'It is a fortunate thing for thee, you will have only one boot to clean in future.'
The Percy Anecdotes, 1823

. . . Since Russia, by the campaign of 1812 has taught us, first, that an empire of great dimensions is not to be conquered (which might have been easily known before), secondly, that the probability of final success does not in all cases diminish in the same measures as battles, capitals, and provinces are lost (which was formerly an incontrovertible principle with all diplomatists, and therefore made them always ready to enter at once into some bad temporary peace), but that a nation is often strongest in the heart of its country, if the enemy's offensive power has exhausted itself, and with that enormous force the defensive then springs over to the offensive; . . .
Karl von Clausewitz, *On War*, 1832: III

The Smolensk Road. As we rode through the forests, for a long time I couldn't understand why the wind wafted a bad smell from the thickets. At last I asked our driver about it and received an answer that could not be more horrible, spoken with the total indifference of the Russian peasant: 'There's a Frenchman rotting somewhere.'
Nadezhda Durova, *The Cavalry Maiden*, 1836

We are moving by quick marches into the heart of Russia, with an enemy at our heels who believes in all simplicity that we are running to escape him! Fortune blinds. I often think of Starn's prayer before the altar of Odin, when he asks the god to cloud Fingal's mind with the credulity that *presages a great fall!* Despite Napoleon's countless admirers, I make so bold to think that, for one considered such a great genius, he is much too confident both of his luck and his capabilities, too credulous, rash and uninformed. Blind luck, coincidence of circumstance, an oppressed nobility, and a deluded people all helped him take the throne, but he will have difficulty in holding and occupying it worthily. The artillery lieutenant, whose unprecedented luck has cost him both wits and common sense, will soon be remarked through the emperor's robes. On the basis of only geographical information and the dispatches of spies, how could he resolve to come and conquer a vast, rich nation, one famed for the magnanimous spirit and selflessness of its nobility, the unshakable bulwark of the Russian throne, and for its well-ordered host of troops, whose strict discipline and courage, physical strength and sturdy constitution allow them to withstand all hardships: a nation that includes as many peoples as it does climates and, above and beyond all this, is buttressed by its faith and toleration? To see that glorious army retreating without giving battle, retreating so rapidly that it is hard to keep pace with it, and to believe that it is retreating for fear of encountering the enemy? To believe in the timidity of the Russian army within the borders of its native land? To believe and pursue it, trying to overtake it! What horrible blindness! It can lead only to a horrible end.

Nadezhda Durova, *The Cavalry Maiden*, 1836

– Battle of Borodino, 7th September 1812

One Paris night will replace them all.

Napoleon Bonaparte, attributed, surveying the 75,000 casualties after the battle

French authors in particular, and great admirers of Buonaparte . . . have blamed him decidedly because he did not drive the Russian army completely off the field, and use his last reserves to scatter it, because then what was only a lost battle would have been a complete rout. We should be obliged to diverge too far to describe circumstantially the mutual situation of the two Armies; but this much is evident, that when Buonaparte passed the Niemen with his Army the same corps which afterwards fought at Borodino numbered 300,000 men, of whom now only 120,000 remained, he might therefore well be apprehensive that he would not have enough left to march on Moscow, the point on which everything seemed to depend. The victory which he had just gained gave nearly a certainty of taking that capital, for that the Russians would be in a condition to fight a second battle within eight days seemed in the highest degree improbable; and in Moscow he hoped to find peace . . . At Borodino the conqueror preferred to content himself with half a victory, not because the decision appeared doubtful, but because he was not rich enough to pay for the whole.

Karl von Clausewitz, *On War*, 1832, IV

Battle of Dresden, 26th–27th August 1913

I know of no example in war which furnishes clearer evidence that the numbers and morale of an army, important factors as they are, may be outmatched by the weight of one man of genius.

Graf Maximilian Yorck von Wartenburg, *Napoleon as a General*, 1901

Battle of Leipzig, 16th–18th October 1813

Between a battle lost and a battle won the distance is immense and there stand empires.

Napoleon Bonaparte, on the eve of battle

At Jena, Napoleon destroyed not only a feudal army, but the last vestiges of the feudal idea, and out of the ashes arose a national army, which at Leipzig destroyed him. On the corpse-strewn fields by the Elster, present-day Europe writhed out of its medieval shell.

J. F. C. Fuller, *The Decisive Battles of the Western World*, 1954–56

Battle of Waterloo, 18th June 1815

Whatever happens, you and I will do our duty.

Duke of Wellington, to Lord Uxbridge on the eve of battle

Soldiers, we must never be beat; what will they say in England?

Duke of Wellington, attributed

Up, Guards, and at 'em!

Duke of Wellington, attributed

How beautifully the English fight! But they must give way.

Napoleon, attributed

The Guard dies, but never surrenders.

Pierre de Cambronne, attributed

Come and see how a Marshal of France can die!

Marshal Ney, attributed, towards the end of the battle

Lord Uxbridge: I've lost my leg, Egad!
Wellington: Egad, sir, so you have!

Attributed conversation

The nearest run thing that you ever saw.

Duke of Wellington, attributed

I hope to God I have fought my last battle. It is a bad thing to be always fighting. While in the thick of it I am too much occupied to feel anything; but it is wretched just after. It is quite impossible to think of glory.

Duke of Wellington, to Lady Frances Shelley, in Brussels, 19th June 1815

Next to a battle lost, the greatest misery is a battle won.

Duke of Wellington, to Lady Frances Shelley, in Brussels, 19th June 1815

In all my life I have not experienced such anxiety, for I must confess I have never before been so close to defeat.

Duke of Wellington, Letter to his brother, written shortly after Waterloo

Napoleon did not manoeuvre at all. He just moved forward in the old style, and was driven off in the old style.

Duke of Wellington, Letter to Sir William Beresford, 2nd July 1815

Well, Caulaincourt, here is a pretty to-do! A battle lost! How will the country bear this reverse? All the material is lost. It is a frightful disaster. The day was won. The army had performed prodigies; the enemy was beaten at every point; only the English centre still held. Just as all was over the army was seized with panic. It is inexplicable.

Napoleon, 21st June 1815, in *The Memoirs of Caulaincourt*, 1935

The battle of Waterloo was won on the playing fields of Eton.

Duke of Wellington, attributed (although he almost certainly never said this)

But hark! – that heavy sound breaks in once more,
As if the clouds its echo would repeat;
And nearer, clearer, deadlier than before!
Arm! Arm! it is – it is – the cannon's opening roar.

Lord Byron, *Childe Harold's Pilgrimage*, 1812–17

Last noon behind them full of lusty life,
Last eve in Beauty's circle proudly gay,
The midnight brought the signal-sound of strife,
The morn the marshalling in arms, – the day
Battle's magnificently stern array!
The thunder-clouds close o'er it, which when rent
The earth is cover'd thick with other clay,
Which her own clay shall cover, heap'd and pent,
Rider and horse, – friend, foe, – in one red burial blent!

Lord Byron, *Childe Harold's Pilgrimage*, 1812–17

The Life Guards coming up in the rear of the 95th, which distinguished regiment acted as sharp-shooters in front of the line, sustaining and repelling a most formidable onset of the French, called out to them, as if they had been on the parade in the Park, 'Bravo, 95th! do you *lather* them, and we'll *shave* them.'

The Percy Anecdotes, 1823

Serjeant Weir, of the Scots Greys, was pay-serjeant to his troop, and as such might have excused himself from serving in action; but on such a day as the battle of Waterloo, he disdained to avail himself of his privilege, and requested to be allowed to join his regiment in the mortal fray. In one of the charges, he fell mortally wounded, and was left on the field. Corporal Scot, of the same regiment, who lost a leg, asserts, that when the field was searched for the wounded and slain, the body of Serjeant Weir was found *with his name written on his forehead with his own hand, dipped in his own blood!* This his comrade said he was supposed to have done, that his body might be found and recognized, and that it might not be imagined he disappeared with the money of his troop.

The Percy Anecdotes, 1823

I have never heard of a battle in which everybody was killed; but this seemed likely to be an exception, as all were going by turns.

John Kincaid, *Adventures with the Rifle Brigade*, 1830

Meeting an acquaintance of another regiment, a very little fellow, I asked him what had happened to them yesterday. 'I'll be hanged,' says he, 'if I know anything at all about the matter, for I was all day trodden in the mud and galloped over by every scoundrel who had a horse; and, in short, I owe my existence to my insignificance.'

John Kincaid, *Adventures with the Rifle Brigade*, 1830

However highly we must esteem courage and firmness in War, and however little prospect there is of victory to him who cannot resolve to seek it by the exertion of all his power, still there is a point beyond which perseverance can only be termed desperate folly, and therefore can meet with no approbation from any critic. In the most celebrated of all battles, that of Belle-Alliance, Buonaparte used his last reserve in an effort to retrieve a battle which was past being retrieved. He spent his last farthing, and then, as beggar, abandoned both the battlefield and his crown.

Karl von Clausewitz, *On War*, 1832: IV

Again their ravening eagle rose
In anger, wheel'd on Europe-shadowing wings,
And barking for the throne of kings;
Till one that sought but Duty's iron crown
On that loud sabbath shook the spoiler down;
A day of onsets of despair!
Dash'd on every rocky square
Their surging charges foam'd themselves away;
Last, the Prussian trumpet blew;
Thro' the long-tormented air
Heaven flash'd a sudden jubilant ray,
And down we swept and charged and overthrew.
So great a soldier taught us there,
What long-enduring hearts could do
In that world-earthquake, Waterloo!

Alfred Tennyson, 'Ode on the Death of the Duke of Wellington', 1852

Every man meets his Waterloo at last.

Wendell Phillips, speech, 1st November 1859

Waterloo is a battle of the first rank won by a captain of the second.

Victor Hugo, *Les Misérables*, 1862

The British Army is an army of snobs, but the universal snobbery produced here a maximum of good results.

Elie Halévy, *A History of the English People*, 1912

Probably the Battle of Waterloo was won on the playing-fields of Eton, but the opening battles of all subsequent wars have been lost there.

George Orwell, *The Lion and the Unicorn*, 1941

With such subordinates as Grouchy and Ney, Michael and all his angels would have lost the campaign.

J. F. C. Fuller, *The Decisive Battles of the Western World*, 1954–56

The volleys crashed, the Imperial Guard reeled back. The 52nd Foot swung out of the British line and poured a volley into the French flank. The red line swept the blue masses down the slope. Wellington waved his cocked hat towards the enemy, and the whole allied line charged. The wars of the French Revolution and Empire were over.

Correlli Barnett, *Britain and Her Army, 1509–1970*, 1970

Louis XVIII enters Cambrai, 25th June 1815

On the 25th we halted and his pottle belly Majesty, Louis 18th, marched into the loyal town of Cambray . . . No doubt the papers will inform you how Louis 18th entered the loyal city of Cambray, how his loyal subjects welcomed their beloved king, how the best of monarchs wept over the sufferings of his beloved people, how the Citadel surrendered with acclamation of joy to the best of kings, and how his most Christian Majesty effected all this without being accompanied by a single soldier. But the papers will not inform you that the 4th Division and a brigade of Hanoverian Huzzars (red) were in readiness within half a mile of this faithful city, and if the loyal citizens had insulted their king, how it was very probable we should have bayoneted every Frenchman in the place. The people well knew this, and this will account for the sudden change in their loyalty or allegiance from their Idol Napoleon (properly named the Great) to an old bloated poltroon, the Sir John Falstaff of France.

Private Wheeler, 25th June 1815, in *The Letters of Private Wheeler*, ed B. H. Liddell Hart, 1951

WAR OF HAITIAN INDEPENDENCE, 1804

Some doubt the courage of the Negro. Go to Haiti and stand on those fifty thousand graves of the best soldiers France ever had, and ask them what they think of the Negro's sword.

Wendell Phillips, *Address on Toussaint l'Ouverture*, 1861

BARBARY WARS, 1805–16

Why do they send wild young men to treat for peace with old powers?

The Bey of Tunis, August 1815

If the Dey of Algiers should bully and fume,
Or hereafter his claim to this tribute resume,
We'll send him Decatur once more to defy him,
And his motto shall be, if you please, Carpe Diem.

Anonymous, '*Carpe Diem* – Seize the Dey', 1816

WAR OF 1812, 1812–15

If you wish to abandon foreign collision, you had better abandon the ocean.

Henry Clay, in the House of Representatives, 22nd January 1812

Thousands of American citizens, under the safeguard of public law and of their national flag, have been torn from their country and everything dear to them; have been dragged on ships of war of a foreign nation and exposed, under the severities of their discipline, to be exiled to the most distant and deadly climes, to risk their lives in the battles of their oppressors, and to be the melancholy instruments of taking away those of their own brethren.

James Madison, Message to Congress, 1st June 1812

The acquisition of Canada this year, as far as the neighbourhood of Quebec, will be a mere matter of marching.

Thomas Jefferson, Letter to Duane, 4th August 1812

USS *Chesapeake* versus HMS *Shannon*, 1st June 1813

Tell the men to fire faster and not to give up the ship. Fight her till she sinks.

Captain James Lawrence, of the *Chesapeake*, dying words, attributed

Battle of Lake Erie, August 1813

We have met the enemy, and they are ours.

Captain Oliver H. Perry (USN), August 1813

Siege of New Orleans, December 1814–January 1816

By the Eternal, they shall not sleep on our soil!

Andrew Jackson, on learning of British landings, 23rd December 1814

I will hold New Orleans in spite of Urop and all Hell.

Andrew Jackson, attributed

For glory lights the soldier's tomb,
And beauty weeps the brave.

Joseph Rodman Drake, *To the Defenders of New Orleans*, 1814

STORMING OF THE ALAMO, 22nd February 1836

Thermopylae had its messenger of defeat; the Alamo had none.

Graffito, found on the walls of the Alamo, 1836

Remember the Alamo!

Texan slogan

RUSSIAN CAMPAIGNS IN THE CAUCASUS,

early 19th century

How hot the day: only our swords to shade us!
How thick the smoke, how dark the night.
Only our guns to light us!
Oh birds, fly homeward! Give our last greetings to our sisters.
Tell them our only mourners will be ravens:
Our only dirge, the hungry howling wolves.
Tell them we died, sword in hand, in the land of the Giaour
Where the ravens pick our eyes, and the wolves tear our flesh.

'Song of Hamzad', in Leslie Blanch, *The Sabres of Paradise*, 1960

They don't seem to know when they ought to die. Indeed these villains can hardly ever be killed. They are a people without the slightest idea of propriety.

Mikhail Lermontov, *A Hero of Our Time*, 1840

FIRST OPIUM WAR, 1839–42

It appears to your Majesty's slave that we are very deficient in means, and have not the shells and rockets used by the barbarians. We must, therefore, adopt other methods to stop them, which will be easy, as they have opened negotiations.

Kee Shen, written report to the Chinese Emperor, March 1841

CONQUEST OF SIND, 1843

Peccavi. [I have sinned, i.e. Sind]

Sir Charles James Napier, dispatch after the Battle of Hyderabad, 24th March 1843

AMERICAN–MEXICAN WAR, 1846–48

We want room!

Lewis Cass, in the Senate, 11th February 1846

If I were a Mexican, I would tell you, 'Have you not enough room in your own country to bury your dead men? If you come into mine, we will greet you with bloody hands and welcome you to hospitable graves.'

Thomas Corwin, in the Senate, 11th February 1846

Military glory – that attractive rainbow that rises in showers of blood, that serpent's eye that charms to destroy.

Abraham Lincoln, in the House of Representatives, 12th January 1848

Poor Mexico. So far from God and so close to the United States!

Mexican saying

Battle of Buena Vista, 22nd February 1846

My wounded are behind me, and I will never pass them alive.

Zachary Taylor, attributed, refusing to retreat

On fame's eternal camping ground
Their silent tents are spread,
And glory guards with solemn ground
The bivouac of the dead.

Theodore O'Hara, 'The Bivouac of the Dead', 1847

From the Rio Grande's waters to the icy lakes of Maine,
Let all exult, for we have met the enemy again.
Beneath their stern old mountains we have met them in their pride,
And rolled from Buena Vista back the battle's bloody tide.

Albert Pike, 'Battle of Buena Vista', 1854

Capture of Monte(r)rey, 23rd September 1846

Old Zach's at Monterey,
Bring on your Santa Anner;
For every time we raise a gun,
Down goes a Mexicaner.

Anonymous, song, 1846

We were not many, we who stood
Before the iron sleet that day;
Yet many a gallant spirit would
Give half his years, if he but could
Have been with us at Monterey.

Charles Fenno Hoffman, 'Monterey', *c.* 1850

THE CRIMEAN WAR, 1853–56

We have on our hands a sick man, a very sick man.

Tsar Nicholas I, referring to Turkey, in conversation with Sir G. H. Seymour, 1853

The Russian army is a wall which, however far it may retreat, you will always find in front of you.

Antoine Henri Jomini, advising Marshal Canrobert, 1854

I have never been able to join in the popular cry about the recklessness, sensuality and helplessness of the soldiers. On the contrary I should say . . . that I have never seen so teachable and helpful a class as an Army generally. Give them opportunity promptly and securely to send money home and they will use it. Give them schools and lectures and they will come to use them. Give them books and games and amusements and they will leave off drinking. Give them suffering and they will bear it. Give them work and they will do it.

Florence Nightingale, Letter to her sister, March 1856

Hail, ye indomitable heroes, hail!
In spite of all your generals, ye prevail.

Walter Savage Landor, 'The Crimean Heroes', 1856

Overwhelmed by a mass of verbiage, and wrapped up in endless coatings of manifestoes, protocols, and despatches, the real causes of the war with Russia are rather patent to the consciences than admitted by the lips of European politicians. The independence of Turkey was, indeed, menaced by Czar Nicholas; but for that independence, England and France would have cared comparatively little if Turkey had been some distant power whose fate and fortunes could effect in no degree the commerce or the reputation of the allies in the East. France, destitute of material possessions in that quarter of the globe, is ever jealous of her prestige, and anxious to uphold the power of that name which, to the Oriental, embodies the force, the intelligence, the wealth, and the civilization of Europe. England, with a growing commerce in the Levant, and with a prodigious empire still nearer to the rising sun, could never permit the one to be absorbed and the other to be threatened in a new direction by the most aggressive and persistently ambitious state the world has ever seen. With Russia by her side she had not hesitated, in the interests of humanity, to inflict a wound on the independence of Turkey which has been widening and growing deeper every day. But when Russia, impatient of the slowness of the process of decay and death, sought to rend open the wound at once, and to precipitate the end, England and France were bound to stay those insatiable hands, and to prop the falling throne of the Sultans on their bayonets.

W. H. Russell, *The British Expedition to the Crimea*, 1858

The French losses from cholera were frightful. Convinced that there was something radically wrong in the air of the hospital at Varnam the French cleared out of the building, altogether, and resolved to treat their cases in the field. The hospital had been formerly used as a Turkish barrack. It was a huge quadrangular building, like the barracks at Scutari, with a courtyard in the centre . . . About one-third of the building was reserved for our use, the remainder occupied by the French. Although not very old, the building was far from being in thorough repair. The windows were broken, the walls in parts were cracked and shaky, and the floors were mouldering and rotten. Like all places which have been inhabited by Turkish soldiers for any time, the smell of the buildings was abominable. Men sent in there with fevers and other disorders were frequently attacked with the cholera in its worst form, and died with unusual rapidity, in spite of all that could be done to save them. I visited the hospital, and observed that a large train of araba carts, filled with sick soldiers, were drawn up by the walls. There were thirty-five carts, with three or four men in each. These were sick French soldiers sent in from camps, and waiting till room could be found for them in the hospital. A number of soldiers were sitting down by the roadside, and here and there the moonbeams flashed brightly off their piled arms. The men were silent; not a song, not a laugh! A gloom, seldom seen among French troops, reigned amid these groups of grey-coated men, and the quiet that prevailed was only broken now and then by the moans and cries of pain of the poor sufferers in the carts. Observing that about fifteen arabas without any occupants were waiting in the square, I asked a *sous-officier* for what purpose they were required. His answer, sullen and short, was – *'Pours les morts – pour les Français décédés, Monsieur.'*

W. H. Russell, *The British Expedition to the Crimea*, 1858

He [Lord Aberdeen] drew down war by suffering himself to have an undue horror of it.

A. W. Kinglake, *The Invasion of the Crimea*, 1877

The Crimean War is one of the bad jokes of history.

Philip Guedalla, *The Two Marshals*, 1943

Two things saved this small, odd, rather absurd British Army, challenging so far from home a gigantic empire, from immediate defeat and then total disaster. First, the Russians, with more men in the field and immense potential reserves, were even bigger muddlers than their invaders, and seemed to move in a vague dream of battle. Secondly, and not for the first or last time, the British owed almost everything to the courage, obstinacy and superb discipline of the regular infantryman.

J. B. Priestley, *Victoria's Heyday*, 1974

Battle of Balaclava, 25th October 1854

Magnificent! – but it isn't war.

Pierre Bosquet, watching the charge of the Light Brigade

A feat of chivalry, fiery with consummate courage, and bright with flashing courage.

Benjamin Disraeli, in the House of Commons, 15th December 1855

. . . the glorious catastrophe . . .

W. H. Russell, *The British Expedition to the Crimea*, 1858

It appeared that the Quartermaster-General, Brigadier Airey, thinking that the Light Cavalry had not gone far enough in front . . . when the enemy's horse had fled, gave an order in writing to Captain Nolan, 15th Hussars, to take to Lord Lucan, directing his Lordship 'to advance' his cavalry nearer the enemy. A braver soldier than Captain Nolan the army did not possess. He was known to all his arm of the service for his entire devotion to his profession, and his name must be familiar to all who take interest in our cavalry for his excellent work on our drill and system of remount and breaking horses. I had the pleasure of his acquaintance, and I know he entertained the most exalted opinions respecting the capabilities of the English horse soldier. Properly led, the British Hussar and Dragoon could in his mind break squares, take batteries, ride over columns of infantry, and pierce any other cavalry in the world as if they were made of straw. He thought they had not had the opportunity of doing all that was in their power, and that they had missed even such chances as had been offered to them – that, in fact, they were in some measure disgraced . . . He is now dead and gone. God forbid I should cast a shade on the brightness of his honour, but I am bound to state what I am told occurred when he reached his Lordship . . . When Lord Lucan received the order from Captain Nolan, and had read it, he asked, we are told, 'Where are we to advance to?' Captain Nolan pointed with his finger to the line of the Russians, and said, 'There are the enemy, and there are the guns', or words to that effect, according to the statements made after his death.

W. H. Russell, *The British Expedition to the Crimea*, 1858

At ten minutes past eleven our Light Cavalry advanced. The whole Brigade scarcely made one effective regiment, according to the numbers of continental armies; and yet it was more than we could spare. As they rushed toward the front, the Russians opened on them from the guns in the redoubt on the right, with volleys of musketry and rifles. They swept proudly past, glittering in the morning sun in all the pride and splendour of war. We could scarcely believe the evidence of our senses! Surely that handful of men were not going to charge an army in position? Alas, it was but too true – their desperate valour knew no bounds, and far indeed was it removed from its so-called better part – discretion.

W. H. Russell, *The British Expedition to the Crimea*, 1858

Half a league, half a league,
   Half a league onward,
All in the valley of Death
   Rode the six hundred.

'Forward, the Light Brigade!
Charge for the guns!' he said:
Into the valley of Death
  Rode the six hundred.

'Forward the Light Brigade!'
Was there a man dismay'd?
Not tho' the soldier knew
  Some one had blunder'd:
Theirs not to make reply,
Theirs not to reason why,
Theirs but to do and die:
Into the valley of Death
  Rode the six hundred.

Cannon to right of them,
Cannon to left of them,
Cannon in front of them
  Volley'd and thunder'd;
Storm'd at with shot and shell,
Boldly they rode and well,
Into the jaws of Death,
Into the mouth of Hell
  Rode the six hundred.

Flash'd all their sabres bare,
Flash'd as they turn'd in air
Sabring the gunners there,
Charging an army, while
  All the world wonder'd:
Plung'd in the battery-smoke
Right thro' the line they broke;
Cossack and Russian
Reel'd from the sabre-stroke
  Shatter'd and sunder'd.
Then they rode back, but not
  Not the six hundred.

Alfred Tennyson, 'The Charge of the Light Brigade', 1854

When can their glory fade?
O the wild charge they made!
  All the world wonder'd.
Honour the charge they made!
Honour the Light Brigade,
  Noble six hundred.

Alfred Tennyson, 'The Charge of the Light Brigade', 1854

INDIAN MUTINY, 1857–59

Entrench, entrench, entrench . . .

Sir Henry Lawrence, dying orders, during the Siege of Lucknow, 4th July 1857

On 28 November the Commander-in-Chief, Sir Colin Campbell, reached Cawnpore, where another battle had been in progress, with the British troops faring badly. As Campbell arrived at the bridge of boats across the Ganges an officer said to him, 'Thank God you have come, sir. The troops are at their last gasp.'

Campbell glared at him. 'How dare you say, sir, of Her Majesty's troops that they are ever at their last gasp!'

John Laffin, *Tommy Atkins: the Story of an English Soldier*, 1966

AMERICAN CIVIL WAR, 1861–65

Resolved: That the compact which exists between the North and the South is a covenant with death and an agreement with hell, involving both parties in atrocious criminality, and should be immediately annulled.

William Lloyd Garrison, Resolution passed by the Massachusetts Anti-Slavery Society, 27th January 1843

No sir, you dare not make war on cotton. No power on earth dares make war upon it. Cotton is king.

James Henry Hammond, addressing the Senate, March 1858

'A house divided against itself cannot stand.' I believe this government cannot endure, permanently half slave and half free. I do not expect the Union to be dissolved – I do not expect the house to fall – but I do expect it will cease to be divided. It will become all one thing, or all the other. Either the opponents of slavery will arrest the further spread of it, and place it where the public mind shall rest in the belief that it is in the course of ultimate extinction; or its advocates will push it forward, till it shall alike become lawful in all states, old as well as new – North as well as South.

Abraham Lincoln, speech at Springfield, Illinois, 1858

You had better, all you people of the South, prepare yourself for a settlement of this question. It must come up for settlement sooner than you are prepared for it, and the sooner you commence that preparation, the better for you. You may dispose of me very easily: I am nearly disposed of now. But this question is still to be settled – this negro question, I mean.

John Brown, after he was taken at Harper's Ferry, 19th October 1859

Save in the defence of my native State, I never desire again to draw my sword.

Robert E. Lee, Letter to Winfield Scott, 20th April 1861

Leaped to their feet, a thousand men,
Their voices echoing far and near;
'We go, we care not where or when;
Our country calls us, we are here!'

Anonymous, in *Harper's Weekly*, 27th April 1861

A reckless and unprincipled tyrant has invaded your soil. Abraham Lincoln, regardless of all moral, legal and constitutional restraints, has thrown his Abolition hosts among you, who are murdering and imprisoning your citizens, confiscating and destroying your property, and committing other acts of violence and outrage too shocking and revolting to humanity to be ennumerated.

P. G. T. Beauregard, Proclamation to the People of Virginia, 1st June 1861

This is essentially a people's contest . . . It is a struggle for maintaining in the world that form and substance of government whose leading object is to elevate the condition of men – to lift artificial weights from all shoulders – to clear the paths of laudable pursuit for all – to afford all an unfettered start, and a fair chance, in the race of life.

Abraham Lincoln, Message to Congress, 4th July 1861

If we are surrounded, we must cut our way out as we cut our way in.

Ulysses Grant, at Belmont, Missouri, 7th November 1861

'All quiet along the Potomac,' they said,
'Except, now and then a stray picket
Is shot as he walks on his beat to and fro
By a rifleman hid in the thicket.'

Ethel Lynn Beers, 'The Picket Guard', 1861

All quiet on the Potomac tonight,
No sound save the rush of the river,
While soft falls the dew on the face of the dead –
The picket's off duty forever.

Ethel Lynn Beers, 'The Picket Guard', 1861

Yet if God wills that it continue till all the wealth piled by the bondsman's 250 years of unrequited toil shall be sunk, and until every drop of blood drawn with the lash shall be paid by another drawn by the sword, as was said 3,000 years ago, so still it must be said, that the judgments of the Lord are true and righteous altogether.

Abraham Lincoln, Inaugural Address, 1862

You appear much concerned at my attacking on Sunday. I am greatly concerned, too; but I felt my duty to do it.

'Stonewall' Jackson, Letter to his Wife, March 1862

It is called the Army of the Potomac but it is only McClellan's bodyguard . . . If McClellan is not using the army, I should like to borrow it for a while.

Abraham Lincoln, in Washington DC, 9th April 1862

My headquarters will be in the saddle.

Major General John Pope, Press statement, on taking charge of the Army of the Potomac, June 1862

Never take counsel of your fears.

'Stonewall' Jackson, advice to Major Hotchkiss, 18th June 1862

We are coming, Father Abraham, three hundred thousand more,
From Mississippi's winding stream and from New England's shore,
We leave our ploughs and workshops, our wives and children dear,
With hearts too full for utterance, with but a single tear.

James Sloan Gibbons, song, 16th July 1862

Not only does economy, but naval success, dictate the wisdom and expediency of fighting with iron against wood.

Stephen R. Mallory, Letter, 1862, referring to the ironclad USS *Merrimack*

Mine eyes have seen the glory of the coming of the Lord:
He is trampling out the vintage where the grapes of wrath are stored;
He hath loosed the fatal lightning of His terrible swift sword:
His truth is marching on.

I have seen Him in the watch-fires of a hundred circling camps,
They have builded Him an altar in the evening dews and damps;
I can read His righteous sentence by the dim and flaring lamps:
His day is marching on.

I have read a fiery gospel writ in burnished rows of steel:
'As ye deal with my contemners, so with you my grace shall deal;
Let the Hero, born of woman, crush the serpent with his heel,
Since God is marching on.'

He has sounded forth the trumpet that shall never call retreat;
He is sifting out the hearts of men before His judgement seat:
Oh, be swift, my soul, to answer Him! Be jubilant, my feet!
Our God is marching on.

In the beauty of the lilies Christ was born across the sea,
With a glory in his bosom that transfigures you and me:
As he died to make men holy, let us die to make men free,
While God is marching on.

Julia Ward Howe, 'The Battle Hymn of the Republic', 1862

You have confidence in yourself, which is valuable, if not an indispensable quality. You are ambitious, which, within reasonable bounds, does good rather than harm; I think that during General Burnside's command of the Army you have taken counsel of your ambition and thwarted him as much as you could, in which you did a great wrong to the country and to a most meritorious and honorable brother officer. I have heard, in such a way as to believe it, of your recently saying that both the Army and the Government needed a dictator. Of course it was not for this, but in spite of it, that I have given you the command.

Only those generals who gain successes can set up as dictators. What I now ask of you is military success, and I will risk the dictatorship.

Abraham Lincoln, Letter to Joseph Hooker, 26th January 1863

I much fear that the spirit which you have decided to infuse into the Army of criticizing their commander and withholding confidence from him will now turn upon you. I shall assist you as far as I can to put it down. Neither you nor Napoleon, if he were alive again, could get any good out of an army while such a spirit prevails in it; and now beware of rashness. Beware of rashness, but with energy and sleepless vigilance go forward and give us victories.

Abraham Lincoln, Letter to Joseph Hooker, 26th January, 1863

There is no better way of defending a long line than by moving into the enemy's territory.

Robert E. Lee, Letter to J. R. Jones, 21st March 1863

We must make this campaign an exceedingly active one. Only then can a weaker country cope with a stronger; it must make up in activity what it lacks in strength.

'Stonewall' Jackson, Letter, April, 1863

A rich man's war and a poor man's fight.

Draft Rioteers' Slogan, New York City, July 1863 [Those who presented $300 were exempted from service]

[War] should be pure and simple as applied to the belligerents. I would keep it so, till all the traces of the war are effaced; till those who appealed to it are sick and tired of it, and come to the emblem of our nation, and sue for peace. I would not coax them, or meet them half-way, but make them so sick of war that generations would pass away before they would again appeal to it.

W. T. Sherman, Letter to H. W. Halleck, 17th September 1863

Yes, we'll rally round the flag, we'll rally once again,
Shouting the battle-cry of Freedom,
We will rally from the hillside, we'll gather from the plain,
Shouting the battle-cry of Freedom.

George Frederick Root, *Battle-cry of Freedom*, 1863

My opinion is that the Northern States will manage somehow to muddle through.

John Bright, attributed, *c.* 1863

I have not seen in this war a cavalry command of 1,000 that was not afraid of the sight of a dozen infantry bayonets.

W. T. Sherman, remark made to J. B. Steedman, January 1864

We of the North are beyond all question right in our cause, but we are not bound to ignore the fact that the people of the South have prejudices which form part of their nature, and which they cannot throw off without an effort of reason or the slower process of natural change. The question then arises, Should we treat as absolute enemies all in the South who differ from us in opinion or prejudice, kill or banish them, or should we give them time to think and gradually change their conduct so as to conform to the new order of things which is slowly and gradually creeping into their country?

When we take up arms to resist a rightful authority, we are compelled to use like force, because all reason and argument cease when arms are resorted to. When the provisions, forage, horses, mules, wagons, etc., are used by our enemy, it is clearly our right and duty to take them also, because otherwise they might be used against us. In like manner all houses left vacant by an inimical people are clearly our right, and as such are needed as storehouses, hospitals and quarters.

But the question arises as to dwellings used by women, children and non-combatants. So long as non-combatants remain in their houses and keep to their accustomed peaceful business, their opinions and prejudices can in no wise influence the war, and therefore should not be noticed; but if any one comes out into the public streets and creates disorder, he or she should be punished, restrained, or banished to the rear or front, as the officer in command adjudges. If the people, or any of them, keep up a correspondence with parties in hostility, they are spies, and can be punished according to law with death or minor punishment . . . The people of the South having appealed to *war*, are barred from appealing for protection to our constitution, which they have practically and publicly defied.

W. T. Sherman, Letter to R. M. Sawyer, 31st January 1864

If slavery is not wrong, nothing is wrong.

Abraham Lincoln, Letter to A. G. Hodges, 4th April 1864

I propose to fight it out on this line if it takes all summer.

Ulysses Grant, dispatch from Spottsylvania, 11th May 1864

Fight anything that comes!

W. T. Sherman, to General J. B. McPherson, Atlanta, 11th May 1864

I worked night and day for twelve years to prevent the war, but I could not. The North was mad and blind, and would not let us govern ourselves, and so the war came. Now it must go on until the last man of this generation falls in his tracks and his children seize his musket and fight our battles.

Jefferson Davies, to J. F. Jacques and J. R. Gilmore, 17th July 1864

I begin to regard the death and mangling of a couple of thousand men as a small affair, a kind of morning dash, . . .

W. T. Sherman, Letter to his Wife, July 1864

If the people raise a howl against my barbarity and cruelty, I will answer that war is war, and not popularity-seeking. If they want peace, they and their relatives must stop the war.

W. T. Sherman, Letter to H. W. Halleck, 4th September 1864

Until we can repopulate Georgia, it is useless for us to occupy it; but the utter destruction of its roads, houses and people will cripple their military resources. I can make this march, and make Georgia howl.

W. T. Sherman, in Atlanta, wire to Ulysses Grant, 9th September 1864

You who, in the midst of peace and prosperity, have plunged a nation into war – dark and cruel war – who dared and badgered us to battle, insulted our flag, seized our arsenals and forts that were left in the honorable custody of peaceful ordnance sergeants, seized and made 'prisoners of war' the very garrisons sent to protect your people against negroes and Indians, long before any overt act was committed by the (to you) hated Lincoln government; tried to force Kentucky and Indiana into rebellion, spite of themselves; falsified the vote of Louisiana; turned loose your privateers to plunder unarmed ships; expelled Union families by the thousands, burned their houses, and declared, by an act of your Congress, the confiscation of all debts due Northern men for goods had and received! Talk thus to the Marines, but not to me, who have seen these things.

W. T. Sherman, Letter to John B. Hood, 10th September 1864

You might as well appeal against the thunderstorm as against these terrible hardships of war.

W. T. Sherman, Letter to the Mayor of Atlanta, 12th September 1864

I shall always respect war hereafter. The cost of life, the dreary havoc of comfort and time, are overpaid by the vistas it opens of eternal life, eternal law, reconstructing and uplifting society, – breaks up the old horizon, and we see through the rifts a wider vista.

R. W. Emerson, Letter to Thomas Carlyle, 26th September 1864

I am short a cheekbone and an ear, but I am able to whip all hell yet.

Colonel John M. Corse, reporting to Sherman from Allatoona, 6th October 1864

I have been shown in the files of the War Department a statement to the Adjutant General of Massachusetts that you are the mother of five sons who have died gloriously on the field of battle. I feel how weak and fruitless must be any words of mine which should attempt to beguile you from the grief of a loss so overwhelming. But I cannot refrain from tendering you the consolation that may be found in the thanks of the Republic they died to save. I pray that our heavenly Father may assuage the anguish of your bereavement, and leave you only the cherished memory of the loved and the lost, and the solemn pride that must be yours to have laid so costly a sacrifice upon the altar of freedom.

Abraham Lincoln, Letter to Mrs Lydia Bixbey, 21st November 1864

I will soon commence on London County, and let them know there is a God in Israel.

P. H. Sheridan, wire to W. M. Halleck, 26th November 1864

Beat! beat! drums! – blow! bugles! blow
Through the windows – through doors – bust like a
ruthless force,
Into the solemn church, and scatter the congregation,
Into the school where the scholar is studying;
Leave not the bridegroom quiet – no happiness must he now have
with his bride,
Nor the peaceful farmer any peace, ploughing his field or
gathering his grain
So fierce you whirr and pound you drums – so shrill you
bugles blow.

Walt Whitman, 'Beat! Beat! Drums!', from *Drum-Taps*, 1865

Bring the good old bugle, boys, we'll sing another song,
Sing it with a spirit that will start the world along,
Sing it as we used to sing it – fifty thousand strong,
While we were marching through Georgia.

Henry Clay Work, 'Marching Through Georgia' (song), 1865

If I had the power, I would arm every wolf, panther, catamount and bear in the mountains of America, every crocodile in the swamps of Florida, every negro in the South, every devil in Hell, clothe him in the uniform of the Federal Army, and then turn them loose on the rebels of the South and exterminate every man, woman and child south of Mason and Dixon's Line.

W. P. Brownlow, speech in New York, 1866

Put a man in a hole, and a good battery on a hill behind him, and he will beat off three times his number, even if he is not a very good soldier.

Theodore Lyman, 1869, in *Meade's Headquarters 1863–1865*, 1922

I was too weak to defend, so I attacked.

Robert E. Lee, attributed

Under the sod and the dew,
Waiting the judgement-day;
Under the laurel, the Blue,
Under the willow, the Grey.

Francis Miles Finch, 'The Blue and the Grey', *c.* 1880

Such was the war. It was not a quadrille in a ball-room. Its interior history will not only never be written – its practicality, minutiae of deeds and passions, will never even be suggested. The actual soldier of 1862–'65, North and South, with all his ways, his incredible dauntlessness, habits, practices, tastes, language, his fierce friendship, his appetite, rankness, his superb strength and animality, lawless gait, and a hundred unnamed lights and shades of camp, I say, will never be written – perhaps must not and should not be.

Walt Whitman, *Specimen Days*, 1882

In one of the fights before Atlanta, a rebel soldier, of large size, evidently a young man, was mortally wounded top of the head, so that the brains partially exuded. He lived three days, lying on his back on the spot where he first dropt. He dug with his heel in the ground during that time a hole big enough to put in a couple of ordinary knapsacks. He just lay there in the open air, and with little intermission kept his heel going night and day. Some of our soldiers then moved him to a house, but he died in a few minutes.

Walt Whitman, *Specimen Days*, 1882

In the South, the war is what AD is elsewhere; they date from it.

Mark Twain, *Life on the Mississippi*, 1883

Had the South had a people as numerous as it was warlike, and a navy commensurate with its other resources as a sea power, the great extent of its sea-coast and its numerous inlets would have been elements of great strength.

Alfred Thayer Mahan, *The Influence of Sea Power Upon History*, 1890

The only war in modern times as to which we can be sure, first, that no skill and patience of diplomacy could have avoided it, and second, that preservation of the American Union and abolition of negro slavery were two vast triumphs of good by which even the inferno of war was justified.

Lord Morley, quoted in J. T. Winterich's Introduction (1951) to Stephen Crane's *Red Badge of Courage*

I see no results of this great conflict which justify the tremendous sacrifices which we as a nation were required to make. I see only an enormous waste of life and property, the vindication of right by might, and the substitution of one form of injustice by another.

Henry Miller, *The Air-Conditioned Nightmare*, 1945

The first of the unlimited industrial wars was the Civil War in America. It was the first great conflict of the steam age, and the aim of the Northern, or Federal, States was unconditional surrender – that is, total victory. Its character was, therefore, that of a crusade, and because of this, as well as because it put to the test the military developments of the Industrial Revolution, it opened a radically new chapter in the history of war.

J. F. C. Fuller, *The Decisive Battles of the Western World*, 1954–56

It was the railroad and the river steamboat which robbed the great battlefield victories of finality. It was these devices, managed by telegraphic communications, which made it possible promptly to repair the terrible casualties of the major battles, to re-supply and re-equip, to draw reinforcements from another theatre to plug the gaps which the enemy opened up, to manoeuver not only armies but groups of armies so as to prevent defeat from turning into destruction.

Walter Millis, *Arms and Men: a Study of American Military History*, 1958

The transcending facts of the American Civil War are the military genius of Robert E. Lee and the naval superiority of the North. Behind all the blood and sacrifice, behind the movements of armies and pronouncements of political leaders, the war was essentially a conflict between these two strategic forces. Lee's tactical opponent was the Army of the Potomac, but his strategic rival was the Union Navy.

John D. Hayes, *Sea Power in the Civil War*, 1961

A century is a long time. The Confederate flag is often just confetti in careless hands now.

Jonathan Daniels, *The South Today*, 1965

Two months after marching through Boston,
half the regiment was dead;
at the dedication,
William James could almost hear the bronze Negroes breathe.

Their monument sticks like a fishbone
in the city's throat.
Its Colonel is as lean
as a compass-needle.

He has an angry wrenlike vigilance,
a greyhound's gentle tautness;
he seems to wince at pleasure,
and suffocate for privacy.

He is out of bounds now. He rejoices in man's lovely,
peculiar power to choose life and die –
when he leads his black soldiers to death,
he cannot bend his back.

Robert Lowell, 'For the Union Dead', 1965

The men of 1860–61 allowed an academic argument about an 'imaginary Negro in an impossible place' to end in a bloody Civil War.

Peter J. Parish, *The American Civil War*, 1975

What happened on the field of battle had become more than ever the tip of the military iceberg. The great submerged mass was a matter of equipment, supply, transport and communications, of individual power, and technical skill, and also of public opinion, civilian morale, and sheer will to resist. War had become a matter of management and organization more than individual heroism or feats of derring-do. A policy of attrition by the stronger side ultimately wore out the weaker. This was now the way of reaching a military decision less spectacular and dramatic than the old, but ultimately more relentless and inescapable. It was all summed up in a few words written in 1863 by one of the organization men of the new warfare, Quartermaster-General Meigs: 'It is exhaustion of men and money that finally terminates all modern wars.'

Peter J. Parish, *The American Civil War*, 1975

Attack on Fort Sumter, April 1861

It will require the exercise of the full powers of the Federal Government to restrain the fury of the noncombatants.

Winfield Scott, attributed

Sometimes gunpowder smells good.

Ralph Waldo Emerson, quoted in Robert Debs Heinl Jr, *Dictionary of Military and Naval Quotations*, 1966

First Battle of Bull Run, 21st July 1861

Then, sir, we will give them the bayonet!

'Stonewall' Jackson, quoted in the *Charleston Mercury*, 25th July 1861

The Virginia Military Institute will be heard from today.

'Stonewall' Jackson, attributed

All battles, and their results, are far more matters of accident than is generally thought: but this was throughout a casualty, a chance. Each side supposed it had won, till the last moment. One had, in point of fact, just as much right to be routed as the other. By a fiction, or series of fictions, the national forces at the last moment exploded in a panic and fled from the field.

Walt Whitman, *Specimen Days*, 1882

The army which went forth to Bull Run, freighted with the hope of a loyal people, was simply a chain of weak links.

Emery Upton, *The Military Policy of the United States*, 1904

Sinking of USS *Cumberland*, 8th March 1862

And there, while thread will hang to thread,
Oh let the ensign fly!
The noblest constellation set
Against the Northern sky.

George Henry Boker, 'The *Cumberland*', 1862

Battle of Kernstown, 23rd March 1862

Lay me down and save the Flag!

Colonel James A. Mulligan, last command

Battle of Shiloh, 6th–7th April 1862

A case of Southern dash against Northern pluck and endurance.

Ulysses Grant, *Memoirs*, 1894

Battle of Fredericksburg, 13th December 1862

It is well that war is so terrible: we would grow too fond of it.

Robert E. Lee, comment passed to James Longstreet, 13th December 1862

Battle of Antietam (Sharpsburg), 17th December 1862

Sharpsburg was artillery hell.

Stephen D. Lee, attributed

Battle of Murfreesboro, 31st December 1862

Some of us must die. Cross yourselves and march forward.

W. S. Rosecrans, attributed

Battle of Gettysburg, 1st–3rd July 1863

Major, tell my father that I died with my face to the enemy.

Colonel I. E. Avery, attributed, 2nd July 1863

Never mind, General, all this has been my fault, it is I that have lost this fight, and you must help me out of it the best you can.

Robert E. Lee, to General C. M. Wilcox, following Pickett's Charge, 3rd July 1863

We have met on a great battlefield of that war. We have come to dedicate a portion of that battlefield as a final resting-place for those who here gave their lives that that nation might live. It is altogether fitting and proper that we should do this. But in a larger sense we cannot dedicate, we cannot hallow this ground. The brave men, living and dead, who struggled here have consecrated it far above our poor power to add or detract. The world will little note, nor long remember, what we say here, but it cannot forget what they did here.

Abraham Lincoln, the Gettysburg Address, 19th November 1863

'Tis Pickett's charge at Gettysburg:
How terrible it is to see
Great armies making history:
Long lines of musket belching flame!
No need of gunners taking aim
When from that thunder cloud of smoke
The lightning kills at every stroke!
If there's a place resembling hell,
'Tis where, 'mid shot and bursting shell,
Stalks Carnage arm in arm with Death,
A furnace-blast in every breath,
On Pickett's charge at Gettysburg.

Fred Emerson Brooks, 'Pickett's Charge', date unknown

In a previous battle [General Ewell] had lost one of his legs, but prided himself on the efficiency of the wooden one which he used in its place. As we rode together, a body of Union soldiers, posted behind some fences and buildings on the outskirts of the town, suddenly opened a brisk fire. A number of Confederates were killed and wounded, and I heard the ominous thud of a Minié ball as it struck General Ewell at my side. I quickly asked: 'Are you hurt, sir?' 'No, no,' he replied; 'I am not hurt. But suppose the ball had struck you; we would have had the trouble of carrying you off the field, sir. You see how much better fixed for a fight I am than you are. It don't hurt a bit to be shot in a wooden leg.'

John B. Gordon, *Reminiscences of the Civil War*, 1904

[on Pickett's Charge:] There it was, for the last time in this war, perhaps for the last time anywhere, the grand pageantry and colour of war in the old style, beautiful and majestic and terrible.

Bruce Catton, *Glory Road*, 1952

I was just an ordinary fellow, with an ordinary fellow's interest in the Civil War, until I spent two days at Gettysburg. Now I think I could lecture at the War College.

Philip Hamburger, *An American Notebook*, 1965

Surrender of Vicksburg, 4th July 1863

Let the only walls the foe shall scale
Be ramparts of the dead!

Paul Hamilton Hayne, 'Vicksburg', 1863

The Father of Waters again goes unvexed to the sea.

Abraham Lincoln, Letter to J. C. Conkling, 26th August 1863

Battle of Mobile Bay, 5th August 1864

Damn the torpedoes! Four bells, Captain Drayton, go ahead!
David Farragut, Order, 5th August 1864

The sea upon the bar is smooth
Yet perilous the path
Where Gaines' and Morgan's bristling guns
Belch forth their rebel wrath.
And, close behind, their ironclads
Loom in the breaking day;
But Farragut is leading us
And we will clear the way.
Anonymous, in *Army and Navy Journal*, 3rd September 1864

Sherman enters Savannah, 22nd December 1864

I beg to present you as a Christmas gift, the city of Savannah with 150 guns and plenty of ammunition, and also about 25,000 bales of cotton.
General W. T. Sherman, dispatch to President Lincoln, December 1864

Battle of Appomattox, 9th April 1865

The war is over. The rebels are our countrymen again.
Ulysses Grant, in an effort to silence the cheers of his victorious troops, 9th April 1965

There is nothing left for me but to go and see General Grant, and I would rather die a thousand deaths.
Robert E. Lee, to his staff, before meeting Grant at Appomattox Court House, 9th April 1865

Whatever General Lee's feelings were I do not know. As he was a man of much dignity, with an impassable face, it was impossible to say whether he felt inwardly glad that the end had finally come, or felt sad over the result and was too manly to show it.
Ulysses Grant, *Memoirs*, 1885

AMERICAN–INDIAN WARS, 18th to early 20th centuries

Indians spurr'd on by our inveterate Enemys the French, are the only Brutes and Cowards in the Creation who were ever known to exercise their Cruelties upon the Sex, and to scalp and mangle the poor sick Soldiers and defenceless Women.
Lord Amherst, General Order, 1758

We must act with vindictive earnestness against the Sioux, even to their extermination, men, women, and children. Nothing less will reach the root of the case.
W. T. Sherman, quoted in Robert Debs Heinl Jr, *Dictionary of Military and Naval Quotations*, 1966

Strategy, when practised by Indians, is called treachery.

Unknown U S Cavalry Officer, attributed, *c.* 1865

The only good Indians I ever saw were dead.

P. H. Sheridan, attributed, 1869

If I were an Indian, I would certainly prefer to cast my lot . . . to the free open plains rather than submit to the confined limits of a reservation, there to be the recipient of the blessed benefits of civilization with its vices thrown in.

George Armstrong Custer, 1874, in S. E. Morison, *The Oxford History of the American People*, 1965

I am tired of fighting. Our chiefs are killed. The old men are all dead. It is the young men who say yes or no. He who led the young men is dead. It is cold and we have no blankets. The little children are freezing to death. My people, some of them, have run away to the hills and have no blankets, no food. No one knows where they are – perhaps freezing to death. I want to have time to look for my children and see how many of them I can find. Maybe I shall find them among the dead. Hear me, my chiefs. I am tired. My heart is sick and sad. From where the sun now stands I will fight no more, forever.

Chief Joseph, Surrender Speech, October 1877

We took away their country and their means of support, broke up their mode of living, their habits of life, introduced disease and decay among them and it was for this and against this they made war. Could anyone expect less?

P. H. Sheridan, 1878, in Thomas C. Leonard, *Above the Battle*, 1978

When I was young I walked all over this country, east and west, and saw no other people than the Apaches. After many summers I walked again and found another race of people had come to take it. How is it? Why is it that the Apaches wait to die – that they carry their lives on their fingernails? They roam over the hills and the plains and want the heavens to fall on them. The Apaches were once a great nation; they are now but few, and because of this they so carry their lives on their fingernails . . .

Chief Cochise, in Dee Brown, *Bury My Heart at Wounded Knee*, 1970

Forward! If any man is killed I'll make him a corporal.

Adna R. Chaffee, during the Kiowa–Comanche campaign of 1874

ABYSSINIAN EXPEDITION of 1868

They brought the elephant of Asia to convey the artillery of Europe to dethrone one of the kings of Africa, and to hoist the standard of St George upon the mountains of Rasselas.

Benjamin Disraeli, in the House of Commons, 1868

THE FRANCO–PRUSSIAN WAR, 1870–71

Above all the plan of the war was based on the resolve to attack the enemy at once, wherever found, and keep the German forces so compact that a superior force could always be brought into the field. By whatever special means these plans were to be accomplished was left to the decision of the hour; the advance to the frontiers alone was pre-ordained in every detail.

Helmuth von Moltke, *The Franco–Prussian War of 1870–71*, 1891

What our sword has won in half a year, our sword must guard for half a century.

Helmuth von Moltke, *The Franco–Prussian War of 1870–71*, 1891

The main weakness and strength of the two armies lay not in their armaments, but in their respective General Staffs. In the French . . . the lack of an efficient General Staff was one of the main causes of Napoleon I's ultimate ruin. This was little appreciated in France after 1815, and when war broke out in 1870 we find that the officers of the General Staff of the Second Empire were mere popinjays and clerks, either young 'bloods' out of touch with the army or greybeards overwhelmed by the minutiae of routine. So far did Marshal Bazaine distrust his General Staff that he forbade its officers to appear on the battlefield, and instead of them he used his Personal Staff, as Napoleon had done 60 years before.

J. F. C. Fuller, *The Decisive Battles of the Western World*, 1954–56

Battle of Sedan, 1st September 1870

We are in a chamber-pot and we are going to be shat upon.

General Ducrot, on the eve of battle, in Docteur Sarazin, *Récits sur la dernière guerre franco-allemande*, 1887

Our superiority over the enemy was so overwhelming that we suffered no loss at all. The batteries fired as if at practice.

Prince Kraft zu Hohenlohe-Ingelfingen, *Letters on Artillery*, 1888

Never speak of it, but always remember it.

Léon Gambetta, attributed

RUSSO–TURKISH WAR of 1877–78

We don't want to fight, but, by jingo, if we do,
We've got the ships, we've got the men, we've got the money too.

G. W. Hunt, music hall song, 1878

THE BRITISH ARMY, *c.* 1880

The feeling that it was a disgrace to a family for one of its members to go for a soldier died hard. Although the gradual reform of conditions of army life and discipline had put an end to a rank-and-file of felons, drunks, and pathological outcasts, the army was still recruited mostly from the very poorest and most ignorant. The army was, in a real sense, the only welfare service provided by the British state for the rescue of such unfortunates.

Correlli Barnett, *Britain and Her Army 1509–1970*, 1970

BRITISH RULE IN INDIA, 19th century

The English are as brave as lions, they are splendid sepoys, and very nearly equal to us. A Gurkha soldier, after the capture of Bhurtpore, 1827, attributed

If the facilities for washing were as great as those for drink, our Indian Army would be the cleanest body of men in the world.

Florence Nightingale, *Observations on Evidence Contained in Stational Reports Submitted to the Royal Commission on the Sanitary State of the Army in India*, 1863

Sacred To The Memory Of
Captain Maurice James Butler,
Royal Irish Rifles.
Accidentally Shot Dead By His
Batman On The Fourth Day Of
April, 1882
'Well Done, Thou Good And
Faithful Servant'

Epitaph, in Miles Noonan, *Tales From the Mess*, 1983

Admirers of improvisation in the field of veterinary technique will wish to unite in respect for the unnamed farrier of the Royal Horse Artillery who at Umballa in 1898 used a fire-engine to give an enema to an elephant.

Miles Noonan, *Tales From the Mess*, 1983

[See also above, Indian Mutiny, p. 277]

THE BURMA WAR, 1883–85

Boh da Thone was a warrior bold:
His sword and his Snider were bossed with gold.

And the Peacock Banner his henchmen bore
Was stiff with bullion, but stiffer with gore.

He shot at the strong and slashed at the weak
From the Salween scrub to the Chindwin teak:

He crucified noble, he sacrificed mean,
He filled old ladies with kerosene:

While over the water the papers cried,
'The patriot fights for his countryside!'

Rudyard Kipling, 'Ballad of Boh da Thone', 1888

THE SUDAN WAR, 1892–98

Battle of Omdurman, 2nd September 1898

It was now half-past six. The flags seemed still very distant, the roar very faint, and the thud of our first gun was almost startling. It may have swung forward, and a mass of white flying linen swung forward with it too. They came very fast, and they came very straight; and then presently they came no farther. With a crash the bullets leaped out of the British rifles. It began with the Guards and Warwicks – section volleys at 2000 yards; then, as the Dervishes edged rightwards, it ran along to the Highlanders, the Lincolns, and to Maxwell's Brigade. The British stood up in double rank behind their zariba; the blacks lay down in their shelter-trench; both poured out death as fast as they could load and press a trigger. Shrapnel whistled and Maxims growled savagely. From all the line came perpetual fire, fire, fire and shrieked forth in great gusts of destruction.

And the enemy? No white troops would have faced that torrent of death for five minutes, but the Bagarra and the blacks came on. The torrent swept into them and hurled them down in whole companies . . . It was the last day of Mahdism, and the greatest. They could never get near, and they refused to hold back. By now the ground before us was all white with dead men's drapery. Rifles grew red-hot; the soldiers seized them by slings and dragged them back to the reserve to change to cool ones. It was not a battle, but an execution.

George Warrington Steevens, *With Kitchener to Khartoum*, 1898

But the cockpit of the fight was Macdonald's. The British might avenge his brigade; it was his to keep it and to kill off the attack. To meet it he turned his front through a complete half-circle, facing successively south, west and north. Every tactician in the army was delirious in his praise: the ignorant correspondent was content to watch the man and his blacks. 'Cool as on parade' is an old phrase; Macdonald Bey was very much cooler. Beneath the strong, square-hewn face you could tell that the brain was working as if packed in ice. He sat solid on his horse, and bent his black brows towards the green flag and the Remingtons. Then he turned to a galloper with an order, and cantered easily up to a battalion commander. Magically the rifles hushed, the stinging powder smoke wiped away, and the companies were rapidly threading back and forward, round and round, in and out, as if it were a figure of a dance. In two minutes the brigade was together again in a new place . . . Macdonald's jaw gripped and hardened as the flame spurted out again, and the whitey-brown cloud quivered and stood still. He saw everything; knew what to do; knew how to do it. At the fire he was ever brooding watchfully behind his firing-line; at the cease-fire he was instantly in front of it: all saw him, and knew that they were being nursed to triumph.

George Warrington Steevens, *With Kitchener to Khartoum*, 1898

THE SPANISH–AMERICAN WAR, 1898

You furnish the pictures and I'll furnish the war.

William Randolph Hearst, cable to Frederic Remington, in Cuba, March 1898

While we are conducting war, and until its conclusion, we must keep all we get; when the war is over we must keep what we want.

William McKinley, memorandum, 1898

We've taken up the white man's burden
Of ebony and brown;
Now will you kindly tell us, Rudyard,
How we may put it down?

Anonymous, contemporary

Rough-tough, we're the stuff! We want to fight and we can't get enough!

Motto of the 'Rough Riders' (1st US Cavalry Regiment)

The Spanish–American War was not a great war. A large number of our troops took the hazard of watermelons in Georgia and Florida, and fought the malaria and mosquitos, but very few Spanish . . .

James L. Slayden, in the House of Representatives, 1906

An hour or two at Manila, an hour or two at Santiago, and the maps of the world were changed.

Albert Smith Barker, quoted in Robert Debs Heinl Jr, *Dictionary of Military and Naval Quotations*, 1966

Battle of Manila Bay, 1st May 1898

The battle of Manila Bay was one of the most important ever fought. It decided that the United States should start in a direction in which it had never travelled before. It placed the United States in the family of great nations.

Bradley A. Fiske, Letter to Mark Sullivan, 1925

[See also Part III: Dewey, p. 411]

Battle of Santiago de Cuba, 3rd July 1898

Don't cheer, boys – the poor devils are dying.

John W. Philip, as his ship, the USS *Texas*, passed the burning Spanish cruiser *Vizkaya*

PHILIPPINE INSURRECTION, 1899–1904

Damn, damn, damn the Filipinos!
Cross-eyed, kakiak ladrones!
Underneath the starry flag
Civilize 'em with a Krag,
And return us to our own beloved homes.

US soldiers' song, *c.* 1900

Oh, I want to know, who's the boss of this show?
Is it me, or Emilio Aguinaldo?

US soldiers' song, 1901, referring to William Howard Taft, then Governor-General of the Philippines

Zamboanga, Mindanao,
From the transport you look damn well,
But before I'd serve again in Zamboanga
I'd rather serve a hitch in Hell.

US soldiers' song, *c.* 1901

A man who is good enough to shed his blood for his country is good enough to be given a square deal afterwards,

Theodore Roosevelt, at Springfield, Illinois, 4th July 1903

THE BOER WAR, 1899–1902

They have asked for my trousers, and I have given them; for my coat, and I have given that also; now they want my life, and that I cannot give.

Paulus Krüger, speech in Raad, 7th September 1899

We are not interested in the possibilities of defeat.

Queen Victoria, in conversation with Arthur Balfour, December 1899

You entered into these two republics for philanthropic purposes and remained to commit burglary

David Lloyd George, in the House of Commons, 25th July 1900

They throw in Drummer Hodge, to rest
Uncoffined – just as found:
His landmark is a kopje-crest
That breaks the veldt around;
And foreign constellations west
Each night above his mound.

Young Hodge the Drummer never knew –
Fresh from his Wessex home –
The meaning of the broad Karoo,
The Bush, the dusty loam,
And why uprose to nightly view
Strange stars amid the gloam.

Yet portion of that unknown plain
Will Hodge for ever be;
His homely Northern breast and brain
Grow to some Southern Tree,
And strange-eyed constellations reign
His stars eternally.

Thomas Hardy, 'Drummer Hodge', *c.* 1901

The General got 'is decorations thick
(The men that backed 'is lies could not complain),
The Staff 'ad DSOs till we was sick,
An' the soldier – 'ad to do his work again!

Rudyard Kipling, 'Stellenbosch', 1903

Out of that bungled, unwise war
An alp of unforgiveness grew.

William Plomer, 'The Boer War', 1932

Before the war, and especially before the Boer War, it was summer all the year round.

George Orwell, *Coming Up for Air*, 1939

In this war the old terror of a visible foe gave way to the paralysing sensation of advancing on an invisible one, which fostered the suspicion that the enemy was everywhere. A universal terror, rather than a localized danger, now enveloped the attacker, while the defender, always ready to protect himself by some rough earth or stone-work, was enabled through the rapidity of rifle-fire to use extensions unheard of in past fighting, and in consequence to overlap every frontal attack.

J. F. C. Fuller, *The Decisive Battles of the Western World*, 1954–56

While the British Empire was mostly acquired at a period when the Colonial Office . . . occupied haphazard premises in Downing Street, a new phase of colonial policy began when the department moved into buildings actually designed for the purpose. This was in 1875 and the structure was well designed as a background for the disasters of the Boer War.

C. Northcote Parkinson, *Parkinson's Law*, 1958

The war had been essentially fought to prevent the Boers establishing a Dutch republic over all southern Africa, including Cape Colony, and instead to extend British sovereignty over the existing Dutch Republics. The results of this generous political settlement made by Britain in 1907 was that fifty-four years later, the whole region became a Boer republic.

Correlli Barnett, *Britain and Her Army 1509–1970*, 1970

Haig soon settled into the voyage, which was unique in the fact that his fellow passengers included Boer soldiers, among them two nephews of Paul Kruger, the President of the Transvaal. The irony of men travelling together for seventeen days in order to fight each other on the other side of the world apparently escaped Haig's notice.

Gerard J. De Groot, *Douglas Haig 1861–1928*, 1988

Siege of Mafeking, October 1899–17th May 1900

I was returning to my hotel one afternoon in the first week of May, and saw outside my room several white men looking at something on the ground. When I arrived I saw that the 'something' was a little Kafir boy of about twelve years who lay on the ground, a living skeleton in the agonies of death. The commissariat officer was among those who watched him, and fate threw open the miserable rag that covered the boy's chest and displayed his little bones protruding, as though to say to the official, 'The lad dies of hunger'. Anything more depressing than the sight of these struggling remains of humanity it would be impossible to imagine. Hunger weakened us; it killed the wretched natives.

Emerson Neilly, *Besieged with B.P.*

Siege of Ladysmith, 2nd November 1899–27th February 1900

Relieve us, in Heaven's name, good countrymen, or we die of dullness.

George Warrington Steevens, in the *Ladysmith Lyre*, December 1899

Battle of Stormberg, 10th December 1899

And there was General Gatacre, whose performance at the Battle of Stormberg Junction was singularly lacking in panache. To capture *his* objective, Gatacre settled for a night march followed by a dawn attack. Not only did he not know the route but he succeeded in forgetting to bring along the one man who did, a certain Captain of Intelligence. As the result of the appointment of two 'guides' (who knew no more than he did), dawn found him and his army behind the hills he was supposed to be in front of. After some moments of consternation, during which he lost all sense of direction, the general resolutely faced his army the wrong way with their backs to the enemy.

Having recovered from the novel experience of being attacked by an army which appeared to be moving in reverse, the Boers opened fire with such devastating results that within half an hour Gatacre's force was in full retreat. When finally they reached their original starting-line they were delighted to find they had suffered only 90 casualties. Their euphoria was shortlived, for a second count revealed that 'by a mere oversight' 600 British soldiers had been left behind on the enemy-held hills. Since nobody had told them to retreat, they became prisoners of the Boers.

Norman F. Dixon, *On the Psychology of Military Incompetence*, 1976

WORLD WAR ONE, 1914–18

If the iron dice roll, may God help us.

Theobald von Bethmann-Hollweg, in the German Reichstag, 1914

That night [3rd August 1914], as the lamps were being lit in the summer dusk, [Viscount] Grey, standing in the windows of his room at the Foreign Office overlooking St James's Park, said to a friend: 'The lamps are going out all over Europe; we shall not see them lit again in our lifetime.'

G. M. Trevelyan, *Grey of Fallodon*, 1937

Just for the word 'neutrality', a word which in wartime has so often been disregarded – just for a scrap of paper, Great Britain is going to make war on a kindred nation who desires nothing better than to be friends with her.

Theobald von Bethmann-Hollweg, to Sir Edward Goschen, 4th August 1914

It is my Royal and Imperial Command that you should concentrate your energies for the immediate present upon one single purpose, that is that you address all your skill and all the valour of my soldiers to exterminate first, the treacherous English, [and] walk over General French's contemptible little army.

Kaiser Wilhelm II, Order issued 19th August 1914

The War That Will End War

H. G. Wells, title of a book, 1914

The immediate object of fighting is to kill and go on killing, until there is nothing left to kill.

Comment attributed to an unknown French officer, 1914

The only law in France today is to win or die. I repeat my formal request, that you place in the highest positions only men who are young, energetic, and decided to win at any price; eliminate the old fossils without pity.

Adolphe Messimy, imploring Marshal Joffre, 24th August 1914, in Joffre, *Memoirs*, 1932

I feel my own life all the more precious and more dear in the presence of this deflowering of Europe. While it is true that the guns will effect a little useful weeding, I am furious with chagrin to think that the Minds, which were to have excelled the civilization of two thousand years, are being annihilated – and bodies, the product of aeons of Natural Selection, melted down to pay for political statues.

Wilfred Owen, Letter, 28th August 1914

They shall not grow old, as we that are left grow old:
Age shall not weary them nor the years condemn.

Laurence Binyon, 'For the Fallen', September 1914

I cannot get any sense of an enemy – only of a disaster.

D. H. Lawrence, Letter to Edward Marsh, October 1914

The maxim of the British people is 'Business as usual'.

Winston Churchill, speaking at the Guildhall, 9th November 1914

If I should die, think only this of me:
  That there's some corner of a foreign field
That is for ever England. There shall be
  In that rich earth a richer dust concealed;
A dust whom England bore, shaped, made aware,
  Gave, once, her flowers to love, her ways to roam,
A body of England's, breathing English air,
  Washed by the rivers, blest by suns of home.

Rupert Brooke, 'The Soldier', 1914

We who strike the enemy where his heart beats have been slandered as 'baby-killers' and 'murderers of women' . . . What we do is repugnant to us too, but necessary. Very necessary. Nowadays there is no such animal as a non-combatant: modern warfare is total warfare. A soldier cannot function at the front without the factory worker, the farmer, and all the other providers behind him. You and I, Mother, have discussed this subject, and I know you understand what I say. My men are brave and honourable. Their cause is holy, so how can they sin while doing their duty? If what we do is frightful, then may frightfulness be Germany's salvation.

Captain Peter Strausser, 1915, in Aaron Norman, *The Great Air War*, 1968

As re the workmen who are said to get drunk now, I expect that the New Army has taken away a very large number of the best workers, so that many who were only occasional workers (because of their taste for Drink) have now to work full time. Their presence or absence was hardly noticed until the need for a full output of work was rendered necessary by the war. I don't suppose it would be possible to make such people sober by any regulations. The best thing, in my opinion, is to punish some of the chief offenders . . . Take and shoot two or three of them, and the 'Drink habit' would cease I feel sure. These sub-people don't care what the King or anyone else does – they mean to have their drink.

Douglas Haig, Letter to Lady Haig, 10th April 1915

There is such a thing as a man being too proud to fight.

Woodrow Wilson, speech at Philadelphia, 10th May 1915

The torpedo that sank the *Lusitania* also sank Germany in the opinion of mankind.

New York Nation, May 1915

There is a price which is too great to pay for peace, and that price can be put into one word. One cannot pay the price of self-respect.

Woodrow Wilson, speech at Des Moines, Iowa, 1st February 1916

What did you do in the Great War, Daddy?

British Recruiting Poster, *c.* 1916

I have a rendezvous with Death,
At some disputed barricade.

Alan Seeger, 'I Have A Rendezvous With Death', 1916

Time swims before me, making as a day
  A thousand years, while the broad ploughland oak
  Roars mill-like and men strike and bear the stroke
  Of war as ever, audacious or resigned,
And God still sits aloft in the array
  That we have wrought him, stone-deaf and stone-blind.

Edward Thomas, 'February Afternoon', 1916

The world must be made safe for democracy.

Woodrow Wilson, Address to Congress, 2nd April 1917

When a war is waged by two opposing groups of robbers for the sake of deciding who shall have a freer hand to oppress more people, then the question of the origin of the war is of no real economic or political significance.

V. I. Lenin, in *Pravda*, 26th April 1917

Aunt Maria: Do you know I actually once saw the Kaiser riding through the streets of London as bold as brass. If I'd known then what I know now I'd have told a policeman.

Cartoon caption, *Punch*, November 1917

Please God – let there be victory, before the Americans arrive.

Douglas Haig, diary entry, 1917

If any question why we died,
Tell them, because our fathers lied.

Rudyard Kipling, 'Epitaphs of War', 1914–18

This is really a platoon commanders' war.

Douglas Haig, diary entry, 29th July 1918

What I dread is that Germany doesn't know that she is licked. Had they given us another week, we'd have *taught* them.

John J. Pershing, 1918, in Donald Smythe, 1986

To conquer the world with arms is only to make a temporary conquest; to conquer the world by earning its esteem is to make a permanent conquest.

Woodrow Wilson, in Congress, 11th November 1918

Thank God this is over and we can get back to real soldiering again.

Soldiers' saying, after the Armistice of 1918

What is our task? To make Britain a fit country for heroes to live in.

David Lloyd George, speech, 24th November 1918

Even in theory the gas mask is a dreadful thing. It stands for one's first flash of insight into man's measureless malignity against man.

Reginald Farrer, *The Void of War*, 1918

The first hundred years are the hardest.

US Expeditionary Force saying, 1918

We drove the Boche across the Rhine,
The Kaiser from his throne.
Oh, Lafayette, we've paid our debt,
For Christ's sake, send us home.

US Army song, 1919, during the occupation of the Rhineland.

And he'd come home again to find it more
Desirable than ever it was before.
How right it seemed that he should reach the span
Of comfortable years allowed to man!
Splendid to eat and sleep and choose a wife,
Safe with his wound, a citizen of life.
He hobbled blithely through the garden gate,
And thought: 'Thank God they had to amputate!'

Siegfried Sassoon, 'The One-Legged Man', 1916

'Good morning! Good morning!' the General said
When we met him last week on the way to the Line.
Now the soldiers he smiled at are most of 'em dead,
And we're cursing his staff for incompetent swine.
'He's a cheery old card,' grunted Harry to Jack
As they slogged up to Arras with rifle and pack.
But he did for them both with his plan of attack.

Siegfried Sassoon, 'The General', 1917

I see them in foul dug-outs, gnawed by rats,
And in the ruined trenches, lashed with rain,
Dreaming of things they did with balls and bats,
And mocked by hopeless longing to regain

Bank-holidays, and picture-shows, and spats,
  And going to the office in the train.
Siegfried Sassoon, 'Dreamers', 1917

You love us when we're heroes, home on leave,
Or wounded in a mentionable place.
You worship decorations; you believe
That chivalry redeems the war's disgrace.
You make us shells. You listen with delight,
By tales of dirt and danger fondly thrilled.
You crown our distant ardours while we fight,
And mourn our laurelled memories when we're killed.
You can't believe that British troops 'retire'
When hell's last horror breaks them, and they run,
Trampling the terrible corpses – blind with blood.
  O German mother dreaming by the fire,
While you are knitting socks to send your son
His face is trodden deeper in the mud.
Siegfried Sassoon, 'Glory of Women', 1917

When you are standing at your hero's grave,
Or near some homeless village where he died,
Remember, through your heart's rekindling pride,
The German soldiers who were loyal and brave.
Men fought like brutes; and hideous things were done;
And you have nourished hatred, harsh and blind.
But in that Golgotha perhaps you'll find
The mothers of the men who killed your son.
Siegfried Sassoon, 'Reconciliation', 1918

To have built up successfully in the very midst of war a great new Army on a more than Continental scale, capable of beating the best troops of the strongest military nation in pre-war days, is an achievement of which the whole Empire may be proud.
Douglas Haig, in *Sir Douglas Haig's Despatches*, ed. J. H. Boraston, 1919

This war, in its inception, was a commercial and industrial war. It was not a political war.
Woodrow Wilson, 1919, in J. F. C. Fuller, *The Conduct of War, 1789–1961*, 1961

The war we have just been through, though it was shot through with terror, is not to be compared with the war we would have to face next time.
Woodrow Wilson, 1919, in John Dos Passos, *Mr Wilson's War*, 1963

His wild heart beats with painful sobs
His strain'd hands clench an ice-cold rifle
his aching jaws grip a hot parch'd tongue
his wide eyes search unconsciously.

He cannot shriek.

Blood saliva
dribbles down his shapeless jacket.

I saw him stab
and stab again
a well-killed Boche.

This is the happy warrior,
this is he . . .

Herbert Read, *The Happy Warrior*, 1919

There was nothing very new to learn about this war or the end it was fought for; England had destroyed, as in each preceding century, a trade rival.

John Maynard Keynes, *The Economic Consequences of the Peace*, 1920

This book is not about heroes. English poetry is not yet fit to speak of them.

Nor is it about deeds, or lands, nor anything about glory, honour, might, majesty, dominion, or power, except War.

Above all I am not concerned with Poetry.

My subject is War, and the pity of War.

The Poetry is in the pity.

Yet these elegies are to this generation in no sense consolatory. They may be to the next. All a poet can do today is warn. That is why the true Poets must be truthful.

Wilfred Owen, Preface to his *Poems*, 1920

Then Abram bound the youth with belts and straps,
And builded parapets and trenches there,
And stretched forth the knife to slay/his son.
When lo! an angel called him out of heaven,
Saying, Lay not thy hand upon the lad,
Neither do anything to him. Behold,
A ram, caught in a thicket by its horns;
Offer the Ram of Pride instead of him.
But the old man would not so, but slew his son,
And half the seed of Europe, one by one.

Wilfred Owen, 'The Parable of the Old Man and the Young', in *Poems*, 1920

What passing-bells for these who die as cattle?
  Only the monstrous anger of the guns,
  Only the stuttering rifles' rapid rattle
Can patter out their hasty orisons.
No mockeries now for them; no prayers nor bells,
  Nor any voice of mourning save the choirs, –
The shrill, demented choirs of wailing shells;
  And bugles calling for them from sad shires.

Wilfred Owen, 'Anthem for Doomed Youth', in *Poems*, 1920

Move him into the sun –
Gently its touch awoke him once,
At home, whispering of fields unsown.
Always it woke him, even in France,
Until this morning and this snow.
If anything might rouse him now
The kind old sun will know.

Wilfred Owen, 'Futility', in *Poems*, 1920

Oh, Death was never enemy of ours!
We laughed at him, we leagued with him, old chum.
No soldier's paid to kick against his powers.
We laughed, knowing that better men would come,
And greater wars; when each proud fighter brags
He wars on Death – for lives; not men – for flags.

Wilfred Owen, 'The Next War', in *Poems*, 1920

The World War was only a point on the graph curve showing the evolution of the character of war: at that point the graph curve makes a sharp swerve showing the influence of entirely new factors. For this reason clinging to the past will teach us nothing useful for the future, for that future will be radically different from anything that has gone before. The future must be approached from a new angle.

Giulio Douhet, *The Command of the Air*, 1921

The foolish doctrine was preached to the public through innumerable agencies that Generals and Admirals must be right on war matters, and civilians of all kinds must be wrong. These erroneous conceptions were inculcated billion-fold by the newspapers under the crudest forms. The feeble or presumptuous politician is portrayed cowering in his office, intent in the crash of the world on Party intrigues or personal glorification, fearful of responsibility, incapable of aught save shallow phrase-making. To him enters the calm, noble, resolute figure of the great Commander by land or sea, resplendent in uniform, glittering with decorations, irradiated with the lustre of the hero, shod with the science and armed with the panoply of war. This stately figure, devoid of the slightest thought of self, offers his clear far-sighted guidance and counsel for vehement action or artifice or wise delay. But his advice is rejected; his sound plans put aside; his courageous initiative baffled by political chatterboxes and incompetents. As well, it was suggested, might a great surgeon, about to operate with sure science and the study of a lifetime upon a desperate case, have his arm jogged or his hand impeded, or even his lancet snatched from him, by some agitated relation of the patient. Such was the picture presented to the public, and such was the mood which ruled.

Winston Churchill, *The World Crisis, 1916–1918*, 1923

The Tank was the beginning of the bullet-proof army.

Winston Churchill, *The World Crisis, 1916–1918*, 1923

It was . . . a fundamental mistake to ridicule the worth of the enemy, as the Austrian and German comic papers made a chief point of doing in their propaganda. The very principle here is a mistaken one: for, when they came face to face with the enemy, our soldiers had quite a different impression. Therefore, the mistake had disastrous results. Once the German soldier realized what a tough enemy he had to fight he felt that he had been deceived by the manufacturers of the information which had been given him. Therefore, instead of strengthening and stimulating his fighting spirit, this information had quite the contrary effect. Finally, he lost heart.

Adolf Hitler, *Mein Kampf*, 1924–26

As wounded men may limp through life, so our war minds may not regain the balance of their thoughts for decades.

Frank Moore Colby, *The Colby Essays*, 1926

On the score of courage, patriotism, sacrifice and death, we had been deceived and with the first bullets we recognized at once the falsity of anecdote, history, literature, art, the gossip of veterans, and public speeches.

Jean Norton Cru, *Du Témoignage*, 1931

. . . The lecturer's voice still battered on my brain. 'The bullet and the bayonet are brother and sister.' 'If you don't kill him, he'll kill you.' 'Stick him between the eyes, in the throat, in the chest.' 'Don't waste good steel. Six inches are enough. What's the use of a foot of steel sticking out at the back of a man's neck? Three inches will do for him; when he coughs, go and look for another.'

Siegfried Sassoon, *Memoirs of an Infantry Officer*, 1931

In the face of gas, without protection, individuality was annihilated; the soldier in the trench became a mere passive recipient of torture and death. A final stage seemed to be reached in the whole tendency of modern scientific warfare to depress and make of no effect individual bravery, enterprise and skill.

C. R. M. F. Crutwell, *A History of the Great War*, 1934

Here dead we lie because we did not choose
  To live and shame the land from which we sprung.
Life, to be sure, is nothing much to lose,
  But young men think it is, and we were young.

A. E. Housman, *More Poems*, 1936

. . . The General said to me: 'The War Office is very nervous about an invasion, there are five million (or whatever the number was) sheep in Sussex, Kent, and Surrey. When the enemy land, they will at once be moved by route march to Salisbury Plain.' I knew that this was an impossible task, and that Sir John Moore had proclaimed it as such in 1805. But there was no arguing over it, so I spent days and days working out march tables for sheep. One day I said to him: 'Do you realize, sir, that should all these sheep be set in movement, every road will be blocked?' 'Of course,' he answered; 'at once arrange to have a number of signposts ready and marked, *Sheep are not to use this road*.' 'But,' I replied, 'what if the less well-educated sheep are unable to read them?'

J. F. C. Fuller, *Memoirs of an Unconventional Soldier*, 1936

Nobody wanted war . . . The nations backed their machines over the precipice.
David Lloyd George, *War Memoirs*, 1936

The Army Chiefs were mostly horsemen.
David Lloyd George, *War Memoirs*, 1936

Men are reluctant to believe that great events have small causes. Therefore, once the Great War started, they were convinced that it must be the outcome of profound forces. It is hard to discover these when we examine the details. Nowhere was there conscious determination to provoke a war. Statesmen miscalculated. They used the instruments of bluff and threat which had proved effective on previous occasions. This time things went wrong. The deterrent on which they relied failed to deter; the statesmen became the prisoners of their own weapons. The great armies, accumulated to provide security and preserve peace, carried the nations to war by their own weight.
A. J. P. Taylor, *The First World War*, 1963

It was often said in 1914, and has been often repeated since: 'mobilization means war'. This was not true. All the Powers except one could mobilize and could yet go on with diplomacy, keeping the armies within their frontiers. Mobilization was a threat of a high order, but still a threat. The Germans, however, had run mobilization and war into one. In this sense, Schlieffen, Chief of the German General Staff from 1892 to 1906, though dead, was the real maker of the First World War. 'Mobilization means war' was his idea. In 1914 his dead hand automatically pulled the trigger.
A. J. P. Taylor, *The First World War*, 1963

Railway trains go faster than men walking. This is the strategical reason why the defence was stronger than the attack throughout the First World War. Defence was mechanized; attack was not.
A. J. P. Taylor, *The First World War*, 1963

The First World War had causes but no objectives.
Correlli Barnett, *The Swordbearers*, 1963

These men [Kitchener's New Army] were of the Victorian breed. They could say – and they did say – as they died in action, 'God bless the old regiment,' and 'Don't let them break the line!' and 'Do your duty, lads, and never mind me,' and 'Leave me; there are others more badly wounded.' One soldier said, when badly hit, 'Goodbye, old man, I'm done for. Tell poor old dad I died at the front. I began a letter to him; you finish it.'

Officers shouted 'Old England for ever! Follow me lads!' Or: 'No surrender, lads, remember the regiment!' Or: 'Bravo men, that was a gallant show!' . . .

And most of the time Victorian discipline prevailed. A soldier lying close by his platoon commander under fire said after a while, 'Sir, may I retire? I have been hit three times.'
John Laffin, *Tommy Atkins, the Story of an English Soldier*, 1966

Lenin was the first to discover that capitalism 'inevitably' caused war; and he discovered this only when the First World War was already being fought. Of course he was right. Since every great state was capitalist in 1914, capitalism obviously 'caused' the First World War; but just as obviously it had caused the previous generation of peace.

A. J. P. Taylor, *The Origins of the Second World War*, 1961

Even now [1914] the Liberal Government decided against conscription, so utterly had the ancient English obligation to bear arms in national defence become eclipsed by the later belief that conscription was incompatible with British liberty. Instead there was a call for volunteers: 'the first hundred thousand', and then as many as could be recruited. Kitchener's personal appeal for men was immortalized in the most famous of all British posters, on which his hooded eyes glared over a pointed finger above the legend: 'Your country needs YOU'.

Correlli Barnett, *Britain and Her Army, 1509–1970*, 1970

The war will not be understood in traditional terms: the machine gun alone makes it so special and unexampled that it simply can't be talked about as if it were one of the conventional wars of history.

Paul Fussell, *The Great War and Modern Memory*, 1975

In terms of the number of lives lost, relative to the ground gained, the actions of the First World War make dismal reading. In the first two hours of the battle of Loos we lost more men than were lost by all the services together in the whole of D-Day 1944. On the first day of the Somme offensive the British Army suffered 57,000 casualties – the biggest loss ever suffered by any army in a single day. And yet, as one historian has put it, to see the ground gained one needs a magnifying glass and large-scale map.

Norman F. Dixon, *On the Psychology of Military Incompetence*, 1976

When Roumania declared war in August 1916, it is said that one of the first army orders, after mobilization, was that only officers above the rank of major were allowed to use make-up.

Ronald Lewin, in *Oxford Book of Military Anecdotes*, ed. Max Hastings, 1987

What that generation of naval and military leaders, no longer young, brought up in Victorian society, and accustomed to a leisurely process of technical and social change, had to face was this:

the first war of aviation, with all the implications of that;
the first real under-sea war, entirely altering the nature of naval power;
the first war of the internal combustion engine, therefore also the first war of the mechanics, a new breed of men in uniform;
the first war of wireless telegraphy;
the first of the two great artillery wars, with all *their* destructive implications;
the first chemical war, using (among other things) poison gas and napalm (flame-throwers, petroleum-based);
the first war of modern mass production, mass logistics, and mass administration (by 1916 British GHQ in France was administering a population bigger than any single unit of control in England, except Greater London);
and much else besides.

All in all, the 'custom-bound clique' had a good deal to think about; its experience was in fact unique; never before or since has so much innovation been packed into such a short space of time.

John Terraine, *The Smoke and the Fire*, 1980

Songs of the First World War

Old soldiers never die;
They only fade away!

Anonymous, British

Brother Bertie went away
To do his bit the other day
With a smile on his lips and his
Lieutenant's pips upon his shoulder bright and gay.
As the train moved out he said,
'Remember me to all the birds.'
And he wagg'd his paw and went away to war
Shouting out these pathetic words:
Goodbye-ee, goodbye-ee.
Wipe the tear, baby dear, from your eye-ee,
Tho' it's hard to part I know,
I'll be tickled to death to go,
Don't cry-ee, don't sigh-ee,
There's a silver lining in the sky-ee!
Bonsoir, old thing! cheerio! chin-chin!
Nahpoo! Toodle-oo! goodbye-ee

R. P. Weston and Bert Lee, British, 1915

Belgium put the kibosh on the Kaiser,
Europe took a stick and made him sore;
And if Turkey makes a stand
She'll get ghurka'd and japanned,
And it won't be Hoch the Kaiser any more.

Anonymous, British, 1915

Hush, here comes a whizzbang,
Hush, here comes a whizzbang,
Now, you soldier men, get down those stairs,
Down in your dugouts and say your prayers.

R. P. Weston, F. R. Barnes and Maurice Scott, 1916

Keep the home fires burning,
While your hearts are yearning . . .

Lena Guilbert Ford, 1915

The bells of hell go ting-a-ling-a-ling
For you but not for me.

Anonymous, British

We'll be over, we're coming over,
And we won't come back till it's over, over there.

George M. Cohan (American), 1917

We're here because we're here because we're here because we're here . . .

Anonymous, American

The Western Front

You will be home before the leaves have fallen from the trees.

Kaiser Wilhelm II, addressing Germans troops leaving for the Front, August 1914

The battlefield is fearful. One is overcome by a peculiar sour, heavy and penetrating smell of corpses. Rising over a plank bridge, you find the middle is supported only by the body of a long-dead horse. Men that were killed last October lie half in swamp and half in the yellow-sprouting beet-fields. The legs of an Englishman, still encased in puttees, stick out of a trench, the corpse being built into the parapet; a soldier hangs his rifle on them. A little brook runs through the trench, and everyone used the water for drinking and washing; it is the only water they have. Nobody minds the pale Englishman who is rotting away a few steps further up.

Rudolph Binding, *A Fatalist at War*, 1915

A chap in our company has a ripping cure for neuralgia, but he isn't going to take out a patent, because it's too risky, and might kill a patient. He was lying in the trenches the other day nearly mad with pain in his face, when a German shell burst close by. He wasn't hit, but the explosion knocked him senseless for a bit. 'Me neuralgia's gone!' says he, when he came around. 'And so's six of your mates!' says me. 'O Cricky,' says he. His name's Palmer, and that's why we call the German shells now 'Palmer's Neuralgia Cure'.

An unnamed soldier, writing home, 1915, in John Laffin, *Tommy Atkins: the Story of an English Soldier*, 1966

In Flanders fields the poppies blow
Between the crosses, row on row
That mark our place; and in the sky
The larks, still bravely singing, fly
Scarce heard amid the guns below.

We are the Dead. Short days ago
We lived, felt dawn, saw sunset glow,
Loved and were loved, and now we lie
In Flanders fields.

Take up our quarrel with the foe:
To you from failing hands we throw
The torch; be yours to hold it high.
If ye break faith with us who die
We shall not sleep, though poppies grow
In Flanders fields.

John McCrae, 'In Flanders Fields', 1915

We would seem to be confronted with the problem that unless we use a great deal of artillery fire we cannot get on, and if we do use it the ground is destroyed . . . Therefore the problem to be solved is how to get forward without too much destruction of the ground.

General William Robertson, memorandum to Douglas Haig, 15th September 1917 (re Flanders)

Nevertheless, except you share
With them in hell the sorrowful dark of hell,
Whose world is but the trembling of a flare,
And heaven but as the highway for a shell,

You shall not hear their mirth:
You shall not come to think them well content
By any jest of mine. These men are worth
Your tears. You are not worth their merriment.

Wilfred Owen, *'Apologia Pro Poemate Meo'*, November 1917

I must say our idea of what American men are like was quite wrong! Those we are working with are quiet, unassuming, practical fellows. Entirely unlike the fashionable Yankees we used to see in London following in the wake of some loud-mouthed American beauty! Personally, I am finding the American men connected with the USA Forces very much like our own officers. I need give them no higher recommendation.

Douglas Haig, Letter to Lady Haig, 8th December 1917

The Garden called Gethsemane
In Picardy it was,
And there the people came to see
The English soldiers pass.

We used to pass – we used to pass
Or halt, as it might be,
And ship our masks in case of gas
Beyond Gethsemane.

The Garden called Gethsemane
It held a pretty lass,
But all the time she talked to me
I prayed my cup might pass.

The officer sat on the chair,
The men lay on the grass,
And all the time we halted there
I prayed my cup might pass.

It didn't pass – it didn't pass –
It didn't pass from me.
I drank it when we met the gas
Beyond Gethsemane.

Rudyard Kipling, 'Gethsemane', 1918

[On the British GHQ at Montreuil] An 'Open Sesame' by means of a special pass was needed to enter this city of Beautiful Nonsense. Below the gateway, up the steep hillside, sentries stood at a white post across the road, which lifted up on pulleys when the pass had been examined by a military policeman in a red cap. Then the sentries slapped their hands on their rifles to the occupants of any motor-car, sure that more staff-officers were going in to perform those duties which no private soldier could attempt to understand, believing they belonged to such mysteries as those of God. Through the narrow streets walked elderly generals, middle-aged colonels and majors, youthful subalterns all wearing red hat-bands, red tabs, and the blue-and-red armlet of G.H.Q., so that colour went with them on their way. Often one saw the Commander-in-Chief starting for an afternoon ride, a fine figure, nobly mounted, with two A.D.C.s and an escort of Lancers. A pretty sight, with fluttering pennons on all their lances, and horses groomed to the last hair. It was prettier than the real thing up in the Salient or beyond the Somme, where dead bodies lay in upheaved earth among ruins and slaughtered trees. War at Montreuil was quite a pleasant occupation for elderly generals who liked their little stroll after lunch, and for young Regular officers, released from the painful necessity of dying for their country.

Philip Gibbs, *Realities of War*, 1920

Only in the trenches (on both sides of No Man's Land) were chivalry and sweet reasonableness to be found.

Charles Edmonds, *A Subaltern's War*, 1929

The Army report confined itself to a single sentence: All quiet on the Western Front.

Erich Maria Remarque, *In Westen Nichts Neues*, 1929

Well, as to that, the nastiest job I've had
Was last year on this very front
Taking the discs at night from men
Who'd hung for six months on the wire
Just over there.
The worst of all was
They fell to pieces at a touch.
Thank God we couldn't see their faces;
They had gas helmets on . . .

Richard Aldington, 'Trench Idyll', 1929

Man, it seemed, had been created to jab the life out of Germans.

Siegfried Sassoon, *Memoirs of an Infantry Officer*, 1931

Having exhausted their own armies, the British and French stood ready to fight to the last American.

Allan Millett, *For the Common Defense*, 1984

The machine gun completed the contrast between the speed with which men could arrive at the battlefield by rail, and the slowness with which they moved once they were there. Indeed they did not move at all. The opposing lines congealed, grew solid. The generals on both sides stared at these lines impotently and without understanding. They went on staring for nearly four years.

A. J. P. Taylor, *The First World War*, 1963

The trenches were the concentration camps of the First World War.

Robert Kee, quoted in John Keegan, *The Face of Battle*, 1976

As a killing agent over long as well as short ranges . . . the bullet was champion. Unlike the musket-ball which, moving at slow speed and without rotating, merely drove a clean path for itself through soft tissue, the high velocity conical bullet, spinning quickly about its long axis, could produce inside the human body a variety of extremely unpleasant results. At best, it left a neat channel with the 'exit' wound the same size as the 'entry'. Should it be caused to 'tumble' inside the body, however, either on hitting bone or for some ballistic reason, its path beyond the point of tumble became very much enlarged and the 'exit' wound – often mistaken by amateurs for the entry – 'explosive' in appearance. The effects of a tumble produced by striking bone were enhanced by the bone's splintering under the impact, its own fragments then becoming secondary projectiles which produced massive damage to tissues round about. Some bullets also set up hydraulic effects, their passage driving body fluids away from the wound track at pressures which surrounding tissues could not withstand. The lower frequency of bullet wounds, noted in the medical statistics, may thus have been due to the bullet's greater lethality, for doctors noted the nature of wounds brought to them for treatment, not those inflicted on the bodies of all soldiers. It is suspicious, for example, that, at one major Casualty Clearing Station, the proportion of bullet wounds of the chest to all other gunshot wounds was, during a year of serious fighting, about three per cent.

John Keegan, *The Face of Battle*, 1976

I lost all count of the shells and all count of time. There was no past to remember or future to think about. Only the present. The present agony of waiting, waiting for the shell that was coming to destroy us, waiting to die.

P. J. Campbell, *In the Cannon's Mouth*, 1979

1914

They have sent me here to manoeuver, but things are not going very brightly. This eternal stretching out in a line is getting on my nerves.

Marshal Foch, September 1914, in André Tardieu, *Avec Foch: Août-Novembre 1914*, 1939

Are there not other alternatives than sending our armies to chew barbed wire in Flanders?

Winston Churchill, Memorandum to the Prime Minister, 24th December 1914

. . . The sense of the tragic futility of it will never quite fade from the minds of those who saw these brave men, dashing across the open to the sound of bugles and drums, clad in the old red caps and trousers which a parsimonious democracy dictated they should wear, although they turned each man into a target. The gallant officers who led them were entirely ignorant of the stopping power of modern firearms, and many of them thought it chic to die in white gloves.

Edward Spears, *Liaison 1914*, 1930

The aspect of the French infantry straggling forward anyhow had profoundly shocked me when I first saw the long columns sprawling all over the road, no two men in step, the capotes unbuttoned, looking much more like a mob than like disciplined men, but it quickly became apparent that although this infantry was not smart to look at, it got there all the same, and that the lack of polish was due more to badly fitting uniforms than to anything else. The French soldier, we were soon to learn, had lost nothing of the wonderful marching powers which had proved so disturbing to us in the days of the Peninsular War.

Edward Spears, *Liaison 1914*, 1930

War correspondents were not allowed anywhere near the front. The British people were not told that the expeditionary force was retreating from Mons; the French were not told that their armies had lost the battle of the frontiers; the Germans were not told that the Schlieffen plan had failed to win the war. The facts, when they gradually came out, only inspired men to further frenzy. Where hard news was lacking, rumour flourished. A hundred thousand (or according to other accounts a million) Russian troops were reported to have landed at Aberdeen, and passed through England on their way to the Western Front. Everyone knew some other person who had seen them; many claimed even to have seen the snow on their boots . . . German soldiers were said to operate disguised as nuns, and could be detected by their hairy legs . . . In England wealthy people, who had installed concrete tennis courts before the war, were suspected of preparing gun-emplacements from which the Germans could bombard London.

A. J. P. Taylor, *The First World War*, 1963

– Retreat from Mons, 23rd August–5th September 1914

Hard pressed on my right. My centre is yielding. Impossible to manoeuvre. Situation excellent. I am attacking.

Ferdinand Foch, telegram to General Joffre, 8 p.m., 8th September 1914, on the eve of the Battle of the Marne

On the night of the 27th I was riding along in the column with two other officers. We had been talking and doing our best to keep from falling asleep on our horses.

As we rode along I became conscious of the fact that, in the fields on both sides of the road along which we were marching, I could see a very large body of horsemen.

These horsemen had the appearance of squadrons of cavalry, and they seemed to be riding across the fields and going in the same direction as we were going, and keeping level with us.

The night was not very dark, and I fancied I could see squadron upon squadron of these cavalrymen quite distinctly.

I did not say a word about it at first, but I watched them for about twenty minutes. The other two officers had stopped talking.

At last one of them asked me if I saw anything in the fields. I then told him what I had seen. The third officer then confessed that he too had been watching these horsemen for the past twenty minutes.

So convinced were we that they were really cavalry that, at the next halt, one of the officers took a party of men out to reconnoitre, and found no one there.

The night then grew darker, and we saw no more.

The same phenomenon was seen by many men in our column. Of course, we were all dog tired and overtaxed, but it is an extraordinary thing that the same phenomenon should be witnessed by so many different people.

'Letter' from 'a distinguished Lieutenant-Colonel', describing the 'Angels of Mons', *Evening News*, 14th September 1914

But there was one thing which, for the men who saw it, dwarfed all else. Hanging up in the open window of a shop, strung from a hook in the cross-beam, like a joint in a butcher's shop, was the body of a little girl, five years old, perhaps. Its poor little hands had been hacked off, and through the slender body were vicious bayonet stabs.

Major A. Corbett-Smith, *The Retreat From Mons, By One Who Shared It*, 1916

Stretched out across the broad expanse of meadows between us and the river was a long line of dots wide apart, and looking through glasses one saw that these dots were infantry advancing, widely extended: English infantry, too, unmistakably. A field battery on our left had spotted them, and we watched their shrapnel bursting over the advancing line. Soon a second line of dots emerged from the willows along the river bank, at least ten paces apart, and began to advance. More of our batteries came into action; but it was noticed that a shell, however well aimed, seldom killed more than one man, the lines being so well and widely extended. The front line had taken cover when the shelling began, running behind any hedges or buildings near by, but this second line kept steadily on, while a third and fourth line now appeared from the river bank, each keeping about two hundred yards distance from the line in front. Our guns now fired like mad, but it did not stop the movement: a fifth and sixth line came on, all with the same wide intervals between men and the same distance apart. It was magnificently done.

Walter Bloem, *The Advance From Mons*, 1930

1915

I suppose that we must now recognize that the French Army cannot make a sufficient break through the German lines of defence to bring about the retreat of the German forces from northern France. If that is so, then the German lines in France may be looked upon as a fortress that cannot be carried by assault, and also cannot be completely invested.

Lord Kitchener, Letter to Sir John French, 2nd January 1915

Ludendorff: The English soldiers fight like lions.
Hoffman: True. But don't we know they are lions led by donkeys.

A. Clark, *The Donkeys*, 1961

There is no doubt as to what the proper course should have been in the Spring of 1915. The regular British Army had suffered heavily in the battles of 1914, and could only be reinforced gradually by volunteers from the United Kingdom and the Dominions, hardly trained as soldiers. The British Army should have been so defeated that it could never develop into an efficient 'million army'. It should have been like a newly-sown field struck by a heavy hailstorm, which never recovers to bear a full crop.

General von Moser, in *Official History: 1915*, 1922–47

... There were issued from Calais alone during the first ten months of 1915, 11,000 prismatic and magnetic compasses, 7,000 watches, 40,000 miles of electric cable, 40,000 electric torches, 3,600,000 yards of flannelette, 1,260,000 yards of rot-proof canvas, 25,000 tents, 1,600,000 waterproof sheets, 12,800 bicycles, 20,000 wheels, 6,000,000 anti-gas helmets, 4,000,000 pairs of horse and wheel shoes, 447,000 Lewis gun magazines, 2,260,000 bars of soap . . .

Official History: 1916, 1922–47

– Battle of Neuve Chapelle, 10th–13th March 1915

Sir John French, to conceal his failure, complained that he was short of shells. The Government in their turn blamed the munition workers, who were alleged to draw high wages and to pass their days drinking in public houses. Legislation was hastily introduced to restrict the hours when public houses were open and, in particular, to impose an afternoon gap when drinkers must be turned out. Those restrictions, still with us, rank with Summer Time as the only lasting effects of the First World War on British life. Anyone who feels thirsty in England during the afternoon is still paying a price for the battle of Neuve Chapelle.

A. J. P. Taylor, *The First World War*, 1963

– First Use of Gas, at Vijfwege, April 1915

The effects of the successful gas attack were horrible. I am not pleased with the idea of poisoning men. Of course the entire world will rage about it first and then imitate us. All the dead lie on their backs with clenched fists; the whole field is yellow.

Rudolph Binding, *A Fatalist At War*, 1915

1916

– Verdun, 21st February–18th December 1916

They shall not pass.

Marshal Pétain, to General de Castelnau, 26th February 1916

I have not got an Army in France, really, but a collection of divisions untrained for the field. The actual fighting Army will be evolved from them.

Douglas Haig, diary entry, 29th March 1916

With a bullet through his head, he fell from an altitude of 9,000 feet, a beautiful death.

Baron Manfred von Richthofen, describing the death of Count von Holck, a German pilot, in a letter, 1st May 1916

I forbid the voluntary evacuation of trenches. The will to stand firm must be impressed on every man in the Army. I hold Commanding Officers responsible for this. The enemy should have to carve his way over heaps of corpses.

General von Below, Order of the Day, 3rd July 1916

Verdun has become a battle of mad men inside a volcano.

Comment supposedly made by a French officer, July 1916

Verdun was the most senseless episode in a war not distinguished for sense anywhere.

A. J. P. Taylor, *The First World War*, 1963

– First Battle of the Somme, 1st July–18th November 1916

Proof given to the world that the Allies are capable of making and maintaining a vigorous offensive and of driving enemy's best troops from the strongest positions has shaken faith of the Germans, of their friends, of doubting neutrals in the invincibility of Germany. Also impressed on the world, England's strength and determination, and the fighting power of the British race.

Douglas Haig, memorandum to William Robertson, 1st August 1916

If two lives or ten lives were required by their commanders to kill one German, no word of complaint ever rose from the fighting troops. No attack, however forlorn, however fatal, found them without ardour. No slaughter, however desolating, prevented them from returning to the charge. No physical conditions however severe deprived their commanders of their obedience and loyalty. Martyrs not less than soldiers, they fulfilled the high purpose of duty with which they were imbued. The battlefields of the Somme were the graveyards of Kitchener's Army.

Winston Churchill, *The World Crisis*, 1923

It was like walking through caramel. At every step the foot stuck fast, and was only wrenched out by a determined effort, bringing away with it several pounds of earth till legs ached in every muscle. No one could struggle through that mud for more than a few yards without rest. Terrible in its clinging consistency, it was the arbiter of destiny, the supreme enemy, paralysing and mocking English and German alike. Distances were measured not in yards but in mud.

Sidney Rogerson, *Twelve Days*, 1933

See that little stream. We could walk to it in two minutes. It took the British a whole month to walk to it – a whole empire walking very slowly, dying in front and pushing forward behind. And another empire walked very slowly backwards a few inches a day, leaving the dead like a million bloody rugs.

F. Scott Fitzgerald, *Tender Is the Night*, 1934

The picture of the British infantry rising from their trenches to be mown down is the only true picture of the Battle of the Somme when set beside that of the German infantry rising from their trenches to be mown down.

John Terraine, *The Smoke and the Fire*, 1980

– First Use of Tanks, Flers, 15th September 1915

A Tank is walking up the High Street of Flers with the British Army cheering behind.

An aviator's message, 15th September 1916

They [tanks] caused a sensation, a sense of excitement, laughter which shook the nation, because of the comicality, the grotesque surprise, the possibility of quicker victory which caught hold of the imagination of people who heard for the first time of those new engines of war, so beast-like in appearance and performance. The vagueness of our descriptions was due to the censorship, which forbade, wisely enough, any technical and exact definition, so that we had to compare them to giant toads, mammoths and prehistoric animals of all kinds.

Philip Gibbs, *Realities of War*, 1920

Public excitement naturally did not die down for some time, and for days many lurid stories about tanks were current. Amongst other 'real truths' were the following:- That the tanks carried a crew of 400 men, were armed with 12-inch guns, had a speed of 30 m.p.h., were constructed in Japan by Swedes, and, – dire insult to the Heavy Section – were officered by airmen who had lost their nerve.

Sir Ernest Swinton, *Eyewitness*, 1932

So the great secret was sold for the battered ruin of a little hamlet on the Somme, which was not worth capturing.

David Lloyd George, *War Memoirs*, 1936

The nervous strain in this first battle of tanks for officers and crew alike was ghastly. Of my company, one officer shot his engine to make it go faster; another shot himself because he thought he had failed to do as well as he ought; two others had what I suppose could be called a nervous breakdown.

Sir Basil Henriques, Letter to *The Times*, 16th September 1976

1917

It is not an army that we must train for war; it is a nation.

Woodrow Wilson, speech, 12th May 1917

Gentlemen, I don't know whether we will make history tomorrow, but we will certainly change geography.

Sir Herbert Plumer, on the eve of blowing up Messines Ridge, 6th June 1917

Evil and the incarnate fiend alone can be master of this war, and no glimmer of God's hand is seen anywhere.

Paul Nash, Letter to his wife, November 1917

The old coat of democracy, never intended for war at Armageddon, was showing white at the seams.

Edward Spears, *Prelude to Victory*, 1939

Exasperated by these unprofitable assaults, and ignorant of tactical considerations, the allied statesmen accused the soldiers of lack of imagination, and set out to recapture mobility by a change of front, as if the locality itself was to blame for the stalemate. What they were unable to appreciate was, that should another locality be found in which the enemy's resistance was less formidable than on the Western Front, it would only be a matter of time before the same tactical conditions prevailed. It was the bullet, spade and wire which were the enemy on *every* front, and their geographical location was purely incidental.

J. F. C. Fuller, *The Conduct of War, 1789–1961*, 1961

– Battle of Arras, 9th April – 5th May 1917

As to the battle of Arras, I know quite well that I am being used as a tool in the hands of the Divine Power, and that my strength is not my own, so I am not at all conceited, and you may rest assured that I am not likely to forget to whom belongs the honour and glory for *all* our good work and success.

Douglas Haig, Letter to Lady Haig, 20th April 1917

– The United States Enters the War, 6th April 1917

The Allies must *not* be beaten. It would mean the triumph of Autocracy over Democracy; the shattering of all our moral standards; and a real, though it may seem remote, peril to our independence and institutions.

Robert Lansing, private memorandum, 27th January 1917

My message today was a message of death for our young men. How strange it seems to applaud that.

Woodrow Wilson, after his speech asking Congress for a declaration of war, April 1917

America . . . is the prize amateur nation of the world. Germany is the prize professional nation.

Woodrow Wilson, August 1917, in John Dos Passos, *Mr Wilson's War*, 1963

The Americans, while keeping their eyes and ears open and accepting our own and French instructors, are set on having their own code of tactics . . . and as they are different the Americans fight better by themselves. Everything has to be, and so is, American. The pride of race is very strong. The Americans are earnest, serious people, even the private soldiers, who have nothing of the devil-may-care light-heartedness of our men. They have come here to do or die and are as keen as mustard, but still very serious and quiet about it all. They are in truth Crusaders.

Colonel Repington, *The First World War*, 1920

It means that we shall lose our heads along with the rest and stop weighing right and wrong.

Woodrow Wilson, quoted in A. J. P. Taylor, *The First World War*, 1963

If the Allies lost the war, the American loans would be lost also. In the last resort, the United States went to war so that America could remain prosperous and rich Americans could grow richer.

A. J. P. Taylor, *The First World War*, 1963

– 3rd Battle of Ypres (Passchendaele), 31st July–10th November 1917

Satisfactory attack this morning – advances made with 11 tanks on one mile of front. All objectives taken, 12 infantry casualties, and 14 men of Tanks hit. Without tanks we would have lost 600!

Douglas Haig, diary entry, 19th August 1917

While I and others were taking supplies into the line at Ypres, we waded through mud all the way. It was very necessary to keep following the leader strictly in line, for one false step to the right or left sometimes meant plunging into dangerous and deep mudpools. One of our men was unfortunate enough to step out of line and fell into one of these mud-holes. Knowing from past experience that quick action was needed if we were to save him from quickly sinking, we got hold of his arms and tried to pull him out. We finally procured a rope and managed to loop it securely under his armpits. He was now gradually sinking until the mud and water reached almost to his shoulders. We tugged at the rope with the strength of desperation in an effort to save him, but it was useless. He was fast in the mud and beyond human aid. Reluctantly, the party had to leave him to his fate, and that fate was – gradually sinking inch by inch and finally dying of suffocation. The poor fellow now knew he was beyond all aid and begged me to shoot him rather than leave him to die a miserable death by suffocation. I did not want to do this, but thinking of the agonies he would endure if I left him to this horrible death, I decided a quick death would be a merciful ending. I am not afraid to say therefore that I shot this man at his own urgent request, thus releasing him from a far more agonizing end.

A private soldier, in Bryan Cooper, *The Ironclads of Cambrai*, 1967

It achieved little except loss – in which again, it repeated the early history of this theatre of war. So fruitless in its results, so depressing in its direction was this 1917 offensive that 'Passchendaele' has come to be like Walcheren a century before, a synonym for military failure.

B. H. Liddell Hart, *History of the First World War*, 1934

The battle of the mud.

David Lloyd George, *War Memoirs*, 1936

Third Ypres was the blindest slaughter of a blind war. Haig bore the greatest responsibility. Some of the mud sticks also to Lloyd George, the man who lacked the supreme authority to forbid the battle.

A. J. P. Taylor, *The First World War*, 1963

– Battle of Cambrai, 20th November–7th December 1917

The day was one of memorable achievement. On a front of over six miles an advance has been made varying from three miles to four. The two strong trench systems, covered by an outpost zone, which formed the Hindenburg Position had been carried in not much more than four hours, a rate of progress which was without precedent on the Western Front . . . It was a triumph for the new tactics which, combined with the secret and meticulous preparation made possible by admirable staff work and the whole-hearted cooperation of all ranks of all arms and services, had produced a surprise of a character well-nigh irresistible. The unregistered bombardment of the artillery had done all that was claimed for it. The tanks had enabled the assault to burst without warning through un-cut wire, to over-run trenches, and to crush well-sited strongpoints which linked up the whole powerful system of defence.

Official History: 1917, 1922–47

Accusing as I do without exception all the great Allied offensives of 1914, 1916 and 1917, as needless and wrongly conceived operations of infinite cost, I am bound to reply to the question – what else could have been done? I answer it, pointing to the Battle of Cambrai, 'this could have been done'. This in many variants, this in larger and better forms ought to have been done, and would have been done if only the generals had not been content to fight machine-gun bullets with the breasts of gallant men, and think that that was waging war.

Winston Churchill, *The World Crisis*, 1923

At Cambrai in 1917, Brigadier-General Hugh Elles, commanding the Tank Corps, proclaimed his intention of leading the corps into battle; which he did, in the tank 'Hilda', flying the Tank Corps flag. It was an admirable gesture, but no more than that. General Elles soon discovered that his only command capacity inside 'Hilda' was to kick the driver's right shoulder if he wanted to turn right, or kick his left shoulder if he wanted to turn left. After quite a short time General Elles realized that, if he wanted to influence the battle at all, he had better leave 'Hilda'; so he got out and walked back to his headquarters, and started being a general again, at the end of several telephone lines.

John Terraine, *The Smoke and the Fire*, 1980

1918

I shall fight before Paris, I shall fight in Paris, I shall fight behind Paris.

Georges Clemenceau, in the Chamber of Deputies, 4th June 1918

None of us will live to see the end of this war.

Lord Northcliffe, attributed, September 1918

There have, naturally, been special champions of various arms, and because armoured warfare became a developing theme in the post-war years and a very important element in the Second World War, tanks have been singled out as the decisive weapon of 1918. This is mythology . . . In the tank actions of the First World War it is not Day 1 that counts, no matter how spectacular its achievements, but Day 2; tanks scored a great success at Cambrai on 20 November 1917, but they lost 179 machines out of 378, and their role on 21 November was accordingly much reduced. It was the same in 1918: for the counterstroke on the Marne on 18 July, General Mangin's Tenth Army had 346 tanks, of which 225 got into action; 102 became casualties, so that on 19 July there were 195 available, of which 50 were hit. These losses, with breakdown and exhaustion, meant that only 32 were available on Day 3. The Battle of Amiens, 8 August, saw the largest deployment of tanks in any British engagement in the war: 534, of which 414 were fighting tanks (Mark Vs and Whippets). On Day 2 (9 August) the number available had dropped to 145, on 10 August it was 85, and on 11 August it had dropped to 38. The battle formally ended on that day, which was just as well, because on 12 August only 6 tanks were fit to fight; . . . the German empire was not going to be overthrown by six tanks.

John Terraine, *White Heat: The New Warfare 1914–18*, 1982

– German Offensive in Picardy, 9th–30th April 1918

Words fail me to express the admiration which I feel for the splendid resistance offered by all ranks of our Army under the most trying circumstances. Many amongst us are now tired. To those I would say that victory belongs to those who hold out the longest . . . There is no other course open to us but to fight it out. Every position must be held to the last man; there must be no retirement. With our backs to the wall, and believing in the justice of our cause, each one of us must fight on to the end. The safety of our homes and the freedom of mankind alike depend on the conduct of each one of us at this critical moment.

Douglas Haig, Order to the British forces in France, 11th April 1918

– Battle of Belleau Wood, 6th–28th June 1918

Retreat hell! We just got here.

Captain Lloyd S. Williams, attributed, 5th June 1918

Come on, you sons of bitches! Do you want to live for ever?

Sergeant Dan Daly, US Marine, leading from the front, 6th June 1918

– Second Battle of the Marne, 15th July 1918

I have lived through the most disheartening day of the whole War, though it was by no means the most dangerous. . . . Our guns bombarded empty trenches; our gas-shells gassed empty artillery positions; only in little folds of the ground, sparsely distributed, lay machine gun posts, like lice in the seams and folds of a garment, to give the attacking force a warm reception.

Rudolph Binding, *A Fatalist At War*, 1929

– Battle of Amiens, 8th August 1918

August 8th, 1918, is a date which grows ever larger on the horizon of the historian. So far as any one event of the campaign in the west can be regarded as decisive, it is the great surprise east of Amiens that occurred on this day. And that decisiveness is above all a proof that the moral element dominates warfare.

B. H. Liddell Hart, *A History of the World War*, 1934

– Collapse of the German Front, from 18th July 1918

In the stage of the wearing-out struggle losses will necessarily be heavy on both sides, for in it the victory is paid. If the opposing forces are approximately equal in numbers, in courage, in morale and in equipment, there is no way of avoiding payment of the price or of eliminating this phase of the struggle. In former battles this stage of the conflict has rarely lasted more than a few days, and has often been completed in a few hours. When armies of millions are engaged, with the resources of great empires behind them, it will inevitably be long. It will include violent crises of fighting which, when viewed separately and apart from the general perspective, will appear individually as great indecisive battles. To this stage belong the great engagements of 1916 and 1917 which wore down the strength of the German armies . . . If the whole operations of the present war are regarded in correct perspective, the victories of the summer and autumn of 1918 will be seen to be directly dependent upon the two years of stubborn fighting that preceded them.

Douglas Haig, *Dispatches*, 1919

Every road was littered with broken-down motor trucks, guns, machine guns and trench mortars. Great stacks of supplies and of military stores of all kinds were abandoned. Every railway line was blocked with loaded trucks which the

Germans had been unable to remove . . . It is beyond dispute that on November 11 the lines of communication immediately behind the German armies had been thrown into complete disorder by the streams of traffic converging on the Meuse bridges, disorder greatly intensified by the attacks of Allied airmen. The German armies, unable to resist on the fighting front, could no longer retreat in good order, partly because of the congestion on the roads and railways behind them, which not only hampered the movements of the troops, but prevented the systematic supply to them of food and ammunition, partly owing to the fact that there were not horses left to draw the transport of the fighting troops.

Sir Frederick Maurice, *The Last Four Months*, 1920

During the night of October 13th–14th the British opened an attack with gas on the front south of Ypres. They used the yellow gas whose effect was unknown to us, at least from personal experience. I was destined to experience it that very night. On a hill south of Werwick, in the evening of October 13th, we were subjected for several hours to a heavy bombardment with gas bombs, which continued throughout the night with more or less intensity. About midnight a number of us were put out of action, some for ever. Towards morning I began to feel pain. It increased with every quarter of an hour; and about seven o'clock my eyes were scorching as I staggered back and delivered the last dispatch I was destined to carry in this war. A few hours later my eyes were like glowing coals, and all was darkness around me.

Adolf Hitler, *Mein Kampf*, 1924–26

On 11 November the Allied peoples burst into rejoicing. All work stopped for the day. Crowds blocked the streets, dancing and cheering. In Trafalgar Square Canadian soldiers lit a bonfire at the plinth of Nelson's column, the marks of which can be seen to this day. As evening fell, the crowds grew more riotous. Total strangers copulated in public – a symbol that life had triumphed over death.

A. J. P. Taylor, *The First World War*, 1963

The Sea War

Our most vulnerable point is our food and oil supply. The submarine has introduced a new method of attacking these supplies. Will feelings of humanity restrain our enemy from using it?

Sir Percy Scott, in *The Times*, July 1914

We shall commence unrestricted U boat warfare on February 1st. Nevertheless we hope to keep the United States neutral. If we should not succeed in this, we shall propose to Mexico an alliance on the following terms: We shall wage war and conclude peace in common. We shall provide general financial support, and stipulate that Mexico shall receive back the territory of New Mexico and Arizona which she lost in 1848. The details will be left to you to carry out. You are instructed to sound [President] Carranza in the strictest confidence, and as soon as war against the United States is certain you will give him a hint to enter into negotiations with Japan on his own initiative requesting her to join us and offering to act as intermediary between Japan and Germany. Draw Carranza's attention to

the fact that the carrying out of unrestricted U boat warfare will make it possible to bring England to her knees and compel her to sue for peace within a few months.
Arthur Zimmerman (German Foreign Secretary), telegram to the German Minister in Mexico, intercepted by British Intelligence, 16th January 1917

The Navy is very old and very wise.
Rudyard Kipling, 'The Fringes of the Fleet', 1915

Brutes they were, and brutes they remain.
Arthur Balfour, October 1918, after learning that the SS *Leinster* had been sunk by a German U-boat

– Battle of Jutland, 31st May 1916

There seems to be something wrong with our bloody ships today, Chatfield.
Sir David Beatty, attributed, upon seeing HMS *Queen Mary* blown up

. . . In the British Navy in the years before the First World War, ship commanders were actively discouraged from gunnery practice because the smoke might mark the paintwork and soil the gleaming decks. The price for this was paid at Jutland.
Norman F. Dixon, *On the Psychology of Military Incompetence*, 1976

The Air War

Oh, it was a good fight, and the Huns were fine sports. One tried to ram me, after he was hit, and only missed by inches. Am indeed looked after by God, but oh! I do get tired of living always to kill, and am really beginning to feel like a murderer.
Captain Albert Ball, in a Letter, 1917

I know that I shall meet my fate
Somewhere among the clouds above;
Those that I fight I do not hate,
Those that I guard I do not love;
My country is Kiltartan Cross,
My countrymen Kiltartan's poor,
No likely end could bring them loss
Or leave them happier than before.
Nor law, nor duty bade me fight,
Nor public men, nor cheering crowds,
A lonely impulse of delight
Drove to this tumult in the clouds;
I balanced all, brought all to mind,
The years to come seemed waste of breath,
A waste of breath the years behind
In balance with this life, this death.
W. B. Yeats, 'An Irish Airman Foresees His Death', 1919

And then after a flight or two I was sent to start Hornchurch air station as a night-flying anti-zeppelin station. I landed there and the aerodrome consisted of a large field full of sheep, an infuriated farmer, and a still more infuriated dog. So when we'd cleared off the sheep and I'd appeased the farmer and been billeted on him, I formed a flight there which contained amongst others Leefe Robinson – and when I was away on a four-day leave doing something much more dangerous, which was getting married, he went up and bagged the first zeppelin.

Sir Arthur Harris, in Gwynne Dyer, *War*, 1986

The Eastern Front

In the West the armies were too big for the country. In the East the country was too big for the armies.

Winston Churchill, *The Eastern Front*, 1931

I forbid myself to use the word 'strategy'. We chop a hole. The rest follows. We did it that way in Russia.

Erich von Ludendorff, quoted in the *Official History: 1918*, 1922–47

– The Battle of Tannenberg, 26th–30th August 1914

The Tsarist army was not crippled by its inferiority in artillery or men; it was crippled by its inability to use its superiority.

Norman Stone, *The Eastern Front*, 1975

Gallipoli, April 1915–January 1916

W.C. [Winston Churchill] is a bigger danger than the Germans by a long way in what is just now imminent in the Dardanelles.

H. A. L. Fisher, Letter to Bonar Law, May 1915

There are poets and writers who see naught in war but carrion, filth, savagery and horror . . . They refuse war the credit of being the only exercise in devotion on the large scale existing in this world. The superb moral victory over death leaves them cold. Each one to his taste. To me this is no valley of death – it is a valley brim full of life at its highest power.

Sir Ian Hamilton, diary entry, 30th May 1915

The sailormen have a real pull over us soldiers in all matters of messing. Linen, plate, glass, bread, meat, wine; of the best are on the spot, always: even after the enemy is sighted, if they happen to feel a sense of emptiness they have only to go to the cold sideboard.

Sir Ian Hamilton, diary entry, 17th June 1915

Damn the Dardanelles. They will be our grave.

Sir John Fisher, to the Dardanelles Committee, 1915

To call this thing a beach is stiff,
It's nothing but a bloody cliff.

John Churchill, 'Y Beach', impromptu lines written soon after the initial landings.

Casualties? What do I care about casualties?

Major-General A. G. Hunter-Weston, attributed, 1915

The Dardanelles operations hang like a millstone about our necks, and have brought upon us the most vast disaster that has happened in the course of the war.

Sir Edward Carson, in the House of Commons, October 1916

For Britain 'Gallipoli' held another, even more serious meaning: this was the last attempt in British history to exercise absolute naval supremacy in the traditional manner. Since the British Empire was founded upon naval might, one might say that the Gallipoli failure marked the beginning of the end of that Empire.

John Terraine, *White Heat: the New Warfare 1914–18*, 1982

The Arab Revolt, 1916–18

I loved you, so I drew these tides of men into my hands
and wrote my will across the sky in stars
To earn you Freedom, the seven-pillared worthy house,
that your eyes might be shining for me
When we came.

Death seemed my servant on the road, till we were near
and saw you waiting:
When you smiled, and in sorrowful envy he outran me
and took you apart:
Into his quietness.

T. E. Lawrence, *Seven Pillars of Wisdom*, 1926: dedicatory verses

The staff knew so much more of war than I did that they refused to learn from me of the strange conditions in which Arab irregulars had to act; and I could not be bothered to set up a kindergarten of the imagination for their benefit.

T. E. Lawrence, *Seven Pillars of Wisdom*, 1926

The textbooks gave the aim in war as 'the destruction of the organized forces of the enemy' by 'the one process, battle'. Victory could only be purchased by blood. This was a hard saying, as the Arabs had no organized forces, and so a Turkish Foch would have no aim; and the Arabs would not endure casualties, so that an Arab Clausewitz could not buy his victory.

T. E. Lawrence, *Science of Guerilla Warfare*, 1929

Mesopotamia

As I write these last words my thoughts return to you who were my comrades, the stubborn and indomitable peasants of Nepal. Once more I hear the laughter with which you greeted every hardship. Once more I see you in your bivouacs or about your fires, on forced march or in the trenches, now shivering with wet and cold, now scorched by a pitiless and burning sun. Uncomplaining, you endure hunger and thirst and wounds, and at last your unwavering lines disappear into the smoke and wrath of battle.

Bravest of the brave, most generous of the generous, never had country more faithful friends than you.

R. L. Turner, eulogising the Gurkhas, in the Foreword to his *Dictionary of the Nepali Language*, 1931

Palestine: Battle of Megiddo, September 1918

Whether it should be regarded primarily as a campaign or as a battle completed by pursuit is a moot question. For it opened with the forces in contact and hence would seem to fall into the category of a battle; but it was achieved mainly by strategic means, with fighting playing a minor part. This fact has tended to its disparagement in the sight of those who are obsessed with the Clausewitzian dogma that blood is the price of victory – and hold, as a corollary, that no victory is worthy of recognition which is not sanctified by a lavish oblation of blood. But Caesar's triumph at Ilerda, Scipio's near Utica, Cromwell's at Preston, and Moltke's, though opportunist rather than sought for, at Sedan, each had the same 'pale pink' complexion. In each, strategy was so effective that fighting was but incidental.

B. H. Liddell Hart, *A History of the World War*, 1934

A more serious 'depreciation' of this final campaign-battle in Palestine lies in the fact that Allenby had a superiority of over two to one in numbers and more in terms of weapon-values. In addition the morale of the Turks had so declined that it is often argued that Allenby had merely to stretch out his hand for the Turkish army, like an overripe plum, to fall into it. There is force in these contentions; but most of the 'crowning mercies' of modern history, from Worcester to Sedan, have seen almost as great a disparity of strength and morale between victors and vanquished. And in 1918 Allenby had to outwit such able commanders as Liman von Sanders and Mustapha Kemal, not such men as those who thrust their heads into the sack at Sedan.

B. H. Liddell Hart, *A History of the World War*, 1934

The Versailles Peace Conference, 1919

Six million young men lie in premature graves, and four old men sit in Paris partitioning the earth.

New York Nation, 1919

Tell me what's right and I'll fight for it.

Woodrow Wilson, to his aides, in John Dos Passos, *Mr Wilson's War*, 1963

This is not peace: it is an armistice for twenty years.

Marshal Foch, attributed

A peace that passeth all understanding. Accept it children, with faith and resignation – and prepare for the next Armageddon.

New York Call, 1919, in Thomas A. Bailey, *Woodrow Wilson and the Lost Peace*, 1944

I had to deal in the peace conference with two men, one of whom thought he was Napoleon [Lloyd George] and the other Jesus Christ [Woodrow Wilson].

Georges Clemenceau, attributed

THE IRISH UPRISING OF 1916

The young men are mad jealous of their leaders for being shot.

An Irish Cabinet Minister, attributed

We know their dream; enough
To know they dreamed and are dead;
And what if excess of love
Bewildered them till they died?
I write it out in a verse –
MacDonagh and MacBride
And Conolly and Pearse
Now and in time to be,
Wherever green is worn,
Are changed, changed utterly:
A terrible beauty is born.
W. B. Yeats, 'Easter 1916', 1921

THE RUSSIAN REVOLUTION, October 1917

The war is relentless: it puts the alternative in a ruthless relief: either to perish, or to catch up with the advanced countries and overtake them.
V. I. Lenin, *The Impending Catastrophe and How to Fight It*, 1917

1st Bolshevik: Let me see: we've made an end of Law, Credit, Treaties, the Army and the Navy. Is there anything else to abolish?
2nd Bolshevik: What about War?
1st Bolshevik: Good! And Peace too. Away with both of 'em.
Cartoon caption, *Punch*, February 1918

A civil war is inevitable. We have only to organize it as painlessly as possible.
Leon Trotsky, speech, quoted in his *History of the Russian Revolution*, 1931

The [absconding Tsarist] army has voted for peace with its feet.
V. I. Lenin, attributed

The revolution does not choose its paths: it made its first steps towards victory under the belly of a Cossack's horse.
Leon Trotsky, *History of the Russian Revolution*, 1931

JAPANESE OCCUPATION OF MANCHURIA, 1931–44

The richest source of power to wage war lies in the masses of the people. It is mainly because of the unorganized state of the Chinese masses that Japan dares to bully us. When this defect is remedied, then the Japanese aggressor, like a mad bull crashing into a ring of flames, will be surrounded by hundreds of millions of our people standing upright, the mere sound of their voices will strike terror into him, and he will be burned to death.
Mao Tse-tung, *On Protracted War*, 1938

He [the Westerner] was accustomed to regard Japan as barbarous for as long she practised the gentle arts of peace; now that she has undertaken massive slaughter in Manchuria, he regards her as civilized.
Okakura Kakuzo, *The Book of Tea*, 1938

THE SPANISH CIVIL WAR, 1936–39

It is better to die on your feet than live on your knees.
'La Pasionara' (Dolores Ibarruri), speech in Paris, 1936

We have four columns advancing on Madrid. The fifth column will rise at the proper time.
Emilio Mola, radio broadcast, October 1936

[Franco's Fascists] will conquer, but they will not convince.
Miguel de Unamuno, said shortly before his death, 1936

At this moment, a shell has just alighted on a house up the street from the hotel where I am typing this. A little boy is crying in the street. A militiaman has picked him up and is comforting him. There was no one killed on our street, and the people who started to run slow down and grin nervously. The one who never started to run at all looks at the others in a superior way, and the town we are living in now is called Madrid.
Ernest Hemingway, 'A Brush with Death', 30th September 1937

Up the Tortosa road, planes were diving and machine-gunning. German planes are absolutely methodical though. They do their job, and, if you are a part of their job, you're out of luck. If you are not included in their job, you can go very close to them and watch them as you can watch lions feeding. If their orders are to strafe the road on their way home, you will get it. Otherwise, when they are finished with their job on their particular objective, they go off like bank clerks, flying home.
Ernest Hemingway, 'Tortosa Calmly Awaits Assault', 18th April 1938

. . . In the circumstances the militias could not have been much better than they were. A modern mechanized army does not spring up from the ground, and if the Government had waited until it had trained troops at its disposal, Franco would never have been resisted. Later it became the fashion to descry the militias and therefore to pretend that the faults were the result of the equalitarian system. Actually, a newly raised draft of militia was an undisciplined mob not because the officers called the private 'Comrade' but because raw troops are *always* an undisciplined mob. In practice the democratic 'revolutionary' type of discipline is more reliable than might be expected. In a workers' army discipline is theoretically voluntary. It is based on class-loyalty, whereas the discipline of a bourgeois conscript army is based ultimately on fear.
George Orwell, *Homage to Catalonia*, 1938

George Kopp, on his periodic tours of inspection, was quite frank with us. 'This is not a war,' he used to say, 'it is a comic opera with an occasional death.'
George Orwell, *Homage to Catalonia*, 1938

The difficult passwords which the army was using at this time were a minor source of danger. They were those tiresome double passwords in which one word has to be answered by another. Usually they were of an elevating and revolutionary nature, such as *Cultura-progreso*, or *Seremos-invencibles*, and it was often impossible to get illiterate sentries to remember these highfalutin' words. One night, I remember, the password was *Cataluna-eroica*, and a moon-faced peasant-lad named Jaime Domenech approached me, greatly puzzled, and asked me to explain.

'*Eroica* – what does *eroica* mean?'

I told him it meant the same as *valiente*. A little while later he was stumbling up the trench in the darkness, and the sentry challenged him.

'*Alto! Cataluna!*'

'*Valiente!*' yelled Jaime, certain that he was saying the right thing.

Bang!

However, the sentry missed him. In this war everyone always did miss everyone else, when it was humanly possible.

George Orwell, *Homage to Catalonia*, 1938

The fighting had barely started when the newspapers of the Right and Left dived simultaneously into the same cesspool of abuse. We all remember the *Daily Mail*'s poster: 'REDS CRUCIFY NUNS', while to the *Daily Worker* Franco's Foreign Legion was 'composed of murderers, white-slavers, dope-fiends, and the offal of every European country'. As late as October 1937 the *New Statesman* was treating us to tales of Fascist barricades made of bodies of living children (a most unhandy thing to make barricades with), and Mr Arthur Bryant was declaring that 'the sawing-off of a Conservative tradesman's legs' was 'a commonplace' in loyalist Spain. The people who write that kind of stuff never fight; possibly they believe that to write it is a substitute for fighting. It is the same in all wars; the soldiers do the fighting, the journalists do the shouting, and no true patriot ever gets near a front-line trench, except on the briefest of propaganda-tours. Sometimes it is a comfort to me to think that the aeroplane is altering the conditions of war. Perhaps when the next great war comes we may see that sight unprecedented in all history, a jingo with a bullet-hole in him.

George Orwell, *Homage to Catalonia*, 1938

The shells the Fascists were firing at this period [early 1937] were wretchedly bad . . . There were the usual romantic tales of sabotage in the Fascist factories and unexploded shells in which, instead of the charge, there was found a scrap of paper saying: 'Red Front', but I never saw one. The truth was that the shells were hopelessly old; someone picked up a brass fuse-cap stamped with the date, and it was 1917. The Fascist guns were of the same make and calibre as our own, and the un-exploded shells were often reconditioned and fired back. There was said to be one old shell with a nickname of its own which travelled daily to and fro, never exploding.

George Orwell, *Homage to Catalonia*, 1938

And I remember Spain
At Easter ripe as an egg for revolt and ruin
Though for a tripper the rain
Was worse than the surly or the worried or the haunted faces
With writings on the walls –
Hammer and sickle, Boicot, Viva, Muerra; . . .

Louis MacNeice, *Autumn Journal*, 1939

If your picture wasn't any good, you're not standing close enough.

Robert Capa (war photographer), quoted in Trevor Royle, *War Report*, 1987

Honour forever to the International Brigade!
They are a song in the blood of all true men.

Hugh MacDiarmid, 'The International Brigade', 1938

On that arid square, that fragment nipped off from hot
Africa, soldered so crudely to inventive Europe,
On that tableland scored by rivers,
Our fever's menacing shapes are precise and alive.

W. H. Auden, 'Spain 1937', 1940

The stars are dead; the animals will not look:
We are left alone with our day, and the time is short and
History to the defeated
May say Alas but cannot help or pardon.

W. H. Auden, 'Spain 1937', 1940

I have praised the *Causa* of the Republic of Spain on the slightest provocation for twenty years, and I am tired of explaining that the Spanish Republic was neither a collective of blood-slaughtering Reds nor a cat's-paw of Russia. Long ago I also gave up repeating that the men who fought and those who died for the Republic, whatever their nationality and whether they were Communists, anarchists, Socialists, poets, plumbers, middle-class professional men, or the one Abyssinian prince, were brave and disinterested, as there were no rewards in Spain. They were fighting for us all, against the combined force of European Fascism. They deserved our thanks and our respect and got neither.

Martha Gellhorn, *The Face of War*, 1986

Battle of the Jarama, February 1937

There's a valley in Spain called Jarama
It's a place that we all know too well,
For 'tis there that we wasted our manhood,
And most of our old age as well.

Charles Donnelly, untitled, 1937

Death stalked the olive trees
Picking his men
His leaden finger beckoned
Again and again.

John Lepper, in *Poems for Spain*, ed. Stephen Spender and John Lehmann, 1939

THE SECOND WORLD WAR 1939–45

Mankind has grown strong in eternal struggles and it will only perish through eternal peace.

Adolf Hitler, *Mein Kampf*, 1924–26

When you think about the defence of England you no longer think of the chalk cliffs of Dover. You think of the Rhine. That is where our frontier lies today.

Stanley Baldwin, in the House of Commons, 30th July 1934

We can do without butter, but, despite all our love of peace, not without arms. One cannot shoot with butter.

Joseph Goebbels, speech in Berlin, 17th January 1936

After all, they are only going into their own back garden.

Lord Lothian, 1936, after Hitler's reoccupation of the Rhineland, in Winston Churchill, *The Second World War*, 1948–54

How horrible, fantastic, incredible it is that we should be digging trenches and trying on gas-masks here because of a quarrel in a far-away country between people of whom we know nothing!

Neville Chamberlain, radio broadcast, 27th September 1938

I believe it is peace for our time . . . Peace with honour.

Neville Chamberlain, radio broadcast, after the Munich Agreement

We have sustained a defeat without a war.

Winston Churchill, after the Munich Agreement, 5th October 1938

Winston is back.

Admiralty message, sent to all ships and shore stations, 3rd September 1939, marking Churchill's reappointment as First Lord of the Admiralty

This nation will remain a neutral nation, but I cannot ask that every American remain neutral in thought as well . . . Even a neutral cannot be asked to close his mind or his conscience.

Franklin D. Roosevelt, radio address, 3rd September 1939

We have at this moment to distinguish carefully between running an industry or a profession, and winning the war.

Winston Churchill, memorandum to the First Sea Lord, 8th October 1939

For each and all, as for the Royal Navy, the watchword should be, 'Carry on, and dread nought.'

Winston Churchill, in the House of Commons, 6th December 1939

A lot of our destroyers and small craft are bumping into one another under the present hard conditions of service. We must be very careful not to damp the ardour of officers in the flotillas by making heavy weather of occasional accidents. They should be encouraged to use their ships with wartime freedom, should feel they will not be considered guilty of unprofessional conduct, if they have done their best and something or other happens.

Winston Churchill, note to the First Sea Lord, 24th September 1939

It must not be forgotten that defeat of the U-boats carries with it the sovereignty of all the oceans of the world.

Winston Churchill, to the French Admiralty, November 1939

Whatever may be the reason – whether it was that Hitler thought he might get away with what he had got without fighting for it, or whether it was that after all the preparations were not sufficiently complete – however, one thing is certain: he missed the bus.

Neville Chamberlain, speech to the Conservative and Unionist Association, 4th April 1940

In three weeks England will have her neck wrung like a chicken's.

General Weygand, April 1940, quoted in Winston Churchill, *The Second World War*, 1948–54

You ask: 'What is our aim?' I can answer in one word: 'Victory!' Victory at all costs, victory in spite of all terror, victory however long and hard the road may be; for without victory there is no survival.

Winston Churchill, in the House of Commons, 13th May 1940

Our security is not a matter of weapons alone. The arm that wields them must be strong, the eye that guides them clear, the will that directs them indomitable.

Franklin D. Roosevelt, message to Congress, 16th May 1940

We shall fight on for ever and ever and ever.

Winston Churchill, message to Paul Reynaud after the fall of France, 1940

Mr Churchill ought perhaps, for once, to believe me when I prophesy that a great Empire will be destroyed which it was never my intention to destroy or even to harm.

Adolf Hitler, to the Reichstag, 19th July 1940

We shall defend every village, every town and every city. The vast mass of London itself, fought street by street, could easily devour an entire hostile army; and we would rather see London laid in ruins and ashes than that it should be tamely and abjectly enslaved.

Winston Churchill, radio broadcast, 14th July 1940

I have told you once and I will tell you again – you boys will not be sent into any foreign wars.

Franklin D. Roosevelt, campaign speech, 1940

The Navy can lose us the war, but only the Air Force can win it. Therefore, our supreme effort must be to gain overwhelming mastery in the air.

Winston Churchill, to his War Cabinet, 3rd September 1940

Death and sorrow will be the companions of our journey; hardship our garment; constancy and valour our only shield.

Winston Churchill, in the House of Commons, 8th October 1940

We are waiting for the long-promised invasion. So are the fishes.

Winston Churchill, radio broadcast to France, 21st October 1940

The core of our defence is the faith we have in the institutions we defend.
Franklin D. Roosevelt, speech at Dayton, 12th October 1940

The best immediate defense of the United States is the success of Great Britain defending itself.
Franklin D. Roosevelt, at a Press conference, 17th December 1940

We must be the great arsenal of Democracy.
Franklin D. Roosevelt, Address to the American People, 29th December 1940

Give us the tools, and we will finish the job.
Winston Churchill, broadcast address to President Roosevelt, 9th February 1941

If we see that Germany is winning the war we ought to help Russia, and if Russia is winning we ought to help Germany, and in that way let them kill as many as possible.
Harry S. Truman, quoted in the *New York Times*, 24th July 1941

I ask you to look at the map of Europe today and see if you can suggest any way in which we could win this war if we entered it.
Charles Lindbergh, speech in New York, 1941

When you see a rattlesnake poised to strike, you do not wait until he has struck before you crush him.
Franklin D. Roosevelt, radio broadcast, 11th September 1941

Nothing is more dangerous in war time than to live in the temperamental atmosphere of a Gallup poll, always feeling one's pulse and taking one's temperature.
Winston Churchill, in the House of Commons, 30th September 1941

We are all in it – all the way.
Franklin D. Roosevelt, radio broadcast of 7th December 1941

I repeat that the United States can accept no result save victory, final and complete.
Franklin D. Roosevelt, radio broadcast, 9th December 1941

'In three weeks England will have her neck wrung like a chicken.' Some chicken! Some neck!!
Winston Churchill, in the Canadian Senate, 30th December 1941

Believe! Obey! Fight!
Italian war slogan, probably coined by Benito Mussolini, *c.* 1941

Don't let's be beastly to the Germans,
Do let's be beastly to the Huns.
Noël Coward, song, 1941

Loose talk can cost lives.
US poster, 1941

Careless talk costs lives.
British poster, 1941

Never before have we had so little time in which to do so much.

Franklin D. Roosevelt, radio broadcast, 22nd February 1942

We have not yet lost this war, but we are overdrawn on the Bank of Miracles.

W. J. Brown, quoted in the *Observer*, 16th August 1942

The mine issues no official communiqué.

Admiral William V. Pratt, in *Newsweek*, 5th October 1942

I have not become the King's First Minister to preside over the liquidation of the British Empire.

Winston Churchill, in the House of Commons, 9th November 1942

This is not the end. It is not even the beginning of the end. But it is, perhaps, the end of the beginning.

Winston Churchill, at Mansion House, 10th November 1942, after victory in Egypt

A Russian state from the Urals to the North Sea can be no great improvement over a German state from the North Sea to the Urals.

Nicholas J. Spykman, *The United States and the Balance of Power*, 1942

One job that I really funked
Was when Fat Riley bunked
From a Jerry leaguer on a getaway.
We found him blind, with both hands gone.
When we got him back inside the lines
He'd only say,
Over and over, 'the mines, the mines, the mines'.
It's the lucky ones get dead:
He's still alive. I wonder if his wife understands
You can't even shoot yourself without your hands.

J. G. Meddemmen, 'L.R.D.G.', 1942

Do not despair
For Johnny-head-in-air;
He sleeps as sound
As Johnny underground.

Fetch out no shroud
For Johnny-in-the-cloud;
And keep your tears
For him in after years.

Better by far
For Johnny-the-bright-star,
To keep your head,
And see his children fed.

John Pudney, 'For Johnny', in *Dispersal Point, and other air poems*, 1942

No more, alas, the head-tossed foam, the fretful foot that pawed:
Oh glory that was Tetrarch's might, oh drabness that is Ford!

E. F. Gosling, *Mechanization*, *c.* 1942

The problems of victory are more agreeable than those of defeat, but they are still no less difficult.

Winston Churchill, in the House of Commons, 11th November 1942

We shall never be rough and heartless when it is not necessary, that is clear. We Germans, who are the only people in the world who have a decent attitude towards animals, will also assume a decent attitude towards these human animals.

Heinrich Himmler, speech, 4th October 1943

How easy it is to make a ghost.

Keith Douglas, 'How To Kill', 1943, in *Alamein to Zem-Zem*, 1944

Agnostic: so the ticket on the bed
along with army number name and rank
as guide for priest or parson in a ward
of pole and canvas wounded men and sand,
the clergy heedful of that pothook scrawl
of nurse who checked the spelling as she wrote
and then forgot on pocketing the pen,
blood having levelled or exalted all.

She's neither time nor space to write below:
'This casualty retains implicitly faith
in timeless pulse of life, a shadow-tide
evading creed and microscope, beyond
analysis in plasm sap and egg,
a gut conviction deep below belief
and therefore credible. He harbours doubt
of God in nightgown and prophetic voice
invariably male, and fancy dress
performances of strictly human rite –
but now, confused by pain, depends upon
a mothering nurse who cannot spell.'

Charles Smith, 'Field Hospital', *c.* 1943

Older men declare war. But it is youth that must fight and die.

Herbert Hoover, at the Republican National Convention, Chicago, 27th June 1944

There's one thing you men can say when it's all over and you're home once more. You can thank God that twenty years from now when you're sitting by the fireside with your grandson on your knee, and he asks you what you did in the war, you won't have to shift him to the other knee, cough and say, 'I shovelled crap in Louisiana.'

George S. Patton, 1944, quoted in John Ellis, *The Sharp End of War*, 1980

The responsibility of the great states is to serve and not to dominate the world.

Harry S. Truman, message to Congress, 16th April 1945

What will be the position in a year or two, when the British and American Armies have melted and the French has not yet been formed on any major scale, when we may have a handful of Divisions, mostly French, and when Russia may choose to keep two or three hundred on active service? An iron curtain is drawn down upon their front. We do not know what is going on behind.

Winston Churchill, telegram to President Truman, 12th May 1945

From my mother's sleep I fell into the State,
And I hunched in its belly till my wet fur froze.
Six miles from earth, loosed from its dream of life,
I woke to black flak and the nightmare fighters.
When I died they washed me out of the turret with a hose.

Randall Jarrell, 'The Death of the Ball Turret Gunner', 1945

A thousand years shall pass and this guilt of Germany shall not have been erased.

Obergrüppenführer Hans Frank, attributed

It [the first V2 rocket to fall on London, 8.9.44] was very successful, but it fell on the wrong planet.

Wernher von Braun, attributed

Hitler's dictatorship was the first dictatorship of an industrial state in the age of modern technology, a dictatorship which deployed to perfection the instruments of technology to dominate its own people . . . By means of such instruments of technology as the radio and public-address systems, eighty million persons could be made subject to the will of one individual. Telephone, teletype, and radio made it possible to transmit the commands of the highest levels directly to the lowest organs where because of their high authority they were executed uncritically. Thus many officers and squads received their evil commands in this direct manner. The instruments of technology made it possible to maintain a close watch over all citizens and to keep criminal operations shrouded in a high degree of secrecy. To the outsider this state apparatus may look like the seemingly wild tangle of cables in a telephone exchange; but like such an exchange it could be directed by a single will. Dictatorships of the past needed assistants of high quality in the lower ranks of the leadership also – men who could think and act independently. The authoritarian system in the age of technology can do without such men. The means of communication alone enable it to mechanize the work of the lower leadership. Thus the type of uncritical receiver of orders is created.

Albert Speer, addressing the International Military Tribunal at Nuremberg, 1946

One day President Roosevelt told me that he was asking publicly for suggestions about what the war should be called. I said at once 'the Unnecessary War.'

Winston Churchill, *The Second World War*, 1948–54

I have often wondered what would have happened if two hundred thousand German storm troopers had actually established themselves ashore . . . I intended to use the slogan, 'You can always take one with you.'

Winston Churchill, *The Second World War*, 1948–54

When I look back on all these worries I remember the story of the old man who said on his deathbed that he had had a lot of trouble in his life, most of which had never happened.

Winston Churchill, *The Second World War*, 1948–54

The size of the sea is so vast that the difference in size of a convoy and the size of a single ship shrinks in comparison almost to insignificance. There was in fact very nearly as good a chance of a convoy of forty ships in close order slipping unperceived between patrolling U-boats as there was for a single ship; and each time this happened, forty ships escaped instead of one. Here then was the key to the success of the convoy system against U-boats.

Winston Churchill, *The Second World War*, 1948–54

I said that the world must be made safe for at least fifty years. If it was only for fifteen or twenty years then we should have betrayed our soldiers.

Winston Churchill, *The Second World War*, 1948–54

As I observed last time, when the war of the giants is over the wars of the pygmies will begin.

Winston Churchill, *The Second World War*, 1948–54

I opposed and protested every step in the policies which led us into the Second World War. Especially in June, 1941, when Britain was safe from German invasion due to Hitler's diversion to attack Stalin, I urged that the gargantuan jest of all history would be our giving aid to the Soviet government. I urged we should allow these two dictators to exhaust each other. I stated that the result of our assistance would be to spread Communism over the whole world. I urged that if we stood aside the time would come when we could bring lasting peace to the world. I have no regrets. The consequences have proved that I was right.

Herbert Hoover, radio broadcast, 10th August 1954

In Germany, the Nazis came for the Communists, and I didn't speak up because I was not a Communist. Then they came for the Jews and I didn't speak up because I was not a Jew. Then they came for the trade unionists and I didn't speak up because I was not a trade unionist. Then they came for the Catholics and I was a Protestant so I didn't speak up. Then they came for me . . . and by that time there was no one to speak up for anyone.

Martin Niemöller, quoted in W. Neil, *Concise Dictionary of Religious Quotations*, 1975

War in 1944–1945 was still basically a matter of flesh and blood.

L. F. Ellis and A. E. Warhurst, *Victory in the West*, 1968

During the years of military victory Hitler had associated largely with the circle of generals around him. With the approaching end of his rule he visibly withdrew into the intimate clique of old party members with whom he had launched out on his career. Night after night he sat with Goebbels, Ley, and Bormann for a few hours. No one was admitted to these gatherings, no one knew what they were talking about, whether they were reminiscing about their beginnings or talking about the end and what would come after it. I listened in vain for at least a single feeling remark about the future of the defeated nation. They grasped at every straw, made much of even the vaguest signs of a turning point; yet they were in no way prepared to regard the fate of the entire nation as nearly important as their own. 'We will leave nothing but a desert to the Americans, English and Russians' – this was the standard close to any discussion of the matter.

Albert Speer, *Inside the Third Reich*, 1969

The British contribution to the Second World War reflected the decline in Britain's relative power. The British *helped* the Russians and Americans to beat Germany, and *helped* the Americans to beat the Japanese; they took the major part only in defeating Italy.

Correlli Barnett, *Britain and Her Army 1509–1970*, 1970

Capable of an almost vertical dive onto its target, the Stuka was intended to induce terror as well as inflict damage, and the rising whine of its accelerating engine was supplemented by a high-pitched siren fitted, it is said, at Hitler's personal suggestion.

Bryan Perrett, *A History of Blitzkrieg*, 1983

We didn't worry too much about not hitting the military targets we were after. Really, I suppose one thought we were at war with Germany and so long as we dropped our bombs we were doing some damage somewhere, although the ruling was that if we couldn't see our target we were to bring our bombs back, but nobody did this . . .

Rupert Oakley, pilot, in Gwynne Dyer, *War*, 1986

The U.S. Army concluded during World War II that almost every soldier, if he escaped death or wounds, would break down after 200 to 240 'combat days'; the British, who rotated their troops out of the front line more often, reckoned 400 days, but they agreed breakdown was inevitable. The reason that about only one sixth of the casualties were psychiatric was that most combat troops did not survive long enough to go to pieces.

Gwynne Dyer, *War*, 1986

The War in Europe

The hand that held the dagger has struck it into the back of its neighbour.

Franklin D. Roosevelt, address, following Italy's declaration of war against France, 10th June 1940

Our first line of defence against invasion must be as ever the enemy's ports.

Winston Churchill, minute to Chiefs of Staff Committee, 5th August 1940

It should be inferred in every case of resistance to the German occupying forces, no matter what the individual circumstances, that it is of communist origin. The death penalty of 50 to 100 Communists should generally be regarded as suitable atonement for one German soldier's life.

Field Marshal Keitel, order, 1941

Investigation seems to show that having one's house demolished is most damaging to morale. People seem to mind it more than having their friends or even relatives killed. At Hull, signs of strain were evident, though only one tenth of the houses were demolished. On the above figures we should be able to do ten times as much harm to each of the fifty-eight principal German towns. There seems little doubt that this would break the will of the people.

Lord Cherwell, 1942, quoted in Max Hastings, *Bomber Command*, 1979

The 'Führer aller Germanen' has been talking to wounded soldiers. Listening-in to it was pitiful. Question and answer went something like this:

'My name is Heinrich Scheppel.'

'Wounded where?'

'Near Stalingrad.'

'What kind of wound?'

'Two feet frozen off and a broken joint in the left arm.'

This is exactly what the frightful puppet show on the radio was like. The wounded seemed to be proud of their wounds – the more the better. One of them felt so moved at being able to shake hands with the Führer (that is, if he still had a hand!) that he could hardly get the words out of his mouth.

Anne Frank, *The Diary of a Young Girl*, 1952: 19th March 1943

It takes twenty minutes for a medium tank to incinerate; and the flames burn slowly, so figure it takes ten minutes for a hearty man within to perish. You wouldn't even be able to struggle for chances are both exits would be sheeted with flame and smoke. You would sit, read *Good Housekeeping*, and die like a dog.

Nat Frankel, 1944, quoted in John Ellis, *The Sharp End of War*, 1980

I don't care if the guy behind that gun is a syphilitic prick who's a hundred years old – he's still sitting behind eight foot of concrete and he's still got enough fingers to pull triggers and shoot bullets.

Anonymous US infantryman, 1945, in C. Whiting, *Bloody Achen*, 1976

Dig a hole in your back garden while it is raining. Sit in the hole while the water climbs up round your ankles. Pour cold mud down your shirt collar. Sit there for forty-eight hours, and, so there is no danger of your dozing off, imagine that a guy is sneaking round waiting for a chance to club you on the head or set your house on fire. Get out of the hole, fill a suitcase full of rocks, pick it up, put a shotgun in your other hand, and walk down the muddiest road you can find. Fall flat on your face every few minutes, as you imagine big meteors streaking down to sock you . . . Snoop around until you find a bull. Try to figure a way to sneak around him without letting him see you. When he does see you, run like hell all the way back to your hole in the back yard, drop the suitcase and shotgun, and get in. If you repeat this performance every three days for several months you may begin to understand why an infantryman gets out of breath.

Bill Mauldin, *Up Front*, 1945

All the German generals to whom I talked were of the opinion that the Allied Supreme Command had missed a great opportunity of ending the war in the autumn of 1944. They agreed with Montgomery's view, that this could best have been achieved by concentrating all possible resources on a threat in the north, towards Berlin.

B. H. Liddell Hart, *The Other Side of the Hill*, 1951

The air raids carried the war into our midst. In the burning and devastated cities we daily experienced the direct impact of the war. And it spurred us to do our utmost.

Neither did the bombings and the hardships that resulted from them weaken the morale of the populace. On the contrary, from my visits to the armament plants and my contacts with the man on the street I carried away the impression of growing toughness. It may well be that the estimated loss of 9 per cent of our production capacity was amply balanced out by increased effort.

Our heaviest expense was in fact the elaborate defensive measures. In the Reich and in the western theatres of war the barrels of ten thousand antiaircraft guns were pointed toward the sky. The same guns could have well been employed in Russia against tanks and other ground targets. Had it not been for this new front, the airfront over Germany, our defensive strength against tanks would have been almost doubled, as far as equipment was concerned. Moreover, the antiaircraft force tied down hundreds of thousands of young soldiers. A third of the optical industry was busy producing gunsights for the flak batteries. About half of the electronics industry was engaged in producing radar and communications networks for defense against bombing. Simply because of this, in spite of the high level of the German electronics and optical industries, the supply of our frontline troops with modern equipment remained far behind that of the Western armies.

Albert Speer, *Inside the Third Reich*, 1969

– The Jewish Holocaust

In my eyes the charge against Judaism became a grave one the moment I discovered the Jewish activities in the Press, in art, in literature and the theatre. All unctuous protests were now more or less futile. One needed only to look at the posters announcing the hideous productions of the cinema and theatre, and study the names of the authors who were highly lauded there in order to become permanently adamant on Jewish questions. Here was a pestilence, with which the public were being infected. It was worse than the Black Plague of long ago. And in what mighty doses this poison was manufactured and distributed. Naturally the lower the moral and intellectual level of such an author of artistic products, the more inexhaustible his fecundity. Sometimes it went so far that one of these fellows, acting like a sewage pump, would shoot his filth directly in the face of other members of the human race. In this connection we must remember there is no limit to the number of such people. One ought to realize that for one Goethe, Nature may bring into existence ten thousand such despoilers who act as the worst kind of germ-carriers in poisoning human souls. It was a terrible thought, and yet it could not be avoided, that the greater number of the Jews seemed specially destined to play this shameful part.

Adolf Hitler, *Mein Kampf*, 1924–26

Should the Jew, with the aid of his Marxist creed, triumph over the people of this world, his Crown will be the funeral wreath of mankind, and this planet will once again follow its orbit through ether, without human life on its surface, as it did millions of years ago.

Adolf Hitler, *Mein Kampf*, 1924–26

It will be the task of the People's State to make the race the centre of the life of the community. It must make sure that the purity of the racial strain will be preserved. It must proclaim the truth that the child is the most valuable possession a people can have. It must see to it that only those who are healthy beget children; that there is only one infamy, namely, for parents that are ill or show hereditary defects to bring children into the world and that in such cases it is a high honour to refrain from doing so.

Adolf Hitler, *Mein Kampf*, 1924–26

I decide who is a Jew.

Karl Lüger, quoted in Alan Bullock, *Hitler*, 1971

I hereby commission you to carry out all preparations with regard to . . . a total solution of the Jewish question in those territories of Europe which are under German influence.

Hermann Goering, written instruction to Reinhard Heydrich, 31st July 1941

Another improvement that we made . . . was that we built our gas-chambers to accommodate two thousand people at one time.

Rudolph Hess, quoted in Alan Bullock, *Hitler*, 1971

Yesterday the Germans, with the help of the Jewish police, rounded up young Jewish girls, and women both young and old, and also men with and without beards on the streets and in particular among the occupants of 38 Dzielna Street. Two lorry-loads of Germans, airforce, S S and men from other units, as well as a smaller vehicle with officers in it, drew up at the entrance of 38 Dzielna Street. First of all they photographed all the young girls – incidentally, they had picked out girls and women who were particularly respectable-looking and expensively dressed. Then they pushed all the Jewish men and women into the bath-house that is in the corner of the courtyard of the above-mentioned building. Once inside they photographed all the women again. Then they forced the men and women to strip completely naked. German officers divided them into pairs made of one from each sex from among the Jews. They matched young girls to old men, and conversely, young boys with old women. Then they forced the two sexes to commit a sexual act. These scenes . . . were filmed with special apparatus that had been brought in for that purpose.

Abraham Lewin, journal entry 13th May 1942, in *A Cup of Tears*, 1988

The filming that the Germans carried out in the [Warsaw] ghetto continues. Today they set up a film-session in Szulc's restaurant at the corner of Leszno and Nowolipki Streets. They brought in Jews they had rounded up, ordinary Jews and well-dressed Jews, and also women who were respectably dressed, sat them down at the tables and ordered that they be served with all kinds of food and drink at the expense of the Jewish community: meat, fish, liqueurs, white pastries and other delicacies. The Jews ate and the Germans filmed. It is not hard to imagine the motivation behind this. Let the world see the kind of paradise the Jews are living in. They stuff themselves with fish and goose and drink liqueurs and wine. These despicable scenes went on for several hours.

Abraham Lewin, journal entry 19th May 1942, in *A Cup of Tears*, 1988

I know an old Jew, grey with age, about 80 years old. This old man was hit by a terrible misfortune last winter: he had an only son aged 52 who died of typhus. He had no other children. The son is dead. He hadn't remarried and had lived together with his son. A few days ago I visited the old man. As I was saying goodbye to him (he is still in complete command of his faculties), he burst into tears and said to me I want to live to see the end of the war and then live for just another half hour longer.

Abraham Lewin, journal entry 5th June 1942, in *A Cup of Tears*, 1988

Dear Kitty,

I've only got dismal and depressing news for you today. Our many Jewish friends are being taken away by the dozen. These people are treated by the Gestapo without a shred of decency, being loaded into cattle trucks and sent to Westerbork, the big Jewish camp in Drente. Westerbork sounds terrible: only one washing cubicle for a hundred people and not nearly enough lavatories. There is no separate accommodation. Men, women and children all sleep together. One hears of frightful immorality because of this; and a lot of women, and even girls, who stay there any length of time are expecting babies.

Anne Frank, *The Diary of a Young Girl*, 1952: 9th October 1942

A Jewish young man, who was a policeman, told me the following illustrative story: the Christians are being given packed meat (in cans). We also received a ration. Among the Polish masses there is a rumour that this meat has been made from our flesh, that is, from the flesh of Jews who have been murdered.

Abraham Lewin, journal entry 22nd November 1942, in *A Cup of Tears*, 1988

In terms of the number of victims, Hitler has murdered an entire people. There are many peoples in Europe who number fewer than the number of our martyrs. The Danes and the Norwegians are no more than three million. The Lithuanians, the Letts and the Estonians have far fewer. The Swedes – six million. The Slovaks fewer than two million, and so on. And Hitler has already killed five, six million Jews. Our language has no words with which to express the calamity and disaster that has struck us.

Abraham Lewin, journal entry 29th December 1942, in *A Cup of Tears*, 1988

The feeling that one gets is that the Germans want to drown the disaster that must come to them in a sea of innocent blood.

Abraham Lewin, journal entry 11th January 1943, in *A Cup of Tears*, 1988

All the newspapers are full of the invasion and are driving people mad by saying that 'In the event of the English landing in Holland, the Germans will do all they can to defend the country; if necessary they will resort to flooding.' With this, maps have been published, in which the parts of Holland that will be under water are marked. As this applied to large parts of Amsterdam, the first question was, what shall we do if the water in the streets rises to one meter? The answers given by different people vary considerably.

'As walking or cycling is out of the question, we shall have to wade through the stagnant water.'

'Of course not, one will have to try and swim. We shall all put on bathing suits and caps and swim under water as much as possible, then no one will see that we are Jews.'

Anne Frank, *The Diary of a Young Girl*, 1952: 3rd February 1944

Who has inflicted this upon us? Who has made us Jews different from all other people? Who has allowed us to suffer so terribly up till now? It is God that has made us as we are, but it will be God, too, who will raise us up again. If we bear all this suffering and there are still Jews left, when it is over, then Jews, instead of being doomed, will be held up as an example. Who knows, it might even be our religion from which the world and all peoples learn good, and for that reason and that reason only do we have to suffer now. We can never become just Netherlanders, or just English, or representatives of any country for that matter, we will always remain Jews, but we want to, too.

Anne Frank, *The Diary of a Young Girl*, 1952: 11th April 1944

I don't believe that the big men, the politicians and the capitalists alone, are guilty of the war. Oh no, the little man is just as guilty, otherwise the peoples of the world would have risen in revolt long ago. There's in people simply an urge to destroy, an urge to kill, to murder and rage, and until all mankind, without exception, undergoes a great change, wars will be waged, everything that has been built up, cultivated, and grown will be destroyed and disfigured, after which mankind will have to begin all over again.

Anne Frank, *The Diary of a Young Girl*, 1952: 3rd May 1944

Now we were at the crematorium. 'You will put a handkerchief over your nose,' the guide said. There, suddenly, but never to be believed, were the bodies of the dead. They were everywhere. There were piles of them inside the oven room, but the SS had not had time to burn them. They were piled outside the door and alongside the building. They were all naked, and behind the crematorium the ragged clothing of the dead was neatly stacked, shirts, jackets, trousers, shoes, awaiting sterilization and further use. The clothing was handled with order, but the bodies were dumped like garbage, rotting in the sun, yellow and nothing but bones, bones grown huge because there was no flesh to cover them, hideous, terrible, agonizing bones, and the unendurable smell of death.

Martha Gellhorn, 'Dachau', May 1945, in *The Face of War*, 1986

Yet ideas can be true, although men die:
For we have seen a myriad faces
Ecstatic from one lie,

And maps can really point to places
Where life is evil now.
Nanking. Dachau.

W. H. Auden, 'Sonnets from China', 1945: xii

No punishment has ever possessed enough power of deterrence to prevent the commission of crimes. On the contrary, whatever the punishment, once a specific crime has appeared for the first time, its reappearance is more likely than its initial emergence could have been.

Hannah Arendt, *Eichmann in Jerusalem: A Report on the Banality of Evil*, 1963

– The Fall of France, 1940

France has lost the battle but she has not lost the war.

Charles de Gaulle, 1940

Hitler claimed total credit for the success of the campaign in the West. The plan for it came from him, he said. 'I have again and again,' he told us, 'read Colonel de Gaulle's book on methods of modern warfare employing fully motorized units, and I have learned a great deal from it.'

Albert Speer, *Inside the Third Reich*, 1969

– Dunkirk, 26th May–4th June 1940

We shall not flag or fail. We shall go on to the end, we shall fight in France, we shall fight in the seas and oceans, we shall fight with growing confidence and growing strength in the air, we shall defend our island, whatever the cost may be, we shall fight on the beaches, we shall fight on the landing grounds, we shall fight in the fields and in the streets, we shall fight in the hills; we shall never surrender.

Winston Churchill, in the House of Commons, 4th June 1940

Our great-grandchildren, when they learn how we began this war by snatching glory out of defeat . . . may also learn how the little holiday steamers made an excursion to hell and came back glorious.

J. B. Priestley, radio broadcast, 5th June 1940

The Mosquito Armada as a whole was unsinkable. In the midst of our defeat glory came to the Island people, united and unconquerable; and the tale of the Dunkirk beaches will shine in whatever records are preserved of our affairs.

Winston Churchill, *The Second World War*, 1948–54

We must be very careful not to assign to this deliverance the attributes of a victory. Wars are not won by evacuations.

Winston Churchill, *The Second World War*, 1948–54

When so much was uncertain, the need to recover the initiative glared forth.

Winston Churchill, *The Second World War*, 1948–54

– Battle of Britain, 10th July–12th October 1940

Let us therefore brace ourselves to our duties, and so bear ourselves that, if the British Empire and its Commonwealth last for a thousand years, men will still say, 'This was their finest hour'.

Winston Churchill, in the House of Commons, 18th June 1940

Learn to get used to it. Eels get used to skinning.

Winston Churchill, apropos the Blitz, notes for a speech, 20th June 1940

The universe is so vast and so ageless that the life of one man can only be justified by the measure of his sacrifice.

V. A. Rosewarne, Letter to his mother, published in *The Times*, 18th June 1940

Never in the field of human conflict was so much owed by so many to so few.

Winston Churchill, in the House of Commons, 20th August 1940

Still falls the Rain –
Dark as the world of man, black as our loss –
Blind as the nineteen hundred and forty nails
Upon the Cross.

Edith Sitwell, referring to the Blitz, 'Still Falls the Rain', 1940

Far out on the grey waters of the North Sea and the Channel coursed and patrolled the faithful, eager flotillas peering through the night. High in the air soared the fighter pilots, or waited serene at a moment's notice around their excellent machines. This was a time when it was equally good to live or die.

Winston Churchill, *The Second World War*, 1948–54

The Battle of Britain was won. The Battle of the Atlantic had now to be fought.

Winston Churchill, *The Second World War*, 1948–54

– British Withdrawal from Crete, 1st June 1941

It takes the Navy three years to build a ship. It would take three hundred to rebuild a tradition.

Sir Andrew Browne Cunningham, resisting plans for the Royal Navy to abandon soldiers stranded on Crete, May 1941

– Bombing of Hamburg, July 1943

It was as if I was looking into what I imagined to be an active volcano . . . There were great volumes of smoke and, mentally, I could sense the great heat. Our actual bombing was like putting another shovelful of coal into the furnace.

Martin Middlebrook, *The Battle of Hamburg*, 1980

– Allied Invasion of Sicily, from 9th July 1943

Battle is the most magnificent competition in which a human being can indulge. It brings out all that is best; it removes all that is base.

George S. Patton, to the officers of the 45th Division, 27th July 1943

– Allied Landing at Salerno, 9th–16th September 1943

In one case the trapped crew [of a tank] had been broiled in such a way that a puddle of fat had spread from under the tank and this was quilted with brilliant flies of all descriptions and colours.

Norman Lewis, *Naples 44*, 1978

– Allied Forces in Italy, winter of 1943/44

One never saw masses of men assaulting the enemy. What one observed, in apparently unrelated patches, was small, loose bodies of men moving down through narrow defiles or over steep inclines, going methodically from position to position between long halts and the only continuous factor was the roaring and crackling of the big guns. One felt baffled at first by the unreality of it all. Unseen groups of men were fighting other men that they rarely saw.

E. Sevareid, *Not So Wild a Dream*, 1946

– Allied Landing at Anzio, 22nd January 1944

I had hoped that we were hurling a wildcat onto the shore, but all we had got was a stranded whale.

Winston Churchill, *The Second World War*, 1948–54

The whole affair has a strong odor of Gallipoli and apparently the same amateur was still on the coach's bench.

General John P. Lucas, in Martin Blumenson, *Anzio*, 1963

– Battle of Cassino, 29th February–11th May 1944

We Polish soldiers, for our freedom and yours, have given our souls to God, our bodies to the soil of Italy and our hearts to Poland.

Inscription at the Polish Cemetery, Cassino

– The Allies take Rome, 4th June 1944

It was most thoughtful of you as an old Harrovian to capture Rome on the Fourth of June.

Harold Macmillan, telegram to General Alexander, 4th June 1944

– D-Day (Operation Overlord), 6th June 1944, and subsequent Allied Reoccupation of Normandy

We're getting killed on the beaches – let's go inshore and get killed.

US officer, Omaha Beach, June 1944, in John Ellis, *The Sharp End of War*, 1980

Our chiefs of staff are convinced of one thing. The way to kill the most Germans with the least loss of American soldiers, is to mount one great big invasion and then slam 'em with everything we've got. It makes sense to me. It makes sense to Uncle Joe. It makes sense to all our generals, and always has, ever since the beginning of the war.

Franklin D. Roosevelt, 1944, in Elliott Roosevelt, *As He Saw It*, 1946

The whole of this difficult question, how to divide military resources between the Normandy invasion and the invasion of Southern France, only arises out of the absurd shortages of the LSTs. How it is that the plans of two great empires like Britain and the United States should be so much hamstrung and limited by a hundred or so of these particular vessels will never be understood by history.

Winston Churchill, Letter to General Marshall, 1944

We are in the position of a testator who wishes to leave the bulk of his fortune to his mistress. He must, however, leave something to his wife, and his problem is to decide how little he can in decency set apart for her.

Sir Charles Portal, on the demands made upon British Bomber Command by Operation Overlord, 1944, in Anthony Verrier, *Bomber Offensive*, 1968

Overpaid, oversexed, and over here.

British saying, 1944, apropos the build-up of American forces in Britain.

Those of our troops who were not wax-grey with seasickness, fighting it off, trying to hold on to themselves before they had to grab the steel side of the boat, were watching the *Texas* with looks of surprise and happiness. Under the steel helmets they looked like pikemen of the Middle Ages to whose aid in battle had suddenly come some strange and unbelievable monster.

Ernest Hemingway, in *Collier's*, 22nd July 1944

History now was old K-ration boxes, empty foxholes, the drying leaves on the branches that were cut for camouflage. It was burned German vehicles, burned

German tanks, many burned German Panthers and some burned Tigers, German dead along the roads, in the hedges and in the orchards, German equipment scattered everywhere, German horses roaming the fields, and our own wounded and our dead passing back strapped two abreast on top of the evacuation jeeps. But mostly history was getting where we were to get on time and waiting there for others to come up.

Ernest Hemingway, in *Collier's*, 4th November 1944

We sure liberated the hell out of this place.

Anonymous US soldier, in a Normandy village, June 1944, in Max Miller, *The Far Shore*, 1945

For the United States and Great Britain, the fruits of the battle of Normandy were apples of Sodom, which turned to ashes as soon as they were plucked. Hitler and his legions were destroyed, and in their stead stood Stalin and his Asiatic hordes. Because 'Victory – victory at all costs!' had been the western allies' aim, and because of their insistence that 'it was to be the defeat, ruin and slaughter of Hitler, to the exclusion of all other purposes, loyalties and aims,' Stalin, the supreme realist, whose strategy had throughout kept in step with his policy, had been able to impose his messianic cult upon Estonia, Latvia, Lithuania, part of Finland, Poland, eastern and central Germany, a third of Austria, Czechoslovakia, Yugoslavia, Hungary, Rumania, and Bulgaria. Vienna, Prague, and Berlin, the vertebrae of Europe, were his, and except for Athens, so was every capital in eastern Europe . . . A thousand years of European history had been rolled back. Such were the fruits of the battle of Normandy, fructified by inept strategy and a policy of pure destruction.

J. F. C. Fuller, *The Decisive Battles of the Western World*, 1954–56

It wasn't too bad for us sailors, but I think one of the main reasons why Normandy was such a great success was that the soldiers would rather have fought thousands of Germans than go back into those boats and be sea-sick again.

R. McKinlay, in A. McKee, *Caen: Anvil of Victory*, 1966

In the no-man's land between the two sides, in the deserted farmsteads, there were plenty of fowls if you could catch them. I couldn't. These chickens, as soon as they saw anybody in battledress, however much he whistled disinterest, scrambled up the nearest rampart, and you could not get after them without revealing yourself in a field of machinegun fire. But I discovered a flock of geese, and I broke my penknife trying to slaughter the first. When I had at last killed them all and loaded them into my jeep for my hungry colleagues, I was covered from top to tail with feathers. A soldier looking like one out of a Giles wartime cartoon climbed out of a slit trench and said to me balefully, 'Them was laying eggs.'

Macdonald Hastings, *Gamebook*, 1979

– Battle of Arnhem, 17th September 1944

'Not in vain' may be the pride of those who survived and the epitaph of those who fell.

Winston Churchill, in the House of Commons, 28th September 1944

To have turned the enemy flank in the north, seizing the bridge-heads on the way, would have demanded daring of high order in conception, in leadership in the field, and in execution. The conception of such a plan was impossible for a man of Montgomery's innate caution . . . In fact, Montgomery's decision to mount the operation aimed at the Zuider Zee was as startling as it would have been for an elderly and saintly Bishop suddenly to decide to take up safe-breaking and begin on the Bank of England.

R. W. Thompson, *Montgomery the Field-Marshal*, 1969

– Battle of the Bulge, 16th December 1944–16th January 1945

They've got us surrounded again, the poor bastards.

Colonel Creighton Abrams, U S Army, attributed

– German Surrender, 7th May 1945

A splendid moment in our great history and in our small lives.

Winston Churchill, radio broadcast, 7th May 1945

The Russian Front

I cannot forecast to you the action of Russia. It is a riddle wrapped in a mystery inside an enigma. But perhaps there is a key. That key is Russian national interest.

Winston Churchill, radio broadcast, 1st October 1939

You know, Ribbentrop, if I made an agreement with Russia today, I'd still break it tomorrow – I just can't help it.

Adolf Hitler, in conversation with his Foreign Minister, November 1939

When Barbarossa commences, the world will hold its breath and make no comment.

Adolf Hitler, to General Franz Halder, 1940

The German army in fighting Russia is like an elephant attacking a host of ants. The elephant will kill thousands, perhaps even millions, of ants, but in the end their numbers will overcome him, and he will be eaten to the bone.

Bernd von Kleist, in Alan Clark, *Barbarossa*, 1965

It is hardly too much to say that the campaign against Russia has been won in fourteen days.

Franz Halder, diary entry, 3rd July 1941

In the case of a forced retreat of Red Army units, all rolling stock must be evacuated; to the enemy must not be left a single engine, a single railway carriage, not a single pound of grain nor one gallon of fuel . . . In occupied regions conditions must be made unbearable for the enemy and all his accomplices. They must be hounded and annihilated at every step and all their measures frustrated.

Joseph Stalin, Address to the Russian People, 3rd July 1941

So far as strategy, policy, foresight and competence are arbiters Stalin and his commissars showed themselves at this moment [July 1941] the most completely outwitted bunglers of the Second World War.

Winston Churchill, *The Second World War*, 1948–54

An additional obstruction was that every time a difficulty arose in the rear, Kluge stopped the advance until it had been overcome. Here it may be observed that, like a jockey, a bold tank general should have his eyes fixed on the winning post, and not, like a cautious transport leader, on the tail of his convoy.

J. F. C. Fuller, *The Decisive Battles of the Western World*, 1954–56

Whether 10,000 Russian females fall from exhaustion while digging an antitank ditch interests in me only in so far as the antitank ditch for Germans is finished.

Heinrich Himmler, addressing S S officers, 1941, quoted in Martha Gellhorn, *The Face of War*, 1986

A Tsar once remarked that two of the best generals in his army were named January and February. If he had lived to see the era of mechanized war he might have commented that October and March were pretty impressive fellows too, for in October the first torrential winter rains reduced the roads to bottomless quagmires, while the Spring thaw had precisely the same effect.

Bryan Perrett, *A History of Blitzkrieg*, 1983

– Russian Counter-Offensive of 1941

Every man must fight back where he stands. No falling back where there are no prepared positions in rear.

Adolf Hitler, General Order, 19th December 1941

The advance of a Russian Army is something that Westerners can't imagine. Behind the tank spearheads rolls on a vast horde, largely mounted on horses. The soldier carries a sack on his back, with dry crusts of bread and raw vegetables collected on the march from fields and villages. The horses eat the straw from the house-roofs – they get very little else. The Russians are accustomed to carry on for as long as three weeks in this primitive way, when advancing. You can't stop them, like an ordinary army, by cutting their communications, for you rarely find any supply columns to strike.

General von Manteuffel, in B. H. Liddell Hart, *The Other Side of the Hill*, 1951

– Battle of Stalingrad, August 1942–February 1943

The duty of the men at Stalingrad is to be dead.

Adolf Hitler, remark at a luncheon conference, January 1943

A defeat for Europe as a whole.

F. O. Miksche, *Unconditional Surrender*, 1952

The War In Africa

We have finished the job, what shall we do with the tools?

Emperor Haile Selassie of Abyssinia, telegram to Winston Churchill, 1941

A pint of sweat will save a gallon of blood.

George S. Patton, to American forces at Casablanca, 8th November 1942

Tell them from me they are unloading history.

Winston Churchill, telegram to the Port Commandant of Tripoli, 24th February 1943

– Battle of El Alamein, October 23rd–24th 1942

Before Alamein we never had a victory. After Alamein we never had a defeat.

Winston Churchill, *The Second World War*, 1948–54

The War Against Japan (The Pacific War), 1941–45

Before we're through with them, the Japanese language will be spoken only in hell.

William F. Halsey, attributed, *c.* 1943

When you go home
Tell them of us, and say,
For your tomorrow
We gave our today.

Inscription on the British war memorial at Kohima (India), 1944

We call Japanese soldiers fanatics when they die rather than surrender, whereas American soldiers who do the same thing are heroes.

Robert M. Hutchins, lecture at the University of Chicago, June 1945

If the Battle of Waterloo was won on the playing fields of Eton, the Japanese bases in the Pacific were captured on the beaches of the Caribbean.

Holland M. Smith, *Coral and Brass*, 1949

Hitler's fate was sealed. Mussolini's fate was sealed. As for the Japanese, they would be ground to powder. All the rest was merely the proper application of overwhelming force.

Winston Churchill, *The Second World War*, 1948–54

There was only one kind of Japanese casualty – the dead.

United States Army in World War II (Official History), 1951

– Japanese Attack on Pearl Harbor, 7th December 1941

My Peruvian Colleague told a member of my staff that he had heard . . . that the Japanese military forces planned, in the event of trouble with the United States, to attempt a surprise mass attack on Pearl Harbor . . . he added that although the project seemed fantastic the fact that he had heard it from many sources prompted him to pass on the information.

Joseph Grew (US ambassador to Japan), telegram to the Secretary of State, 27th January 1941

Praise the Lord and pass the ammunition.

Lieutenant-Commander H. M. Forgy, during the Japanese attack on Pearl Harbor, 7th December 1941

Yesterday, December 7th, 1941 – a date which will live in infamy – the United States of America was suddenly and deliberately attacked by naval and air forces of the Empire of Japan.

Franklin D. Roosevelt, message to Congress, 8th December 1941

The British are such clever propagandists they might well have cooked up the story.

Congresswoman Jeanette Rankin, voting against the US Declaration of War against Japan

I fear we have only awakened a sleeping giant, and his reaction will be terrible.

Admiral Yamamoto, December 1941, quoted in the *Listener*, 9th September 1976

The only thing to do now is to lick hell out of them.

Senator Burton K. Wheeler, comment made shortly after the bombing of Pearl Harbor, December 1941

It becomes still more difficult to reconcile Japanese action with prudence or even with sanity. What kind of people do they think we are?

Winston Churchill, speaking to Congress, 24th December 1941

Remember Pearl Harbor!

US Slogan

– Japanese take the Philippines: Battle of Bataan-Corregidor, 10th January 1942

There are no atheists in foxholes.

W. T. Cummings (chaplain), sermon on Bataan, March 1942

We're the battling bastards of Bataan,
No mama, no papa, no Uncle Sam,
No aunts, no uncles, no cousins, no nieces,
No pills, no planes, no artillery pieces.
And nobody gives a damn.

Anonymous, contemporary

I shall return.

Douglas MacArthur, leaving the Philippines, 11th March 1942

It was bitter for us not to be able to land a million men from a thousand ships in the Philippine Islands.

Franklin D. Roosevelt, State of the Union Address, 1942

– Battle of the Coral Sea, 8th Mary 1942

Scratch one flat-top.

Commander Robert Dixon, radio report, apropos the sinking of the Japanese carrier HIMJS *Shoko*, 7th May 1942

– Japanese Conquest of Burma, 16th January–20th May 1942

We got run out of Burma, and it is humiliating as hell.

Joseph W. Stilwell, Press statement, 25th May 1942

Jackie, you dropped your Field Marshal's baton into the Sittang River.

William Slim, remark made to Major-General J. G. Smyth following the demolition of the Sittang Bridge, February 1942

The dominant feeling of the battlefield is loneliness.

William Slim, addressing the 10th Indian Infantry Division, June 1942

On the last day of the nine hundred mile retreat I stood on a bank beside the road and watched the rearguard march into India. All of them, British, Indian and Gurkha, were gaunt and ragged as scarecrows. Yet, as they trudged behind their surviving officers in groups pitifully small they still carried their arms and kept their ranks, they were still recognizable as fighting units. They might look like scarecrows, but they looked like soldiers too.

William Slim, *Defeat Into Victory*, 1956

Defeat is bitter. Bitter to the common soldier, but trebly bitter to his general. The soldier may comfort himself with the thought that, whatever the result, he has done his duty faithfully and steadfastly, but the commander has failed in *his* duty if he has not won victory – for that *is* his duty. He has no other comparable to it.

William Slim, *Defeat Into Victory*, 1956

In terms of discomfort and endurance, the Burma front was the only Second-World-War equivalent of Great-War trench life faced by the British army.

Correlli Barnett, *Britain and Her Army 1509–1970*, 1970

– Battle of Santa Cruz Islands, 26th October 1942

Attack repeat attack.

William F. Halsey, signal to the South Pacific Force immediately prior to the engagement.

– Battle of Midway, 4th June 1942

Midway could not have been won if our Hawaii shipyards had not performed a backbreaking miracle repairing the carrier *Yorktown* . . . accomplishing in three days a job that today would probably take the average shipyard three years – and then be done sloppily, with extravagant cost overruns.

Charles Peters, in *Washington Monthly*, December 1981

– Battle for Guadalcanal, July 1942–January 1943

And when he gets to Heaven,
To St Peter he will tell:
'One more Marine reporting, Sir –
I've served my time in Hell.'

Inscription on the grave of US Marine Pfc. Cameron, 1942

Goddamn it, you'll never get the Purple Heart hiding in a foxhole! Follow me!

Lieutenant-Colonel Henry P. Crowe, attributed, 13th January 1943

Guadalcanal is no longer merely the name of an island. It is the graveyard of the Japanese Army.

Major-General Kiyotake Kawaguchi, attributed, 1943

I have observed the Japs often get short of ammunition. They cut bamboo and crack it together to simulate rifle fire to draw our fire. They ain't supermen; they're just tricky bastards.

Joseph S. Stankus, in *Marine Corps Reader*, ed. C. H. Metcalf, 1944

Long may the tale be told in the great Republic.

Winston Churchill, *Closing the Ring*, 1951

It was all good Robert Mitchum stuff. The Japanese lost in excess of 20,000 men, though as in New Guinea a moiety died of malaria and other jungle diseases. They also lost what chance they had of winning the war. For the Solomon Islanders it was a confusing experience. The scenes of destruction they had witnessed were on a scale that was strictly fantastic. They were also treated to another miraculous spectacle: white men upon occasion taking orders from black men, in the ranks of the American forces. The black G.I. was not a phenomenon any Briton or Australian had prepared them for.

Justin Wintle, *Heat Treatment*, 1988

– British Reconquest of Burma, June 1943–3rd May 1945

The vulnerable artery is the line of communications winding through the jungle. Have no L. of C. on the jungle floor. Bring in the goods like Father Christmas, down the chimney.

Orde Wingate, advocating air-borne supplies, the Myitkyina area, 1943

We have inflicted complete surprise on the enemy. All our columns are inserted in the enemy's guts.

Orde Wingate, Order of the Day, 3rd Indian Division, 11th March 1944

Armies do not win wars by means of a few bodies of super-soldiers, but by the average quality of their standard units . . . Any well-trained infantry battalion should be able to do what a commando can do; in the Fourteenth Army they could and did.

William Slim, *Defeat Into Victory*, 1956

When I asked a man in his foxhole or sitting beside the track what he was, he would often, instead of answering 'I am a Lancashire Fusilier', or 'an FOO's signaller', or 'Bren gunner of this section', say, 'I am four and two', or 'Three and ten'. He meant that was the number of years and months he served in the Far East, and the unspoken question in his eyes was, 'How many more?' I could not answer him. . . .

William Slim, *Defeat Into Victory*, 1956

To obviate [the] danger of coughs giving away gun positions, 'coughing piquets' were established some 500 yards away. All notorious coughers were obliged to go there, with the knowledge that any night-prowling Japs were likely to fire on them first. This largely cured the early morning coughing to which the Indians were so prone!

S. T. Clarke, in H. Maule, *Spearhead General*, 1961

The Gurkha swung his kukri with a deft cutting sideways movement.

'Ja! missed,' cried the German.

'Try shaking your head,' retorted the Gurkha.

E. D. Smith, *Johnny Gurkha*, 1985

– Allied Forces Liberate the Philippines, from 20th October 1944

Our ships have been salvaged and are retiring at high speed toward the Japanese fleet.

William F. Halsey, scotching a rumour that the Third Fleet had been defeated, 26th October 1944

I see that the old flagpole still stands. Have your troops hoist the Colors to its peak, and let no enemy ever haul them down.

Douglas MacArthur, to Colonel George M. Jones, at Corregidor, 2nd March 1945

– The Kamikaze

The purity of youth will usher in the Divine Wind.

Vice-Admiral Onishi, inscription, 1944

If only we might fall
Like cherry blossoms in the Spring –
So pure and radiant!

Haiku by an unknown kamikaze pilot, February 1945

On our last sortie we shall wear regular flight uniforms and a headband bearing the rising sun. Snow-white scarves give a certain dash to our appearance.

Lieutenant Hayashi, Letter to his mother, 1945

Now that I set off on my last attack
I can never feel alone,
For my mother's band
Is safely tied about my waist.

Matsuo Tomio, poem written before his death at twenty-one, 1945

– Battle of Iwo Jima, 19th February–26th March 1945

The raising of that flag on Suribachi means a Marine Corps for the next five hundred years.

James Forrestal, as the US Marines raised their colours on Mt Suribachi, 23rd February 1945

Among the men who fought on Iwo Jima, uncommon valor was a common virtue.

C. W. Nimitz, Pacific Fleet communiqué, 16th March 1945

Your mouth is a vacuum and speech is remote and any sound from it would be a turgid groan. Your mind looks at itself and it shrinks away and wonders whether or not to stand bravely or run and hide. Feelings, senses and physical motion are faint and far off, and all existence is a rushing wind in your ear.

Peter Bowman, *Beach Head*, 1946

– Hiroshima, 6th August 1945

Little Boy

Name given to the bomb dropped on Hiroshima

We have resolved to endure the unendurable and suffer what is insufferable.

Emperor Hirohito, shortly after the bomb was dropped, August 1945

Everything fell, and Miss Sasaki lost consciousness. The ceiling dropped suddenly and the wooden floor above collapsed in splinters and the people up there came down and the roof above them gave way; but principally and first of all, the bookcases right behind her swooped forward and the contents threw her down, with her left leg horribly twisted and breaking underneath her. There, in the tin factory, in the first moment of the atomic age, a human being was crushed by books.

John Hersey, *Hiroshima*, 1946

Mrs Nakamura and her children were among the first to arrive, and they settled in the bamboo grove near the river. At once they were nauseated and began vomiting, and they retched the whole day. Others were also nauseated; they all thought (probably because of the strong odour of ionization, an 'electric smell' given off by the bomb's fission) that they were sick from a gas the Americans had dropped.

John Hersey, *Hiroshima*, 1946

The day before the bomb, I went for a swim. In the morning I was eating peanuts. I saw a light. I was knocked to my little sister's sleeping place. When we were saved I could only see as far as the tram. My mother and I started to pack our things. The neighbours were walking around burned and bleeding. Hataya-san told me to run away with her. I said I wanted to wait for my mother. We went to the park. A whirlwind came. At night a gas tank burned and I saw the reflection in the river. We stayed in the park one night. Next day I went to Taiko Bridge and met my girl friends Kikuki and Murakami. They were looking for their mothers. But Kikuki's mother was wounded and Murakami's mother, alas, was dead.

Toshio Nakamura, aged ten, school essay, in John Hersey, *Hiroshima*, 1946

My own feeling was that in being the first to use it, we had adopted an ethical standard common to the barbarians of the Dark Ages . . . Employment of the atomic bomb will take us back in cruelty towards noncombatants to the days of Genghis Khan.

William D. Leahy, *I Was There*, 1950

We knew the world would not be the same. A few people laughed. A few people cried. Most people were silent. I remembered the line from the Hindu scripture – the Bhagavad-gita. Vishnu is trying to persuade the prince that he should do his duty, and to impress him, takes on his multi-armed form and says, 'Now I am become Death, the destroyer of worlds.' I suppose we all felt that, one way or another.

Robert Oppenheimer, quoted in Gwynne Dyer, *War*, 1986

I saw a perfectly outlined city, clear in every detail, coming in. The city was roughly about four miles in diameter. By that time we were at our bombing altitude of thirty-two thousand feet. The navigator came up – looking over my shoulder, he said: 'Yes, that's Hiroshima, there's no doubt about it.' We were so well on the target that the bombardier says: 'I can't do anything, there's nothing to do.' He says: 'It's just sitting there.'

Colonel Paul Tibbetts, pilot of the Enola Gay, in Gwynne Dyer, *War*, 1986

– Nagasaki, 9th August 1945

Big Boy

Name given to the bomb dropped on Nagasaki

A rain of ruin the like of which has never been seen on earth.

Leaflet dropped on Nagasaki a few days before the bombing, warning its people about the use of an atomic weapon

Somebody said, Play it again Uncle Sam, and he did.

1960s joke

– Japanese Surrender, 15th August 1945

The enemy have begun to employ a new and most cruel bomb, the power of which to damage is indeed incalculable, taking the toll of many innocent lives. Should we continue to fight, it would not only result in an ultimate collapse and obliteration of the Japanese nation, but it would also lead to the total extinction of human civilization.

Emperor Hirohito, radio broadcast, 15th August 1945

Cease firing, but if any enemy planes appear, shoot them down in a friendly fashion.

William F. Halsey, message to the 3rd Fleet, 15th August 1945

NUCLEAR WEAPONS and THE COLD WAR, from 1945

Some day science may have the existence of mankind in its power and the human race commit suicide by blowing up the world.

Henry Adams, Letter, 1862

It is not probable that war will ever absolutely cease until science discovers some destroying force so simple in its administration, so horrible in its effects, that all art, all gallantry, will be at an end, and battles will be massacres which the feelings of mankind will be unable to endure.

W. Winwood Reade, *The Martyrdom of Man*, 1872

War to the hilt between communism and capitalism is inevitable. Today, of course, we are not strong enough to attack. Our time will come in twenty or thirty years. To win, we shall need the element of surprise. The bourgeoisie will have to be put to sleep. So we shall begin by launching the most spectacular peace movement on record. There will be electrifying overtures and unheard-of concessions. The capitalist countries, stupid and decadent, will rejoice to co-operate in their own destruction. They will leap at another chance to be friends. As soon as their guard is down, we shall smash them with our clenched fists.

Dmitri Zacharevichi Manuilsky, Address to the Lenin School of Political Warfare, 1931

Now we are all sons of bitches.

Kenneth Bainbridge, remark made after first atomic test, 1945

At first it was a giant column that soon took the shape of a supramundane mushroom.

William L. Laurence, describing the first atomic explosion, quoted in the *New York Times*, 26th September 1945

Aside from being tremendous it was one of the most aesthetically beautiful things I have ever seen.

Donald Hornig, in *The Decision to Drop the Bomb*

There is an iron curtain across Europe.

St Vincent Troubridge, in the *Sunday Empire News*, 21st October 1945

We are not dealing simply with a military or scientific problem but with a problem in statecraft and ways of the human spirit.

Report on the Control of Atomic Energy, (the 'Smith' Report) March 1946

Thus far the chief purpose of our military establishment has been to win wars. From now on its chief purpose must be to avert them. It can have almost no other useful purpose.

Bernard Brodie, *The Absolute Weapon: Atomic Power and World Order*, 1946

The atom bomb is a paper tiger which the U.S. reactionaries use to scare people. It looks terrible, but in fact it isn't. Of course, the atom bomb is a weapon of mass slaughter, but the outcome of a war is decided by the people, not by one or two new types of weapon.

Mao Tse-tung, in conversation with Anna Louise Strong, August 1946

The physicists have known sin; and this is a knowledge which they cannot lose.

J. Robert Oppenheimer, speech at the Massachusetts Institute of Technology, 25th November 1947

Although the war is over, we are in the midst of a cold war which is getting warmer.

Bernard M. Baruch, to the Senate War Investigation Committee, 24th August 1948

If we embrace this escape from reality, the Myth of the Atomic Bomb, we will drift into the belief that we Americans are safe in the world, safe and secure, because we have this devastating weapon – this and nothing more. We will then tend to relax when we need to be eternally vigilant.

David Lilienthal, Commencement Address, Michigan State College, June 1949

The Atomic Age is here to stay – but are we?

Bennett Cerf, quoted in the *Observer*, 12th February 1950

The way to win an atomic war is to make certain it never starts.

Omar Bradley, quoted in the *Observer*, 20th April 1952

Man has wrested from nature the power to make the world a desert or to make the deserts bloom. There is no evil in the atom; only in men's souls.

Adlai Stevenson, speech at Hartford, Connecticut, 18th September 1952

By carrying destruction to a suicidal extreme, atomic power is stimulating and accelerating a reversion to the indirect methods that are the essence of strategy – since they endow war with intelligent properties that raise it above the brute application of force.

B. H. Liddell Hart, *Strategy*, 1954

The terror of the atom age is not the violence of the new power but the speed of man's adjustment to it – the speed of his acceptance. Already bombproofing is on approximately the same level as mothproofing.

E. B. White, *The Second Tree from the Corner*, 1954

It may well be that we shall by a process of sublime irony have reached a state in this story where safety will be the sturdy child of terror, and survival the twin brother of annihilation.

Winston Churchill, in the House of Commons, 1st March 1955

If you are scared to go to the brink, you are lost.

John Foster Dulles, quoted in *Life* magazine, 16th January 1956

Whether you like it or not, history is on our side. We will bury you.

Nikita Khrushchev, in the Kremlin, 26th November 1956

We can lose the world, one parcel of real estate after another, while we wait for a shot that may never be fired.

Arthur W. Radford, speech, 1956

Can one guess how great will be the toll of human casualties in a future war? Possibly it would be a third of the 2,700 million inhabitants of the entire world – i.e., only 900 million people. Of course it is most terrible. But even half would not be so bad . . . If a half of humanity were destroyed, the other half would remain but imperialism would be destroyed entirely and there would be only Socialism in all the world.

Mao Tse-tung, speech in Moscow, 1957

I have no faith in the so-called controlled use of atomic weapons. There is no dependable distinction between tactical and strategic situations. I would not recommend the use of any atomic weapon, no matter how small, when both sides have the power to destroy the world.

Charles R. Brown, speaking in Washington, 1958

If I had only known I would have become a watchmaker.

Alfred Einstein, attributed

The new and terrible dangers created by man can only be controlled by man.

John F. Kennedy, at the University of California, 2nd November 1959

In the future, if nuclear weapons are unleashed there will be no front and no rear.

Nikita Khrushchev, speaking in Moscow, August 1961

There is no presumption more terrifying than that of those who would blow up the world on the basis of their personal judgement of a transient situation.

George F. Kennan, comment made to the Press after returning from Belgrade, August 1961

Mankind must put an end to war or war will put an end to mankind.

John F. Kennedy, at the UN General Assembly, 25th September 1961

Young officers of all Services must learn terrain or learn Russian.

Major-General Alden Sibley, Naval War College lecture, February 1962

Peace does not rest in charters and covenants alone. It lies in the hearts and minds of the people. And if it is cast out there, then no act, no pact, no treaty organization can ever hope to preserve it. So let us not rest all our hopes for peace on parchment and paper – let us strive also to build peace in the hearts and minds of our people.

John F. Kennedy, addressing the UN General Assembly, 20th September 1963

We have genuflected before the god of science only to find that it has given us the atomic bomb, producing fears and anxieties that science can never mitigate.

Martin Luther King, *Strength To Love*, 1963

Victory is no longer a truth. It is only a word to describe who is left alive in the ruins.

Lyndon B. Johnson, in New York, 6th February 1964

The master myth of the cold war is that the Communist bloc is a monolith, composed of governments which are not really governments at all, but organized conspiracies . . . all equally resolute and implacable in their determination to destroy the free world.

James William Fulbright, in the US Senate, 27th March 1964

Make no mistake. There is no such thing as a conventional nuclear weapon.

Lyndon B. Johnson, in Detroit, August 1964

We have the power to knock any society out of the twentieth century.

Robert McNamara, in the Pentagon, 1964

Here is our difference with the Communists – and our strength. They would use their skills to forge new chains of tyranny. We would use ours to free men from the bonds of the past.

Lyndon B. Johnson, Message to Congress, 14th January 1965

You may reasonably expect a man to walk a tightrope safely for ten minutes; it would be unreasonable to do so without accident for two hundred years.

Bertrand Russell, in D. Bagley, *The Tightrope Men*

It is not enough to ban nuclear weapons, for nuclear weapons can always be manufactured again. The thing you have to ban is war.

Bertrand Russell, quoted in Caroline Moorehead, *Troublesome People*, 1987

We are, to put it mildly, in a mess, and there is a strong chance that we shall have exterminated ourselves by the end of the century. Our only consolation will have to be that, as a species, we have had an exciting term in office.

Desmond Morris, *The Naked Ape*, 1967

No country without an atom bomb could properly consider itself independent.

Charles de Gaulle, quoted in the *New York Times*, 12th May 1968

Man is preceded by forest, succeeded by desert.

Graffito, Paris, May 1968

The arms race is based on an optimistic view of technology and a pessimistic view of man.

I. F. Stone, in *The New York Review of Books*, 27th March 1969

Our failure to pursue the possibilities of atomic warfare can be partly traced to ideological reasons. Hitler had great respect for Philipp Lenard, the physicist who had received the Nobel Prize in 1920 and was one of the few early adherents of Nazism among the ranks of the scientists. Lenard had instilled the idea in Hitler that the Jews were exerting a seditious influence in their concern with nuclear physics and the relativity theory. To his table companions Hitler occasionally referred to nuclear physics as 'Jewish physics' – citing Lenard as his authority for this. This view was taken up by Rosenberg. It thus becomes clearer why the Minister of Education was not inclined to support nuclear research.

Albert Speer, *Inside the Third Reich*, 1969

A further grim truth is that the only way so far devised of shortening a war of mass armies based on mass populations has been the invention of a weapon of mass extermination.

John Terraine, *The Smoke and the Fire*, 1980

Species extinction could be expected for most tropical plants and animals and for most terrestrial vertebrates of north temperate regions, a large number of plants, and numerous freshwater and some marine organisms . . . Whether any people would be able to persist for long in the face of highly modified biological communities; novel climates; high levels of radiation; shattered agricultural, social and economic systems; extraordinary psychological stresses; and a host of other difficulties is open to question. It is clear that the ecosystem effects alone resulting from a thermonuclear war could be enough to destroy the current civilization in at least the Northern Hemisphere.

Paul R. Ehrlich *et al.*, 'The Long-Term Biological Consequences of Nuclear Warfare', in *Science*, December 1983

In almost any realistic case involving nuclear exchanges between the superpowers, global environmental changes sufficient to cause an extinction event equal to or more severe than that at the close of the Cretaceous [Period] when the dinosaurs and many other species died out are likely. In that event, the possibility of the extinction of Homo Sapiens cannot be excluded.

Paul R. Ehrlich *et al.*, 'The Long-Term Biological Consequences of Nuclear Warfare', in *Science*, December 1983

I don't think there'll be an Armageddon war, but I'll put it this way. There has never been any weapon yet invented or perfected that hasn't been used.

General Bruce Holloway, in Michael Parfitt, *The Boys Behind the Bombs*, 1983

THE WAR OF INDONESIAN INDEPENDENCE, 1945–49

It is the idea of *Merdeka* that has got them, though it is hard to find out exactly what they think this *Merdeka* – Freedom – will mean. Naked, potbellied children stand along the roadside and pipe *'Merdeka'*, raising their clenched fists in salute. Coolies put down their loads and say *'Merdeka'* as you would say 'Hi, Mac'. Neat, pretty Javanese young ladies, selling subscriptions for nonexistent newspapers in the cafés, smile and say *'Merdeka'* politely, like saying 'Good-bye' or 'Delighted to have met you'. It is an immensely successful word. It sounds cheerful and appeals to everyone.

'What are you going to do, once you've got *Merdeka*, Johnny?' someone asked. You do find yourself peevishly wishing the Indonesians would be practical. 'How are you going to make your country run?'

'Oh I see,' said Johnny, still happy as a lark. 'As soon as we have our freedom, we will let the Dutch stay and help us.'

Martha Gellhorn, 'Java Journey', 1946

THE VIETNAM WARS, 1945–75

You may kill ten of my men for every one I kill of yours, but even at those odds, you will lose and I will win.

Ho Chi Minh, *c.* 1948 (to the French)

. . . The Three Manys and the Three Fews – Much Work, Much Responsibility, Much Reprimand; and Little Authority, Little Material Advantage, and Little Reward.

Hoang Duy, comment on the organisation of the Viet Minh forces, attributed, *c.* 1952

Diplomacy has rarely been able to gain at the conference table what cannot be gained or held on the battlefield.

Walter Bedell Smith, speaking on his return from the Geneva Conference on Indo-China, 1954

The troops will march in, the bands will play, the crowds will cheer, and in four days everyone will have forgotten. Then we will be told to have to send in more troops. It's like taking a drink. The effect wears off, and you have to take another.

John F. Kennedy, in conversation with Arthur Schlesinger, 1961, in Stanley Karnow, *Vietnam: A History*, 1983

The struggle of our people exceeds the imagination. It has astonished us, too.

Pham Van Dong, speaking in June 1964

Aggression unchallenged is aggression unleashed.

Lyndon B. Johnson, broadcast after Vietcong attack on US ships, in the Gulf of Tonkin, 4th August 1964

We still seek no wider war.

Lyndon B. Johnson, television broadcast, 4th August 1964

All Vietnam is not worth the life of a single American boy.

Senator Ernest Gruening, speaking in Congress, 6th August 1964

Once on the tiger's back, we cannot be sure of picking the place to dismount.

George Ball, in a White House memorandum, October 1964

We are not about to send American boys nine or ten thousand miles away from home to do what Asian boys ought to be doing for themselves.

Lyndon B. Johnson, television broadcast, 21st October 1964

I have asked the Commanding General, General Westmoreland, what more he needs to meet this mounting aggression. He has told me. And we will meet his needs. We will stand in Vietnam.

Lyndon B. Johnson, broadcast, 28th July 1965

I feel like a hitch-hiker on a Texas highway in the middle of a hail storm; I can't run, I can't hide, and I can't make it go away.

Lyndon B. Johnson, summer 1965

My solution to the problem would be to tell [the Viet Cong] they've got to draw in their horns and stop their aggression or we're going to bomb them back into the Stone Age.

Curtis E. LeMay, *Mission With LeMay*, 1965

A plume of white rises in the midst of dense tropical forest, with a Bird Dog spotter plane in attendance. Route 16 is to the right; beyond is a large settlement of red-tiled houses.

Two F105 jets appear over the horizon in formation, split, then one passes over the smoke, dropping the trail of silver, fish-shaped canisters. After four seconds' silence, light orange fire explodes in patches along an area fifty yards wide by three-quarters of a mile long. Napalm.

The trees and bushes burn, pouring dark oily smoke into the sky. The second plane dives and fire covers the entire strip of dense forest.

'Aaaaah,' cries the General. 'Nice. Nice. Very neat. Come in low, let's see who's left down there.'

'How do you know for sure the Viet Cong snipers were in that strip you burned?'

'We don't. The smoke position was a guess. That's why we zapp the whole forest.'

'But what if there was someone, a civilian, walking through there?'

'Aw come, son, you think there's folks just sniffing flowers in tropical vegetation like that? With a big operation on hereabouts? Anyone left down there, he's Charlie Cong all right.'

I point to a paddy field full of peasants less than half a mile away.

'That's different, son. We know they're genuine.'

The pilot shouts: 'General, half-right, two running for that bush.'

'I see them. Down, down, goddam you.'

In one movement he yanks his M16 off the hanger, slams in a clip of cartridges and leans right out of the door, hanging on his seatbelt to fire one long burst in the general direction of the bush.

Nicholas Tomalin, in the *Sunday Times*, 5th June 1966

All the noises of this war have an unaccountably Texan ring.

Nicholas Tomalin, in the *Sunday Times*, 5th June 1966

The Great Society has been shot down on the battlefield of Vietnam.

Martin Luther King, slogan, 1967

We used to get our footwear free from Mr Michelin; now we get them free from Mr Firestone.

North Vietnamese joke, *c.* 1967, referring to 'Ho Chi Minh Sandals'

Though I walk through the Valley of Death, I will fear no evil – 'cos I'm the meanest mother in the valley.

US Army saying, *c.* 1967

There may be a limit beyond which many Americans and much of the world will not permit the United States to go. The picture of the world's greatest superpower killing or seriously injuring one thousand non-combatants a week, while trying to pound a tiny backward nation into submission on an issue whose merits are hotly disputed, is not a pretty one.

Robert McNamara, White House memo, 1967, from *The Pentagon Papers*, 1972

The war in Vietnam is by no means exclusively American business; it is everyone's business. It is a small war and may be our ultimate chance to learn that we can no longer afford even small wars. The anthropologists' definition of man as a weapon-making animal should be modernized to read: man is an animal enslaved by his weapons. We pay for our weapons first and pay for our real needs with the left-over cash. Year after year, every nation economizes on money for life in order to spend more on weapons and still the weapons are futile. B-52's, each carrying thirty tons of bombs, do not crush the Vietnamese who continue to carry little home-made bombs on bicycles. Nothing will protect anyone from H-bombs. Overkill is surely the most lunatic word and fact the world has ever known. Perhaps we have finally reached the moment of truth when we must decide which is obsolete, war or the human race.

Martha Gellhorn, *The Face of War*, 1986: 'Conclusion, 1967'

Reserve Officers' Training Corps students at the University of California, compared with student draft resisters, were found to have experienced strict childhood discipline in relation to a dominant father-figure. They showed a strong concern about proving their masculinity, used more alcohol, felt powerless to influence their country's actions, felt troubled about their sexual inadequacy, defined independence as loss of self-control, preferred a well-ordered and structured environment, admitted being self-centred and egotistical, felt shy with girls but boasted to their fellows of their sexual conquests, claimed little real intimacy with and poor relationships with the opposite sex, admitted treating females as objects, tended to seek dominance-submission relationships, and were relatively aggressive, impulsive, irresponsible and non-intellectual, with a poorly developed conscience.

W. Eckhardt, 'Psychology of war and peace', in *Journal of Human Relations*, XVI, 1968

To win in Vietnam, we will have to exterminate a nation.

Dr Benjamin Spock, *Dr Spock on Vietnam*, 1968

We are in the wrong place, fighting the wrong war.

Senator Mike Mansfield, in Congress, March 1968

Growth statistics, offered everywhere, on bicycle ownership, irrigation, rice harvests, maternity clinics, literacy are the answer to the 'war of destruction', which began 7 February 1965; a bombed oak putting out new leaves is a 'reply' to the air pirates of the Air Force and the Seventh Fleet. All communist countries are bent on furnishing growth statistics (it is their form of advertising), but with Hanoi this is something special, carrying a secondary meaning – defiance. On a big billboard in the city center, the number of US planes shot down is revised forward almost daily in red paint – 2,818, they claimed when I left, and the number keeps growing. In villages, the score is kept on a blackboard. Everything they build is dated, down to the family wells in a hamlet – a means of visibly recording progress, like penciling the heights of children, with the dates opposite, on a door. And each date has a clear significance in the story of resistance: 1965 or 1966, stamped on a well, proclaims that it was built *in spite of* the air pirates.

Mary McCarthy, *Hanoi*, 1968

Nor – excuse me – is it unthinkable that the US Navy or the Air Force would consider bombing a zoo. The model leper colony at Quyn Lap was bombed not just once – which might have been an accident – but thirty-nine times; I have seen photographs of the pandemonic scenes as doctors and attendants sought to carry lepers to safety on their backs and on stretchers – limbs wasted to stumps, arms ending in knobs. One hundred and sixty secluded buildings, housing more than 2,000 lepers, were demolished (I apologize for using North Vietnamese statistics, but the Americans have not supplied any); the first raid netted 139 dead, some, it is said, machine-gunned as they scattered. 'But what could be the motive?' Americans protest. 'What is the *point* of bombing a model leper colony?' I do not know the motive but I know the result: the surviving lepers have been distributed to ordinary district and provincial hospitals, where they are, to put it mildly, a problem, a pathetic menace to public health. If you bomb lepers, why draw the line at captive lions and tigers, who could be quite a menace, too?

Mary McCarthy, *Hanoi*, 1968

One awkwardness for a Western writer in a Communist country is that he is committed to a tradition of freshness, of making it new. In antiquity, originality was not so highly valued, and it has occurred to me that the set phrases of North Vietnamese diction are really Homeric epithets. Compare 'the insolent wooers', 'the long-haired Achaeans', 'cloud-gathering Zeus', 'the hateful Furies' with 'the American aggressors', 'the American imperialists', 'the war of destruction', 'the air pirates'. And no doubt, too, they are Oriental ideograms; some, like the 'just cause', are the same in the South as in the North, though with different referents, of course. There is also a prescribed, quite angry Marxist language in the Eastern European countries, but behind the Iron Curtain, as opposed to the Bamboo, it is not a *spoken* language; the *Izvestia* correspondent in the Thong Nhat Hotel used the ordinary vernacular when he drew up a chair to our table, like party members in Warsaw, Cracow, Budapest, but probably when he wrote for his paper he used the official language, just as a man in the Middle Ages wrote Latin and spoke in the vulgar tongue.

Mary McCarthy, *Hanoi*, 1968

No normal person, set down in a North Vietnamese rice field beside an anti-aircraft unit manned by excited boys and girls, could help being thrilled, whereas in the South, beside an artillery battery, surrounded by sandbags, you share the sullen gloom of the population and the sardonic resentment of the soldiers.

Mary McCarthy, *Hanoi*, 1968

Hey, hey, LBJ, how many kids did you kill today?

Anti-war chant, *c.* 1968

Q: What's the difference between the Boy Scouts and the Marines?
A: The Boy Scouts are led by adults.

War joke, *c.* 1968

My son who valiant flies the sky,
Has killed eleven men,
And he will leave the earth at dawn
To fly and kill again.
The neighbours say that he will get
A shining cross to wear,
They talk as if eleven men
Weren't cross enough to bear.

Broadside, no. 89, 1968

The conventional army loses if it does not win, the guerilla wins if he does not lose.

Henry Kissinger, 'The Vietnam Negotiations', in *Foreign Affairs*, January 1969

Our rivers, our mountains, our men
will always remain;
The Yanks defeated, we will build our country
ten times more beautiful.

Ho Chi Minh, last poem, written on 10th May 1969

The only monuments to this war will be the dead, the maimed, the despairing and the forlorn.

Letter from the International Voluntary Services Agency to President Johnson, September 1969

I can't believe that a fourth-rate power like Vietnam doesn't have a breaking point.

Henry Kissinger, in a conversation with his staff, autumn 1969

And so tonight, to you, the great silent majority of my fellow Americans – I ask for your support. Let us be united for peace. Let us be united against defeat. Because let us understand: North Vietnam cannot defeat or humiliate the United States. Only Americans can do that.

Richard Nixon, television broadcast, 3rd November 1969

I call it the Madman Theory. I want the North Vietnamese to believe I've reached the point where I might do *anything* to stop the war. We'll just slip the word to them that 'For God's sake, you know, Nixon is obsessed about Communism. We can't restrain him when he's angry – and he has his hand on the nuclear button.' They'll believe any threat of force that Nixon makes because it's Nixon.

Richard Nixon, 1969, in H. R. Halderman, *The Ends of Power*, 1978

If, when the chips are down, the world's most powerful nation, the United States of America, acts like a pitiful helpless giant, the forces of totalitarianism and anarchy will threaten free nations and free institutions throughout the world.

Richard Nixon, television broadcast, 30th April 1970

When I read about an American soldier firing a clip of tracer bullets into a group of women and children in some Mekong hamlet, I feel a quiet thrill of pride. The vivid description of a fighter-bomber snarling across the hills near Khe Sanh, spraying napalm, sends a surge of patriotism coursing through my veins. An eyewitness account of bombs wrenching at rice paddies along the Ho Chi Minh Trail stirs me like a cry of bugles. After all, it's our war, too. The bullets for that soldier's weapon may have ridden in a De Havilland Caribou built at Malton, Ontario; that napalm-spraying fighter-bomber was almost certainly equipped with a Canadian-made Marconi Doppler Navigation System; those bombs along the Ho Chi Minh Trail may have been made from dynamite shipped out of Valleyfield, Quebec, and disgorged by a bombing computer fashioned in Rexdale, Ontario.

Why should the Americans have all the glory? We do our part, too.

Walter Stewart, *Shrug: Trudeau in Power*, 1971

The Special Forces have done so much for nothing for so long that now we are expected to do everything for nothing for ever.

Ed Sprague, 1971, in James Fenton, 'The Fall of Saigon', *Granta 15*, Spring 1985

The U.S. First Infantry Division has carved its divisional insignia with defoliants in a stretch of jungle – a giant poisonous graffito.

Frances Fitzgerald, *Fire in the Lake*, 1972

The French and the Americans tried to stop the revolution, and in doing so they created an interregnum of violence unparalleled in Vietnamese history. In the end the Vietnamese may reject them and their intervention as an organism rejects a foreign body. As one Vietnamese scholar told a Frenchman, 'If you want so much to be in Vietnam, just wait a bit and perhaps in your next reincarnation you will be born Vietnamese.'

Frances Fitzgerald, *Fire in the Lake*, 1972

I don't have a broom long enough to reach Taiwan, and you don't have a broom long enough to reach Saigon.

Mao Tse-tung, in conversation with Pham Van Dong, Peking 1973

Canada helps make our napalm and then takes in our deserters. Canada has both ends of a dirty stick and ends up with both hands dirty.

Anonymous American, in *The Toronto Star*, 3rd December 1973

. . . let saigons . . .
be saigons . . .

Roger McGough, 'Poem for President Nixon', 1973

One American in Qui Nhon, a lugubrious construction worker, said to me once: 'There's a captain I know who's done two tours of duty and he regards this country with passionate hatred, I mean hatred. He's really worked at it. He says, and I've got to kind of agree with him, that the only solution to this country is to withdraw all the Americans, and then to plaster the whole goddam place with nukes. Then after it was all over he'd take up an airplane with two monkeys, a male and a female, attached to two parachutes. And just before throwing them out of the plane he'd say: "This time, don't fuck it up!"'

Richard West, *Victory in Vietnam*, 1974

The last crusade.

Chester Cooper, quoted in the *Daily Telegraph*, 4th April 1975

We'd all heard about the man in the Highlands who was 'building his own gook', parts were the least of his troubles. In Chu Lai some Marines pointed a man out to me and swore to God they'd seen him bayonet a wounded NVA and then lick the bayonet clean. There was a famous story, some reporters asked a door gunner, 'How can you shoot women and children?' and he'd answered, 'It's easy, you just don't lead 'em so much.' Well, they said you needed a sense of humour, there you go, even the VC had one. Once after an ambush that killed a lot of Americans, they covered the field with copies of a photograph that showed one more young, dead American, with the punch line mimeographed on the back, 'Your X-rays have just come back from the lab and we think we know what your problem is.'

Michael Herr, *Dispatches*, 1977

'Listen,' Mayhew said. 'Maybe you better go and see the chaplain.'

'Real good,' Orrin said. 'What's that cocksucker gone do for me?'

'Maybe you could get an emergency leave.'

'No,' someone said. 'There's gotta be a death in the family before you'll get out like that.'

'Oh, don't worry,' Orrin said. 'There's gone be a death in my family. Just soon's I git home.' And then he laughed.

Michael Herr, *Dispatches*, 1977

There was a special Air Force outfit that flew defoliation missions. They were called the Ranch Hands, and their motto was, 'Only we can prevent forests.'

Michael Herr, *Dispatches*, 1977

A twenty-four-year-old Special Forces captain was telling me about it. 'I went out and killed one VC and liberated a prisoner. Next day the major called me in and told me I'd killed fourteen VC and liberated six prisoners. You want to see the medal?'

Michael Herr, *Dispatches*, 1977

We were walking across 57th Street one afternoon and passed a blind man carrying a sign that read, MY DAYS ARE DARKER THAN YOUR NIGHTS. 'Don't bet on it, man,' the ex-medic said.

Michael Herr, *Dispatches*, 1977

Vietnam was what we had instead of happy childhoods.

Michael Herr, *Dispatches*, 1977

A few graphic newspaper photographs and TV shots of American troops setting fire to thatched-roof huts were enough to convince many that 'search and destroy' operations were laying waste to the land.

William C. Westmoreland, 'A War of Attrition', in *The Lessons of Vietnam*, ed. D. D. Frizzel and W. S. Thompson, 1977

General Westmoreland's strategy of attrition also had an important effect on our behavior. Our mission was not to win terrain or seize positions, but simply to kill: to kill Communists and to kill as many of them as possible. Stack 'em like cordwood. Victory was a high body-count, defeat a low kill-ratio, war a matter of arithmetic. The pressure on unit commanders to produce enemy corpses was intense, and they in turn communicated it to their troops. This led to such practices as counting civilians as Viet Cong. 'If it's dead and Vietnamese, it's VC,' was a rule of thumb in the bush. It is not surprising, therefore, that some men acquired a contempt for human life and a predilection for taking it.

Philip Caputo, *A Rumour of War*, 1977

I could not come down from the high produced by the action. The fire-fight was over, except for a few desultory exchanges, but I did not want it to be over. So, when a sniper opened up from a tree line beyond the village, I did something slightly mad. Ordering the platoon to train their rifles on the tree line, I walked up and down the clearing, trying to draw the sniper's fire.

'When he opens up, every man put five rounds rapid into the tree line,' I said, walking back and forth and feeling as invulnerable as an Indian wearing his ghost shirt.

Nothing happened.

I stopped walking and, facing the tree line, waved my arms. 'C'mon, Charlie, hit me, you son of a bitch,' I yelled at the top of my lungs, 'HO CHI MINH SUCKS. FUCK COMMUNISM, HIT ME, CHARLIE.'

Some of the marines started laughing, and when I heard one of them mutter, 'That stocky little fucker's crazy,' I started laughing too. I was crazy. I was soaring high, very high in a delirium of violence.

'C'mon and hit me, Charlie,' I yelled again, firing a burst into the tree line with my carbine. 'YOU SON OF A BITCH, TRY AND HIT ME. FUCK UNCLE HO. HANOI BY CHRISTMAS.'

I was John Wayne in *Sands of Iwo Jima.* I was Aldo Ray in *Battle Cry.*

Philip Caputo, *A Rumour of War*, 1977

Vietnam was as much a laboratory experiment as a war.

John Pilger, *Do You Remember Vietnam?*, TV documentary, 3rd October 1978

From 1969 Vietnam brought a grim new word in the military lexicon – 'fragging': in plain English, murder. The term fragging derived from the use of a fragmentation weapon, usually a hand-grenade, as the surest way of dispatching an unpopular officer. Between 1969 and 1971, according to Congressional data, the total number of 'fragging incidents' – including actual attempts at murder and intimidation – was 730, and eighty-three officers were killed this way. But these figures do not include assaults on officers with other weapons – rifles or knives – and by one official estimate there was sufficient evidence in only ten per cent of suspected 'fraggings' to warrant investigation. The ratio of violence against officers in Vietnam was believed to be almost fifteen times as great as in the grim trench-warfare of World War I.

Michael Maclear, *Vietnam: The Ten Thousand Day War*, 1981

It is hard to escape the conclusion that Commander in Chief Richard Nixon, through his doubling of the war years without military objective, left a once proud army morally shattered. The American public would finally judge Nixon for his administration's political degeneracy; the demoralization of the military was probably no less dangerous.

Michael Maclear, *Vietnam: The Ten Thousand Day War*, 1981

One of the hardest things for me to really adjust to in my mind was to step off an air-conditioned plane where I'd just watched a first-run movie and hear this stewardess say 'Have a nice war'.

James Webb, in Michael Maclear, *Vietnam: The Ten Thousand Day War*, 1981

The most spectacular development was the coming of age of the helicopters. It saved innumerable lives through air evacuation. It gave us a battlefield mobility that we never dreamed of years previously.

William C. Westmoreland, in Michael Maclear, *Vietnam: The Ten Thousand Day War*, 1981

The final effect was of a moron wandering through a foreign land, or a blind man wandering through a foreign land. Vietnam was like walking a maze: you didn't know where the maze was leading. You would leave a point and walk blindly through some hedgerow, take a right and then a left and then a right, and you would end up sometimes back where you started. No sense of progression. And all along the way mines were going off – feet going, legs going, balls going.

Tim O'Brien, in Michael Maclear, *Vietnam: The Ten Thousand Day War*, 1981

'You know,' [Colonel] Summers told a North Vietnamese colonel after the war, 'you never defeated us on the battlefield.' To which his Communist counterpart replied, 'That may be so, but it is also irrelevant.'

Stanley Karnow, *Vietnam: A History*, 1983

Vietnam is still with us. It has created doubts about American judgement, about American credibility, about American power – not only at home, but throughout the world. It has poisoned our domestic debate. So we paid an exorbitant price for the decisions that were made in good faith and for good purpose.

Henry Kissinger, in Stanley Karnow, *Vietnam: A History*, 1983

Whenever you turned round, you'd be taking it in the solar plexus. Then the enemy would disappear, and you'd end up taking out your frustrations on the civilians. The way we operated, any Vietnamese seen running away from Americans was a Vietcong suspect, and we could shoot. It was standard operating procedure. One day I shot a woman in a rice field because she was running – just running away from the Americans. And I killed her. Fifty-five or sixty years old, unarmed, and at the time I didn't even think twice about it.

William Erhart, in Stanley Karnow, *Vietnam: A History*, 1983

You never knew who was the enemy and who was the friend. They all looked alike. They all dressed alike. They were all Vietnamese. Some of them were Vietcong. Here's a woman of twenty-two or twenty-three. She is pregnant, and she tells an interrogator that her husband works in Danang and isn't a Vietcong. But she watches your men walk down a trail and get killed or wounded by a booby trap. She knows the booby trap is there, but she doesn't warn them. Maybe she placed it herself. It wasn't like the San Francisco Forty-Niners on one side of the field and the Cincinnati Bengals on the other.

E. J. Banks, in Stanley Karnow, *Vietnam: A History*, 1983

The Huey was the taxicab of the war. You could spend days with one aviation unit fragging missions all over the Corps: eagle lifts, reacting to small units under fire, resupply runs and dustoffs; when there were too many WIA or KIA you got left behind on the ground. Occasionally you got to ride a hog gunship, the armoured sportscar of the inventory – but they rarely set you down. I knew a hog driver that flew on acid who would leave his visiting card on his kill: 'The Psychedelic Killer has struck again!' But Command never did suss his ID.

Tim Page, *Nam*, 1983

There were a million ways, and then some, that people and other living things could be dealt with, a soldier of fortune catalogue. One Air Force unit, whose task was to defoliate the place, also destroyed all the staple food crops, trying to deny Charlie the wherewithal to survive; they had the motto, 'We Prevent Forests'. The whole country started to look like a leper from the air, a series of gross malformed swimming holes, barren scrags of what once were majestic 300-feet mahogany trees. The 40-ton tracked vehicles did marvels for the eco-structure of the ancient paddy irrigation system; water buffaloes, who always got nervous at the scent of a white man, got greased at the slightest snuffle. The very air and water started to take on a total polluted glint, a deathly hue in which the Vietnamese were supposed to enjoy the benefits of a free democratic way of life. Nowhere was there purity; even sleep became a luxury, and few of us liked living underground.

Tim Page, *Nam*, 1983

It was the only war I reported on the wrong side.

Martha Gellhorn, *The Face of War*, 1986

You really had a mentality in the U.S. Army in Vietnam which had very little to do with war and fighting in the conventional historical sense. The officers and men quite frequently were more involved in typing and driving trucks around than they were in fighting, and in many cases it meant that the morale of a unit was not that of a fighting unit; it was an administrative unit that happened to get people killed up in the front of it. There eventually developed a considerable difference in the attitudes of the front-line soldiers versus the people in the rear, who were usually given various nicknames by the people in front, like remfs – rear-echelon motherfuckers.

Tom Tulenko, in Gwynne Dyer, *War*, 1986

This is going to sound really strange, but there's a love relationship that is nurtured in combat because the man next to you – you're depending on him for the most important things you have, your life, and if he lets you down you're either maimed or killed. If you make a mistake the same thing happens to him, so the bond of trust has to be extremely close, and I'd say this bond is stronger than almost anything, with the exception of parent and child. It's a hell of a lot stronger than man and wife – your life is in his hands, you trust that person with the most valuable thing you have. And you'll find that people who pursue the aphrodisiac of combat or whatever you want to call it are there because they're friends, the same people show up in the same wars time and again.

John Early, in Gwynne Dyer, *War*, 1986

Battle of Dien Bien Phu, 13th March–7th May 1954

Was there a chance of relief? Was Red General Giap's army as worn out as the garrison? Or would the outcome be the simple probability – death or Red captivity in one of three bitter ways: a sudden, crushing onset in the dark, or death by the thousand cuts of a siege, or surrender with the honors of war? These were the lurking uncertainties in the dusk of Dien Bien Phu.

Time magazine, 3rd May 1954

There is no doubt that if the American air force had been heavily involved, as was proposed to me by the Pentagon, and as President Eisenhower had not dared to do, Dien Bien Phu would certainly have been saved. The US would not have had to become involved later as it was obliged to do.

General Henri Navarre, in Michael Maclear, *Vietnam: The Ten Thousand Day War*, 1981

It was shaped – as the waiting Viet Minh described it – like a frying pan.

Michael Maclear, *Vietnam: The Ten Thousand Day War*, 1981

In the French medical catacombs the scene was nightmarish. The underground hospital had been extended until it reached close to the now disused graveyard. There came a day when the wounded found large white worms from the graves crawling amid their bandages. 'We could see legs with maggots,' says Bigeard, 'but the doctor left them on because, he said, "I think it prevents gangrene."'

Michael Maclear, *Vietnam: The Ten Thousand Day War*, 1981

. . . Colonel Charles Piroth was a one-armed gunnery expert who had predicted that 'no Vietminh cannon will be able to fire three rounds before being destroyed by my artillery.' At dawn on March 15th, 1954, two days after the Vietminh had wiped out the second of three key French artillery positions, Piroth pulled the safety pin out of a grenade with his teeth and blew himself to bits, having said the evening before, 'I am completely dishonored.'

Stanley Karnow, *Vietnam: A History*, 1983

The Ho Chi Minh Trail

One US Special Forces soldier, Ivan Delbyk, who went on commando raids, says that 'at times the Ho Chi Minh Trail was so busy it was like the Long Island expressway – during rush hour.' Another Special Forces officer, Captain Dave Christian, says from experience, 'Well, it wasn't one trail. There were thousands of trails, thousands of rest spots along the way where enemy troops could seek refuge and build up – and I have to commend them: the NVA were some super soldiers.' But back in the US people would keep asking him, 'Why don't we just plug up the Ho Chi Minh Trail?'

Michael Maclear, *Vietnam: The Ten Thousand Day War*, 1981

The United States Bombs North Vietnamese Oil Installations at Vinh, August 1964

I didn't just screw Ho Chi Minh; I cut his pecker off.

Lyndon B. Johnson, 4th August 1964

The Tet Offensive, early 1968

What the hell is going on? I thought we were winning this war.

Walter Cronkite, inadvertent broadcast remark, 1st February 1968

If I've lost Walter Cronkite I've lost Mr Average Citizen.

Lyndon B. Johnson, attributed remark made in the Oval Office, February 1968

It was undoubtedly a *tour de force*: the spectacle of an enemy force dispersed and unseen, everywhere hunted unremittingly, suddenly materializing, to strike simultaneously in a hundred places throughout the country.

Time magazine, 9th February 1968

We had to destroy it to save it.

US Army officer's comment after the destruction of Ben Tre, in South Vietnam

This was the first struggle fought on television in everybody's living-room every day. What would have happened in World War II if Guadalcanal and the Anzio beach-head and the Battle of the Bulge or the Dieppe raid were on television and the other side was not doing the same thing? War is an obscene blot on the face of the human race. But whether ordinary people, who prefer peace to war in any country, whether ordinary people can sustain a war effort under that kind of daily hammering is a very large question.

Dean Rusk, in Michael Maclear, *Vietnam: The Ten Thousand Day War*, 1981

In all honesty, we didn't achieve our main objective, which was to spur uprisings throughout the south. Still, we inflicted heavy casualties on the Americans and their puppets, and that was a big gain for us. As for making an impact in the United States, it had not been our intention – but it turned out to be a fortunate result.

General Tran Do, in Stanley Karnow, *Vietnam: A History*, 1983

– Siege of Khe Sanh, 21st January–7th April 1968

We had a man who caught an artillery round. A shell came right into this man's trench, and what they had to send home would probably fit into a handkerchief.

Anthony Astuccio, in Michael Maclear, *Vietnam: The Ten Thousand Day War*, 1981

Massacre at My Lai, 16th March 1968

No big deal, Sir.

Lieutenant W. L. Calley, in George Walton, *The Tarnished Shield: A Report on Today's Army*, 1973

If there was any concurrence among former members of Calley's platoon in Vietnam, it is the amazement that the army considered Calley officer material.

Seymour Hersh, *My Lai 4: A Report on the Massacre and its Aftermath*, 1970

Several old men were stabbed with bayonets and one was thrown down a well to be followed by a hand grenade. Some women and children praying outside of the local temple were killed by shooting them in the back of the head with rifles. Occasionally a soldier would drag a girl, often a mere child, to a ditch where he would rape her. One GI is said to have thrown a grenade into a hootch where a girl of five or six lay that he had just raped. The young were slaughtered with the same impartiality as the old. Children barely able to walk were picked off at point blank range.

George Walton, *The Tarnished Shield: A Report on Today's Army*, 1973

Bombing and Invasion of Cambodia, 1969–74

I would rather be a one-term President and do what I believe is right than to be a two-term President at the cost of seeing America become a second-rate power and to see this nation accept the first defeat in its proud 190-year history.

Richard Nixon, television broadcast, 30th April 1970

The South Vietnamese are wandering all over Cambodia protecting the government while we, in turn, are in South Vietnam protecting the South Vietnamese.

Melvin Laird, comment made in the Pentagon, May 1970

Now with respect to Cambodia, it is another curious bit of mythology. People usually refer to the bombing of Cambodia as if it had been an unprovoked, secretive US action. The fact is that we were bombing North Vietnamese troops that had invaded Cambodia, that were killing many Americans from these sanctuaries, and we were doing it with the acquiescence of the Cambodian government, which never once protested against it, and which, indeed, encouraged us to do it. I may have a lack of imagination, but I fail to see the moral issue involved and why Cambodian neutrality should apply to only one country. Why is it moral for the North Vietnamese to have 50,000 to 100,000 troops in Cambodia, why should we let them kill Americans from their territory, and why, when the government concerned never once protested, and indeed told us that if we bombed unpopulated areas that they would not notice, why in all these conditions is there a moral issue?

Henry Kissinger, interview with *Die Zeit*, autumn 1976

One day Henry Kissinger will write his memoirs. And we will all go out and buy them. And there will be a chapter on Cambodia. And I will write a footnote on every page.

Robert Keeley, remark made at a dinner party given by John Gunther Dean, 6th April 1975

In his February 9 [1969] cable, Abrams had asked for a single attack to destroy COSVN headquarters. But once the decision had been made in principle that Communist violations of Cambodia's neutrality justified aggressive reciprocal action, it was not difficult to repeat the performance. The first mission had not been discovered by the press, nor had Cambodia protested. Indeed, it would now have been hard for the White House to insist on only one attack: Base 353 was, according to Abrams' headquarters, the Military Assistance Command, Vietnam (MACV), only one of fifteen Communist sanctuaries.

Over the next fourteen months 3,630 B-52 raids were flown against suspected Communist bases along different areas of Cambodia's border. Breakfast was followed by 'Lunch', Lunch by 'Snack', Snack by 'Dinner', Dinner by 'Dessert', Dessert by 'Supper' as the program expanded to cover one 'sanctuary' after another. Collectively the operation was known as 'Menu'.

William Shawcross, *Sideshow: Kissinger, Nixon and the Destruction of Cambodia*, 1979

Even the ordinary White House staff was somewhat alarmed. Kissinger was asked at a meeting whether the invasion did not expand the war. 'Look,' he replied, 'we're not interested in Cambodia. We're only interested in it not being used as a base.' The wider justifications he cited dealt with the superpower relations. 'We're trying to shock the Soviets into calling a Conference,' he said, 'and we can't do this by appearing weak.' William Safire asked if it did not breach the Nixon Doctrine, and Kissinger replied, 'We wrote the goddam doctrine, we can change it.' At the end of the meeting Haig stood up and shouted, 'The basic substance of all this is that we have to be tough.' That was indeed a point. Another, as Kissinger instructed his staff, was that 'We are all the President's men.'

William Shawcross, *Sideshow: Kissinger, Nixon and the Destruction of Cambodia*, 1979

Much of the tactical bombing of the country was controlled by American spotter planes known as FACs (Forward Air Control planes). Their job was to call the 'strike birds' or bombers into targets. Because American ground advisers were forbidden, the United States trained Cambodian soldiers to liaise with the pilots from the ground. They were known as FAGs (Forward Air Guides), and they spoke either a little French or a little English and were equipped by the United States with FM radios on which they could speak either to the 'strike birds' or to the spotter planes above. They developed a close rapport with their American counterparts in the sky, and together the FAGs and the FACs actually controlled many battles. The American pilot was often able to see just what a situation was, and he frequently gave encouragement and instructions, through his FAG, to the ground-unit commander, to whom the Cooper-Church amendment denied such help. (Problems arose after the Communists captured or bought the radio sets and started to ask pilots to bomb FANK positions, and jammed the wave bands by shouting or playing Radio Peking down them.)

William Shawcross, *Sideshow: Kissinger, Nixon and the Destruction of Cambodia*, 1979

[See also below, p. 380]

Fall of Saigon, 29th April 1975

These events, tragic as they are, portend neither the end of the world nor of America's leadership in the world.

Gerald Ford, speech in New Orleans, 23rd April 1975

At noon on the 29th the signal came – first a prearranged weather report: 'It is 105 degrees and rising,' said a solemn announcer; then a further code, Bing Crosby singing 'I'm Dreaming of a White Christmas' – repeated every fifteen minutes. American officials, businessmen and journalists dropped everything and ran.

Michael Maclear, *Vietnam: The Ten Thousand Day War*, 1981

ISRAEL'S WAR OF INDEPENDENCE, 1948–49

The disadvantages under which the Israeli Army operated during the War of Independence – its weakness in manpower, its lack of modern weapons, and the necessity to fight on many fronts at the same time – evolved a military philosophy based on flexibility, the use of surprise and innovation. Fighting by night became almost second nature to the Israeli forces, because darkness neutralized to a degree the advantages enjoyed by the Arab forces. Indeed the Israeli attacks . . . were nearly all mounted at night. Speed, commando-type operations, the use of outflanking manoeuvres – all these combined to emphasize the character and mode of operation of the emerging Israeli armed forces. Coupled with this was a flexibility of thought that encouraged the leader in battle to adapt himself to the vicissitudes of war at a moment's notice and to take advantage of changing circumstances in the field. A rigid approach and over-dependence on higher command had no place in the Israeli forces. Thus emerged the Israel Defence Forces, which was to become a major military factor in the Middle East, a factor that would not only be of local significance but would also become an important strategic element in the region.

Chaim Herzog, *The Arab–Israeli Wars*, 1982

THE KOREAN WAR, 1950–53

The amphibious landing is the most powerful tool we have.

Douglas MacArthur, in Tokyo, 23rd August 1950

United Nations forces are now being attacked from the safety of a privileged sanctuary.

Harry S. Truman, Press statement, 15th November 1950

[The Americans] have never studied or been taught defence. They appear only to have studied mechanized and mechanical advances at great speed. They do not understand locality defence in depth or all-round defence. They do not like holding defensive positions. They have been trained for very rapid withdrawals. Americans do not understand infiltration and feel very naked when anybody threatens their flank or rear.

Sir Robert Mansergh, secret report to the British Chiefs of Staff, March 1951

Here we fight Europe's war with arms while the diplomats there still fight with words.

Douglas MacArthur, Letter to Joseph Martin, 6th April 1951

This strategy would involve us in the wrong war, at the wrong place, at the wrong time, and with the wrong enemy.

Omar N. Bradley, to the Senate Committee on Armed Services and Foreign Relations, contemplating conflict with China, 15th May 1951

It is fatal to enter any war without the will to win it.

Douglas MacArthur, radio broadcast, 7th July 1952

That job requires a personal trip to Korea. I shall make that trip. Only in that way could I learn best how to serve the American people in the cause of peace. I shall go to Korea.

Dwight Eisenhower, presidential campaign pledge, Detroit, 24th October 1952

The Korean War began in a way in which wars often begin. A potential aggressor miscalculated.

John Foster Dulles, speech in St Louis, 2nd September 1953

One only jumps from a smaller conflict to a larger stalemate at greater expense.

Omar N. Bradley, remark made during the Korean War, quoted in Max Hastings and Simon Jenkins, *The Battle for the Falklands*, 1983

Korea was the prep school for Vietnam.

James Cameron, *Point of Departure*, 1967

To back away from this challenge, in view of our capacity for meeting it, would be highly destructive of the power and prestige of the United States.

Dean Acheson, *Present at the Creation*, 1969

I favoured using one [atomic] bomb in one unoccupied area – say, The Punchbowl. Pop it off. Say to the communists: 'Come off of this stuff and get out.' The Korean War was our first real national vacillation, the first evidence of the great decline in our will as a nation to make a real hard decision.

Colonel Ellis Williamson, interview with Max Hastings, May 1985

I think wars are designed for twenty-three-year-olds. I enjoyed it very much – it was the time of my life.

Flight-Lieutenant Roy Watson (RAF), interview with Max Hastings, October 1985

It seems impossible to gain any worthwhile insights into the North Korean view of the war, as long as Kim Il Sung presides over a society in which the private possession of a bicycle is considered a threat to national security.

Max Hastings, *The Korean War*, 1987

It was the familiar intelligence problem, of distinguishing 'signals' from 'noise'. The 'noise', that summer of 1950, came in the form of communist threats that seemed to touch every quarter of the globe: on the occupation boundaries in Europe, at Trieste and in the oilfields of the Middle East, among the Huk guerillas of the Philippines, on the borders of Greece and Yugoslavia. Korea was indeed recognized, in the war departments of the West, as a possible point of confrontation with the communists. But it lay near the bottom of a long list of prospective battlefields.

Max Hastings, *The Korean War*, 1987

Korea put the CIA on the map.

Max Hastings, *The Korean War*, 1987

The Defence of the Pusan Perimeter, August–September 1950

There are no lines behind which we can retreat. This is not going to be a Dunkirk or Bataan. A retreat to Pusan would result in one of the greatest butcheries in history. We must fight to the end. We must fight as a team. If some of us die, we will die fighting together.

General Walton H. Walker, Order of the Day, 29th July, 1950

Battle of Inchon, 15th–19th September 1950

I can almost hear the ticking of the second hand of destiny. We must act now or we will die . . . We shall land at Inchon, and I shall crush them.

Douglas MacArthur, at a meeting with his commanders, Tokyo, 23rd August 1950

I know that this operation will be sort of helter-skelter. But the 1st Marine Division is going to win the war by landing at Inchon.

Douglas MacArthur, in conversation with O. P. Smith, August 1950

What seemed to be a tank ashore sent some quick resentful fire back but it soon stopped. Later we found that one ship had tossed a hundred and sixty rounds of ammunition at the tank before it had finished it; the economics of plenty in action.

James Cameron, in *Picture Post*, 7th October 1950

There was quite a lot of Inchon still standing. One wondered how. There were quite a number of citizens still alive. They came stumbling from the ruins – some of them sound, some of them smashed – numbers of them quite clearly driven into a sort of numbed dementia by the night of destruction. They ran about, capering crazily or shambling blankly, with a repeated automatic gesture of surrender. Some of them called out as we passed their one English phrase, as a kind of password: 'Sank you!' 'Sank you!'; and the irony of that transcended the grotesque into the macabre.

James Cameron, *Point of Departure*, 1967

The Chinese Counter-Attack, from December 1950

We had a saying – Red Army's two legs better than Kuomintang's four wheels. Life was very hard, but the atmosphere was very good, because we were full of hope.

Li Hebei, in Max Hastings, *The Korean War*, 1987

Gentlemen. We are not retreating. We are merely advancing in another direction.

O. P. Smith, Press conference, 4th December 1950

THE BRITISH FLEET AIR-ARM, 1950s

The Batsman is my shepherd, I shall not crash.
He maketh me to land on flat runways.
He bringeth me in off rough waters,
He restoreth my confidence.
Yea, though I come stalling into the deck at sixty knots
I shall fear no evil,
For he is with me.
His arms and his bats comfort me.
He prepareth a deck before me in the presence of mine enemies.
He attacheth my hook to the wire.
My deck space runneth over.

Anonymous version of Psalm 23, British Fleet Air Arm. *c.* 1952

CUBAN REVOLUTION, (1953)–1959

History will absolve me.

Fidel Castro, after an unsuccessful assault on the Moncada Barracks, 26th July 1953

THE SUEZ CRISIS, 1956

We are not at war with Egypt. We are in an armed conflict.

Anthony Eden, in the House of Commons, 4th November 1956

During the last few weeks I have felt that the Suez Canal was flowing through my drawing room.

Clarissa Eden, attributed

THE CUBAN MISSILE CRISIS, 1962

We're eyeball to eyeball, and the other fellow just blinked.

Dean Rusk, remark made in early October 1962

We will not act prematurely or unnecessarily risk the costs of world-wide nuclear war in which even the fruits of victory would be ashes in our mouths. But neither will we shrink from that risk at any time it must be faced.

John F. Kennedy, television broadcast, 22nd October 1962

They talk about who won and who lost. Human reason won. Mankind won.

Nikita Khrushchev, quoted in the *Observer*, 11th November 1962

In the military operations of Cuba President Kennedy did not look for military victory, he sought to change Mr Khrushchev's mind, and he succeeded.

Sir Peter Gretton, speech at the Royal United Services Institution, April 1965

GENOCIDE: INDONESIAN OCCUPATION OF IRIAN JAYA, from 1962

Let the rats run into the jungle so that the chickens may breed in the coop.

Indonesian Army slogan, 1981

One of the more bizarre forms of persecution has involved pigs. Pigs have a special status among nearly all Melanesians, from New Guinea to Fiji. They are sacred animals, to be eaten only on certain occasions as offerings to the ancestors. In a sense, the health of a village is reflected in the health of this livestock. Yet it is known that the Indonesian authorities have deliberately introduced infected pigs into remote villages, to destroy morale.

Justin Wintle, *Heat Treatment*, 1988

THE US MILITARY: mid to late 20th century

We shall pay any price, bear any burden, meet any hardship, support any friend, oppose any foe to assure the survival and the success of liberty.

John F. Kennedy, Inaugural Address, 21st January 1961

The Americans have become too liberal to fight.

Nikita Khrushchev, 1962, in T. W. Wolfe, *Soviet Power and Europe 1945–70*, 1970

The United States, as the world knows, will never start a war. We do not want a war. We do not now expect a war. This generation of Americans has already had enough – of war and hate and oppression. We shall be prepared if others wish it. We shall be alert to try to stop it. But we shall also do our part to build a world of peace where the weak are safe and the strong are just.

John F. Kennedy, speech in Washington DC, June 1963

A European soldier, when he steals, will steal a package or even a carton of cigarettes. But Americans, nothing but a whole train and all of its contents will do!

Ashley Montagu, *The American Way of Life*, 1967

There were B-36s, B-50s, B-52s, B-58s, B-70s. Now they are starting it all over again with a bomber called the B-1. Besides the manned bombers we have C-5As, F-111s, ICBMs, MIRVs and so on. Some members of Congress will vote for almost anything with initials.

Eugene McCarthy, *The Hard Years*, 1975

The Russians can give you arms, but only the United States can give you a selection.

Anwar el-Sadat, in *Newsweek*, 17th January 1977

THE SIX DAY WAR, 5th–10th June 1967

The existence of Israel is an error which must be rectified.

President of Iraq, broadcast, 31st May 1967

If we do not win we have nowhere to come back to.

Colonel Shmuel Gonen, to the Israeli Seventh Armoured Division, June 1967

Kill the Jews wherever you find them. Kill them with your hands, with your nails and teeth.

King Hussein of Jordan.

This is the second great day in my life. The first was when I immigrated to Israel.

David Ben-Gurion, at the Wailing Wall, Jerusalem, 8th June 1967

General [Moshe] Dayan once said that he would rather advance running in bare feet than walk in slippers; we were barefoot perhaps but we were able to advance fast.

Yael Dayan, *A Soldier's Diary: Sinai 1967*, 1967

[Wednesday 7th June] A few minutes later we heard the sentence which shook us all – *The Old City of Jerusalem is ours.*

Did I say fatigue? Minefield, late night, Sinai-desert – all disappeared. Suddenly there was the Temple Mount and the Wailing Wall and a heart too small to contain the thought. Was it joy that brought tears from the toughest soldiers? Pride? Sense of history? Religion? All I know is that this brilliance was cried out, and it sparked like electricity from convoy to convoy.

Yael Dayan, *A Soldier's Diary: Sinai 1967*, 1967

For six days, following an old tradition, this labour continued, and on the seventh ceased.

Lionel Davidson, *Smith's Gazelle*, 1968

Although Israeli units can be extremely smart on a ceremonial parade, there is very little discipline in the normal sense. Officers are often called by their first names amongst their men, as amongst their colleagues; there is very little saluting; there are a lot of unshaven chins; there are no outward signs of respect for superiors; there is no word in Hebrew for 'Sir'. A soldier genuinely feels himself to be the equal of his officer – indeed of any officer – yet in battle he accepts military authority without question. I cannot explain. I cannot begin to understand how, or why it works. All my own military experience in the British and American Armies has taught me that first-class discipline in battle depends on good discipline in the barracks. Israel's Army seems to refute that lesson.

Robert Henriques, quoted in Y. Allon, *The Making of Israel's Army*, 1970

I stood in silence facing the Wall. Then I took a small notebook out of my pocket, wrote a few words, and, following the Jewish tradition of centuries when pilgrims would press their written pleas and prayers in the crevices of the Wall, I folded the note and thrust it into an opening between the ashlars. Moshe Pearlman, my special assistant, was somewhat surprised and asked what I had written. Without speaking I wrote again: 'May peace descend upon the whole House of Israel.'

Moshe Dayan, *Story of My Life*, 1976

I think that if Israel did not exist, the Arab leaders would have to invent it. It is the single imaginary enemy that unifies all their people. The Moslems of the Middle East quarrel among themselves, mistrust, assassinate, plot coups, change alliances, kill each other with ferocious energy; they can agree on nothing except their nourishing hatred for the Jews of Israel.

Martha Gellhorn, *The Face of War*, 1986

RUSSIAN OCCUPATION OF CZECHOSLOVAKIA, August 1968

Russian Circus In Town – Do Not Feed The Animals!

Grafitto found in Prague, 1968

YOM KIPPUR (or OCTOBER) WAR, 1973

If we lose this war, I'll start another in my wife's name.

Moshe Dayan, attributed

The United States' announcement was more worrying. Commenting on the outbreak of hostilities in the Middle East, a White House spokesman said that President Nixon had been 'closely following the situation since the early hours of the morning'. Morning in Washington was afternoon in the Middle East. The announcement was being made three hours after the Egyptian-Syrian attack without the slightest hint that it was the Arabs who had started the war. When our representative in Washington reported to the U.S. government that the Arabs had launched their invasion, he was told the Arabs claimed it was we who had attacked them. In Washington, of course, they knew the truth, knew from the beginning that we had not started the war. Perhaps they thought we should have done a bit more than simply 'not start'!

Moshe Dayan, *Story of My Life*, 1976

As for the fighting standard of the Arab soldiers, I can sum it up in one sentence: they did not run away. In the past flight was a common characteristic of the Arab armies. Not all. Not immediately. But as far as one can generalize it can be said that when they were hit and badly mauled and their front was broken wide open, they would raise their hands – and their heels. Not this time. Now, in the Yom Kippur War, even when they suffered heavy casualties and recognized that the battle was lost, they did not run; they withdrew.

Moshe Dayan, *Story of My Life*, 1976

The fact that the surprise attack had taken place on Yom Kippur facilitated the mobilization of Israel's reserves, as most of them were either in the synagogues at prayer or at home. Thus a nation at prayer rushed to units and assembly areas, changing prayer shawls for battle kit on the way. Israel was again fighting for its existence.

Chaim Herzog, *The Arab-Israeli Wars*, 1982

CAMBODIA: THE REIGN OF THE KHMER ROUGE, 1975–78

One must trust completely in the *Angka*, because the Organization has as many eyes as a pineapple and cannot make mistakes.

Ith Sarin, *Regrets for the Khmer Soul*, 1970

To preserve you is no benefit, to destroy you is no loss.

Khmer Rouge slogan

'When did you first come to know about Pol Pot?' I asked a Cambodian. He said, 'When I came home from the rice field one day I saw my two-year-old child lying dead in a heap of ashes with a half-finished piece of pumpkin soaked in blood in his mouth and my wife dying of a head wound. She was panting and whispering to me – "Try to find the murderer of our son and revenge me and our son." Then, I found out about Pol Pot.'

Report in a Vietnamese newspaper, 30th September 1978, quoted in William Shawcross, *Sideshow: Kissinger, Nixon and the Destruction of Cambodia*, 1979

Our government has succeeded perfectly in establishing authority and order. Fighting exists only in the minds of some ugly Cambodians in Thailand and Paris. They fight from their nightclubs there.

Norodom Sihanouk, during a Press Conference in Paris, 1978

There are only two men responsible for the tragedy in Cambodia today, Mr Nixon and Dr Kissinger. Lon Nol was nothing without them and the Khmer Rouge were nothing without Lon Nol. Mr Nixon and Dr Kissinger gave the Khmer Rouge involuntary aid because the people had to support the Communist patriots against Lon Nol. By expanding the war into Cambodia, Nixon and Kissinger killed a lot of Americans and many other people, they spent enormous sums of money – $4 billion – and the results were the opposite of what they wanted. They demoralized America, they lost all of Indochina to the Communists, and they created the Khmer Rouge.

Norodom Sihanouk, in William Shawcross, *Sideshow: Kissinger, Nixon and the Destruction of Cambodia*, 1979

In Cambodia, the imperatives of a small and vulnerable people were consciously sacrificed to the interests of strategic design. For this reason alone the design was flawed – sacrifice the parts and what becomes of the whole? The country was used to practice ill-conceived theories and to fortify a notion of American credibility that could in fact only be harmed by such actions. Neither the United States nor its friends nor those who are caught helplessly in its embrace are well served when its leaders act, as Nixon and Kissinger acted, without care. Cambodia was not a mistake; it was a crime.

William Shawcross, *Sideshow: Kissinger, Nixon and the Destruction of Cambodia*, 1979

One man shall smile one day and say goodbye.
Two shall be left, two shall be left to die.

One man shall give his best advice.
Three men shall pay the price.

One man shall live, live to regret.
Four men shall meet the debt.

One man shall wake from terror to his bed.
Five men shall be dead.

One man to five. A million men to one.
And still they die. And still the war goes on.

James Fenton, 'Cambodia', 1982

What appeared as a weakness – the communists' inability to proclaim straightforwardly who they were because Sihanouk was their movement's figurehead – proved a master strategy. The Khmer Rouge did not appear to be a radical alternative to what had come before, merely a new variation on familiar Cambodian politicians. Thus the Cambodian people followed the initial instructions of the Khmer Rouge when the war ended, obeyed their drastic orders in 1975, and marched into a life more miserable than they could imagine.

Elizabeth Becker, *When the War Was Over*, 1986

The Khmer Rouge allowed the world to know as little as possible about their methods and ambitions. Their silence was mysterious, even sinister. The first stories about life under their rule, told by Cambodians who managed to escape to Thailand, were fantastic and made the regime sound like a monstrous abomination. Refugees said Cambodians wearing eyeglasses were killed because the Khmer Rouge thought only intellectuals wore eyeglasses. They said beautiful young women were forced to marry deformed Khmer Rouge veterans. They said all toys were banned, that there were no more kites flying in the sky. They said there were no dogs left in the country because starving people had killed them all for food.

These were exaggerations, but they were exaggerations such as are fables, based on a truth too awful to explain. The eyeglass fable reflected how the Khmer Rouge had targeted intellectuals as dangerous and killed thousands simply for having an education. The story of beautiful women and deformed soldiers was the mythological version of how the state had taken control over marriages and outlawed sex and romance outside marriage, often murdering offenders. The toys and the kites appropriately represented the loss of childhood for Cambodia's youngsters, who had to work like adults and were given no time for a rudimentary education. And the disappearance of the dogs symbolized the disappearance of food for many people.

Elizabeth Becker, *When the War Was Over*, 1986

Now we could see that he had worked himself up into a rage. He approached the pile of struggling monkeys, and killed them one by one without a word. The meeting froze. Comrade Tek was a new man. He dispatched each monkey with a blow to the back of the skull. As he did so, people straightened their backs.

'And now,' he said, 'I'll show you the way I used to kill the Lon Nol soldiers when we caught them, and the way to get the liver out.' He laid the last monkey flat on the ground. In the light of the bonfire I could see its watery eyes. 'If you don't know the right place to cut,' he continued, with emphasis, 'you won't get the whole thing out in one.'

He made a cut to the stomach. Then he pressed hard on the incision with both hands. The monkey screeched. The liver came out whole. Comrade Tek then slit the animal's throat. He said, 'If it had been a man, I would have put my foot in the cut to get the right pressure – otherwise the liver never comes out properly.' He held the liver in his hand, and for a brief moment we could smell it. What he was saying sounded like no more than an anecdote to him. Every time I think of it I imagine my father was killed in the same way.

Someth May, *Cambodian Witness*, 1986

As I reached the canteen, I saw that something was up. Usually people were sitting at the tables, waiting for their soup. That day, everyone was gathering in silence to the side of the canteen hut. I went closer and peered through the crowd.

There I saw a lamentable sight. The teacher – the sister of the woman whom I had buried the day before – was crying, lying with one cheek on the muddy ground. She was almost naked, and her face was badly bruised. Her arms and legs too were black and blue. Her daughter was sitting beside her, her face a blank, staring round in shock.

'What happened?' I asked.

The story came from many mouths, whispered in low voices, for the Khmer Rouge were already waving us toward the tables. The woman had eaten the flesh of her dead sister. She'd been caught with a piece of human flesh in her pot. That explained, of course, why the corpse had been covered up so carefully. The Khmer Rouge had beaten and kicked the woman all morning, until she lost consciousness.

Transfixed with horror, not at the woman's action, but at what had led to it, I stared at this awful sight, a woman driven to cannibalism, and the frightened child beside her. Meanwhile the Khmer Rouge were telling us: 'Move on! Do not pity this ogress!'

Pin Yathay, *Stay Alive, My Son*, 1987

[See also – The Vietnam Wars: Bombing and Invasion of Cambodia, p. 371.]

THE IRAN–IRAQ WAR, 1980–(1989)

We are not the kind of people to bow to Khomeini. He has wagered to bend us and we have wagered to bend him. We shall see who will bend the other.

Saddam Hussein, in Nineveh, 15th April 1980

It is not a question of a fight between one government and another. It is a question of an invasion by an Iraqi non-Moslem Ba'thist against an Islamic country, and this is a rebellion by blasphemy against Islam.

Ayatollah Rouhollah Khomeini, in Tehran, 20th October 1980

Khomeini is not a man of religion. Whoever describes him as such is fanatical, stupid and understands nothing of politics. Khomeini is a politician. When he realizes he is losing more than he is gaining, he will establish peace.

Saddam Hussein, in Baghdad, 4th November 1982

The day we put, with the grace of God, a victorious end to the imposed war, no other country would dare attack us.

Hashemi Rafsanjani, in Tehran, 1st February 1985

The Algerian revolution took one million lives out of fourteen million people. We are fifty million. It is still very early for us to put aside our arms and refrain from the holy defence which is one of our mandatory duties . . .

Musavi Ardebili, Tehran, 9th October 1987

Now that the Khomeini government in Iran has been deprived of the chance to export its revolution through force of arms, it has no option but to develop revolutionary Islamic fundamentalism socially and economically in one country to provide a model to other Muslim states.

Dilip Hiro, *The Longest War: the Iran–Iraq Military Conflict*, 1989

AFGHANISTAN WAR, from 1981

Wake up! It's time to be a martyr in Kabul!

Rebel folksong, *c.* 1982

THE FALKLANDS WAR, 1982

Q: What are ten thousand sheep doing in the hold of the *QE2*?
A: War-brides for the Falklands task force!

Contemporary joke

The BBC were on board [HMS *Glamorgan*] and grandiosed everything out of all proportion. (Antarctic wind, force nine gales, terrific disruption done, disrupted entire Argentine war effort, etc.). Mostly, they sat drinking the wardroom beer and were sick in their heads: the weather was in fact quite good.

Lieutenant David Tinker, diary entry, quoted in Trevor Royle, *War Report*, 1987

The tabloid press, with the undeniably courageous exception of the *Daily Mirror*, was continuing to run pages of near-hysterical war-mongering. 'Haig Double Faults Again,' the *Daily Mail* cried with evident glee. 'No Surrender' demanded the *Express*. The *Sun* tried the obscenity *'Stick It Up Your Junta!'* in response to a peace proposal. Fleet Street's yearning for an old-fashioned sea battle was equalled only by its suspicion that the Foreign Office might be conspiring to cheat it of one. 'Let's End the War of Politics,' said the *Daily Star* in frustration. The distance of the impending encounter from Britain and from civilian casualties seemed to induce a reckless aversion to peace. At one point, Downing Street became so alarmed that lobby correspondents were urged to persuade their editors to acknowledge the risks the task force was running.

Max Hastings and Simon Jenkins, *The Battle for the Falklands*, 1983

The British were awed by the courage of the Argentine pilots, flying suicidally low to attack, then vanishing amid flushes of pursuing Sea Cat, Blowpipe, Rapier, racing across the sky behind them. Alone among the enemy's three services, the air force seemed highly motivated and utterly committed to the battle. 'We should have been able to work out that any nation which produces first-class Formula One racing drivers is also likely to turn out some pretty good pilots,' said *Arrow*'s doctor sardonically between attacks.

Max Hastings and Simon Jenkins, *The Battle for the Falklands*, 1983

Unlike in Vietnam, where soldiers were only minutes by helicopter from the most modern hospitals, Falklands wounded had to lie out, often for hours, before helicopters could get to them. Medical training on the voyage south enabled their mates to keep them alive during this waiting. Every man knew basic major road accident-type first aid – techniques for stopping massive bleeding, external heart massage, mouth to mouth resuscitation and putting up drips, either intravenous or intra-rectal, introducing a new cry onto the modern battlefield: 'Medic, Medic . . . shove it up my arse for goodness sake!'

Hugh McManners, *Falklands Commando*, 1984

Now, in the comfort of normal surroundings with time to reflect, Operation Corporate (as the whole operation was termed) seems like a dream that happened to other people. It was like stepping through a looking glass – but once on the other side there was no guarantee of getting back. The first time I allowed myself to think realistically of getting back home was a few days after the Argentine surrender, but even then I did not count on it until I was in the comfort and warmth of HMS *Intrepid* watching video films of Wimbledon.

Hugh McManners, *Falklands Commando*, 1984

The Sinking of the *General Belgrano*, 2nd May 1982

Britain may not rule the waves, but she certainly waives the rules.

Jorge Herrera Vegas, comment made at the United Nations, 4th May 1982

The British Defence Secretary, John Nott, later argued that the old cruiser presented an immediate threat to Woodward's task force. The Argentinians admit that she was providing aircraft direction for their air force. Some naval officers suggest that criticism of the decision to attack the ship merely betrays 'wetness' or inability to grasp the realities of war. It may be years, if ever, before we know whether Admiral Anaya ever intended an early concerted surface attack which might have hurt the British, but which could have entirely destroyed the Argentinian fleet in the process. What is incontrovertible is that the British strategic purpose was to defeat the enemy's air and sea forces before the amphibious landing force was committed. To achieve this, it was vital to seize the earliest opportunity to remove one or more major Argentine surface threats from the battlefield. 'You have got to start something like this by showing that you're bloody good and you're determined to win,' said a senior British commander forcefully.

Max Hastings and Simon Jenkins, *The Battle for the Falklands*, 1983

The Battle for Port Stanley, 11th–14th June 1982

Two and a quarter hours after the firefight began, although 45 Commando was still exposed to constant shelling from the Argentine artillery, they had seized the summits of Two Sisters, and pulled back from the crest line to await the coming of dawn. Andrew Whitehead looked in wonderment at the strength of the positions the enemy had abandoned. 'With 120 men,' he said, 'I could have died of old age holding these hills.'

Max Hastings and Simon Jenkins, *The Battle for the Falklands*, 1983

Walking into the hotel was the fulfilment of a dream, a fantasy that had filled all our thoughts for almost three months. 'We never doubted for a moment that the British would come,' said the proprietor, Desmond King. 'We have just been waiting for the moment.' It was like liberating an English suburban golf club.

Max Hastings, Press dispatch, 14th June 1982

PART THREE: PERSONALITIES

Quotations about commanders, captains and others, arranged alphabetically by name

[Note: This section is not strictly speaking an anthology of biographical quotations. It does not include many famous quotations about the figures included. It only includes quotations that have a military bearing.]

ALARIC, King of the Goths, 370–410

An Italian hermit, whose zeal and sanctity were respected by the barbarians themselves, encountered the victorious monarch, and boldly denounced the indignation of Heaven against the oppressors of the earth: but the saint himself was confounded by the solemn asseveration of Alaric, that he felt a secret and preternatural impulse, which directed, and even compelled, his march to the gates of Rome. He felt that his genius and his fortune were equal to the most arduous enterprises; and the enthusiasm which he communicated to the Goths, insensibly removed the popular, and almost superstitious, reverence of the nations for the majesty of the Roman name.

Edward Gibbon, *The History Of The Decline And Fall Of The Roman Empire*, 1776–88, xxxi

ALCIBIADES, *c.* 450–404 BC

He had a great position among the citizens and was devoted to horse-racing and other pleasures which outran his means. And in the end his wild courses went far to ruin the Athenian state. For the people feared the extremes to which he carried his lawless self-indulgence, and the far-reaching purposes which animated him in all his actions. They thought that he was aiming at a tyranny and set themselves against him. And therefore, although his talents as a military commander were unrivalled, they entrusted the administration of the war to others, because they personally objected to his private life; and so they speedily shipwrecked the state.

Thucydides, *The Peloponnesian Wars*, 401 BC: Bk VI

. . . The most complete example of genius without principle that history produces, the Bolingbroke of antiquity . . .

E. S. Creasy, *The Fifteen Decisive Battles of the World*, 1851

ALEXANDER THE GREAT (of Macedon), 365–323 BC

But some may say, that while you endured toil and fatigue, I have acquired those things as your leader without myself sharing the toil and the fatigue. But who is there of you who knows that he has endured greater toil for me than I have for him? Come now! Whoever of you has wounds, let him strip and show them, and I will show mine in turn; for there is no part of my body, in front at any rate, remaining free from wounds; nor is there any kind of weapon used either for close combat or for hurling at the enemy, the traces of which I do not bear on my person. For I have been wounded with the sword in close fight, I have been shot with arrows, and I have been hit with missiles projected from engines of war; and though of ten times I have been hit with stones and bolts of wood for the sake of your lives, your glory, and your wealth, I am still leading you as conquerors over all the land and sea, all rivers, mountains and plains.

On himself, addressing his army towards the end of his campaigns, in Arrian, *The Anabasis of Alexander*, *c.* 160: Bk VII

Take this son of mine away and teach him the poems of Homer.

Philip of Macedon, attributed

A tomb now suffices him for whom the whole world was not enough.

Epitaph of Alexander the Great

Alexander no doubt did all that a soldier ought to do in battle, and that is not his least title to fame. But if Manlius Torquatus had been opposed to him in the field, would he have been inferior to him in this respect, or Valerius Corvus, both of them distinguished as soldiers before they assumed command? Would the Decii, who, after devoting themselves, rushed upon the enemy, or Papirius Cursor with his vast physical courage and strength? Would the clever generalship of one young man have succeeded in baffling the whole senate, not to mention individuals, that senate of which he, who declared that it was composed of kings, alone formed a true idea? Was there any danger of his showing more skill than any of these whom I have mentioned in choosing the site for his camp, or organising his commissariat, or guarding against surprises, or choosing the right moment for giving battle, or disposing his men in line of battle and posting his reserves to the best advantage? He would have said that it was not with Darius that he had to do, dragging after him a chain of women and eunuchs, wrapped up in purple and gold, encumbered with all the trappings of state. He found him an easy prey rather than a formidable enemy and defeated him without loss, without being called to do anything more daring than to show a just contempt for the idle show of power. The aspect of Italy would have struck him as very different from the India he traversed in drunken revelry with an intoxicated army; he would have seen in the passes of Apulia and the mountains of Lucania the traces of the recent disaster which befell his house when his uncle Alexander, King of Epirus, perished.

Livy, *The History of Rome*, from 29 BC: Bk IX

Darius now sent an embassy to Alexander, bearing a letter, in which he offered to pay ten thousand talents as a ransom for his wife and children, and proposed that Alexander should receive all the territory west of the Euphrates, and become his ally and son-in-law. Alexander laid this proposal before his friends, and when Parmenio said, 'I should accept it, if I were Alexander.' – 'So would I,' replied Alexander, 'if I were Parmenio.'

Plutarch, *Lives: Alexander*, *c.* 110

Hannibal was in great difficulties and straits in Italy, and yet yielded a very unwilling obedience when summoned home to protect Carthage, while Alexander merely sneered at the news of the battle between Agis and Antipater, observing, 'It appears, my friends, that while we have been conquering Darius here, there has been a battle of mice in Arcadia.'

Plutarch, *Lives: Agesilaus*, *c.* 110

He was very clever in recognizing what was necessary to be done, even when it was a matter still unnoticed by others; and very successful in conjecturing from the observation of facts what was likely to occur. In marshalling, arming and ruling an army he was exceedingly skilful; and very renowned for rousing the courage of his soldiers, filling them with hopes of success, and dispelling their fear in the midst of danger by his own freedom of fear. Therefore even what he had to do in secret he did with the greatest boldness. He was also very clever in getting the start of his enemies, and snatching from them their advantages by secretly forestalling them, before any one even feared what was about to happen.

Arrian, *The Anabasis of Alexander*, c. 160: Bk VII

. . . He said that the kings of the Persians and the Medes called themselves Great Kings without any right, since they did not rule the larger part of Asia. Some say that he was meditating a voyage thence into the Euxine Sea, to Scythia and the Lake Maeotis (the Sea of Azov); while others assert that he intended to go to Sicily and the Iapygian Cape, for the fame of the Romans spreading far and wide was now exciting his jealousy. For my own part I cannot conjecture with any certainty what were his plans; and I do not care to guess. But this I think I can confidently affirm, that he meditated nothing small or mean; and that he would never have remained satisfied with any of the acquisitions he had made, even if he had added Europe to Asia, or the islands of the Britons to Europe; but would still have gone on seeking unknown lands beyond those mentioned.

Arrian, *The Anabasis of Alexander*, c. 110, Bk VII

For it was a witty and truthful rejoinder which was given by a captured pirate to Alexander the Great. The king asked the fellow, 'What is your idea, in infesting the sea?' And the pirate answered, with uninhibited insolence, 'The same as yours, in infesting the earth! But because I do it with a tiny craft, I'm called a pirate; because you have a mighty navy, you're called an emperor.'

St Augustine, *City Of God*, 427: IV.v

Fluellen: I think it is in Macedon where Alexander is porn. I tell you, captain, if you look in the maps of the 'orld, I warrant you sall find, in the comparisons between Macedon and Monmouth, that the situations, look you, is both alike. There is a river in Macedon, and there is also moreover a river in Monmouth: it is called Wye at Monmouth; but it is out of my prains what is the name of the other river; but 'tis all one, 'tis as alike as my fingers is to my fingers, and there is salmons in both. If you mark Alexander's life well, Harry of Monmouth's life is come after it indifferent well; for there is figures in all things. Alexander, – God knows, and you know, – in his rages, and his furies, and his wraths, and his cholers, and his moods, and his displeasures, and his indignations, and also being a little intoxicates in his prains, did, in his ales and his angers, look you, kill his pest friend, Cleitus.

William Shakespeare, *Henry V*, 1600, Act IV sc. vii

With a small army, but distinguished for its intrinsic perfection, he overthrew the decayed fabric of the Asiatic States; without rest, and regardless of risks, he traverses the breadth of Asia, and penetrates into India. No republics could do this. Only a King, in a certain measure his own condottiere, could get through so much so quickly.

Karl von Clausewitz, *On War*, 1832: V.iii

. . . Although the rapidity and extent of Alexander's conquests have through all ages challenged admiration and amazement, the grandeur of genius which he displayed in his schemes of commerce, civilization, and of comprehensive union and unity among nations, has, until lately, been comparatively unhonoured. This long continued depreciation was of early date. The ancient rhetoricians – a class of babblers, a school for lies and scandal, as Niebuhr justly termed them – chose among the stock themes for their common-places, the character and exploits of Alexander. They had their followers in every age; and, until a very recent period, all who wished to 'point a moral or adorn a tale', about unreasoning ambition, extravagant pride, and the formidable frenzies of free will when leagued with free power, have never failed to blazon forth the so-called madman of Macedonia as one of the most glaring examples.

E. S. Creasy, *The Fifteen Decisive Battles of the World*, 1851

There has been no illustrious captain who did not possess taste and a feeling for the heritage of the human mind. At the root of Alexander's victories one will always find Aristotle.

Charles de Gaulle, *The Army of the Future*, 1934

Most historians have had their own Alexander, and a view of him which is one-sided is bound to have missed the truth. There are features which cannot be disputed; the extraordinary toughness of a man who sustained nine wounds, breaking an ankle bone and receiving an arrow through his chest and the bolt of a catapult through his shoulder. He was twice struck on the head and neck by stones and once lost his sight from such a blow. The bravery which bordered on folly never failed him in the front line of battle, a position which few generals since have considered proper; he set out to show himself a hero, and from the Grancius to Multan he left a trail of heroics which has never been surpassed and is perhaps too easily assumed among all his achievements. There are two ways to lead men, either to delegate all authority and limit the leader's burden or to share every hardship and decision and to be seen to take the toughest labour, prolonging it until every other man has finished. Alexander's method was the second, and only those who have suffered the first can appreciate why his men adored him; they will also remember how lightly men talk of a leader's example, but how much it costs both the will and the body to sustain it.

Robin Lane Fox, *Alexander the Great*, 1973

Harold Rupert Leofric George, Earl ALEXANDER of Tunis, 1891–1969

He had almost every quality you could wish to have, except that he had the average brain of the average English gentleman. He lacked that little extra cubic centimetre which produces genius. If you recognize that, it's perhaps a greater tribute to what he did achieve by leadership, courage and inspiring devotion in those who served under him.

Earl Mountbatten, in Nigel Nicolson, *Alex*, 1973

The Dominion's most industrious gadabout.

Time magazine, October 1946

If Montgomery was the Wellington, Alexander was certainly the Marlborough of this war [Second World War].

Harold Macmillan, *The Blast of War*, 1967

ALFRED, King of England, 849–901

Not long after venturing from his concealment, he hazarded an experiment of consummate art. Accompanied only by one of his most faithful adherents, he entered the tent of the Danish King under the disguise of a minstrel; and being admitted as a professor of the mimic art, to the banqueting room, there was no object of secrecy that he did not minutely attend to with both eyes and ears. Remaining there several days, till he had satisfied his mind on every matter which he wished to know, he returned to Ethelingai; and assembling his companions, pointed out the insolence of the enemy and the easiness of their defeat.

William of Malmesbury, *History of the Kings of England*, *c.* 1120

When Alfred observed this symptom of successful resistance in his subjects, he left his retreat; but before he would assemble them in arms, or urge them to any attempt, which, if unfortunate, might, in their present despondency, prove fatal, he resolved to inspect, himself, the situation of the enemy, and to judge of the probability of success. For this purpose he entered their camp under the disguise of a harper, and passed unsuspected through every quarter. He so entertained them with his music and facetious humours, that he met with a welcome reception; and was even introduced to the tent of Guthrum, their prince, where he remained some days. He remarked the supine security of the Danes, their contempt of the English, their negligence in foraging and plundering, and their dissolute wasting of what they gained by rapine and violence. Encouraged by these favourable appearances, he secretly sent emissaries to the most considerable of his subjects, and summoned them to a rendezvous, attended by their warlike followers, at Brixton, on the borders of Selwood forest. The English, who had hoped to put an end to their calamities by servile submission, now found the insolence and rapine of the conqueror more intolerable than all past fatigues and dangers; and at the appointed day, they joyfully resorted to their prince.

David Hume, *The History of England*, 1754–62: vol. i

There was no English Armour left,
Nor any English thing,
When Alfred came to Athelney
To be an English King.

G. K. Chesterton, *Ballad of the White Horse*, 1911

Edmund Henry Hynman, Viscount ALLENBY, 1861–1936

Allenby was so great that the comprehension of our littleness came slow to him.

T. E. Lawrence, quoted in Norman F. Dixon, *On the Psychology of Military Incompetence*, 1976

The last of the Paladins.

Sir Ronald Storrs, *Orientations*, 1937

ARMINIUS (HERMANN), d. AD 19

. . . The deliverer of Germany without doubt he was, and one who assailed the Roman state, not like other kings and leaders, in its infancy, but in the pride of imperial elevation; in single encounters sometimes victorious, sometimes defeated, but not worsted in the general issue of the war: he lived thirty-seven years; twelve he was in possession of power; and, amongst barbarous nations, his memory is still celebrated in their songs; his name is unknown in the annals of the Greeks, who only admire their own achievements; nor is he very much celebrated among us Romans, whose habit it is to magnify men and feats of old, but to regard with indifference the examples of modern prowess.

Tacitus, *The Annals*, *c.* 115: Bk II

It was part of the subtle policy of Rome to confer rank and privileges on the youth of the leading families in the nations which she wished to enslave. Among other young German chieftains, Arminius and his brother, who were the heads of the noblest house in the tribe of the Cherusci, had been selected as fit objects for the exercise of this insidious system. Roman refinements and dignities succeeded in denationalizing the brother, who assumed the Roman name of Flavius, and adhered to Rome throughout all her wars against his country. Arminius remained unbought by honours or wealth, uncorrupted by refinement or luxury. He aspired to and obtained from Roman enmity a higher title than ever could have been given him by Roman favour.

E. S. Creasy, *The Fifteen Decisive Battles of the World*, 1851

Benedict ARNOLD, 1741–1801

Our troops by Arnold thoroughly were bang'd,
  And poor St André was by Arnold hang'd.
To George a Rebel, to the Congress Traitor,
  Pray what can make the name of Arnold greater?
By one bold treason more to gain his ends
  Let him betray his new adopted friends.

Anonymous, early 19th century

ARTEMESIA, fl. 480 BC

Of the lower officers I shall make no mention, since no necessity is laid upon me; but I must speak of a certain leader named Artemesia, whose participation in the attack upon Greece, notwithstanding that she was a woman, moves my special wonder.

Herodotus, *Histories*, *c.* 450 BC: Bk VII

My men have behaved like women, my women like men.

Xerxes, after the Battle of Salamis, 480 BC, in Herodotus, *Histories*, *c.* 450 BC: Bk VII

ATTILA (the 'Hun'), mid-5th century

Terrific was his semblance, in no mould
Of beautiful proportion cast; his limbs
Nothing exalted, but with sinews braced
Of Chalybaean temper, agile, lithe,
And swifter than the roe; his ample chest
Was over-brow'd by a gigantic head,
With eyes keen, deeply sunk, and small, that gleam'd
Strangely in wrath as though some spirit unclean
Within that corporal tenement install'd
Look'd from its windows, but with temper'd fire
Beam'd mildly on the unresisting. Thin
His beard and hoary; his flat nostrils crown'd
A cicatrized, swart visage, – but withal
That questionable shape such glory wore
That mortals quail'd beneath him.

Ascribed to Herbert of Cherbury, in E. S. Creasy, *The Fifteen Decisive Battles of the World*, 1851

The religious arts of Attila were not less skilfully adapted to the character of his age and country. It was natural enough, that the Scythians should adore, with peculiar devotion, the god of war; but as they were incapable of forming either an abstract idea, or a corporeal representation, they worshipped their tutelar deity under the symbol of an iron cimeter. One of the shepherds of the Huns perceived, that a heifer, who was grazing, had wounded herself in the foot, and curiously followed the track of the blood, till he discovered, among the long grass, the point of an ancient sword, which he dug out of the ground, and presented to Attila. That magnanimous, or rather that artful, prince accepted, with pious gratitude, this celestial favour; and as the rightful possessor of the *sword of Mars*, asserted his divine and infeasible claim to the dominion of the earth.

Edward Gibbon, *The History Of The Decline And Fall Of The Roman Empire*, 1776–88: xxxiv

His body was solemnly exposed in the midst of the plain, under a silken pavilion; and the chosen squadrons of the Huns, wheeling round in measured evolutions, chanted a funeral song to the memory of a hero, glorious in his life, invincible in his death, the father of his people, the scourge of his enemies, and the terror of the world. According to their national custom, the barbarians cut off a part of their hair, gashed their faces with unseemly wounds, and bewailed their valiant leader as he deserved, not with the tears of women, but with the blood of warriors.

Edward Gibbon, *The History Of The Decline And Fall Of The Roman Empire*, 1776–88: xxxv

Austerely sober in his private life – severely just on the judgement-seat – conspicuous among a nation of warriors for hardihood, strength and skill in every martial exercise – grave and deliberate in counsel, but rapid and remorseless in execution – he gave safety and security to all who were under his dominion, while he waged a warfare of extermination against all who opposed or who sought to escape from it. He watched the national passions, the prejudices, the creeds, and the superstitions of the varied nations over which he ruled, and of those which he sought to reduce beneath his sway: all these feelings he had the skill to turn to his own account. His own warriors believed him to be the inspired favourite of their deities, and followed him with fanatic zeal: his enemies looked upon him as the pre-appointed minister of heaven's wrath against themselves; and though they believed not in his creed, their own made them tremble before him.

E. S. Creasy, *The Fifteen Decisive Battles of the World*, 1851

As the greatness of Alexander may be judged from his legend, so may the horror of Attila be translated from his.

J. F. C. Fuller, *The Decisive Battles of the Western World*, 1954–56

Octavius Caesar AUGUSTUS, 63 BC–AD 14

Having entered into a confederacy with Antony and Lepidus, he brought the war at Philippi to an end in two battles, although he was at that time weak, and suffering from sickness. In the first battle he was driven from his camp, and with some difficulty made his escape to the wing of the army commanded by Antony. And now, intoxicated with success, he sent the head of Brutus to be cast at the foot of Caesar's statue, and treated the most illustrious of the prisoners not only with cruelty, but with abusive language; insomuch that he is said to have answered one of them who humbly intreated that at least he might not remain unburied, 'That will be in the power of the birds.'

Suetonius, *Lives of the Twelve Caesars*, *c.* 117

. . . It was reserved for Augustus, to relinquish the ambitious design of subduing the whole earth, and to introduce the spirit of moderation into public councils. Inclined to peace by his temper and situation, it was easy for him to discover, that Rome, in her present exalted situation, had much less to hope than to fear from the chance of arms; and that, in the prosecution of remote wars, the undertaking became every day more difficult, the event more doubtful, and the possession more precarious, and less beneficial.

Edward Gibbon, *The History Of The Decline And Fall Of The Roman Empire*, 1776–88, i

In spite of the glamour of his age, he was a splendid rather than an heroic figure. Though not lacking in courage or in pertinacity, as a leader of men he cannot compare with Julius Caesar. He was a tolerant opportunist who, by means of his policy of *divide et impera*, became the managing director rather than the monarch of his Empire. He believed in Rome as a great business, a vast monopoly, and looked upon states and frontiers as bonds and securities. He lacked the power to electrify men and to compel them to accomplish the seemingly impossible which distinguished the man of genius from the merely great . . . As the frontiers were closed, simultaneously were closed down with them all intellectual and moral endeavour: adventures of the mind and soul ceased with the cessation of the adventures of the body.

J. F. C. Fuller, *The Decisive Battles of the Western World*, 1954–56

AURELIAN (Lucius Domitius Aurelianus), *c.* 215–75

A single instance will serve to display the rigour, and even cruelty, of Aurelian. One of the soldiers had seduced the wife of his host. The guilty wretch was fastened to two trees forcibly drawn towards each other, and his limbs were torn asunder by their sudden separation. A few such examples impressed a salutary consternation. The punishments of Aurelian were terrible; but he had seldom occasion to punish more than once the same offence.

Edward Gibbon, *The History Of The Decline And Fall Of The Roman Empire*, 1776–88, xi

Pierre Terrail de BAYARD, *c.* 1473–1524

Chevalier sans peur et sans reproche.
[Knight without fear and without reproach.]

Traditional soubriquet

It was said of Bayard by military men of his time, that he assaulted like a greyhound, defended himself like a lion, and retreated like a wolf, which always retires from its pursuers with its face towards them . . . At the siege of Mézières, which town he defended, the Comte de Nassau summoned him to surrender it. 'Nay,' replied he, 'if I must march out of the place, it shall be over a bridge of the dead bodies of the enemy.'

The Percy Anecdotes, 1823

Oh for a knight like Bayard
Without reproach or fear;
My light glove on his casque of steel,
My love-knot on his spear.

John Greenleaf Whittier, 'The Hero', 1846

Sir William Carr BERESFORD, 1768–1854

Wellington paid the greatest tribute to him when he declared that if he were removed by death or illness he would recommend Beresford to succeed him, not because he was a great general, but because he alone could 'feed an army'.

Henry Morse Stephens, in *The Dictionary of National Biography*, 1885–1901

Chief BLACK HAWK, 1767–1838

I fought hard. But your guns were well aimed. The bullets flew like birds in the air, and whizzed by our ears like the wind through the trees. My warriors fell around me; it began to look dismal. I saw my evil day at hand. The sun rose dim on us in the morning, and at night it sank in a dark cloud, and looked like a ball of fire. That was the last sun that shone on Black Hawk. His heart is dead, and no longer beats quick in his bosom. He is now a prisoner to the white men; they will do with him as they wish. But he can stand torture and is not afraid of death. He is no coward. Black Hawk is an Indian.

On himself, surrendering to General H. Atkinson, 1833, in T. C. McLuhan, *Touch The Earth*

Robert BLAKE, 1599–1657

Rest here in peace the sacred dust
Of valiant Blake, the good, the just,
Belov'd of all on every side;
England's honours, once her pride,
Rome's terror, Dutch annoyer,
Truth's defender, Spain's destroyer.

Bring no dry eyes unto this place;
Let not be seen in any case
A smiling or an unsad face.
Kindle desires in every breast
Eternally with him to rest.

George Harrison, Epitaph Acrostic, 1657

Gebhard Leberecht von BLÜCHER, 1742–1819

That drunken Hussar.

Napoleon Bonaparte, attributed

BOADICEA (BOUDICCA), Queen of the Iceni, d. AD 60

. . . the British warrior queen,
Bleeding from the Roman rods,
Sought, with an indignant mien,
Counsel of her country's gods.

William Cowper, 'Boadicea', 1786

Although, as a Stoic, Seneca officially despised riches, he amassed a huge fortune . . . Much of this he acquired by lending money in Britain; according to Dio, the excessive rates of interest that he exacted were among the causes of revolt in that country. The heroic Queen Boadicea, if this is true, was heading a rebellion against capitalism, as represented by the philosophic apostle of austerity.

Bertrand Russell, *History of Western Philosophy*, 1946

Toby: Celia, you couldn't – you couldn't possibly play Boudicca.
Celia: Of course I could.
Toby: She was – er – she was a wild, primitive, uninhibited woman who was responsible for the massacre of over seventy thousand crack Roman soldiers whilst clad only in three bits of fur and some blue paint.
Celia: So that's why you want Sylvie Bell to play it.
Toby: No, no. I'm exaggerating. I don't think the parents are quite ready for that. The point I'm making, Celia, is that Boudicca – although very little is known about her really, except through Tacitus who was somewhat prejudiced – none the less, she was a woman of the earth, shall we say?
Celia: She was a queen.
Toby: Well. Not in the sense you mean. Tribal leader.

Celia: She was. She was royal. And, with respect, Sylvie Bell – well, she's hardly what you'd call blue-blooded, is she?
Toby: Neither are you.
Celia: I'm a good deal bluer than she is, I can tell you. My great, great, great, great, great grandfather was a falconer.

Alan Ayckbourn, *Intimate Exchanges: A Pageant*, 1982

Marshal BOUCICAUT, Jean II le Meingre, 1366–1421

He executed a somersault fully armed, except for his bascinet, and whilst dancing he was armed with a mail coat. Item, he leapt onto a courser without placing his foot in the stirrup, fully armed. Item, with a strong man mounted on a great horse, he leapt from the ground onto his shoulders by taking the sleeve in one hand and without any other hold. Item, placing one hand on the saddle pommel of a great courser and the other near the horse's ears, seizing the mane, he leapt from the ground through his arms and over the horse. Item, if two walls were an arm's length apart and as high as a tower, he could climb to the top without slipping on ascent or descent, simply using the strength of his arms and legs, without any other assistance. Item, wearing a coat of mail he ascended the under side of a great ladder placed against a wall to the top without using his feet, simply jumping with both hands from rung to rung and, then, taking off his coat, he did this with one hand until he was unable to ascend any higher.

Anonymous, *Le Livre des faicts du bon messire Jean le Meingre, dit Boucicaut, marshal de France et gouverneur de Gennes*, 15th century

John BROWN, 1800–59

Let no man pray that Brown be spared. Let Virginia make him a martyr. Now, he has only blundered. His soul was noble: his work miserable. But a cord and a gibbet would redeem all that, and round up Brown's failure with a heroic success.

Henry Ward Beecher, quoted in Oswald Garrison Villard, *John Brown*, 1910

Was John Brown justified in his attempt? Yes, if Washington was in his, if Warren and Hancock were in theirs. If men are justified in striking a blow for freedom, when the question is one of a three penny tax on tea, then, I say, they are a thousand times more justified, when it is to save fathers, mothers, wives and children from the slave-coffle and the auction block, and to restore them their God-given rights.

William Lloyd Garrison, in the *Liberator*, 16th December 1859

The death of Brown is more than Cain killing Abel: it is Washington slaying Spartacus.

Victor Hugo, *A Word Concerning John Brown in Virginia*, December 1859

John Brown's body lies a-mouldering in the grave,
But his soul is marching on.

C. S. Hall, 'John Brown's Body', 1859

I speak for the slave when I say that I prefer the philanthropy of Captain Brown to that philanthropy which neither shoots me nor liberates me.

Henry David Thoreau, *A Plea for Captain John Brown*, 1859

John Brown is dead, he will not come again,
A stray ghost-walker with a ghostly gun.

Stephen Vincent Benét, *John Brown's Body*, 1928

Out of John Brown's strong sinews the tall skyscrapers grow,
Out of his heart the chanting buildings rise,
Rivet and girder, motor and dynamo,
Pillar of smoke by day and fire by night,
The steel-faced cities reaching at the skies,
The whole rotating and enormous cage
Hung with hard jewels of electric light,
Smoky with sorrow, black with splendor, dyed
Whiter than damask for a crystal bride
With metal suns, the engine-handed Age,
The genie we have raised to rule the earth,
Obsequious to our will
But servant-master still,
The tireless serf already half a god – . . .

Stephen Vincent Benét, *John Brown's Body*, 1928

When John Brown stretched forth his arm the sky was cleared – the armed hosts of freedom stood face to face over the chasm of a broken union, and the clash of arms was at hand.

Frederick Douglas, speech at Harper's Ferry, May 1882

Thomas Robert BUGEAUD de la Piconnerie, 1784–1849

L'as-tu vue,
La casquette, la casquette,
L'as-tu vue
La casquette de Père Bugeaud?
[Have you seen it, the helmet, the helmet, the helmet of Old Man Bugeaud?]

Soldiers' song, *c.* 1831

Sir Redvers Henry BULLER, 1839–1908

Buller was a characteristic British personality. He looked stolid. He said little, and what he said was obscure.

Winston Churchill, *My Early Life*, 1930

John BYNG, 1704–57

In this country [Britain] it is thought proper to kill an admiral from time to time, to encourage the others.

Voltaire, *Candide*, 1759

Gaius Julius CAESAR, 100–44 BC

He longed for great power, an army, a new war to give his merit scope.

Sallust, *The Conspiracy of Catiline*, c. 41 BC

Further-Spain fell to his lot as quaestor; when there, as he was going about the circuit of the province, by commission from the praetor, for the administration of justice, and had reached Gades, seeing a statue of Alexander the Great in the temple of Hercules, he sighed deeply, as if weary of his sluggish life, for having performed no memorable actions at an age at which Alexander had already conquered the world. He, therefore, immediately sued for his discharge, with the view of embracing the first opportunity, which might present itself in The City, of entering on a more exalted career. In the stillness of the night following, he dreamt that he lay with his own mother; but his confusion was relieved, and his hopes were raised to the highest pitch, by the interpreters of his dream, who expounded it as an omen that he should possess universal empire; for that the mother who in his sleep he had submissive to his embraces, was no other than the earth, the common parent of all mankind.

Suetonius, *Lives of the Twelve Caesars*, c. 117

He was perfect in the use of arms, an accomplished rider, and able to endure fatigue beyond all belief. On a march, he used to go to the head of his troops, sometimes on horseback, but oftener on foot, with his head bare in all kinds of weather. He would travel post in a light carriage without baggage, at the rate of a hundred miles a day; and if he was stopped by floods in the rivers, he swam across, or floated on skins inflated with wind, so that he often anticipated intelligence of his movements.

Suetonius, *Lives of the Twelve Caesars*, c. 117

He was never deterred from any enterprise, nor retarded in the prosecution of it, by superstition. When a victim, which he was about to offer in sacrifice, made its escape, he did not therefore defer his expedition against Scipio and Juba. And, happening to fall, upon stepping out of the ship, he gave a lucky turn to the omen, by exclaiming, 'I hold thee fast, Africa!'

Suetonius, *Lives of the Twelve Caesars*, c. 117

Sometimes, after a great battle ending in victory, he would grant [his troops] relaxation from all kinds of duty, and leave them to revel at pleasure; being used to boast, 'that his soldiers fought nothing the worse for being well oiled.'

Suetonius, *Lives of the Twelve Caesars*, c. 117

So great were the good-will and devotion of Caesar's soldiers to him, that those who under other generals were in no way superior to ordinary soldiers, were invincible and irresistible and ready to meet any danger for Caesar's glory. An instance of this is Acilius, who in the sea-fight of Messalia boarded one of the enemy's ships and had his right hand cut off with a sword, but he still kept hold of his shield with his left hand and striking at the faces of the enemy drove all to flight and got possession of the vessel. Another instance was Cassius Scaeva, who in the fight at Dyrrachium had one eye destroyed by an arrow, his shoulder transfixed with one javelin and his thigh with another, and on his shield he had received the blows of one hundred and thirty missiles. In this plight he called to the enemy as though he designed to surrender himself, and two of them accordingly approached him, but with his sword he lopped off one man's shoulder and wounding the other in the face, put him to flight, and finally he escaped himself with the aid of his friends.

Plutarch, *Lives: Caesar*, *c.* 110

He generally slept in chariots or in litters, making even his repose a kind of action; and in the daytime he used to ride in a vehicle to the garrisons, cities and camps, with a slave by his side, one of those who were expert at taking down what was dictated on a journey, and a single soldier behind him armed with a sword.

Plutarch, *Lives: Caesar*, *c.* 110

His expedition against the Britanni was notorious for its daring; for he was the first who entered the western Ocean with an armament and sailed through the Atlantic sea, leading an army to war; and by attempting to occupy an island of incredible magnitude, which furnished matter of much dispute to numerous writers, who affirmed that the name and the accounts about it were pure invention, for it never existed and did not then exist, he extended the Roman supremacy beyond the inhabited world.

Plutarch, *Lives: Caesar*, *c.* 110

. . . Caesar forthwith advanced against the man with three legions and fighting a great battle near Zela drove Pharnakes in flight from Pontus, and completely destroyed his army. In reporting to one of his friends at Rome, Amantius, the celerity and rapidity of this battle, he wrote only three words: 'I came, I saw, I conquered'. In the Roman language the three words (Veni, Vidi, Vici) ending in the like form of verb, have a brevity which is not without effect.

Plutarch, *Lives: Caesar*, *c.* 110

Cassius: Why, man, he doth bestride the narrow world
Like a Colossus; and we petty men
Walk under his huge legs, and peep about
To find ourselves dishonourable graves.
Men at some time are masters of their fates:
The fault, dear Brutus, is not in our stars,
But in ourselves, that we are underlings.

William Shakespeare, *Julius Caesar*, 1599: Act I sc ii

Antony: O! pardon me, thou bleeding piece of earth,
That I am meek and gentle with these butchers;
Thou art the ruins of the noblest man
That ever lived in the tide of times.
Woe to the hand that shed this costly blood!
Over thy wounds now do I prophesy,
Which like dumb mouths do ope their ruby lips
To beg the voice and utterance of my tongue,
A curse shall light upon the limbs of men;
Domestic fury and fierce civil strife

Shall cumber all the parts of Italy;
Blood and destruction shall be so in use,
And dreadful objects so familiar,
That mothers shall but smile when they behold
Their infants quarter'd with the hands of war;
All pity chok'd with custom of fell deeds:
And Caesar's spirit, ranging for revenge,
With Ate by his side come hot from hell,
Shall in these confines with a monarch's voice
Cry 'Havoc!' and let slip the dogs of war;
That this foul deed shall smell above the earth
With carrion men, groaning for burial.
William Shakespeare, *Julius Caesar*, 1599: Act III sc i

Antony: Friends, Romans, countrymen, lend me your ears;
I come to bury Caesar, not to praise him.
The evil that men do lives after them,
The good is oft interred with their bones.
William Shakespeare, *Julius Caesar*, 1599: Act III sc ii

Antony: But yesterday the word of Caesar might
Have stood against the world; now lies he there,
And none so poor to do him reverence.
William Shakespeare, *Julius Caesar*, 1599: Act III sc ii

Antony: . . . But were I Brutus,
And Brutus Antony, there were an Antony
Would ruffle up your spirits, and put a tongue
In every wound of Caesar, that should move
The stones of Rome to rise and mutiny.
William Shakespeare, *Julius Caesar*, 1599: Act III sc ii

Great Julius, on the mountain bred,
A flock perhaps, or herd had led;
He that the world subdued had been
But the best wrestler on the green.
Edmund Waller, 'To Zelinda', 1645

Ask why from Britain Caesar would retreat?
Caesar himself might whisper he was beat.
Why risk the world's great empire for a punk?
Caesar perhaps might answer, he was drunk.
Alexander Pope, *Moral Essays*, 1731–35

One Caesar lives; a thousand are forgot.
Edward Young, *Night Thoughts*, 1742–45

What millions died – that Caesar might be great!
Thomas Campbell, 'The Pleasures of Hope', 1798

Caius Caesar CALIGULA, 12–41

Only once in his life did he take an active part in military affairs, and then not from any set purpose, but during his journey to Mevania, to see the grove and the river of Clitumnus. Being recommended to recruit a body of Batavians, who attended him, he resolved upon an expedition into Germany. Immediately he drew together several legions, and auxiliary forces from all quarters, and made every where new levies with the utmost vigour. Collecting supplies of all kinds, such as had never been assembled on the like occasion, he set forward on his march, and pursued it sometimes with so much haste and precipitation, that the pretorian cohorts were obliged, contrary to custom, to pack their standards on horses and mules, and so follow him. At other times he would march so slow and luxuriously, that he was carried in a litter by eight men; ordering the roads to be swept by the people of the neighbouring towns, and sprinkled with water to lay the dust.

Suetonius, *Lives of the Twelve Caesars*, c. 117

CARATACUS (Caractacus), mid-1st century AD

. . . He was delivered up in chains in the ninth year after the commencement of the war in Britain. Whence his renown overpassing the limits of the isles, spread over the neighbouring provinces, and became celebrated even in Italy; where all longed to behold the man who, for so many years, had defied the Roman arms: not even at Rome was the name of Caratacus unassociated with fame; and the emperor, while exalting his own glory, added to that of the vanquished. For the people were summoned to see him, as a rare spectacle; and the praetorian bands stood under arms in the field before their camp.

Tacitus, *The Annals*, c. 115: Bk XII

James Thomas Brudenell, Lord CARDIGAN, 1797–1868

Lord Cardigan was not unique in lavishing an attention upon the appearance of his troops which, in a more enlightened age, might be reserved for the ladies of the Miss World competition.

Norman F. Dixon, *On the Psychology of Military Incompetence*, 1976

Sir Edward (Henry) CARSON, 1854–1935

My only great qualification for being put in charge of the Navy is that I am very much at sea.

On himself, 1916, in H. Montgomery Hyde, *Carson*, 1953

Marcus Aurelius CARUS, d. 283

The Persians expressed their desire of being introduced to the presence of the Roman emperor. They were at length conducted to a soldier, who was seated in the grass. A piece of stale bacon and a few hard pease composed his supper. A coarse woollen garment of purple was the only circumstance that announced his dignity. The conference was conducted with the same disregard of courtly elegance. Carus, taking off a cap which he wore to conceal his baldness, assured the ambassadors, that, unless their master acknowledged the superiority of Rome, he would speedily render Persia as naked of trees, as his own head was destitute of hair.

Edward Gibbon, *The History Of The Decline And Fall Of The Roman Empire*, 1776–88, xii

Edith Louisa CAVELL, 1865–1915

I realize that patriotism is not enough. I must have no hatred or bitterness towards anyone.

Last words, 12th October 1915

CHARLEMAGNE (CHARLES THE GREAT of France), *c.* 742–814

Then appeared the iron king, crowned with his iron helm, with sleeves of iron mail on his arms, his broad breast protected by an iron byrnie, an iron lance in his left hand, his right free to grasp his unconquered sword. His thighs were guarded with iron mail, though other men are wont to leave them unprotected that they may spring the more lightly on their steeds. And his legs, like those of all his host, were protected by iron greaves. His shield was plain iron, without device or colour. And round him and before him and behind him rode all his men, armed as nearly like him as they could fashion themselves; so iron filled the fields and the ways, and the sun's rays were in every quarter reflected from iron.

Chronicle of St Gall, describing Charles in Italy, 814

His military renown must be tried by the scrutiny of his troops, his enemies, and his actions. Alexander conquered with the arms of Philip, but the *two* heroes who preceded Charlemagne, bequeathed him their name, their examples, and the companions of their victories. At the head of his veteran and superior armies, he oppressed the savage or degenerate nations, who were incapable of confederating for their common safety; nor did he ever encounter an equal antagonist in numbers, in discipline, or in arms. The science of war has been lost and revived with the arts of peace; but his campaigns are not illustrated with any siege or battle of any singular difficulty and success; and he might behold, with envy, the Saracen trophies of his grandfather.

Edward Gibbon, *The History Of The Decline And Fall Of The Roman Empire*, 1776–88, xlix

CHARLES XII of Sweden, 1682–1718

Ten years of unbroken success – and two hours of mismanagement!

The Duke of Marlborough, attributed, on hearing of Charles XII's defeat at Poltava in 1709

On what foundations stands the Warrior's Pride?
How just his hopes let *Swedish Charles* decide;
A Frame of Adamant, a Soul of Fire,
No Dangers fright him, and no Labours tire;

O'er Love, o'er Fear, extends his wide Domain,
Unconquer'd Lord of Pleasure, and of Pain;
No Joys to him pacific Scepters yield,
War sounds the Trump, he rushed to the Field;
Behold surrounding Kings their Pow'rs combine,
And One capitulate, and One resign;
Peace courts his Hand, but spreads her Charms in vain;
'Think Nothing gain'd, he cries, till nought remain,
On *Moscow's* Walls till *Gothic* Standards fly,
And all be Mine beneath the Polar Sky.'
The March begins in Military State,
And Nations on his Eye suspended wait;
Stern Famine guards the solitary Coast,
And Winter barricades the Realms of Frost;
He comes, nor Want nor Cold his Course delay; –
Hide, blushing Glory, hide *Pultowa's* Day:
The vanquish'd Hero leaves his broken Bands,
And shews his Miseries in distant Lands;
Condemn'd a needy Supplicant to wait,
While Ladies interpose, and Slaves debate.
But did not Chance at length her Error mend?
Did no subverted Empire mark his End?
Did rival Monarchs give the fatal Wound?
Or hostile Millions press him to the Ground?
His Fall was destin'd to a barren Strand,
A petty Fortress, and a dubious Hand;
He left the Name, at which the World grew pale,
To point a Moral, or adorn a Tale.

Samuel Johnson, *The Vanity Of Human Wishes*, 1749

Sir Winston Leonard Spencer CHURCHILL, 1874–1965

Like a good many other Generals at this time [the Boer War], French disapproved of me. I was that hybrid combination of subaltern and widely-followed war-correspondent which was not unnaturally obnoxious to the military mind.

On himself, *Great Contemporaries*, 1937

I have always been against the Pacifists during the quarrel, and against the Jingoes at its close.

On himself, *My Early Life*, 1930

I would say to the House, as I said to those who have joined the Government: I have nothing to offer but blood, toil, tears and sweat.

On himself, in the House of Commons, 13th May 1940

I have never accepted what many people have kindly said, namely that I inspired the nation. It was the nation and the races dwelling all around the globe that had the lion heart. I had the luck to be called upon to give the roar.

On himself, Eightieth Birthday Speech, November 1954

Winston may in your eyes and in those with whom he had to work have faults, but he has the supreme quality which I venture to say very few of your present future Cabinet possess – the power, the imagination, the deadliness, to fight Germany.

Clementine Churchill, Letter to H. H. Asquith, May 1915

He has spoilt himself by reading about Napoleon.

David Lloyd George, in Frances Stevenson, diary, 19th May 1917

5 November 1940. The Prime Minister makes a statement after Question Time. He is rather grim. He brings home to the House as never before the gravity of our shipping losses and the danger of our position in the Eastern Mediterranean. It has a good effect. By putting the grim side foremost he impresses us with his ability to face the worst. He rubs the palms of his hands with five fingers extended up and down the front of his coat, searching for the right phrase, indicating cautious selection, conveying almost medicinal poise. If Chamberlain had spoken glum words such as these the impression would have been one of despair and lack of confidence. Churchill can say them and we all feel, 'Thank God we have a man like this!' I have never admired him more. Thereafter he slouches into the smoking room and reads the *Evening News* intently, as if it were the only source of information available to him.

Harold Nicolson, *Diaries and Letters, 1939–45*, 1971

Winston is always expecting rabbits to come out of empty hats.

Lord Wavell, in Henry Channon, Diary, 30th May 1943

I think that the first time I ever deeply disliked Winston and realised the depths of selfish brutality to which he could sink, was when he told me, not only that he was getting rid of Wavell from the Middle East, but why. He walked up and down his room, chin sunk on chest, glowering ferociously, and muttering, 'I wanted to show my power!' over and over.

R. W. Thompson, in *Churchill and Morton: Correspondence between Major Sir Desmond Morton and R. W. Thompson*, ed. R. W. Thompson, 1976

His inspirational quality owed its dynamic force to the romantic world of phantasy in which he had his true being.

Anthony Storr, *Churchill's Black Dog and Other Phenomena of the Human Mind*, 1989

George Rogers CLARK, 1752–1818

I am a man and a warrior – not a counselor. I carry war in my right hand, and in my left, peace.

On himself, in William English, *Conquest of the Country Northwest of the River Ohio*

Karl von CLAUSEWITZ, 1780–1831

The Germans interpret their new national colours – black, red and white – by the saying, 'Durch Nacht und Blut zur Licht' ('Through night and blood to light') and no work yet written conveys to the thinker a clearer conception of all that the red streak in their flag stands for than this deep and philosophical analysis of 'War' by Clausewitz.

Colonel J. J. Graham, Introduction to his 1908 translation of *On War.*

Clausewitz's influence is not dead. The philosophy of *On War* is the philosophy of Bismarck's Blood and Iron and the philosophy of *Mein Kampf.*

US Military Academy pamphlet, *Clausewitz, Jomini, Schlieffen*, 1951

The Mahdi of mass and mutual destruction.

B. H. Liddell Hart, *The Ghost of Napoleon*

Clausewitz' great achievement was in having made people *aware* of the way war can be used as an arm of national policy in the sense of accepting its legitimacy. In his day the question of the legitimacy of war did not arise. In our day this question is forced upon us. The disciples of Clausewitz in effect plead for 'recognizing' war as an arm of national policy in the sense of accepting its legitimacy. And since war in the nuclear age has become a political absurdity, a vast amount of discussion is devoted to theorizing about 'limited' wars, controlled escalation, the game of threats, self-terminating 'nuclear exchanges' and the like. All this investment of intellectual effort seems to be motivated to a considerable degree by a determination to preserve the struggle for power as the theoretical bedrock of political reality.

Anatol Rapoport, 'Concluding Remarks' to the Penguin edition of *On War*, 1968

CLOVIS, *c.* 466–511

The mind of Clovis was susceptible of transient fervour: he was exasperated by the pathetic tale of the passion and death of Christ; and, instead of weighing the salutary consequences of that mysterious sacrifice, he exclaimed, with indiscreet fury, 'Had I been present at the head of my valiant Franks, I would have revenged his injuries.'

Edward Gibbon, *The History Of The Decline And Fall Of The Roman Empire*, 1776–88, xxxviii

Oliver CROMWELL, 1599–1658

I had rather have a plain russet-coated captain that knows what he fights for, and loves what he knows, than which you call a gentleman and is nothing else.

On himself, September 1643, in Thomas Carlyle, *The Letters and Speeches of* Oliver Cromwell, 1845

I am a poor weak creature yet accepted to serve the Lord and His people. Indeed . . . ye know not me, my weakness, my immoderate passions, and everyway unfitness for my work; yet the Lord, who will have mercy on whom He will, does as you see.

On himself, June 1645, in Thomas Carlyle, *The Letters and Speeches of Oliver Cromwell*, 1845

A Caesar he ere long to Gaul,
To Italy an Hannibal,
And to all States not free
Shall Clymacterick be.

Andrew Marvell, 'An Horatian Ode upon Cromwell's Return from Ireland', 1650

'You do well,' said he, 'to charge us with the guilt of blood; but we think there is good return for what hath been shed.'

Edmund Ludlow, interview with Cromwell, August 1656

Cromwell, our chief of men, who through a cloud,
Not of war only, but of detractions rude,
Guided by faith and matchless fortitude,
To peace and truth thy glorious way has ploughed,
And on the neck of crowned Fortune proud
Has reared God's trophies, and his work pursued,
While Darwen stream with blood of Scots imbrued,
And Dunbar field resounds thy praises loud,
And Worcester's laureate wreath. Yet much remains
To conquer still; peace hath her victories
No less renowned than war: new foes arise,
Threatening to bind our souls with secular chains:
Help us to free conscience from the paw
Of hireling wolves whose gospel is the maw.

John Milton, 'To the Lord General Cromwell', 1652

His Grandeur he deriv'd from Heaven alone,
For he was great e'er fortune made him so,
And Wars like Mists that rise against the Sun
Made him but greater seem, not greater grow.

John Dryden, 'Heroick Stanzas consecrated to the Memory of His Highness Oliver', 1659

Oliver Cromwell had certainly this afflatus. One that I knew that was at the Battle of Dunbar, told me that Oliver was carried on with a divine impulse; he did Laugh so excessively as if he had been drunk; his Eyes sparkled with Spirits. He obtain'd a great Victory; but the action was said to be contrary to Human Prudence. The same Fit of Laughter seized Oliver Cromwell just before the Battle of Naseby; as a Kinsman of mine, and a great favourite of his, Colonel J.P. then present, testified. Cardinal Mazerine said, That he was a Lucky Fool.

John Aubrey, *Miscellanies, c.* 1690

Sylla was the first of victors; but our own
The sagest of usurpers, Cromwell; he
Too swept off senates while he hewed the throne
Down to a block – immortal rebel! See
What crimes it costs to be a moment free
And famous through all ages.

Lord Byron, *Childe Harold's Pilgrimage*, 1812–17; Canto IV

Cromwell kept his fanatics in order in their own way; for when one of them waited upon him, as he said, in the name of the Lord, to know the destination of one of his fleets, Cromwell said, 'My good friend, the Lord shall know, for thou shalt go with the fleet.' He immediately gave orders for having him stowed in the hold of one of the vessels then under sailing orders; and actually sent him out, thus confined, with the expedition.

The Percy Anecdotes, 1823

George Armstrong CUSTER, 1839–76

Cut off from aid, abandoned in the midst of incredible odds, waving aloft the sabre which had won him victory so often; the pride and glory of his comrades, the noble Custer fell: bequeathing to the nation his sword, to his comrades an example, to his friends a memory, and to his beloved a hero's name.

Lawrence Barrett, in Frederick Whittaker, *A Complete Life of General George A. Custer*, 1876

CYRUS THE GREAT of Persia, *c.* 585–529 BC

I considered that herdsmen are the rulers of oxen, and horse-feeders of horses; and that, in general, all those called overseers of animals may properly be accounted the rulers of the animals of which they have the charge. I thought that I perceived all these herds more willing to obey their keepers than men their governors; for the herds go the way that their keepers direct them; they feed on those lands to which their keepers drive them, and abstain from those from which they repel them; and they suffer their keepers to make what use they please of the profits that arise from them. Besides, I never saw a herd conspiring against its keeper, either with a view of not obeying him, or of not allowing him to enjoy the advantages arising from them; for herds are more refractory towards strangers than they are towards their keepers, and those who make profits of them; but men conspire against none sooner than against those whom they perceive attempting to rule them. While I was reflecting upon these things, I came to this judgement upon them: that to man, such is his nature, it was easier to rule every other sort of creature than to rule man. But when I considered that there was Cyrus the Persian, who had rendered many men, many cities, and many nations, obedient to him, I was then necessitated to change my opinion, and to think that to rule men is not among the things that are impossible, or even difficult, if a person undertakes it with understanding and skill.

Xenophon, *Cyropaedia*, *c.* 360 BC, I.i

They then went off to their tents, and, on their way, observed among themselves how retentive a memory Cyrus had, and how, as he gave his orders to those to whom he assigned their places, he addressed each of them by name. This Cyrus was enabled to do by giving his attention to it; for he thought it very strange, if, while artificers know the names of their tools, each in his own art, and a physician knows the names of all the instruments and medicines that he uses, a general should be so foolish as not to know the names of the commanders under him, whom he must necessarily use as his instruments whenever he wishes to seize any post, to keep on guard, to encourage his men, or to strike terror into the enemy; and when he desired to do honour to any one, he thought it became him to address him by name. He was of the opinion, too, that those who thought themselves known to their commander, would thus be more eager to be seen performing some honourable action, and more anxious to abstain from doing anything that was disgraceful.

Xenophon, *Cyropaedia*, *c.* 360 BC, V.iii

Jefferson DAVIS, 1808–89

Oh, the muskets they may rattle,
And the cannon they may roar,
But we'll fight for you, Jeff Davis,
Along the Southern shore.

Anonymous, *c.* 1865

There is no doubt that Jefferson Davis and other leaders of the South have made an army; they are making, it appears, a navy; and they have made what is more than either, they have made a nation.

W. E. Gladstone, speech at Newcastle, 7th October 1862

Moshe DAYAN, 1915–81

On my visits to the front, I wore Israeli army fatigue without any badges of rank, green shirt and trousers, paratroop boots, and a wind-jacket. The problem was a hat, but I solved that one before the war. When I returned from my 1966 Vietnam visit, I adopted a somewhat doubtful form of headgear of the kind worn by Vietnamese rear-echelon privates engaged in service duties – cooks, sanitary orderlies, and so on. It laid no claims to elegance, but it could be crumpled and shoved in a pocket when not needed, and it looked no worse when taken out and put on the head. The one article of apparel I was careful about was my dust goggles. I never moved without them, for when the socket of my missing eye gets dry, I suffer severe headaches. I also try to keep my right eye protected. Just as well for an eye accident not to happen more than once.

Moshe Dayan, *Story of My Life*, 1976

George DEWEY, 1837–1917

Oh dewy was the morning
Upon the first of May,
And Dewey was the admiral
Down in Manila Bay,
And dewy were the Regent's eyes,
The orbs of royal blue,
And dew we feel discouraged;
I dew not think we dew.

Eugene Fitch Ware, in the *Topeka Daily Capital*, 3rd May 1898

Sir Francis DRAKE, 1540–96

He was more skilful in all poyntes of Nauigation, then any that euer was before his time, in his time, or since his death, he was also of a perfect memory, great Observation, Eloquent by Nature, Skilfull in Artillery, Expert and apt to let blood, and giue Physicke unto his people according to the Climate, he was low of stature, of strong limbs, broad breasted, round headed, browne hair, full Bearded, his eyes round, large and cleare, well fauoured, fayre, and of a cheerefull countenance.

John Stow, *Annales*, 1580

Drake he's in his hammock an' a thousand mile away
(Capten, art tha' sleepin' there below?)
Slung away between the round shot in Nombre Dios Bay
An' dreamin' arl the time o' Plymouth Hoe.

Henry Newbolt, 'Drake's Drum', 1896

EDWARD I of England, 1239–1307

The longbow comes to the front only in the wars of Edward I, and its predominance in later English wars is directly due to the king's own action. Edward, after much experience, found that more advantage might be got from a judicious combination of cavalry and infantry armed with missile weapons, than from the use of horsemen alone. We have no signs that he had learned this at the time of Lewes and Evesham, but it appears clearly enough during the Welsh wars. In expeditions among the hills of Gwynedd the horseman was often useless; he could not storm crags or scramble down ravines. Welsh fighting was mainly work for infantry, and the king – as his conduct in the Evesham campaign had shown – was ready to learn in the school of war. Having come to know the strength and the weakness of infantry as well as of mailed knighthood, he was quite capable of combining his lessons.

Charles Oman, *A History of the Art of War in the Middle Ages*, 1928

To win his battles, all he had to do was to beat the French knights, and whereas the French feudal tactics were to dismount one's opponent and to hold him to ransome, Edward's were very definitely more to kill. His tactics were 'modern' more than feudal in idea, and the longbow, adopted by his grandfather from the Welsh, enabled him to base them on missile power as well as shock.

J. F. C. Fuller, *The Decisive Battles of the Western World*, 1954–56

EDWARD VIII, 1894–1972

I don't mind your being killed, but I do object to your being taken prisoner.

Lord Kitchener, to Edward as Prince of Wales, in Lord Esher, Journal, 18th December 1914

EDWIN (Eadwine), King of Northumbria, 585–633

So peaceful was it in those parts of Britain under King Edwin's jurisdiction that the proverb still runs that a woman could carry her newborn babe across the island from sea to sea without any fear of harm. Such was the king's concern for the welfare of his people that in a number of places where he had noticed clear springs adjacent to the highway he ordered posts be erected with brass bowls hanging from them, so that travellers could drink and refresh themselves. And so great was the people's affection for him, and so great was the awe in which he was held, that no one wished or ventured to use these bowls for any other purpose.

Bede, *Ecclesiastical History of the English People*, 731

Dwight David EISENHOWER, 1890–1969

Ike is the best damn general the British have got.

George S. Patton, attributed

It was imperative for him to establish harmony between his leading generals, and this he did admirably. But it was equally imperative in order to win the war in the shortest time and at the least cost, that strategy should not be subordinated to concord. Because he failed to understand this, as a general-in-chief he was more of a co-ordinator than a commander. In order to keep his turbulent barons occupied and tranquil he cut the strategic cake into slices and gave each a slice to eat; in so doing he violated the principle of concentration and prolonged the war.

J. F. C. Fuller, *The Decisive Battles of the Western World*, 1954

I read a very interesting quote by Senator Kerr of Oklahoma. In summing up Ike, he said 'Eisenhower is the only living unknown soldier.' Even this is giving him all the best of it.

Groucho Marx, Letter to Goodman Ace, 19th July 1960

President Eisenhower's whole life is proof of the stark but simple truth – that no one hates war more than one who has seen a lot of it.

Richard M. Nixon, media broadcast, Moscow, August 1959

Complex human societies depend for the final decisions of war and peace on a group of elderly men any sensible plant personnel manager . . . would hesitate to hire. Here we have at the top a cardiac case whose chief interest is in getting away from his job as often as possible for golf and bridge.

I. F. Stone, 'What the Berlin Crisis Really Shows', 9th March 1959

ELIZABETH I of England, 1533–1603

I know I have the body of a weak and feeble woman, but I have the heart and stomach of a king, and of a King of England too, and think foul scorn that Parma, or Spain, or any prince of Europe should dare to invade the borders of my realm; to which, rather than any dishonour shall grow by me, I myself will take up arms, I myself will be your general, judge, and rewarder of every one of your virtues in the field.

On herself, addressing troops at Tilbury, 1588

I am more afraid of making a fault in my Latin than of the Kings of Spain, France, Scotland, the whole House of Guise, and all their confederates.

On herself, in F. Chamberlin, *The Sayings of Queen Elizabeth*, 1924

Quintus FABIUS MAXIMUS Rullianus ('Cunctator'), 4th century BC

In Italy the masterly inaction of Fabius had for a short while stemmed the tide of Roman disasters. It was a cause of grave anxiety to Hannibal, for he realized that the Romans had chosen for their commander-in-chief a man who conducted war on rational principles, and not by trusting to chance. But amongst his own people, soldiers and civilians alike, his tactics were viewed with contempt, especially after a battle had been brought about owing to the rashness of the Master of the Horse in the Dictator's absence which would be more correctly described as fortunate rather than as successful. Two incidents occurred which made the Dictator still more unpopular. One was due to the crafty policy of Hannibal. Some deserters had pointed out to him the Dictator's landed property and after all the surrounding buildings had been levelled to the ground he gave orders for that property to be spared from fire and sword and all hostile treatment whatever in order that it might be thought that there was some secret bargain between them. The second cause of the Dictator's growing unpopularity was something which he himself did, and which at first bore an equivocal aspect because he had acted without the authority of the senate, but ultimately it was universally recognized as redounding very greatly to his credit. In carrying out the exchange of prisoners it had been agreed between the Roman and the Carthaginian commanders, following the precedent of the first Punic war, that whichever side received back more prisoners than they gave should strike a balance by paying two and half pounds of silver for each soldier they received in excess of those they gave. The Roman prisoners restored were two hundred and forty-seven more than the Carthaginians. The question of this payment had been frequently discussed in the senate, but as Fabius had not consulted that body before making the agreement there was some delay in voting the money. The matter was settled by Fabius sending his son Quintus to Rome to sell the land which had been untouched by the enemy; he thus discharged the obligation of the State at his own private expense.

Livy, *The History of Rome*, from 29 BC; Bk XXII

Thomas, Lord FAIRFAX, 1612–71

For General they chose Sir Thomas Fairfax . . . This man was chosen because they supposed to find him a man of no quickness of Parts, of no Elocution, of no suspicious plotting Wit, and therefore one that Cromwell could make use of at his pleasure. And he was acceptable to sober Men, because he was Religious, Faithful, Valiant, and of a grave, sober, resolved Disposition; very fit for Execution, and neither too Great, nor too Cunning to be Commanded by Parliament.

Richard Baxter, *Reliquiae Baxterianae*, 1696

Fairfax, whose name in arms through Europe rings
Filling each mouth with envy, or with praise,
And all her jealous monarchs with amaze,
And rumours loud, that daunt remotest kings,

Thy firm, unshak'n vertuè ever brings
  Victory home, though new rebellions raise
  Thir Hydra heads, and the fals North displaies
  Her brok'n league, to impe their serpent wings,
O yet a nobler task awaites thy hand;
  For what can Warr, but endless warr still breed,
  Till Truth, and Right from Violence be freed,
And Public Faith clear'd from the shamefull brand
  Of Public Fraud. In vain doth Valoiur bleed
  While Avarice and Rapine share the land.

John Milton, 'On the Lord General Fairfax at the Siege of Colchester', 1648

Taller, some say, when he is in the field than at home.

Joshua Sprigge, *Anglia Rediviva*, 1647

I have observed him at councils of war that he hath said little but hath ordered things expressly contrary to the judgement of his council; and in action in the field I have seen him so highly transported that scarce anyone durst speak a word to him and he would seem more like a man distracted and furious than of his ordinary mildness and so far different temper.

Bulstrode Whitelocke, *Memorials of English Affairs*, 1682

David Glasgow FARRAGUT, 1801–70

Oh, never through all time shall be forgot
His last brave deed, now told by every lip,
When on he sailed, amid a storm of shot,
Lashed in the rigging of his staunched old ship.

Anonymous, in *Harper's Weekly*, 10th September 1864

The Sea King of the Sovereign West
  Who made his mast a throne!

Oliver Wendell Holmes, 'A Toast to the Vice-Admiral', 1864

Sir John FASTOLFE, *c.* 1378–1459

Nor is our Comedian [Shakespeare] excusable, by some alteration of his name, writing him Sir John Falstafe, (and making him the property of pleasure for King Henry the fifth to abuse) seeing the vicinity of sounds intrench on the memory of that worthy Knight, and few do heed the inconsiderable difference in spelling of their names.

Thomas Fuller, *The History of the Worthies of England*, 1622

John Arbuthnot FISHER, Lord, 1841–1920

Fear God and Dread Nought.

Fisher's motto

[Fisher's] great claim to fame is that he succeeded in making us think.

Admiral Sir Sidney Freemantle, in a Letter to A. J. Marder, 1946

In an age when patronage and privilege was still exclusive and tenacious, Fisher brashly fought his way through to become at the age of sixty-three the controller of the most powerful single force of destruction in the world.

Richard Hough, *Fisher, First Sea Lord*, 1969

Ferdinand FOCH, 1851–1929

. . . Only a frantic pair of moustaches.

T. E. Lawrence, Letter to Basil Liddell Hart, April 1932

He was, in his own words, '[the] conductor of an opera who beats time well'.

A. J. P. Taylor, *The First World War*, 1963

When asked which of two officers of equal rank should salute the other first, Foch made the famous reply: 'The most polite.'

Georges Roditi, *The Spirit of Perfection*, 1988

Andrew Hull FOOTE, 1806–63

He prays like a saint, and fights like the devil.

Rear Admiral Francis H. Gregory, in Robert Debs Heinl Jr, *The Dictionary of Military and Naval Quotations*, 1966

Benjamin FRANKLIN, 1706–90

The history of our Revolution will be one continued lie from one end to the other. The essence of the whole will be that Dr Franklin's electrical rod smote the earth and out sprang George Washington. That Franklin electrified him with his rod – and thenceforward these two conducted all the policy, negotiations, legislatures, and war.

John Adams, Letter to Benjamin Rush, 4th April 1790

FREDERICK WILLIAM I of Prussia, 1688–1740

. . . The mind of Frederic William was so ill regulated that all his inclinations became passions, and all his passions partook of the character of moral and intellectual disease. His parsimony degenerated into sordid avarice. His taste for military pomp became a mania, like that of the Dutch burgomaster for tulips, or that of a member of the Roxburghe Club for Caxtons. While the envoys of the Court of Berlin were in a state of such squalid poverty as moved the laughter of foreign capitals, while the food placed before the princes and princesses of the blood-royal of Prussia was too scanty to appease hunger, and so bad that even hunger loathed it, no price was thought too extravagant for tall recruits. The ambition of the King was to form a brigade of giants, and every country was ransacked by his agents for men above the ordinary stature. These researches were not confined to Europe. No head that towered above the crowd in the bazaars of Aleppo, of Cairo, or of Surat, could escape the crimps of Frederic William. One Irishman, more than seven feet high, who was picked up in London by the Prussian ambassador, received a bounty of near thirteen hundred pounds sterling, very much more than the ambassador's salary. This extravagance was the more absurd, because a stout youth of five feet eight, who might have been procured for a few dollars, would in all probability have been a more valuable soldier. But to Frederic William this huge Irishman was what a brass Otho, or a Vinegar Bible, is to a collector of a different kind.

T. B. Macaulay, *Essays: Frederic the Great*, 1846

On May 31, 1740, Frederick William I died, and when those around him sang the hymn, 'Naked I came into the world and naked I shall go', he had just sufficient strength to mutter, 'No, not quite naked; I shall have my uniform on.'

J. F. C. Fuller, *The Decisive Battles of the Western World*, 1954–56

FREDERICK THE GREAT (Frederick II of Prussia), 1712–86

He fiddles and fights as well as any man in Christendom.

Voltaire, Letter to Sir Edward Fawkenden, June 1742

The King of Prussia is a mischievous rascal, a base friend, a bad ally, a bad relation and a bad neighbour: in fact, the most dangerous and evil-disposed prince in Europe.

William Pitt, Letter, May 1756

What distinguishes Frederick the most is not his skill in manoeuvring, but his audacity. He carried out things I never dared to do. He abandoned his line of operations, and often acted as if he had no knowledge whatsoever of the art of war.

Napoleon Bonaparte, on St Helena, *c.* 1816

At the head of a small State, which was like other States in most things, and only ahead of them in some branches of administration; he could not be an Alexander, and, as Charles XII, he would only, like him, have broken his head. We find, therefore, in the whole of his conduct of War, a controlled power, always well balanced, and never wanting in energy, which in the most critical moments rises to astonishing deeds, and the next moment oscillates quietly on again in subordination to the play of the most subtil political influences. Neither vanity, thirst for glory, nor vengeance could make him deviate from his course, and this course alone it is which brought him to a fortunate termination of the contest,

Karl von Clausewitz, *On War*, 1832: III.i

Frederick the Great was right when he said that if his nightcap knew what was inside his head he would throw it in the fire.

Antoine Henri de Jomini, *Précis de l'Art de la Guerre*, 1838

'Why did you leave me?' said the King [to a deserter]. 'Indeed, your Majesty,' replied the grenadier, '. . . things are going very badly with us.' 'Come, come,' rejoined Frederick, 'let us fight another battle today: if I am beaten, we will desert together tomorrow.'

Thomas Campbell, *Frederick the Great: His Court and Times*, 1846

In the midst of all the great King's calamities, his passion for writing indifferent poetry grew stronger and stronger. Enemies all around him, despair in his heart, pills of corrosive sublimate hidden in his clothes, he poured forth hundreds upon hundreds of lines, hateful to gods and men, the insipid dregs of Voltaire's Hippocrene, the faint echo of the lyre of Chaulieu. It is amusing to compare what he did during the last months of 1757, with what he wrote during the same time. It may be doubted whether any equal portion of the life of Hannibal, of Caesar, or of Napoleon, will bear a comparison with that short period, the most brilliant in the history of Prussia and of Frederic. Yet at this very time the scanty leisure of the illustrious warrior was employed in producing odes and epistles, a little better than Cibber's and a little worse than Hayley's.

T. B. Macaulay, *Essays: Frederic the Great*, 1846

The head of Frederick is a bank you cannot easily break by coming on it for plans: such a creature for impromptu plans, and unexpected dashes swift as the panther's, I have hardly known, – especially when you squeeze him into a corner, and fancy he is over with it!

Thomas Carlyle, *Frederick the Great*, 1858–65

Frederick the Great had a mule that went on 27 campaigns with him – and after 27 campaigns it still remained a mule.

Elihu Root (U S Secretary of War), attributed

A mixture of Puck and Machiavelli welded together on the anvil of Vulcan by the hammer of Thor.

J. F. C. Fuller, *The Decisive Battles of the Western World*, 1954–56

John Charles FRÉMONT, 1813–90

I fancied I could see Frémont's men, hauling the cannon up the savage battlements of the Rocky Mountains, flags in the air, Frémont at the head, waving his sword, his horse neighing wildly in the mountain wind, with unknown and unnamed empires at every hand.

Joaquin Miller, *Overland in a Covered Wagon*, 1930

John Denton Pinkstone FRENCH, Earl of Ypres, 1852–1925

Anyone can work him up into a sort of mad suspicion, so that he falls an easy prey to the people around him.

Sir John Fisher, Letter to Lord Stamfordham, December 1915

These are terrible times that we have been passing through, and our difficulties and anxieties have been greatly added to by having at the head of the Army in France a general who is not only very ignorant of the principles of the higher leading of a large Army but is also lacking in the necessary temperament! He is so hot tempered and excitable – like a bottle of soda water in suddenness of explosion – that he is quite incapable of thinking over a serious situation and coming to a reasoned decision.

Douglas Haig, Letter to his wife, 16th December 1916

His normal apoplectic expression, combined with the tight cavalryman's stock which he affected in the place of collar and tie, gave him an appearance of being perpetually on the verge of choking, as indeed he often was, emotionally if not physically.

Barbara Tuchman, *The Guns of August*, 1962

GENGHIS KHAN, *c.* 1162–1227

When Jenghiz-Khan died in 1227, his dominions stretched from Korea to Persia and from the Indian Ocean to the plains of Siberia. No other man has created so vast an empire. It is impossible to explain his success by some theory that the Mongols had any economic urge for expansion; it can only be said that they were a suitable instrument for an expansionist leader. Jenghiz was the architect of his destiny. But he himself remains mysterious. In appearance, we are told, he was tall and vigorous, with eyes like a cat's. It is certain that his physical endurance was great. It is certain, too, that his personality profoundly impressed everyone who had dealings with him. His skill as an organizer was superb; and he knew how to choose men and how to handle them. He had genuine respect for learning, and was always ready to spare a scholar's life; but unfortunately few of his victims were given time to prove their scholarship.

Steven Runciman, *A History of the Crusades*, 1951–54: vol. III

Chief GERONIMO, 1829–1909

I don't fight Mexicans with cartridges. I fight them with rocks, and keep my cartridges to fight the white soldiers.

On himself, in Britton Davis, *The Truth About Geronimo*, 1929

Once I moved about like the wind. Now I surrender to you and that is all.

On himself, to General Crook, 1889, in Alexander B. Adams, *Geronimo*, 1971

Hermann GOERING (Göring), 1893–1946

When I talk with Goering, it's like a bath in steel for me; I feel fresh afterward.

Adolf Hitler, in Albert Speer, *Inside the Third Reich*, 1969

Charles George GORDON (of Khartoum), 1833–86

It is quite painful to see men tremble so when they come to see me, that they cannot hold the match to their cigarette.

On himself, diary entry, November 1884

He has an immense name in Egypt – he is popular at home. He is a strong but sensible opponent of slavery. He has a small bee in his bonnet.

Lord Granville, Letter to W. E. Gladstone, November 1883

A man who habitually consults the Prophet Isaiah when he is in a difficulty is not apt to obey the orders of anyone.

Lord Cromer, Letter to Lord Granville, 1884

The man isn't worth the camels.

General Buller, responding to a suggestion that Gordon be rescued at Khartoum

Too late, too late to save him.
In vain, in vain they tried.
His life was England's Glory,
His death was England's pride.

Anonymous, written soon after Gordon's death

The man of England, circled by the sands.

George Meredith, Epigram, 1887

Ulysses Simpson GRANT, 1822–85

The truth is I am more of a farmer than a soldier. I take little or no interest in military affairs, and, although I entered the army thirty-five years ago and have been in two wars, in Mexico as a young lieutenant, and later, I never went into the army without regret and never retired without pleasure.

On himself, in conversation with Otto von Bismarck, in W. E. Woodward, *Meet General Grant*

How is it that Grant, who was behind at Fort Henry, drunk at Donelson, surprised at Shiloh, and driven back from Oxford, Miss., is still in command?

Murat Halstead, Letter to Salmon P. Chase, 19th February 1863

You just tell me the brand of whiskey Grant drinks: I would like to send a barrell of it to my other generals.

Abraham Lincoln, as reported in the *New York Herald*, 26th November 1863

Since Vicksburg they have not a word to say against Grant's habits. He has the disagreeable habit of not retreating before irresistible veterans.

Mary Chestnut, diary entry, 1st January 1864

He is a scientific Goth, resembling Alaric, destroying the country as he goes and delivering the people over to starvation. Nor does he bury his dead, but leaves them to rot on the battlefield.

John Tyler, Letter to Sterling Price, 7th June 1864

When Grant once gets possession of a place, he holds on to it as if he had inherited it.

Abraham Lincoln, Letter to Benjamin F. Butler, 22nd June 1864

We all thought Richmond, protected as it was by our splendid fortifications and defended by our army of veterans, could not be taken. Yet Grant turned his face to our Capital, and never turned it away until we had surrendered. Now, I have carefully searched the military records of both ancient and modern history, and have never found Grant's superior as a general. I doubt if his superior can be found in all history.

Robert E. Lee, in James Grant Wilson, *General Grant*, 1895

Grant stood by me when I was crazy, and I stood by him when he was drunk, and now we stand by each other.

W. T. Sherman, attributed, *c.* 1870

I knew him as a cadet at West Point, as a lieutenant of the Fourth Infantry, as a citizen of St Louis, and as a growing general all through the bloody Civil War. Yet to me he is a mystery and I believe he is a mystery to himself.

W. T. Sherman, in Warren W. Hassler Jnr, *Commanders of the Army of the Potomac*, 1957

And if asked what state he hails from,
This our sole reply shall be,
'From near Appomattox Court-house,
With its famous apple-tree.'

Charles Graham Halpine, 'A Bumper To Grant', 1869

How history repeats itself
You'll say when you remember Grant,
Who, in his boyhood days, once sought
Throughout the lexicon for 'can't'.

Harriet Prescott Spofford, 'Grant', 1871

How those old Greeks, indeed, would have seized on him! A mere plain man – no art, no poetry – only practical sense, ability to do, or try his best to do, what devolv'd upon him. A common trader, money-maker, tanner, farmer of Illinois – general for the republic, in its terrific struggle with itself, in the war of attempted secession – President following, (a task of peace, more difficult than the war itself) – nothing heroic, as the authorities put it – and yet the greatest hero. The gods, the destinies, seem to have concentrated upon him.

Walt Whitman, *Specimen Days*, 1882

Grant was five feet eight inches and slightly stooped. He had cold blue eyes and a big jaw hidden behind a scrubby, messy light brown beard which went well with his scrubby, messy uniform.

Herbert Agar, in Lord Longford, *Abraham Lincoln*, 1974

His was the heavy hand, and his
The service of the despot blade;
His the soft answer that allayed
War's giant animosities.

Ambrose Bierce, 'The Death of Grant', 1892

The iron shackles which Lincoln declared should be loosed from the limbs and souls of the black slaves, Grant, with his matchless army, melted and destroyed in the burning glories of the war.

William McKinley, speech on Grant's birthday, 1893

I always liked the way Grant said he knew what the other generals would do because after all they had been to school at West Point together and the Mexican War together and the others acted like generals but he acted like he knew just what the generals opposite him would do because that one had always been like that at West Point and after all what can anybody change to, they have to be what they are and so Grant always knew what to do.

Gertrude Stein, *Everybody's Autobiography*, 1937

The greatest general of the North was U.S. Grant, who is not to be confused with U.S. Mail or U.S. Steel. In a picture of the Northern generals, all of whom had identical untidy black whiskers, he is usually the one in the center with his coat unbuttoned.

Richard Armour, *It All Started With Columbus*, 1961

Nathanael GREENE, 1742–86

There are few generals that have run oftener, or more lustily than I have done. But I have taken care not to run too far, and commonly have run as fast forward as backward, to convince the Enemy that we were like a Crab, that could run either way.

On himself, to Henry Knox, 18th July 1781

Sir Richard GRENVILLE, 1542–91

And the sun went down, and the stars came out far over the summer sea,
But never a moment ceased the fight of the one and the fifty-three,
Ship after ship, the whole night long, their high-built galleons came,
Ship after ship, the whole night long, with her battle-thunder and flame;
Ship after ship, the whole night long, drew back with her dead and her shame.
For some were sunk and many were shatter'd, and so could fight us no more –
God of battles, was ever a battle like this in the world before?

For he said, 'Fight on! Fight on!'
Tho' his vessel was all but a wreck;
And it chanced that, when half of the short summer night was gone,
With a grisly wound to be drest he had left the deck,
But a bullet struck him that was dressing it suddenly dead,
And himself he was wounded again in the side and the head,
And he said, 'Fight on! Fight on!'

Alfred Tennyson, 'The Revenge', 1880

GUSTAVUS ADOLPHUS II, King of Sweden, 1594–1632

I recognize no one above me, except God and the sword of the conqueror.

On himself, attributed, *c.* 1631

Consider the great Gustavus Adolphus! In eighteen months he won one battle, lost a second, and was killed in the third. His fame was won at a bargain price!

Napoleon Bonaparte, Letter to Gaspar Gourgaud, 1818

The first modern army that could not have been defeated by Alexander the Great was probably the army of Gustavus Adolphus.

Colonel T. N. Depuy, in Gwynne Dyer, *War*, 1986

His main contribution to his art was that he was the first general during the modern age who realized that mobility is founded upon discipline, and discipline upon efficient administration and leadership.

J. F. C. Fuller, *The Decisive Battles of the Western World*, 1954–56

Douglas HAIG, Earl, 1861–1928

He was devoid of the gift of intelligible and coherent expression.

David Lloyd George, *War Memoirs*, 1936

Brilliant to the top of his army boots.

David Lloyd George, attributed

It is indeed strange that the man whose stubbornness in the offensive had all but ruined us on the Somme should from August 1918 onwards have become the driving force of the Allied armies. Yet this was so and it must stand to his credit, for no man can deny that during the last hundred days of the war he fitted events as a hand fitted a glove.

J. F. C. Fuller, *Memoirs of an Unconventional Soldier*, 1931

He might be, he surely was, unequal to the prodigious scale of events; but no one else was discerned as his equal or his better.

Winston Churchill, quoted in John Terraine, *The Western Front*, 1954

Haig had a first-rate General Staff mind.

Lord Haldane, *An Autobiography*, 1929

His war diary is a self-revealing document: frank, truthful, egotistical, self-confident and malicious. His spear knew no brother.

Max Beaverbrook, *Men of Power*, 1956

With the publication of his Private Papers in 1952, he committed suicide twenty-five years after his death.

Max Beaverbrook, *Men of Power*, 1956

Now Haig had immense influence at the Palace. The King relied upon him. Without doubt, he was the Keeper of the Palace Gates.

Max Beaverbrook, *Men of Power*, 1956

We may not like the psychological basis of Haig's imperturbability. We may condemn the system that moulded him. But it could not have been a 'small' man who bore that massive responsibility, and worked out his behaviour by the creed of a world in whose destruction he himself was taking, unwittingly, a major part.

John Terraine, in *New Statesman and Nation*, 1952

His was the only army of the great nations at war which did not break.

Sir John Kennedy, in *The Scotsman*, 15th August 1959

Haig failed perhaps to see that a dead man cannot advance, and that to replace him is only to provide another corpse.

E. K. G. Sixsmith, *British Generalship in the Twentieth Century*, 1970

From beginning to end his handling of Third Ypres betokened an obstinacy of statuesque proportions.

Norman F. Dixon, *On the Psychology of Military Incompetence*, 1976

In World War I Douglas Haig butchered the flower of British youth in the Somme and Flanders without winning a single victory.

William Manchester, *American Caesar: Douglas MacArthur 1880–1964*, 1979

Nathan HALE, 1755–76

I only regret that I have had but one life to lose for my country.

On himself, before being executed as a spy, 22nd September 1776

Henry Wager HALLECK, 1815–72

Originates nothing, anticipates nothing, takes no responsibility, plans nothing, suggests nothing, is good for nothing.

Gideon Welles, diary entry, 1862

HANNIBAL, 247–183 BC

There was a story widely current that when, after bringing the African war to a close, [Hamilcar] was offering sacrifices before transporting his army to Spain, the boy Hannibal, nine years old, was coaxing his father to take him with him, and his father led him up to the altar and made him swear with his hand laid on the victim that as soon as he possibly could he would show himself the enemy of Rome.

Livy, *The History of Rome*, from 29 BC: Bk XXI

No sooner had Hannibal landed in Spain than he became a favourite with the whole army. The veterans thought they saw Hamilcar restored to them as he was in his youth; they saw the same determined expression, the same piercing eyes, the same cast of features. He soon showed, however, that it was not his father's memory that helped him most to win the affections of the army. Never was there a character more capable of the two tasks so opposed to each other of commanding and obeying; you could not easily make out whether the army or its general were more attached to him. Whenever courage and resolution were needed Hasdrubal never cared to entrust the command to anyone else; and there was no leader in whom the soldiers placed more confidence or under whom they showed more daring. He was fearless in exposing himself to danger and perfectly self-possessed in the presence of danger. No amount of exertion could cause him either bodily or mental fatigue; he was equally indifferent to heat and cold; his eating and drinking were measured by the needs of nature, not by appetite; his hours of sleep were not determined by day or night, whatever time was not taken up with active duties was given to sleep and rest, but that rest was not wooed on a soft couch or in silence, men often saw him lying on the ground amongst the sentinels and outposts, wrapped in his military cloak. His dress was in no way superior to that of his comrades; what did make him conspicuous were his arms and his horses. He was by far the foremost both of the cavalry and the infantry, the first to enter the fight and the last to leave the field.

Livy, *The History of Rome*, from 29 BC: Bk XXI

Hannibal knew how to gain a victory, but not how to use one.

Plutarch, *Lives*: *c.* AD 100

By many degrees, the greatest soldier on record.

Duke of Wellington, attributed

[See also: Scipio Africanus, pp. 455–56]

Ernest Miller HEMINGWAY, 1899–1961

During this epoch I was addressed by the guerilla force as 'Captain'. This is a very low rank to have at the age of forty-five years, and so, in the presence of strangers, they would address me, usually, as 'Colonel'. But they were a little upset and worried by my very low rank, and one of them, whose trade for the past year had been receiving mines and blowing up German ammunition trucks and staff cars, asked confidentially, 'My Captain, how is it that with your age and your undoubted long years of service and your obvious wounds (caused by hitting a static water tank in London) you are still a captain?'

'Young man,' I told him, 'I have not been able to advance in rank due to the fact that I cannot read or write.'

On himself, in *Collier's*, 30th September 1944

HENRY I of England, 1068–1135

The king praises no one whom he has not resolved to ruin.

Bishop Blouet, in Henry of Huntingdon's *History of England*, 1154

HENRY V of England, 1387–1422

Owre kyng went forth to Normandy
With grace and myyt of chivalry;
The God for hym wrouyt marvelously . . .

Anonymous ballad, in *Percy's Reliques of Ancient English Poetry*, 1765

HEPHAESTION, late 4th century BC

Alexander's grief for him exceeded all reasonable measure. He ordered the manes of all the horses and mules to be cut off in sign of mourning, he struck off the battlements of all the neighbouring cities, crucified the unhappy physician, and would not permit the flute or any other musical instrument to be played throughout his camp, until a response came from the oracle of Ammon bidding him honour Hephaestion and offer sacrifice to him as to a hero. To assuage his grief he took to war, and found consolation in fighting and man-hunting. He conquered the tribe called Kossaei, and slew their entire male population, which passed for an acceptable offering to the manes of Hephaestion.

Plutarch, *Lives: Alexander*, *c.* 110

James Butler HICKOK ('Wild Bill'), 1837–76

He is said never to have killed a man except in self-defense, but he was defending himself almost constantly.

Richard Armour, *It All Started With Columbus*, 1961

Paul von HINDENBURG, 1847–1934

Here the General slept before the battle of Tannenberg; here also the General slept after the battle; and between you and I, during the battle too.

Max Hoffman, attributed

. . . The wooden titan.

A. J. P. Taylor, *The First World War*, 1963

Adolf HITLER, 1899–1945

Who says I am not under the special protection of God?

On himself, attributed, after an attempt on his life in July 1944

I thank heaven for a man like Adolf Hitler, who built a front line of defence against the anti-Christ of Communism.

Frank Buchman, in *New York World-Telegram*, 25th August 1936

We're going to string old Hitler
From the very highest bough
Of the biggest aspidistra in the world.

Gracie Fields, 'The Biggest Aspidistra' (song)

You do your worst, and we will do our best.

Winston Churchill, speaking at the Civil Defence Services' Luncheon, 14th July 1941

I have only one purpose, the destruction of Hitler, and my life is much simplified thereby. If Hitler invaded Hell I would make at least a favourable reference to the Devil in the House of Commons.

Winston Churchill, *The Second World War*, 1948–54

Hitler was a man who usually could no more break away from a preconceived idea than Joan of Arc could abandon her angelic voices.

J. F. C. Fuller, *The Decisive Battles of the Western World*, 1954–56

The people Hitler never understood, and whose actions continued to exasperate him until the end of his life, were the British.

Alan Bullock, *Hitler*, 1971

In politics, as in grammar, one should be able to tell substantives from adjectives. Hitler was a substantive; Mussolini only an adjective. Hitler was a nuisance; Mussolini was bloody. Together, a bloody nuisance.

Salvador de Madariaga, attributed

There he sat, a voluntary prisoner with his view of the Untersberg where, legend has it, Emperor Charlemagne still sleeps, but will one day arise to restore the past glory of the German Empire. Hitler naturally appropriated this legend for himself: 'You see the Untersberg over there. It is no accident that I have my residence opposite it.'

Albert Speer, *Inside the Third Reich*, 1969

Amateurishness was one of Hitler's dominant traits. He had never learned a profession and basically had always remained an outsider to all fields of endeavour. Like many self-taught people, he had no idea what real specialized knowledge meant. Without any sense of the complexities of any great task, he boldly assumed one function after another. Unburdened by standard ideas, his quick intelligence sometimes conceived unusual measures which a specialist would not have hit on at all. The victories of the early years of the war can literally be attributed to Hitler's ignorance of the rules of the game and his layman's delight in decision-making. Since the opposing side was trained to apply rules which Hitler's self-taught, autocratic mind did not know and did not use, he achieved surprises. These audacities, coupled with military superiority, were the basis of his early successes. But as soon as setbacks occurred he suffered shipwreck, like most untrained people. Then his ignorance of the rules of the game was revealed as another kind of incompetence, then his defects were no longer strengths. The greater the failures became, the more obstinately his incurable amateurishness came to the fore. The tendency to wild decisions had long been his forte; now it speeded his downfall.

Albert Speer, *Inside the Third Reich*, 1969

A racing tipster who only reached Hitler's level of accuracy would not do well for his clients.

A. J. P. Taylor, *The Origins of the Second World War*, 1961

Hitler's achievements as supreme commander in the Second World War were inferior to his achievements as an ordinary soldier in the First.

J. Strawson, *Hitler As Military Commander*, 1971

HO CHI MINH, 1890–1969

Ho Chi Minh himself, according to rumor, is in a safe place in the country; that is why he has not been available to recent visitors to Hanoi. Imagination situates him in a cavern, like Frederick Barbarossa, waiting for his country's need to summon him back. In fact, on his return to what was then Indochina, in 1940, and again at the end of World War II, he *was* living in a cave beside a mountain brook, at Pac Bo, near the Chinese border. In the Musuem of the Revolution, you are shown photographs of the cave, and his few simple possessions, relics of the hegira, are on exhibit, the most touching being his 'suitcase', a small flat reed basket; he traveled light. With his many changes of name, which seem to signify so many protean incarnations, he is a legendary figure, a fitting place spirit or *genius loci*. The whole saga now being enacted of the dispersal bears his imprint: *mobility*, *simplicity*, *privation*, resourcefulness. The Vietnamese Revolution has recovered its lyricism by returning to its primal myth of Ho's cave; the bombers furnished the inspiration.

Mary McCarthy, *Hanoi*, 1968

HORATIUS COCLES, 6th century BC

On the appearance of the enemy the country people fled into the City as best they could. The weak places in the defences were occupied by military posts; elsewhere the walls and the Tiber were deemed sufficient protection. The enemy would have forced their way over the Sublician bridge had it not been for one man, Horatius Cocles. The good fortune of Rome provided him as her bulwark on that memorable day. He happened to be on guard at the bridge when he saw the Janiculum taken by a sudden assault and the enemy rushing down from it to the river, whilst his own men, a panic-stricken mob, were deserting their posts and throwing away their arms. He reproached them one after another for their cowardice, tried to stop them, appealed to them in heaven's name to stand, declared that it was in vain for them to seek safety in flight while leaving the bridge open behind them, there would very soon be more of the enemy on the Palatine and the Capitol than there were on the Janiculum. So he shouted to them to break down the bridge by sword or fire, or by whatever means they could, he would meet the enemies' attack so far as one man could keep them at bay. He advanced to the head of the bridge. Amongst the fugitives, whose backs alone were visible to the enemy, he was conspicuous as he fronted them armed for fight at close quarters. The enemy were astounded at his preternatural courage. Two men were kept by a sense of shame from deserting him – Sp. Lartius and T. Herminius – both of them men of high birth and renowned courage. With them he sustained the first tempestuous shock and wild confused onset, for a brief interval. Then, whilst only a small portion of the bridge remained and those who were cutting it down called upon them to retire, he insisted upon these, too, retiring. Looking round with eyes dark with menace upon the Etruscan chiefs, he challenged them to single combat, and reproached them all with being slaves of tyrant kings, and whilst unmindful of their own liberty coming to attack that of others. For some time they hesitated, each looking round upon the others to begin. At length shame roused them to action, and raising a shout they hurled their javelins from all sides on their solitary foe. He caught them on his outstretched shield, and with unshaken resolution kept his place on the bridge with firmly planted foot. They were just attempting to dislodge him with a charge when the crash of the broken bridge and the shout which the Romans raised at seeing the work completed stayed the attack by filling them with sudden panic. Then Cocles said, 'Tiberius, holy father, I pray thee to receive into thy propitious stream these arms and this thy warrior.' So, fully armed, he leaped into the Tiber, and though many missiles fell over him he swam across in safety to his friends: an act of daring more famous than credible with posterity.

Livy, *The History of Rome*, from 29 BC: Bk I

Charles, Lord HOWARD OF EFFINGHAM, Earl of Nottingham, 1536–1624

Certainly he that will happily perform a fight at sea must be skilful in making choice of vessels to fight in: he must believe that there is more belonging to a good man of war, upon the waters, than great daring; and must know, that there is a great deal of difference between fighting loose or at large and grappling. The guns of a slow ship pierce as well, and make as great holes, as those in a swift. To clap ships together, without consideration, belongs rather to a madman than to a man of war; for by such an ignorant bravery was Peter Strossie lost at the Azores, when he fought against the Marquis of Santa Cruz. In like sort had the Lord Charles Howard, Admiral of England, been lost in the year 1588, if he had not been better advised, than a great many malignant fools were, that found fault with his demeanour.

Sir Walter Raleigh, *Historie of the World*, 1614

Richard, Earl HOWE, 1726–99

Admiral Lord Howe, when a captain, was once hastily awakened in the middle of the night by the lieutenant of the watch, who informed him with great agitation, that the ship was on fire near the magazine. 'If that be the case,' said he, rising leisurely to put on his clothes, 'we shall soon hear a farther report in the matter.'

The Percy Anecdotes, 1823

ISABELLA I of Spain, 1451–1504

The queen, seeing that the majority of her gentle men rode mules and when it was necessary to arm and ride on horseback they were the least dexterous in the world, considering that there was a daily expectation of war with the French or the Moors or against both of them at the same time, ordered that no-one, however great he was, unless he was a priest or ecclesiastic, should ride a mule but a horse and that the horses should stand fifteen hands or more, in order to be better suited to war, and she even forced her husband, the king, to do this and ordered that those living on the borders of France should ride in our fashion and those who were neighbours of the Moors should ride short-stirruped.

Antoine de Lalaing, *c.* 1501, in L. P. Gachard, *Collection des voyages des souverains des Pays-Bas*, 1876

'Captain' JACK, *c.* 1835–73

I am but one man. I am the voice of my people. Whatever their hearts are, that I talk. I want no more war. You deny me the right of the white man. My skin is red; my heart is a white man's heart; but I am a Modoc. I am not afraid to die. I will not fall on the rocks. When I die, my enemies will be under me. Your soldiers began on me when I was asleep on Lost River. They drove us to these rocks, like a wounded deer.

On himself, in Dee Brown, *Bury My Heart at Wounded Knee*, 1970

Thomas Jonathan JACKSON, ('Stonewall'), 1824–63

There is Jackson, standing like a stone wall. Let us determine to die here, and we will conquer.

Brigadier General Bernard Bee, addressing his troops at the first Battle of Bull Run, 21st July 1862

I never saw one of Jackson's couriers approach without expecting an order to assault the North Pole.

Richard S. Ewell, during the campaign of 1862

Such an executive officer the sun never shone on. I have but to show him my design, and I know that if it can be done it will be done. No need for me to send for or watch him. Straight as the needle to the pole he advances to the execution of my purpose.

Robert E. Lee, in G. F. R. Henderson, *Stonewall Jackson and the American Civil War*, 1898

You are better off than I am, for while you have lost your left, I have lost my right arm.

Robert E. Lee, note to Jackson lying mortally wounded after Chancellorsville, 4th May 1863

Stonewall Jackson, wrapped in his beard and his silence.

Stephen Vincent Benét, *John Brown's Body*, 1928

John Rushworth, Earl JELLICOE, 1859–1935

Jellicoe was the only man on either side who could lose the [First World] war in an afternoon.

Winston Churchill, *The World Crisis*, 1923–29

He fought to make a German victory impossible rather than a British victory certain.

Cyril Falls, *The First World War*, 1960

Sailor with a flawed cutlass.

Correlli Barnett, *The Swordbearers*, 1963

Sir John JERVIS, Earl St VINCENT, 1735–1823

Where I would take a penknife, Lord St Vincent takes a hatchet.

Lord Nelson, attributed

My Old Oak.

George IV, attributed

St JOAN OF ARC (Jeanne d'Arc), 1412–31

. . . The Bellona of the European commonwealth of states . . .

E. S. Creasy, *The Fifteen Decisive Battles of the World*, 1851

Joan appeared at the camp of Blois clad in a new suit of brilliant white armour, mounted on a stately black war-horse, and with a lance in her right hand, which she had learned to wield with skill and grace. Her head was unhelmeted, so that all could behold her fair and expressive features, her deep-set and earnest eyes, and her long black hair, which was parted across her forehead, and bound by a ribbon behind her back. She wore at her side a small battle-axe, and the consecrated sword, marked on the blade with five crosses, which had at her bidding been taken for her from the shrine of St Catherine at Fierbois. A page carried her banner, which she had caused to be made and embroidered, as her Voices enjoined. It was white satin, strewn with fleur-de-lis; and on it were the words JHESUS MARIA, and the representation of the Saviour in his Glory. Joan afterwards generally bore her banner herself in battle; she said that though she loved her sword much, she loved her banner forty times as much; and she loved to carry it because it could not kill any one.

E. S. Creasy, *The Fifteen Decisive Battles of the World*, 1851

Joseph-Jacques-Césaire JOFFRE, 1852–1931

To sum up Joffre, it might be said that the war was very nearly lost with him, but that it would almost certainly have been lost without him.

Alistair Horne, *The Price of Glory*, 1962

Joffre himself was a skilful politician, though hardly an inspired general. He flamboyantly dismissed some of his subordinates, and listened patiently to visiting ministers. Moreover he invented a brilliant justification for his own existence: he alone had the prestige and influence to dominate France's allies, particularly to keep the British faithful to the Western Front. His critics accepted this argument. In this curious way, the French, who had little faith in Joffre, kept him as Commander-in-Chief because they thought that this would please the Allies; and the Allies, who had no great faith in Joffre, conformed to his wishes because they thought that this would please the French.

A. J. P. Taylor, *The First World War*, 1963

Lyndon Baines JOHNSON, 1908–73

When someone asked him later why he had not involved the public more in the question of Vietnam, he was told: 'If you have a mother-in-law with only one eye and she has it in the centre of her forehead, you don't keep her in the living-room.'

D. Halberstram, *The Best and the Brightest*, 1972

'If he had "lost" Vietnam,' he told Doris Kearns years later, 'there would be Robert Kennedy out in front leading the fight against me, telling everybody that I had betrayed John Kennedy's commitment to South Vietnam. That I had let a democracy fall into the hands of the Communists. That I was a coward. An unmanly man. A man without a spine. Oh, I could see it coming all right. Every night when I fell asleep I would see myself tied to the ground in the middle of a long, open space. In the distance I could hear the voices of thousands of people. They were all shouting and running toward me: "Coward! Traitor! Weakling!".'

Stanley Karnow, *Vietnam: A History*, 1983

John Paul JONES, 1747–92

I have not drawn my sword in our glorious cause for hire, but in support of the dignity of human nature and the divine feelings of philanthropy. I hoisted with my own hands the flag of freedom the first time it was displayed on board the *Alfred* in the Delaware; and I have attended it ever since with veneration on the ocean.

On himself, in Lincoln Lorenz, *John Paul Jones: Fighter for Freedom and Glory*

'Out booms! Out booms!' our skipper cried,
'Out booms and give her sheet!'
And the swiftest keel that was ever launched
Shot ahead of the British fleet.
And amidst a thundering shower of shot,
With stunsails hoisting away,
Down the North Channel Paul Jones did steer
Just at the break of day.

Anonymous, *c.* 1782

JULIAN (The 'Apostate': Falavius Claudius Julianus), 332–63

The retired scholastic education of Julian, in which he had been more conversant with books than with arms, with the dead than with the living, left him in profound ignorance of the arts of war and government; and when he awkwardly repeated some military exercise which it was necessary for him to learn, he exclaimed with a sigh, 'O Plato, Plato, what a task for a philosopher!' Yet even this speculative philosophy, which men of business are too apt to despise, had filled the mind of Julian with the noblest precepts, and the most shining examples; had animated him with the love of virtue, the desire of fame, and the contempt of death. The habits of temperance recommended in the schools, are still more essential in the severe discipline of a camp.

Edward Gibbon, *The History Of The Decline And Fall Of The Roman Empire*, 1776–88, xix

The remains of Julian were interred at Tarsus in Cilicia; but his stately tomb, which arose in that city, on the banks of the cold and limpid Cydnus, was displeasing to the faithful friends, who loved and revered the memory of that extraordinary man. The philosopher expressed a very reasonable wish, that the disciple of Plato might have reposed amidst the groves of the academy; while the soldier exclaimed in bolder accents, that the ashes of Julian should have been mingled with those of Caesar, in the field of Mars, and among the ancient monuments of Roman virtue. The history of princes does not very frequently renew the example of a similar competition.

Edward Gibbon, *The History Of The Decline And Fall Of The Roman Empire*, 1776–88: xxiv

John Fitzgerald KENNEDY, 1917–63

It was involuntary. They sank my boat.

On himself, when asked how he became a war hero, in Arthur M. Schlesinger, *A Thousand Days*, 1965

Characteristically, the world at large believes that if JFK were alive there would be no war in Vietnam. The myth-makers have obscured the fact that it was JFK who began our active participation in the war when, in 1961, he added to the six hundred American observers the first of a gradual build-up of American troops, which reached twenty thousand at the time of his assassination. And there is no evidence that he would not have persisted in that war, for, as he said to a friend shortly before he died, 'I have to go all the way with this one.' He could not suffer a second Cuba and hope to maintain the appearance of Defender of the Free World at the ballot box in 1964.

Gore Vidal, 'The Holy Family', in *Esquire*, April 1967

Horatio Herbert KITCHENER, Earl of Khartoum and Broome, 1850–1916

You could imagine the character just the same as if all the externals were different. He has no age but the prime of life, no body but one to carry his mind, no face but one to keep his brain behind. The brain and the will are the essence and the whole of the man – a brain and a will so perfect in their workings that, in the face of extremest difficulty, they never seem to know what struggle is. You cannot imagine the Sirdar otherwise than as seeing the right thing to do and doing it. His precision is so inhumanly unerring, he is more like a machine than a man. You feel that he ought to be patented and shown with pride at the Paris International Exhibition. British Empire: Exhibit No. 1, *hors concours*, the Sudan Machine.

George Warrington Steevens, *With Kitchener to Khartoum*, 1898

Lord K, is playing hell with its lid off at the War Office – What the papers call 'standing no nonsense' but which often means 'listening to no sense'.

Lady Jean Hamilton, diary entry, 12th August 1914

This molten mass of devouring energy.

Lord Curzon, in Norman F. Dixon, *On the Psychology of Military Incompetence*, 1976

The great armies that he called into being are his living monument, and no nobler monument has been raised to man.

Obituary in *The Times*, 1916

The great poster.

Margot Asquith, in A. J. P. Taylor, *English History 1914–45*, 1965

Henry KNOX, 1750–1806

The resources of his genius supplied the deficit of means.

George Washington, to the Continental Congress after the Battle of Yorktown, 1781

James LAWRENCE, 1781–1813

He had no more dodge in him than the mainmast.

Stephen Decatur, attributed comment upon learning of Lawrence's death in the action between USS *Chesapeake* and HMS *Shannon*.

T(homas) E(dward) LAWRENCE ('of Arabia'), 1888–1935

. . . I drew these tides of men into my hands
And wrote my will across the sky in stars.

On himself, dedicatory verses to *The Seven Pillars of Wisdom*, 1926

I was an Irish nobody. I did something. It was a failure. And I became an Irish nobody again.

On himself, in Percy Wyndham Lewis, *Blasting and Bombadiering*, 1937

A callow and terrified Marbot, placed in command of a sardonic Napoleon at Austerlitz and Jena, would have felt much as your superiors must in command of Lawrence the great.

George Bernard Shaw, Letter to Lawrence, 17th December 1922

Lawrence can bear comparison with Marlborough or Napoleon in that vital faculty of generalship, the power of grasping instantly the picture of the ground and situation, of relating the one to the other, and the local to the general. Indeed there is much to suggest that his topographical and geographical sense was more remarkable than theirs.

B. H. Liddell Hart, *T. E. Lawrence*, 1934

. . . He had none of a gentleman's instincts, strutting about Peace Conferences in Arab dress.

Henry ('Chips') Channon, diary, 25th May 1935

Lawrence licentiate to dream and to dare.

Sir Ronald Storrs, *Orientations*, 1937

There are those who have tried to dismiss his story with a flourish of the Union Jack, a psychoanalytical catchword or a sneer; it should move our deepest admiration and pity. Like Shelley and like Baudelaire, it may be said of him that he suffered, in his own person, the neurotic ills of an entire generation.

Christopher Isherwood, *Exhumations*, 1966

Robert Edward LEE, 1807–70

Strike the tent!

Last words, 12th October 1870

Lee is the only man I know whom I would follow blindfold.

'Stonewall' Jackson, in a Letter of May 1862

An angel's heart, an angel's mouth,
Not Homer's, could alone for me
Hymn well the great Confederate South,
Virginia first, and Lee!

Philip Stanhope Worsley, verse inscribed in a copy of his translation of Homer sent to Lee in January 1864

His Virginia was to him the world . . . He stood at the front porch battling with the flames whilst the kitchen and the house were burning, sure in the end to consume the whole.

W. T. Sherman, in the *North American*, March 1887

He was a foe without hate, a friend without treachery, a soldier without cruelty, and a victim without murmuring. He was a public officer without vices, a private citizen without wrong, a neighbour without hypocrisy, and a man without guilt. He was Caesar without his ambition, Frederick without his tyranny, Napoleon without his selfishness and Washington without his reward.

Benjamin H. Hill, in Robert Debs Heinl Jr, *The Dictionary of Military and Naval Quotations*, 1966

Here was a man who failed grandly, a man who said that 'human virtue should be equal to human calamity', and showed that it could be equal to it, and so, without pretense, without display, without self-consciousness, left an example that future Americans may study with profit as long as there is an America.

Gamaliel Bradford, in Margaret Sanborn, *Robert E. Lee: The Complete Man*

If I were on my deathbed, and the President should tell me that a great battle was to be fought for the liberty or slavery of the country, and asked my judgement as to the ability of a commander, I would say with my dying breath, let it be Robert E. Lee.

General Winfield Scott, in Burke Davis, *They Called Him Stonewall*, 1954

Sir Basil Henry LIDDELL HART, 1895–1970

If a soldier advocates any new idea of real importance he builds up such a wall of obstruction – compounded by resentment, suspicion and inertia – that the idea only succeeds at the sacrifice of himself: as the wall finally yields to the pressure of the new idea it falls and crushes him.

On himself, *Memoirs*, 1965

Equally unambiguous was the treatment meted out to Liddell Hart, a man described by the press as 'the most important military thinker of the age of mechanization in any country'. Over the years Liddell Hart produced a number of articles and books on mechanization, on new infantry tactics, and on the strategic and tactical use of armour. His efforts encountered extreme hostility and resistance from the British General Staff. When he submitted his essay on 'Mechanization of the Army' for a military competition, it was rejected in favour of an essay on 'Limitations of the Tank'. The judges were a field-marshal, a general and a colonel.

Unfortunately Liddell Hart's entry was not entirely lost to view. Along with other products of his pen, it was enthusiastically studied by Hitler's Panzer General, Guderian, and became required reading for the German General Staff.

Norman F. Dixon, *On the Psychology of Military Incompetence*, 1976

David, Earl LLOYD GEORGE of Dwyfor, 1863–1945

With so much dishonour, you might have brought us a little peace.

Lord Hugh Cecil, commenting on Lloyd George's Irish Policy, 1916, in David Cecil, *The Cecils of Hatfield House*, 1973

LOUIS XIV of France, 1638–1715

I have loved war too well.

On his deathbed, attributed

LYSANDER of Sparta, fl. 407 BC

He indeed laughed at those who said that the race of Herakles ought not to make war by strategem, saying, 'Where the lion's skin will not protect us, we must sew the fox's skin to it.'

Plutarch, *Lives: Lysander*, *c.* 110

In all the other cities, too, an indiscriminate massacre of the popular party took place, as Lysander not only put to death his own personal enemies, but also those persons against whom any of his friends in each city might happen to have a grudge. Wherefore Eteokles the Lacedaemonian was thought to have spoken well, when he said that 'Greece could not have borne two Lysanders.'

Plutarch, *Lives: Lysander*, *c.* AD 110

Douglas MacARTHUR, 1880–1964

If the historian of the future should deem my service worthy of some slight notice, it would be my hope that he mention me not as commander engaged in campaigns and battles, even though victorious in American arms, but rather as one whose sacred duty it became, once the guns were silenced, to carry to the land of our vanquished foe the solace and hope and faith of Christian morals.

On himself, Address to a Joint Section of Congress, 19th April 1951

Today marks my final roll call with you, but I want you to know that when I cross the river my last conscious thoughts will be of The Corps, and The Corps, and The Corps.

On himself, at the US Military Academy at West Point, 12th May 1962

My first recollection is that of a bugle call.

On himself, quoted in the New York *Herald Tribune*, 6th April 1964

Let him go, let him go, we are the braver,
Stain his hands with our blood, dye them forever.
Recall, oh ye kinsmen, how he left us to die,
Starved and insulted by his infamous lie;
How he seduced us with boasts of defense;
How he traduced us with plans of offense.
When his publicity chairman presides,
Vaunts his fame as high as the Bay of Fundy tides –
Recollect bonus boys gassed out by him,

Remember Bataan boys sacrificed for him.
Try him, Tribunal of Public Opinion,
Brothers, condemn him through our dominion;
Then when he stands before Judges Olympian,
Quakes at his final court-martial: oblivion.

'Aquill Penn', 'The Lost Leader', written in a Japanese POW camp, June 1943

I fired him because he wouldn't respect the authority of the President. That's the answer to that. I didn't fire him because he was a dumb son of a bitch, although he was, but that's not against the law for generals. If it was, half to three quarters of them would be in jail.

Harry S. Truman, on MacArthur's removal from Korea, in Merle Miller, *Plain Speaking: An Oral Biography of Harry S. Truman*, 1974

Almost at the very moment yesterday that the news of General MacArthur's relief was coming over the radio at the divisional command post on the western front where I have been spending a few days, a terrific wind blew across the camp site, leveling a couple of tents. A few minutes later, a hailstorm lashed the countryside. A few hours after that, there was a driving snowstorm. Since the weather had been fairly springlike for the previous couple of weeks, the odd climatic goings on prompted one soldier to exclaim, 'Gee, do you suppose he really is God after all?'

E. J. Kahn, in *The New Yorker*, 24th April 1951

By the grace of God and a few Marines,
MacArthur returned to the Philippines.

Marine Corps song

There wasn't a dry eye on the Democratic side of the House, nor a dry seat on the Republican side.

Congressman Joseph Martin, on MacArthur's farewell address to Congress, April 1951

We heard God speak here today. God in the flesh, the voice of God.

Congressman Dewey Short, responding to the same speech, April 1951

It [the jockeying for position among MacArthur's subordinates] reminds me of the poker games in Shanghai . . . where the cuspidor was put on the center of the table because no one dared look away to spit.

Jay Luvaas, ed., *Dear Miss Em*, 1972

I had kept a very careful watch on MacArthur's strategy in the Pacific and the more I saw of it the more impressed I had become. The masterly way in which he had jumped from point to point leaving masses of Japanese to decay behind him had filled me with admiration, whereas any ordinary general might have eaten up penny packets of Japanese till he had such indigestion that he could proceed no further.

Lord Alanbrooke, in Arthur Bryant, *Triumph of the West*, 1959

Oh yes, I studied dramatics under him for twelve years.

Dwight Eisenhower, in Quentin Reynolds, *By Quentin Reynolds*, 1964

'In reply to your question with reference to the integration of the Inchon Campaign and Wolfe's Quebec operation,' General MacArthur wrote to my father in 1959, 'so much time has elapsed since then that I would hesitate to attempt a categorical reply. That I have read and studied your father's account in *Great Captains Unveiled* is unquestionable . . . The most indispensable attribute of the great Captain is imagination.' Wolfe, we know, was a well read general; 'I had it from Xenophon,' he explained at Louisbourg – while Xenophon had discussed matters with Socrates, who gave him the benefit of his own military experience.

Adrian Liddell Hart, Introduction to B. H. Liddell Hart, *The Sword and the Pen*, 1978

Alfred Thayer MAHAN, 1840–1914

It is not the business of a naval officer to write books.

Rear Admiral F. H. Ramsay, endorsing an unfavourable fitness report, 1893

Mahan, the maritime Clausewitz, the Schlieffen of the sea.

Barbara W. Tuchman, *The Guns of August*, 1962

Marcus Claudius MARCELLUS, *c* 268–208 BC

Hannibal himself said that he feared Fabius as a schoolmaster, but regarded Marcellus as an antagonist, for the former prevented him doing any mischief, while the latter might make him suffer some.

Plutarch, *Lives: Marcellus*, *c.* 110

Gaius MARIUS, *c.* 157–96 BC

. . . The consul saw to everything in person, as though he had no subordinates in charge, going round to every section of the army and distributing praise and reprimands as they were deserved. Always fully armed and on the alert himself, he compelled the soldiers to follow his example. The precautions taken on the march were observed in the fortifications of each camp. Legionary cohorts were detailed to keep watch at the gates, auxiliary cavalry to patrol outside, and others to mount guard on top of the rampart. Marius went the rounds in person, not because he feared that his orders might not be carried out, but because he thought the soldiers would do the work more willingly if their commander took his fair share. On this and other occasions during the war he maintained discipline by appealing to his soldiers' honour, rather than by punishment. Many said he did this to increase his popularity. Others suggested that, accustomed as he was since childhood to a laborious life, he actually took pleasure in what other people call hardships. Be that as it may, he could not, by enforcing the most rigorous discipline, have served the state with more success or with more distinction.

Sallust, *The Jugurthine War*, 42 BC

John Churchill, Duke of MARLBOROUGH, 1650–1722

Dost thou recall to mind with joy, or grief,
Great Marlborough's actions, that immortal chief,
Whose slightest trophy rais'd in each campaign,
More than suffic'd to signalize a reign?

William Congreve, 'A Letter to Lord Viscount Cobham', *c.* 1705

'Twas then great Marlbro's mighty soul was prov'd,
That in the shock of charging hosts unmov'd,
Amidst confusion, horror and despair,
Examin'd all the dreadful scenes of war;
In peaceful thought the field of death survey'd,
To fainting squadrons sent the timely aid,
Inspir'd repuls'd battalions to engage,
And taught the doubtful battle where to rage.

Joseph Addison, 'The Campaign', 1704

He had to a degree above all the other generals of his time that calm courage in the midst of tumult, that serenity of soul in danger, which the English call a cool head, and it was perhaps this quality, the greatest gift of nature for command, which formerly gave the English so many advantages over the French in the plains of Cressy, Poitiers and Agincourt.

Voltaire, *Age of Louis XIV*, 1751

England's reproach and her pride: her pride for his noble achievements,
Her reproach for the wrongs he endured.

Robert Southey, *A Vision of Judgement*, 1821

And glory long has made the sages smile;
'Tis something, nothing, words, illusion, wind –
Depending more upon the historian's style
Than on the name a person leaves behind:
Troy owes to Homer what whist owes to Hoyle:
The present century was growing blind
To the great Marlborough's skill in giving knocks,
Until his late Life by Archdeacon Coxe.

Lord Byron, *Don Juan*, 1818–24: canto iii

At the siege of Nimeguen, Marlborough, then a very young man, attracted the notice of the celebrated Turenne, who from that period spoke of him by the familiar title of 'the handsome Englishman', and shortly afterwards put his spirit to the test. A lieutenant-colonel having scandalously abandoned, without resistance, a station which he was enjoined to defend to the last extremity, Turenne exclaimed, 'I will bet a supper and a dozen of claret, that my handsome Englishman will recover the post with half the number of men that the officer commanded who has lost it.' The wager was instantly accepted, and the event justified the confidence of the general; for Captain Churchill, after a short but desperate resistance, expelled the enemy and maintained the post.

The Percy Anecdotes, 1823

He is perhaps the only instance of a man of real greatness who loved money for money's sake.

J. R. Green, *A Short History of the English People*, 1874

It was Marlborough who first taught us to be proud of our standing army as a national institution, and the spirit of confidence which pervaded Wellington's army in the Peninsula, and to a still more remarkable degree shows itself now in Queen Victoria's army, may be said to have been born at Blenheim, baptized at Ramilies, and confirmed at Oudenarde.

Lord Wolseley, *Life of Marlborough*, 1894

He never rode off any field except as a victor. He quitted war invincible; and no sooner was his guiding hand withdrawn than disaster overtook the armies he had led.

Winston Churchill, *Marlborough*, 1933

In Marlborough's fashion of war-making there was emphatically no nonsense. He never wasted a man or a movement; he never executed a single manoeuvre for show; he never, either in words or deeds, indulged in gasconading. Probably no man ever had such a superhuman business as he had put on his shoulders in the the business of at once fighting half Europe and keeping the other half in fighting order.

George Saintsbury, *Life of Marlborough*, 1885

Marlborough's talents had no flaw. As a strategist he saw clearly and simply the great issues – the relationship of war and policy, the interdependence between one theatre and another, the inter-relation between sea-power and land war. He constantly outwitted his enemies, one success paving the way for the next. As an organizer, he made a nonsensical military system work. His care for his troops, his understanding of them, led to his nickname of 'Corporal John'. On the battlefield his grasp of confused tactical situations was uncannily clear and accurate: he kept cool and thought fast. To all these qualities he added unflexing will and resolution, and unflagging energy. And yet his personality remains elusive. There is none of the pungent individuality conveyed by Wellington's correspondence and conversation; none of the brisk anecdotes told about Wellington. Marlborough presented a smooth, perfect, flawless surface of ability.

Correlli Barnett, *Britain and Her Army 1509–1970*, 1970

George Catlett MARSHALL, 1880–1959

In a war unparalleled in magnitude and horror, millions of Americans gave their country outstanding service. General of the Army George C. Marshall gave it victory.

Harry S. Truman, speech, 16th November 1945

George Brinton McCLELLAN, 1826–85

If I gave McClellan all the men he asks for, they could not find room to lie down.

Abraham Lincoln, in Carl Sandburg, *Abraham Lincoln: The Prairie Years and the War Years*, 1926

My dear McClellan,
If you don't want to use the army, I should like to borrow it for a while.
Yours respectfully,
Abraham Lincoln.

Carl Sandburg, *Abraham Lincoln: The Prairie Years and the War Years*, 1926

So McClellan sent a telegram to Lincoln one day: 'Have captured two cows. What disposition should I make of them?' And Lincoln: 'Milk 'em, George.'

Carl Sandburg, *Abraham Lincoln: The Prairie Years and the War Years*, 1926

An admirable engineer, but he seems to have a special talent for the stationary engine.

Abraham Lincoln, attributed

King MINOS of Crete, *c.* 100 BC

Minos is the first to whom tradition ascribes the possession of a navy.

Thucydides, *History of the Peloponnesian Wars*, *c.* 404 BC: Bk I

Helmuth Carl Bernhard von MOLTKE, 1800–91

Moltke may be described as a general on rails, for his system of war was both direct and rigid.

J. F. C. Fuller, *The Decisive Battles of the Western World*, 1954–56

George MONCK, Duke of Albermarle, 1608–70

'Twas at his rising that our day begun;
But he the morning star to Charles our sun.
He took Rebellion rampant by the throat,
And made the canting Quaker change his note.
His hand it was that wrote, (we saw no more)
Exit Tyrannus over Lambert's Door.
Like to some subtle lightning so his words
Dissolved in their scabbards rebels' swords.
He with success the sov'reign skill hath found
To dress the weapon and so heal the wound.
George and his boys, as spirits do they say,
Only by walking scare our foes away.

Robert Wild, *Iter Boreale*, 1660

James Fitzroy Scott, Duke of MONMOUTH, 1649–85

To lure, like Monmouth, associates, and humble followers on fools' errands to their doom can find no defenders.

Winston Churchill, *Marlborough*, 1933

Bernard Law MONTGOMERY (Viscount 'of Alamein'), 1887–1979

I have several times had to resist invitations to enter the political field. I do not think that I would make a good politician. War is a pretty rough and dirty game. But politics!

On himself, *Memoirs*, 1958

I am not a bit anxious about my battles. If I am anxious I don't fight them. I wait until I'm ready.

On himself, attributed

The General was worried and very ill at ease,
He was haunted by the subject of Venereal disease;
For four and forty soldiers was the tale he had to tell
Had lain among the beets and loved not wisely but too well.
It was plain that copulation was a tonic for the bored,
But the gallant British soldier was an innocent abroad;
So 'ere he takes his pleasure with an amateur or whore,
He must learn the way from officers who've trod that path before.
No kind of doubt existed in the Major-General's head
That the men who really knew the game of love from A to Z
Were his Colonels and his Adjutants and those above the ruck,
For the higher up an officer the better he can fuck.
The Colonels and the Majors were not a bit dismayed,
They gave orders for the holding of a Unit Love Parade,
And the Adjutants by numbers showed exactly how it's done,
How not to be a casualty and still have lots of fun.
The Adjutants explained that 'capote' did not mean a cup,
That refreshment horizontal must be taken standing up.
They told the troops to work at Love according to the Rules,
And after digging in to take precautions with their tools.
Now the General is happy and perfectly at ease,
No longer is he troubled with venereal disease,
His problem solved, his soldiers clean (their badge is now a dove),
He has earned the cross of Venus, our General of Love.

Unknown member of the Royal Signal Corps, 'Mars Amatoria', 1940, after Montgomery had issued orders to arrest the spread of venereal infection.

In defeat, unbeatable; in victory, unbearable.

Winston Churchill, in Edward Marsh, *Ambrosia and Small Beer*, 1964

A general who did much with much but not much with little.

Hanson Baldwin, *Battles Lost and Won*, 1963

Montgomery had the knack of creating oases of serenity around him.

R. W. Thompson, *Montgomery the Field Marshal*, 1969

By nature a rather cold, introverted and autocratic individual (a side of him seen by many of his officers), he nevertheless had the good sense to apply a somewhat contrived bonhomie, helped out with packets of cigarettes and numerous cap badges, which undoubtedly did much to ensure high morale and group-mindedness in the troops which he commanded. To many people, whether they like him or not, it must seem totally incomprehensible that Montgomery should have been actually criticized for his quite deliberate showmanship, which probably did more for civilian and military morale than any other act by any other general since the beginning of warfare.

Norman F. Dixon, *On the Psychology of Military Incompetence*, 1976

Throughout his subsequent career, Montgomery continued to show evidence of the unremitting schoolboy in his make-up. A typical instance was the occasion in 1911 when, as battalion sports officer, he was required to organize a friendly football match between men from his regiment and sailors from a visiting German battleship. For diplomatic reasons he was given strict instructions to field a team of mediocre players. In the event, however, he confronted the Germans with the best footballers he could find. The inevitable result was a crushing and embarrassing defeat for the Germans by forty goals to nil. Montgomery's subsequent excuse was: 'I was not taking any risks with the Germans.'

Norman F. Dixon, *On the Psychology of Military Incompetence*, 1976

Sir John MOORE, 1761–1809

To him you may safely look as a most promising officer; he goes to England covered with honourable scars, and were I king of England I would administer a salve.

Sir Ralph Abercrombie, Letter to William Huskisson, 1797

Not a drum was heard, not a funeral note,
As his corpse to the rampart we hurried;
Not a soldier discharged his farewell shot
O'er the grave where our hero we buried.

We buried him darkly at dead of night,
The sods with our bayonets turning;
By the struggling moonbeam's misty light
And the lantern dimly burning.

No useless coffin enclosed his breast,
Not in sheet or in shroud we wound him;
But he lay like a warrior taking his rest,
With his martial cloak around him.

Few and short were the prayers we said,
And we spoke not a word of sorrow;
But we steadfastly gazed on the face that was dead,
And we bitterly thought of the morrow.

We thought, as we hollow'd his narrow bed,
  And smoothed down his lonely pillow,
That the foe and the stranger would tread o'er his head,
  And we far away on the billow!

Lightly they'll talk of the spirit that's gone
  And o'er his cold ashes upbraid him, –
But little he'll rock, if they let him sleep on
  In the grave where a Briton has laid him.

But half of our heavy task was done
  When the clock struck the hour for retiring:
And we heard the distant and random gun
  That the foe was sullenly firing.

Slowly and sadly we laid him down.
  From the field of his fame fresh and gory;
We carved not a line, we raised not a stone –
  But we left him alone with his glory.

Charles Wolfe, 'The Burial of Sir John Moore at Corunna', *c.* 1815

When you are a man, come to me, and I will give you a real sword, for your dear Uncle's sake.

Lady Hester Stanhope, note accompanying a gift of toys to Moore's nephew, John, 1809

His power consisted in laborious application to details, but prov'd to be greatly deficient when task'd by the command of a large Army. His Indecision and Ruinous Retreat (in which they say Thousands were sacrific'd from absolute Fatigue) produc'd everything short of a Mutiny, so that when the Men were congratulated after the Victory by their Officers, they loudly exclaimed, 'No thanks to others! Why didn't we do this before?'

Sir Thomas Lawrence, Letter to Joseph Farrington, 1809

No man, not Cromwell, not Marlborough, not Wellington, had set so strong a mark for good upon the British Army as John Moore.

Sir John Fortescue, *History of the British Army*, 1930

Benito MUSSOLINI, 1883–1945

I have tremendous admiration for Caesar. But . . . I myself belong rather to the class of Bismarcks.

On himself, in conversations with Emil Ludwig

Look at that man's eyes. You will hear more of him later.

Andrew Bonar Law, attributed, 1922

Sawdust Caesar

George Seldes, title of biography, 1932

Mussolini is the biggest bluff in Europe. If Mussolini would have me taken out and shot tomorrow I would still regard him as a bluff. The shooting would be a bluff. Get hold of a good photo of Signor Mussolini some time and study it. You will see the weakness in his mouth which forces him to scowl the famous Mussolini scowl that is imitated by every 19-year-old Fascisto in Italy. Study his past record. Study the coalition that Fascismo is between capital and labour and consider the history of past coalitions. Study his genius for clothing small ideas in big words. Study his propensity for duelling. Really brave men do not have to fight duels, and many cowards duel constantly to make themselves believe they are brave. And then look at his black shirt and his white spats. There is something wrong, even histrionically, with a man who wears white spats with a black shirt.

Ernest Hemingway, in *The Toronto Daily Star*, 27th January 1923

Sir Charles James NAPIER, 1782–1853

The hundred-gun ship has taken the little cock-boat in tow, and it will follow for ever over the ocean of time.

On himself, on being praised by Wellington, 1843

When he went into a campaign he took with him but a piece of soap and a pair of towels; he dined off a hunch of bread and a cup of water. 'A warrior,' said he, 'should not care for wine or luxury, for fine turbans or embroidered shulwars; his talwar should be bright, and never mind whether his papooshes are shiny.' Napier Singh was a lion indeed . . . But this lion, though the bravest of animals, was the most quarrelsome that ever lashed a tail and roared in a jungle.

W. M. Thackeray, *The Tale of Koompanee Jehan*, 1841

NAPOLEON BONAPARTE (Napoleon I), 1769–1821

Waterloo is cast in my teeth . . . I ought to have died in Moscow.

On himself, Letter to Gaspard Gourgaud, 1816

Had I succeeded I should have died with the reputation of the greatest man who ever lived. As it is, although I have failed, I shall be considered as an extraordinary man. I have fought fifty pitched battles, almost all of which I have won. I have framed and carried into effect a code of laws that will bear my name to the most distant posterity.

On himself, Letter to Barry O'Meara from St Helena, March 1817

. . . this horrid disturber of mankind.

Earl St Vincent, in a Letter of 1812

The bullet that is to kill me has not yet been moulded.

On himself, 1814, on being asked by the King of Spain whether he had ever been hit by a cannon-ball.

Thirteen and a half years of success turned Alexander the Great into a kind of madman. Good fortune of exactly the same duration produced the same discord in Napoleon. The only difference was that the Macedonian hero had the good fortune to die.

Stendhal, *A Life of Napoleon*, 1818

I don't care a twopenny damn what becomes of the ashes of Napoleon.
Duke of Wellington, *c.* 1821, attributed

Whose game was empires, and whose stakes were thrones,
Whose table earth – and whose dice were human bones.
Lord Byron, *The Age of Bronze*, 1823

Bonaparte I never saw; though during the Battle of Waterloo we were once, I understand, within a quarter of a mile of each other. I regret it much: for he was a most extraordinary man.
Duke of Wellington, in Samuel Rogers, *Recollections*, 1827

Although too much of a soldier among sovereigns, no one could claim better right to be a sovereign among soldiers.
Walter Scott, *Life of Napoleon*, 1827

His life was the stride of a demi-god, from battle to battle, and from victory to victory.
J. W. von Goethe, in *Conversations with Eckerman*, 11th March 1828

In my youth we used to march and counter-march all the Summer without gaining or losing a square league, and then we went into winter quarters. And now comes an ignorant, hot-headed young man who flies about from Boulogne to Ulm, and from Ulm to the middle of Moravia, and fights battles in December. The whole system of his tactics is monstrously incorrect.
An 'Old German Officer', in T. B. Macaulay, *Essays: Moore's Life of Byron*, 1831

He was sent into this world to teach generals and statesmen what they should avoid. His victories teach what may be accomplished by activity, boldness and skill; his disasters what might have been avoided by prudence.
Antoine Henri de Jomini, *Précis de l'Art de la Guerre*, 1838

On May 16th, 1796, General Bonaparte entered Milan at the head of that young army which shortly before had crossed the Bridge of Lodi and taught the world that after all these centuries Caesar and Alexander have a successor.
Stendhal, *The Charterhouse of Parma*, 1840

His orders had to be executed whatever the means of command. This habit of undertaking everything with insufficient means, this determination not to recognize any impossibilities, this boundless assurance of success, which in the beginning were the causes of our triumphs, in the end became fatal to us.
Blaise de Montesquiou Fézensac, *Souvenirs militaires de 1804 à 1814*, 1863

If utter selfishness, if the reckless sacrifice of humanity to your own interest and passions be vileness, history has no viler name.
Goldwin Scott, *Three English Statesmen*, 1867

In certain respects, Napoleon was the greatest of all soldiers. He had, to be sure, the history of other great captains to profit by; he had not to invent; he had only to improve. But he did for the military art what constitutes the greatest advance in any art, he reduced it to its most simple, perfect form.
T. A. Dodge, *Great Captains*, 1895

To husband his troops; to use them judiciously so that the enemy might be attacked at his weakest point with superior forces; to keep control of his men; even when they were scattered, much as a coachman holds the reins, so that they could be concentrated at a moment's notice; to mark down that portion of the opposing army which he aimed at destroying; to discern the critical point where defeat might be turned into rout; to surprise the enemy by the rapidity of his conceptions and operations – these are a few of the essential elements of Napoleon's military genius.

Ferdinand Foch, quoted in Robert Debs Heinl Jr, *Dictionary of Military and Naval Quotations*, 1966

Horatio, Lord NELSON, 1758–1805

I find few think as I do, but to obey orders is all perfection. What would my superiors direct, did they know what was passing under my nose? To serve my King and to destroy the French I consider as the great order of all, from which little ones spring; and if one of those little ones militate against it, I go back to obey the great order.

On himself, Letter from Palermo, March 1799

I have always been a quarter of an hour before my time, and it has made a man of me.

On himself, attributed

I never set eyes on him, for which I am both sorry and glad, for to be sure I should like to have seen him, but then, all the men in our ship who have seen him are such soft toads, they have done nothing but Blast their Eyes and cry ever since he was killed. God bless you! Chaps that fought like the Devil sit down and cry like a wench.

An unnamed sailor, in Oliver Warner, *A Portrait of Lord Nelson*, 1959

It was Nelson's maxim, that, to negotiate with effect, force should be at hand, and in a situation to act.

Robert Southey, *Life of Nelson*, 1813

Presently, calling [Captain] Hardy back, he said to him in a low voice, 'Don't throw me overboard'; and he desired that he might be buried by his parents, unless it should please the king to order otherwise. Then reverting to his private feelings: 'Take care of poor Lady Hamilton. – Kiss me, Hardy,' said he. Hardy knelt down and kissed his cheek: and Nelson said, 'Now I am satisfied. Thank God I have done my duty.'

Robert Southey, *Life of Nelson*, 1813

. . . [After the Battle of the Nile] the king granted these honourable augmentations to his armourial ensign: a chief undulated, *argent*; thereon waves of the sea; from which a palm-tree issuant, between a disabled ship on the dexter, and a ruinous battery on the sinister, all proper; and for his crest, on a naval crown, *or*, the chelengk, or plume, presented to him by the Turk, with the motto *Palman qui meruit ferat*.

Robert Southey, *Life of Nelson*, 1813

Give of me Nelson only a touch,
And I save it, be it little or much.

Robert Browning, *Nationality in Drinks*, 1845

Rarely has a man been more favoured in the hour of his appearing; never one so fortunate in the moment of his death.

Alfred Thayer Mahan, *Life of Nelson*, 1897

If under the presentiment of the most magnificent of all victories, to be crowned by his own glorious death, a sort of priestly motive led him to dress his person in the jewelled vouchers of his own shining deeds; if thus to have adorned himself for the altar and the sacrifice were indeed vainglory, then affectation and fustian is each more heroic in the great epics and dramas, since in such lines the poet but embodies in verse those exaltations of sentiment that a nature like Nelson's, the opportunity being given, vitalizes into acts.

Herman Melville, *Billy Budd*, 1924

Always in his element and always on his element.

G. M. Trevelyan, *History of England*, 1926

Nelson did not fight in order to carry out a plan, instead he planned in order to carry out a fight, . . .

J. F. C. Fuller, *The Decisive Battles of the Western World*, 1954–56

Florence NIGHTINGALE, 1820–1910

What a comfort it was to see her pass. She would speak to one, and nod and smile to as many more; but she could not do it to all you know. We lay there by the hundreds; but we could feel her shadow as it fell and lay our heads on the pillow again content.

A wounded soldier in the Crimean War, in Cecil Woodham-Smith, *Florence Nightingale*, 1950

You are, I know, well aware of the high sense I entertain of the Christian devotion which you have displayed during this great and bloody war, and I need hardly repeat to you how warm my admiration is for your services, which are fully equal to those of my brave and dear soldiers, whose sufferings you have had the *privilege* of alleviating in so merciful a manner. I am, however, anxious of marking my feelings in a manner which I trust will be agreeable to you, and therefore send you with this letter a brooch, the form and emblems of which commemorate your great and blessed work, and which, I hope, you will wear as a mark of the high approbation of your Sovereign!

Queen Victoria, Letter to Florence Nightingale, January 1856

A Lady with a Lamp shall stand
In the great history of the land,
A noble type of good,
Heroic womanhood.

Henry Wadsworth Longfellow, 'Santa Filomena', 1858

Like Dr Pusey you are a myth in your own lifetime.
Benjamin Jowett, Letter to Florence Nightingale, December 1879

Robert-Georges NIVELLE, 1856–1924

Here at least is a general whose plan I can understand.
David Lloyd George, in C. R. M. F. Crutwell, *History of the Great War, 1914–1918*, 1934

Another point in General Nivelle's favour was that Mr Lloyd George liked the shape of his head. He was a great believer in his own powers as a phrenologist. He often judged men this way; he either liked the shape of a man's head, or he did not, and General Nivelle's cranium found favour in his eyes.
Sir Edward Spears, *Prelude to Victory*, 1939

Sir John OLDCASTLE, Lord Cobham, d. 1417

Stage-poets have themselves been very bold with, and others very merry at, the memory of Sir John Oldcastle; whom they have fancied a boon companion, a jovial roister, and yet a coward to boot, contrary to the credit of all chronicles, owning him a martial man of merit. The best is, Sir John Falstaff hath relieved the memory of Sir John Oldcastle, and of late is substituted buffoon in his place; but it matters as little what petulant poets, as what malicious papists, have written against him.
Thomas Fuller, *Church History of Great Britain*, 1655

Wilfred OWEN, 1893–1918

He is all blood, dirt & sucked sugar stick.
W. B. Yeats, Letter to Dorothy Wellesley, 21st December 1936

George Smith PATTON Jr, 1885–1945

Old Blood 'n' Guts.
Nickname.

Patton was an acolyte to Mars.
Colonel J. J. Farley, attributed, November 1964

He came to one patient who, upon inquiry, stated that he was sick with high fever. The General dismissed him without comment. The next patient was sitting huddled up and shivering. When asked what his trouble was, the man replied, 'It's my nerves,' and began to sob. The General then screamed at him, 'What did you say?' He replied, 'It's my nerves. I can't stand the shelling any more.' He was still sobbing.

The General then yelled at him, 'Your nerves Hell, you are just a Goddamn coward, you yellow son of a bitch.' He then slapped the man and said, 'Shut up that Goddamned crying. I won't have these brave men here who have been shot seeing a yellow bastard sitting here crying.' He then struck at the man again, knocking his helmet liner off and into the next tent. He then turned to the Receiving Officer and yelled, 'Don't admit this yellow bastard, there's nothing the matter with him. I won't have the hospitals cluttered up with these sons of bitches who haven't the guts to fight.'

Ladislas Farago, *Patton: Ordeal and Triumph*, 1966

John PELHAM, 1838–63

The noble, the chivalric, the gallant Pelham, is no more.

J. E. B. Stuart, General Order, 19th March 1863

PERICLES of Athens, *c.* 495–429 BC

In his campaigns he was chiefly remarkable for caution, for he would not, if he could help it, begin a battle of which the issue was doubtful; nor did he wish to emulate those generals who have won themselves a great reputation by running risks, and trusting to good luck. But he ever used to say to his countrymen, that none of them should ever come by their deaths through any act of his.

Plutarch, *Lives: Pericles*, *c.* 110

John Joseph PERSHING, 1860–1948

When the last bugle is sounded, I want to stand up with my soldiers.

On himself, in *The Yanks Are Coming*, 1932

Oh to be in Paris now that Pershing's there!
To hear the waves of welcome that greet him everywhere;
To see the children and the girls a-pelting him with flowers,
And feel that every petal is meant for us and ours.

Anonymous, 1918

The General came in a new tin hat
To the shell-torn front where the war was at.
With a faithful aide at his good right hand,
He made his way to No-Man's-Land.

Arthur Guiterman, 'Pershing at the Front', 1918

Pershing inspired confidence but not affection. Personal magnetism seemed lacking; he won followers and admirers, but not personal worshippers. Plain in word, sane and direct in action, he applied himself to all duty and all work with a manifest purpose, not only of succeeding in what he attempted, but of surpassing, guiding and directing his followers in what was before them.

Roger L. Bullard, in Donald Smythe, *Guerilla Warrior: The Early Life of John J. Pershing*, 1986

He was no tin soldier and certainly no figurine saint.

Donald Smythe, *Guerilla Warrior: The Early Life of John J. Pershing*, 1986

Charles Mordaunt, Earl of PETERBOROUGH, 1658–1735

He sailed with all canvas spread, but without a rudder; he admitted of no rule of duty, and his sole, but unacknowledged end, was the gratification of his inordinate self-esteem.

E. B. G. Warburton, *Life of Charles Mordaunt, Earl of Peterborough*, 1853

The standard of stature in the gallery of the War of Spanish Succession is not so heroic that it could afford without a struggle to part with the one type not drearily commonplace.

William Stebbing, *Peterborough*, 1890

PHILIP II OF MACEDON, *c.* 382–336 BC

You must not imagine that he is a super-human being whose success is unalterably fixed. He has enemies to hate, fear and envy him, even in places very friendly to him. His associates, one must suppose, have the same human feelings as anyone else. But now all this is beneath the surface. It has nowhere to turn because of the slowness, the inactivity of Athens. It is this that I urge you to lay aside. Consider the facts, gentlemen, consider the outrageous lengths to which Philip has gone. He does not offer us a choice between action and inaction. He utters threats, according to my information, in overbearing terms. He is not content to rest on his laurels, but is continually adding to the haul he collects in the net in which he ensnares our hesitant, inactive country. When are we to act? What is to be the signal? When compulsion drives, I suppose. Then what are we to say of the present? In my view the greatest compulsion that can be laid upon free men is their shame at the circumstances in which they find themselves. Do you need to go round and ask each other whether there is any startling news? What could be more startling than a Macedonian fighting a successful war against Athens, and dictating the affairs of Greece. 'Philip is dead', comes one report. 'No, he is only ill', from another. What difference does it make? Should anything happen to Philip, Athens, in her present frame of mind, will soon create another Philip.

Demosthenes, *First Philippic*, 351 BC

A man whose actions and calculations are designed for my capture, is at war with me before he ever discharges a weapon. What events are those whose occurrence would be a danger to this country? The alienation of the Hellespont, the control of Megara and Euboea by an enemy, or a tendency in the Peloponnese to side with Philip. This is the artillery aimed against Athens, and how can the man who erects it be said to be at peace?

Demosthenes, *Third Philippic*, 341 BC

William PITT (the 'Younger'), 1759–1806

And oh! if again the rude whirlwinds should rise,
The dawnings of peace should fresh darkness deform,
The regrets of the good and the fears of the wise
Shall turn to the Pilot who weathered the Storm.

George Canning, 'Song', 1802

POMPEY THE GREAT (Gnaeus Pompeius Magnus), 106–48 BC

But it was the chief thing towards his glory, and what had never happened before to any Roman, that he celebrated his third triumph over the third continent. For though others before him had triumphed three times, Pompeius by having gained his first triumph over Libya, his second over Europe, and this the last over Asia, seemed in a manner to have brought the whole world into his three triumphs.

Plutarch, *Lives: Pompeius*, *c.* 110

Fluellen: It is the greatest admiration in the universal world, when the true and ancient prerogatives and laws of the wars is not kept. If you would take the pains but to examine the wars of Pompey the Great, you shall find, I warrant you, that there is no tiddle-taddle nor pibble-pabble in Pompey's camp; I warrant you, you shall find the ceremonies of the wars, and the cares of it, and the forms of it, and the sobriety of it, and the modesty of it, to be otherwise.

William Shakespeare, *Henry V*, 1600: Act IV sc.i

PONTIAC, d. 1769

There is reason to judge of Pontiac, not only as a savage possessed of the most refined cunning and treachery natural to the Indians, but as a person of extraordinary abilities . . . He keeps two secretaries, one to write for him, and the other to read the letters he receives, and he manages them so as to keep each of them ignorant of what is transacted by the other.

General Thomas Gage, Letter to Lord Halifax, 1764

Ezra Weston Loomis POUND, 1885–1972

I see they call me Mussolini's boy. I only saw the bastard once. No German or Italian was ever in a position to give me an order. So I took none. But a German near my home at Rapallo told me they were paying good money for broadcasts. That was a fatal mistake.

On himself, in Charles Norman, *Ezra Pound*, 1960

Fitzroy James Henry Somerset, Lord RAGLAN, 1788–1855

Hey! Don't take that arm away until I have removed my ring!

On himself, on the surgeon's table after Waterloo, 1815

Not since we landed has Raglan shown one particle of military knowledge . . . I wish they would reinforce us with a new Commander-in-Chief, and put this one in petticoats and send him home.

Robert Portal, Letter to his mother, October 1854

Science and mechanics, which were beginning already to change the whole life of Europe, meant nothing to him. Nor did painting, nor music; nor did books. In fact in the great mass of his personal correspondence only once does he mention having read one. It was *The Count of Monte Cristo*. 'So far as I have got in it,' he confessed, 'I find it is tiresome – very poisonous.'

Christopher Hibbert, *The Destruction of Lord Raglan*, 1961

His chief merit was that, despite his incurable habit throughout the campaign [in Crimea] of referring to the enemy as the 'French', he was admirably adapted to lessen the friction in coalition wars.

David Divine, *The Blunted Sword*, 1964

Instead there was Lord Raglan, a man of sixty-six, once Wellington's military secretary in the Peninsula, a man who had never commanded in the field, and appointed for no much better reason than the feeling that he was the repository of the Wellingtonian spirit. Raglan manifested to a remarkable degree the characteristics of the ideal Victorian gentleman. Unfortunately these virtues do not make for success or survival in a tough world. They did not make for success in the Crimea. It would have been better if Raglan had been a bloody-minded careerist bastard, as were Napoleon III's generals. No driving will-power united the disparate parts of the British military machine.

Correlli Barnett, *Britain and Her Army 1509–1970*, 1970

It was a characteristic of the man that he hated conflict!

Norman F. Dixon, *On the Psychology of Military Incompetence*, 1976

Marcus Atilius REGULUS, 3rd century BC

Marcus Regulus, the Roman Commander-in-Chief, was a prisoner in the hands of the Carthaginians. Since the Carthaginians preferred to have their own prisoners released by the Romans, rather than keep their Roman prisoners, Regulus was the man chosen to be sent to Rome with their deputation, having first bound himself by an oath to return to Carthage if he failed to obtain the result the enemy desired. He proceeded to Rome, and in the Senate successfully urged the rejection of the proposal, since he considered that an exchange of prisoners was not to the advantage of Rome. After the success of his plea he was not forced by his countrymen to return to the enemy, but since he had taken an oath, he voluntarily fulfilled his obligation and the enemy put him to death with every refinement of dreadful torture. They shut him in a narrow box, where he was forced to stand upright, and sharp nails had been fixed on all sides of it, so that he could not lean in any direction without the most horrible suffering; thus they dispatched him by keeping him awake.

St Augustine, *City Of God*, 427: I.xv

Paul REVERE, 1735–1818

Paul Revere was more than a figure on horseback, more than a great silversmith, bell-caster, powder-maker and shrewd leader of Boston's artisans. He was the handyman of the Revolution. He helped to plant the Tree of Liberty, and lived to enjoy the fruits.

G. Donald Dallas, *The Spirit of Paul Revere*

RICHARD I of England, 1157–99

But this king, amongst all the princes of the Christian name that the round circle of the world embraces, alone is worthy of the honour of a leader and the name of a king, for he began his work well, he continued it even better, and if he remains with you a while longer, he will finish it perfectly.

Safadin (Saladin's brother), in Richard of Devizes, *Chronicle*

. . . If heroism be confined to brutal and ferocious valour, Richard Plantagenet will stand high among the heroes of the age. The memory of *Coeur de Lion*, of the lion-hearted prince, was long dear and glorious to his English subjects; and, at a distance of sixty years, it was celebrated in proverbial sayings by the grandsons of the Turks and Saracens, against whom he had fought: his tremendous name was employed by the Syrian mothers to silence their infants; and if a horse suddenly started from the way, his rider was wont to exclaim, 'Dost thou think king Richard is in that bush?'

Edward Gibbon, *The History Of The Decline And Fall Of The Roman Empire*, 1776–88: lix

Coeur-de-lion was not a theatrical popinjay with greaves and steel-cap on it, but a man living upon victuals.

Thomas Carlyle, *Past and Present*, 1843

His tale is told with the implication that his departure for the crusade was something like the escapade of a schoolboy running away to sea. It was, in this view, a pardonable or lovable prank; whereas in truth it was more like a responsible Englishman now going to the Front. Christendom was nearly one nation, and the Front was the Holy Land.

G. K. Chesterton, *A Short History of England*, 1920

He was a bad son, a bad husband and a bad king, but a gallant and splendid soldier.

Steven Runciman, *A History of the Crusades*, 1951–54: vol. III

Sir William Robert ROBERTSON, 1860–1933

Sir William Robertson was the first British general to have risen from the ranks; and he maintained a barrack-room roughness. He met heretical suggestions with the unswerving answer: 'I've 'eard different.' He told Lloyd George: 'It is a waste of time explaining strategy to you. To understand my explanation you would have had to have my experience.'

A. J. P. Taylor, *The First World War*, 1963

Erwin ROMMEL, 1891–1944

Germany produces many ruthlessly efficient generals: Rommel stood out amongst them because he had overcome the innate rigidity of the German military mind and was a master of improvisation.

Sir Claude Auchinleck, in Norman F. Dixon, *On the Psychology of Military Incompetence*, 1976

Theodore ROOSEVELT, 1858–1919

Our hero is a man of peace,
 Preparedness he implores;
His sword within his scabbard sleeps,
 But mercy, how it snores!

McLandburgh Wilson, 'A Man of Peace'

Prince RUPERT, Count Palatinate of the Rhine, 1619–82

A man who hath had his hand very deep in the blood of many innocent men.
Oliver Cromwell, Letter to David Lesley, 14th August 1650

Rupert that knew not fear, but health did want,
Kept state, suspended in a *chaise-volante*;
All save his head shut in that wooden case,
He showed but like a broken weatherglass;
But arm'd in a whole lion cap-a-chin
Did represent the Hercules within.
Dear shall the Dutch his twinging anguish know
And feel what valour whet with pain can do.
Andrew Marvell, 'Second Advice to a Painter', 1666

Lord George Germain, Viscount SACKVILLE, 1716–85

Sackvilles alone anticipate defeat,
And ere they dare the battle, sound retreat.
Charles Churchill, *The Candidate*, 1764

SALADIN, 1137–93

. . . His perusal of the Koran on horseback, between the approaching armies, may be quoted as a proof, however ostentatious, of piety and courage.
Edward Gibbon, *The History Of The Decline And Fall Of The Roman Empire*, 1776–88: lix

Of all the great figures of the Crusading era Saladin is the most attractive. He had his faults. In his rise to power he showed a cunning and a ruthlessness that fitted ill with his later reputation. In the interests of policy he never shrank from bloodshed; he slew Reynald of Chatillon, whom he hated, with his own hand. But when he was severe it was for the sake of his people and his faith.
Steven Runciman, *A History of the Crusades*, 1951–54: vol. III

In spite of his power and his victories he was a quiet modest man. Many years later a legend reached the ears of the Frankish writer, Vincent of Beauvais, that when he lay dying he summoned his standard-bearer and bade him go round Damascus with a rag from his shroud set upon a lance calling out that the Monarch of all the East could take nothing with him to the tomb save this cloth.
Steven Runciman, *A History of the Crusades*, 1951–54: vol. III

Publius Cornelius SCIPIO Aemilianus AFRICANUS, 185–129 BC

As to the soubriquet of Africanus, whether it was conferred upon him by the devotion of his soldiers or by popular breath, or whether as in the recent instances of Sulla the Fortunate and Pompey the Great it originated in the flattery of his friends, I cannot say for certain. At all events, he was the first commander-in-chief who was ennobled by the name of the people he had conquered. Since his time men who have won far smaller victories have in imitation of him left splendid inscriptions on their busts and illustrious names to their families.

Livy, *The History of Rome*, from 29 BC: Bk XXX

. . . Africanus asked Hannibal whom he considered to be the greatest commander, and the reply was, 'Alexander of Macedon, for with a small force he routed innumerable armies and traversed the most distant shores of the world which no man ever hoped to visit.' Africanus then asked him whom he would put second, and Hannibal replied, 'Pyrrhus; he was the first who taught how to lay out a camp, and moreover no one ever showed more cleverness in the choice of positions and the disposition of his troops. He possessed, too, the art of winning popularity to such an extent that the nations of Italy preferred the rule of a foreign king to that of the Roman people who had so long held the foremost place in the country.' On Scipio's again asking him whom he regarded as the third, Hannibal, without any hesitation, replied, 'Myself'. Scipio smiled and asked, 'What would you say if you had vanquished me?' 'In that case,' replied Hannibal, 'I should say that I surpassed Alexander and Pyrrhus, and all other commanders in the world.' Scipio was delighted with the turn which the speaker had with true Carthaginian adroitness given to his answer, and the unexpected flattery it conveyed, because Hannibal had set him apart from the ordinary run of military captains as an incomparable commander.

Livy, *The History of Rome*, from 29 BC: Bk XXXV

Sir Percy SCOTT, 1853–1924

I don't care if he drinks, gambles, and womanizes; he hits the target.

Sir John Fisher, *c.* 1908

Winfield SCOTT, 1786–1866

Old Fuss and Feathers.

Nickname

He understands nothing, appreciates nothing, and is ever in my way.

George B. McClellan, in William S. Myers, *A Study in Personality: George Brinton McClellan*, 1934

Not even the gorgeously bedizened marshals of Napoleon wore their plumes, sashes, aiguilettes and glittering uniforms with more complacency than did this republican soldier whose imposing and symmetrical form was so well set off by such martial embellishments.

Charles W. Elliott, *Winfield Scott: The Soldier and the Man*, 1937

SHAKA (Chaka/Tshaka), 1787–1828

Shaka's particular genius lay in his meticulous personal attention to detail, and sheer hard work. If at all possible he always insisted on inspecting everything himself. In every one of his critical battles he insisted on personally reconnoitring the ground and the disposition of the enemy forces. He invariably checked all reports by procuring collateral evidence. He was a firm believer in the maxim, 'it is the man's eye which makes the cow grow fat'.

E. A. Ritter, *Shaka Zulu*, 1958

Another example of his flexibility and refusal to be dominated by tradition was Shaka's banning of sandals for his fighting men. By making them run barefoot, a considerable and by no means popular break with tradition, he invested his army with a speed of movement far in excess of that achieved by his enemies. The displeasure he incurred through this innovation was hardly reduced by an order to his warriors that they should harden their feet on a parade-ground strewn with thorns. Those who hesitated to follow his example in this painful initiation were instantly clubbed to death.

Norman F. Dixon, *On the Psychology of Military Incompetence*, 1976

William Tecumseh SHERMAN, 1820–91

Sherman, hurrah, we'll go with him,
Wherever it may be
Through Carolina's cotton fields
Or Georgia to the sea

Anonymous, song, *c.* 1864

You have accomplished the most gigantic undertaking given to any general in this war, and with a skill and ability that will be acknowledged in history as unsurpassed if not unequalled.

Ulysses Grant, congratulating Sherman on the capture of Atlanta, letter, September 1864

Unsated still in his demoniac vengeance he sweeps over the country like a simoon of destruction.

The Macon Telegraph, 5th December 1864

We drink to twenty years ago,
When Sherman led our banner;
His mistresses were fortresses,
His Christmas gift – Savannah!

George B. Corkhill, proposing a toast, Washington, 8th February 1883

This the soldier brave enough to tell
The glory-dazzled world that War is hell:
Lover of peace, he looks beyond the strife,
And rides through hell to save his country's life.

Henry van Dyke, lines written for inscription on a statue of Sherman, but never used

No man of action has more completely attained the point of view of the scientific historian, who observes the movements of mankind with the same detachment as a bacteriologist observes bacilli under a microscope and yet with a sympathy that springs from his own common manhood. In Sherman's attainment of that philosophic pinnacle, soaring above the clouds of ignorance and passion, lies the explanation of much that seems perplexing in his character – the dispassionateness of an impulsive man, the restfulness of a restless man, the patience of an impatient man, the sympathy of a relentless man.

B. H. Liddell Hart, *Sherman: Soldier, Realist, American*, 1959

Sherman must rank as the first of the modern totalitarian generals. He made war universal, waged it on his enemy's people and not only on armed men, and made terror the linchpin of his strategy. To him more than to any other man must be attributed the hatred that grew out of the Civil War.

J. F. C. Fuller, *The Decisive Battles of the Western World*, 1954–56

Sir Philip SIDNEY, 1554–86

As he was putting the bottle to his mouth, he saw a poor soldier carried along, who had eaten his last at the same Feast, ghastly casting up his eyes at the bottle. Which Sir Philip perceiving, took it from his head before he drank, and delivered it to the poor man with these words, Thy necessity is yet greater than mine. And when he had pledged this poor soldier, he was presently carried to Arnheim.

Fulke Greville, *Life of Sidney*, describing the Battle of Zutphen (22nd September 1586), 1652

. . . lord of the stainless sword . . .

Algernon Swinburne, *Astrophel*, 1889

SITTING BULL, 1830–90

When I was a boy the Sioux owned the world; the sun rose and set on their land; they sent ten thousand men to battle. Where are the warriors today? Who slew them? Where are our lands? Who owns them? What white man can say I ever stole his land or a penny of his money? Yet, they say I am a thief. What white woman, however lonely, was ever captive or insulted by me? Yet they say I am a bad Indian. What white man has ever seen me drunk? Who has ever come to me hungry and unfed? Who has ever seen me beat my wives or abuse my children? What law have I broken? Is it wrong for me to love my own? Is it wicked for me because my skin is red? Because I am a Sioux; because I was born where my father lived; because I would die for my people and my country?

On himself, in T. C. McLuhan, *Touch The Earth*

William Joseph, Viscount SLIM, 1891–1970

By good fortune in the game of military snakes and ladders, I found myself a general.

On himself, *Unofficial History*, 1959

He did not subscribe to the idea that the average soldier's thought dwelt merely on the discomfort and unpleasantness of the country to which he had been sent to fight. He believed that be they British, Indian, Gurkha or African, if they were told the reasons for fighting, the justice of the cause and the importance of beating the enemy, they would respond with enthusiasm. To this end he spent a great deal of time visiting units, talking to them informally in their lines, and encouraged his subordinates to do the same. Naturally, he did not confine these talks to this theme, but interpolated subjects of a more general personal nature such as rations, pay, leave, mails and beer, combining these with the necessary amount of humour. 'There was no brass hat about him', wrote General Messervy.

G. Evans, *Slim*, 1969

Success did not inflate him nor misfortune depress him.

Sir Claude Auchinleck, in Norman F. Dixon, *On the Psychology of Military Incompetence*, 1976

SPARTACUS, d. 71 BC

As fresh men from both sides kept coming up to help their comrades, Spartacus, seeing that he must fight, arranged all his army in order of battle. When his horse was brought to him, he drew his sword and said, that if he won the battle he should have plenty of fine horses from the enemy, and if he was defeated he should not want one; upon which he killed his horse . . .

Plutarch, *Lives: Crassus*, *c.* 110

Albert SPEER, 1905–81

Speer is not one of the flamboyant and picturesque Nazis. Whether he has any other than conventional political opinions at all is unknown. He might have joined any other political party which gave him a job and a career. He is very much the successful average man, well-dressed, civil, noncorrupt, very middle-class in his style of life, with a wife and six children. Much less than any other of the German leaders does he stand for anything particularly German or particularly Nazi. He rather symbolizes a type which is becoming increasingly important in all belligerent countries: the pure technician, the classless bright young man without background, with no other original aim than to make his way in the world and no other means than his technical and managerial ability. It is the lack of psychological and spiritual ballast, and the ease with which he handles the terrifying technical and organizational machinery of our age, which makes the slight type go extremely far nowadays . . . The Hitlers and Himmlers we may well get rid of, but the Speers, whatever happens to this particular special man, will long be with us.

The *Observer*, 9th April 1944

King STEPHEN of England, 1097–1154

He was a man of great renown in the practice of arms, but for the rest almost an incompetent, except that he was rather inclined to evil.

Walter Map, *De Nugis Curialium*, 1192

Joseph Warren STILWELL, 1883–1946

Lean to the point of gauntness, perpetually squinting through steel-rimmed glasses as a result of a near-blinded eye injury in a World War I explosion, profane, irascible, well disciplined in body, undisciplined in tongue, Stilwell was totally lacking in the art of diplomatic finesse. A man with a compulsion to speak and damn the consequences, he sounded off against colleagues and superiors with a zest that caused momentary amusement but ultimate dislike. The nickname 'vinegar Joe', applied in affection, became a damaging trademark.

Forrest C. Pogue, *George C. Marshall: Ordeal and Hope 1939–1942*, 1968

Giles Lytton STRACHEY, 1880–1932

Lytton was unfit [for service], but instead of allowing himself to be rejected by the doctors preferred to appear before a military tribunal as a conscientious objector. He told us of the extrordinary impression caused by an air-cushion he inflated in court as a protest against the hardness of the benches. Asked by the chairman the usual question: 'I understand, Mr Strachey, that you have a conscientious objection to war?', he replied (in his curious falsetto voice): 'Oh no, not at all, only to *this* war.' And to the chairman's other stock question, which had previously never failed to embarrass the claimant: 'Tell me, Mr Strachey, what would you do if you saw a German soldier trying to violate your sister?' he replied with an air of noble virtue: 'I would try to get between them.'

Robert Graves, *Goodbye to All That*, 1929

James Ewell Brown (Jeb) STUART, 1833–64

The Confederate lion, the shaking of whose mane and angry roar kept the Jackal North in a perpetual terror.

The *Richmond Examiner*, 17th May 1864

His horse furniture and equipment were polished leather and bright metal, and he liked to wear a red rose in his jacket when the roses bloomed, and a love knot of red ribbon when flowers were out of season. His soft, fawn-colored hat was looped up on the right with a gold star, and adorned with a curling ostrich feather. His boots sported little knightly spurs of gold – admiring ladies, even those who never saw him in their lives, sent him such things. He went conspicuous all gold and glitter, in the front of great battles and in a hundred little cavalry fights, which killed men just as dead as Gettysburg.

John W. Thomason Jr, *Jeb Stuart*, 1930

Lucius Cornelius SULLA (Sylla), 138–78 BC

When Sulla, as I have said, reached Africa and presented himself at Marius's camp with his cavalry, he had no knowledge or experience of war. Yet in a short space of time he became the most skilful soldier in the army. He spoke in a friendly manner to the men and granted favours to many of them, sometimes without even waiting to be asked. Unwilling to accept favours himself if he could avoid it, he repaid those he did accept more promptly than any loan; for himself, he expected no return from those whom he benefited, but rather sought to have as many as possible indebted to him. He could converse on subjects both grave and gay with the humblest, spent much time with the men at their work, on the march and on guard duty, and all the time refrained from the crooked conduct of seekers after popularity – for he never blackened the reputation of the consul or of any honest man. His sole concern was that no one should be his superior, and very few his equals, in counsel or in action. Such a character and such behaviour quickly endeared him to Marius and the troops.

Sallust, *The Jugurthine War*, *c.* 42 BC

Zachary TAYLOR, 1784–1850

I think I hear his cheerful voice,
'Oh column! Steady! Steady!'
So handy and so prompt was he,
We called him Rough and Ready.

Anonymous rhyme, *c.* 1837

TECUMSEH, 1768–1813

My heart is a stone: heavy with sadness for my people; cold with the knowledge that no treaty will keep the whites out of our lands; hard with the determination to resist as long as I live and breathe. Now we are weak and many of our people are afraid. But hear me: a single twig breaks, but the bundle of twigs is strong. Someday I will embrace our brother tribes and draw them into a bundle and together we will win our country back from the whites.

On himself, in T. C. McLuhan, *Touch The Earth*

I am the maker of my own fortune, and Oh! that I could make that of my Red People, and of my country, as great as the conceptions of my mind, when I think of the spirit that rules the universe. I would not then come to Governor Harrison to ask him to tear up the treaty, and to obliterate the landmark, but I would say to him, 'Sir, you have liberty to return to your own country.'

On himself, in T. C. McLuhan, *Touch The Earth*

THEMISTOCLES, *c.* 524–460 BC

The Greeks now, not doubting what the Athenians told them, made ready for the coming fight. At the dawn of day, all the men-at-arms were assembled together, and speeches were made to them, of which the best was that of Themistocles; who throughout contrasted what was noble with what was base, and bade them, in all that came within the range of man's nature and constitution, *always* to make choice of the nobler part.

Herodotus, *Histories*, *c.* 450 BC: Bk VIII

Eurybiades, on account of the prestige of Sparta, held the chief command of the fleet, but was unwilling to risk a battle, preferring to weigh anchor and sail to the Isthmus where the land army of the Peloponnesians was assembled. The project was opposed by Themistokles; and it was on this occasion that he made use of the following well-known saying: When Eurybiades said to him, 'Themistokles, in the public games they whip those who rise before their turn.' 'True,' said Themistokles, 'but they do not crown those who lag behind.'

Plutarch, *Lives: Themistocles*, *c.* AD 110

Once, when he was made admiral of the Athenian fleet, he put off all the necessary business of his office until the day appointed for sailing, in order that he might have a great many dealings with various people all at once, and so appear to be a person of great influence and importance. And when he saw the corpses floating in the sea with gold bracelets and necklaces, he himself passed them by, but pointed them out to a friend who was following, saying, 'Do you pick them up and keep them; for you are not Themistokles.'

Plutarch, *Lives: Themistocles*, *c.* AD 110

Emperor THEODOSIUS I (the 'Great'), 347–95

. . . Theodosius has deserved the singular commendation, that his virtues always seemed to expand with his fortune: the season of his prosperity was that of his moderation; and his clemency appeared the most conspicuous after the danger and the success of the civil war.

Edward Gibbon, *The History Of The Decline And Fall Of The Roman Empire*, 1776–88: xxvii

But the painful virtue which claims the merit of victory, is exposed to the danger of defeat; and the reign of a wise and merciful prince was polluted by an act of cruelty, which would stain the annals of Nero or Domitian. Within the space of three years the inconsistent historian of Theodosius must relate the generous pardon of the citizens of Antioch, and the inhuman massacre of the people of Thessalonica.

Edward Gibbon, *The History Of The Decline And Fall Of The Roman Empire*, 1776–88: xxvii

The genius of Rome expired with Theodosius.

Edward Gibbon, *The History Of The Decline And Fall Of The Roman Empire*, 1776–88: xxix

Julian THOMPSON, b. 1934

The man of the match [i.e. the Falklands War].

Major-General Jeremy Moore, quoted in Trevor Royle, *War Report*, 1987

THUCYDIDES, *c.* 460–395 BC

My history is an everlasting possession, not a prize composition which is heard and forgotten.

On himself, *History of the Peloponnesian Wars*, *c.* 404 BC, Bk I

There is a special impropriety in combining the fictions of later writers with the narrative of Thucydides, who stands alone absolutely among the historians, not only of Hellas, but of the world, in his impartiality and love of truth.

Benjamin Jowett, Introduction to his translation of Thucydides, 1881

Semyon Konstantinovich TIMOSHENKO, 1895–1970

He turned, and his great shadow on the wall
Swayed like a tree. His eyes grew cold as lead.
Then, in a rage of love and grief and pity,
He made the pencilled map alive with war.

Sidney Keyes, 'Timoshenko', 1942

Henri de La Tour d'Auvergne, vicomte de TURENNE, 1611–75

The enemy came. He was beaten. I am tired. Good night.

On himself, at the Battle of Tünen, 14th June 1658

Some old soldiers going to be shot for a breach of discipline, as passing by Marshal Turenne, pointed to the scars on their faces and breasts. What speech could come up to this? It had the desired effect. The marshal instantly staid the execution, and gave the men a free pardon.

The Percy Anecdotes, 1823

Cornelius VAN TROMP, 1629–91

Van Tromp was an Admiral bold,
The Dutchman's pride was he,
And he cried, 'I'll reign on the rolling main,
As I do on the Zuyder Zee!'

Traditional, 19th century

Queen VICTORIA of Great Britain, 1819–1901

You never saw anybody so entirely taken up with military affairs as she is.

Lord Panmure, Letter to Lord Raglan, 1855

Oh if the Queen were a man, she would like to go and give those horrid Russians whose word one cannot trust such a beating.

On herself, Letter to Benjamin Disraeli, January 1878

George WASHINGTON, 1732–99

I heard the bullets whistle; and believe me, there is something charming in the sound.

On himself, after Great Meadows, Letter to his mother, 3rd May 1754

When we assumed the soldier, we did not lay aside the citizen.

On himself, at the Provincial Congress of New York, 26th June 1775

These are high times when a British general is to take counsel of a Virginia buckskin.

General Edward Braddock, 1755, in Charles Fenno Hoffman, *A Winter in the West*, 1853

He has been beaten whenever he was engaged; and this, if left to befall him again, is a problem which, I believe, most military men are utterly at a loss to solve.
Anonymous contributor, *The Gentleman's Magazine*, August 1778

Who conquered with his suffering bands,
And grew immortal by distress.
Philip Freneau, *Occasioned by Washington's Arrival at Philadelphia*, 1795

A Citizen, first in war, first in peace, first in the hearts of his countrymen.
Henry Lee, in the House of Representatives, 26th December 1799

Washington the brave, the wise, the good,
Supreme in war, in council and in peace, . . .
From the inscription on Washington's tomb

. . . the Cincinnatus of the West,
Whom envy dared not hate,
Bequeathed the name of Washington,
To make men blush there was but one!
Lord Byron, 'Ode To Napoleon Buonaparte', 1814

Nothing but a plain old soldier,
An old revolutionary soldier,
But I've handled a gun
Where noble deeds were done,
For the name of my commander was George Washington.
Stephen Collins Foster, 'I'm Nothing But A Plain Old Soldier', 1863

Soldier and statesman, rarest unison . . .
James Russell Lowell, 'Under The Old Elm', 1875

Mother of states and undiminished men,
Thou gavest us a country, giving him.
James Russell Lowell, 'Under The Old Elm', 1875

Simple and brave, his faith awoke
Ploughmen to struggle with their fate;
Armies won battles when he spoke,
And out of Chaos sprang the state.
Robert Bridges, 'Washington', in *Poetical Works*, 1912

Archibald Percival WAVELL, 1883–1950

There is no need for your son to go into the Army: he is really quite intelligent.
The Headmaster of Winchester, to Wavell's father, attributed

The only one who showed a touch of genius was Wavell.
Erwin Rommel, *The Rommel Papers*, 1953: xxiii

Anthony WAYNE, 1745–96

General Wayne had a constitutional attachment to the sword, and this cast of character had acquired strength from indulgence.

Henry Lee, quoted in Robert Debs Heinl Jr, *Dictionary of Military and Naval Quotations*, 1966

Gideon WELLES, 1802–78

Retire, O Gideon, to an onion farm,
Ply any trade that's innocent and slow.
Do anything, where you can do no harm.
Go anywhere you fancy – only go.

Anonymous rhyme, *Leslie's* magazine, June 1862

Sir Arthur Wellesley, Duke of WELLINGTON, 1769–1852

It is a bad thing always to be fighting. While in the thick of it I am too much occupied to feel anything; but it is wretched just after. It is quite impossible to think of glory. Both mind and feelings are exhausted. I am wretched even at the moment of victory, and I always think that next to a battle lost, the greatest misery is a battle gained.

On himself, in Lady Frances Shelley, *Diary 1787–1817*, 1912

I have been passing my life in guessing what I might meet with beyond the next hill, or around the next corner.

On himself, in conversation with J. W. Croker, 1845

The only thing I am afraid of is fear.

On himself, in Earl of Stanhope, *Notes of Conversations with Wellington 1831–51*, 1888

The real reason why I succeeded . . . is because I was always on the spot – I saw everything, and did everything myself.

On himself, quoted in J. F. C. Fuller, *The Decisive Battles of the Western World*, 1954–56

That long-nosed bugger that beats the French.

An English soldier, *c.* 1811

We would rather see his long nose in a fight than a reinforcement of 10,000 men a day.

Captain John Kincaid, in Michael Glover, *Wellington as Military Commander*, 1968

I should pronounce him to be a man of little genius, without generosity, and without greatness of soul.

Napoleon Bonaparte, Letter to Barry E. O'Meara, 20th September 1817

You are 'the best of cut-throats' – do not start;
The phrase is Shakespeare's, and not misapplied:
War's a brain-spattering, windpipe-slitting art,
Unless her cause by Right be sanctified.

If you have acted *once* a generous part,
  The World, not the World's masters, will decide,
And I shall be delighted to learn who,
Save you and yours, have gained by Waterloo?

I am no flatterer. You've supped full of flattery.
  They say you like it too; 'tis no great wonder:
He whose life has been assault and battery
  At last may get a little tired of thunder;
And swallowing eulogy much more than satire he
  May like being praised for every lucky blunder,
Called saviour of the nations – not yet saved,
And Europe's liberator – still enslaved.

I've done. Now go and dine from off the plate
  Presented by the Prince of the Brazils,
And send the sentinel before your gate
  A slice or two from your luxurious meals:
He fought, but has not fed so well of late.
  Some hunger too they say the people feels.
There is no doubt that you deserve your ration,
But pray give back a little to the nation.

Lord Byron, *Don Juan*, 1818–24: Canto IX

Great Chieftain, who takest such pains
  To prove – what is granted *nem. con.* –
With how mod'rate a portion of brains
  Some heroes contrive to get on.

Thomas Moore, 'Dog-Day Reflections', 1819

If England should require her army again, and I should be with it, let me have 'Old Nosey' to command. Our interests would be sure to be looked into, we should never have occasion to fear an enemy. There are two things we should be certain of. First, we should always be as well supplied with rations as the nature of the service would admit. The second is we should be sure to give the enemy a d—d good thrashing. What can a soldier desire more?

Private Wheeler, *The Letters of Private Wheeler*, ed. B. H. Liddell Hart, 1951

Warriors carry the warrior's pall, . . .

Alfred Tennyson, 'Ode on the Death of the Duke of Wellington', 1852

For this is England's greatest son,
He that gain'd a hundred fights,
Nor ever lost an English gun;
This is he that far away
Against the myriads of Assaye
Clash'd with his fiery few and won;
And underneath another sun,
Warring on a later day,

Round affrighted Lisbon drew
The treble works, the vast designs
Of his labour'd rampart-lines,
Where he greatly stood at bay,
Whence he issued forth anew,
And ever great and greater grew,
Beating from the wasted vines
Back to France her banded swarms,
Back to France with countless blows,
Till o'er the hills her eagles flew
Beyond the Pyrenean pines,
Followed up in valley and glen
With blare of bugle, clamour of men,
Roll of cannon and clash of arms,
And England pouring on her foes.
Such a war had such a close.
Again their ravening eagle rose
In anger, wheel'd on Europe-shadowing wings,
And barking for the thrones of kings;
Till one that sought but Duty's iron crown
On that loud sabbath shook the spoiler down;
A day of onsets of despair!
Dash'd on every rocky square
Their surging charges foam'd themselves away;
Last, the Prussian trumpet blew;
Thro' the long-tormented air
Heaven flash'd a sudden jubilant ray,
And down we swept and charged and overthrew.
So great a soldier taught us there,
What long-enduring hearts could do
In that world-earthquake Waterloo!

Alfred Tennyson, 'Ode on the Death of the Duke of Wellington', 1852

It makes me burn to have been a soldier.

Cardinal Newman, on reading Wellington's *Dispatches*, in B. H. Liddell Hart, *The Sword and the Pen*, 1978

Lady Salisbury asked which was the greatest military genius, Marlborough or Napoleon? [Wellington replied:] 'Why, I don't know – it is very difficult to tell. I can hardly conceive anything greater than Napoleon at the head of an army – especially a French army. Then he had one prodigious advantage – he had no responsibility – he could do whatever he pleased; and no man ever lost more armies than he did. Now with me the loss of every man told. I could not risk so much; I knew that if I ever lost five hundred men without the clearest necessity, I should be brought upon my knees to the bar of the House of Commons.'

Earl of Stanhope, *Notes of Conversations with Wellington 1831–51*, 1888

I observed to the Duke that his previous experience and trial of war in the Dutch campaign must have been very useful to him. 'Why – I learnt what one ought not to do, and that is always something.'

Earl of Stanhope, *Notes of Conversations with Wellington 1831–51*, 1888

It is fortunate for Britain that Wellington was at once a great humanitarian and a great disciplinarian.

G. M. Trevelyan, *British History in the Nineteenth Century and After*, 1938

It was probably fortunate that he rather than Moore fought the Peninsular War. Moore was a grim, priggish, prickly Scot, whose relations with such worldly people as politicians was bad. Wellington was an aristocrat, a broadminded man of the world, who had been a Member of Parliament and had served as Chief Secretary in Ireland. His relations with the government at home were generally excellent, despite his battles with it over particular questions. He and Castlereagh enjoyed special accord. As a soldier, too, Wellington was very different from Moore; an iron disciplinarian where Moore had been something of a scout-master; a stronger character with a cooler nerve. He was also a patient, longheaded practical strategist. Above all, Wellington was a master of the problems of supply and movement over long distances in a barren country; this he had learned in India. The secret of his victories was to be found not only in brisk orders on the battlefield but in dreary correspondence about bullock-carts and mules.

Correlli Barnett, *Britain and Her Army 1509–1970*, 1970

William Childs WESTMORELAND, b. 1914

My own interview with General Westmoreland had been hopelessly awkward. He'd noticed that I was accredited to *Esquire* and asked me if I planned to be doing 'humoristical' pieces. Beyond that, very little was really said. I came away feeling as though I'd just had a conversation with a man who touches a chair and says, 'This is a chair', points to a desk and says, 'This is a desk'.

Michael Herr, *Dispatches*, 1977

A tall, erect, handsome West Pointer with narrow eyes and a chiseled chin, he had earned a chestful of ribbons during World War II and in Korea, and he exuded the same virtuous resolve he had displayed as an eagle scout during his boyhood in South Carolina. But Johnson had not chosen him for his physique or his purity. Westy was a corporation executive in uniform, a diligent, disciplined organization man who would obey orders.

Stanley Karnow, *Vietnam: A History*, 1983

James Abbot McNeil WHISTLER, 1834–1903

'What!' exclaimed the examiner: 'you do not know the date of the Battle of Buena Vista? Suppose you were to go out to dinner, and the company began to talk of the Mexican War, and you, a West Point man, were asked the date of the battle, what would you do?' 'Do? Why, I should refuse to associate with people who could talk of such things at dinner!'

Hesketh Pearson, *Lives of the Witnesses*, 1962

WILLIAM I of England (the 'Conqueror') 1027–86

If anyone desires to know what kind of man he was or in what honour he was held or how many lands he was lord over, then shall we write of him as we have known him, who have ourselves seen him and at one time dwelt in his court. King William, of whom we speak, was a man of great wisdom and power, and surpassed in honour and in strength all those who had gone before him. Though stern beyond measure to those who opposed his will, he was kind to those good men who loved God. On the very spot where God granted him the conquest of England he caused a great abbey to be built; and settled monks in it and richly endowed it.

The Anglo-Saxon Chronicle

That he was ever able to establish his authority was due to his masterful character, his indomitable will, and his unalterable purpose. A man of steel, he could be brutal or lenient as it paid him to be so, but never merciful when it did not. He would tolerate no opposition; his will was law, and he would not be thwarted, whether by overlord, vassal, or pope. He was a great administrator and an able soldier, who based his strategy on striking at the towns and castles of his enemy and on winning possession of them by intimidation rather than by assault. In his hands devastation was the decisive weapon, and he used it with annihilative effect; he showed no feeling for the wretched peasantry he exterminated.

J. F. C. Fuller, *The Decisive Battles of the Western World*, 1954–56

WILLIAM III of Britain, 1650–1702

There is one certain means by which I can be sure never to see my country's ruin: I will die in the last ditch.

On himself, attributed

Thomas Woodrow WILSON, 1856–1924

Mr Wilson's name among the Allies is like that of the rich uncle, and they have accepted his manners out of respect for his means.

The *London Morning Post*, 1919

Mr Wilson bores me with his Fourteen Points; why, God Almighty only has ten.

Georges Clemenceau, attributed

How can I talk to a fellow who thinks himself the first man in two thousand years to know anything about peace on earth?

Georges Clemenceau, in Thomas A. Bailey, *Woodrow Wilson and the Lost Peace*, 1944

James WOLFE, 1727–59

Mad, is he? then I hope he will *bite* some of my other generals.

George II, in Beckles Wilson, *Life and Letters of James Wolfe*, 1909

The sons of earth, the proud giants of old,
Have broke from their darksome abodes;

And such is the news, that in heaven 'tis told,
They're marching to war with the gods.
A council was held in the chamber of Jove,
And this was the final decree,
That Wolfe should be call'd to the armies above,
And the charge was intrusted to me.

To the plains of Quebec with the orders I flew,
He begg'd for a moment's delay;
And cried, O forbear! Let me victory hear,
And then the command I'll obey.
With a darkening film I encompass'd his eyes,
And convey'd him away in an urn,
Lest the fondness he bore for his own native shore
Should tempt him again to return.

Thomas Paine, 'Death of General Wolfe', 1775

What he accomplished was done in the years when the ordinary mortal is learning his business; he was to war what William Pitt, the son of the great commoner who sent him to Quebec, was later to politics, what Keats was to literature.

Edward Salmon, *General Wolfe*, 1909

XERXES I of Persia, *c.* 519–465 BC

He showed such overbearing arrogance as to think it a slight thing to subdue the land of Greece, and to desire to leave a memorial higher than human pride can reach. He did not give way until he had planned and helped to force into being a design which is the common talk of the world, how with his army he sailed over the mainland and marched on foot across the sea, when he bridged the Hellespont and drove a canal through Athos.

Isocrates, *Panegyricus*, 300 BC

In gay Hostility, and barb'rous Pride,
With half Mankind embattled at his Side,
Great Xerxes comes to seize the certain Prey,
And starves exhausted Regions in his Way;
Attendant Flatt'ry counts his Myriads o'er,
Till counted Myriads sooth his Pride no more;
Fresh Praise is try'd till Madness fires his Mind,
The Waves he lashes, and enchains the Wind;
New Pow'rs are claimed, new Pow'rs are still bestow'd,
Till rude Resistance lops the spreading God;
The daring Greeks deride the Martial Shew,
And heap their Vallies with the gaudy Foe;
Th'insulted Sea with humbler Thoughts he gains,
A single Skiff to speed his Flight remains;
Th'incumber'd Oar scarce leaves the dreaded Coast
Through purple Billows and a floating Host.

Samuel Johnson, 'The Vanity Of Human Wishes', 1749

Frederick Augustus, Duke of YORK, 1763–1827

Oh, the brave old Duke of York,
He had ten thousand men;
He marched them up to the top of the hill,
And he marched them down again.
And when they were up, they were up,
And when they were down, they were down,
And when they were only half-way up,
They were neither up nor down.

Nursery rhyme, traditional

ACKNOWLEDGEMENTS

My debt to Lieutenant-Colonel M. J. G. Martin and Professor Calvin Christman is acknowledged in the Foreword to this book. I must also thank Dilip Hiro, my publishers and editors John Curtis and Joyce Seltzer, Carol Johnson for her copy-editing, my agent Michael Sissons, and Merlynna Hashim for some gallant typing.

Inevitably in a compilation of this kind many different sources have been consulted. As well as the standard dictionaries of quotations I have found two volumes to be particularly helpful. The first, a *Dictionary of Military and Naval Quotations*, edited by Colonel Robert Debs Heinl Jr and published by the United States Naval Institute in 1966, although somewhat mandarin in tone and somewhat out of date, indicated many leads that would otherwise have been missed. The second, *The Oxford Book of Military Anecdotes*, edited by that doughty war correspondent Max Hastings and published by OUP in 1985, as well as being a pleasure in itself, again directed some of my reading. Except for some very well-known passages which demanded inclusion I have endeavoured to avoid overlapping with Mr Hastings' work.

Inevitably too I have quoted much material which is still in copyright. Where I have overstepped the bounds of fair-play I am grateful to publishers, copyright-holders and authors for their kindness in allowing me to reprint extracts, viz.:
'Sonnets from China', from the *Collected Poems of W. H. Auden*, and 'Spain 1937' from *The English Auden*, by permission of Faber and Faber Ltd and Random House Inc.; 'The Pageant', from *Intimate Exchanges* by Alan Ayckbourn, by permission of Margaret Ramsay Ltd; *Britain and Her Army*, by Correlli Barnett, by permission of David Higham Associates Ltd, on behalf of Macmillan's; *When the War Was Over*, by Elizabeth Becker, by permission of Simon & Schuster Inc.; St Augustine's *City of God*, in the translation of Henry Bettenson © 1972, by permission of Penguin Books Ltd; *A Rumour of War*, by Philip Caputo, by permission of Macmillan; *The Second World War*, by Winston S. Churchill, by permission of Cassell plc; *The Battle of Malden*, in the translation of Kevin Crossley-Holland © 1965, published by Macmillan & Co. Ltd, by permission of Rogers, Coleridge & White Ltd; *Story of My Life*, by Moshe Dayan, by permission of George Weidenfeld & Nicolson Ltd; *On the Psychology of Military Incompetence*, by Norman F. Dixon, by permission of the author, Jonathan Cape Ltd, and Basic Books Inc.; *War*, by Gwynne Dyer, by permission of the Bodley Head on behalf of the author; *Patton: Ordeal and Triumph*, by Ladislas Farago, by permission of George Weidenfeld & Nicolson Ltd; 'Cambodia', from *In Memory of War*, by James Fenton, by permission of the Peters, Fraser & Dunlop Group Ltd; *Diary of a Young Girl*, by Anne Frank, by permission of Doubleday, a division of Bantam, Doubleday, Dell Publishing Group Inc.; *The Decisive Battles of the Western World*, by J. F. C. Fuller, by permission of David Higham Associates Ltd; *The Anglo-Saxon Chronicle*, in the translation of N. Garmonsway, by permission of J. M. Dent & Son Ltd; *The Face of War*, by Martha Gellhorn, by permission of © the author and the Virago Press; Lucan's *Pharsalia*, in the translation by Robert Graves, by permission of A. P. Watt Ltd on behalf of the Executors of the Estate of Robert Graves; Sallust's *The Jugurthine War* and *Conspiracy of Catiline*, in the translation of S. A. Handford © 1963, by permission of Penguin Books Ltd; *The Korean War*, by Max Hastings, by permission of Michael Joseph Ltd; *The Battle for the Falklands*, by © Max Hastings and Simon Jenkins by permission of Michael Joseph Ltd; *By-Line: Ernest Hemingway*, by Ernest Hemingway, © 1967 Mary Hemingway, by permission of Charles Scribner's Sons, an imprint of Macmillan Publishing Company; *Dispatches*, by Michael Herr, by permission of Alfred Knopf Inc.; *Hiroshima*, by John Hersey, by permission of Alfred Knopf Inc.; *The Arab–Israeli Wars*, by Chaim Herzog © 1982, by permission of Cassell plc; *Vietnam: A*

History by Stanley Karnow, by permission of Viking Penguin Inc.; Confucius's *Analects*, in the translation of D. C. Lau © 1979, by permission of Penguin Books Ltd; Lao Tzu's *Tao Te Ching*, in the translation of D. C. Lau © 1963, by permission of Penguin Books Ltd; *A Cup of Tears* by Abraham Lewin, by permission of Basil Blackwell Ltd; *Wellington: The Years of the Sword*, by Elizabeth Longford, by permission of George Weidenfeld & Nicolson Ltd; 'For the Union Dead', by Robert Lowell © 1960, 1964, by permission of Farrar Straus and Giroux Inc. and Faber and Faber Ltd; *Autumn Journal*, by Louis MacNeice, by permission of Faber & Faber Ltd and David Higham Associates Ltd; Leo Tolstoy's *War and Peace*, in the translation of Louise and Aylmer Maude, by permission of Oxford University Press; *Vietnam: The Ten Thousand Day War*, by Michael Maclear, by permission of Eyre Methuen Ltd; *Cambodian Witness*, by Someth May, by permission of the Peters, Fraser & Dunlop Group Ltd; *Hanoi*, by Mary McCarthy, by permission of A. M. Heath & Co. Ltd; 'Poem for President Nixon', by Roger McGough, by permission of the author and Inter-Action Trust Ltd; *Homage to Catalonia*, by George Orwell, by permission of A. M. Heath & Co. Ltd on behalf of the late Sonia Orwell and Martin Secker and Warburg, and Harcourt Brace Jovanovich Inc.; *Nam*, by Tim Page, by permission of Thames & Hudson Ltd; 'For Johnny', by John Pudney, from *Collected Poems*, by permission of David Higham Associates; *A History of the Crusades*, by Steven Runciman, by permission of the author and Cambridge University Press; *Collected Poems* of Siegfried Sassoon, by permission of George T. Sassoon; *Greek Political Oratory*, in the translation of A. N. W. Saunders © 1970, by permission of Penguin Books Ltd; *Sideshow*, by William Shawcross, by permission of André Deutsch Ltd; 'Field Hospital', by Charles Smith, from the *Oasis* collection of World War II poetry, by permission of J. M. Dent & Sons Ltd; *Inside the Third Reich*, by Albert Speer, by permission of George Weidenfeld & Nicolson Ltd; *The First World War: An Illustrated History*, by A. J. P. Taylor, by permission of Hamish Hamilton Ltd and G. P. Putnam and Sons; *White Heat* and *The Smoke and the Fire*, by John Terraine, by permission of Sidgwick & Jackson Ltd; 'The General Goes Zapping Charlie Cong', by Nicholas Tomalin, published in *The Times* of 5th June 1966, by permission of © Times Newspapers Ltd; *The Poetry and Career of Li Po*, by Arthur Waley, by permission of Unwin Hyman Ltd.; *Heat Treatment*, by Justin Wintle, by permission of J. M. Dent & Son Ltd; *Stay Alive, My Son*, by Pin Yathay, by permission of Bloomsbury Publishing Ltd and the Free Press; 'An Irish Airman Foresees His Death', 'Easter 1916', 'Leda and the Swan' and 'The Valley of the Black Pig', by W. B. Yeats, from his *Collected Poems*, by permission of A. P. Watt Ltd, on behalf of Michael B. Yeats and Macmillan and Co. Ltd; Nadezhda Durova's *The Cavalry Maiden*, in the translation of Mary Fleming Zirin, by permission of Angel Books, London.

J.W.

INDEX OF AUTHORS

MAIN INDEX

This Index gives page references to proper names. Page numbers in **bold** refer to main headings and sub-headings. An asterisk (*) indicates that the subject also occurs in the preceding Author Index. Where an author is not referred to in any quotation, he or she does not appear in this index.